GREGG Transcription

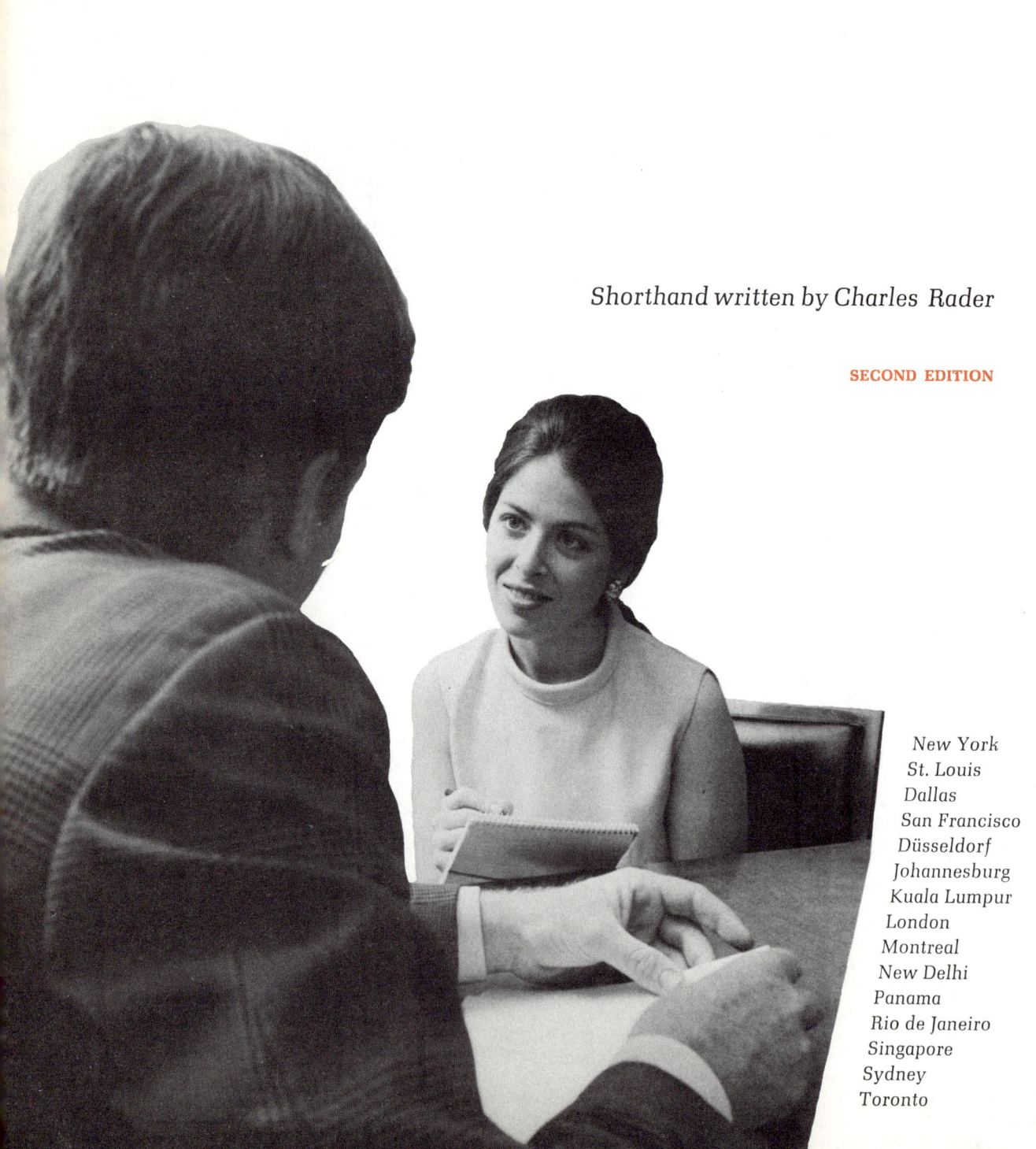

Shorthand written by Charles Rader

SECOND EDITION

New York
St. Louis
Dallas
San Francisco
Düsseldorf
Johannesburg
Kuala Lumpur
London
Montreal
New Delhi
Panama
Rio de Janeiro
Singapore
Sydney
Toronto

 Transcription

Diamond Jubilee Series

Louis A. Leslie

Charles E. Zoubek

GREGG DIVISION / McGRAW-HILL BOOK COMPANY

ACKNOWLEDGMENTS

The authors wish to express their appreciation to the following people for their valuable assistance in the preparation of *Gregg Transcription, Diamond Jubilee Series, Second Edition*:

   The teachers who have shared with the authors their experience with the first edition.

   Mrs. Madeline S. Strony, for her guidance and encouragement.

   Mr. Charles Rader, for the beautiful shorthand and for the supervision of the production of the book.

   Betty Binns, the designer, who was responsible for the physical attractiveness of the book.

   Mrs. Mary Louise Intorrella and Mr. Jerome Edelman, members of the Gregg staff, who contributed so much to the production of the book.

   Mr. Martin Bough of *Fundamental Photographs*, who took the pictures.

   Miss Bambi Hammil, who directed the taking of the pictures.

   King Typographic Service Corp., which set the type and R. R. Donnelley and Sons Company, which printed the book.

GREGG TRANSCRIPTION, DIAMOND JUBILEE SERIES, SECOND EDITION

Copyright © 1972, 1963, 1956 by McGraw-Hill, Inc. All Rights Reserved.
Copyright 1950 by McGraw-Hill, Inc. All Rights Reserved.
Printed in the United States of America. No part of this publication may be reproduced, stored in a retrieval system, or transmitted, in any form or by any means, electronic, mechanical, photocopying, recording, or otherwise, without the prior written permission of the publisher.

4 5 6 7 8 9 0 DODO 0 9 8 7 6 5

ISBN 07-037262-4

Preface

Gregg Transcription, Diamond Jubilee Series, Second Edition, makes a very vital contribution to the student's stenographic training. It teaches him to combine his skills in shorthand and typewriting and his knowledge of the mechanics of English into the production of mailable letters—letters that are accurately transcribed, accurately typed, attractively placed on the letterhead, and free from spelling and punctuation errors.

Objectives

Gregg Transcription, Diamond Jubilee Series, Second Edition, is designed to meet these objectives:

1   To review the principles of Gregg Shorthand.

2   To develop further the student's ability to construct outlines under the stress of dictation.

3   To develop further the student's mastery and understanding of words.

4   To develop the student's ability to spell and punctuate.

5   To develop further the student's command of the mechanics of English.

6   To teach the student to place letters attractively on letterheads.

7   To teach the student to handle the problems of office-style dictation.

8   To teach the student efficient dictation and transcription techniques.

Organization

Gregg Transcription, Diamond Jubilee Series, Second Edition, is organized into 4 parts, 16 chapters, and 80 lessons. Each lesson contains sufficient material for a homework assignment of approximately 45 minutes.

Shorthand skill development

The development of shorthand skill continues to receive strong emphasis in *Gregg Transcription.* The following features are devoted to it:

BUILDING SHORTHAND SKILL

Each of the lessons in Part I (Lessons 1-20) contains a Theory Brushup that reviews phrases, word beginnings, word endings, word families, and brief forms.

READING AND WRITING PRACTICE

Each of the 80 lessons contains a Reading and Writing Practice consisting of several up-to-date business letters and memorandums written in shorthand. This Reading and Writing Practice provides a constant automatic review of the principles of Gregg Shorthand and at the same time develops the student's shorthand vocabulary. About 75 percent of the material is new.

The correspondence in each chapter is devoted to a specific business or department of a business.

ACCURACY PRACTICE

A number of accuracy drills are provided to help the student refine his shorthand style to the end that he can read his notes more rapidly and accurately.

RECALL DRILLS

The Recall Drills in the Appendix provide a concentrated review of all the word beginnings and word endings and the phrasing principles of Gregg Shorthand. A few minutes spent on these drills two or three times a week will do much to improve the student's mastery of the principles of the system.

The mechanics of English

In the earlier volumes of the Diamond Jubilee Series, much stress was placed on the development of the student's mastery of the mechanics of the English language. This stress is continued and intensified through the following features of *Gregg Transcription:*

PUNCTUATION

In Chapters 1-4 the punctuation pointers that the student studied earlier in his shorthand course are reviewed. Additional, more advanced punctuation pointers are introduced beginning with Chapter 5.

SPELLING

Marginal Spelling Reminders Words that transcribers often misspell have been indicated in a second color in the shorthand of the Reading and Writing Practice exercises. The correct longhand spelling and syllabication of these words are given in the margins of the shorthand.

Spelling Families In the second lesson of each chapter, beginning with Chapter 6, the student studies a "Spelling Family," which consists of groups of words that contain a common spelling problem. Several illustrations of each family are used in the Reading and Writing Practice.

Similar Words   The first lesson of each chapter, beginning with Chapter 6, contains a Similar-Words Drill in which the student is alerted to the necessity for caution in transcribing words that sound alike or almost alike.

VOCABULARY DEVELOPMENT

Business Vocabulary Builder   Each lesson contains a Business Vocabulary Builder that consists of several words or expressions, selected from the Reading and Writing Practice, with which the student may not be familiar. The words and expressions are defined briefly.

Common Prefixes and Suffixes   These drills deal with the meanings of common prefixes and suffixes. An understanding of these meanings should do much to help the student expand his vocabulary.

Word Chains   The Word Chain drills are also helpful in expanding the student's vocabulary. Each drill consists of a number of words that have a common meaning; yet each word has its own special shade of meaning. The words in the chain are defined and illustrated.

GRAMMAR

A number of the lessons in *Gregg Transcription* contain drills dealing with errors in grammar that the unwary stenographer often makes.

TYPING STYLE

In the Typing Style Studies, the student is taught how to handle numbers, quantities, dates, and addresses in business correspondence. He is also taught how to type titles of books, magazines, newspapers, booklets, etc., in business correspondence.

Transcription techniques

Gregg Transcription describes to the budding stenographer many of the problems he will encounter on the job, and it teaches him techniques with which to dispose of them.

CHAPTER OPENINGS

Each chapter opens with the presentation and discussion of a dictation or transcription problem, beautifully illustrated by photographs especially prepared for *Gregg Transcription*. Through these chapter openings the student learns what to do before he takes dictation, while he is taking dictation, while he is transcribing, and after he has completed transcribing. These discussions, written around the experiences of a mythical secretary, are not only informative but entertaining.

OFFICE-STYLE DICTATION

In the fourth lesson of each chapter, beginning with Chapter 6, the student is introduced to a common office-style dictation problem and is taught how to handle it.

PLACEMENT BY JUDGMENT

Through a simple but effective device, the student is taught how to place letters attractively on a letterhead in the manner of an experienced secretary—by judgment.

Phrasing on the Job In Chapter 15 the student learns how to make the taking of dictation on the job easier by devising special phrases or shortcuts for frequently recurring expressions that are peculiar to the industry or line of business in which his employer is engaged.

Model Letters The student is supplied with several model letters that show him the commonest letter setups used in business.

Supporting materials

Workbook for Gregg Transcription, Diamond Jubilee Series, Second Edition This workbook, correlated lesson by lesson with the text, supplies the student with many opportunities to test his grasp of the nonshorthand elements of transcription. The student who conscientiously completes the lessons in this workbook will be able to approach his first stenographic job with confidence and poise.

Student's Transcript of Gregg Transcription, Diamond Jubilee Series, Second Edition An indispensable aid to the student is the transcript of the Reading and Writing Practice exercises. This transcript not only enables him to complete his assignments in the shortest possible time but provides him with a source of outside dictation.

Dictation for Transcription, Diamond Jubilee Series, Second Edition In the transcription phase of the student's stenographic training, it is vital that he take and transcribe large quantities of new-matter dictation, graded in difficulty and in problems of transcription. *Dictation for Transcription* is the teacher's dictation book which supplies this dictation.

Dictation for Transcription, Diamond Jubilee Series, Second Edition, contains more than 500 letters correlated lesson by lesson with *Gregg Transcription.* The first three letters in each lesson are related to the first three letters of *Gregg Transcription;* the remaining letters of each lesson are related to the same industry or line of business.

The authors of *Gregg Transcription* are confident that this second edition will enable teachers to do an even more effective job of training efficient, accurate transcribers than they have done in the past.

Louis A. Leslie
Charles E. Zoubek

Contents

1 PREDICTATION PREPARATION

Chapter 1	Letters of Request, Acceptance, Refusal, Appreciation	17
Chapter 2	Public Relations	43
Chapter 3	Personnel Relations	69
Chapter 4	Employment	95

2 DICTATION ON THE JOB

Chapter 5	Publishing	120
Chapter 6	Homes and Home Furnishings	146
Chapter 7	Insurance	170
Chapter 8	Automobiles	194

3 TRANSCRIPTION ON THE JOB

Chapter 9	Automation and Office Equipment	218
Chapter 10	Retailing	244
Chapter 11	Travel and Transportation	266
Chapter 12	Paper and Printing	290

4 TRANSCRIPTION ALERTNESS

Chapter 13	Real Estate	316
Chapter 14	Education	344
Chapter 15	Marketing and Sales Promotion	368
Chapter 16	Investments	396

The story of Ellen Gardiner, secretary

Predictation preparation

Here are some of the things that Ellen Gardiner, who is the "heroine" of Gregg Transcription, does before she takes dictation:

1 Organizes her desk, 12

2 Selects reference books, 40

3 Looks after her dictation tools, 64

4 Obtains advance information, 90

Dictation on the job

Ellen Gardiner found that certain techniques are helpful to her and her employer while she is actually taking his dictation. In this part you will learn how Ellen:

5 Uses efficient notebook techniques, 118

6 Adapts herself to different writing positions, 144

7 Handles interruptions in dictation, 168

8 Interrupts her employer tactfully, 192

Transcription on the job

While Ellen is transcribing the dictation of her employer, there are many things that she must keep in mind. For example,

9 How many copies she must make of each letter or memorandum, 216

10 How to make corrections quickly and neatly, 242

11 How to proofread accurately and rapidly, 264

12 How to submit her letters to her employer after she has transcribed them, 288

Transcription alertness

Ellen realized that there was much more to her job than taking dictation and transcribing. She found that she could be of great help to her employer by:

13 Being alert to catch the occasional error that he made in his dictation (Mr. Davis was, after all, only human!), 314

14 Following implied instructions in the letters that he dictated, 342

15 Collecting information that he would need in answering correspondence, 366

16 Composing routine letters for his signature, 394

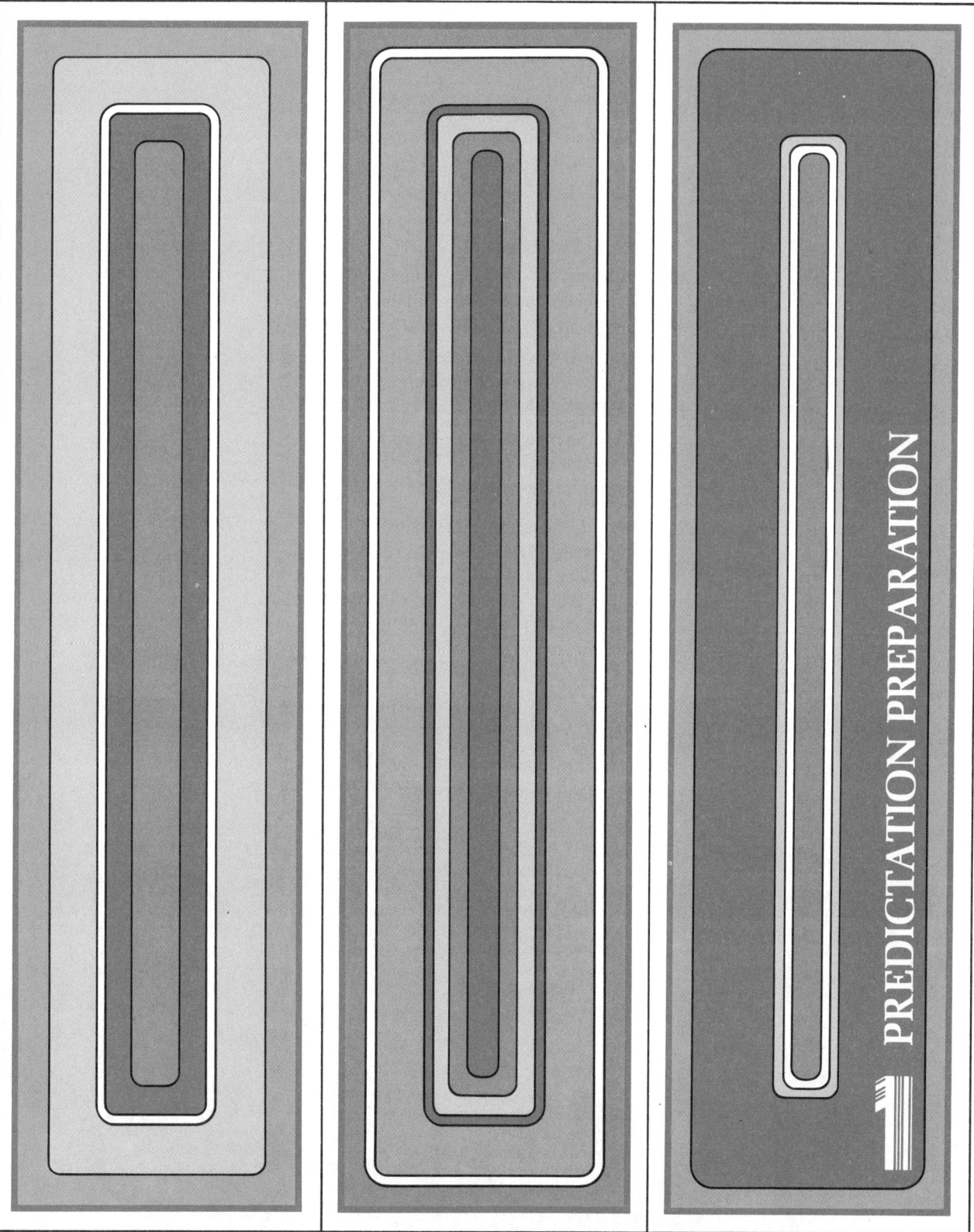

PREDICTATION PREPARATION

1

The secretary's desk

Ellen Gardiner is secretary to Mr. George D. Davis, marketing director for the American Products Company. Mr. Davis thinks very highly of his secretary. "That girl is a wonder," he said to a business associate at luncheon one day. "This morning I dictated fifteen letters to her, and it seemed like no time at all before she had them on my desk, ready to sign. I don't know how she does it."

If Mr. Davis were to investigate "how she does it," it wouldn't take him long to find the answer.

The most important reason why Ellen can produce accurate, attractive letters so rapidly is that her transcribing skills are sharp. She writes shorthand rapidly and legibly; she seldom makes an error as her fingers just dance over the keys of her typewriter; and she has a fair command of grammar, punctuation, and spelling.

Another reason for her high production rate is the way she organizes her work area. Every item she needs in order to

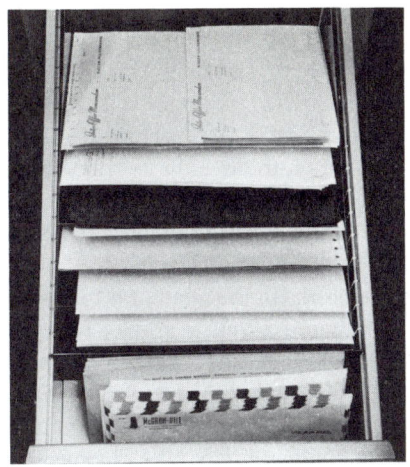

transcribe a letter is efficiently placed so that she can reach it conveniently.

Take her stationery, for example. This she keeps in the middle left-hand drawer of her desk in the following order (from the back of the drawer to the front).

1 Interoffice stationery
2 Letterhead paper
3 Carbon paper and carbon packs
4 Second sheets
5 Onionskin for additional copies
6 Plain bond for second page of two-page letters
7 Envelopes

You can quickly see the advantage of Ellen's system. Most of the material she must transcribe requires either interoffice stationery or a letterhead, a carbon sheet, and at least one copy. Consequently, she has these items placed in her drawer in such a way that she can assemble them without a wasted motion. The envelope, which is the last item she needs, is right in the front of the drawer.

Incidentally, Ellen keeps this drawer open as she transcribes, so that she does not have to open and close it each time she finishes one letter and is ready to start the next.

The large drawer in the center of the desk contains such items as clips, rubber bands, pencils, scissors, a ruler, and other supplies that she may need as she transcribes.

Ellen also has the top of her desk arranged efficiently. There she usually has:

1 A copyholder, conveniently placed by her typewriter so that she can read her notes without eyestrain and so that it will not interfere with the operation of her typewriter.
2 An "in" box in which she places all work that is to be done.
3 An "out" box in which she places all completed work.
4 A number of reference books.
5 A calendar pad.
6 Several pencils.
7 A stapler.
8 A date stamp.
9 A notebook open to a clean page in which she records any instructions Mr. Davis may give her while she is working at her desk.

Of course, you may not have the same type of secretarial desk as Ellen, but whatever the type of desk you find in your office, you will be wise to organize it efficiently.

Punctuation brushup

Your major goal as you work with *Gregg Transcription, Diamond Jubilee Series, Second Edition,* will be to develop your ability to transcribe from your shorthand notes and to produce letters that are mailable. If you are to produce such letters, one of the skills you must possess is the ability to punctuate correctly.

For that reason, in the books in the Diamond Jubilee Series from which you studied earlier, you were given a great deal of drill on the most frequent uses of the comma and other marks of punctuation.

In *Gregg Transcription* you will continue to give attention to punctuation at the same time that you are developing your shorthand speed, improving your ability to spell and to handle the mechanics of the English language, and mastering the other skills that are necessary for rapid transcription.

In Chapters 1-4 you will review the uses of the punctuation marks you have previously studied; beginning with Chapter 5, you will take up additional uses of the comma and also learn how to use the colon correctly.

In *Gregg Transcription,* as in the other books of the Diamond Jubilee Series, you will find each of the punctuation marks squared in color in the Reading and Writing Practice exercises. Directly above each squared punctuation mark will be a brief indication of the reason for the use of that mark.

In the margins of each Reading and Writing Practice exercise, you will find a number of words that have been singled out for special spelling attention.

PRACTICE PROCEDURES

You will derive the greatest benefit from the punctuation and spelling pointers in the Reading and Writing Practice exercises if you follow these practice suggestions:

1   Read each punctuation rule to be sure that you understand its application; then study the illustrative examples.

2   Read the Reading and Writing Practice exercise aloud, if possible. Each time you see a squared punctuation mark, note the reason for its use, which is indicated directly above the squared mark.

3 Make a shorthand copy of the Reading and Writing Practice exercise. As you copy, insert the punctuation marks in your shorthand notes.

4 As you read the Reading and Writing Practice exercises, you will occasionally encounter a shorthand word printed in a second color. That word has been singled out for special spelling attention. It appears in the margin, correctly spelled and syllabicated. Spell the word aloud, if possible, pausing slightly after each syllable.

In Chapter 1 you will review the following common uses of the comma:

, parenthetical

A word or a phrase or a clause that is used parenthetically (that is, a word or a phrase or a clause that is not necessary to the grammatical completeness of the sentence) should be set off by commas.

If the parenthetical expression occurs at the end of a sentence, only one comma is needed.

A better date for me, however, would be July 28.

May I take this opportunity, Mr. Edison, to thank you for your contribution.

We shall take care of your expenses, of course.

Each time a parenthetical expression occurs in the Reading and Writing Practice, it will be indicated in the shorthand as shown in the margin.

par

, apposition

An expression in apposition (that is, a word or a phrase or a clause that identifies or explains other terms) should be set off by commas. When the expression occurs at the end of a sentence, only one comma is necessary.

Our comptroller, Mr. John Quinn, will attend the meeting.

The luncheon will be held on Tuesday, September 25, at the Hotel Edison.

Mr. Smith's latest book, Modern Retailing, has just come off the press.

On April 16 I will be in Cleveland, Ohio.

Each time an expression in apposition occurs in the Reading and Writing Practice, it will be indicated in the shorthand as shown in the margin.

ap ,

, series

When the last member of a series of three or more items is preceded by *and, or,* or *nor,* place a comma before the conjunction as well as between the other items.

Please accept my best wishes for your success, prosperity, and happiness.
I can see him on March 1, on March 18, or on April 10.

Each time a series occurs in the Reading and Writing Practice, it will be indicated in the shorthand as shown in the margin.

ser ,

, conjunction

A comma is used to separate two independent clauses that are joined by a conjunction:

I am proud that you are one of us, and I want you to know that I appreciate your work.
I wish I could be with you on June 15, but I must be in Europe on that date.

Each time this use of the comma occurs in the Reading and Writing Practice, it will be indicated in the shorthand as shown in the margin.

conj ,

, and omitted

When two or more adjectives modify the same noun, they are separated by commas.

He was a quiet, efficient worker.

However, the comma is not used if the first adjective modifies the combined idea of the second adjective plus the noun.

She wore a beautiful green dress.

Each time this use of the comma occurs in the Reading and Writing Practice, it will be indicated in the shorthand as shown in the margin.

and o ,

Chapter 1 / Lesson 1

Letters of request, acceptance, refusal, appreciation

Building shorthand skill

1 THEORY BRUSHUP

The first four chapters of *Gregg Transcription* contain Theory Brushups that are designed to give you a quick recall of the major principles of Gregg Shorthand.

Read each line as rapidly as you can. When you come to an outline that you cannot read, spell it. If the spelling does not give you the meaning at once, refer to the key.

At this stage you should not have to refer to the key very often.

Your reading goal: 1 minute.

Frequent Phrases *Thank*

1

Word Beginning *Re-*

2

Word Ending *-cal*

3

Word Family *-iation*

4

Nt, Nd

5

Brief Forms

6

1 Thank you, thank you for, thank you for your, thank you for your order, to thank you, to thank you for, I thank you, I thank you for.
2 Reports, response, replace, receives, repairs, resign, receipt.
3 Chemical, medical, practical, radical, logical.
4 Association, appreciation, negotiations, depreciation, appropriation, pronunciation.
5 Talent, print, kindness, mind, remind, find.
6 Suggest, suggested, enclose, enclosed, time, timed, timing.

Building transcription skills

2 BUSINESS VOCABULARY BUILDER

In *Gregg Transcription*, you will continue to develop your command of the English language through the Business Vocabulary Builders in each lesson. Remember, the larger your vocabulary, the more easily will you be able to take dictation and transcribe.

Each Business Vocabulary Builder consists of several words or expressions, together with brief definitions, selected from the Reading and Writing Practice. Always study the Business Vocabulary Builder before you begin your work on the Reading and Writing Practice; it will make your work easier.

> **Business vocabulary builder**
>
> **comptroller** (pronounced *con-tro-ler*) An official of a company who examines and supervises expenditures.
>
> **hospitality** Cordial reception of guests.
>
> **dynamic** Forceful; energetic.

Reading and writing practice

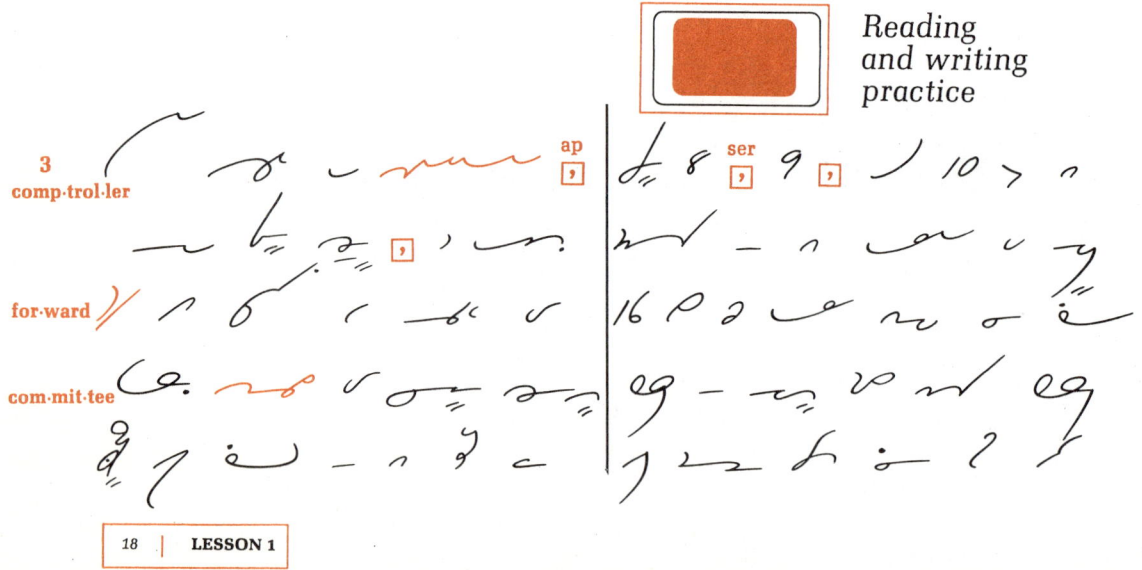

3 comp·trol·ler
for·ward
com·mit·tee

LESSON 1

Flight

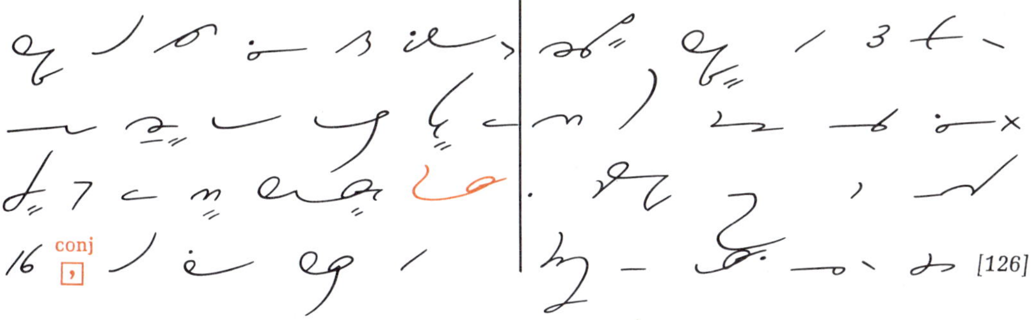

As·so·ci·a·tion
gen·er·ous·ly
ed·i·tor
ac·cept

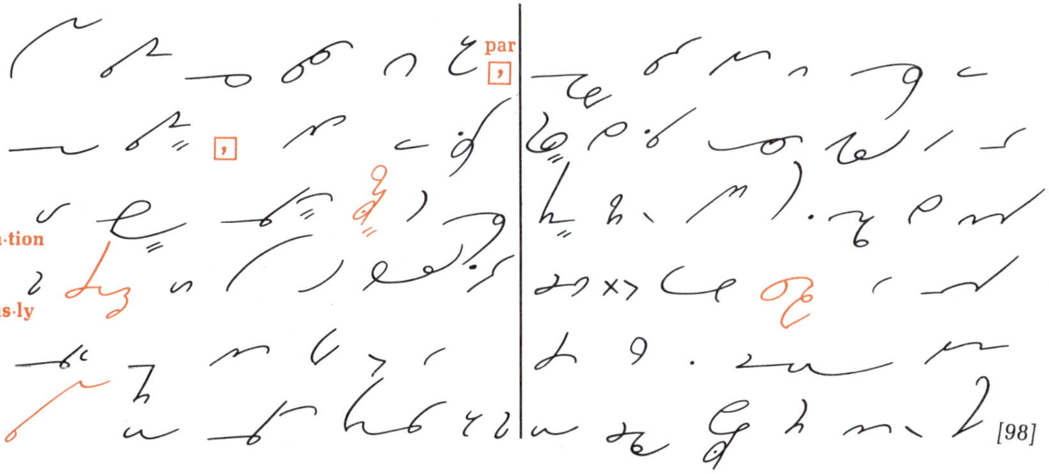

cour·te·sy
guest
be·lieve
ap·pre·ci·ate

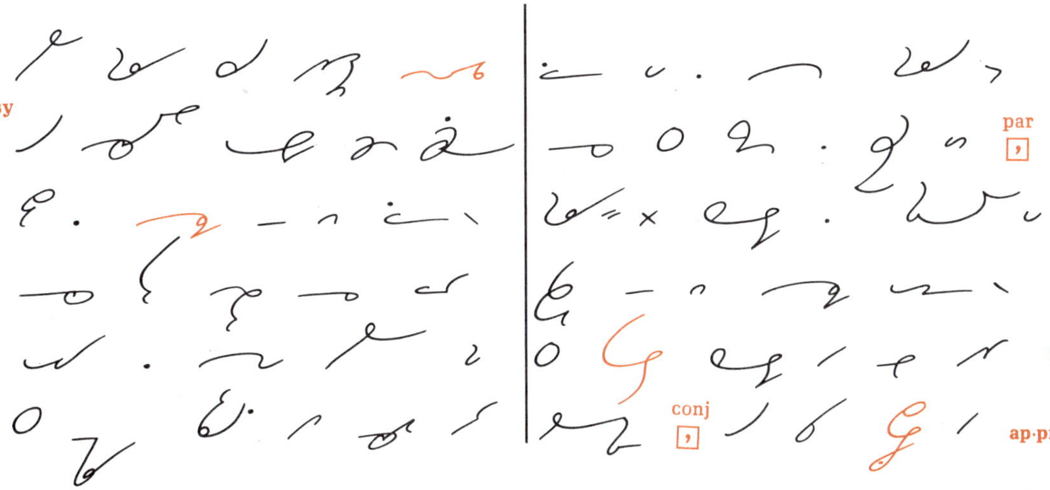

LESSON 1 | 19

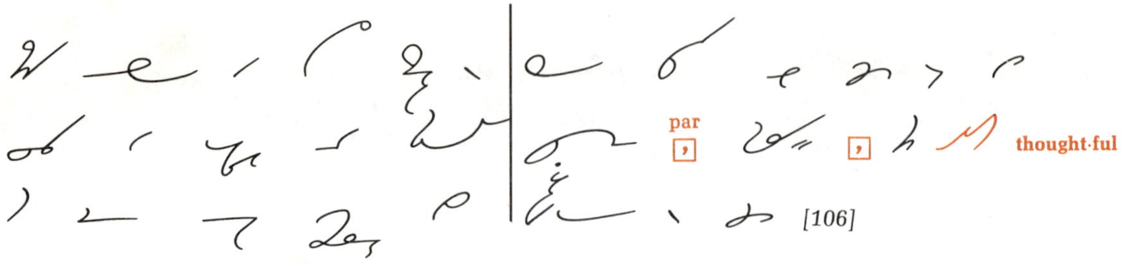

par , thought·ful [106]

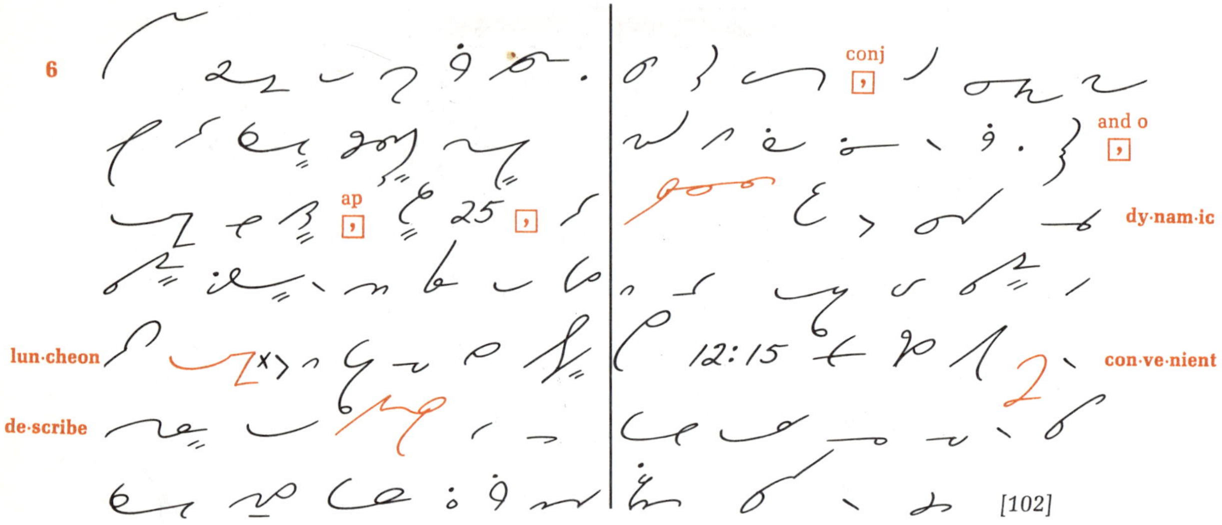

6 conj , and o dy·nam·ic
lun·cheon ap , 25 , con·ve·nient
de·scribe 12:15 [102]

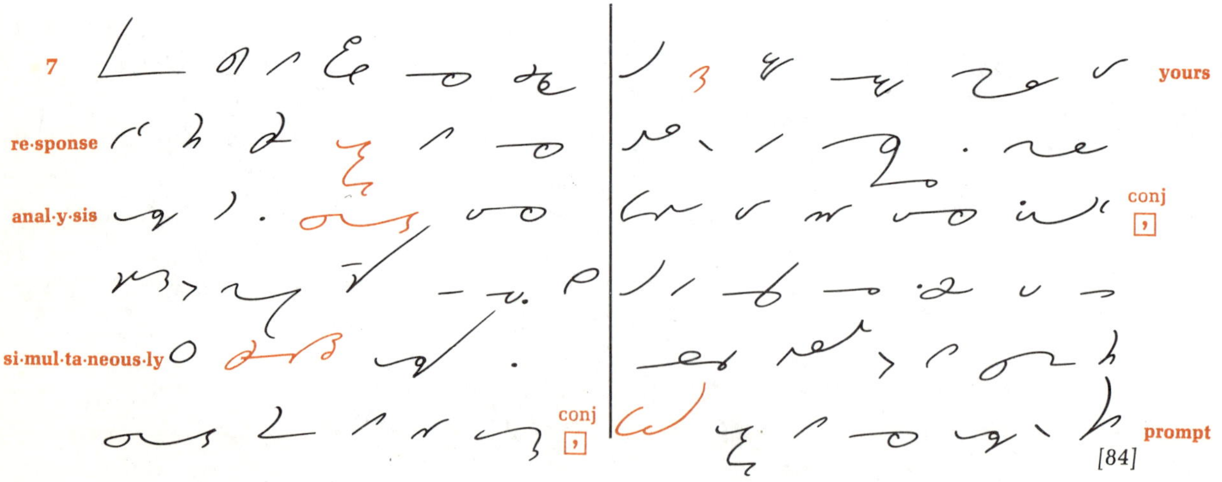

7 yours
re·sponse
anal·y·sis conj ,
si·mul·ta·neous·ly
conj , prompt [84]

20 | LESSON 1

Building shorthand skill

8 THEORY BRUSHUP

Your reading goal: 50 seconds.

Frequent Phrases   To Before a Downstroke

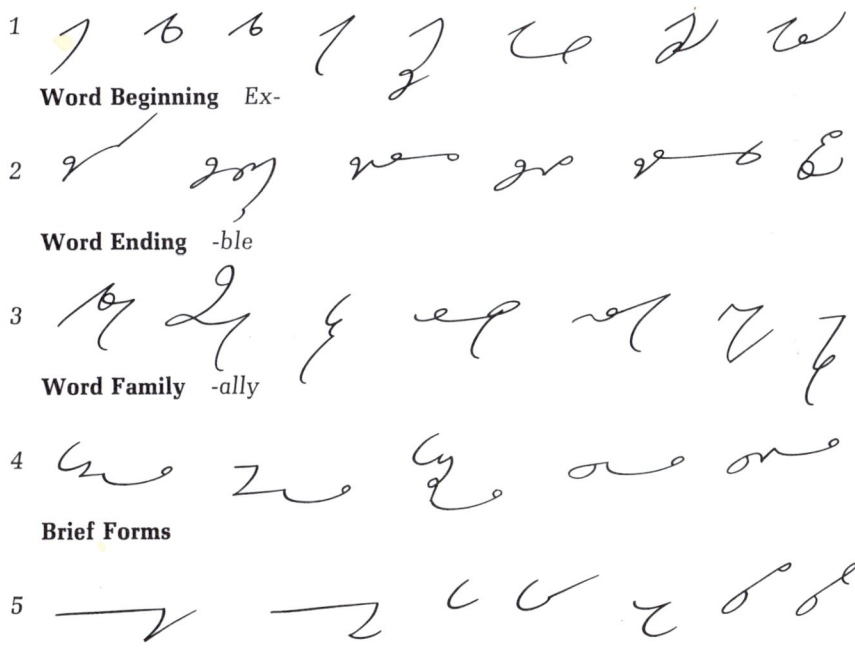

1 To have, to say, to see, to be, to visit, to place, to find, to print.
2 Extend, executives, extremely, exactly, exterminate, expired.
3 Desirable, available, possible, reliable, credible, troubled, enjoyable.
4 Personally, informally, professionally, annually, actually.
5 Manufactured, manufacturer, present, presented, represent, idea, ideas.

AMERICAN ASSOCIATES
203 235-7890
10 BUCHANAN STREET
HARTFORD, CONNECTICUT 06109

January 28, 19--

Mr. James R. Parker
National Publishing Company, Inc.
New York, New York 10077

Dear Mr. Parker:

    Thank you for the material you sent me recently; it arrived on January 12. It is exactly what I wanted, and I appreciate your thoughtfulness in sending it to me.

    As a token of my appreciation, I am sending you a gift that I hope you will like.

                                Sincerely yours,

                                Charles R. Grant

                                Charles R. Grant
                                Sales Manager

CRG:LEA

Short letter—double spaced
Semiblocked style
Standard punctuation

Building transcription skills

9 | Business vocabulary builder

unanimously Completely in agreement.

adjuster One who determines the amount payable on a claim resulting from an accident.

dietitians Persons trained in the science of feeding individuals or groups.

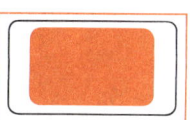

Reading and writing practice

10 *touch, and o, prom·is·ing, fa·cil·i·ties* [73]

11 *res·ig·na·tion*

com·mit·tee
unan·i·mous·ly
hon·or·ary
ges·ture

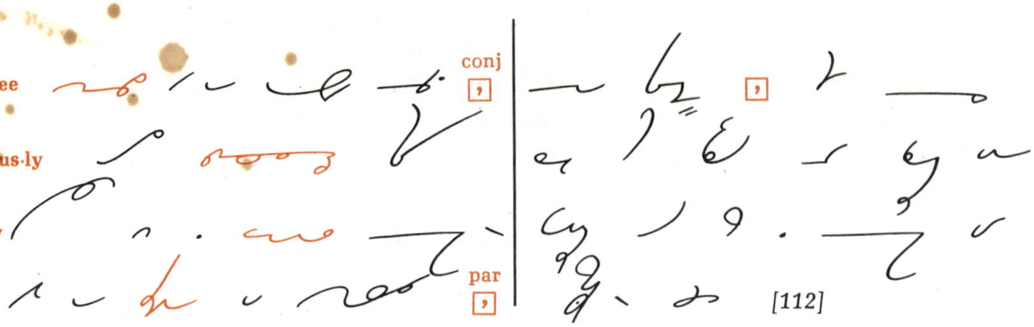

conj
par

[112]

12

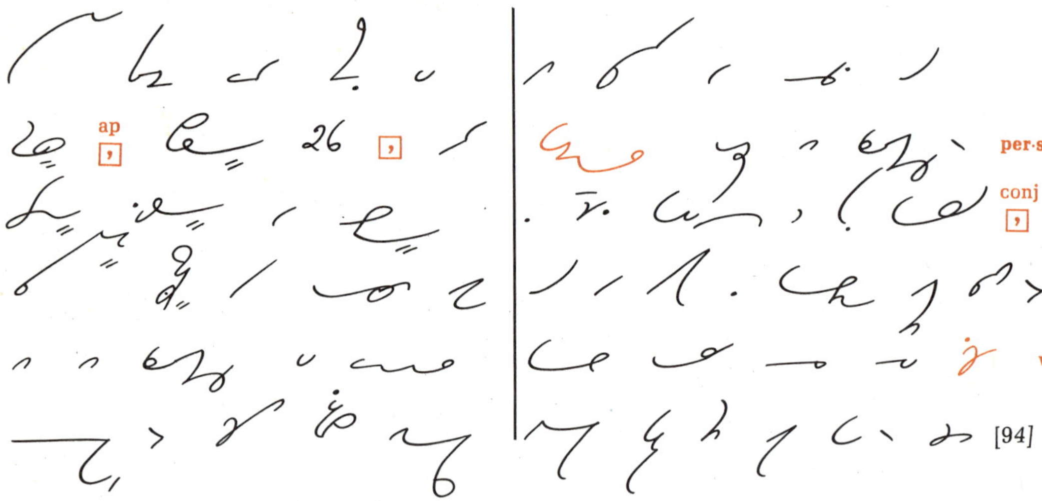

ap
26
per·son·al·ly
conj
wheth·er

[94]

13

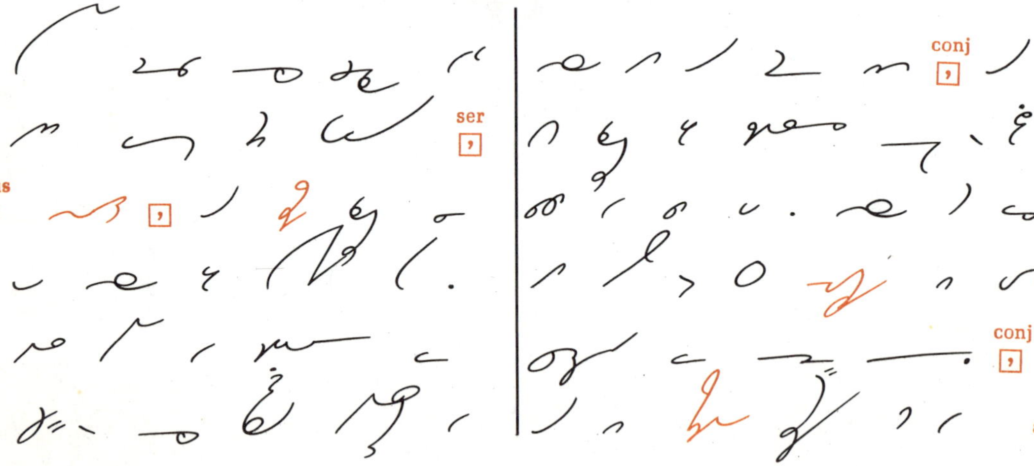

ser
cour·te·ous
ef·fi·cient
conj
no·ti·fied
conj
ad·just·er

LESSON 2 | 25

Building shorthand skill

16   THEORY BRUSHUP

Your reading goal: 50 seconds.

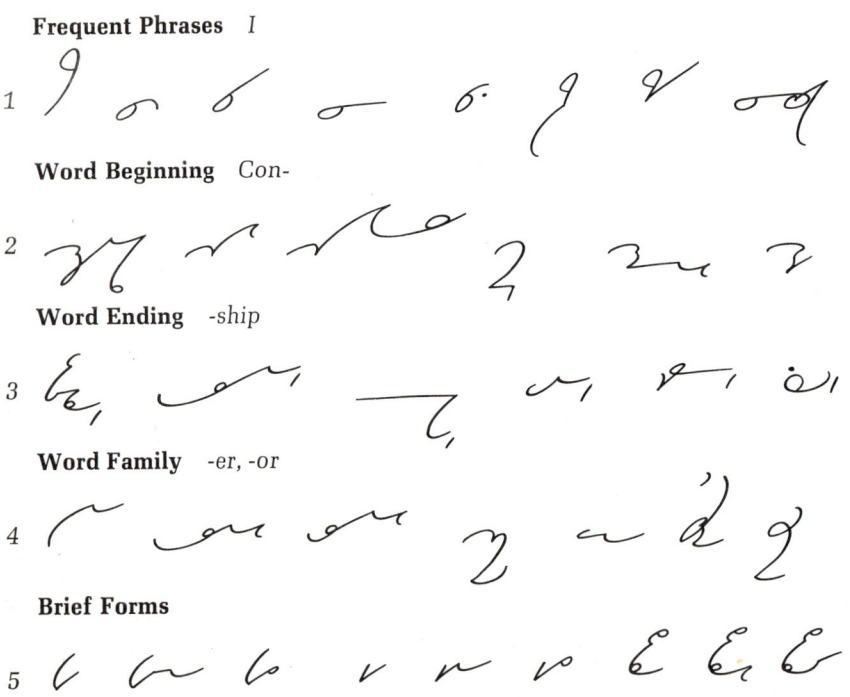

1 I have, I can, I would, I am, I think, I shall be, I should, I might be.
2 Considerably, contains, contemplate, convention, consumers, consist.
3 Sponsorship, leadership, membership, authorship, steamship, hardship.
4 Dinner, letters, readers, covered, honor, supervisor, favor.
5 Part, partner, party, short, shorter, shortly, experience, experiences, experienced.

Building transcription skills

17 Business vocabulary builder

stimulating Arousing; exciting.
nominating committee A group of people who propose a person for an office.
annual Yearly.

Reading and writing practice

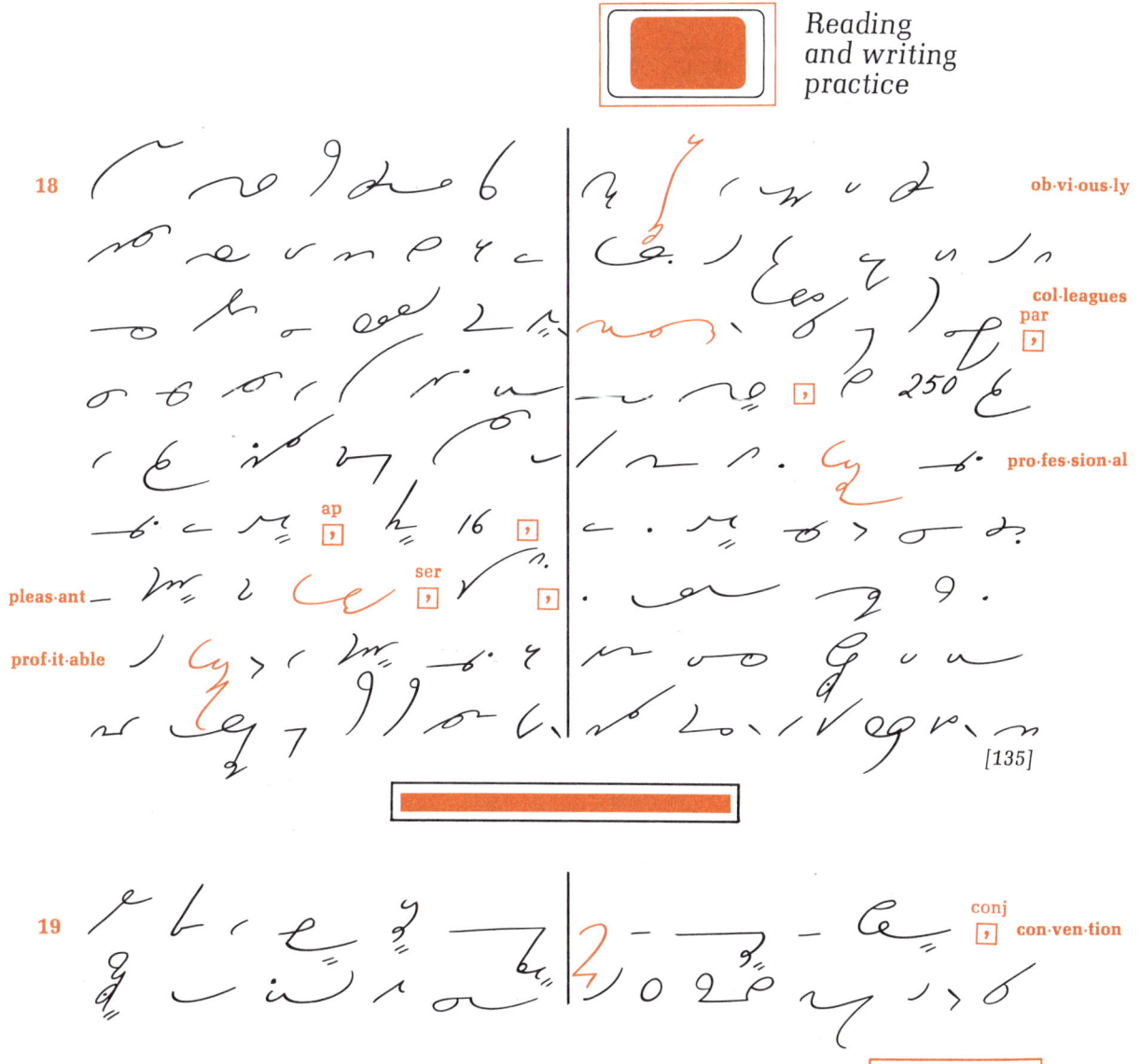

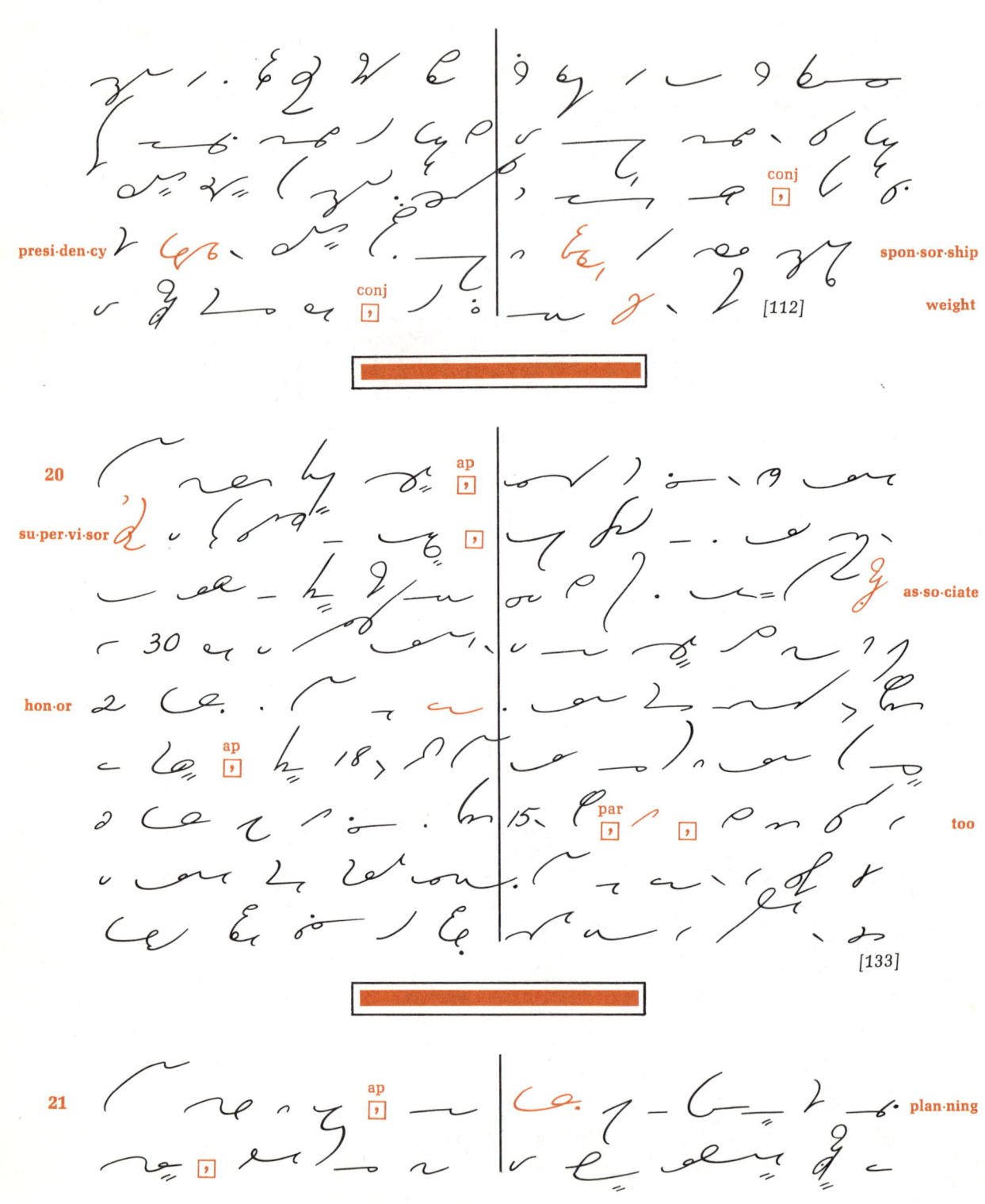

guest — ap — [113] whether, par, arrival

22 — acceptance, par, admission [61]

23 — urban, conjunction, par — commitment [92]

LESSON 3

Letter placement
SHORT LETTERS

Each letter that Ellen Gardiner presents to Mr. Davis to sign is not only accurately transcribed but also attractively placed on the letterhead. Her letters create an immediate good impression on the persons receiving them.

Ellen does not have to consult a placement scale to produce an attractive letter; she has learned to do it by judgment. She glances at her notes and decides that her left-hand margin stop should be set "about here" and her right-hand margin stop "about there." She then types the date, spaces down a number of lines, and is ready to type the inside address. All of this takes only a few seconds.

You, too, will be able to place letters by judgment if you will study the suggestions that follow.

TYPES OF LETTERS

Most one-page letters can be placed in four classifications:

1 Very short letters, containing two or three sentences. These letters may be double-spaced as shown in the model on page 22. Very short letters present no placement problem.
2 Short letters, containing up to approximately 100 words.
3 Average letters, containing 100 to 200 words.
4 Long letters, containing more than 200 words.

PLACING SHORT LETTERS BY JUDGMENT

In this lesson you will learn how to place short letters by judgment. On page 31 you will find Letter No. 23 of *Gregg Transcription* as it was written in shorthand and transcribed by Ellen Gardiner. Her transcript was made on a machine that had elite (small) type. Letter 23 is a short letter containing about 100 words.

You will notice that Ellen's shorthand required a little more than half a column in her notebook. Whenever a letter takes approximately half a column in her notebook, Ellen does three things:

1 She sets her margin stops for approximately 2-inch margins at the left and at the right.
2 She inserts her stationery pack and types the date two lines below the last line of the letterhead. (She *always* types the date at this point, regardless of the length of the letter.)
3 She starts the inside address about 4 inches from the top of the paper.

If she must transcribe on a machine with pica (large) type, she starts the inside address about 3½ inches from the top of the paper. Her margins are again about 2 inches on each side.

YOUR FIRST STEP

As the first step in learning to place letters by judgment, copy Letter 23 in shorthand and see how much space this short letter requires in *your* notebook. If your notes are large, they will require more space than Ellen's did; if they are small, they will require less space. Then, if possible, transcribe the letter from your notes following the three steps given above.

WESTERN SYSTEMS CORP. 483 Market Street, San Francisco, California 94137

Executive Offices

May 20, 19--

Mr. James C. Ellis
Willis College
Baker Street and Davis Avenue
Wilmington, Delaware 19804

Dear Mr. Ellis:

    I sincerely appreciate your invitation to take part in the conference on urban problems to be held on June 18 in conjunction with the meeting of the National Education Association in Dallas.

    I regret, however, that I cannot attend. I have made another commitment for June 18 that I am obliged to keep.

    I hope that you have a very successful conference and that the results of your discussions will be published.

                    Very truly yours,

                    Frank L. Johnson
                    Frank L. Johnson
                    Conference Director

FLJ:JPE

LETTER PLACEMENT 31

Building shorthand skill

24 THEORY BRUSHUP

Your reading goal: 50 seconds.

Phrases Special

1

Word Beginning In-

2

Word Ending -ment

3

Word Family Comm-

4

Brief Forms

5

1 Let us, let us know, as soon as, as soon as possible, I hope, I hope that, I hope you will, we hope.
2 Instead, intend, incomplete, invitation, informal, inspiration, insist.
3 Assignment, treatment, basement, acknowledgment, fundamental.
4 Commencement, comments, common, commitment.
5 Speak, speaking, speaker, willing, willingness, accompany, accompanied, accompanies.

Building transcription skills

25 Business vocabulary builder

resist To oppose; to strive against.

commencement The ceremony at a school during which degrees are conferred.

biographical (*adjective*) Relating to the written history of a person's life.

acutely Critically; crucially.

Reading and writing practice

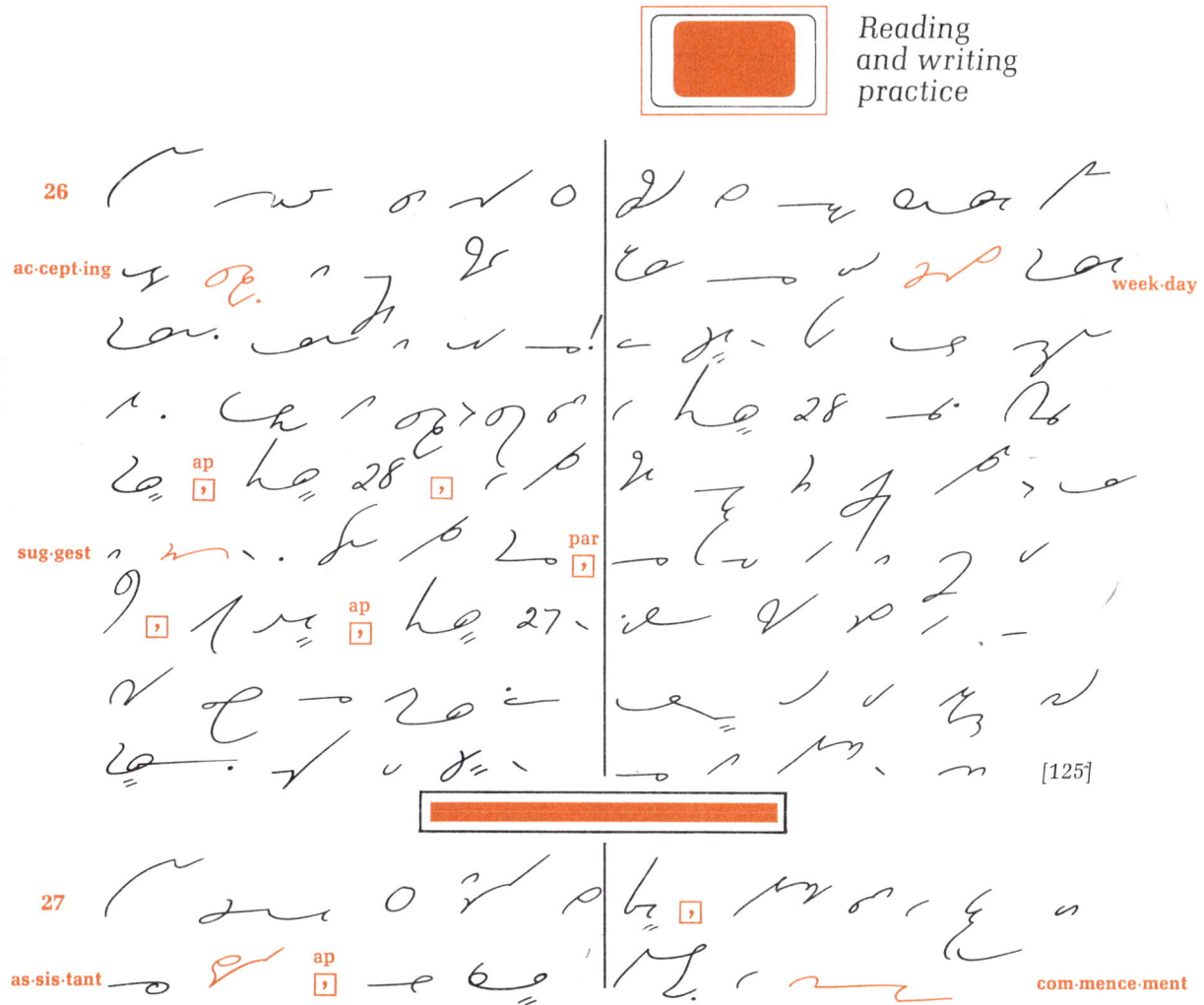

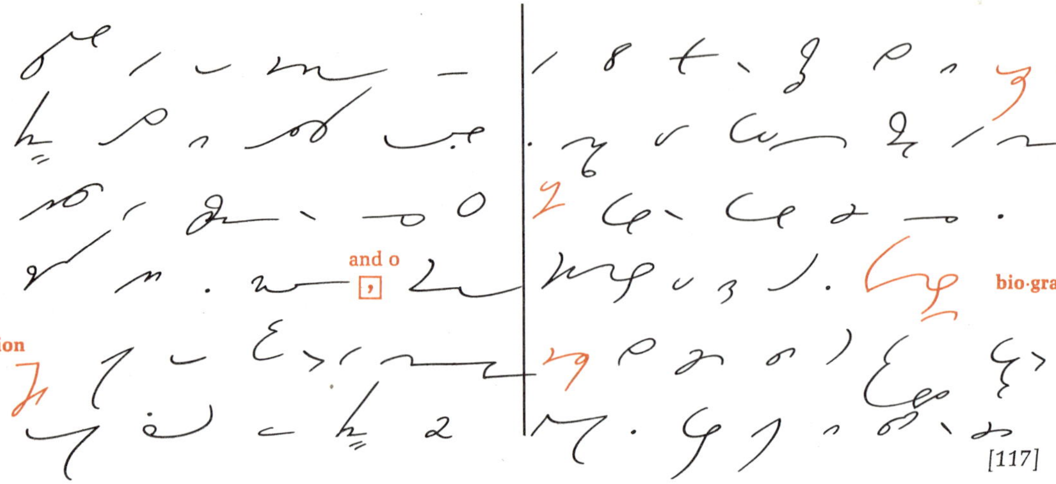

receive

off

and o

biographical

invitation

sketch

[117]

28

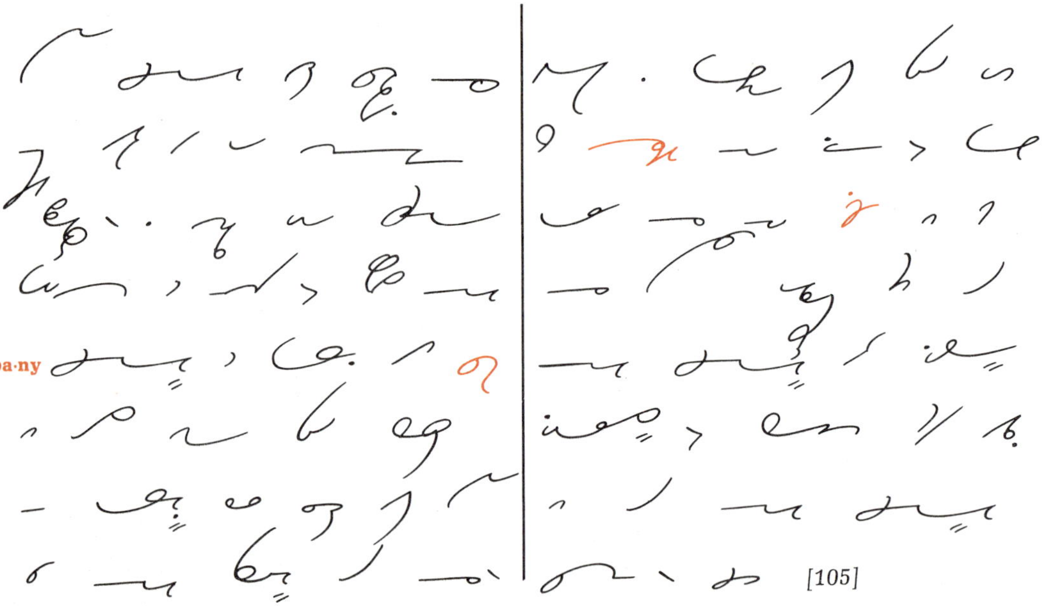

guests

whether

accompany

[105]

29

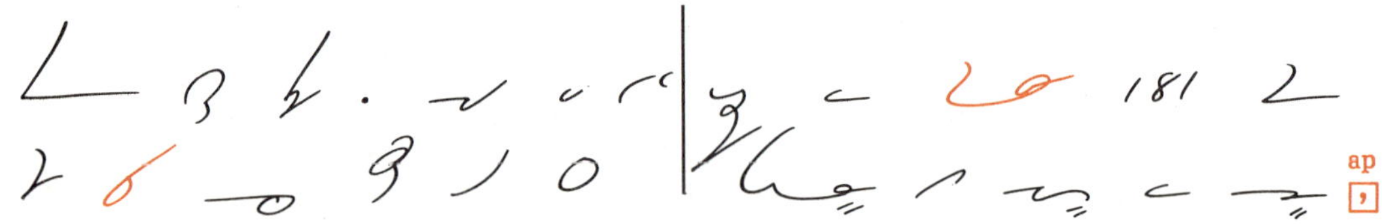

Flight

aid

ap

LESSON 4

acute·ly
breath·ing

stew·ard·ess

wrapped

ox·y·gen

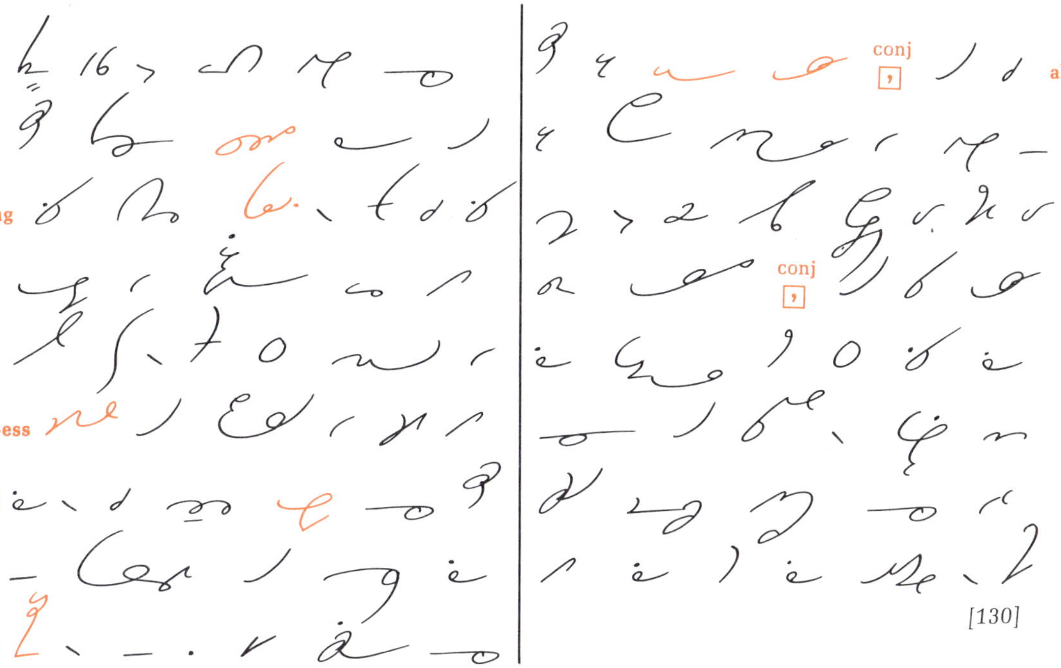

all right

conj

conj

[130]

30
ac·knowl·edge

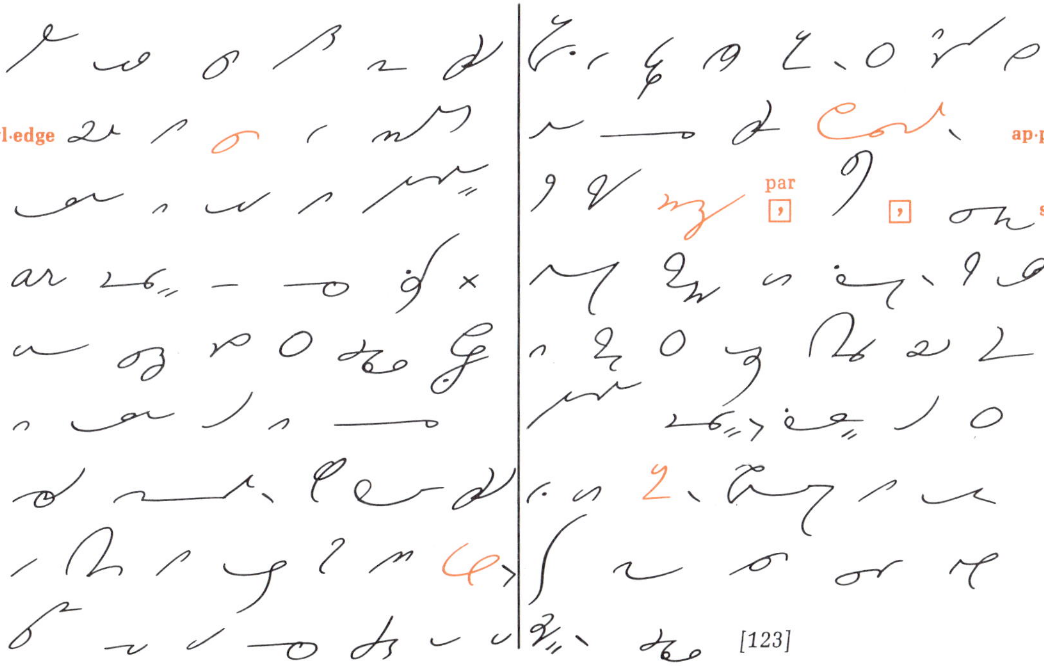

ap·pli·cants

suc·ceed

par

of·ten

praise

[123]

Building shorthand skill

31 **THEORY BRUSHUP**

Your reading goal: 50 seconds.

Phrases You

Word Beginning En-

Word Ending -tion

Word Family Sure

Brief Forms

1. You are, you will, you can be, if you, if you will, you should be, you may be, you might.
2. Enlist, enthusiastic, enforce, engagement, enjoy, enrolled.
3. Mentioned, operation, connection, national, reservation, relationship.
4. Sure, assure, pleasure, measurement, treasure, pressured.
5. Overnight, overtime, overcome, overpaid, understand, underwrite, underneath.

Building transcription skills

32 Business vocabulary builder

chauffeur (verb) To drive.
casually Informally.
hospitalized Placed in a hospital as a patient.

Reading and writing practice

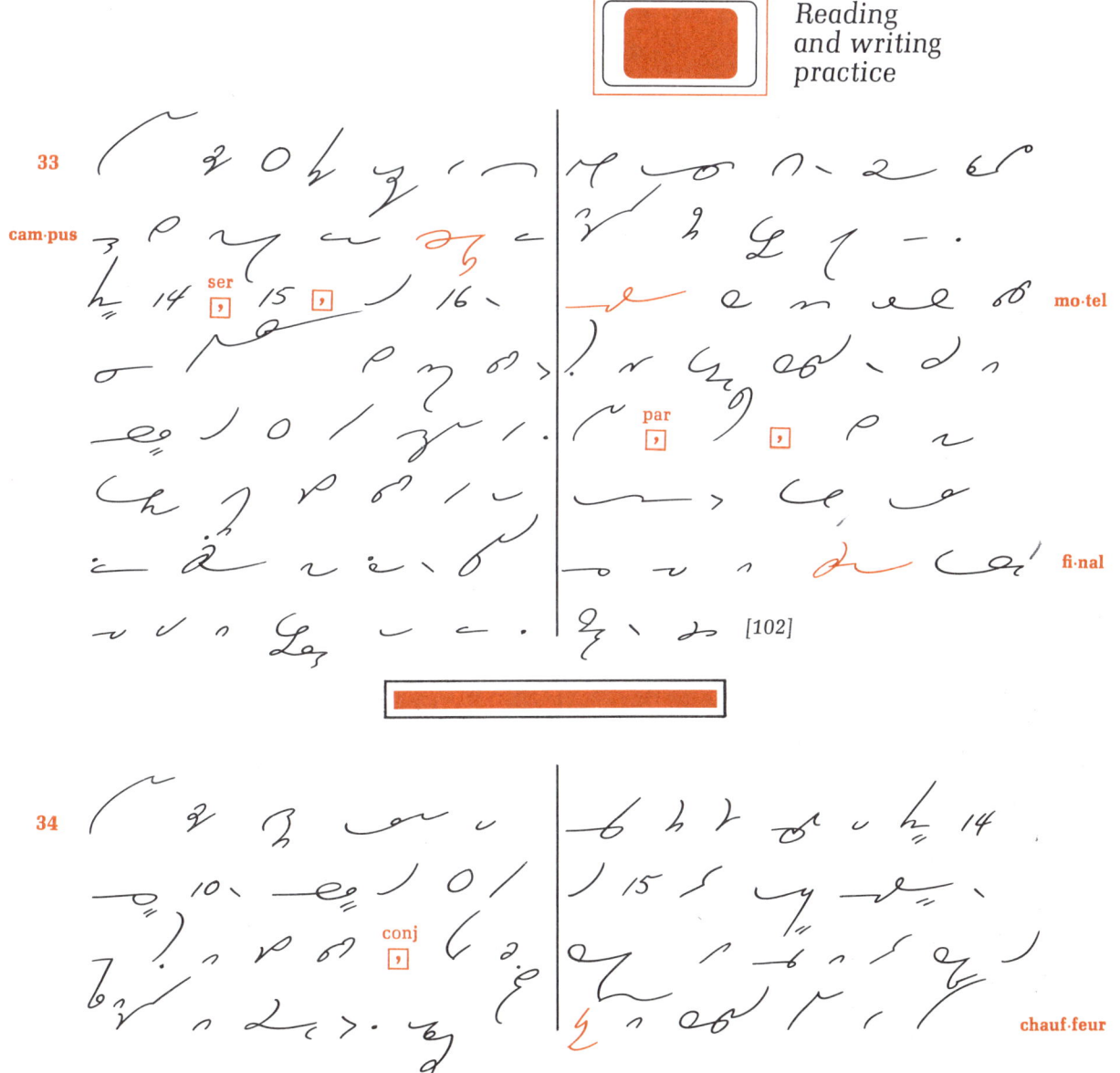

too
steaks

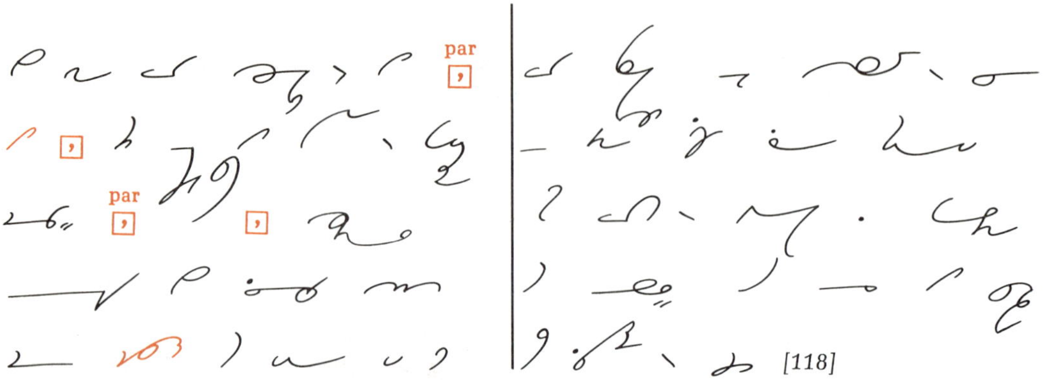

[118]

35
nec·es·sary

in·con·ve·nience

se·ri·ous·ly

en·cour·aged

hos·pi·tal·ized

as·sis·tant

dy·nam·ic

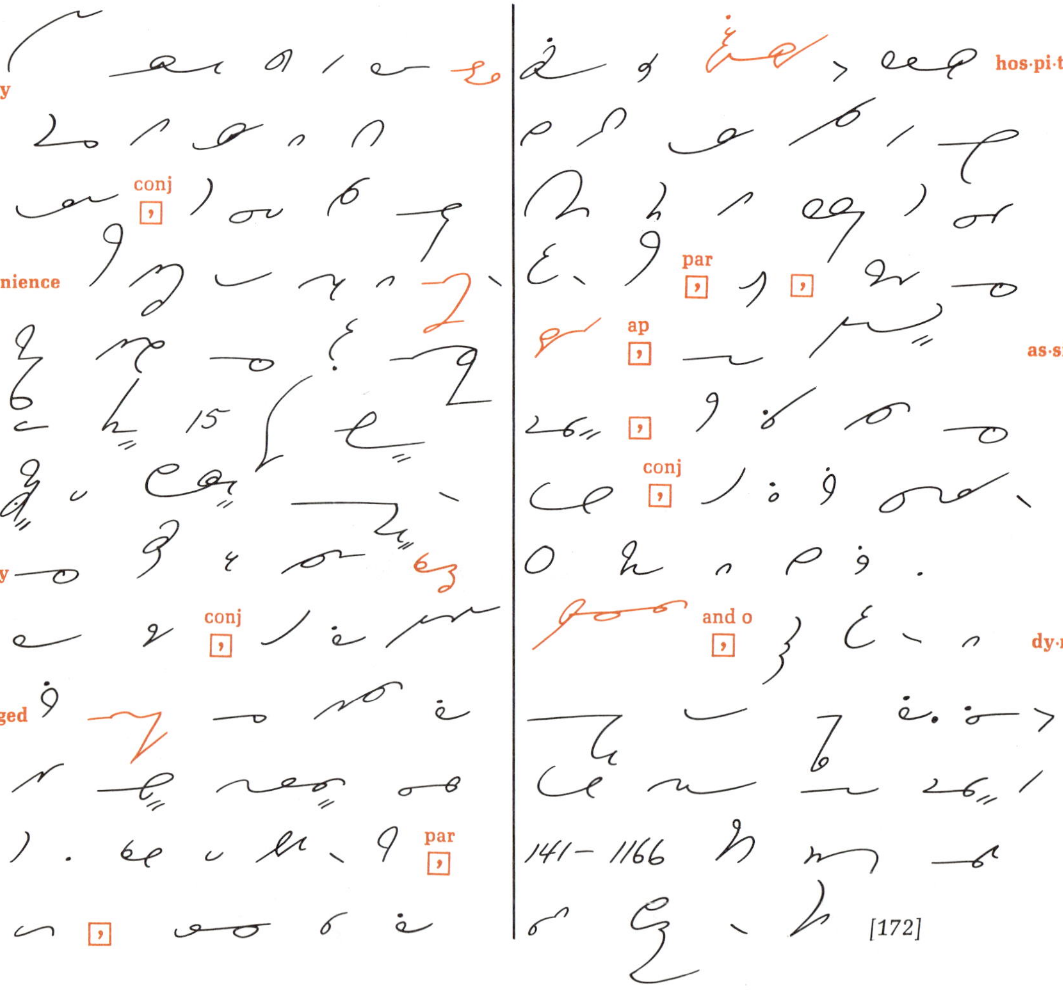

141-1166

[172]

LESSON 5

36 [shorthand] yours, as·sis·tance, en·thu·si·as·tic, ap, lo·cal, ser, ex·pense, sim·i·lar [119]

37 [shorthand] sense, conj, conj [108]

LESSON 5

The secretary's reference books

Mr. Davis congratulated himself on how fortunate he was to have a secretary like Ellen Gardiner. He had just signed a big batch of letters, and in not one of them did he find an incorrectly used word, a misspelled word, or a punctuation mark out of place. Indeed, he is fortunate; many businessmen have grown prematurely gray as a result of errors made by their secretaries in grammar, spelling, punctuation, and word usage.

If you were to ask Ellen the secret of her success, she would tell you frankly that she could always spell fairly well, but that she had never won any spelling contests; that she usually knew when to use a comma and when a semicolon, but not always; that occasionally she wasn't sure whether to use a singular verb or a plural verb. But, she would add, she always knew when she didn't know—and when she didn't know, she would look it up; she never took a chance. What is more, she always knew where to look it up!

If you were to look at Ellen's desk, you would find the following reference books that she uses whenever necessary:

1 20,000 Words. This is the reference book that she uses most frequently. She refers to it when she is in doubt about the way a word is spelled or hyphenated. It is a handy size, and the fact that it contains only spellings and syllabication enables her to find the spelling or hyphenation of any word in a matter of seconds.

Some stenographers keep 20,000 Words with the rest of the reference books at the back of their desks. Ellen, however, keeps hers next to her typewriter, where she can pick it up without any wasted motion.

2 A Dictionary. Ellen uses the dictionary when she comes across a word with which she is unfamiliar or when she has some doubt about its exact meaning or derivation. She does not, however, use it as a spelling or hyphenation reference unless she is looking for some rather unusual word that is not likely to be given in 20,000 Words.

3 Reference Manual for Stenographers and Typists. In her schoolwork, Ellen, of course, mastered all the simple uses of the various punctuation marks, but occasionally she is not sure whether to use a semicolon or a colon or a dash. Sometimes she wonders how to address a minister or an army general. Then again she may not be sure whether to type a number in words or in figures.

She quickly resolves her doubts by referring to her Reference Manual for Stenographers and Typists. No stenographer or secretary should be without this reference book.

4 An Almanac. Ellen consults her Almanac frequently. It contains facts and data on hundreds of subjects—from names of organizations to government expenditures.

5 National ZIP Code Directory. Ellen knows that a letter will reach its destination without delay if the address on the envelope contains the ZIP Code. In most cases she finds the ZIP Code included in the letterhead of the correspondence being answered. When it does not appear there, she obtains it from the National ZIP Code Directory.

The reference books on Ellen's desk are of value to every stenographer or secretary. In addition to these references, however, every secretary keeps on hand other special references that pertain to the particular type of work in which her firm may be engaged. For example, an employee in a travel agency quickly learns that a railroad guide, an airline guide, and a hotel directory are "must" references. A secretary to a lawyer refers often to a law dictionary, and so on.

When the time comes for you to take your place at a stenographer's or secretary's desk, you will be wise to follow Ellen's example: If you are not sure about something, if you don't know, look it up!

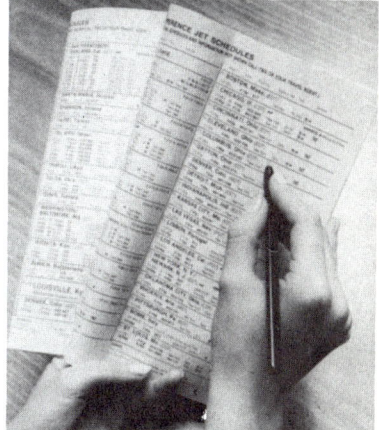

Punctuation brushup

In Chapter 2 you will review the use of commas with introductory expressions and with nonrestrictive clauses.

Introductory commas will be treated under the four headings listed below. Next to each of these headings is the indication that will appear in the Reading and Writing Practice exercises for that use of the comma.

, when clause when ⟨,⟩   **, if clause** if ⟨,⟩

, as clause as ⟨,⟩   **, introductory** intro ⟨,⟩

All introductory dependent clauses beginning with words other than *when, as,* and *if* will be classified as ", introductory."

When the original shipment is located, we will make the necessary adjustments.
As you know, we guarantee our cameras for a year.
If you are in urgent need of the notebooks, wire us.
Unless we receive our supplies soon, we shall be in difficulty.

When the main clause comes first, however, no comma is used between the main clause and the dependent clause.

We shall be in difficulty unless we receive our supplies soon.
Wire us if you are in urgent need of the notebooks.

A comma is also required after introductory words and explanatory expressions such as *frankly, consequently, on the contrary, for instance.*

Frankly, I cannot wait any longer.
On the contrary, you are the one who made the error.

, nonrestrictive

Nonrestrictive, or nonessential, clauses or phrases are set off by commas. A nonrestrictive clause or phrase is one that may be omitted without changing the meaning of the sentence.

restrictive—no commas *All persons who are old enough to vote should register.*
nonrestrictive—commas *John Smith, who is old enough to vote, should register.*

Each time the nonrestrictive use of the comma occurs in the Reading and Writing Practice, it will be indicated in the shorthand as shown in the margin.   nonr ⟨,⟩

42 PUNCTUATION BRUSHUP

Chapter  LESSON

Public relations

Building shorthand skill

38 THEORY BRUSHUP

Your reading goal: 55 seconds.

Phrases *Been*

1

Word Beginning *Com-*

2

Word Ending *-ful*

3

Word Family *Come*

4

Brief Forms

5

---

1 Had been, had not been, he could have been, have been, I have not been, would have been, I should have been.
2 Complaints, compliments, complete, comply, compose, compete.
3 Grateful, thoughtful, thoughtfulness, careful, helpful, helpfully, wishful.
4 Come, become, welcome, outcome, income.
5 Wish, wishes, wished, advertise, advertisement, advertiser, success, successful.

Building transcription skills

39 | Business vocabulary builder

vanity Conceit; empty pride.
diligently With steady, earnest effort.
fertile Productive.
convalescence A period in which a patient gathers strength after an illness.

Reading and writing practice

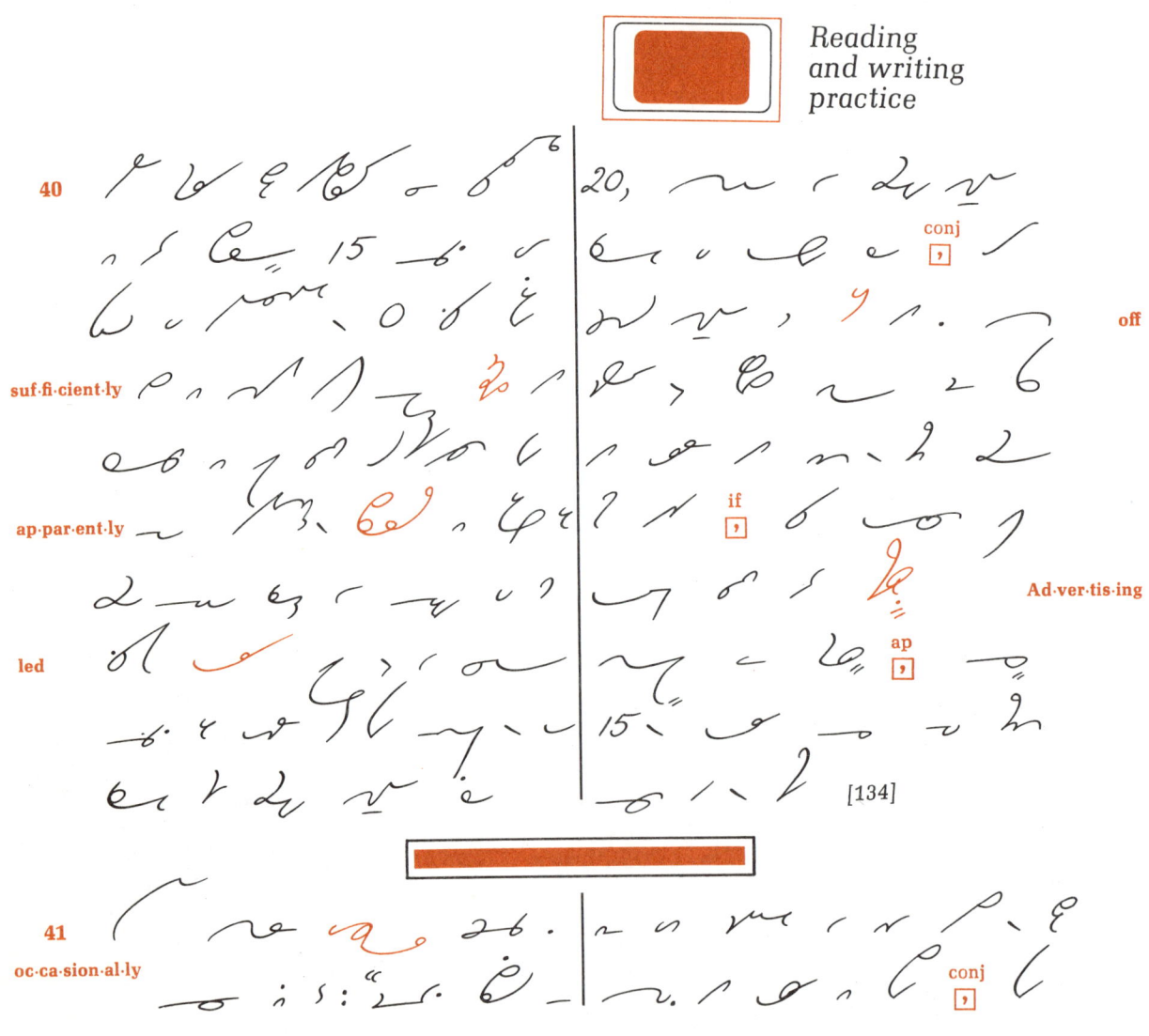

mind / re·ceived / when / com·plaints / par / com·pli·ments / if / and o / grate·ful [129]

42
con·ven·tion / conj / conj / its / com·mit·tee / for·tu·nate / mine [107]

43

of·fered nonr as

de·vel·op·ment and o fer·tile ser af·fec·tion [118]

44

ac·ci·dent ap fel·low's intro

par wor·ry con·va·les·cence conj and o [131]

Building shorthand skill

45 THEORY BRUSHUP

Your reading goal: 50 seconds.

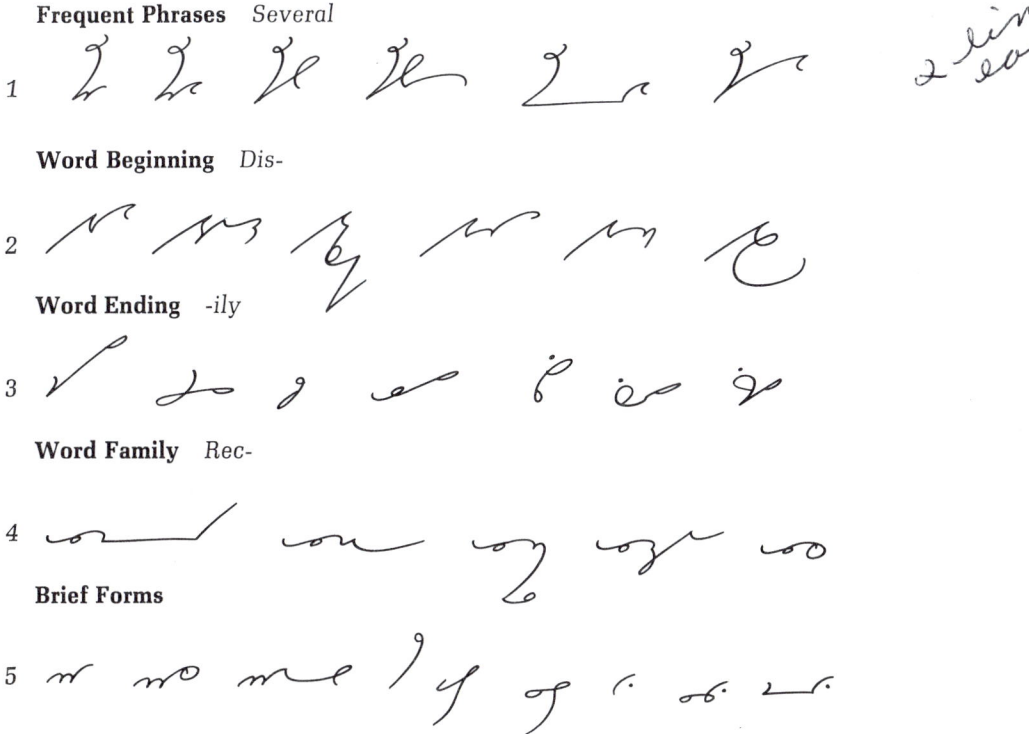

1 Several other, several others, several days, several days ago, several months, several times.
2 Distance, disastrous, discharged, discontinue, discussion, disabled.
3 Steadily, family, easily, readily, happily, heartily, hastily.
4 Recommend, recall, recovery, reconsider, require.
5 Worth, worthwhile, worthless, ever, whatever, whenever, thing, anything, something.

Building transcription skills

46 | Business vocabulary builder

gesture An act performed out of courtesy.
disastrous Causing serious misfortune or suffering.
persuasive Tending to induce a person to believe or do something.

Reading and writing practice

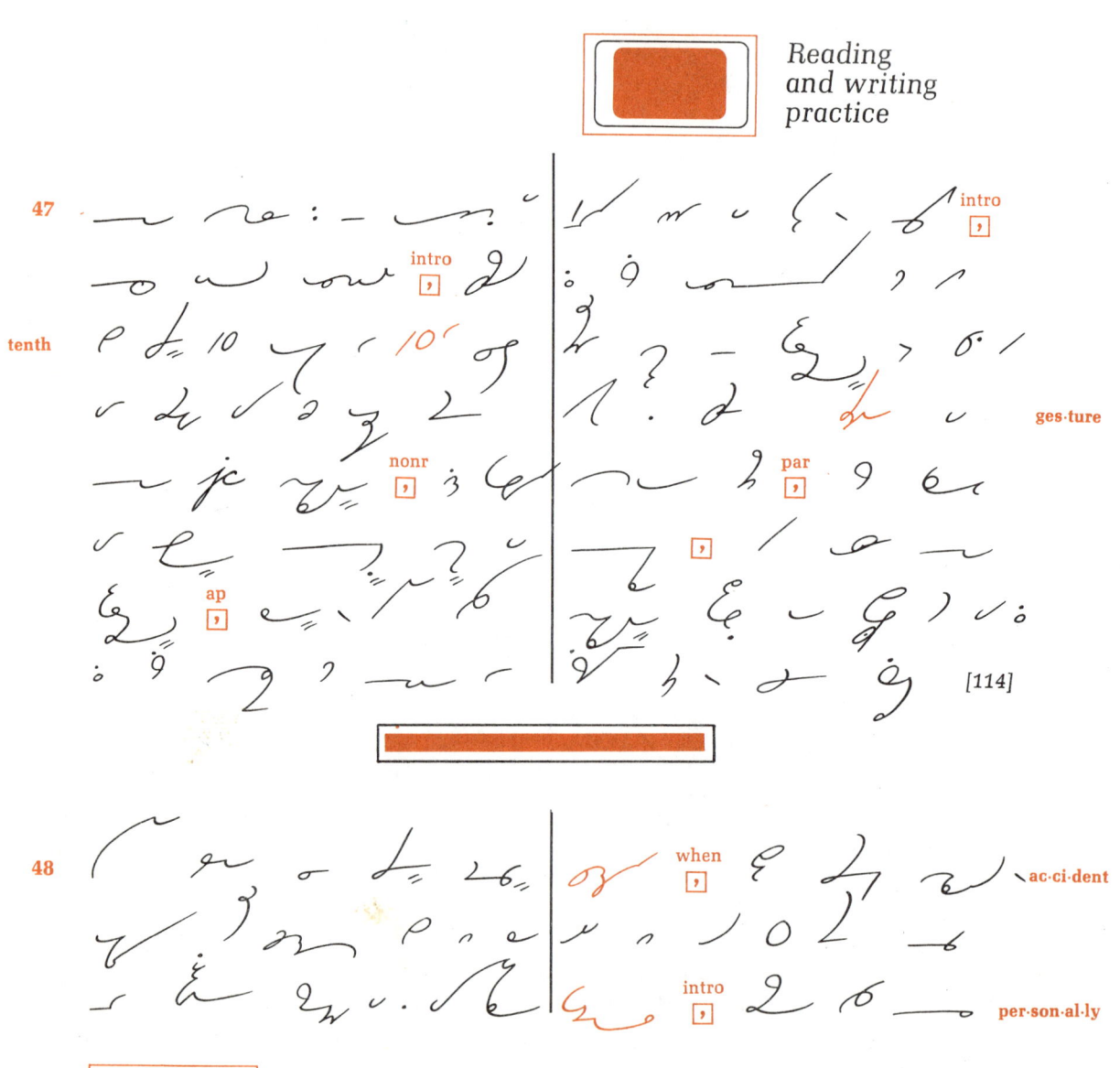

quite
re·lieved   par

                                                                    [96] re·lapse

49   re·as·sure

di·sas·trous

                                                            if

safe·ty
                                                        anx·ious·ly
                  par   [90]

50   and o

                                                  per·sua·sive
                                                      conj
al·ways

anal·y·sis   [74]

LESSON 7 | 49

51

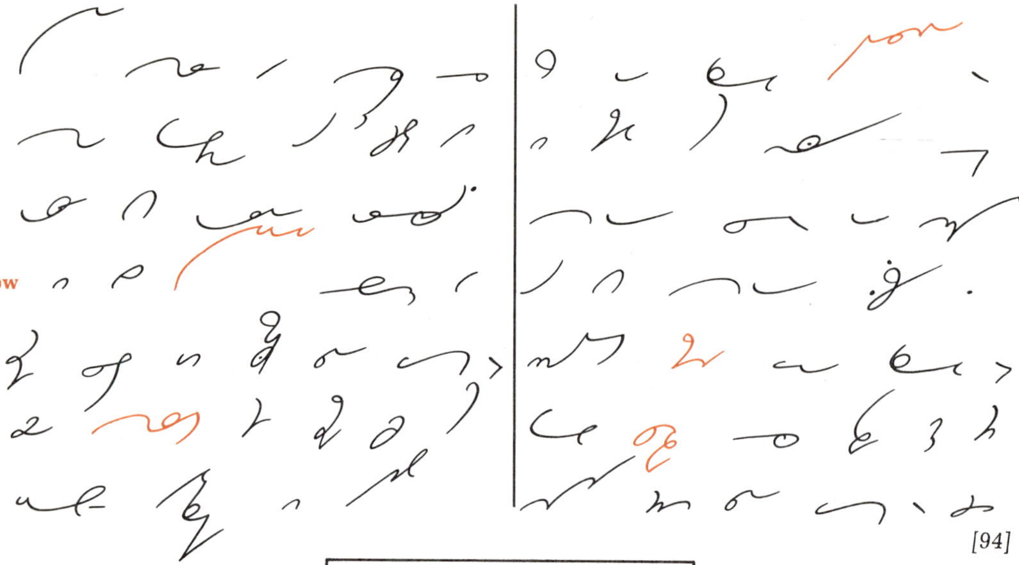

to·mor·row
grate·ful
di·rec·tor
conj
ef·fect
ac·cept
[94]

52

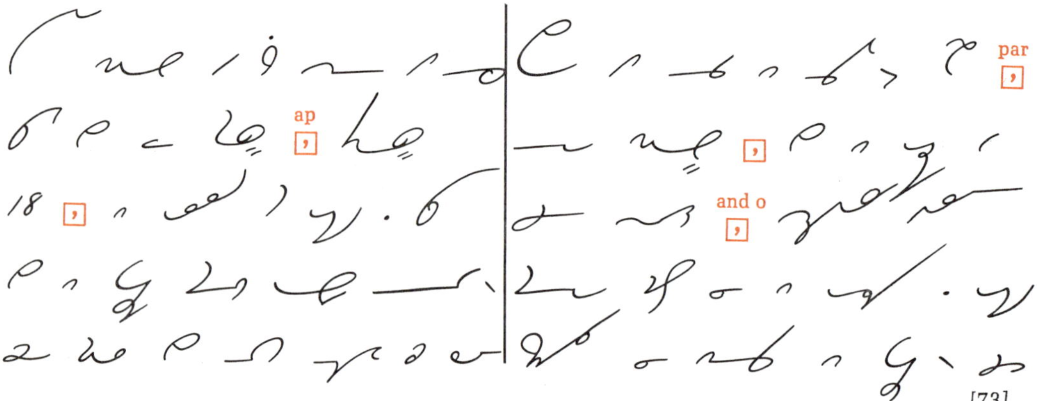

ap
18
par
and o
[73]

53

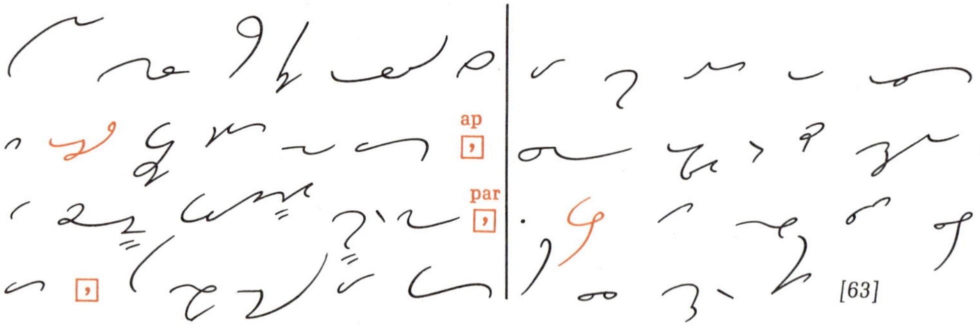

re·cent·ly
ap
par
priv·i·lege
[63]

50 | LESSON 7

Building shorthand skill

54 THEORY BRUSHUP

Your reading goal: 50 seconds.

Frequent Phrases *Omission of Words*

Word Beginnings *Inter-, Enter-*

Word Ending *-ly*

Word Family *Port*

Brief Forms

1 One of the, week or two, one of the most, for a few minutes, some of these, two or three.
2 Interest, interesting, interestingly, uninterested, entertain, entertaining, entertainingly.
3 Uniformly, really, slowly, successfully, rapidly, mostly.
4 Import, export, report, deport, importation, exportation, reportedly.
5 Organize, organization, difficult, difficulties, present, represent, representative.

Building transcription skills

55 Business vocabulary builder

commend Praise.
belated Overdue; tardy.
house organ A magazine or bulletin issued by an organization for its employees.
superb Excellent; splendid.
personable Likable.

Reading and writing practice

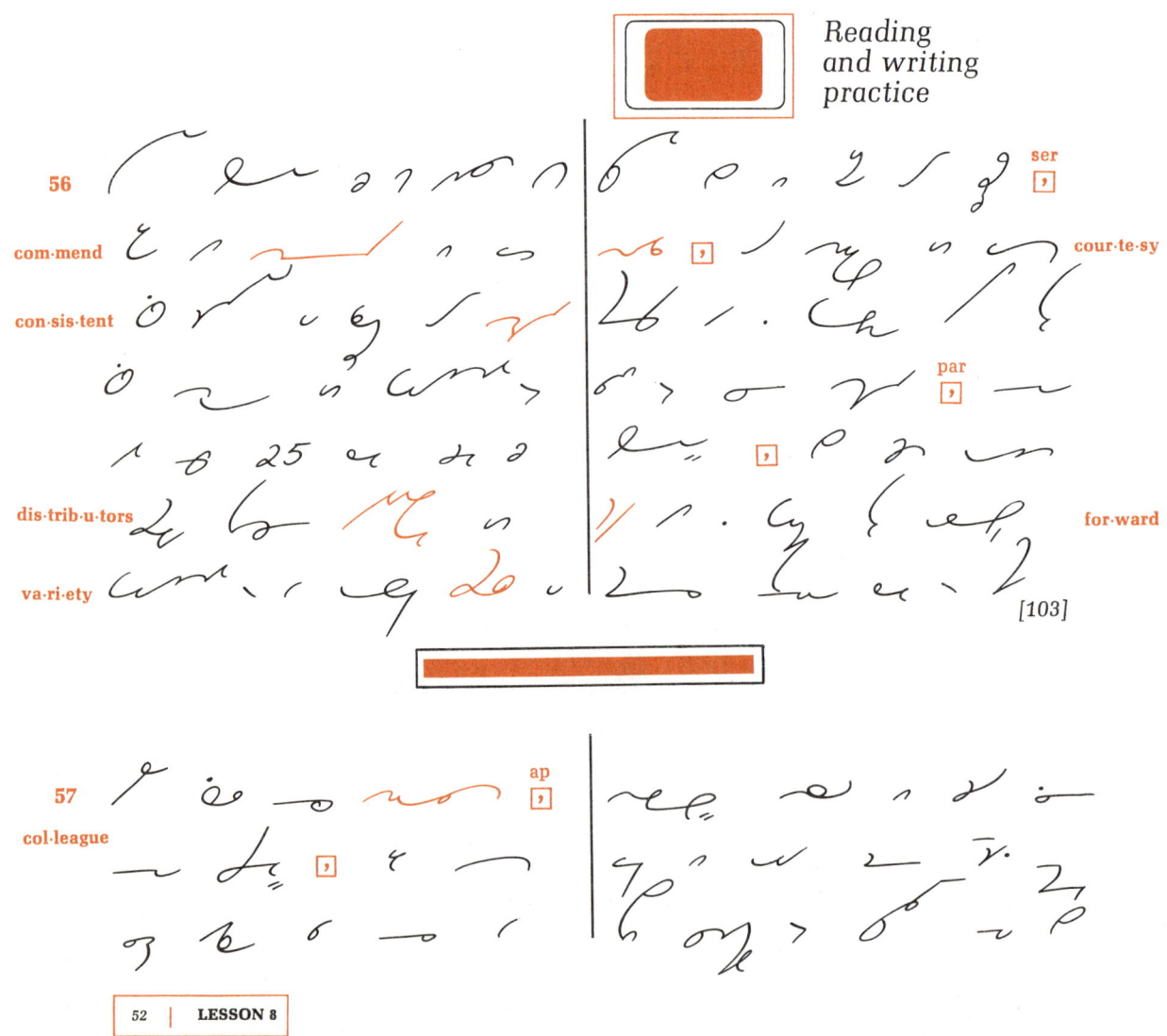

LESSON 8 | 53

59

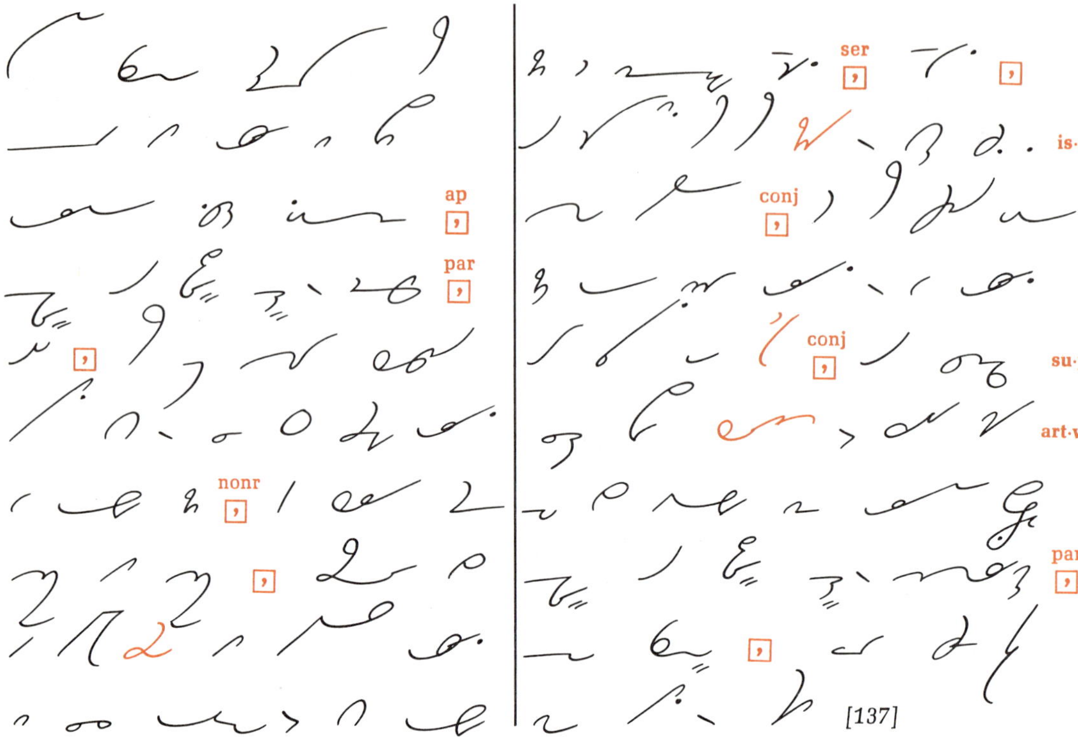

[shorthand content with annotations: ap, par, nonr, fair, ser, is·sued, conj, conj, su·perb, art·work, par] [137]

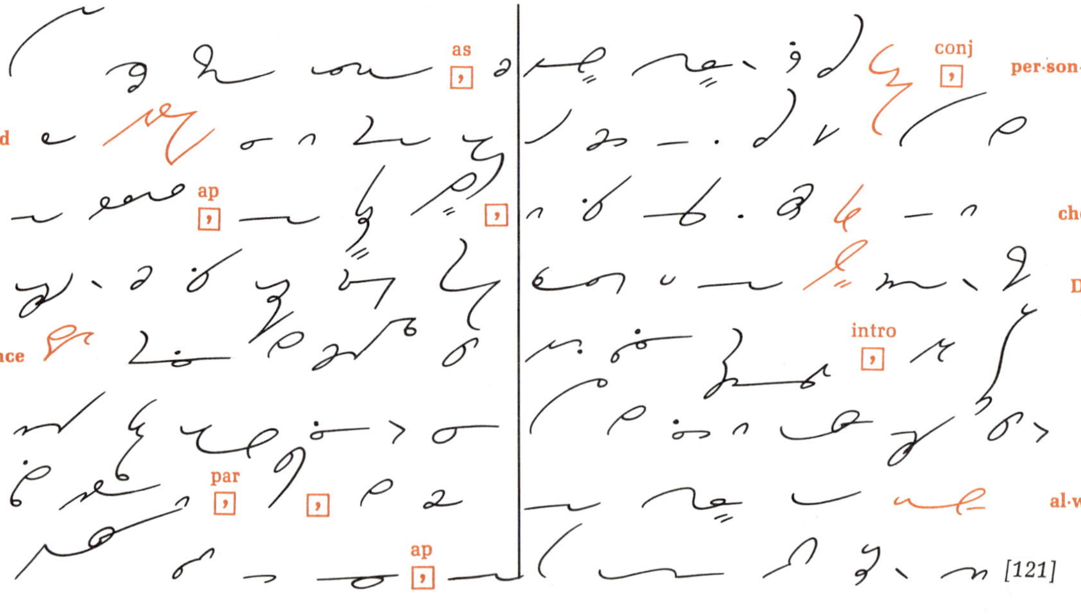

60

[shorthand content with annotations: dis·turbed, as, ap, as·sis·tance, par, ap, conj, per·son·able, choice, Day's, intro, al·ways] [121]

54 | LESSON 8

Building shorthand skill

61　THEORY BRUSHUP

Your reading goal: 50 seconds.

Phrases　Able

1 [shorthand outlines]

Word Beginnings　Em-, Im-

2 [shorthand outlines]

Word Ending　-ther

3 [shorthand outlines]

Word Family　-cate

4 [shorthand outlines]

Brief Forms

5 [shorthand outlines]

1　I would be able, you should be able, he would be able, I will be able, I may be able, you will not be able.
2　Employee, employment, emphasis, impact, improve, imply.
3　Whether, other, either, neither, leather, brother, bother, rather, father.
4　Locate, indicate, dedicate, reciprocate, complicate.
5　Progress, progressive, value, valuable, recognize, recognizes, recognition.

Building transcription skills

62 | Business vocabulary builder | **route** Course; highway.
thesis An essay written by a candidate for an academic degree.
stubbornness Persistence.
optimistic Hopeful.

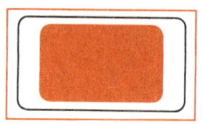

Reading and writing practice

63 [shorthand] son, lo·cat·ing, route [76]

64 [shorthand] re·ceived, re·as·sured

56 | LESSON 9

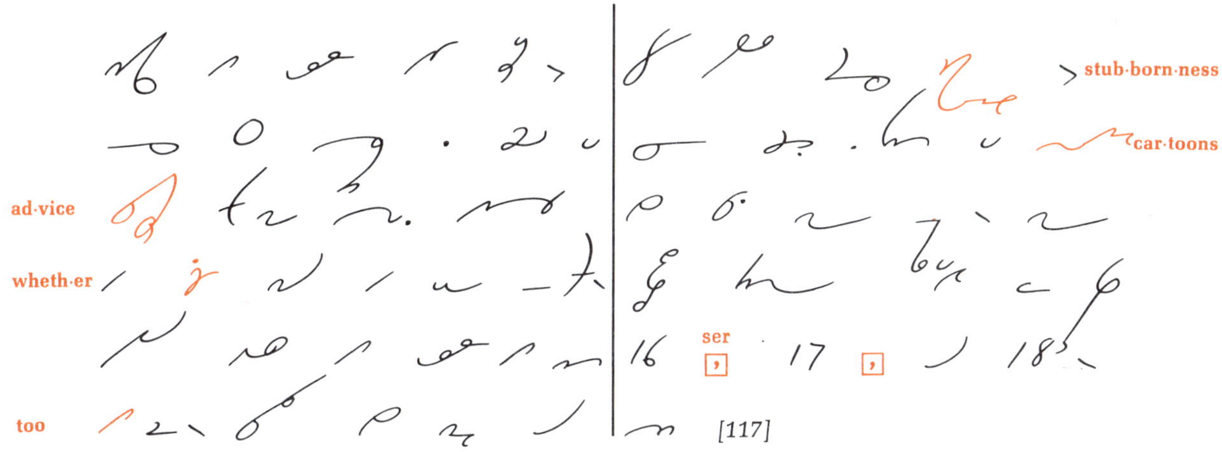

stub·born·ness
car·toons
ad·vice
wheth·er
ser
too
[117]

65 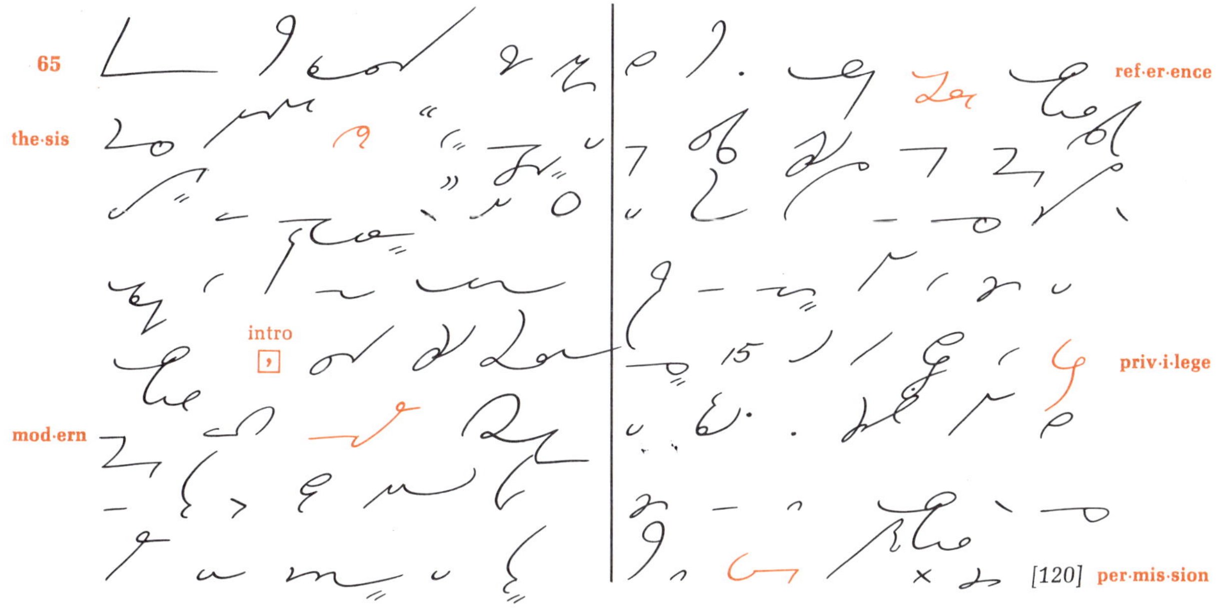
ref·er·ence
the·sis
intro
priv·i·lege
mod·ern
[120] per·mis·sion

66

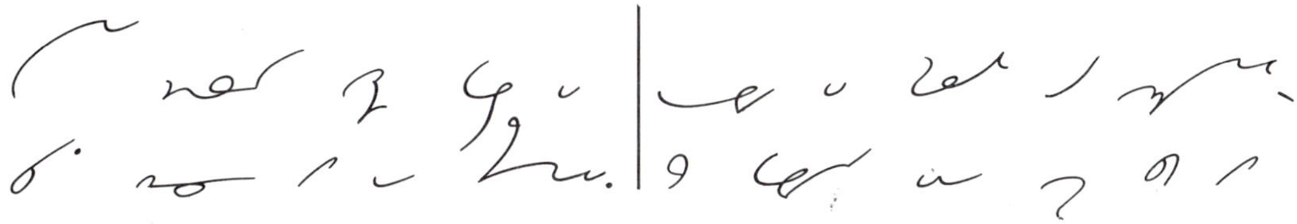

LESSON 9 | 57

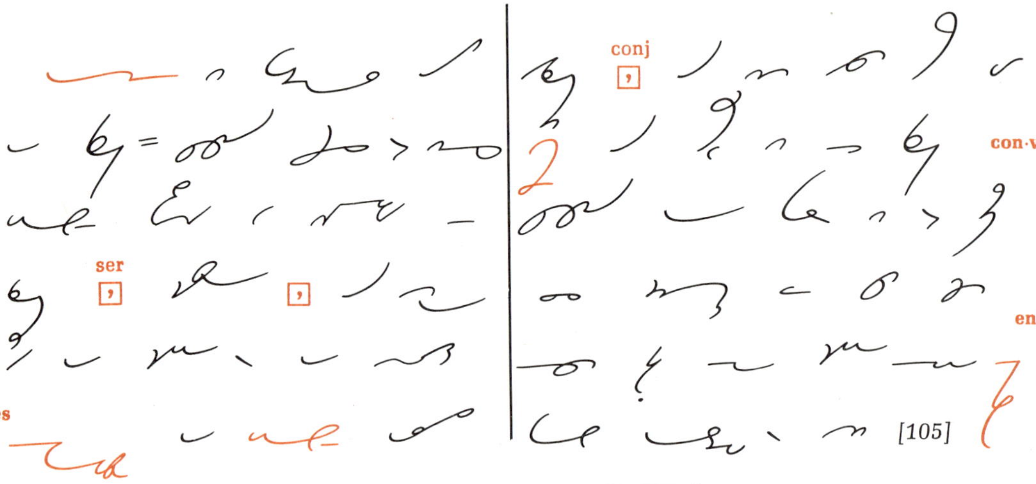

wel·come

ser

em·ploy·ees
al·ways

conj

con·ve·nience

en·joy·able
if

[105]

67

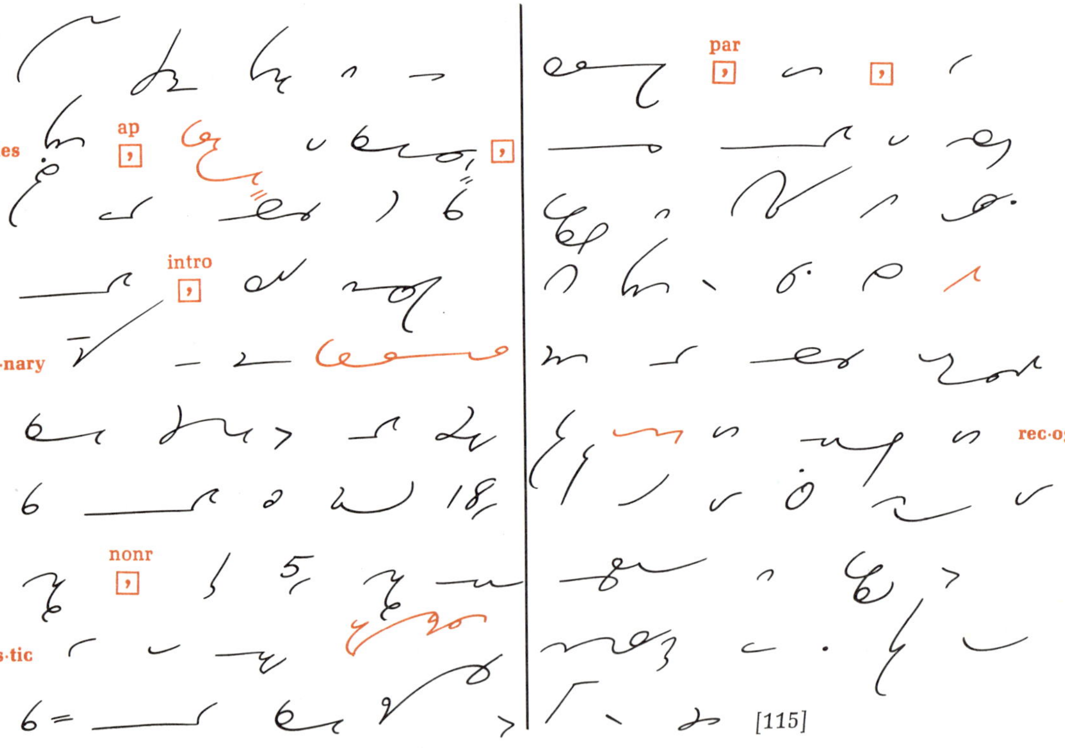

Prin·ci·ples

ap

intro

pre·lim·i·nary

nonr

op·ti·mis·tic

par

its

rec·og·ni·tion

[115]

Building shorthand skill

68 THEORY BRUSHUP

Your reading goal: 50 seconds.

Frequent Phrases *Hope*

Word Beginning *For-*

Word Ending *-lity*

Word Family *-ious*

Brief Forms

---

1 I hope, I hope that, I hope you will, we hope, we hope you are, we hope you will, we hope that, we hope that this.
2 Format, performance, forward, afford, fortune, unfortunate, force.
3 Dependability, facilities, quality, responsibilities, reliability.
4 Serious, curious, various, courteous, discourteous, obviously, furious.
5 Great, greater, business, businesslike, send, sender, sending.

Building transcription skills

69 | Business vocabulary builder | **accommodate** To oblige; to favor.
render To present or submit for payment, action, etc.
pleasurable Agreeable; satisfying.

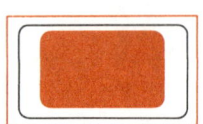 Reading and writing practice

70 [shorthand outlines]

an·noyed
dis·cour·te·ous
apol·o·gies

its
threat·ens

[113]

71 [shorthand outlines]

LESSON 10

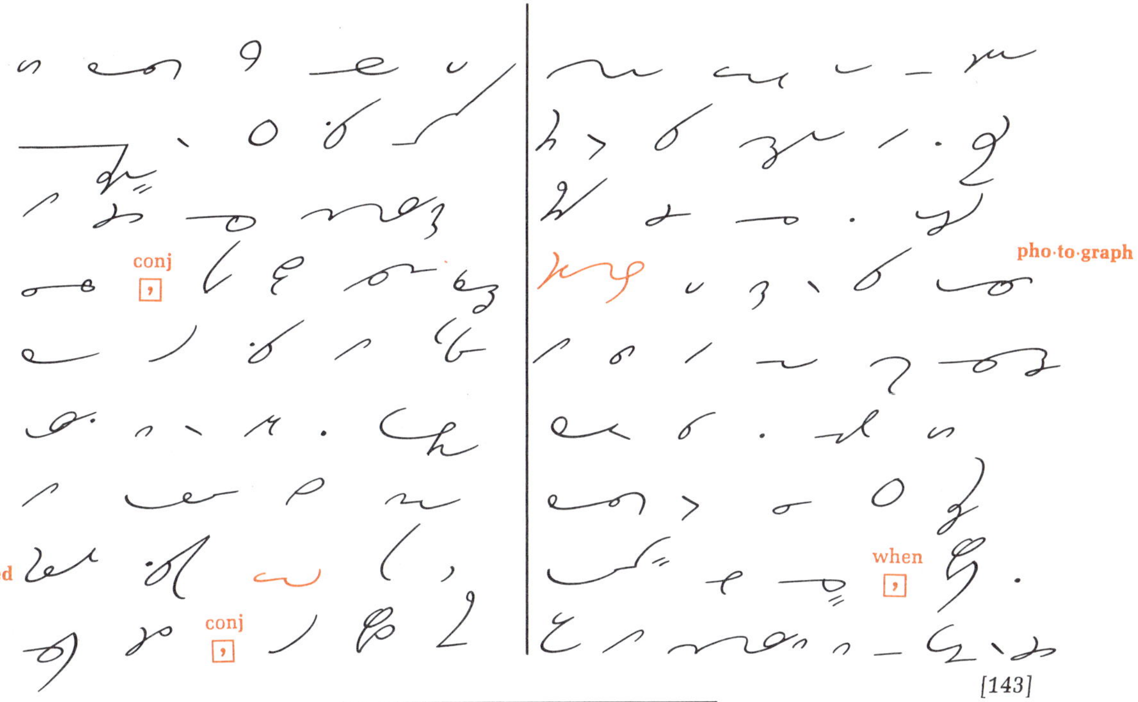

pho·to·graph
conj
hon·ored
when
conj
[143]

72
pleas·ant 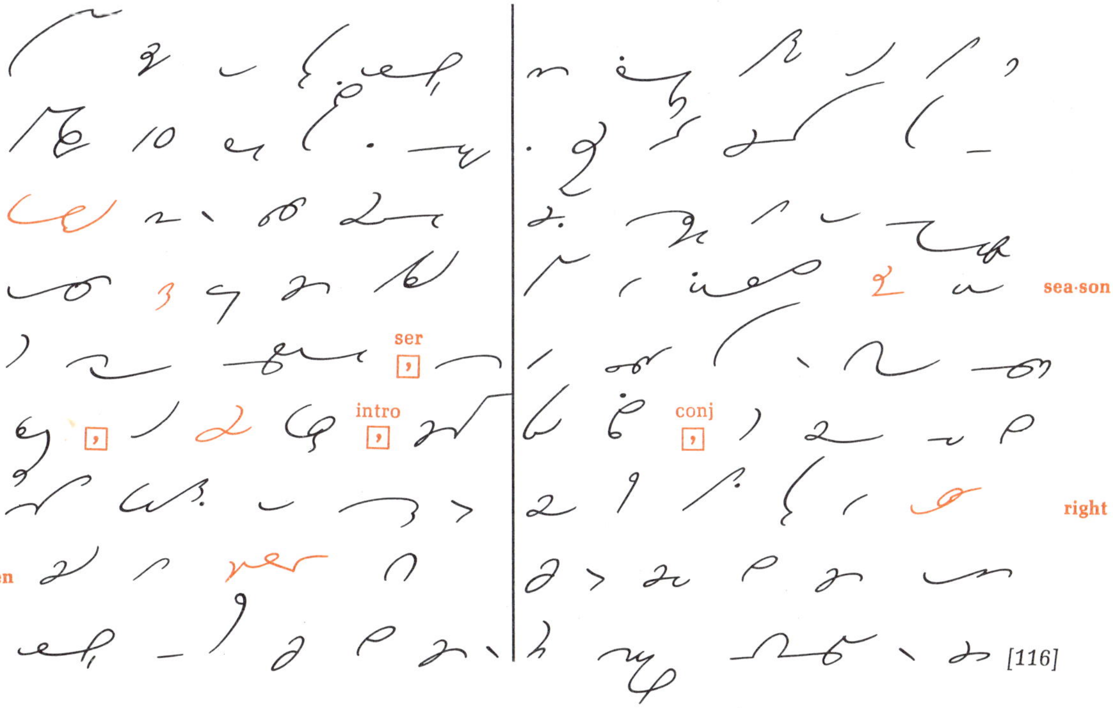
yours
sea·son
ser
fair
intro
conj
right
strength·en
[116]

LESSON 10 | 61

73

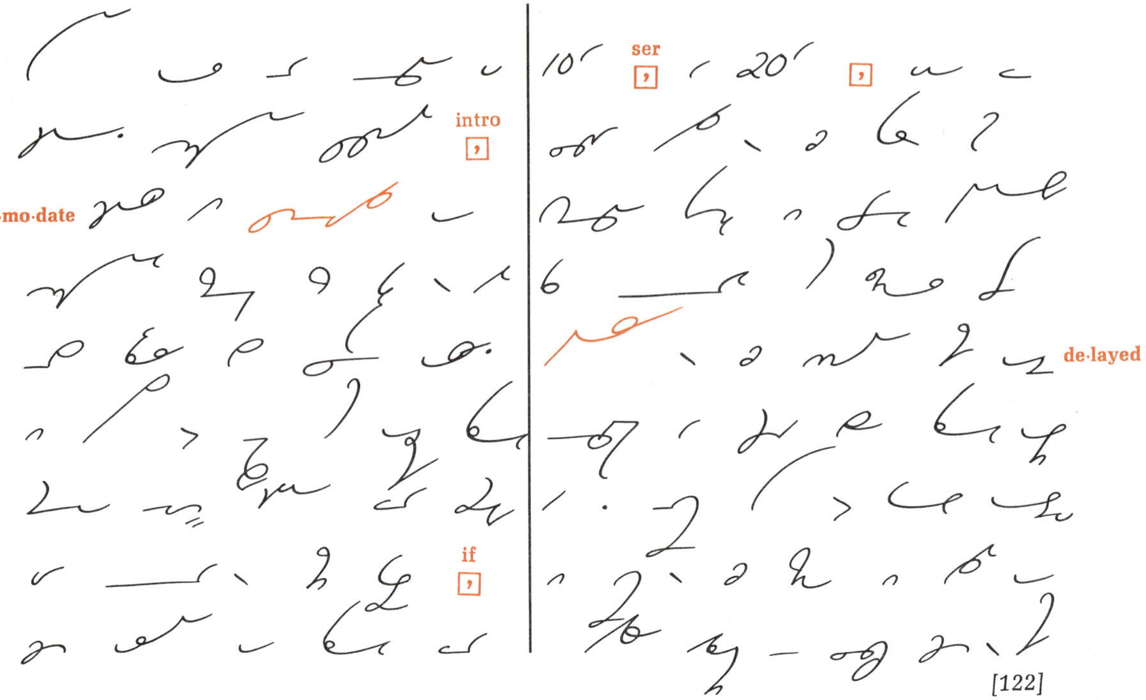

ac·com·mo·date   intro   ser   de·layed

if   [122]

74

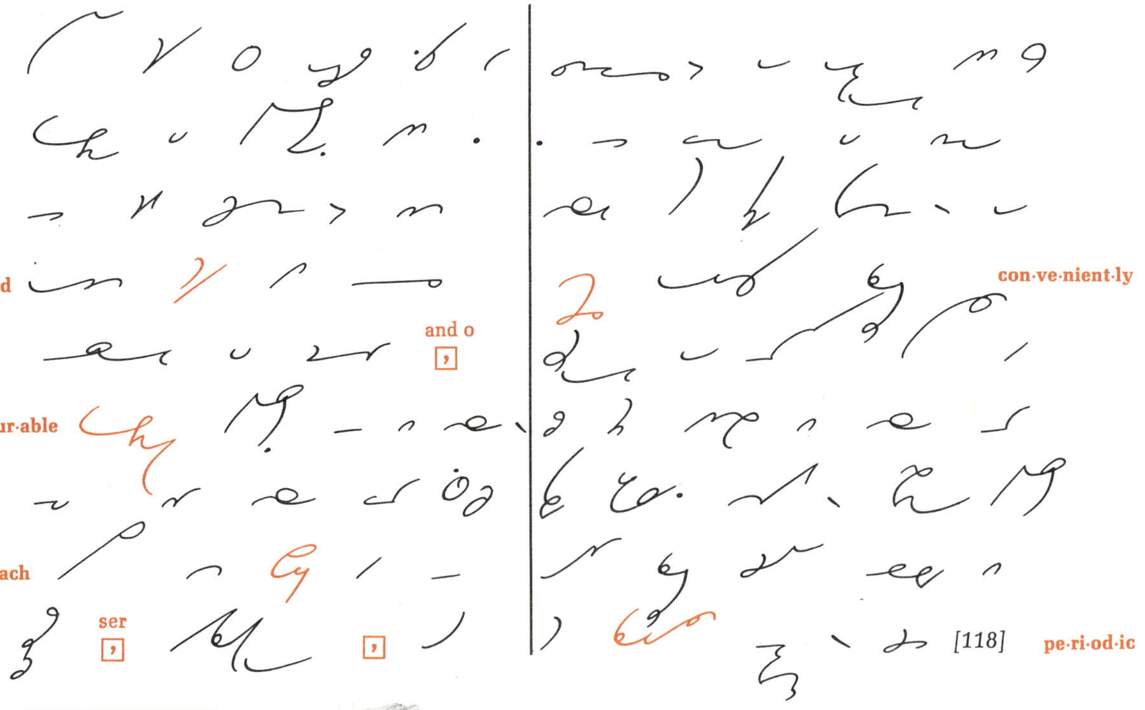

for·ward   and o   con·ve·nient·ly

plea·sur·able

ap·proach   ser   [118]   pe·ri·od·ic

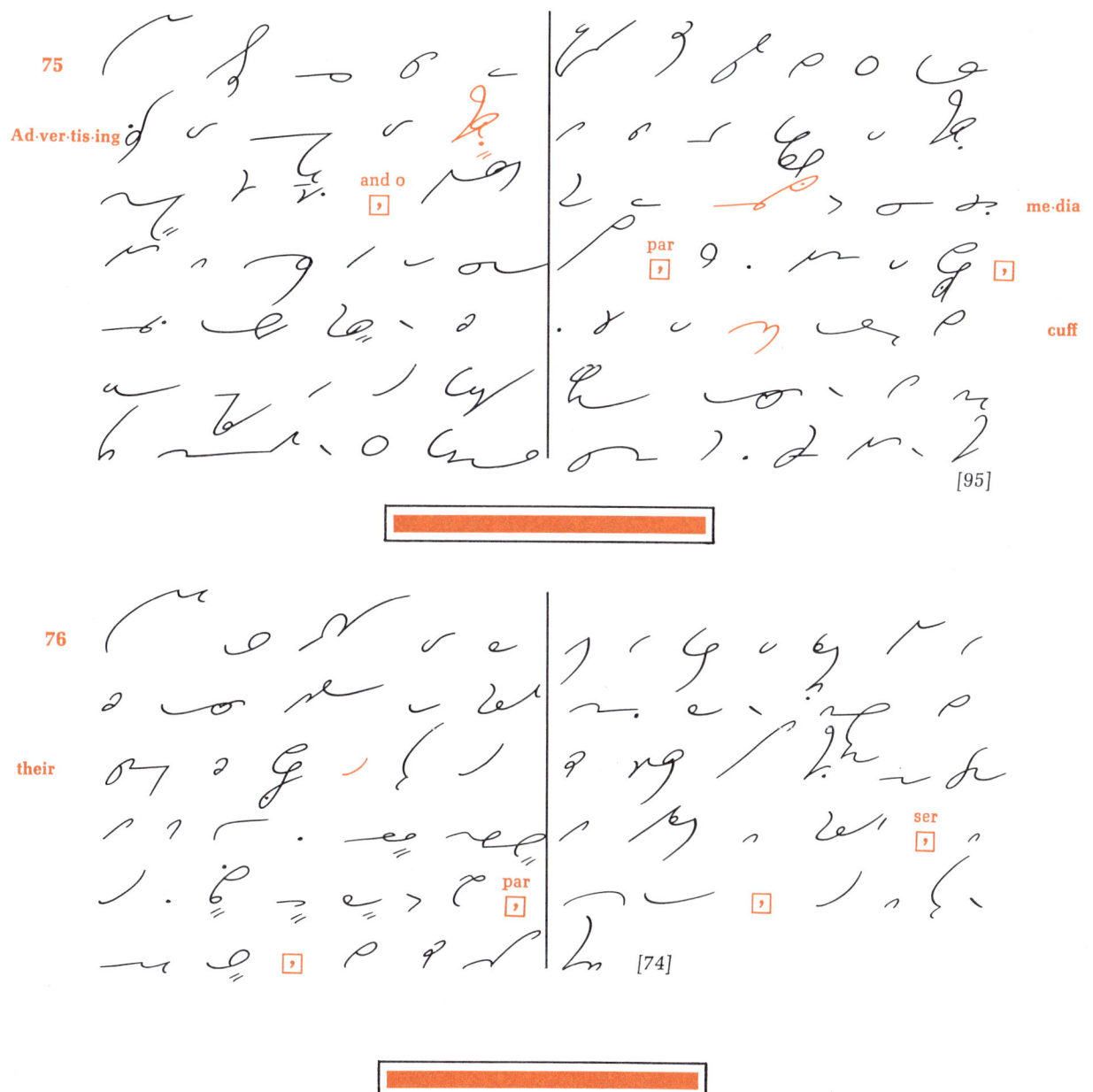

LESSON 10

The secretary's dictation tools

Many times during the day Mr. Davis calls to Ellen, "Miss Gardiner, please take a letter." Often he starts to dictate the moment she sits down, sometimes even before she sits down. A stranger witnessing this scene might think, "My, isn't he inconsiderate. You would think he would at least let the girl sit down before he begins to dictate!"

On the contrary, Mr. Davis is a very thoughtful, considerate person who is highly sensitive to the comfort and welfare of his employees. But he is a busy man, and sometimes in his efforts to make every minute count, he forgets to give his secretary a few moments to "get organized" for dictation at his desk.

The first few times Mr. Davis did this, Ellen was a little flustered, but now she takes it in her stride because she is ready for him! This is what she does each day:

As soon as she arrives at the office in the morning, she checks her dictation tools.

Her notebook

1   She places a rubber band around the pages in her notebook that have already been used. This enables her to turn to the first blank page quickly. (Exception: If there are still pages in her notebook to be

transcribed, she doesn't, of course, place them inside the rubber band—she might forget to transcribe them!)

2 She checks to be sure that she has ample paper left in her notebook for the day's dictation. If she doesn't, she obtains a second notebook and dates it on the cover. Ellen, in the middle of dictation, never has to say, "I must get another notebook; I've run out of paper."

3 She dates the page on the bottom so that she can easily find the dictation of any given day.

Her pen

Some stenographers and secretaries prefer a regular fountain pen with which to take dictation. Ellen, however, uses a ball-point pen with a fine point. She always takes two pens with her, however, just in case one might "run dry" during dictation.

Her pencil

Ellen brings along a colored pencil that she uses to flag important letters and telegrams.

Her folder

Ellen also takes a file folder with her to dictation. In this folder she keeps correspondence and other papers that she wishes to discuss with her employer. She also places in

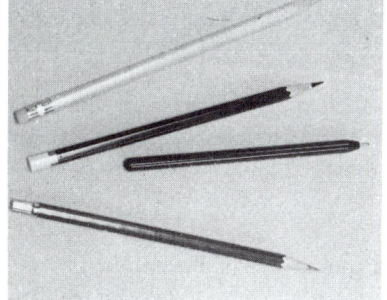

this folder, face down, the letters that her employer hands her after he has dictated answers to them. From these letters she obtains the inside addresses for her transcripts. She always keeps these materials handy so that she can respond immediately when her employer calls her to his office. When that occurs, Ellen places her folder, her notebook—open to a blank page—her colored pencil, and one ball-point pen in her left hand. In her right hand she holds a second ball-point pen, ready to write. (Of course, if Ellen were left-handed, she would place the folder, notebook, colored pencil, and one ball-point pen in her right hand and the second ball-point pen in her left hand.) In that way she is ready to take dictation should Mr. Davis start dictating while she is still walking to his desk.

Looking after her writing tools, however, is not all that Ellen does in the morning. She also cleans the type on her typewriter. If her typewriter needs a new ribbon, she puts one in. In addition, she checks to be sure that she has all the stationery items she will need.

Any one of these predictation preparations may seem minor, but, added together, they save a great deal of time.

Punctuation brushup

In Chapter 3 you will review the following: the use of the period to indicate a courteous request, the hyphen, the apostrophe, and one use of the semicolon.

. courteous request

Very often one businessman may wish to persuade another to take some definite action. He could make his request for action with a direct statement, such as:

I want to hear from you by return mail.

A direct statement of this type, however, might antagonize the reader. Many businessmen, therefore, prefer to make such a request in the form of a question.

Won't you let me hear from you by return mail.

Where a request for definite action is put in the form of a question, a period is used at the end of the sentence.

This is how you can decide whether to use a question mark or a period:

1. If the question calls for an answer in the form of *action,* use a period.
2. If the question calls for a *yes-or-no* answer, use a question mark.

Whenever the period is used in this situation in the Reading and Writing Practice, it will be indicated in the shorthand as shown in the margin.

cr
·

Hyphens

You can quickly decide whether to use a hyphen in compound expressions like *past due* or *well trained* by observing these rules:

1. If a noun follows the expression, use a hyphen.

We are concerned about your past-due *account* (noun).

Whenever a hyphenated expression occurs in the Reading and Writing Practice, it will be called to your attention in the margin thus: **two-page**
hyphenated
before noun

2 If *no* noun follows the compound expression, do *not* use a hyphen.

Your account is past due.

Occasionally these expressions in which a hyphen is not used will be called to your attention thus: **well written**
     no noun,
     no hyphen

3 No hyphen is used in a compound modifier where the first part of the expression is an adverb that ends in *ly*.

He was editor of a widely read magazine.

To be sure that you are not tempted to put a hyphen in expressions of this type, your attention will be called to them in the Reading and Writing Practice thus: **wide·ly used**
     no hyphen
     after ly

The apostrophe

1 A noun that ends in an *s* sound and is followed by another noun is usually a possessive, calling for an apostrophe before the *s* when the word is singular.

This company's advertising is designed for three colors.

2 A plural noun ending in *s* calls for an apostrophe *after* the *s* to form the possessive.

Their employees' wages have been raised.

3 An irregular plural calls for an apostrophe *before* the *s* to form the possessive.

We sell children's toys.

4 The possessive forms of pronouns do not require an apostrophe.

These papers are theirs, *not* ours.

; no conjunction

A semicolon is used to separate two independent, but closely related, clauses when no conjunction is used to connect the clauses.

Mary received an appointment in the personnel department; her sister was not appointed.

The above sentence could be written as two sentences.

Mary received an appointment in the personnel department. Her sister was not appointed.

Because the two thoughts are closely related, however, the use of the semicolon seems more appropriate.

Each time this use of the semicolon occurs in the Reading and Writing Practice, it will be indicated in the shorthand as shown in the margin.

nc
;

Personnel relations

Building shorthand skill

77 THEORY BRUSHUP

Your reading goal: 45 seconds.

Frequent Phrases Special

1

Word Beginning Per-

2

Word Ending -ual

3

Word Family -less

4

Brief Forms

5

1 To know, to make, to me, of course, to do, as soon as, as soon as possible, let us know.
2 Personal, personnel, performance, permit, permission, perfect.
3 Manual, scheduled, actual, annually, equal.
4 Reckless, restless, unless, needless, thoughtless.
5 One, anyone, someone, question, questionable, unquestionable, probable, probably.

Building transcription skills

78 | Business vocabulary builder | **internal injuries** Wounds within the body.
privileged Favored.
authorized (verb) Empowered; justified.

Reading and writing practice

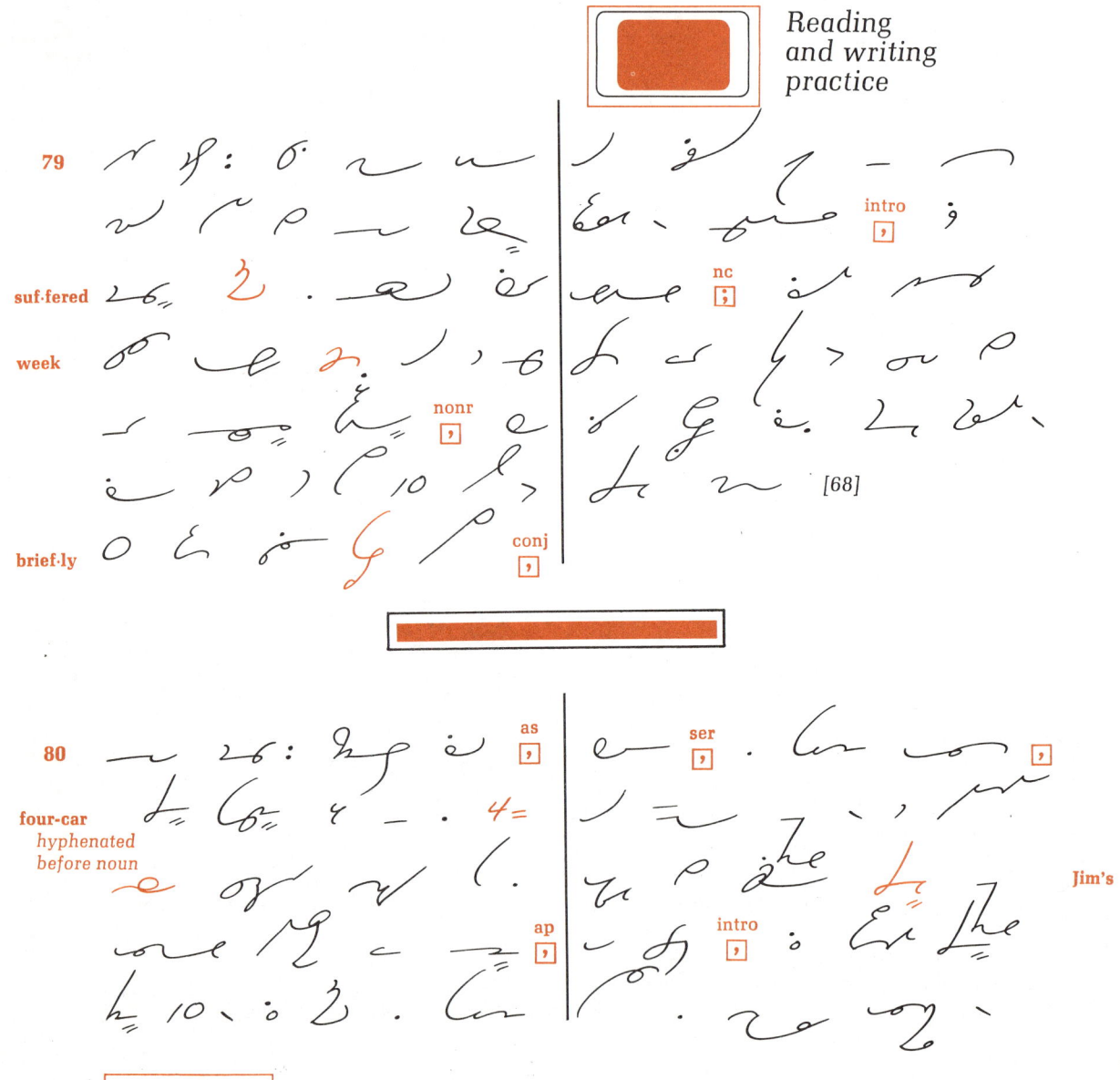

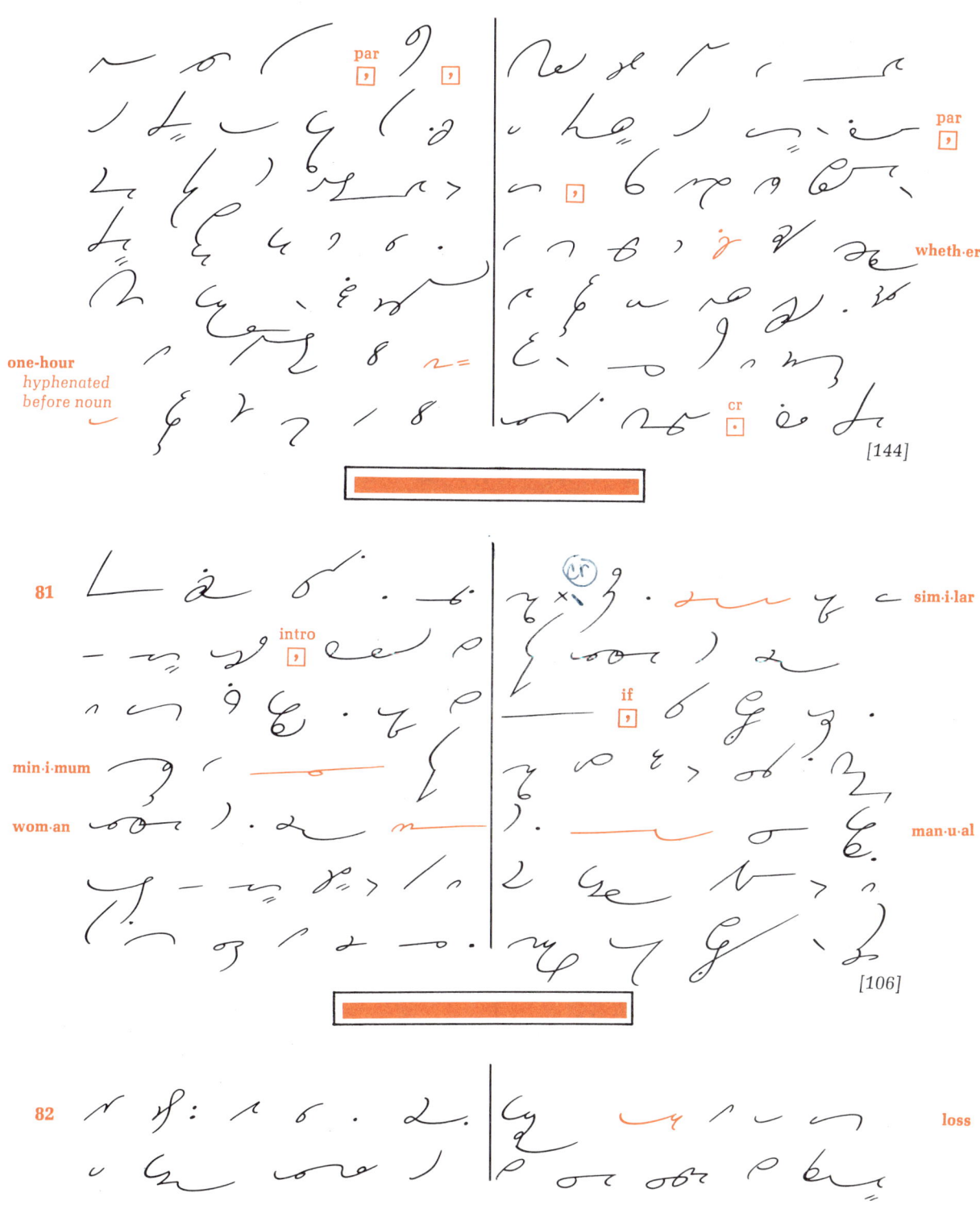

LESSON 11

Building shorthand skill

84 THEORY BRUSHUP

Your reading goal: 45 seconds.

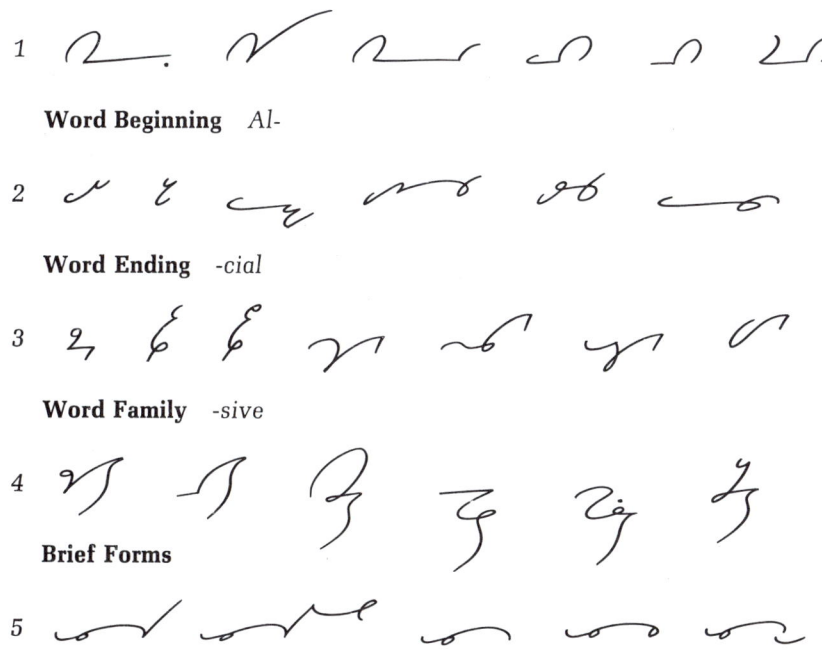

1 This morning, this time, this month, on this, in this, from this.
2 Although, also, almost, altogether, alternate, almanac.
3 Essential, special, especial, confidential, credential, residential, potential.
4 Extensive, intensive, defensive, impressive, comprehensive, offensive.
5 Regard, regardless, regular, regularly, regularity.

Building transcription skills

85

| Business vocabulary builder | **immensely** Tremendously; greatly.
alternatives Choices.
precede To go before; to be earlier than. |

Reading and writing practice

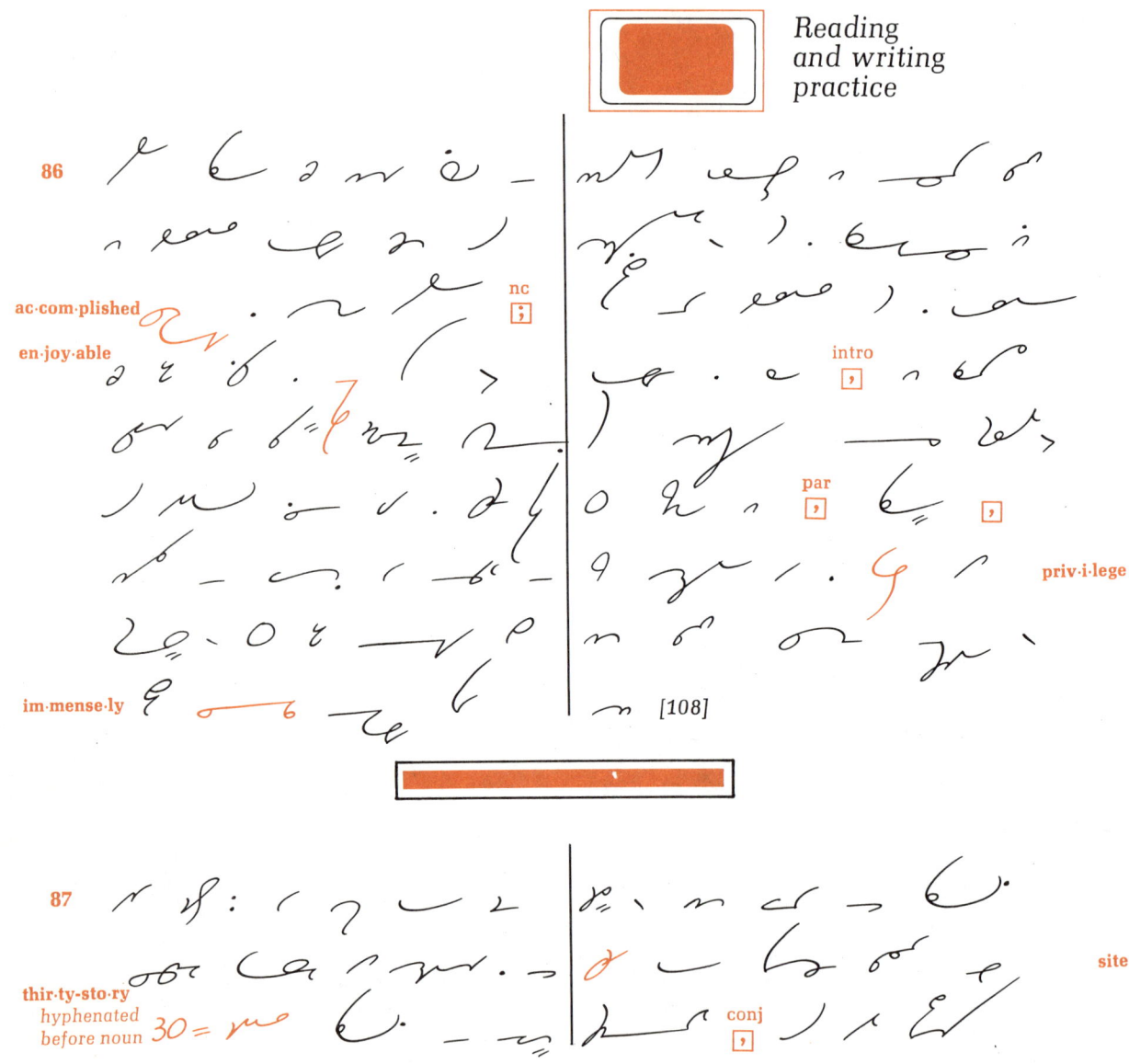

86
ac·com·plished
en·joy·able
im·mense·ly
nc
intro
par
priv·i·lege
[108]

87
thir·ty-sto·ry
hyphenated before noun
conj
site

LESSON 12

LESSON 12

ex·ten·sion [154]

89 hon·ored, im·pres·sive, mar·riage, hus·band's, intro, health, nonr [132]

90 re·ceived, ques·tion·naire [69]

Building shorthand skill

91 THEORY BRUSHUP

Your reading goal: 45 seconds.

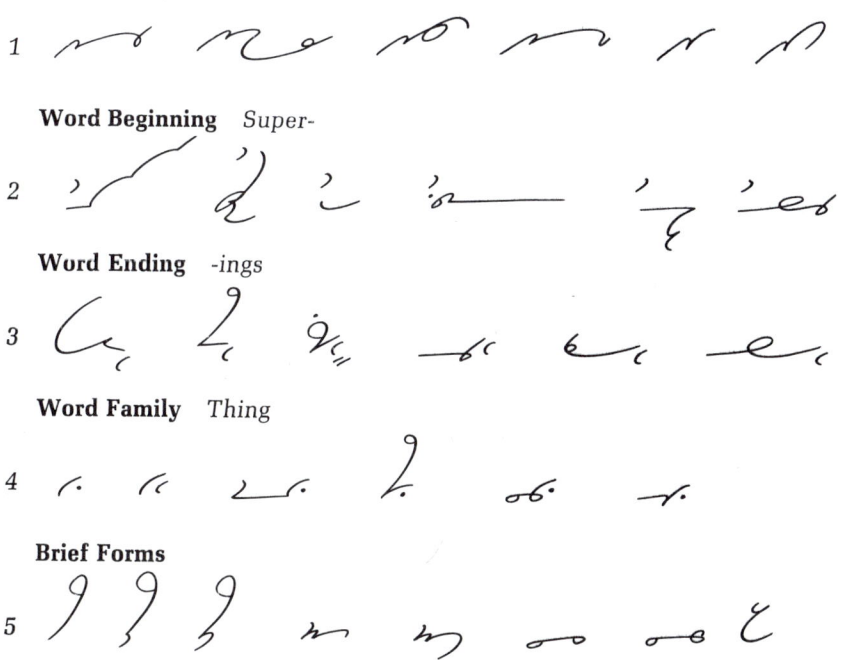

1 To get, to complete, to take, to go, to the, to this.
2 Superintendent, supervisor, superior, superhuman, superimpose, supermarket.
3 Belongings, evenings, Hastings, meetings, ceilings, mailings.
4 Thing-think, things-thinks, something, everything, anything, nothing.
5 Advantage, advantages, advantageous, success, successful, immediate, immediately, opportunity.

Building transcription skills

92

Business vocabulary builder	
precautions	Protective measures.
tuition	The price of, or payment for, instruction.
expeditiously	Promptly; quickly.
unsightly	Not pleasing to the eye.

Reading and writing practice

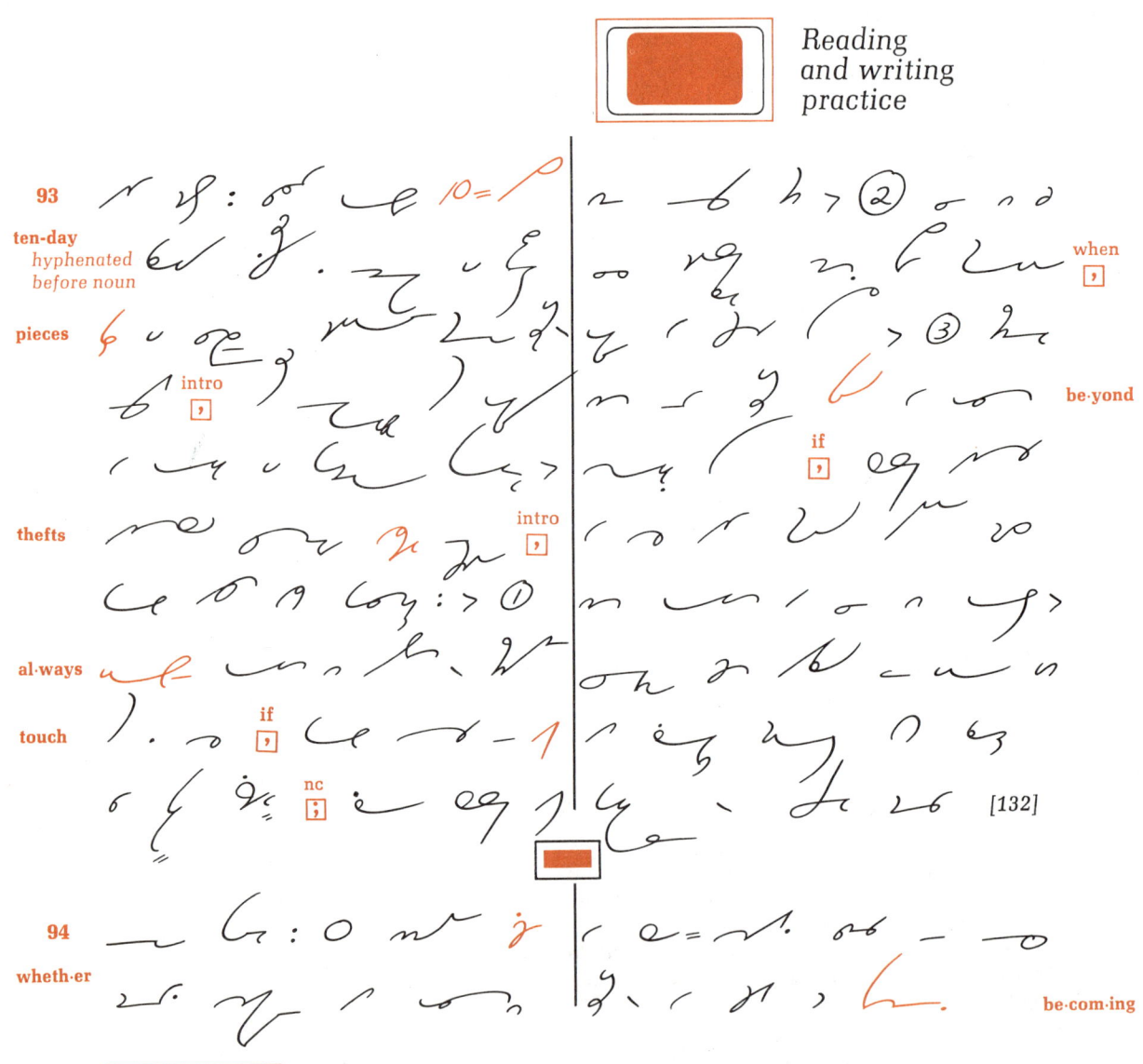

78 | LESSON 13

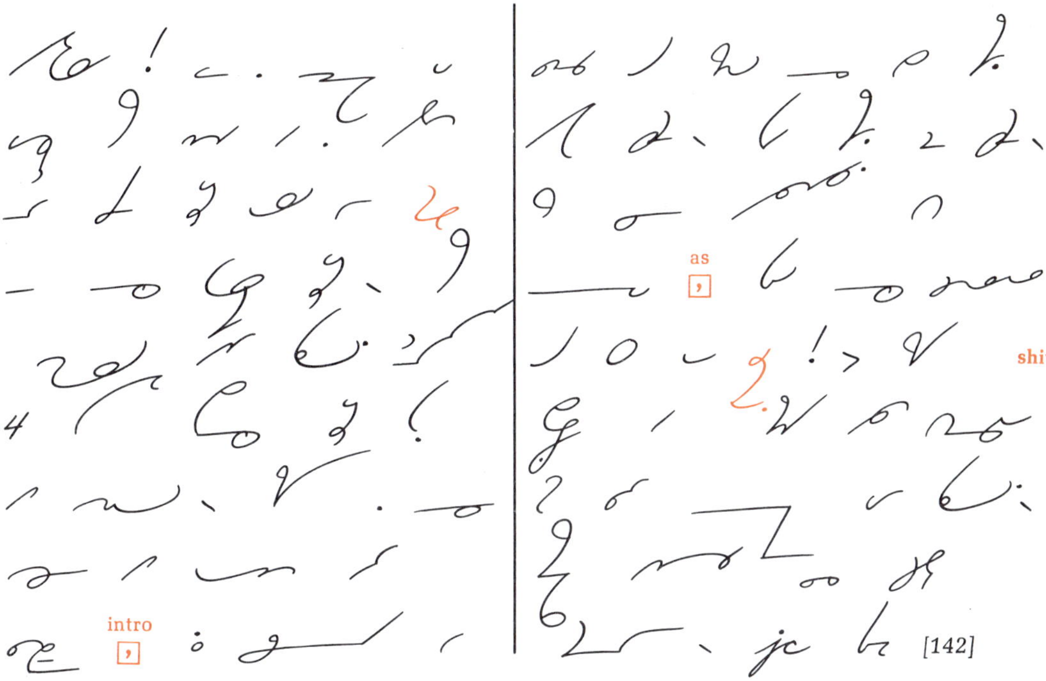

freeze

intro ,

as ,

shiv·er·ing

[142]

95
su·per·vis·or 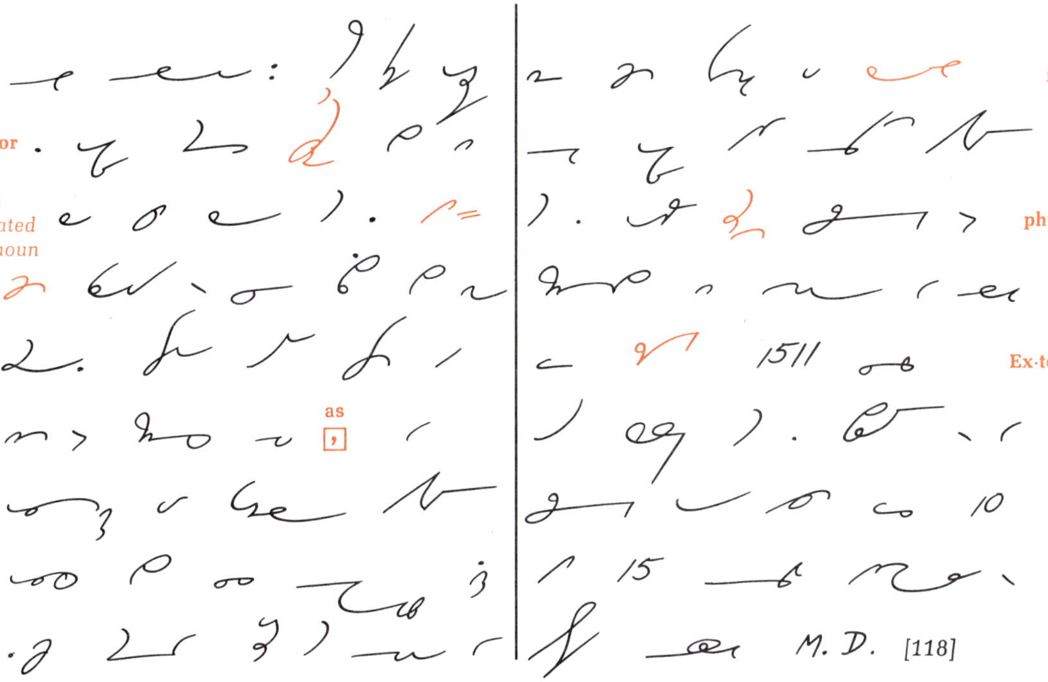
two-week
hyphenated before noun

as ,

ill·ness

phys·i·cal

Ex·ten·sion

1511

15

M. D. [118]

96

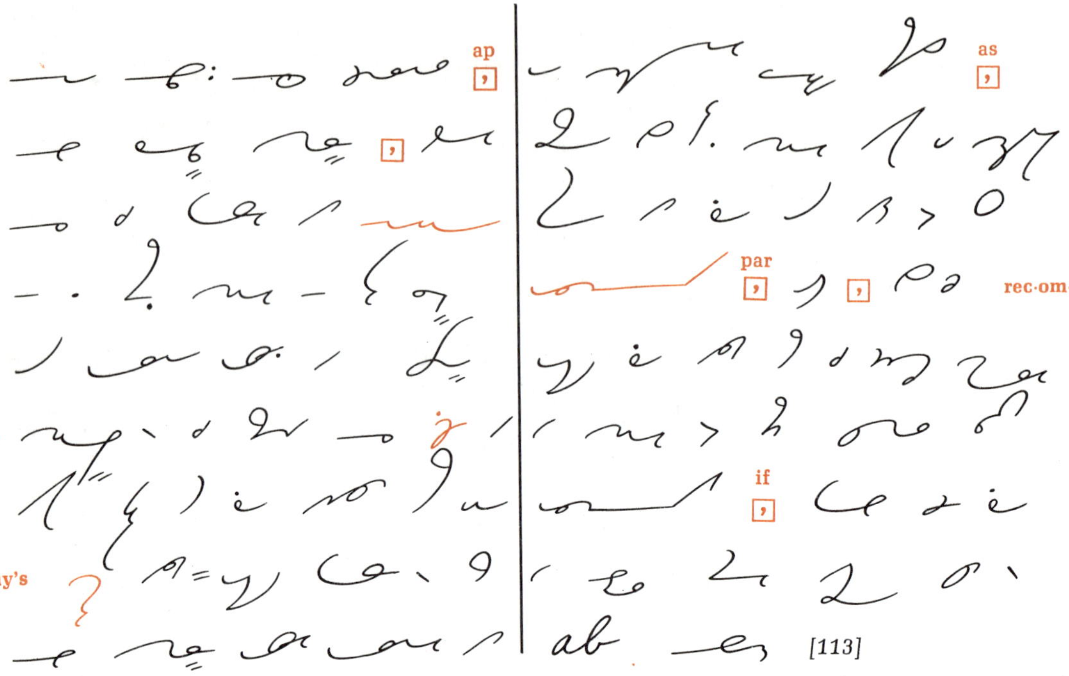

en·roll

wheth·er

com·pa·ny's

ap,
as,
par,
rec·om·mend
if,

[113]

97

to·night

ex·pe·di·tious·ly

in·con·ve·nience

as,
intro,
un·sight·ly
ceil·ings
par,
conj,

[121]

Building shorthand skill

98 **THEORY BRUSHUP**

Your reading goal: 45 seconds.

Frequent Phrases Words Omitted

1

Word Beginning Sub-

2

Word Ending -gram

3

Word Family -quire

4

Brief Forms

5

1 Many of them, one or two, three or four, one of our, some of them, during the past.
2 Substantial, substantially, submit, submission, subscribe, subscriber, subway.
3 Program, programs, programmed, diagram, radiogram.
4 Inquire, require, acquire, esquire, requirements, inquires, inquiries.
5 Request, requested, public, publicly, responsible, responsibility, general, generally.

Building transcription skills

99 Business vocabulary builder
- **instituted** Established; started.
- **discarded** Thrown out.
- **determined** (*adjective*) Firm; decisive.
- **enhance** To make greater (in value or desirability).

Reading and writing practice

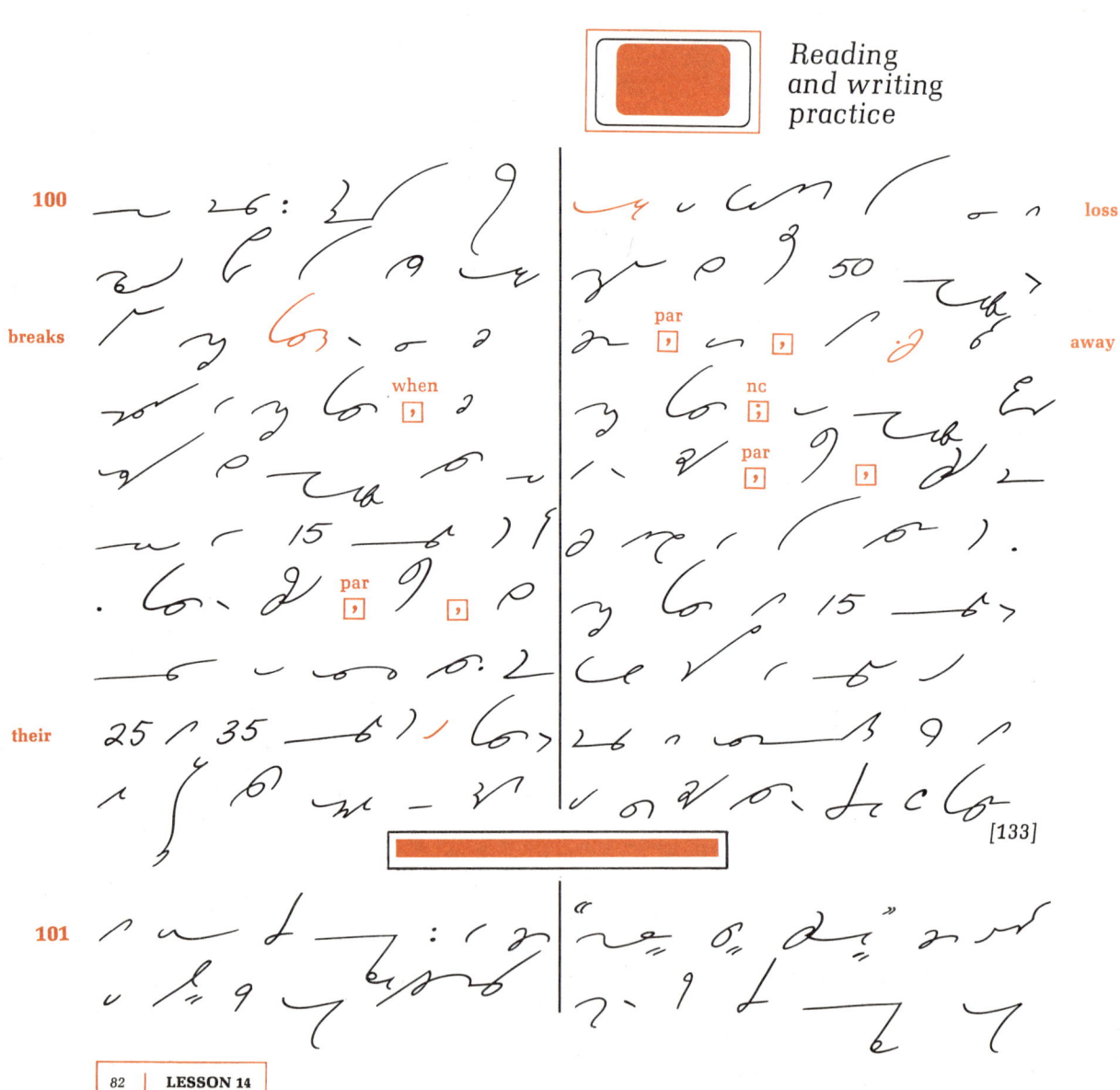

di·vi·sion's

three-draw·er
hyphenated before noun

intro ,

and o ,

well-planned
hyphenated before noun

[137]

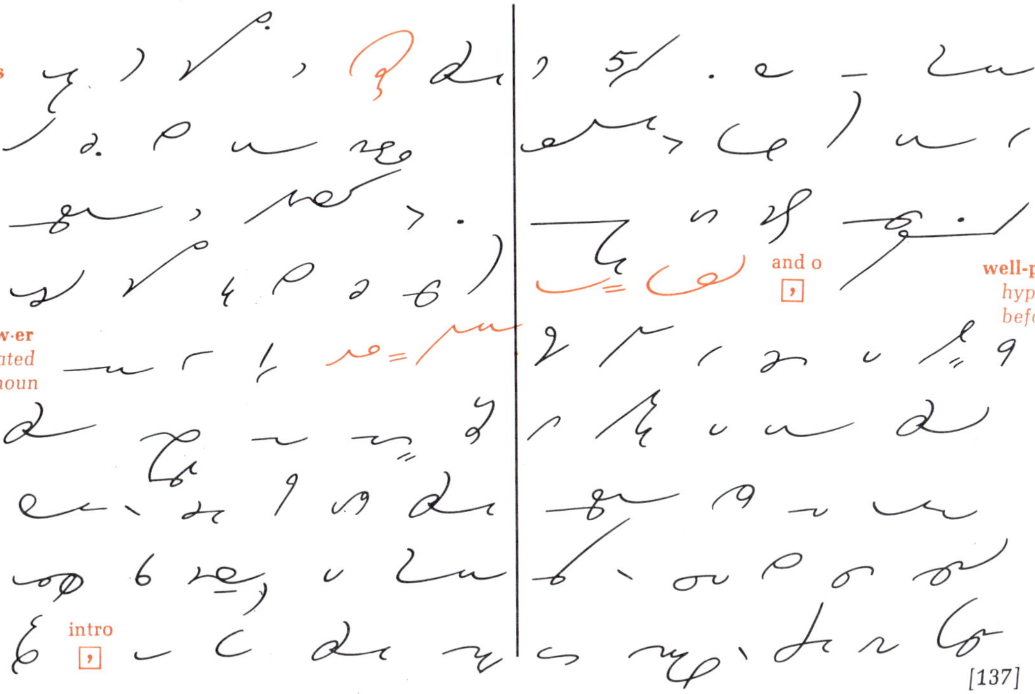

102

per·son·nel

ca·reer

di·rec·tors

ar·ea

conj ,

15-min·ute
hyphenated before noun

role

en·hance

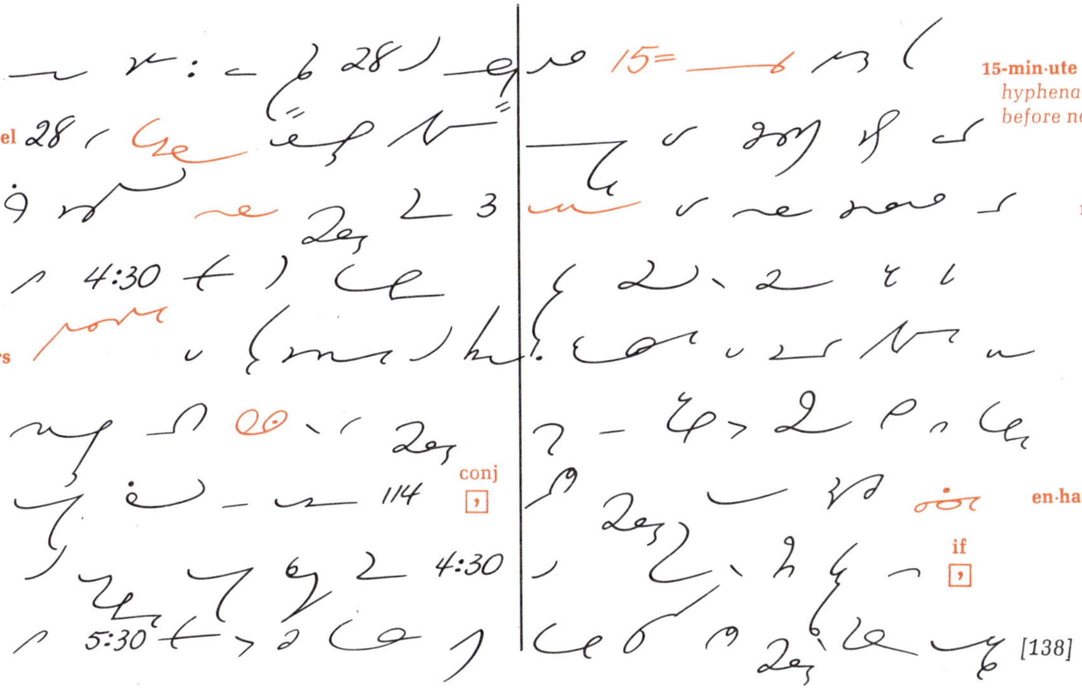

if ,

[138]

103

bus·i·est
oc·cu·py·ing
quite
vis·i·tors
in·qui·ries
urge
greet

[134]

104

two·fold
re·sponse
nev·er·the·less
cat·e·go·ry

[132]

LESSON 14

Building shorthand skill

105 THEORY BRUSHUP

Your reading goal: 45 seconds.

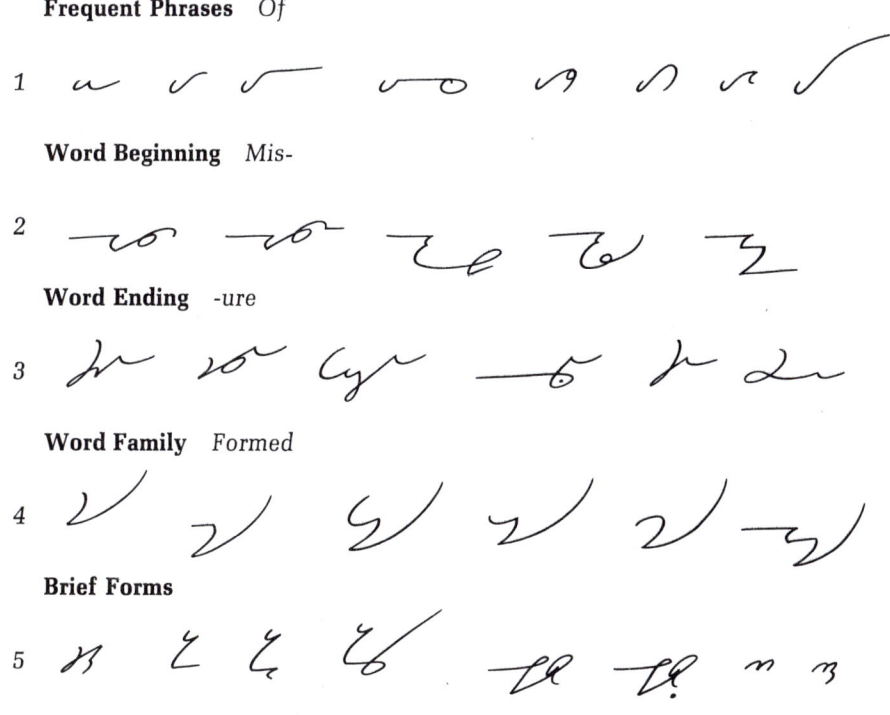

1 Of our, of the, of them, of my, of these, of this, of those, of time.
2 Mistake, mistaken, misplaced, misprint, misinform.
3 Future, stature, procedure, miniature, feature, failure.
4 Formed, informed, performed, reformed, conformed, misinformed.
5 Situations, opinion, opinions, opinionated, merchandise, merchandising, world, worlds.

Building transcription skills

106 | Business vocabulary builder

summary Brief restatement.
auditions Trial performances.
New England Northeast section of the United States.
congenial Cheerful; friendly.

Reading and writing practice

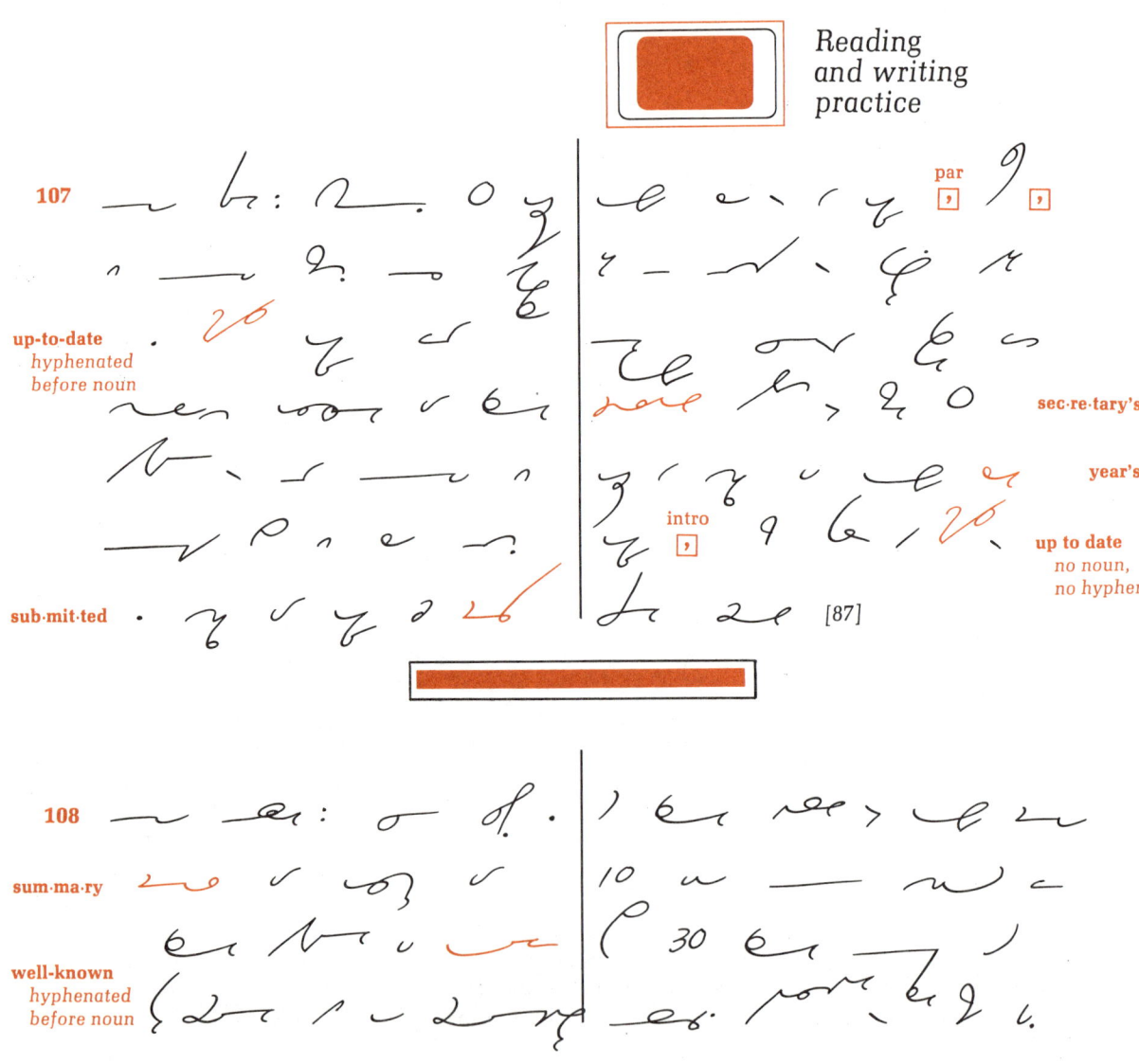

in·ter·viewed

is·su·ing

[intro ,]
[123]

109

re·ferred

writ·er

mer·chan·dise [ser ,]

sup·plies [intro ,]

[intro ,]

[21 intro ,]

of·fered [conj ,]

pro·ce·dures

[129]

LESSON 15 | 87

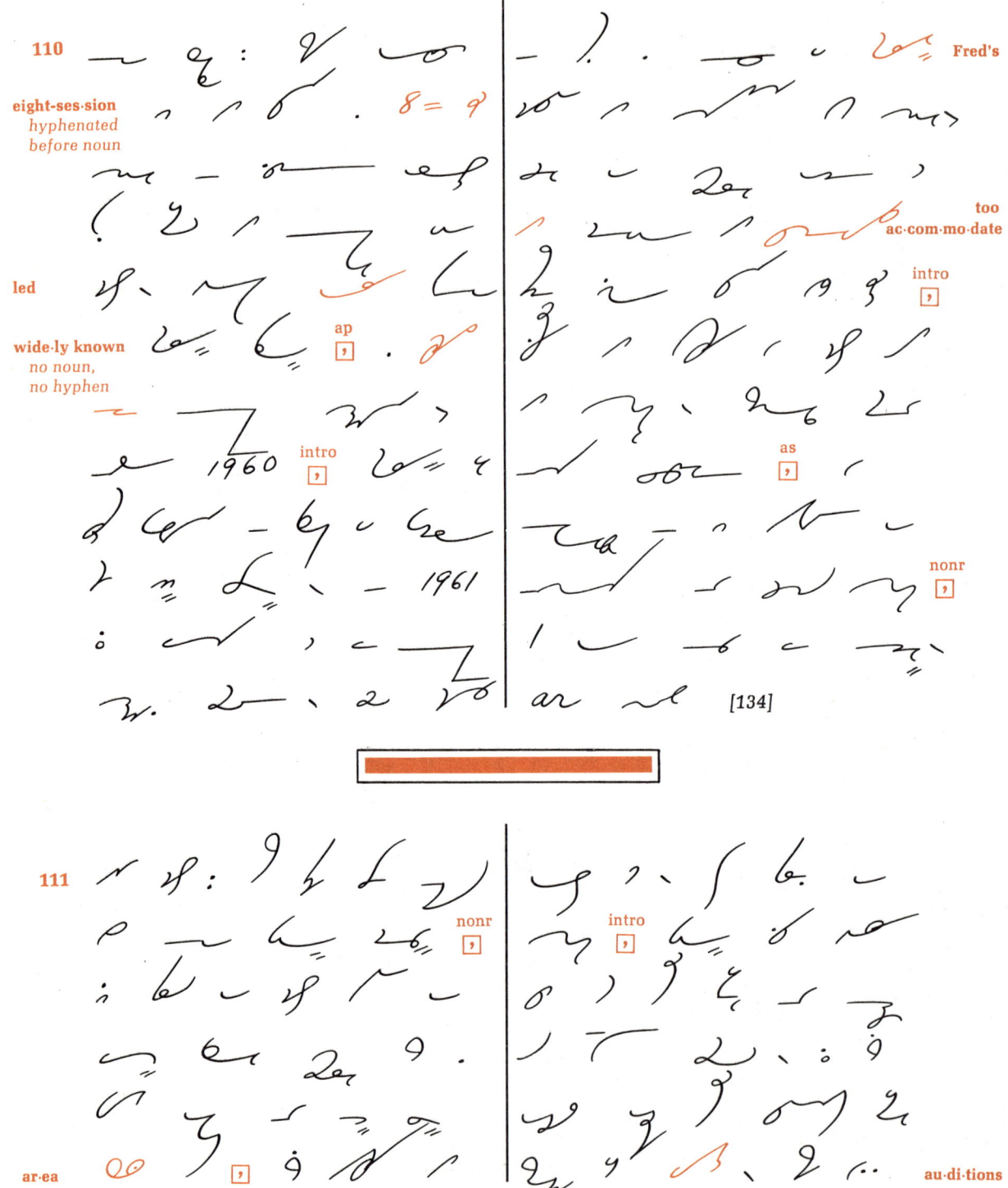

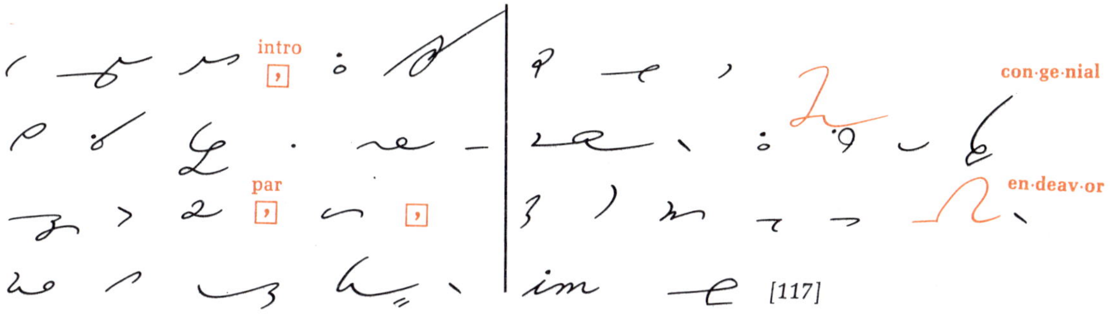

intro , con·ge·nial
par , , en·deav·or
[117]

112 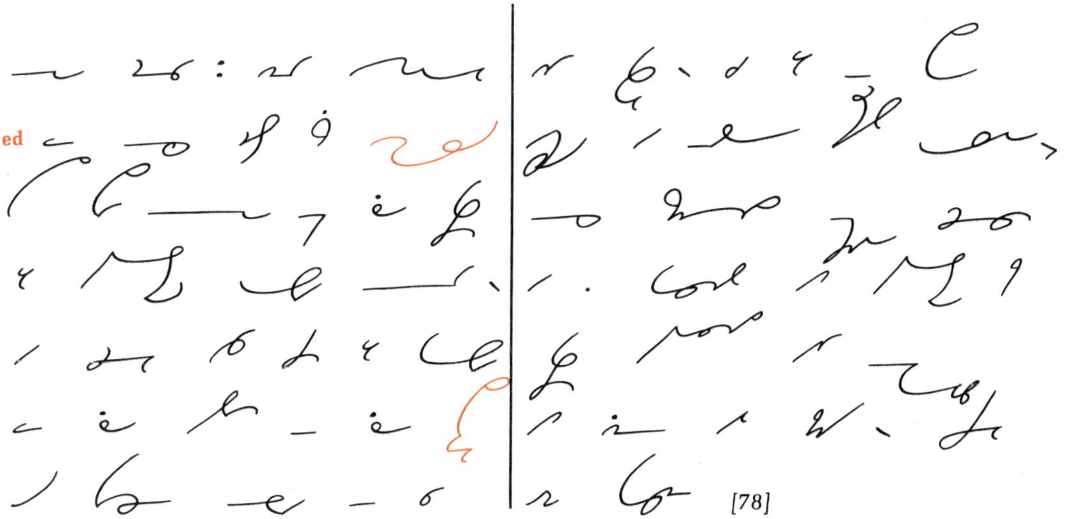
com·plained
ab·sence
[78]

LESSON 15 | 89

Advance information

When you start on your first job, the chances are that you will be somewhat bewildered during the first few days. You will be particularly "jittery" when you take dictation, no matter how considerate and thoughtful your employer may try to be. That is only natural. Remember, however, that the sooner you get over this jitteriness and become adjusted, the sooner will you be of real value to your employer.

Ellen Gardiner, of course, had to go through this adjustment period, but she took steps to help herself adjust. Here is what she did:

On the day Mr. Davis said, "You're hired," she took home the company's style manual and studied it carefully. This manual shows the letter style, salutations, and closings that the company prefers. It also shows the preferred style of interoffice memorandums.

In addition, it gives the company's preferences in spelling. For example, the company prefers enclosed to inclosed, theater to theatre, catalog to catalogue. In punctuation, dashes are to be avoided whenever possible.

All this information Ellen absorbed before she had to transcribe her first letter.

The company by whom you will be hired may be a small one that does not have a style manual. It will then be your job to learn these things by asking questions and by studying copies of previous correspondence. Studying file copies also gives you an opportunity both to learn something about the terms that are peculiar to the business and to familiarize yourself with the names of the persons with whom your employer corresponds.

Ellen also borrowed and browsed through several of the technical magazines that were in her employer's files and thus obtained some insight into the problems of marketing, for which Mr. Davis was responsible in the American Products Company.

Finally, by asking tactful questions of other employees, Ellen learned something about the habits of her employer: he dictated with a cigar in his mouth; he was a rapid, rather than a deliberate, dictator; he preferred to have his stenographer interrupt him during dictation rather than at the end of a letter.

All this preliminary checking helped Ellen gain confidence, and she got over that critical adjustment period successfully and quickly.

Remember that your employer and everyone on his staff will wish to help you succeed. They, too, were beginners once and therefore realize the problems you face. Consequently, never hesitate to ask when you are in doubt, but be sure that you ask at the right time and in a courteous, tactful manner.

Typing style brushup

In Chapter 4 you will review the correct ways of typing addresses, amounts, dates, and expressions of time.

Addresses

1 Always use figures to designate house numbers.

He lived at 600 (not *six hundred*) *Market Street.*

2 Spell out numbers below 11 in street names.

He worked at 330 Fourth Avenue.

3 Use figures in street names over ten.

His address is 18 East 67 Street.

When street addresses occur in the Reading and Writing Practice, they will occasionally be called to your attention in the margin of the shorthand thus: *Transcribe:*
           67 Street

Amounts of money

1 When transcribing whole amounts of dollars in business letters, do not add a decimal point or zeros.

His check for $152 (not *$152.00*) *was lost.*

2 In business letters, use the word *cents* for amounts under $1.

The book cost only 39 cents (not *$.39*).

When amounts such as the above appear in the Reading and Writing Practice, they will occasionally be called to your attention in the margin of the shorthand thus: *Transcribe:*   *Transcribe:*
                                      $8   **7 cents**

Time

1 Use figures in expressing time with *o'clock*. (Remember the apostrophe!)

He came at 10 o'clock (not *ten o'clock*).

2 Use figures in expressing time with *a.m.* and *p.m.*

He left at 9:15 a.m. and returned at 9:30 p.m.

▶ Note: Type *a.m.* and *p.m.* with small letters and no space after the first period.

Occasionally these expressions of time will be called to your attention in the margins of the shorthand thus:

Transcribe: *Transcribe:*
6 o'clock **9 a.m.**
              5 p.m.

Dates

1 If the name of the month precedes the day, do not use *th*, *st*, or *d* after the number. This is the most frequent way that dates are expressed in business letters.

On June 16, 1976, he must retire.

2 If the day precedes the month, *th*, *st*, or *d* should be included.

On the 25th of May he will be able to vote.

When dates appear in the Reading and Writing Practice, they will occasionally be called to your attention in the margin thus:

Transcribe: *Transcribe:*
June 16   **20th**

Commas in numbers

1 When a number contains four or more digits, a comma is used to separate thousands, millions, billions.

$1,000 (not $1000)   167,841   1,321,000   4,500,000,000

2 Commas, however, are *not* used in serial numbers, house or street numbers, telephone numbers, page numbers, and between the digits of a year.

      No. 14568   6314 Third Avenue   546-1161

      page 1212   the year 1978

These uses of the comma in numbers will be called to your attention in the margin of the Reading and Writing Practice thus:

          Transcribe: *Transcribe:*
          $12,000   **No. 4156**

Numbers at the beginning of a sentence

1 Spell out a number that begins a sentence.

Fifty copies of the book were shipped to you yesterday.

2 For consistency, also spell out related numbers.

Twenty or twenty-five (not 25) pages are missing.

Chapter 4 — Lesson 16

Employment

Building shorthand skill

113 THEORY BRUSHUP

Your reading goal: 40 seconds.

Frequent Phrases   As

1

Word Beginning   Tern, Term

2

Word Ending   -ulate

3

Word Family   -ness

4

Brief Forms

5

---

1 As you know, as you will, as you may, as you are, as we have, as well, as it is.
2 Turn, turnover, term, termination, determine, returned.
3 Congratulate, congratulation, formulate, formulated, formulation.
4 Fairness, weakness, frankness, willingness, thoughtfulness, usefulness.
5 Enclose, enclosed, enclosure, object, objection, objective, objected.

Building transcription skills

114 | Business vocabulary builder

overstate Exaggerate.
appraisal Estimation of value.
frankness Sincere, honest expression.

Reading and writing practice

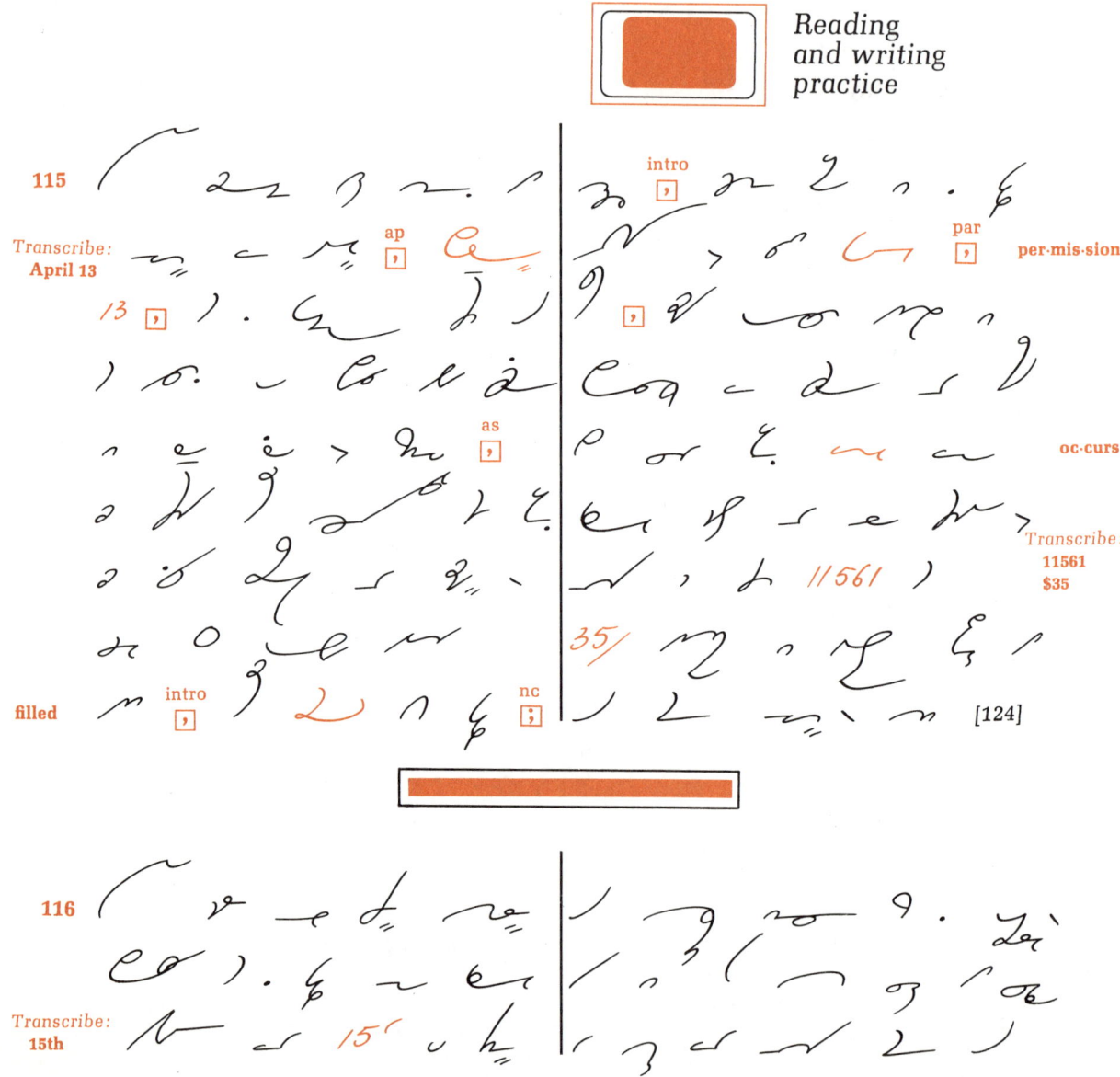

sub·ject's
intro
par
intro
qual·i·fied
ap·prais·al
per·son's
strengths [152] strict

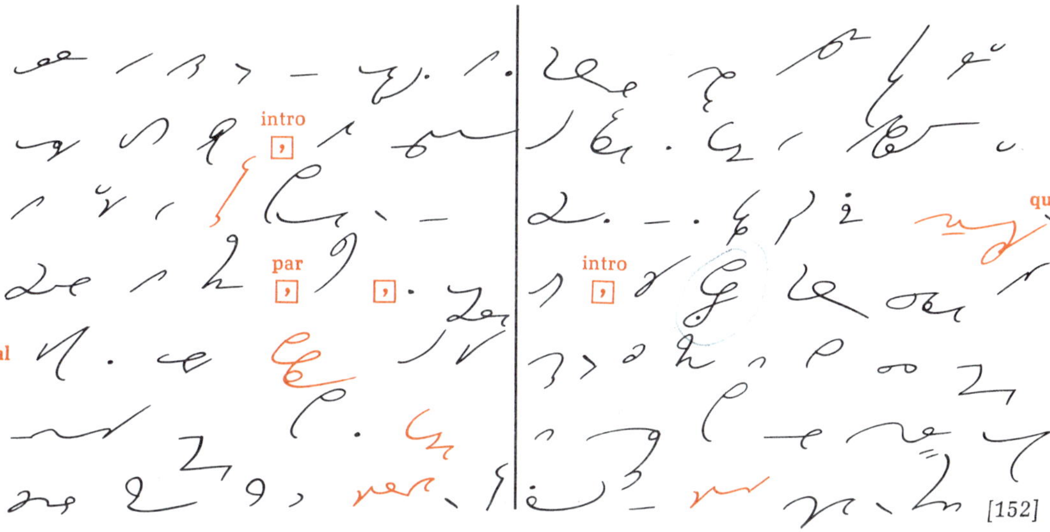

117
bril·liant
ap·ply·ing
nonr
coun·cil
rec·om·men·da·tion
and o
well-trained
hyphenated before noun
if
Transcribe: 1971
conj
[150]

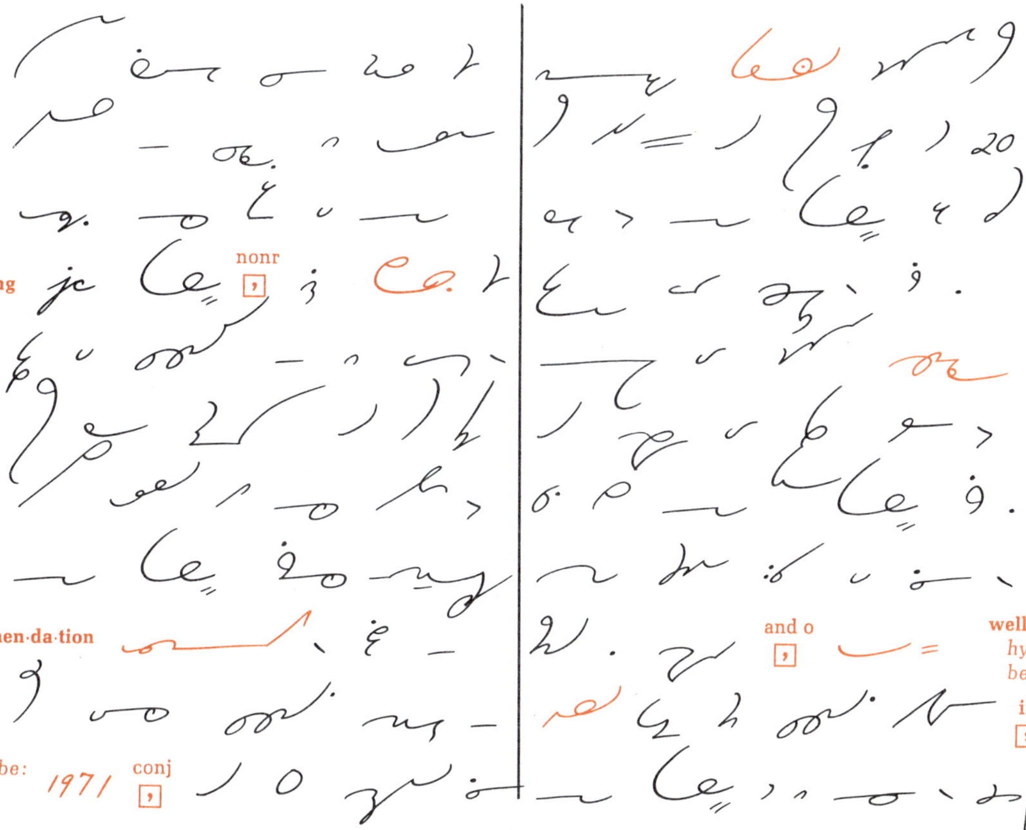

LESSON 16 | 97

118

Transcribe: **April 16**

ap ,

re·ferred

known

intro ,

if ,

Transcribe: **415-1177**

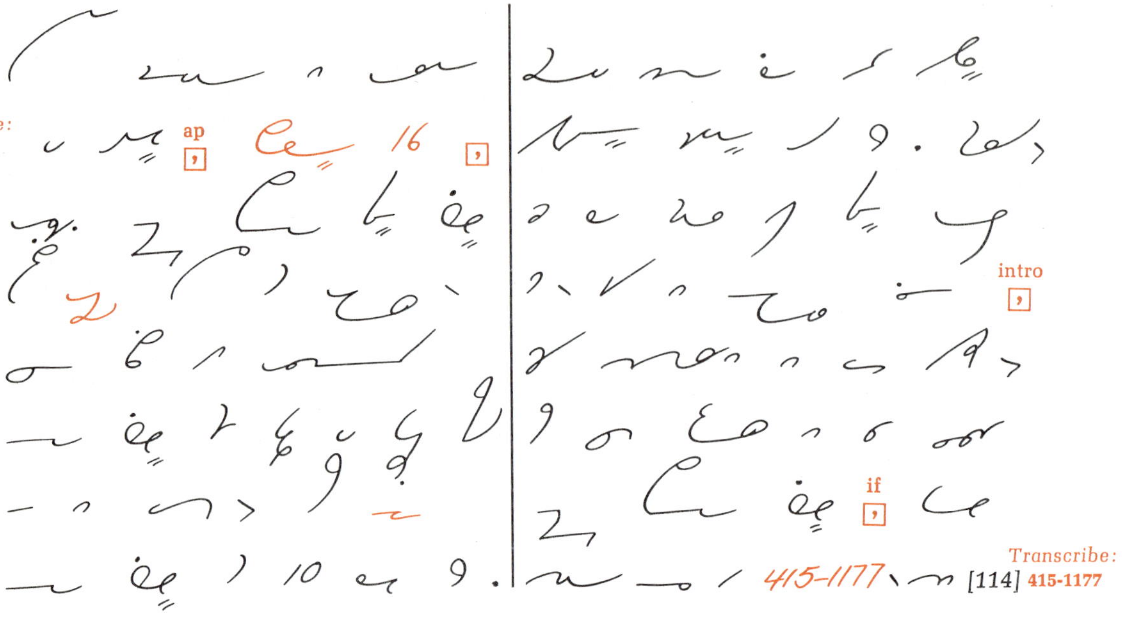

[114]

119

Se·nior

when ,

ad·vance·ment

ser ,

yours

Transcribe: **1514**

Transcribe: **9 a.m.** **5 p.m.**

if ,

if ,

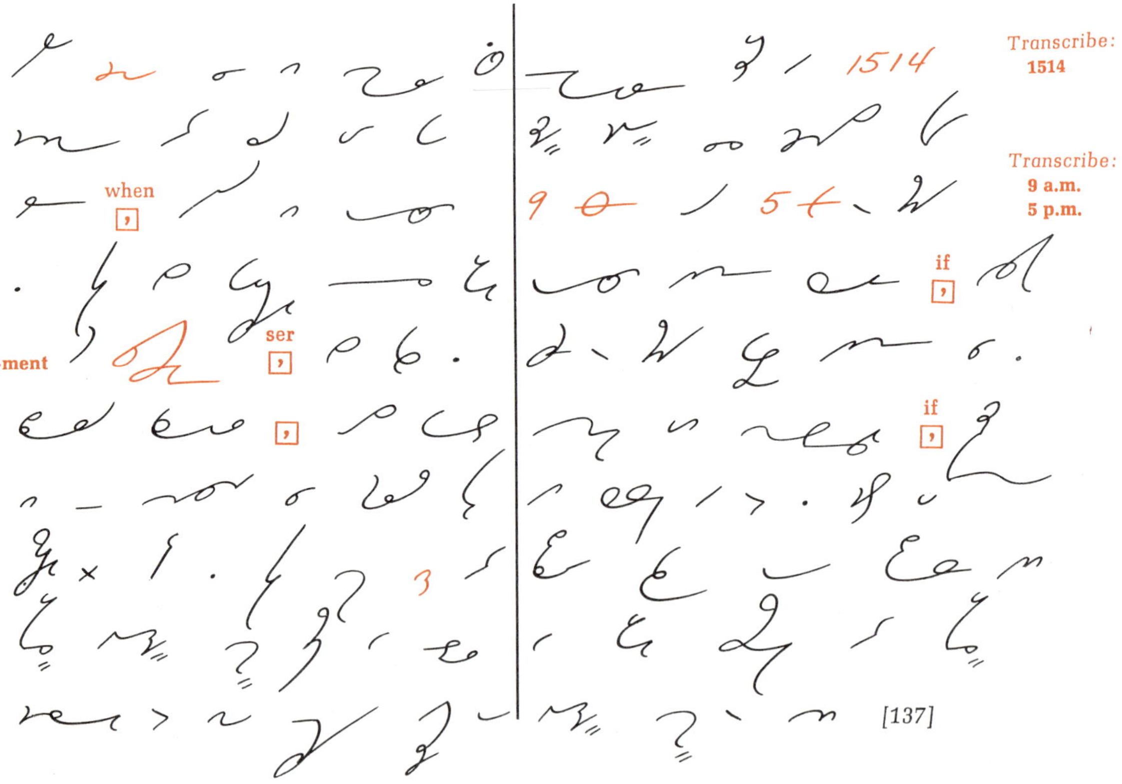

[137]

Building shorthand skill

120 THEORY BRUSHUP

Your reading goal: 40 seconds.

Frequent Phrases *Ago*

Word Beginning *Fur-*

Word Ending *-hood*

Word Family *Pro-*

Brief Forms

1 Months ago, years ago, weeks ago, several days ago, long ago.
2 Further, furthermore, furniture, furnace, furnish, furnished, furnishings, unfurnished.
3 Parenthood, likelihood, motherhood, childhood, neighborhood.
4 Promotion, prompt, profit, prospect, provide, provision, process.
5 Satisfies, satisfied, satisfaction, dissatisfied, part, depart, department.

Building transcription skills

121

Business vocabulary builder	**patent** The exclusive right given to an inventor to make and market his invention.
	established (*adjective*) Recognized.
	reluctance Unwillingness.

Reading and writing practice

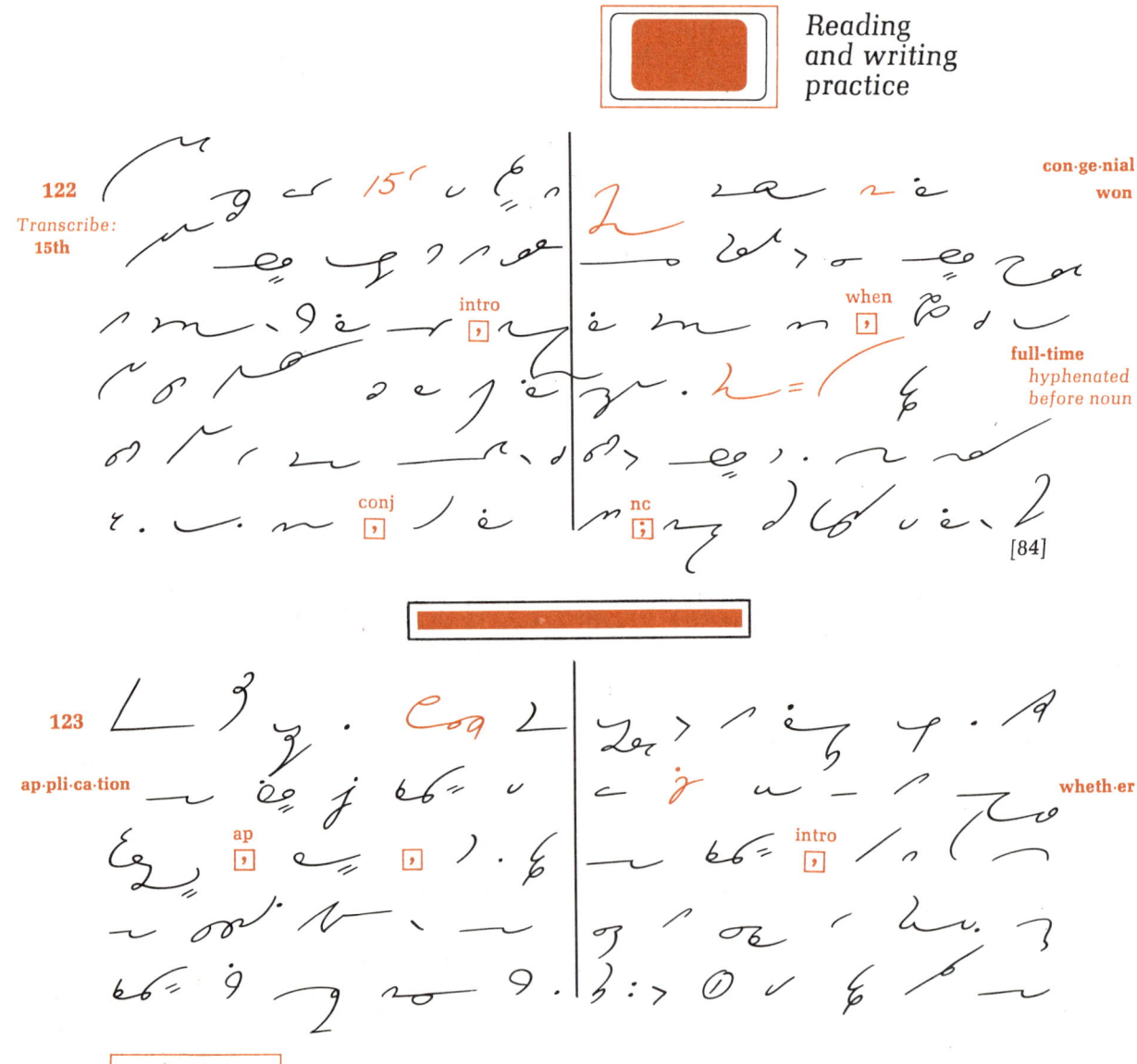

122 Transcribe: 15th

123 ap·pli·ca·tion

per·for·mance conj

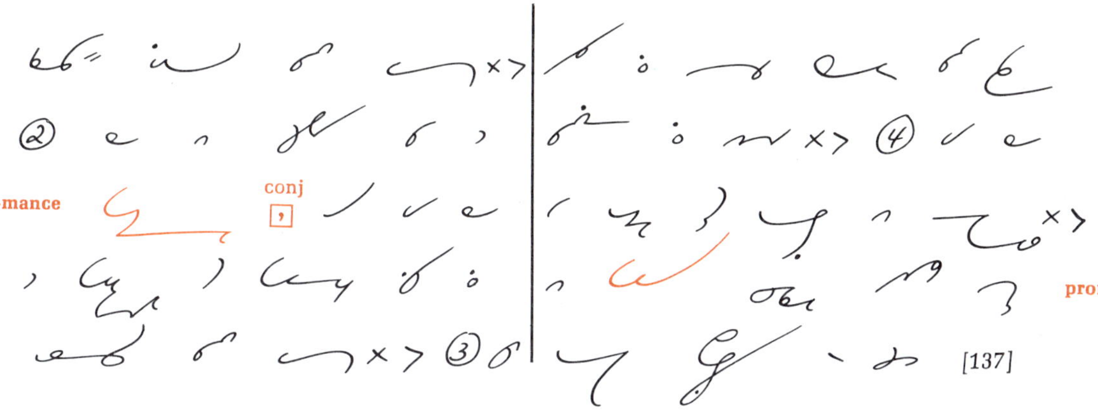

prompt

[137]

124
lun·cheon
Transcribe:
June 16

filled

intro

Transcribe:
$12,000

if

nc

141-1115

intro

de·vice

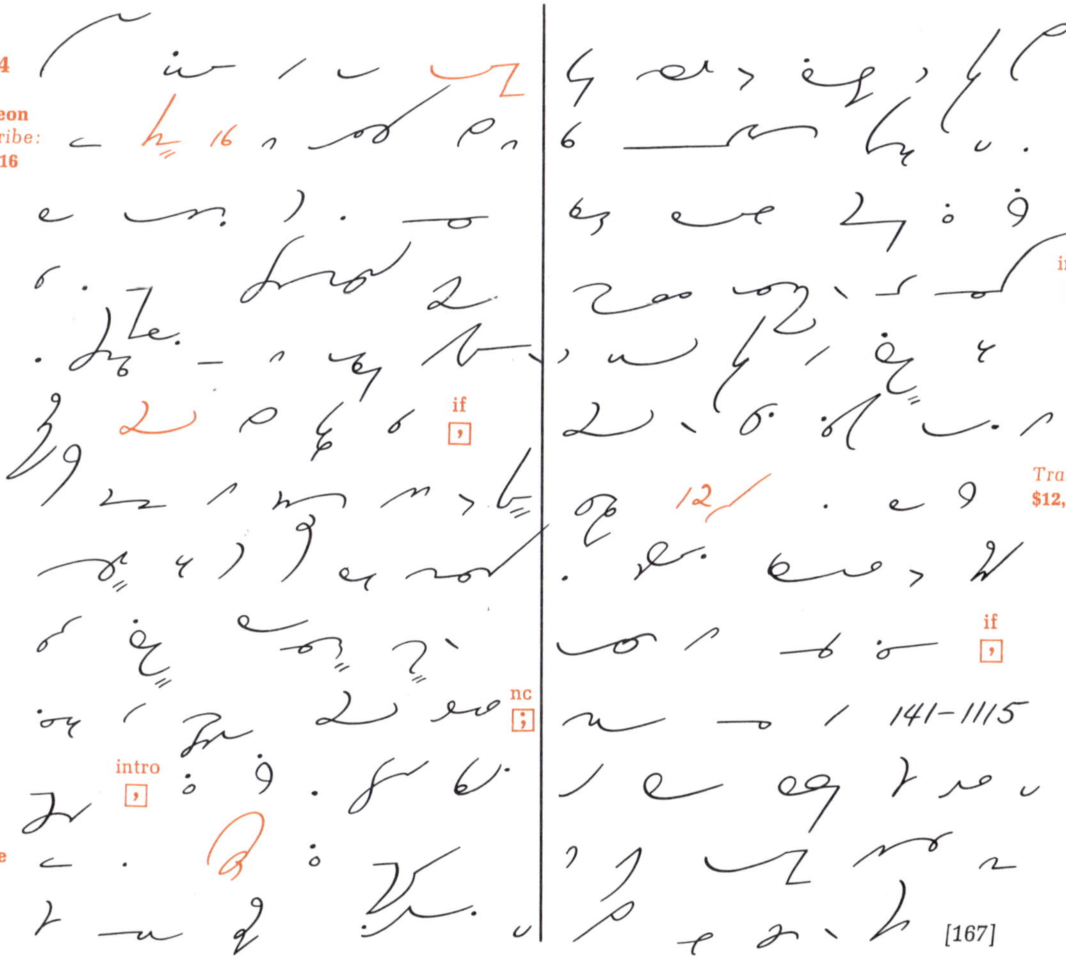

[167]

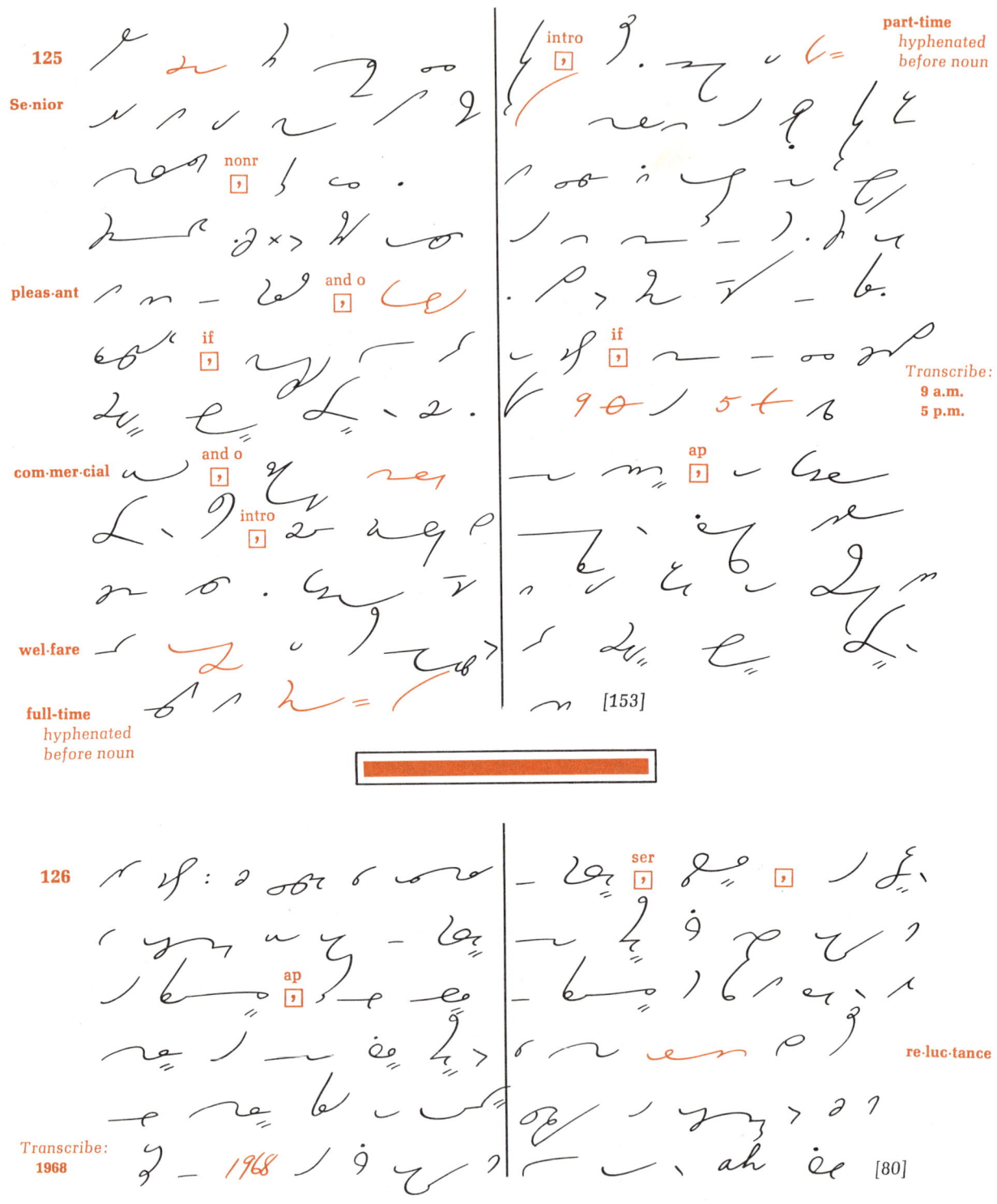

Building shorthand skill

127 THEORY BRUSHUP

Your reading goal: 40 seconds.

Frequent Phrases Words Omitted

1

Word Beginning Be-

2

Word Ending -ification

3

Word Family Point

4

Brief Forms

5

1 Three or four, week or two, one or two, one of them, some of our, in the past, in the future.
2 Because, became, become, beginnings, benefit, beneath, before.
3 Qualifications, modification, gratification, notifications, specifications, ratification.
4 Point, appoint, appointment, appointed, disappoint, reappoint, pointless.
5 Publish-publication, publishes-publications, newspaper, newspapermen, understanding, understands, understandingly.

Building transcription skills

128 | Business vocabulary builder | **likelihood** Probability.
slump A marked decline in business.
prior Earlier; coming before.

Reading and writing practice

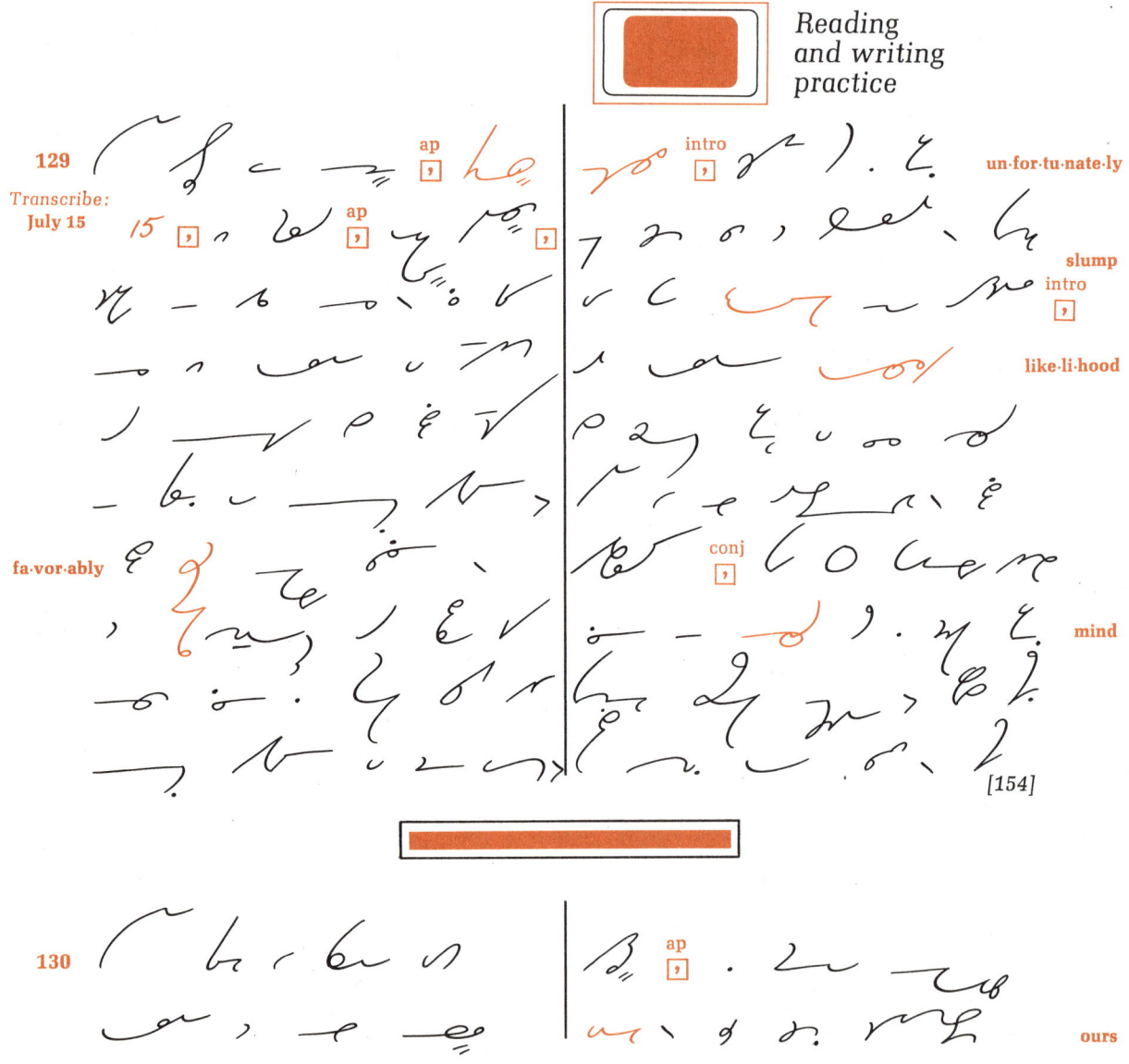

Transcribe: 4151

of·fered

per·son·al

as ,
conj ,

and o ,
if ,

[121]

131

ar·ea

psy·chol·o·gy

ap ,

intro ,

Transcribe: $10,000

— de·scribed

Transcribe: No. 1156

par ,

ac·cept

of·fer·ing

[146]

LESSON 18 | 105

132

Transcribe: **February 18**

ap

em·ploy

nonr

[115]

bach·e·lor's

mas·ter's

intro

taught

Hunt's

133

stew·ard·ess's

ca·reer

if

if

de·vel·op

com·ple·tion

intro

routes

be·gin·ning

[115]

Building shorthand skill

134 THEORY BRUSHUP

Your reading goal: 40 seconds.

Frequent Phrases *He*

Word Beginnings *Electr-, Electric*

Word Endings *-self, -selves*

Word Family *Ent-, Int-, Ant-*

Brief Forms

1 He will, he is, he mentioned, he was, he may, he should, he might, he would.
2 Electronics, electrical, electrician, electric light, electric power.
3 Himself, itself, myself, yourself, themselves, ourselves, yourselves.
4 Entail, entitle, indicate, into, anticipate, anticipation, anticipating.
5 Time, timely, timed, timer, correspond-correspondence, corresponded, correspondent.

Building transcription skills

135 | Business vocabulary builder

reputable Of good standing.
relocated Moved to a new area.
command (noun) Mastery.

 Reading and writing practice

136 [shorthand text with annotations: as·so·ciate, ap, par, ca·pac·i·ty, rea·sons, intro, intro, al·ways, intro, conj, en·gage·ments, rep·u·ta·ble, when, if] [157]

137

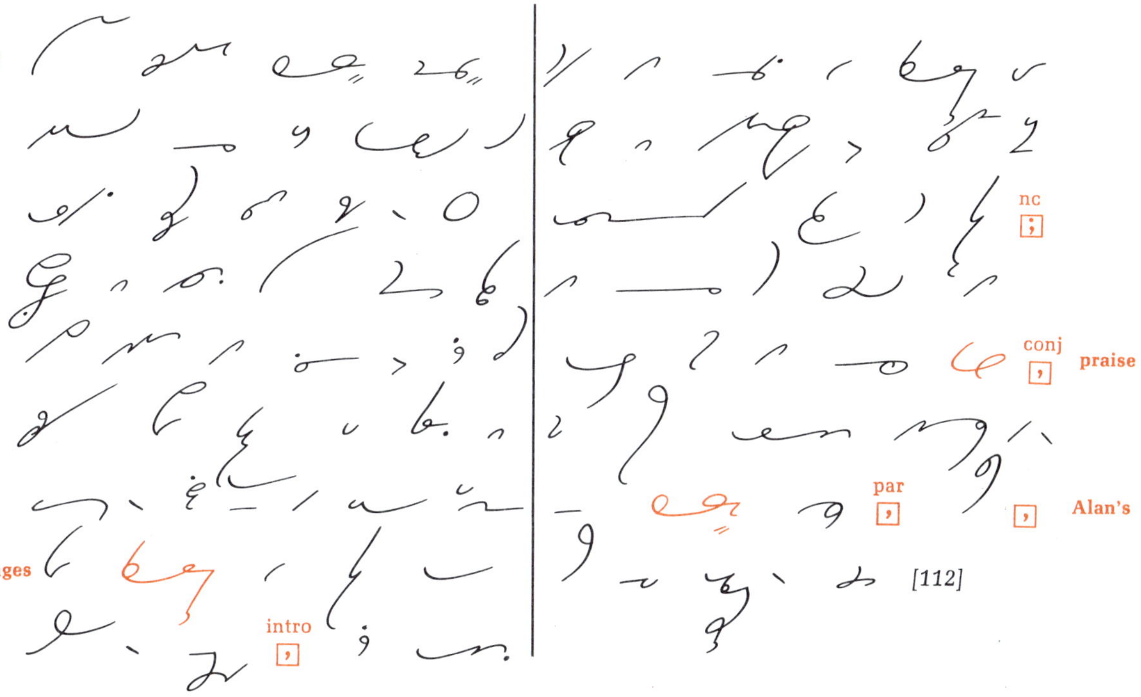

chal·lenges intro nc conj praise par Alan's [112]

138

Transcribe: April 16

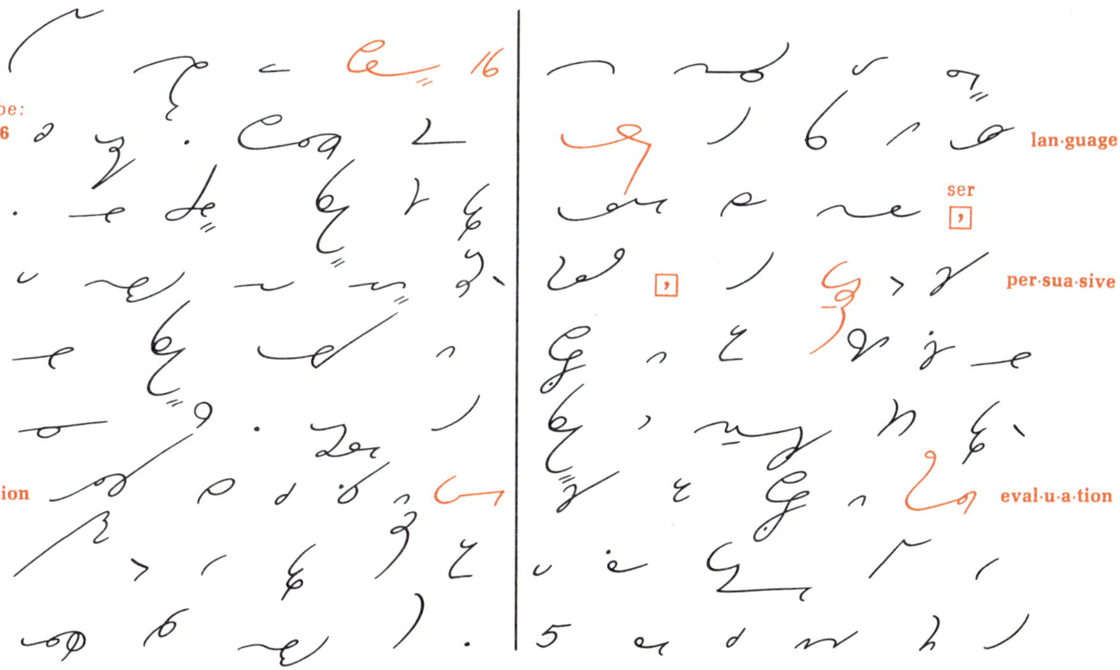

per·mis·sion lan·guage ser per·sua·sive eval·u·a·tion

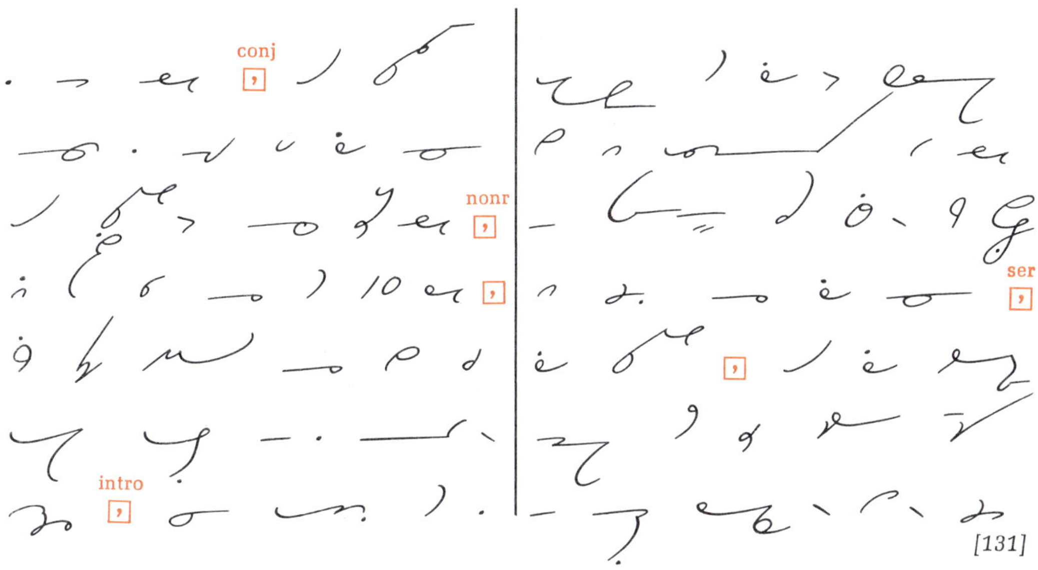
conj
nonr
10
ser
intro
[131]

141

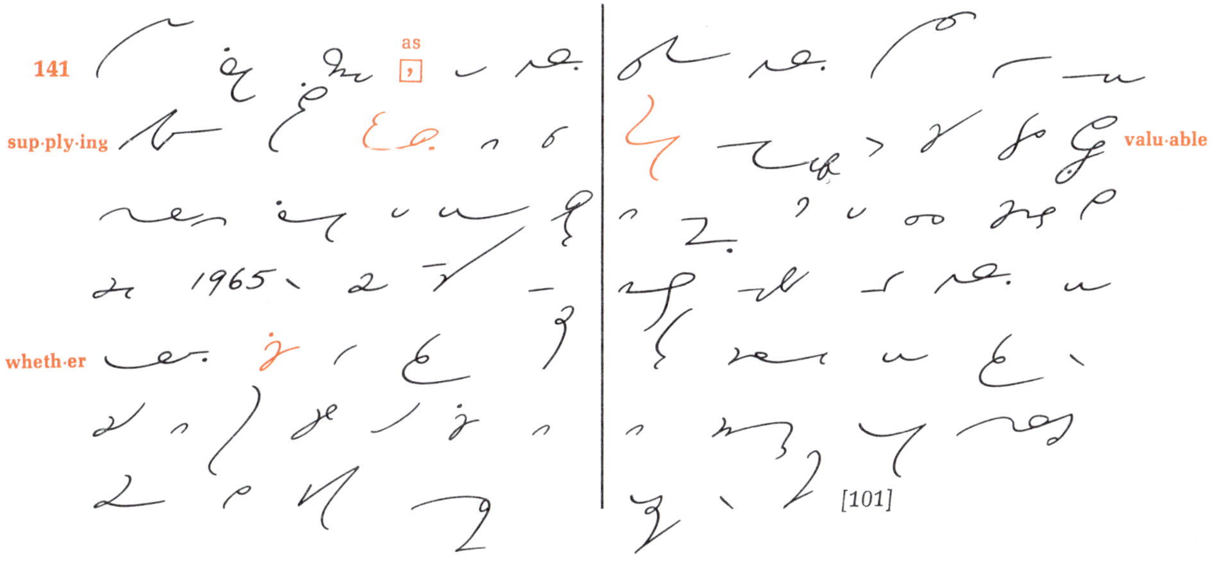
as
sup·ply·ing
valu·able
1965
wheth·er
[101]

Building shorthand skill

142 THEORY BRUSHUP

Your reading goal: 40 seconds.

Frequent Phrases Be

Word Beginning Post-

Word Ending -sume

Word Family Book

Brief Forms

1 Should be, I should be able, I could be, can be, you can be sure, I might be, may not be.
2 Postcard, postal, postpone, postponement, postage, postdate.
3 Consumer, assume, assumed, resume, resumed, presumption.
4 Book, booklet, bookkeeper, bankbook, checkbook, textbook.
5 One, anyone, someone, everyone, regard, regardless.

Building transcription skills

143 | Business vocabulary builder

duration Length of time.
asthma A chronic lung disorder characterized by difficulty of breathing.
entails Includes; involves.
confidential To be kept secret.

Reading and writing practice

144

Transcribe: Fourth

[158]

145

Phoenix, ad·vice, daugh·ter's asth·ma, nonr, ap, when, nonr, par, ser, set·tled [126]

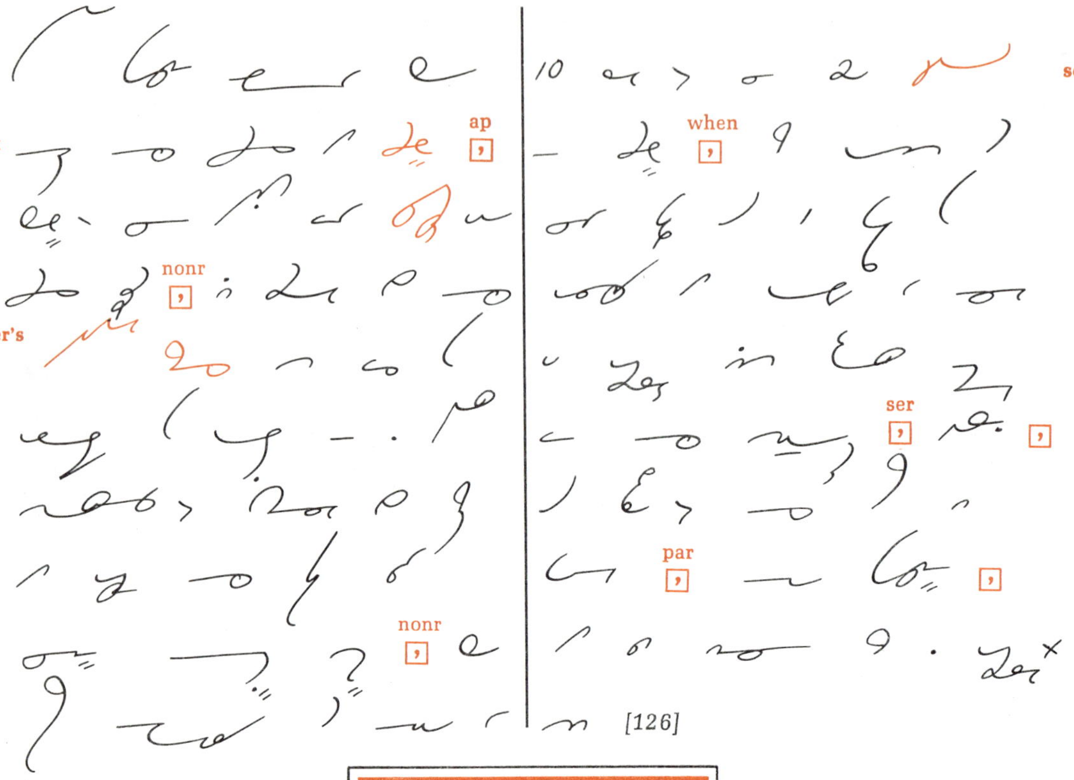

146

sub·mit·ted, im·pressed, par, intro, if, Transcribe: $12,000, en·tails

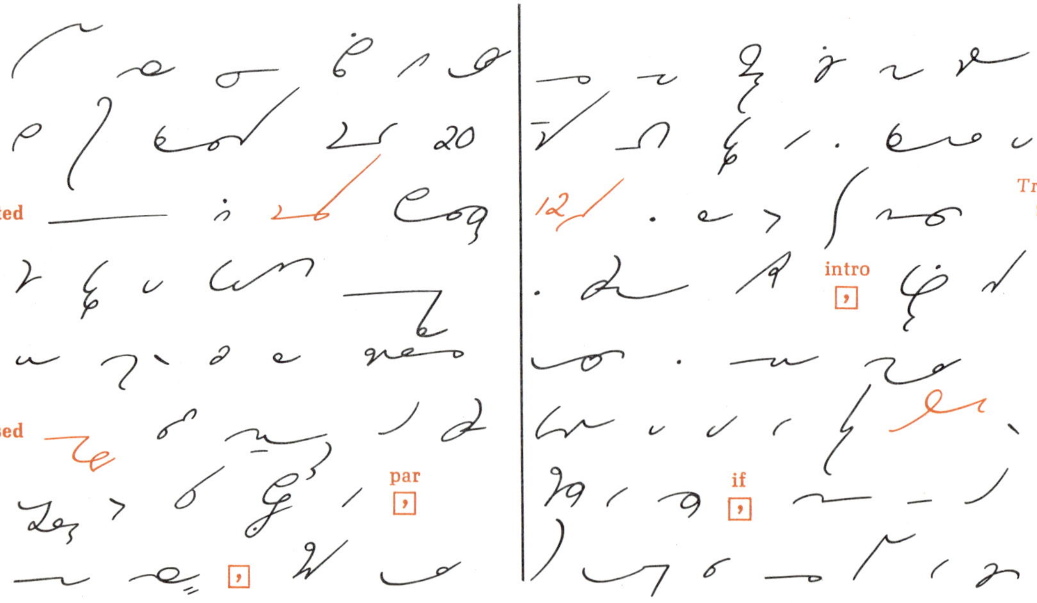

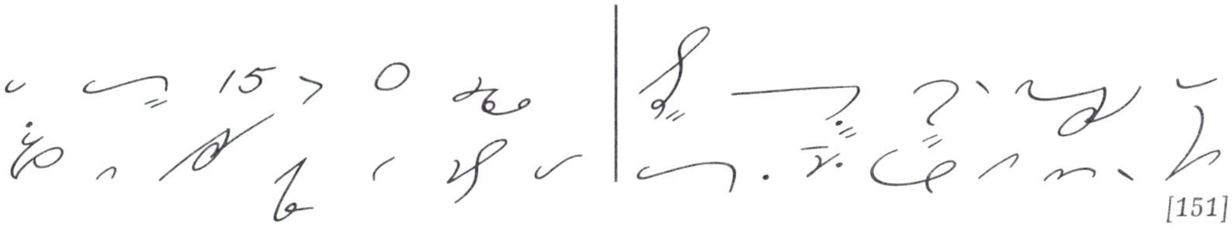

[151]

147 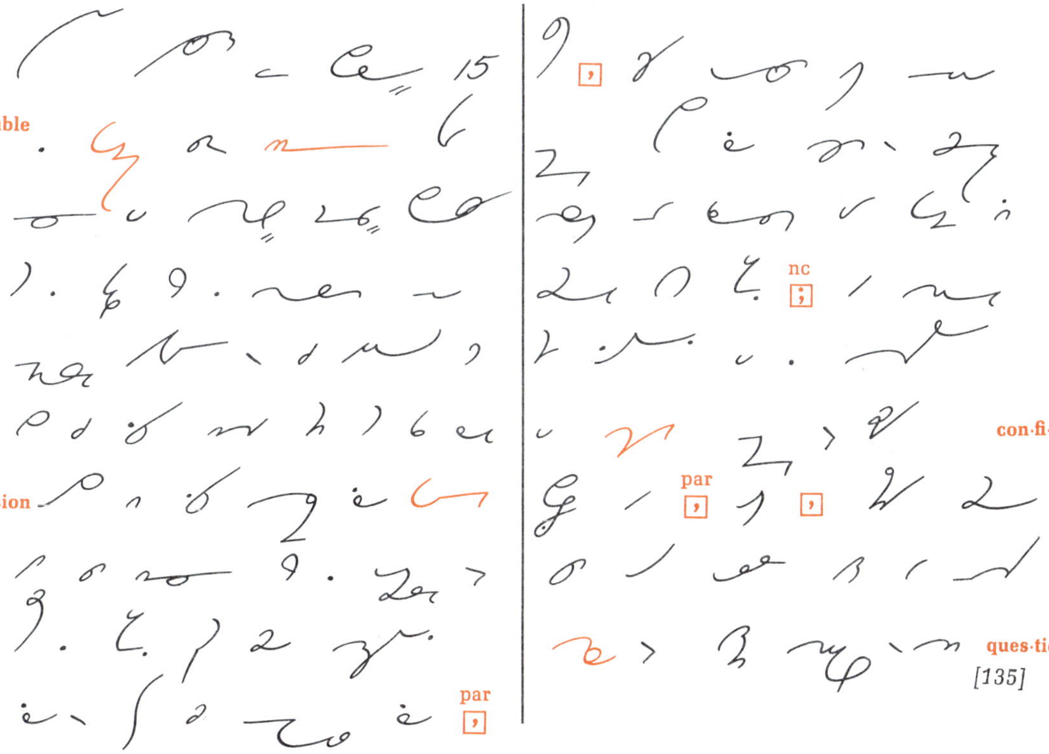
per·son·able wom·an
per·mis·sion
con·fi·den·tial
ques·tion·naire [135]

148 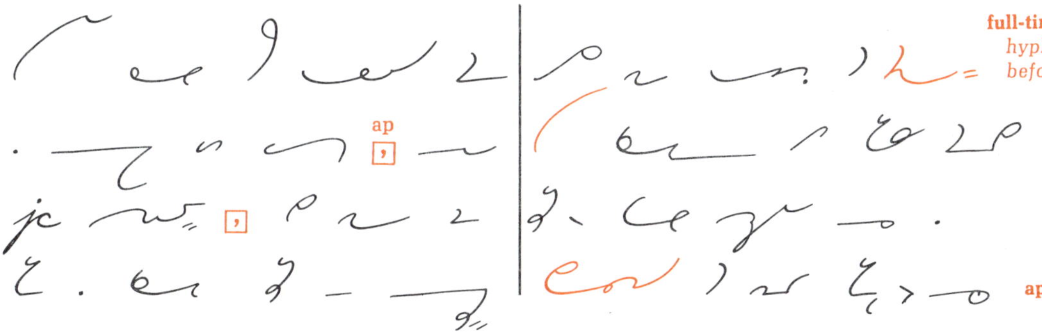
full-time *hyphenated before noun*
ap·pli·cant

LESSON 20

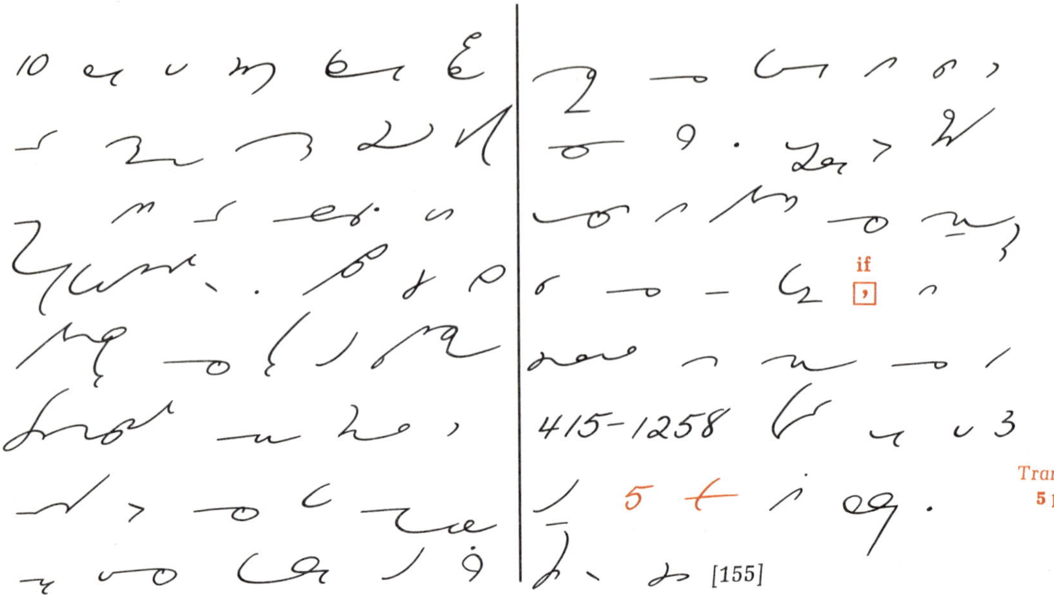

Transcribe:
5 p.m.

[155]

149
well-known
*hyphenated
before noun*

equip·ment

fa·mil·iar

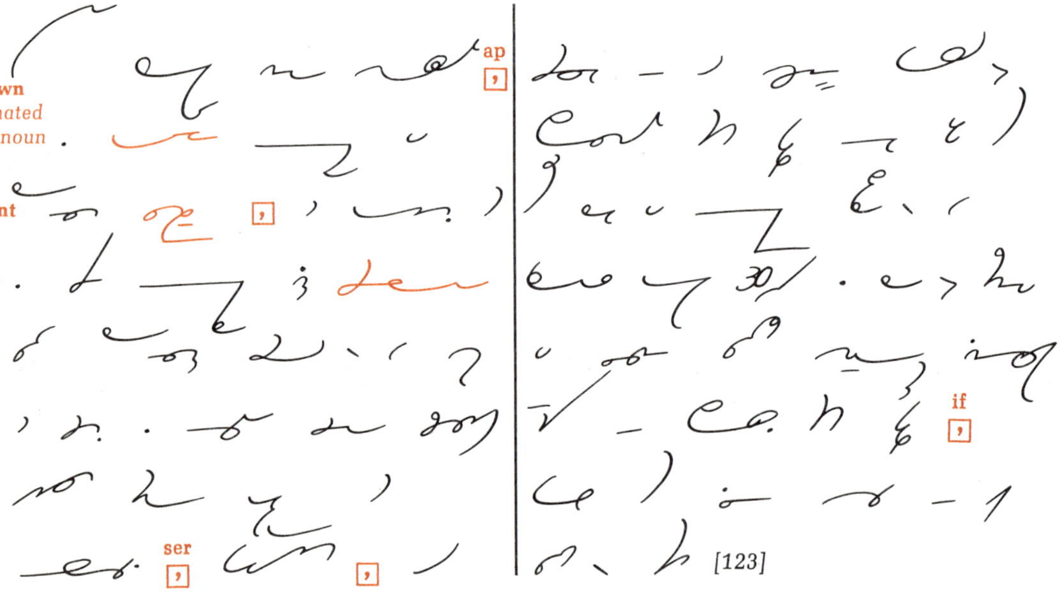

[123]

116 | LESSON 20

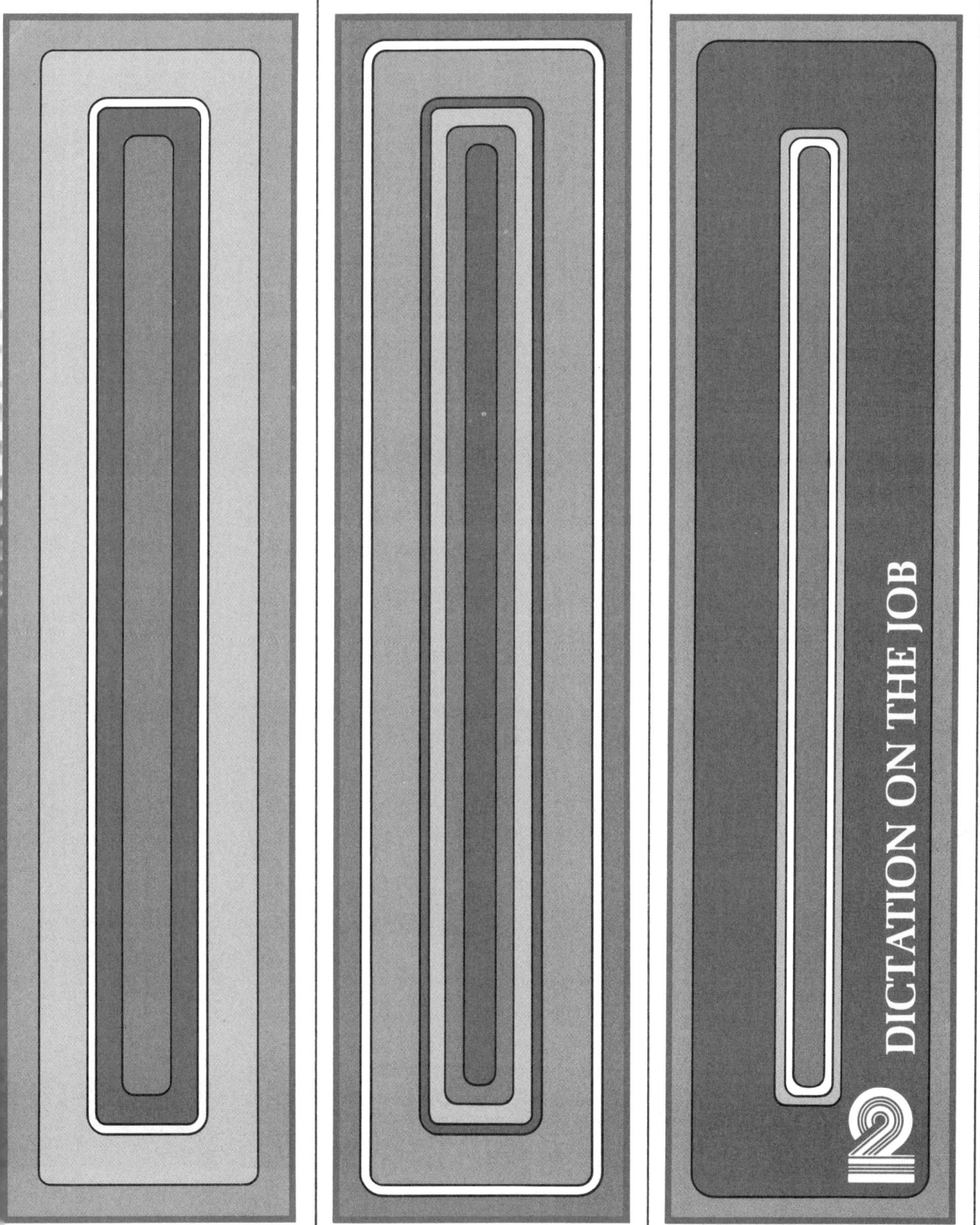

2 DICTATION ON THE JOB

The secretary's notebook techniques

Mr. Davis had been away on a business trip for two weeks, and when he returned to the office, he found a goodly pile of mail on his desk. He read through it quickly, decided what letters he would answer immediately, and buzzed for Ellen. For more than an hour he dictated, one letter after the other. Suddenly he said, "That letter to Mr. Franklin that I dictated earlier—did I tell you to send it airmail, special delivery? Also, I think we should send a carbon to Jones. It is about his account, and I think we should keep him informed about the action we

 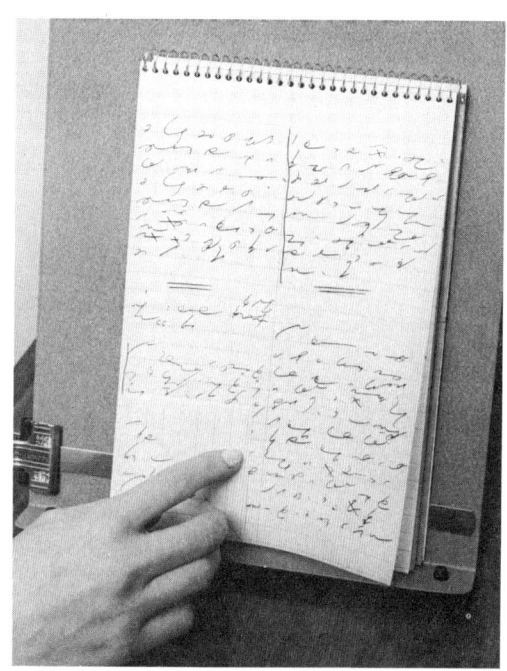

are taking. Be sure both the original and the carbon to Jones get out today." Ellen quickly leafed back to the letter to Mr. Franklin. She found that Mr. Davis had not told her to send it airmail, special delivery—so this is what she did:

1   In the blank space that she left before she began the letter to Mr. Franklin, she wrote in shorthand, "Original: airmail, special delivery. cc: Jones."

2   She then took her colored pencil and drew a heavy line down the page, alongside the letter to Mr. Franklin.

3   She folded over one corner of the notebook page so that she could quickly find the page when she was ready to transcribe.

You can see, of course, why it was so important for Ellen to write these instructions at the head of the letter in her notebook. If she had placed them at the end, she might not have discovered that she had to make two carbon copies until it was too late.

The wise stenographer will always leave several blank lines between letters. When the dictator later gives instructions concerning a letter that was dictated previously, there is space available to write those instructions.

The line drawn with colored pencil next to the shorthand indicates that the letter should be the first, or one of the first, to be transcribed. Telegrams and urgent interoffice memoranda would be marked in the same way.

Folding the corner of a page makes it possible to locate quickly those letters that are to get high priority. This device is especially helpful when a stenographer must take 20, 30, or more notebook pages of dictation at one time, as occasionally happens.

Publishing

Building transcription skills

150 TYPING STYLE STUDY | titles

Books, booklets, magazines, and newspapers. In business letters, titles of books, booklets, magazines, and newspapers are underscored.

Our latest book, <u>Modern Business Practice</u>, just came off the press.

A copy of our booklet, <u>The Duties of a Secretary</u>, is enclosed.

She subscribes to a magazine called <u>Today's Secretary</u>.

I read his speech in yesterday's <u>New York Times</u>.

The first word and all the other main words in a title are capitalized. Words such as *of, a, in, the, and* in the body of the title are not capitalized.

▶ *Caution:* This style is recommended for general business letters; it is the one followed in your textbook.

However, some publishers prefer to have the titles of their publications typed in all caps; others prefer to have them quoted.

151

Business vocabulary builder	**offset** (verb) To balance; to make up for. **refund** To pay back. **in the black** Making a profit.

Reading and writing practice

152

[shorthand outlines with marginal annotations: Groom·ing, ap, Transcribe: $6, suc·cess·ful·ly, roy·al·ty, off·set, Transcribe: 10 percent, if, prompt·ly, agree·able] [143]

153

[shorthand outlines with marginal annotations: ex·ec·u·tives, para·graphs, ap, Smith's Mod·ern]

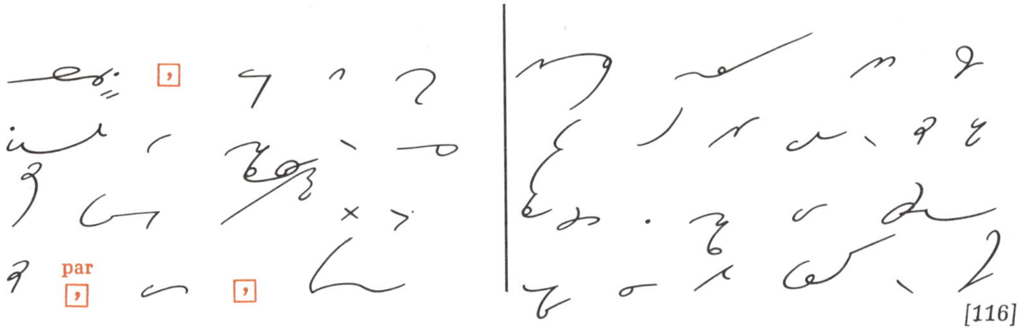

[116]

154
ef·fec·tive·ly 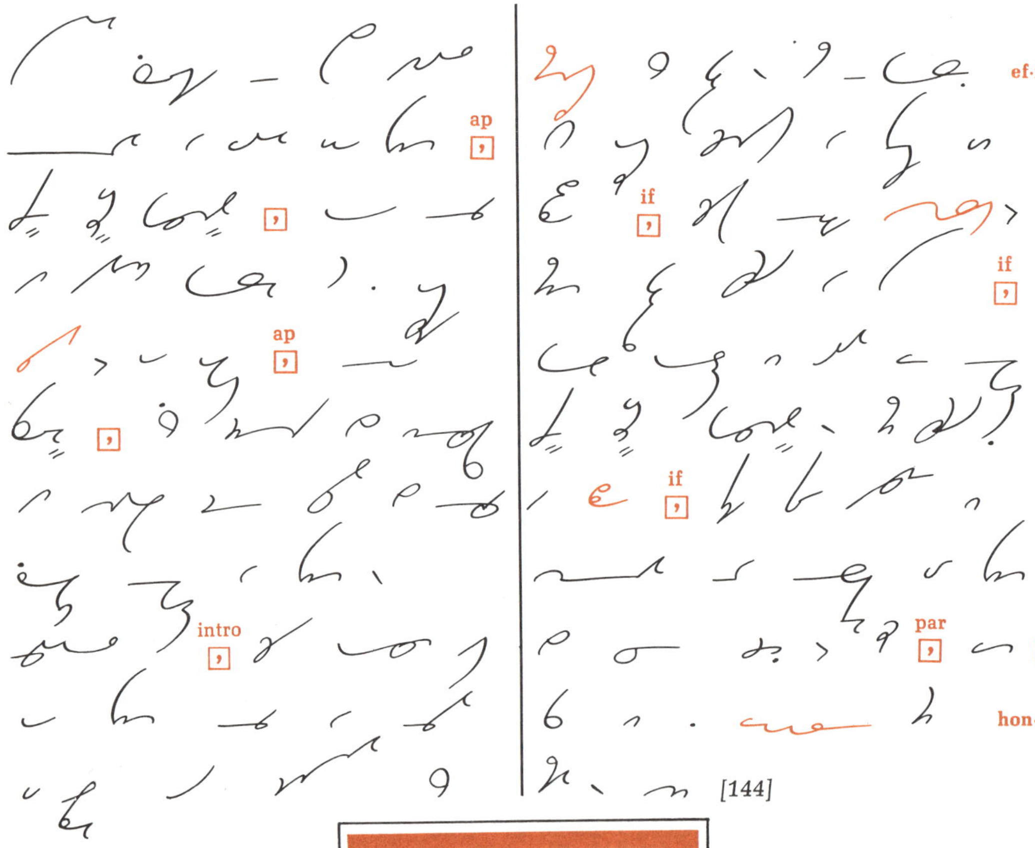
ap
if
grate·ful
edi·tion
ap
if
eas·i·er
intro
par
hon·o·rar·i·um
[144]

155 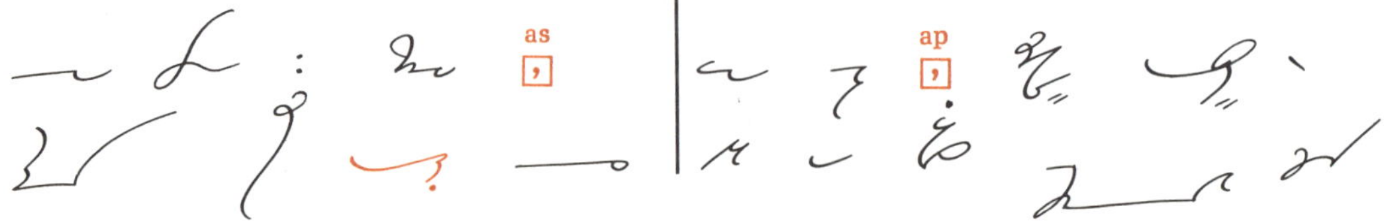
los·ing
as
ap

J. ROBERT JOHNSON CO. • 8992 Belvedere Drive • Seattle • Washington 98117

November 16, 19--

The New York Insurance Company
222 Broadway
New York, New York 10028

                    ATTENTION: Mr. Parsons

Gentlemen:

    This is just a note to tell you how glad we are that we took your advice a few years ago and purchased business-interruption insurance.

    As you know, on May 16 of last year our store was burned to the ground. We could easily have been bankrupted as a result of the fire, which caused considerable damage. Thanks to our policy with your organization, however, everything turned out all right.

    Of course, we obtained temporary quarters quickly. However, we suffered operating losses of more than $50,000. In addition, we had extra expenses amounting to $30,000 for fixtures and other items. We recovered this $80,000 because we had invested in your business-interruption insurance.

    While I am president of our company, we will never be without business-interruption insurance.

              Cordially yours,

              Harold G. Green

              Harold G. Green
              President

HGG:MH

Average-length letter
Semiblocked style,
with attention line
Standard punctuation

LESSON 21

Building transcription skills

157 TYPING STYLE STUDY | titles (concluded)

Articles, chapters, and unpublished manuscripts. The *parts* of complete published works are enclosed in quotation marks. The titles of complete but unpublished works, such as manuscripts and reports, are enclosed in quotation marks.

```
Did you read the article, "A New Beginning," in the
American Magazine?

The last chapter of his book is entitled "Women in the
Business World."
```

The first word and all the other main words in a title are capitalized. Words such as *in, the, and* in the body of the title are not capitalized.

158

Business vocabulary builder	**impact** Effect.
	biography The written story of a person's life.
	abridged Condensed but retaining the general sense of the original.

Reading and writing practice

159

ar·ti·cle

ac·knowl·edg·ing
re·ceipt

[100]

160

Transcribe: 3,000

manu·script

thor·ough·ly

af·fect·ing

length

[146]

161

Sher·iff

LESSON 22

163

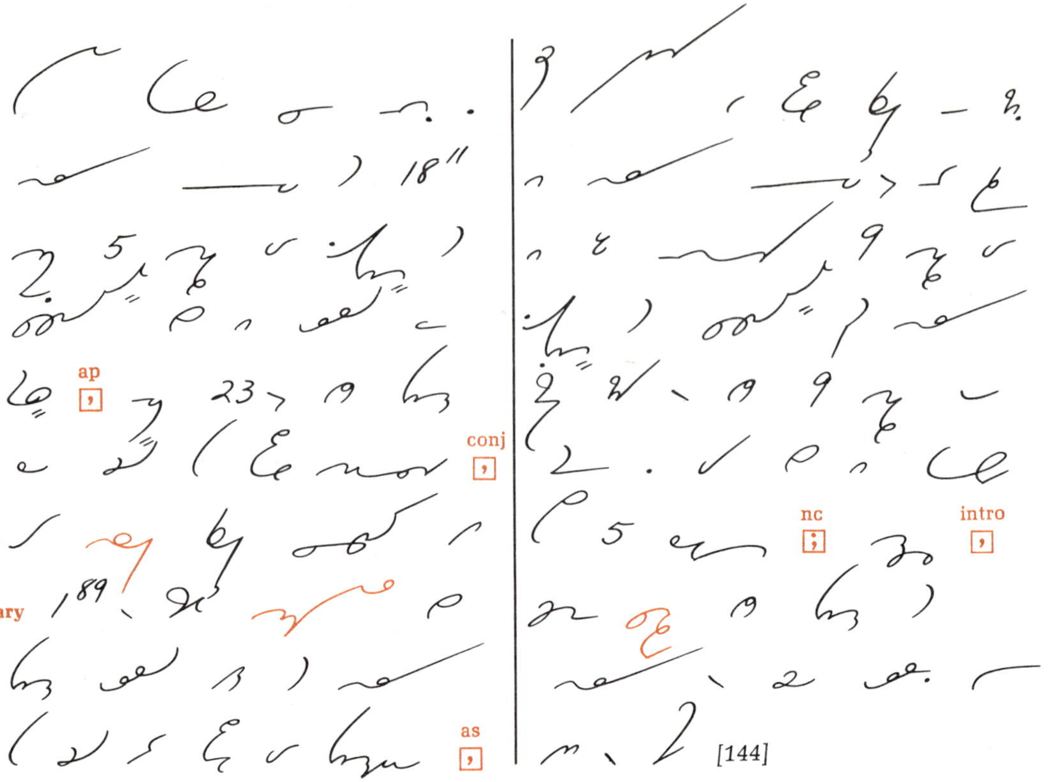

car·riage
cus·tom·ary

ap, 18″, 23, conj, as,

[144]

nc; intro,

ac·cept

164

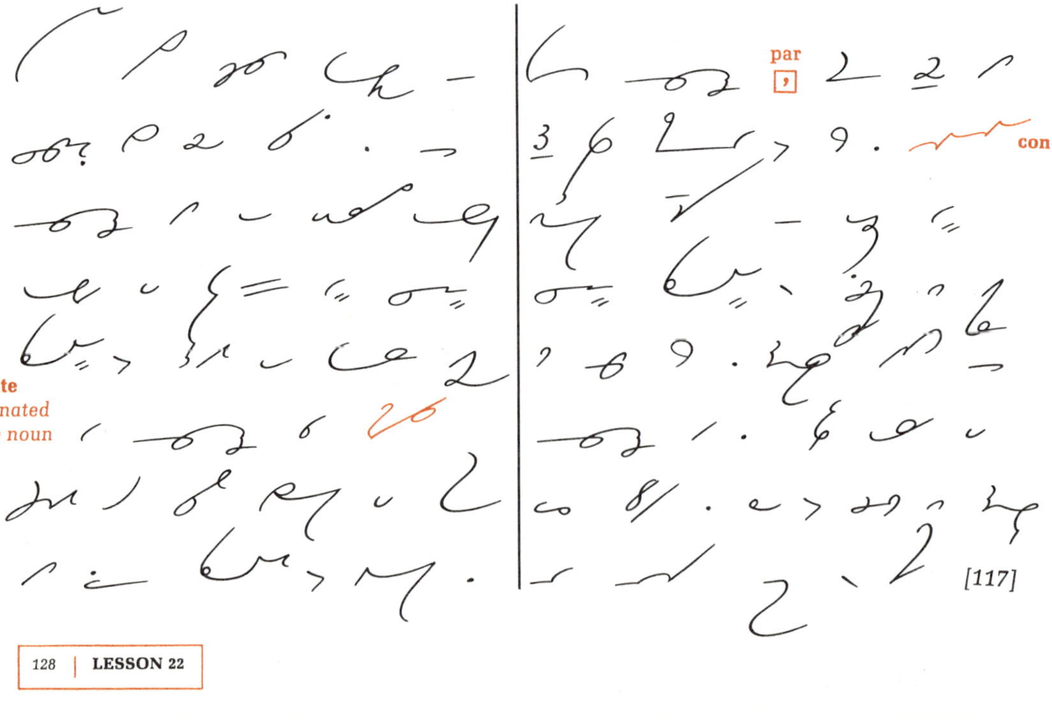

up-to-date
*hyphenated
before noun*

par,

con·trac·tor

[117]

LESSON 22

LESSON 23

Building transcription skills

165 PUNCTUATION PRACTICE | : enumeration

A colon is used after an expression that introduces some following material, such as an explanation of a general statement, a list, or an enumeration.

The paper deals with three subjects: editing, publishing, and printing.
The following topics are discussed in our booklet:
  1. How to write a sales letter
  2. How to write an effective advertisement
  3. How to design an attractive circular

Each time this use of the colon occurs in the Reading and Writing Practice, it will be indicated in the shorthand thus: enu

166

Business vocabulary builder	
proceed	To go ahead.
evaluate	To place a value on; to examine and judge.
salient	Prominent. *important*

Reading and writing practice

167 Build·er's

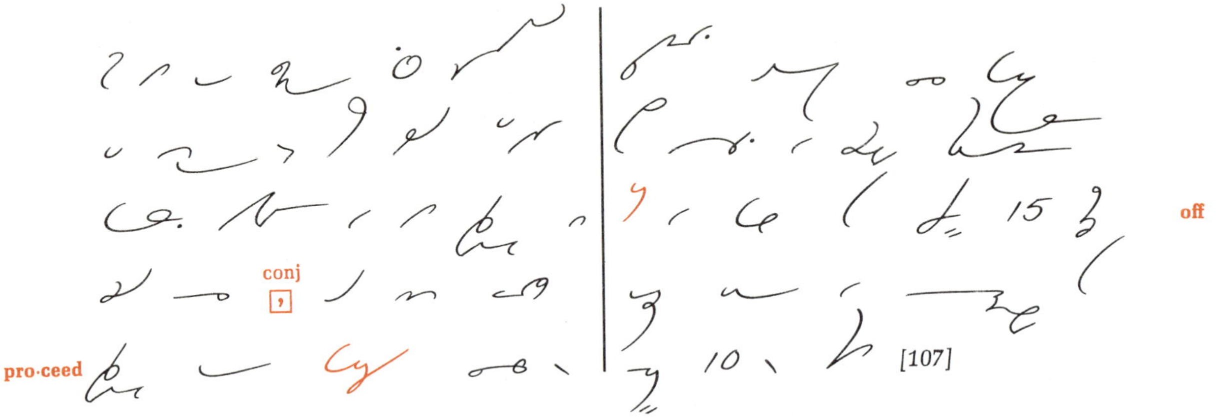

pro·ceed conj off [107]

168 as be·lieve nc enu pam·phlets eval·u·ate when [121]

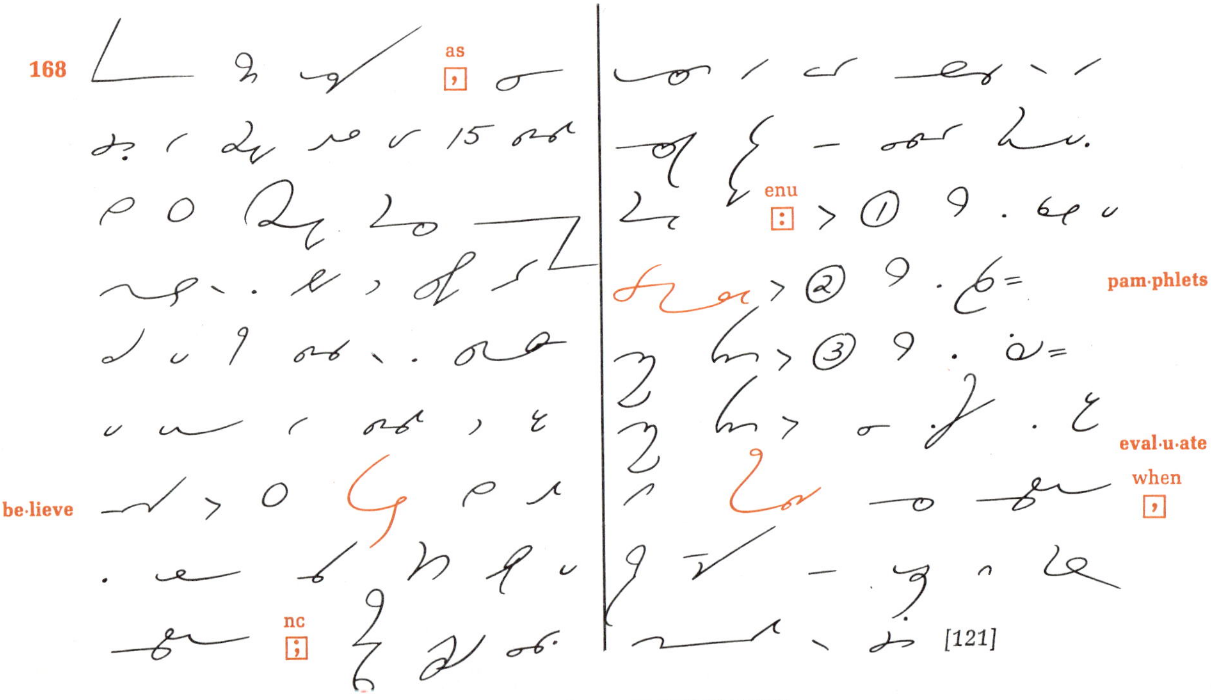

169 wom·en re·ferred

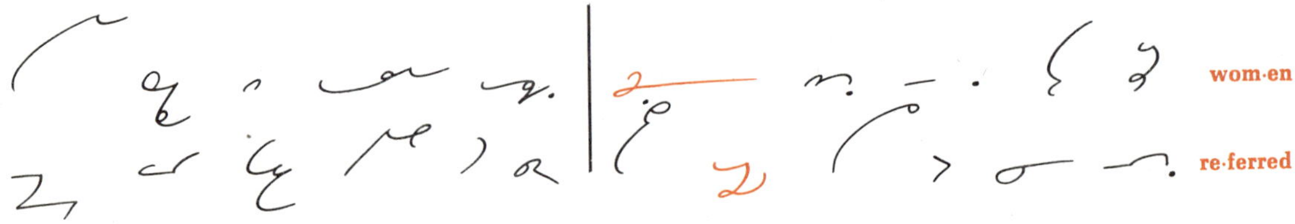

per·son·nel

[101]

170

Pro·ce·dures

suc·cess

ap·proach

LESSON 23

171

pres·ence, ap, sched·ul·ing, nc, al·ready, enu, sa·lient [126]

172 Transcribe: No. 4156 Baker's Psy·chol·o·gy

4156, nonr, intro, es·tab·lished, par, if, enu, rec·om·mend·ing [99]

173

fourth

260-page
hyphenated before noun

fac·tors

ad·just·ment

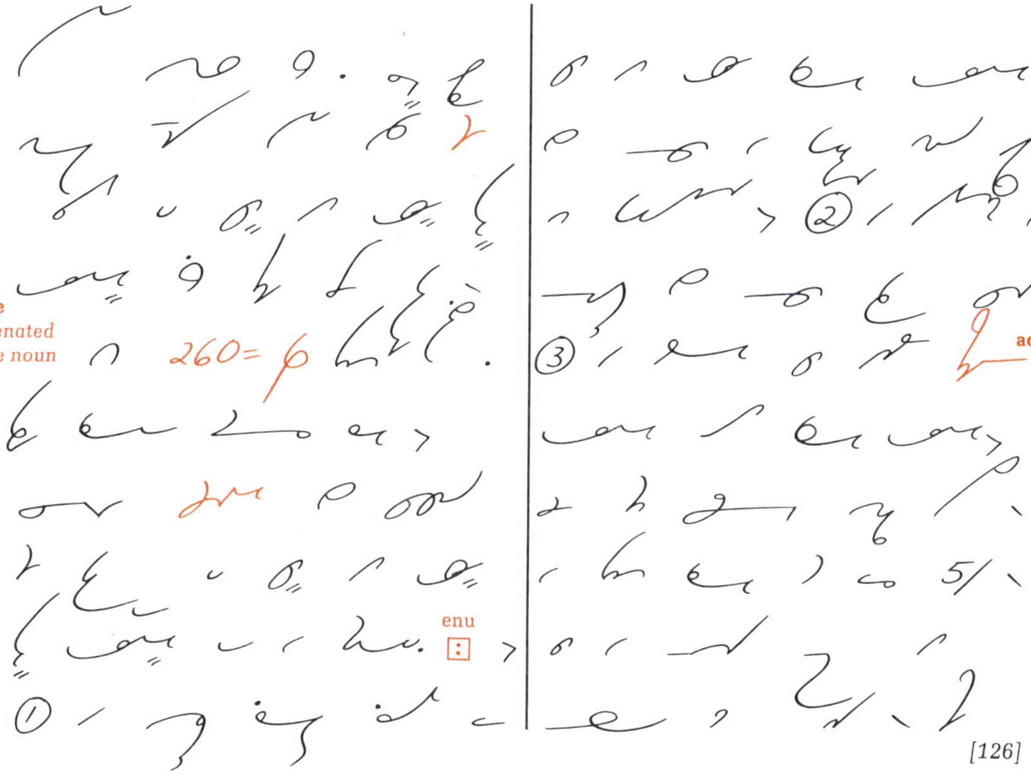

[126]

LESSON 23

Letter placement
AVERAGE LETTERS

By this time you are no doubt getting the "feel" of placing a short letter (up to approximately 100 words) by judgment.

You will now take up the placement of an average-sized letter (one that contains between 100 and 200 words).

On page 135 you will find Letter No. 170 of *Gregg Transcription* as it was written by Ellen Gardiner in her shorthand notebook. You will also find her transcript of that letter, which was made on a typewriter that had elite (small) type. The letter contains about 160 words.

Ellen writes a style of shorthand similar to that in which the letters in this book are written. She required almost an entire column in her notebook for this letter.

Whenever a letter takes approximately one column in her notebook, Ellen does three things:

1 She sets her margin stops for about 1½-inch margins at the left and at the right.

2 She types the date two lines below the last line of the letterhead.

3 She starts the inside address about 3½ inches from the top of the paper.

If she is using a typewriter that has pica (large) type, she starts the inside address about 3 inches from the top of the paper. Her margins are again about 1½ inches on each side.

Make a copy of Letter No. 170 and see how much space this average-sized letter requires in your shorthand notebook. You may require more space than Ellen did if your notes are large and less space if your notes are small. Try to fix in your mind the space you require in your notebook for an average-sized letter; whenever a letter takes that much space in your notebook, you will immediately know where to set your marginal stops and where to begin the inside address. If possible, transcribe Letter No. 170 on the typewriter from your own notes, setting it up by judgment.

▶ *Caution!* When you are taking dictation on the job, you will, of course, have to take into consideration in your letter placement any insertions or deletions that your dictator may make. Even though a letter may fill a full column or more in your notebook, it may still be a "short" letter because of the material that your dictator may have decided to take out during and after dictation.

THE INTERNATIONAL-DETROIT

College of Commerce

BANK OF COMMERCE BUILDING   DETROIT • 48233

June 28, 19--

The Grayson Publishing Company
416 Madison Avenue
New York, New York 10018

Gentlemen:

    I am sending you by express a copy of my manuscript, "Basic Accounting Procedures," which I have developed over a period of years and which I have used in my classes with considerable success. I am sending my materials to you at the suggestion of your representative, Mr. Charles Baker, who expressed great interest in them.

    I think there is a definite need for this type of approach to accounting for the following reasons:

    1. Teachers of accounting have been asking whether I planned to make the materials available in printed form so that they, too, might use them in their classes.

    2. With the interest in accountancy constantly increasing, there should be a big market for these materials.

    If there are any questions I can answer for you after you have had an opportunity to study the manuscript, please let me know.

                    Yours very truly,

                    Charles E. Brock

                    Charles E. Brock
                    Associate Professor

CEB:LE

Building transcription skills

174 PUNCTUATION PRACTICE ❙ **, introducing short quote**

Short quotations are introduced by a comma.

The manager said, "The office will close at 4 o'clock."
He replied, "I cannot accept the position."

Each time this use of the comma occurs in the Reading and Writing Practice, it will be indicated in the shorthand thus: isq

, inside quote

. inside quote

? inside quote

The comma and period are *always* typed inside the final quotation mark.

She said, "I found the book interesting."
My manuscript, "How to Read a Financial Statement," is enclosed.

Question marks are placed inside or outside the final quotation mark according to the sense of the sentence.

She asked, "Did you receive your copy of the book?"

but

Why did she say, "I do not like to work here"?

Semicolons and colons are *always* placed outside the final quotation mark.

Be sure to mark that letter "confidential"; then place the carbon on my desk.
Shipments of the following goods should be marked "fragile": china, glassware, ceramics.

When punctuation is placed inside quotation marks in the Reading and Writing Practice, it will be indicated in the shorthand in the following ways:

iq,   iq.   iq?

175

| Business vocabulary builder | **CPA** Abbreviation for *Certified Public Accountant*.
 habitual Done by habit; customary.
 the bar The legal profession. |

Reading and writing practice

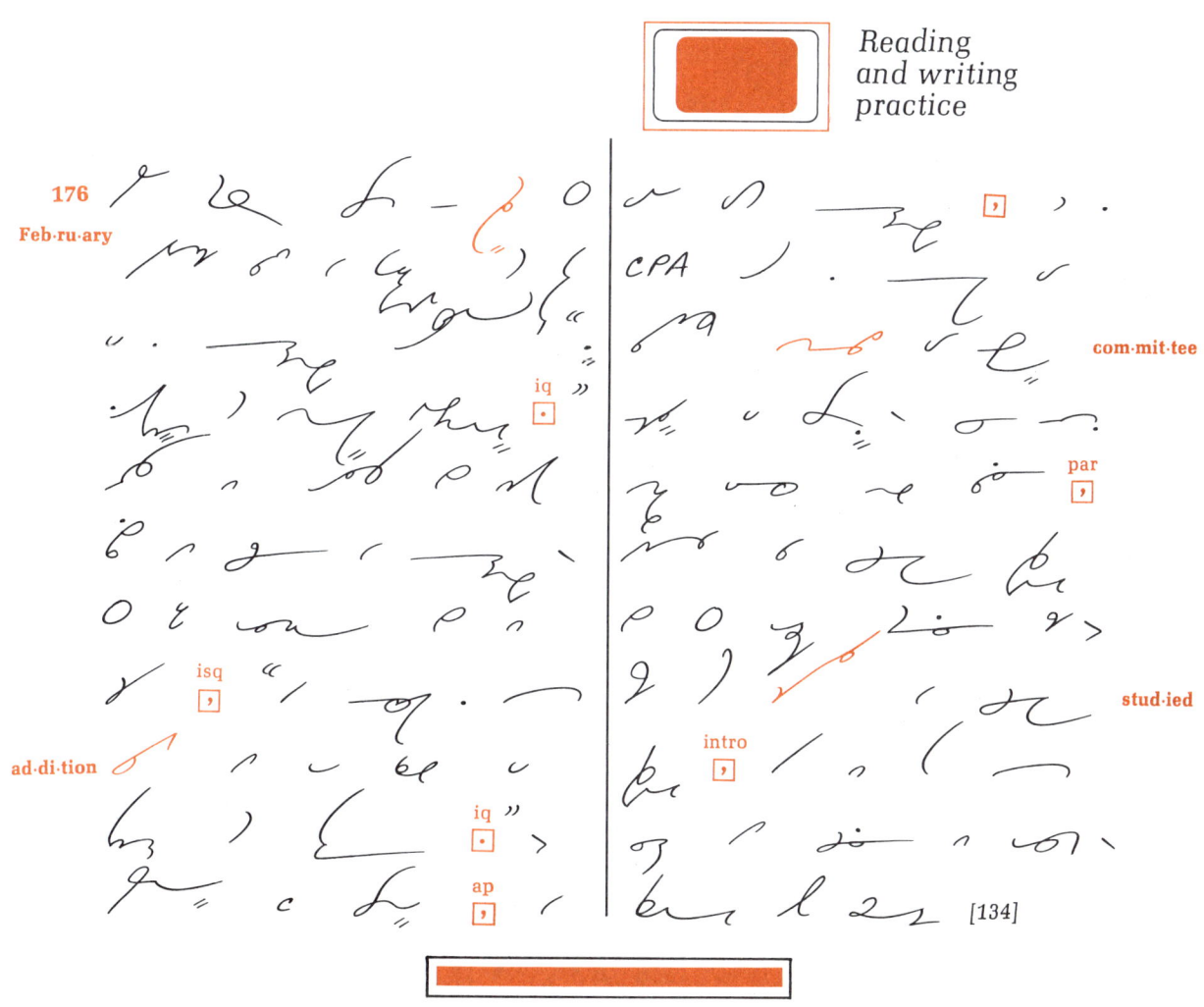

176 Feb·ru·ary, ad·di·tion, isq, iq, ap, CPA, com·mit·tee, par, intro, stud·ied [134]

LESSON 24 | 137

177

178

179

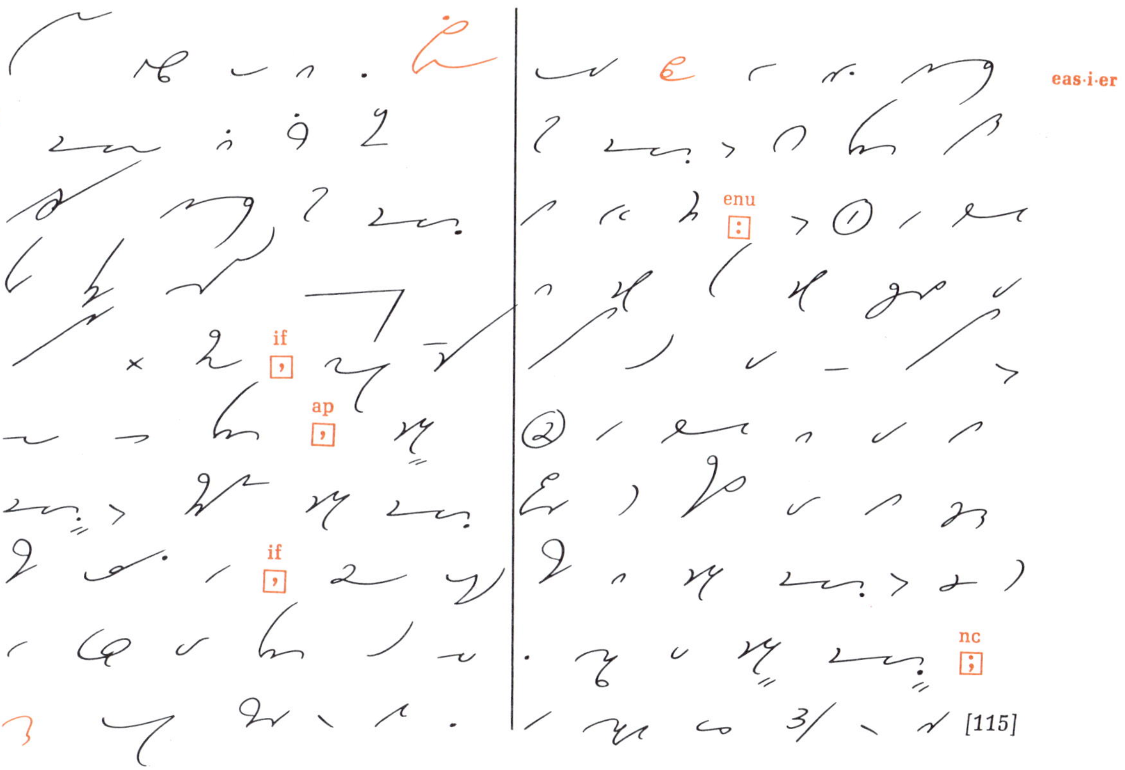

ha·bit·u·al

ques·tions

eas·i·er

180

ad·mis·sion
bar

shin·gle

li·brary

too

LESSON 24 | 139

Building transcription skills

181 PUNCTUATION PRACTICE | **: introducing long quote**

Long quotations are introduced by a colon.

The author said: "I am writing the seventh chapter of my book. If all goes well, I should have the entire manuscript in your hands by May 20."

Each time a long quotation is introduced by a colon in the Reading and Writing Practice, it will be indicated in the shorthand thus: ilq

182

Business vocabulary builder	**textiles** Woven fabrics.
	comply To conform or agree.
	accompany Go along with.

Reading and writing practice

183
se·mes·ter

as·sign·ment

140 | LESSON 25

aids

[84] prac·ti·cal intro

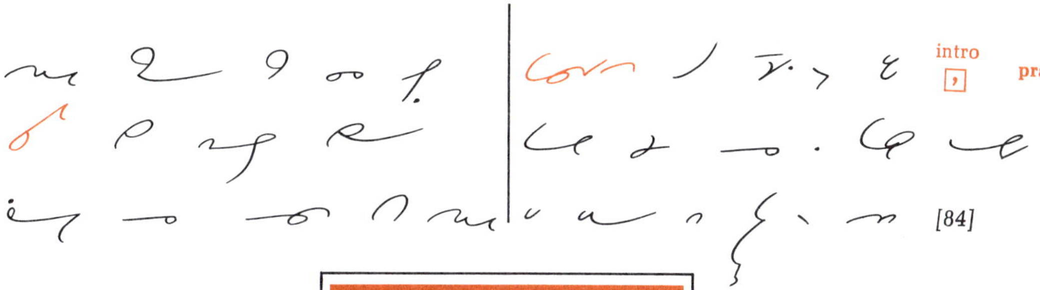

184 Mod·ern

com·mit·tee

ac·com·pa·ny

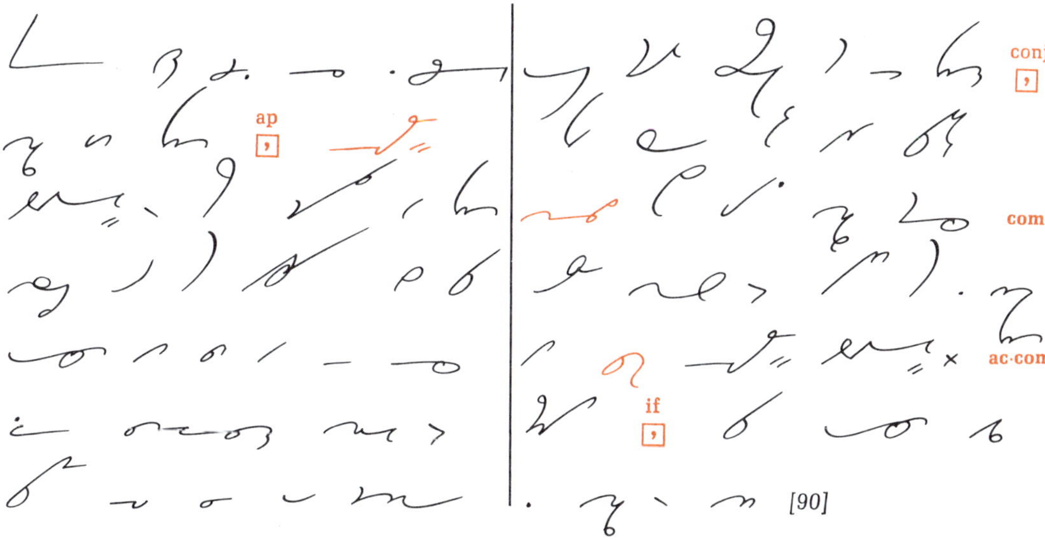

[90] if ap conj

185 flat·tered

man·u·al

guid·ance

enough

intro conj if

LESSON 25

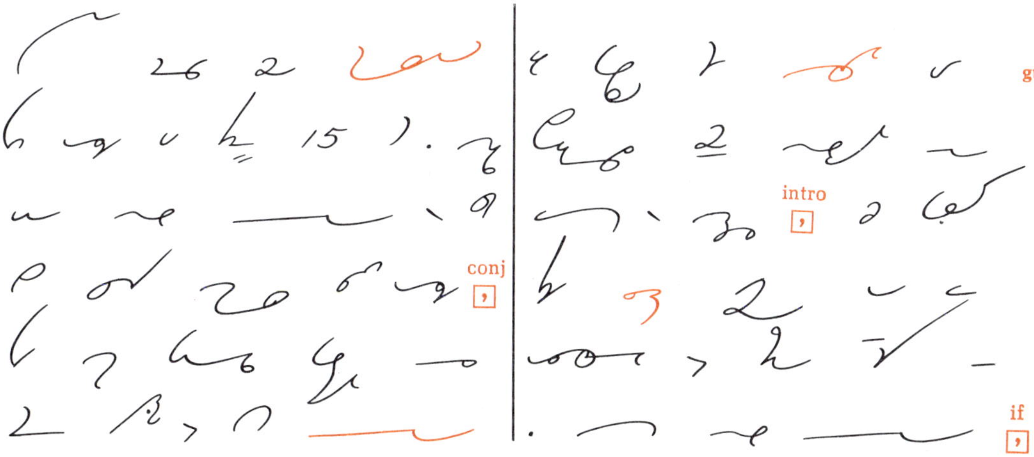

rec·om·mend
Green's 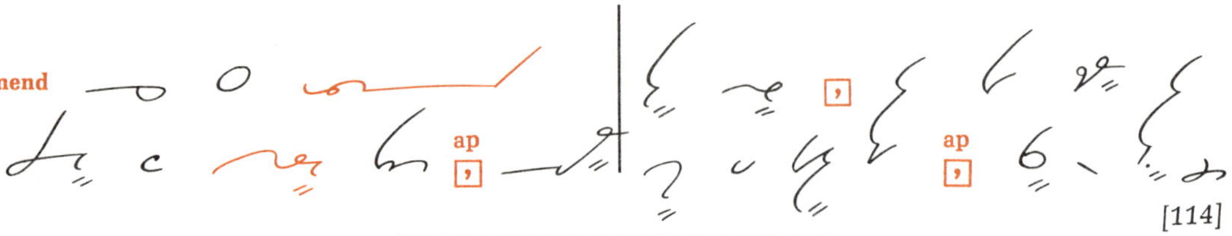
ap
ap
[114]

186
if
sub·scrip·tion
bi·month·ly
par
ilq
par
if
clev·er
Transcribe: $8
of·fer·ing 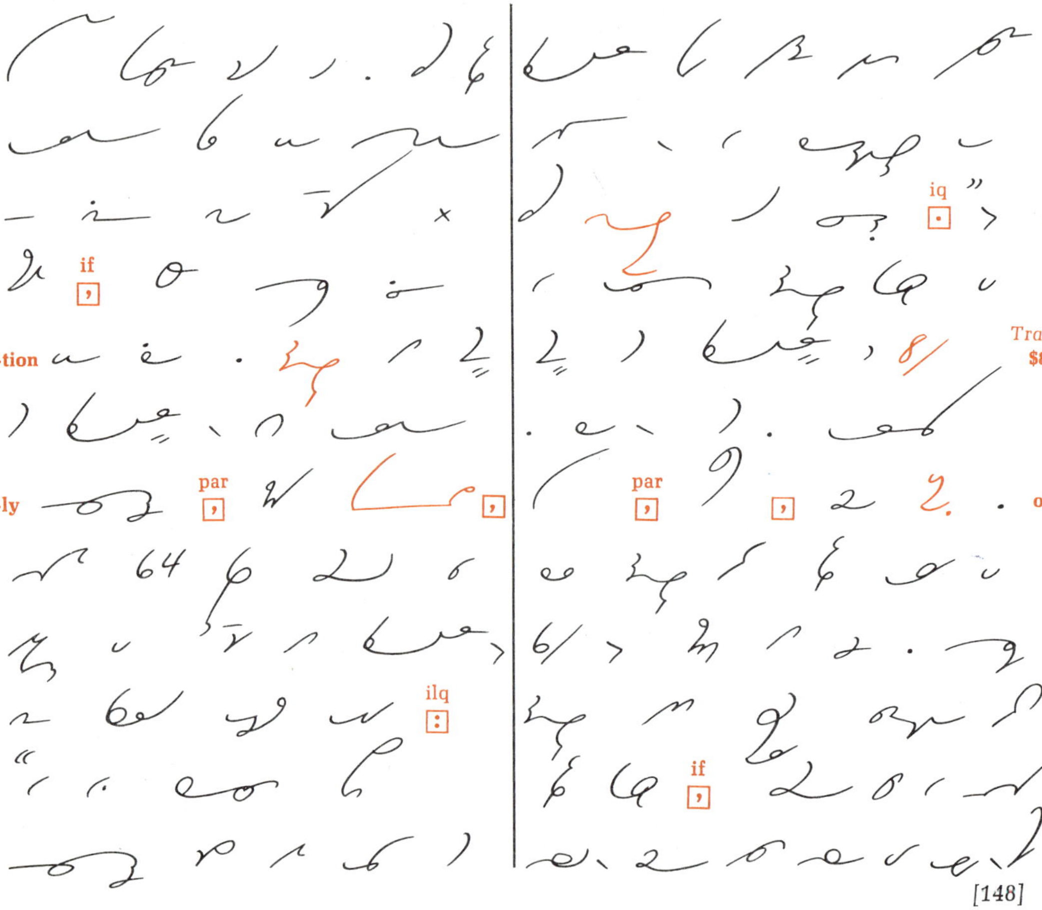
[148]

187
re·cent·ly

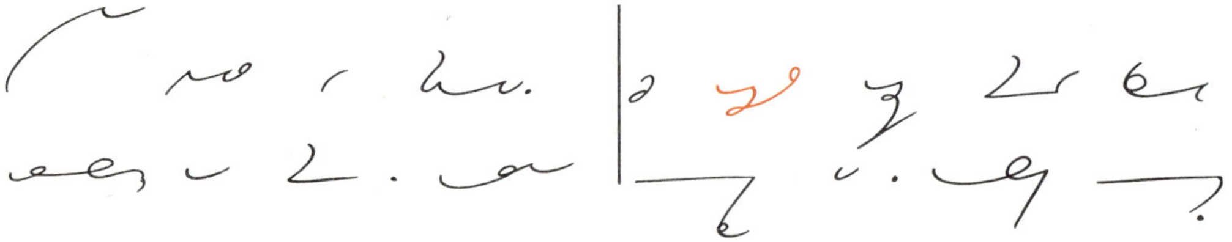

142 | **LESSON 25**

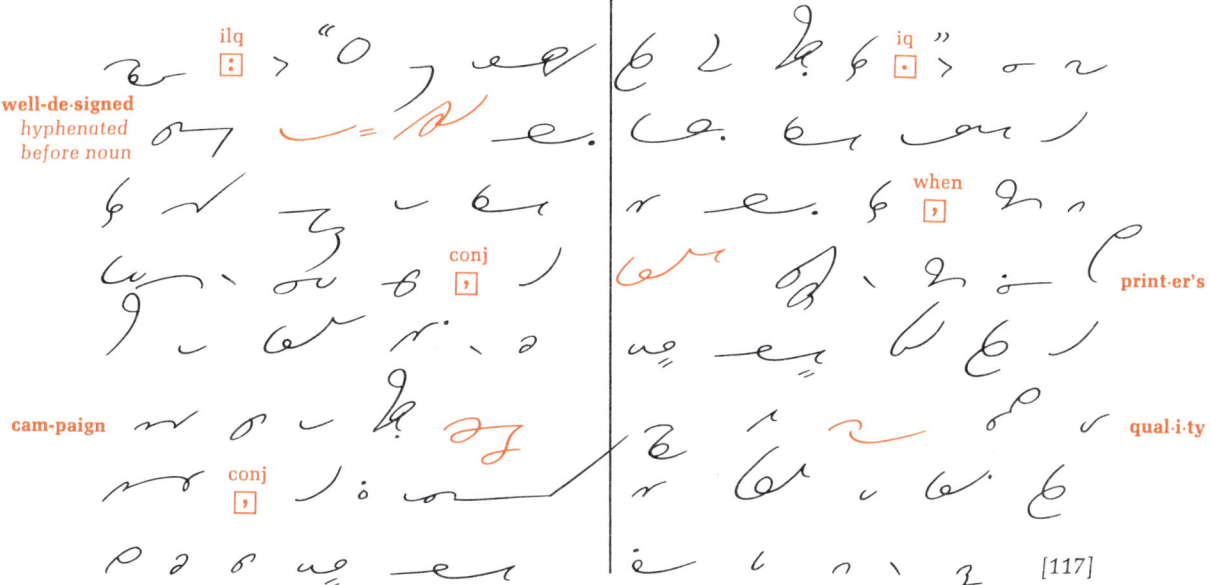

REVIEW TIP

Beginning on page 422 you will find complete lists of the word beginnings and endings, phrases, and brief forms of Gregg Shorthand.

You are already familiar with the words and phrases in those lists, but to be sure that they do not become hazy in your mind, you should review them frequently.

Consequently, plan to set aside a few minutes each day to read from those lists. Time spent on those lists will be time well spent.

After you have read all the lists from left to right, read them again from right to left.

At this stage of your shorthand course, you should be able to read the lists very rapidly.

The secretary's writing positions

When Ellen Gardiner studied shorthand in school, she took dictation under ideal conditions. She had her own comfortable desk and chair, with plenty of room and light. That was as it should be, for Ellen was learning a skill, and her teacher knew that Ellen would progress most rapidly if she practiced under ideal conditions.

Ellen realized, however, that the conditions under which she would have to write when taking dictation on the job might not be ideal. During the first few months on her new job, Ellen counted six different positions in which she had to take dictation. Here they are:

1 The most frequent position, and a fairly comfortable one for Ellen, is writing with her notebook on the ledge of Mr. Davis's desk.

2 Once in a while, however, Mr. Davis has papers or books on the ledge. Not wishing to disturb them, Ellen will write with her notebook on her knee.

3 On a few occasions Ellen can take dictation in real comfort. That is when she can move a chair to the side of the desk opposite Mr. Davis and place her notebook on the desk itself. This does not happen often, however, for Mr. Davis's desk is usually too full of papers and other materials.

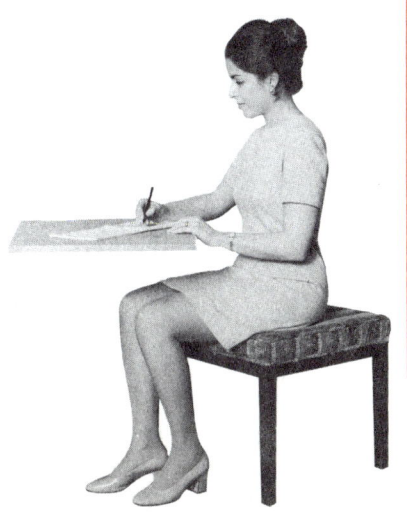

4 On rare occasions Ellen has to write while standing up or even while walking. There was the time, for example, when Mr. Davis had an office full of people and all the chairs were occupied. Mr. Davis called Ellen in and asked her to take a memorandum on an agreement that had been reached. Of course, no employer would ask his secretary to write in a standing position unless it was an emergency.

5 Every month Ellen has the job of taking minutes of the meeting of the board of directors. That is the most difficult shorthand assignment of her job, but, as a compensating factor, she is able to take the minutes under the most comfortable writing conditions—sitting at the head of the table.

6 Finally, Ellen occasionally takes dictation over the telephone. Sometimes she takes an order or makes a few simple notes. Sometimes, she takes entire letters or memoranda. For this purpose she always has handy near the telephone a notebook and a ballpoint pen, for which she reaches almost automatically when she answers the phone.

Homes and home furnishings

Building transcription skills

188 SIMILAR-WORDS DRILL

Words that sound alike and words that sound or look *almost* alike are responsible for many errors that stenographers make when they transcribe. Often they know which word of a similar-sounding pair is the correct one to use in a sentence, but because of carelessness or inattention, they transcribe the incorrect one.

Hereafter, in the first lesson of each chapter you will study a Similar-Words Drill that will call to your attention pairs of words that may lead to mistranscription if you are not wary.

Study the definition of each word carefully. As you read the Reading and Writing Practice of the lesson, watch for the similar words; you will find them used a number of times.

SIMILAR-WORDS DRILL | week, weak

week   Seven days.

I will be gone all week.

weak   Not strong.

The weak water main burst.

189

Business vocabulary builder	**burst** To come open; explode. **concrete** (*noun*) Cement. **negotiate** To confer with another in order to arrive at a settlement.

Reading and writing practice

190

courteous
week
weak

[69]

191

connection
concrete
mine
inspector
garage

[131]

192

week · as · re·pairs · Transcribe: $2,000 · lo·cal · [112]

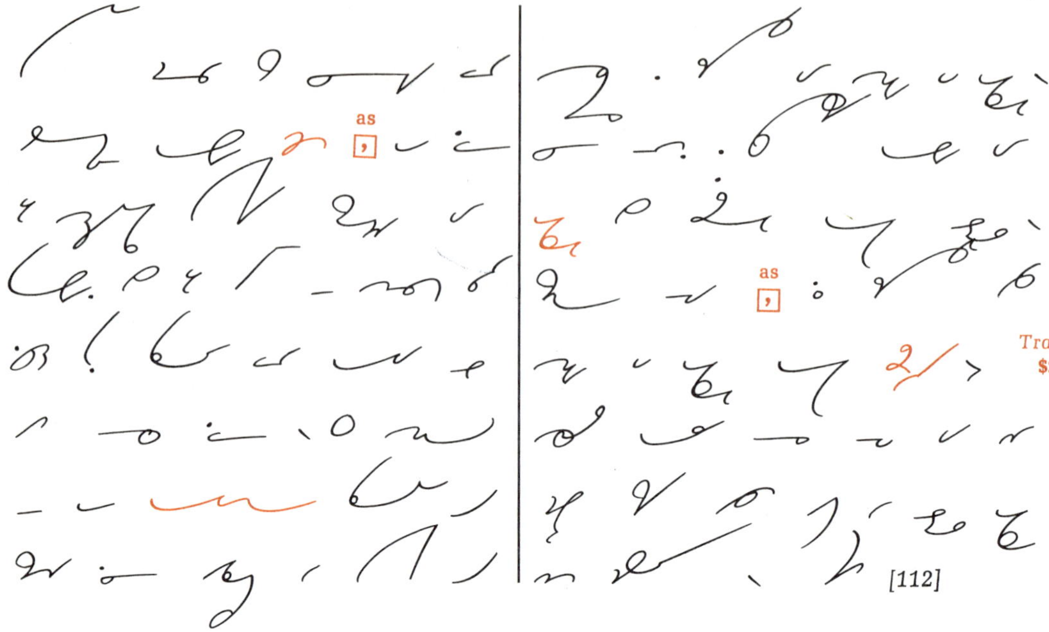

193

con·trac·tor · ac·ci·den·tal·ly · as · intro · ef·fect · per·ma·nent · at·tor·ney · as·so·ci·ate · ap · ne·go·ti·ate · re·vealed · par · [121]

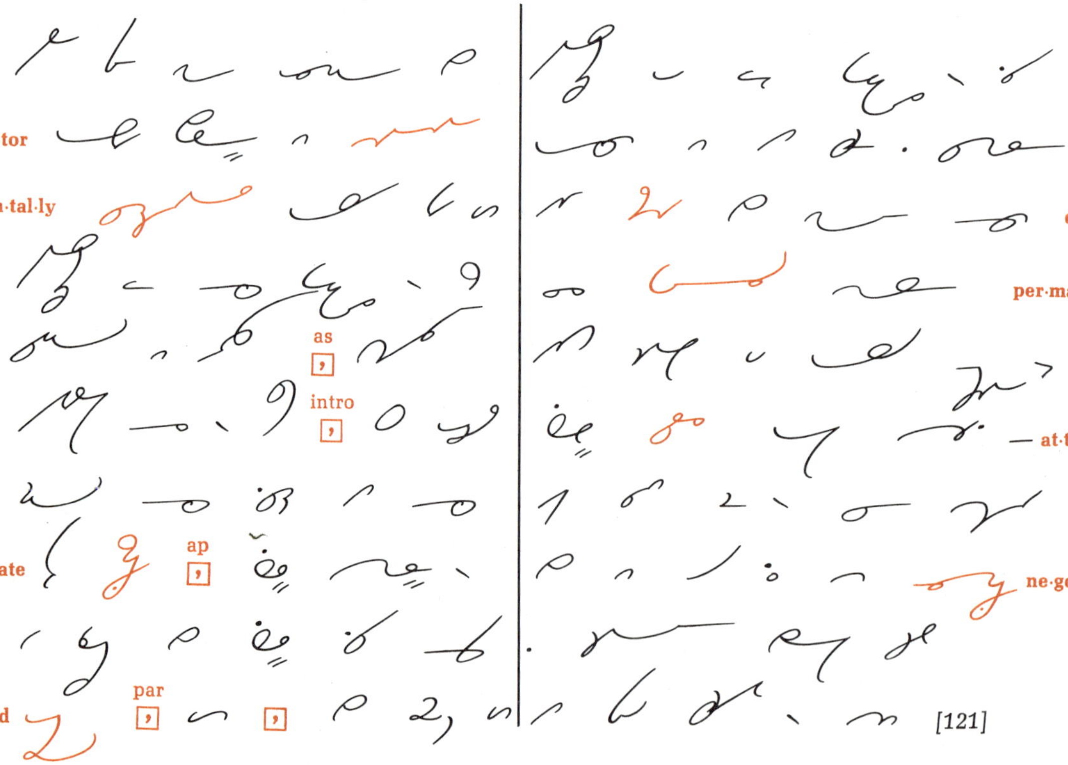

194

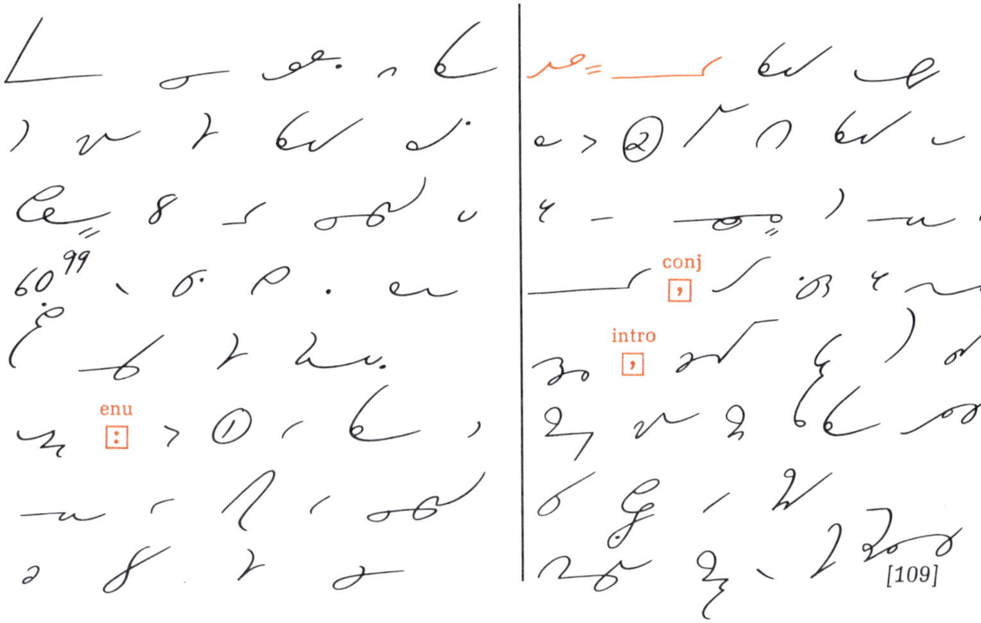

[shorthand content]

enu :

three-month
hyphenated before noun

conj ,

intro ,

[109]

195

[shorthand content]

conj ,

if ,

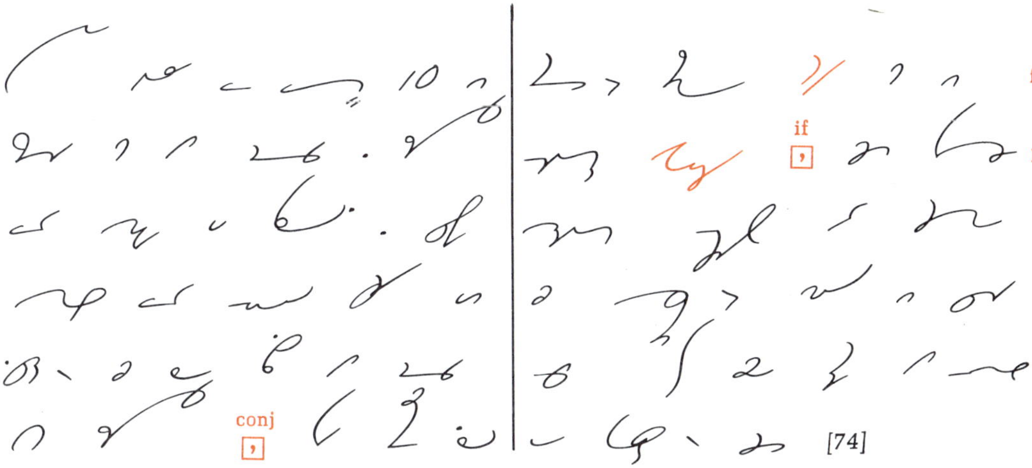

for·ward

pro·ceed

[74]

Building transcription skills

196 SPELLING FAMILIES | **-ense, -ence**

An effective method of improving your ability to spell is to practice words in related groups, or spelling families.

To get the most benefit from these spelling families, follow this procedure, which is recommended by expert teachers of spelling:

1 Look at the word.
2 Pronounce the word.
3 Spell the word.
4 Write or, better still, type the word.

When a word ends with the sound *ens,* be careful; it may be spelled with an *s* or it may be spelled with a *c.*

Practice the following groups, using the procedure described above.

-ense

ex·pense	im·mense	con·dense
in·tense	li·cense	sense
de·fense	pre·tense	of·fense

-ence

ev·i·dence	ref·er·ence	ab·sence
pref·er·ence	con·fer·ence	si·lence
con·fi·dence	com·mence	neg·li·gence

197

Business vocabulary builder	**intensive** Concentrated.
	in transit On the way.
	tranquil Quiet; calm.

150 | LESSON 27

Reading and writing practice

198 [shorthand] sea·son, ex·pe·ri·enc·ing, par, in·ten·sive, intro, urge, freezes [70]

199 [shorthand] intro, con·sul·tant, intro, ap, wide·ly used *no hyphen after ly*, ap·peal, par, li·censed [134]

LESSON 27

200

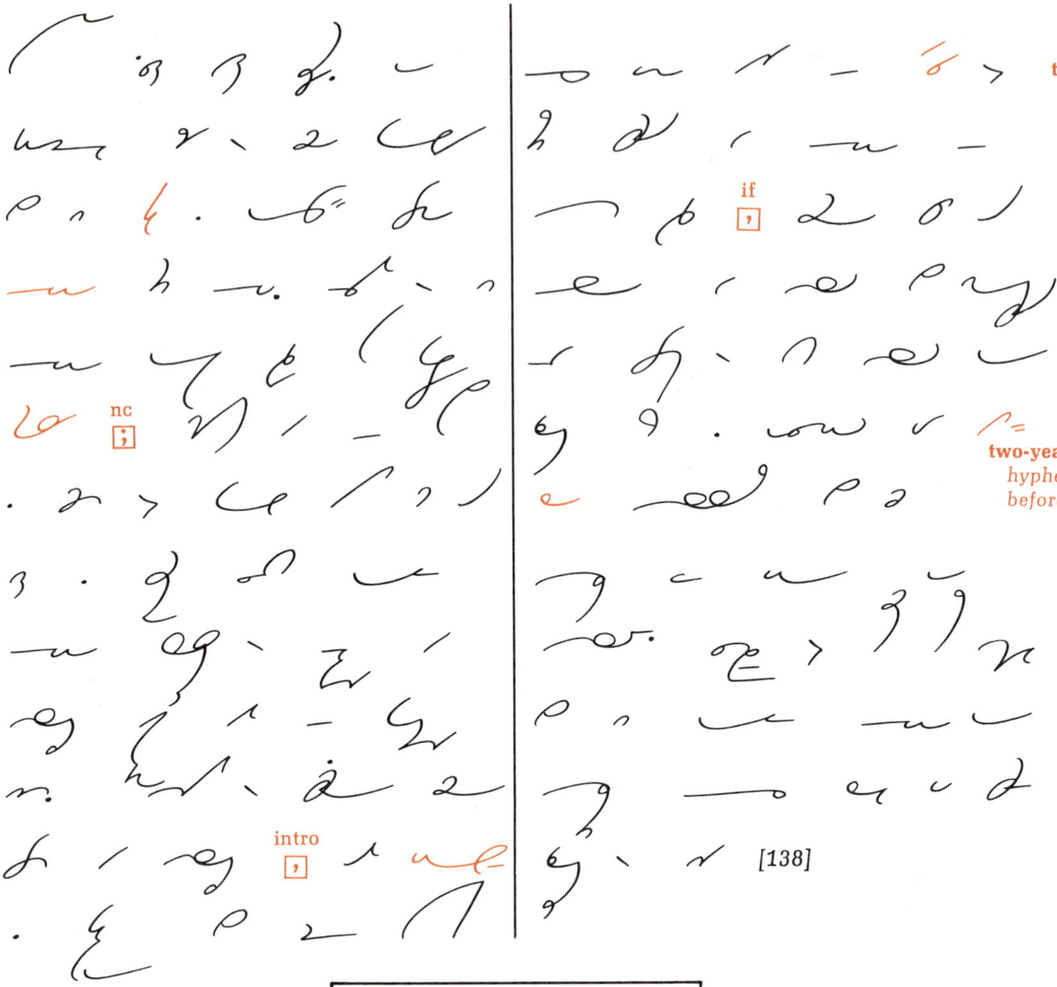

tran·sit
chose
if ,
mow·er
freight
nc ;
two-year
hyphenated before noun
al·ways
intro ,
[138]

201

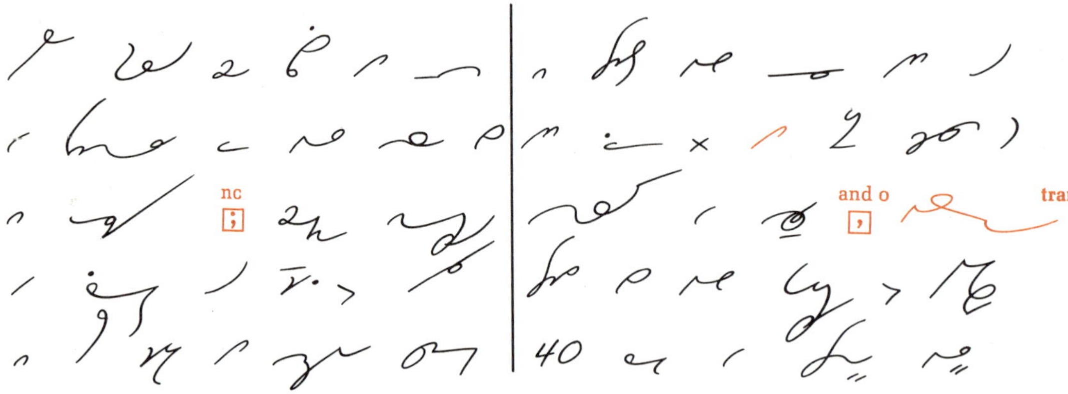

nc ;
too
and o ,
tran·quil

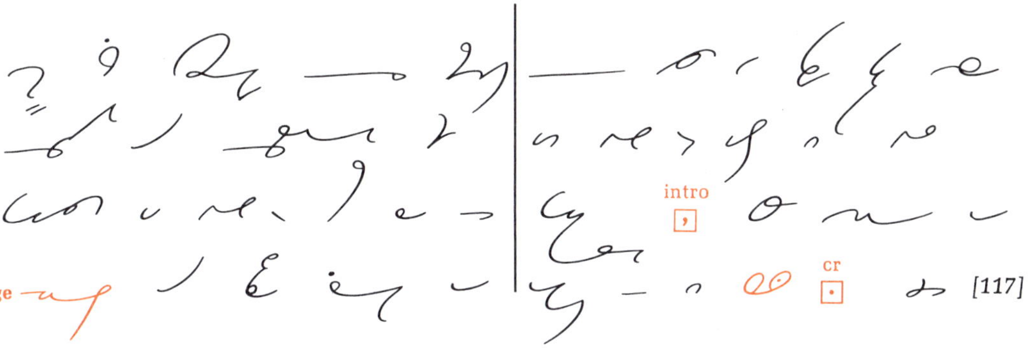

knowl·edge intro cr [117] ar·ea

202 neigh·bor's

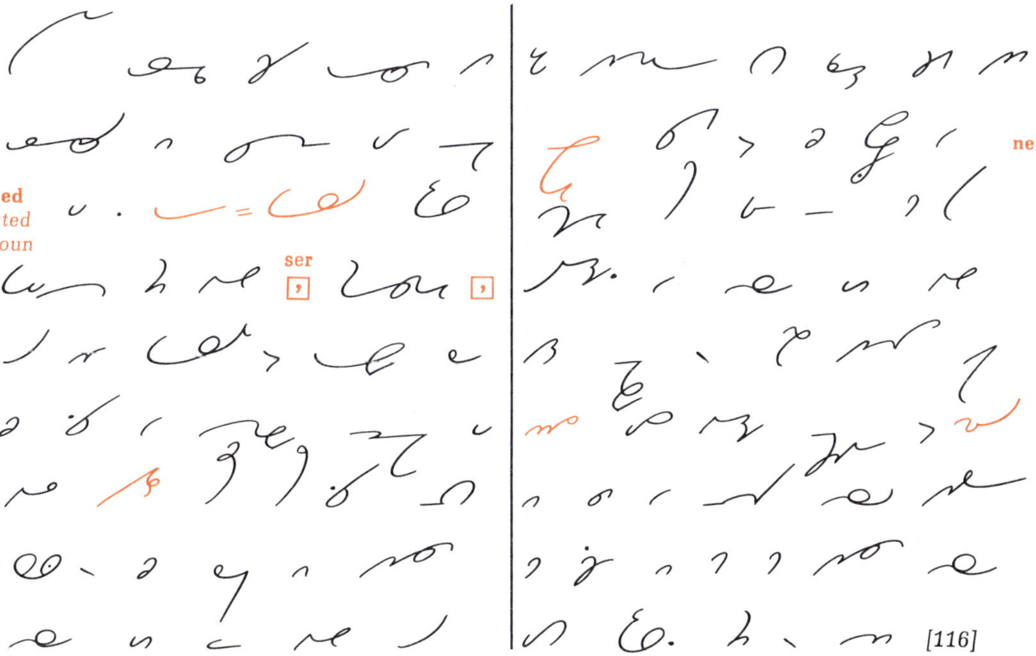

well-planned
*hyphenated
before noun*

ser

dis·eases wor·thy
won't

[116]

203 well written
*no noun,
no hyphen*

of·fi·cial ap conj [36]

LESSON 27 | 153

Building transcription skills

204 ACCURACY PRACTICE

Occasionally, under the stress of rapid writing, you will write an outline that is distorted. In most cases the sense of the sentence will enable you to determine its meaning. However, there are a few outlines—fortunately, very few—that the sense of the sentence will not help you to read if they are distorted. In this Accuracy Practice, and in those that you will find in later lessons, a number of such outlines will be called to your attention so that whenever you have occasion to write them, you can take special pains to execute them with accurate proportion.

Here is the way you should handle each Accuracy Practice:

1 Write the words in Group 1 slowly, watching your proportions carefully.
2 Write the words in Group 1 once again, writing as rapidly as you can while still maintaining accurate proportion.
3 Read and copy the sentence for Group 1 in the Practice Drill.
4 Repeat the same three steps for Groups 2 and 3.

GROUP 1	GROUP 2	GROUP 3
order	say	as
audit	see	if

practice drill

3 [shorthand]

1 The accountant will <u>order</u> the books tomorrow. The accountant will <u>audit</u> the books tomorrow.
2 Can you <u>say</u> whether he made all the changes? Can you <u>see</u> whether he made all the changes?
3 <u>As</u> you are attending the meeting, I shall not have to go. <u>If</u> you are attending the meeting, I shall not have to go.

205 | Business vocabulary builder

postdated Dated later than the actual date.

termites Antlike insects which feed on wood and are highly destructive to trees and wooden structures.

exterminator Person whose occupation is to get rid of insects, vermin, etc.

Reading and writing practice

206
ad·ver·tise·ment
of·fered

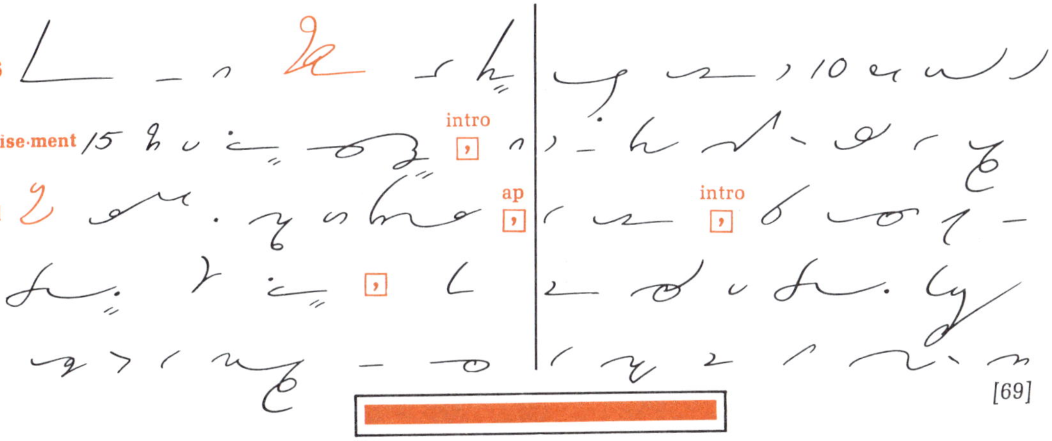

[shorthand] [69]

207
kitch·en
sat·is·fied

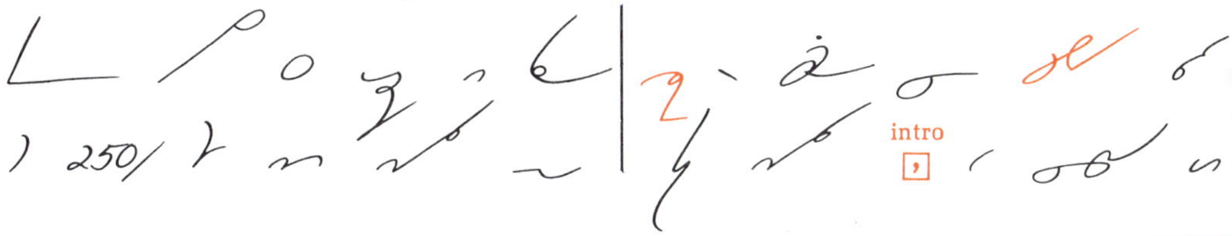

[shorthand]

than [shorthand] when [shorthand] par [shorthand] 150 ap [shorthand] nonr [126]

208
Transcribe:
18 Street

rot·ting

re·spon·si·ble

ex·ter·mi·na·tor

as intro de·struc·tion nc [141]

209 shrink·ing intro enu pop·u·lar·i·ty en·gi·neers conj [137]

210 ser up-to-the-min·ute *hyphenated before noun* best-known *hyphenated before noun* [100]

LESSON 28 | 157

Building transcription skills

211 OFFICE-STYLE DICTATION

When a businessman is answering a routine letter, he will often dictate the entire answer without making any changes or insertions. When he dictates an important letter, where every word is important, he may change words or phrases, transpose sentences, and even revise entire paragraphs. It will be your job to make all these changes and insertions in your notes quickly and in such a way that you will be able to transcribe the letter exactly as the businessman wishes it transcribed.

If you have a good shorthand speed, you will have no difficulty making the transition from the timed dictation that you have been taking in class to the business dictation of your employer. The more shorthand speed you possess, the easier this type of dictation will be for you. In addition, if you are alert, you will soon spot the types of changes that your employer frequently makes and you will develop skill in handling them.

In this chapter and in each chapter hereafter, you will take up one of the more common problems of office-style dictation. Read the explanation of the problem carefully, and study the illustrations that accompany it. Then read the shorthand letter that follows the explanation to see how the problem should be handled in your shorthand notes.

Perhaps your teacher will dictate an occasional letter to you the way a businessman might dictate it. Thus you will have an opportunity to apply the business dictation suggestions that will be presented to you.

OFFICE-STYLE DICTATION | **deletions**

A businessman will occasionally decide to delete—take out—a word or a phrase or even a sentence that he has dictated. For example, he may say:

The pamphlet describes completely the furniture we suggest—take out **completely.**

To indicate this deletion, you would simply strike a heavy downward line through the word thus:

Sometimes he may simply repeat the sentence without the word or phrase that he wishes to omit. He may say:

The enclosed pamphlet describes and illustrates what we have in mind—no, **the enclosed pamphlet describes what we have in mind.**

To indicate this deletion, you would mark out in your notes not only the word *illustrates* but the word *and* as well.

If only one word or short expression is to be taken out, use a heavy downward line; if several words are to be taken out, a wavy line will save time. The dictator may say:

I feel, therefore, that I cannot accept your offer—no, scratch it out.

In your notes you would show this deletion thus:

ILLUSTRATION OF OFFICE-STYLE DICTATION

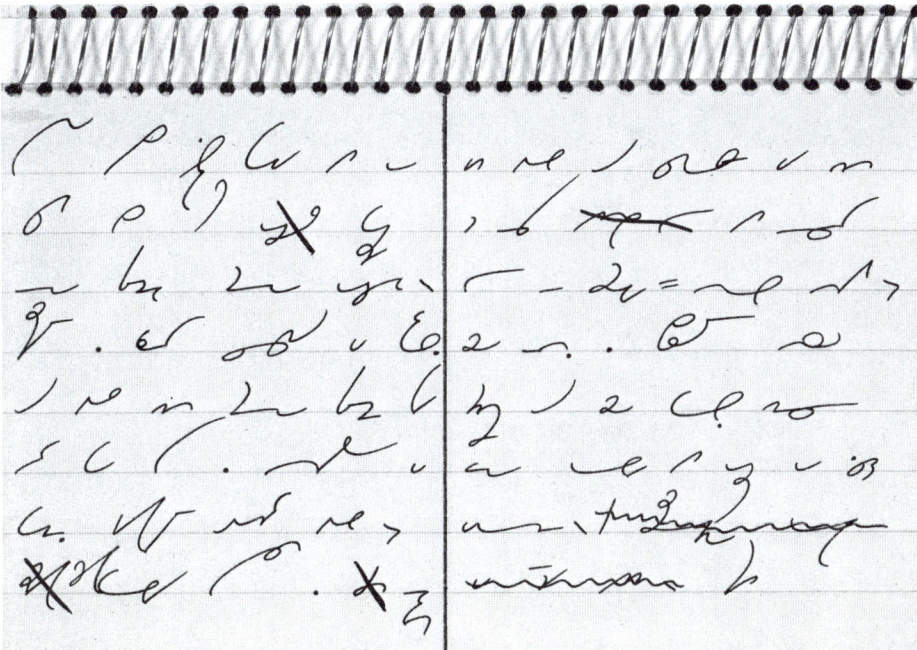

212 Business vocabulary builder

cumbersome Clumsy.
nominal Insignificant.
primary First; main.

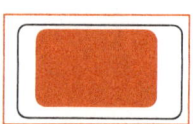
Reading and writing practice

213 [shorthand text with annotations: when, par, ef·fect, sub·stan·tial, and o, when, old-fash·ioned, prompt·ly, fuel, intro, seal·ing] [118]

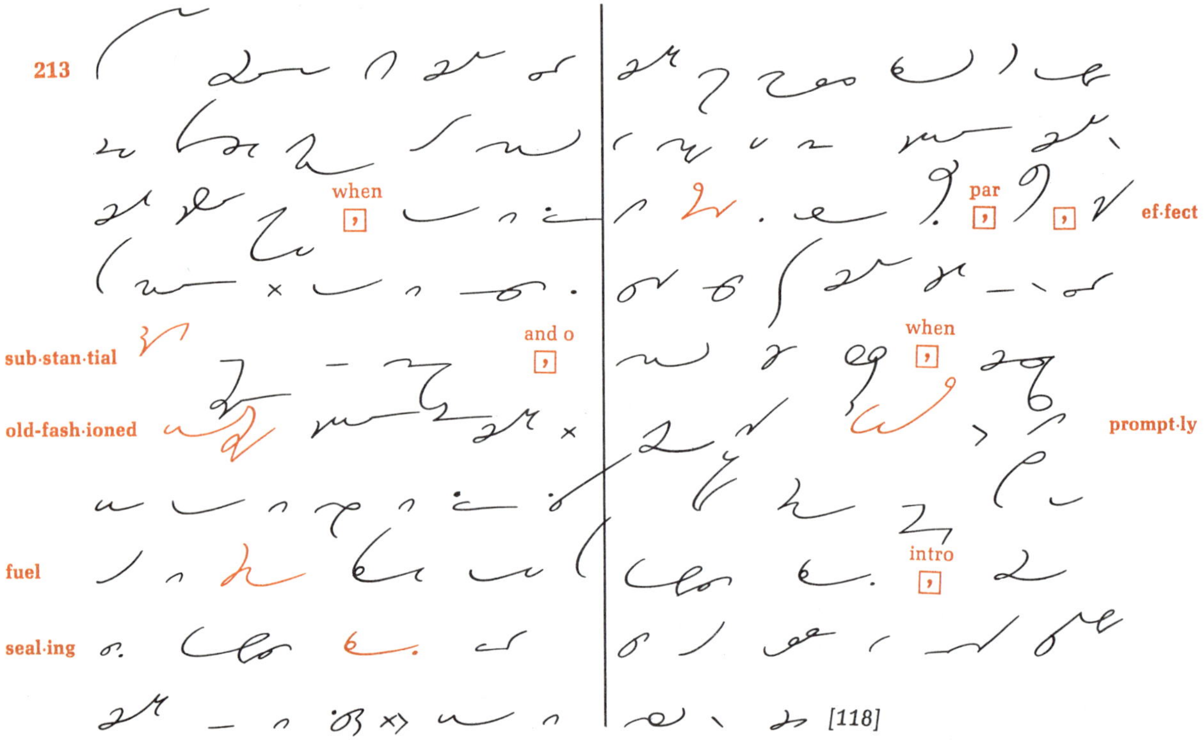

214 [shorthand text]

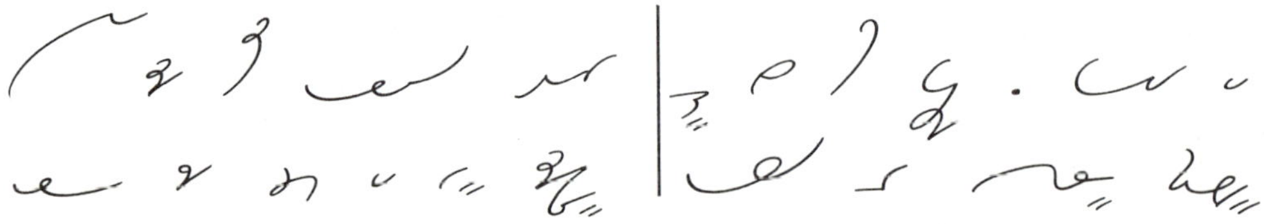

en·hance

well-trained *hyphenated before noun*

rec·om·mend

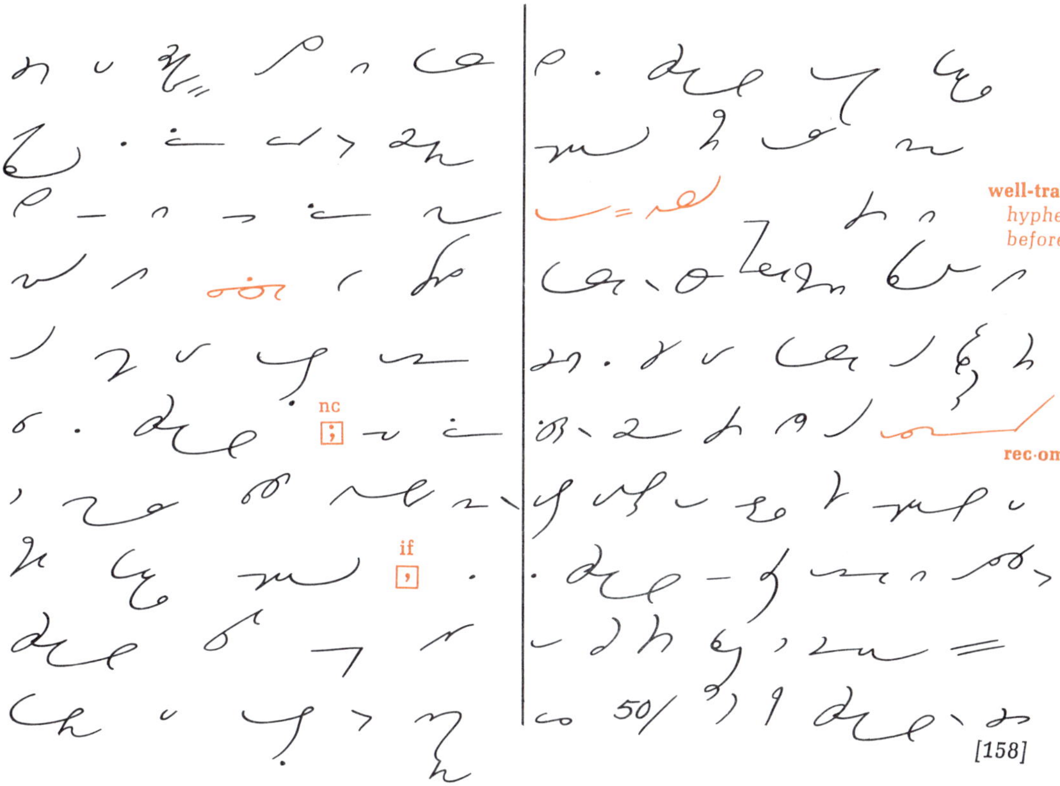

[158]

215

com·pli·ments

print·er's

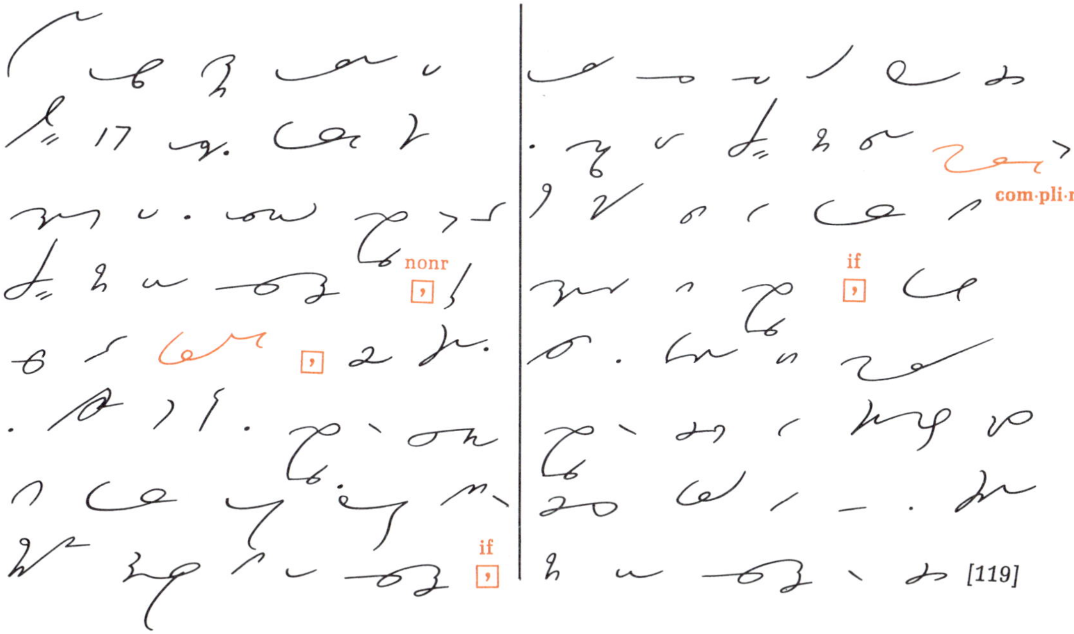

[119]

216

be·lief

their

of·fers

if

to·ward

par

enu

ser

[130]

217

conj

suit·able

mine

when

hard·ware

de·scribes

conj

162 | LESSON 29

pro·ceed [110]

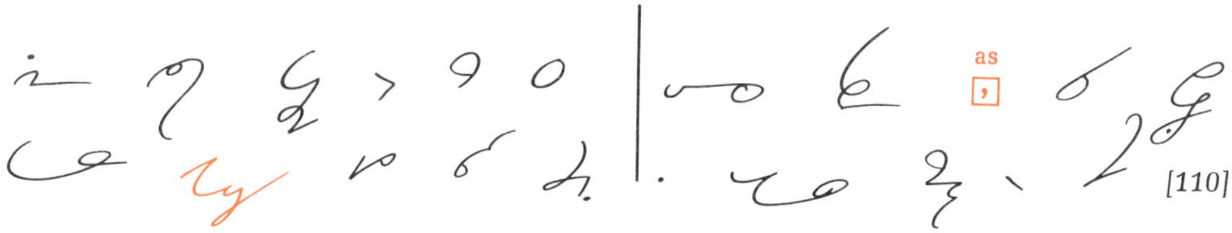

218
son's
fac·to·ry [84] fill·ing

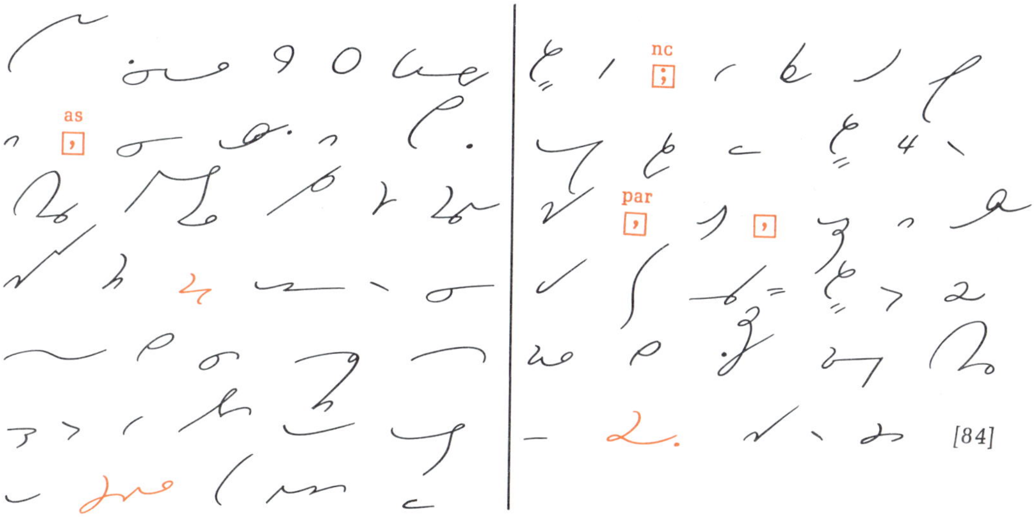

If you are to succeed in the business world, you must learn to follow instructions. The ability to follow instructions is an important step up the promotion ladder.

Building transcription skills

219 COMMON PREFIXES | inter-

A major reason why some students have difficulty gaining shorthand and transcription speed is that their command of words is inadequate; too many words are unfamiliar to them. The more unfamiliar words they encounter in their dictation, the more difficulty they have in developing their shorthand and transcription speed.

Therefore, in the Diamond Jubilee Series strong emphasis has been placed on helping you increase your command of words through Business Vocabulary Builders, Similar-Words Drills, and other devices.

Another effective way to build your vocabulary is to learn the meanings of common prefixes and suffixes. Often a knowledge of the meaning of a prefix or suffix will be sufficient to give you a clue to the definition of a new and unfamiliar word.

In *Gregg Transcription,* you will study the meanings of a number of common prefixes and suffixes and their application to useful business words.

Learn the definition of each prefix or suffix, and add the illustrative words to your vocabulary.

inter- Between; among; in the midst

international Between or among nations.

interrupt To break into or between.

intercity Between or among cities.

intervene To come in between.

intermediate Coming or done between.

220

Business vocabulary builder

home economist One who studies the needs of a family, especially diet, budget, child care, etc.

confirm Verify.

uneventful Without incident.

Reading and writing practice

221 freez·er — ap , when , conj , [73] ad·just

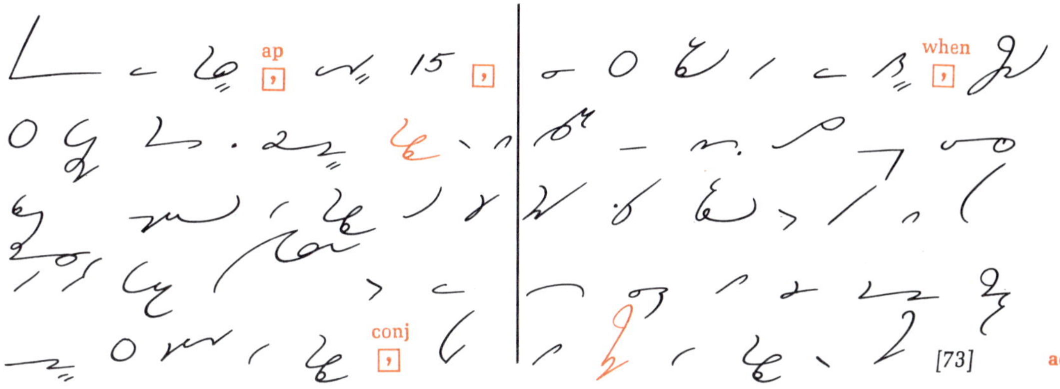

222 wel·come, gen·u·ine, un·doubt·ed·ly, ar·ea, par , as , its, con·ve·nient

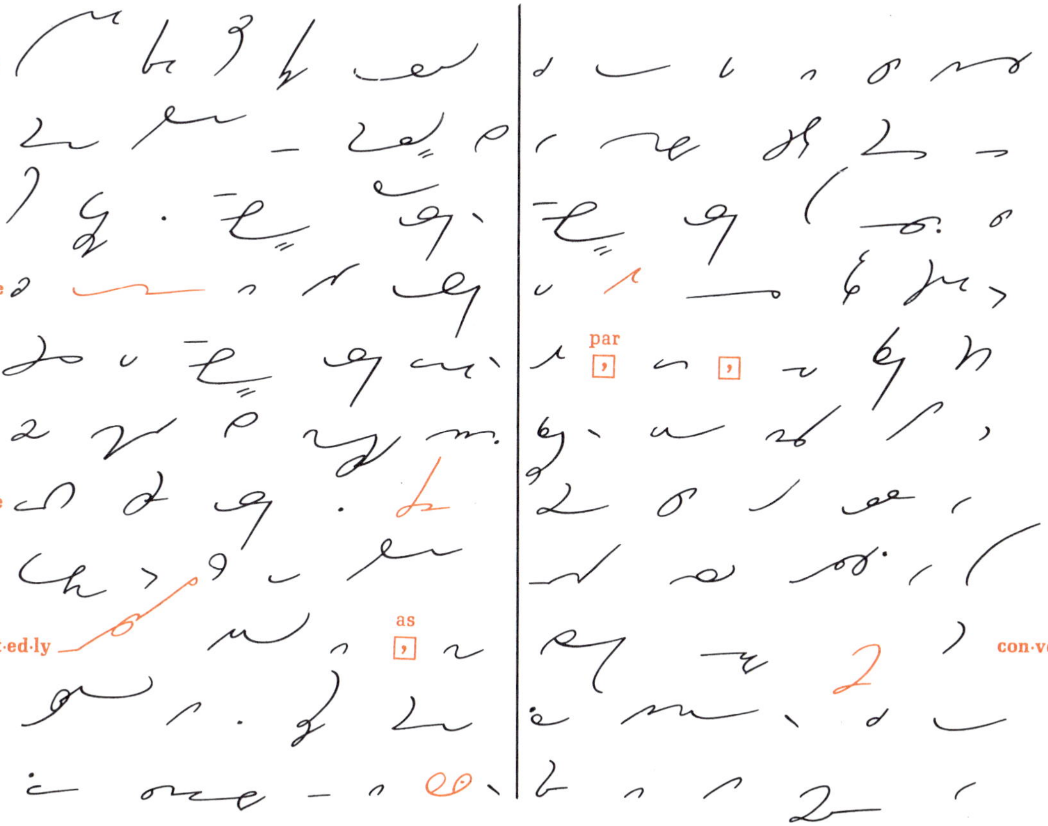

LESSON 30

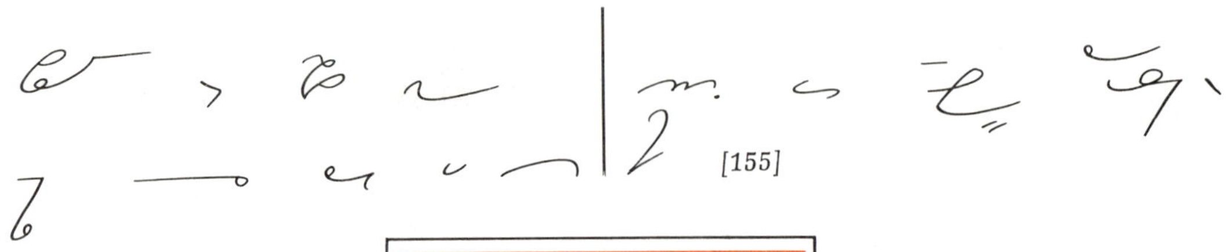

[155]

223

weeks
sea·son

catch

be·ware

equipped

Harper's

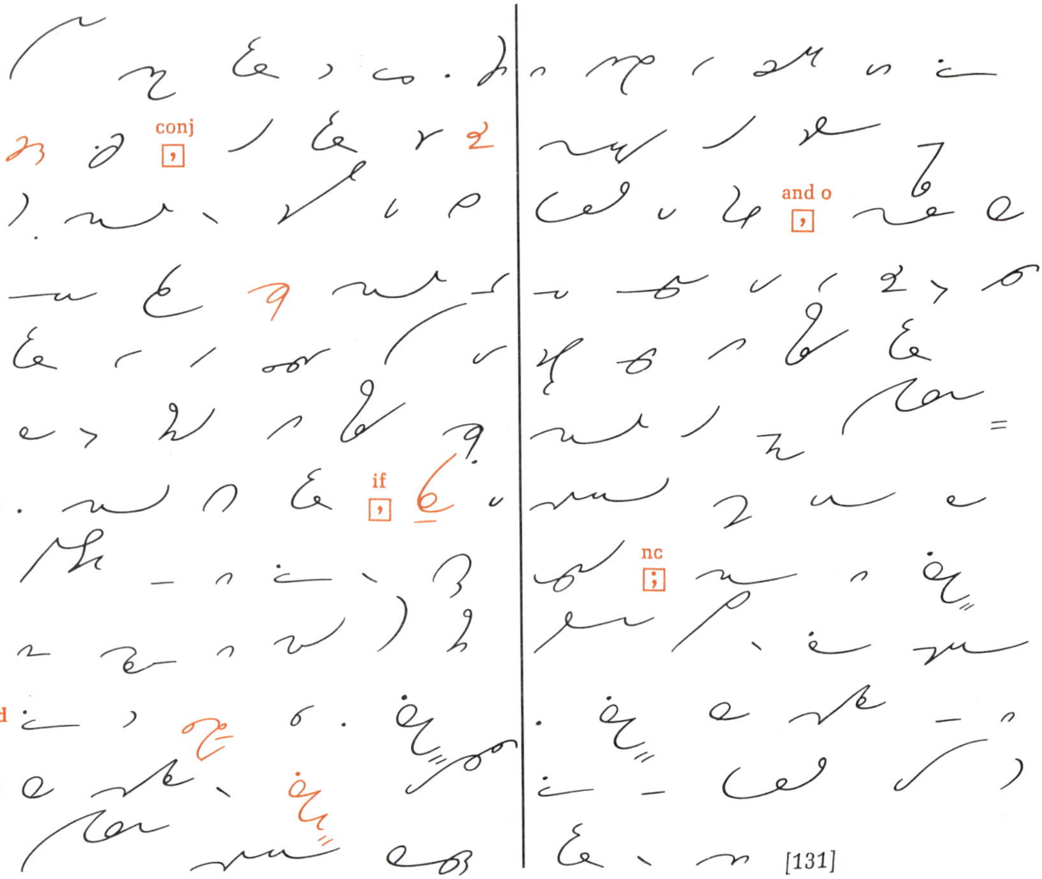

[131]

224

166 | LESSON 30

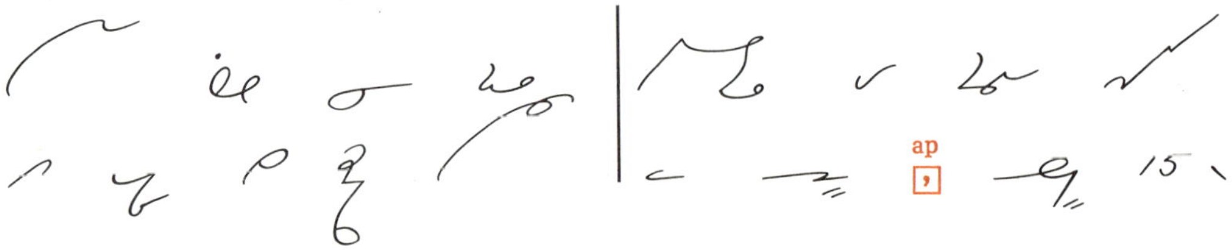

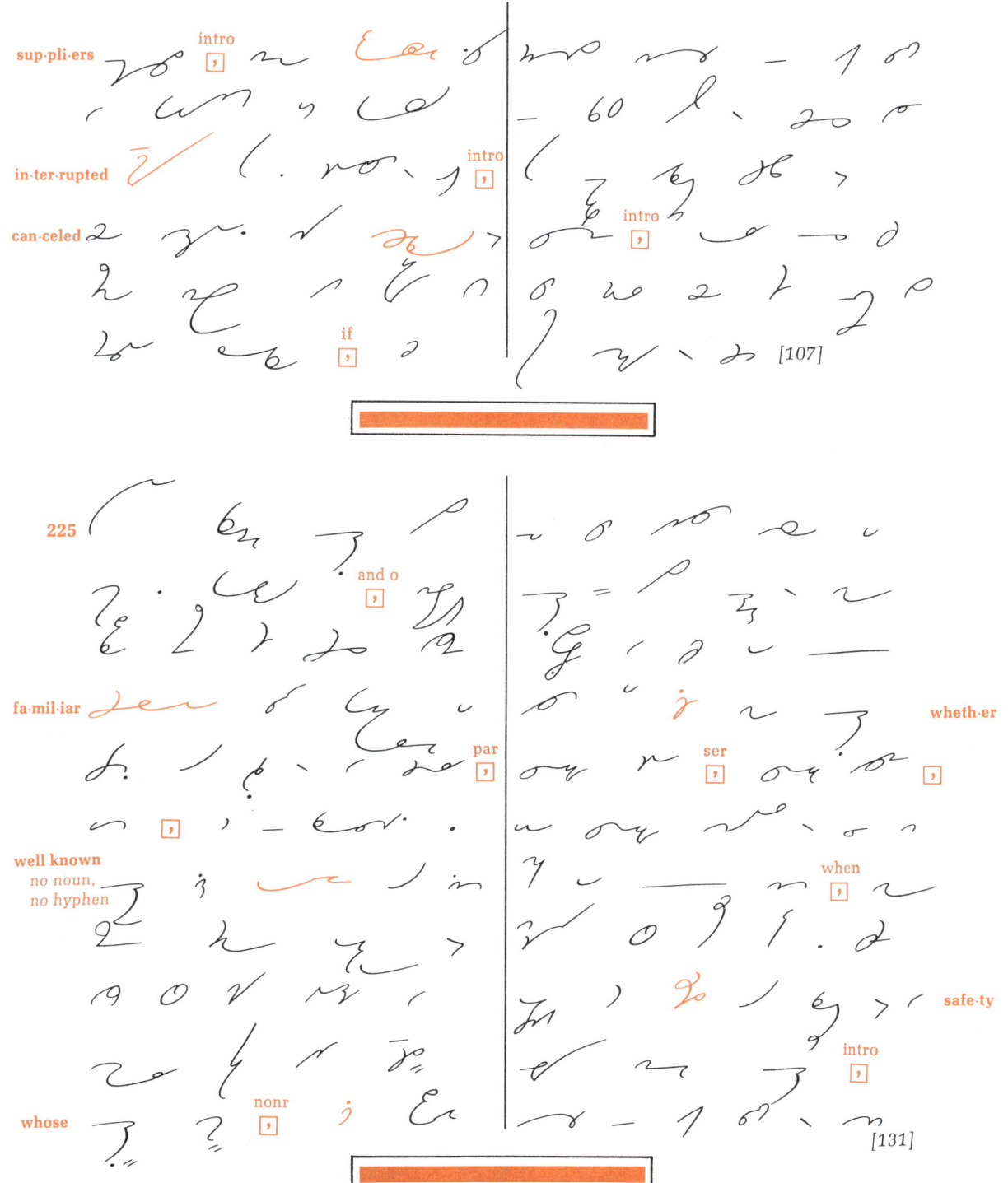

Interruptions in dictation

Mr. Davis, as marketing director of his company, is a busy man. Consequently, during the day he is interrupted in his work many times—even when he is dictating. One day while he was dictating to Ellen, his telephone rang. He was on the phone for only two or three minutes, but in that time Ellen was able to save herself many minutes of transcribing time by:

1 Inserting punctuation in her notes.

2 Improving a number of outlines that might have caused her to hesitate later when she was transcribing.

3 Rereading and "patching up" a sentence that had been dictated rapidly and, consequently, was not written too accurately.

4 Encircling one or two words that she was not sure she could spell correctly.

Then, as soon as Mr. Davis finished his telephone conversation, Ellen read back the last dictated sentence without being asked to do so.

Of course, Ellen didn't have to do all these things; she could

have rested and examined her fingernails or stared out of the window or simply looked bored! But she realized how much easier she could make her transcribing by using the pause profitably.

Often, there will be several interruptions during a dictating period. For example, the dictator may have a visitor with whom he will chat briefly. He may stop for a few moments to fill his pipe. He may read previous correspondence relating to the letter that he is about to answer. All these pauses represent priceless opportunities for the stenographer to simplify her task of transcription.

Ellen does not always sit at her employer's desk during an interruption. Sometimes she realizes that the interruption will be a lengthy one and that she can use her time better doing her regular work. For example, one day Mr. Davis's telephone rang in the middle of dictation, and she heard him say, "Let me tell you about the meeting I attended." She knew that the conversation would take some time; therefore, she returned to her desk and started to transcribe the day's dictation, keeping one eye on her employer.

When she saw him hang up the receiver, she immediately returned to his desk and read back the last sentence that he had dictated.

The experienced stenographer soon comes to welcome these breaks in dictation, especially if her employer dictates for long periods of time. Aside from the opportunity they give her to patch up her notes, they also provide a brief respite from shorthand writing.

Insurance

Building transcription skills

226 SIMILAR-WORDS DRILL | **adverse, averse**

adverse Opposing; unfavorable.

Because of adverse circumstances, I cannot pay my bill at this time.

averse Unwilling.

As my policy has been in force for more than ten years, I am averse to letting it lapse.

227

Business vocabulary builder	**options** Choices. **annually** Yearly. **remainder** What is left.

Reading and writing practice

228 em·ploy·ees

LESSON 31

230 [shorthand] when, yours, widely, discuss, benefit, their, ser, knowledge [134]

231 [shorthand] isq, sufficient, iq, through

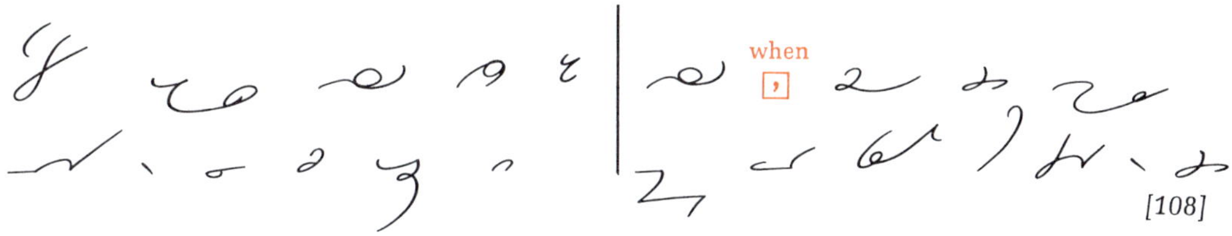

when
[108]

232

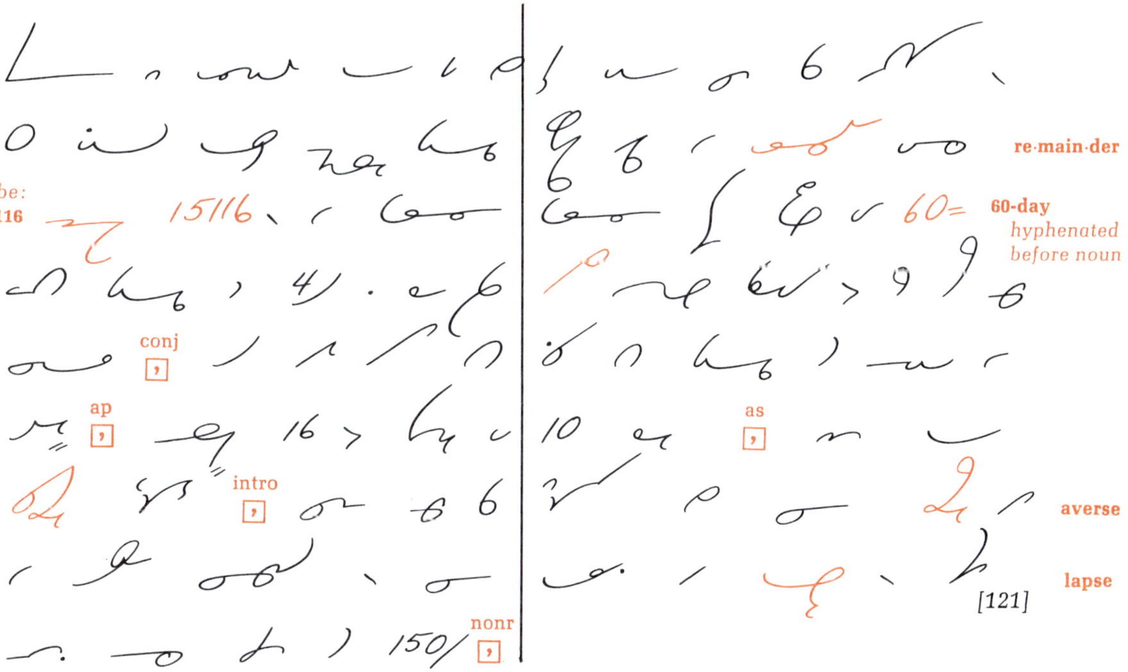

re·main·der
Transcribe:
No. 15116
15116
60-day
hyphenated before noun
60=
conj
ap
as
ad·verse
intro
averse
lapse
[121]
nonr

233

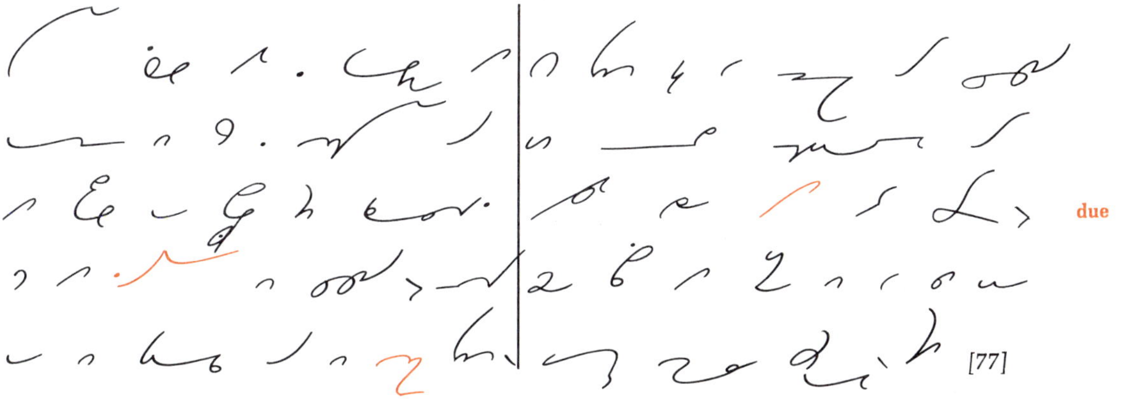

due
han·dle
cou·pon
[77]

Building transcription skills

234 SPELLING FAMILIES | -el, -al, -le

Always think twice when you start to transcribe a word that ends with the sound of *l*; the word may be spelled *-el, -al,* or *-le.*
When in doubt, look it up!

-el

an·gel	la·bel	pan·el
bar·rel	li·bel	par·cel
can·cel	nick·el	tun·nel

-al

| fi·nal | to·tal | per·son·al |
| lo·cal | re·new·al | vi·tal |

-le

an·gle	mid·dle	set·tle
cir·cle	ped·dle	sprin·kle
gam·ble	sam·ple	un·cle

235

| Business vocabulary builder | **jeopardize** To endanger; to risk loss or injury.
reinstate To restore.
urged Pressed. |

Reading and writing practice

236
Transcribe:
No. 15116

cash-sur-ren-der
hyphenated before noun

can-cel-la-tion

conj ,

nonr ,

[78]

237

jeop-ar-dize

intro ,

intro ,

un-pleas-ant

al-lowed

if ,

if ,

bot-tom

ap ,

[118]

LESSON 32 | 175

238

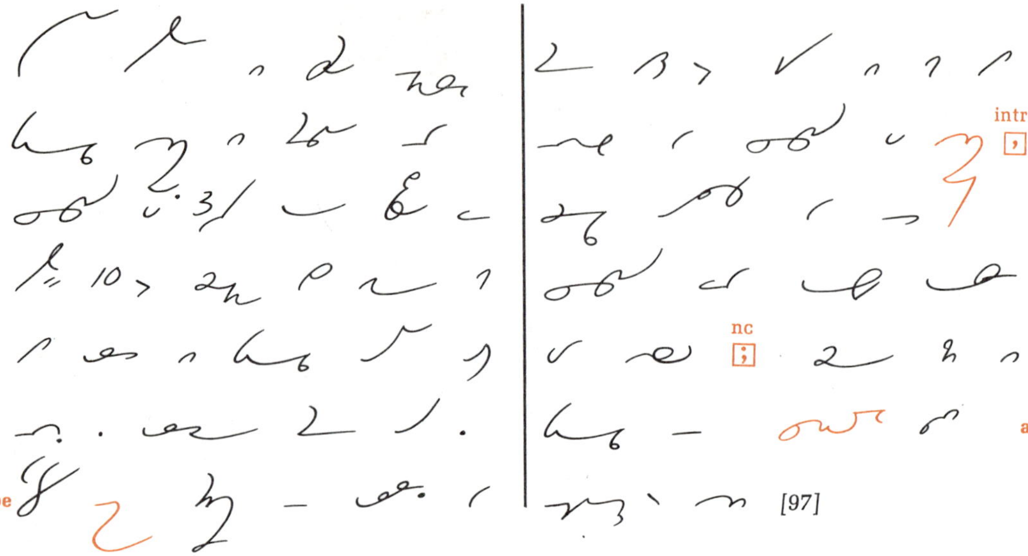

en·ve·lope

intro , **cov·er·age**

nc ;

ac·cor·dance

[97]

239

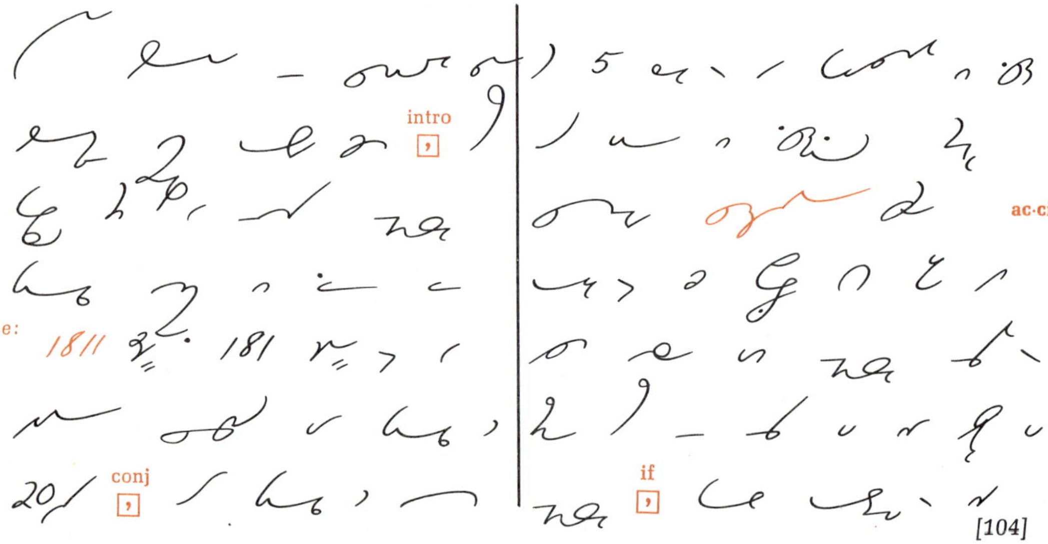

intro ,

ac·ci·den·tal

Transcribe: 1811

conj ,

if ,

[104]

240

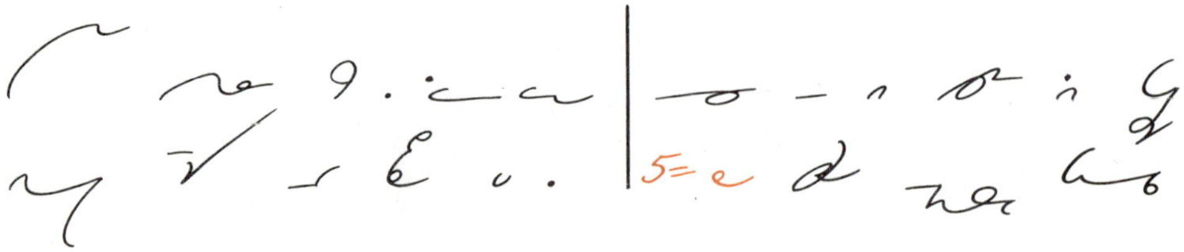

five-year
hyphenated before noun

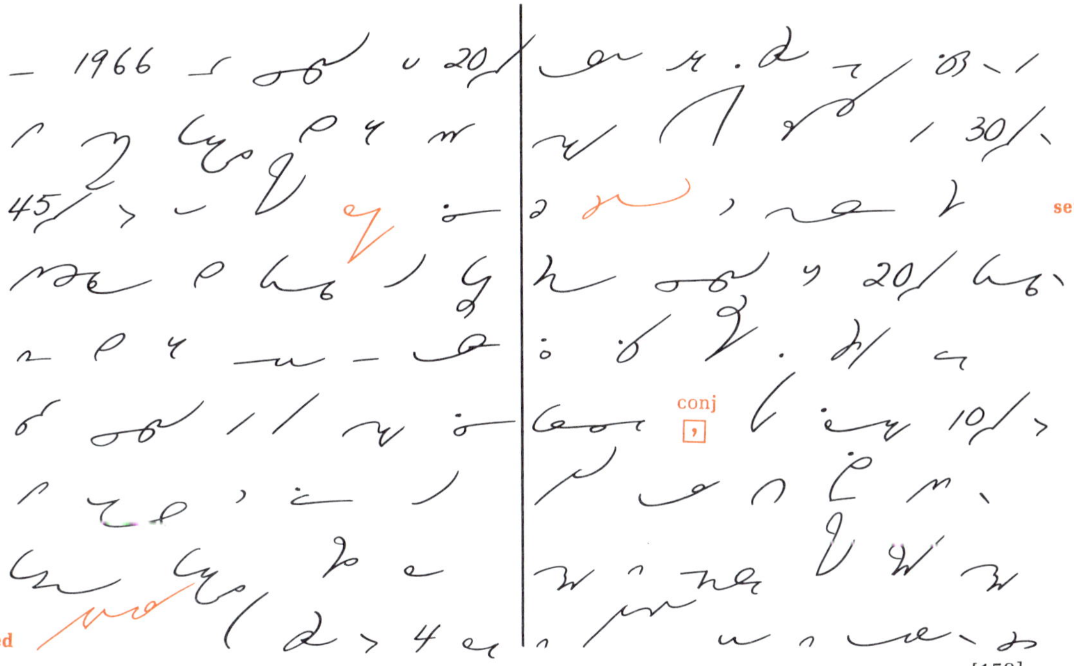

[159]

241

Transcribe: **No. 1170**

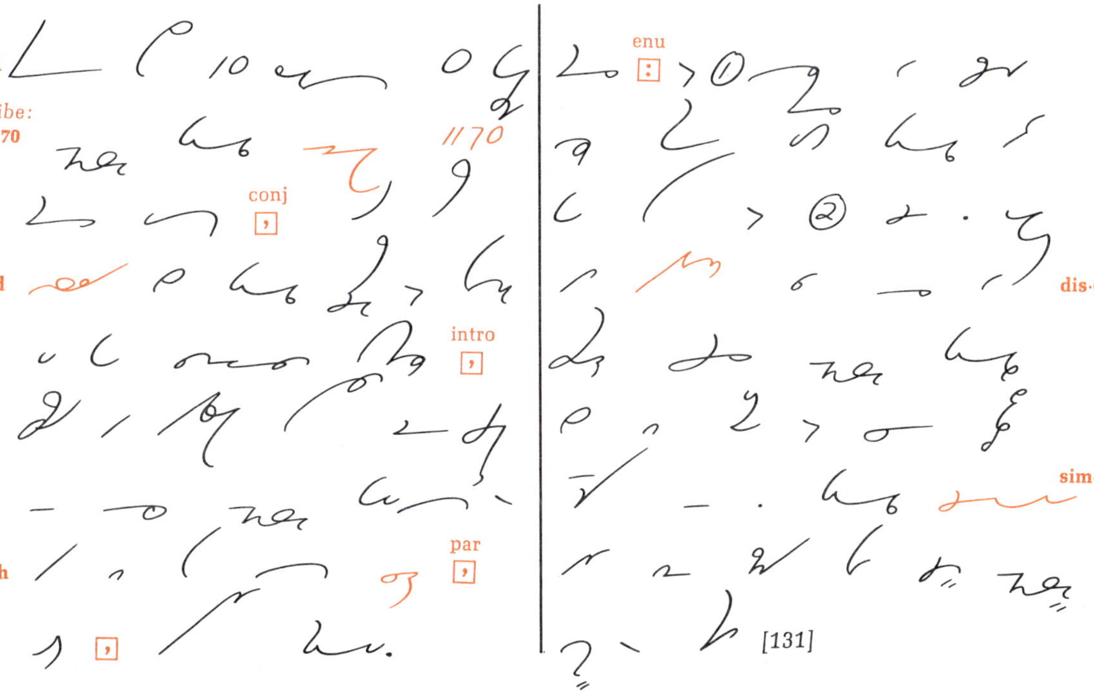

[131]

Building transcription skills

242 GRAMMAR CHECKUP | bring, take

Another important characteristic of the mailable letter is that it contains no errors in grammar. Remember, your employer may occasionally make a mistake in grammar. It is your job, however, to see that the error does not appear in your transcript.

In this Grammar Checkup, and in those that appear in later lessons, you will consider errors that both stenographers and businessmen frequently make.

bring   To carry toward. (*Bring* indicates motion *toward* the speaker.)

I asked him to bring his records when he comes to my office.

take   To carry away from. (*Take* indicates motion *away* from the speaker.)

I will take (not bring) the notebook to him.

243

Business vocabulary builder	
category	A class; a basic classification.
function (noun)	Purpose; assigned duty.
lengthy	Long.

 Reading and writing practice

244 [shorthand]

ac·ci·den·tal·ly   as   li·cense

LESSON 33

[142]

247

[137]

180 | LESSON 33

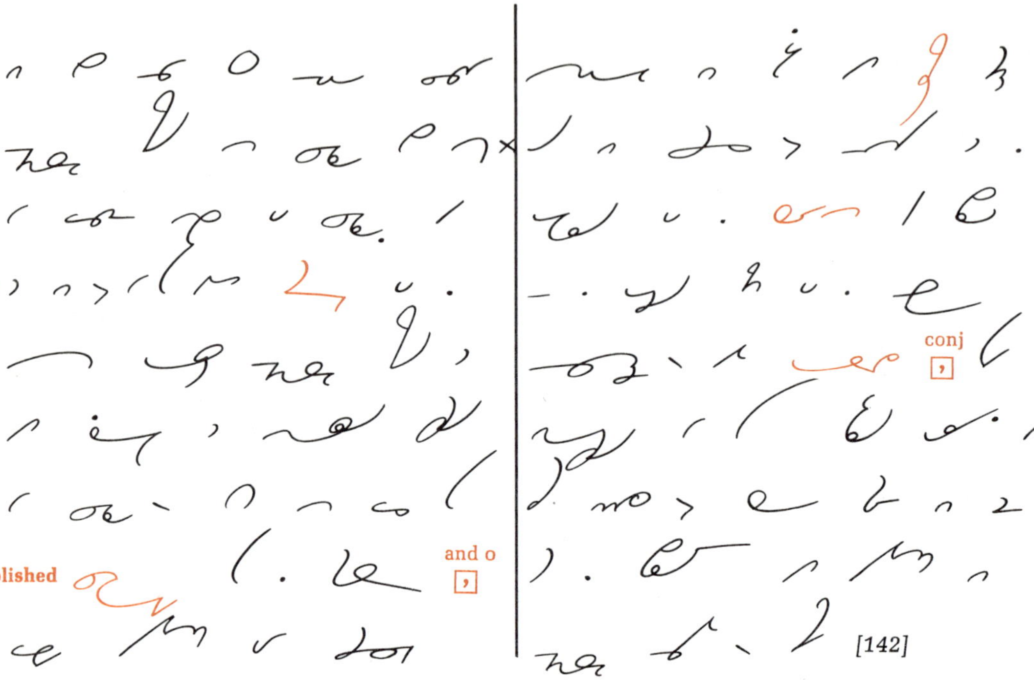

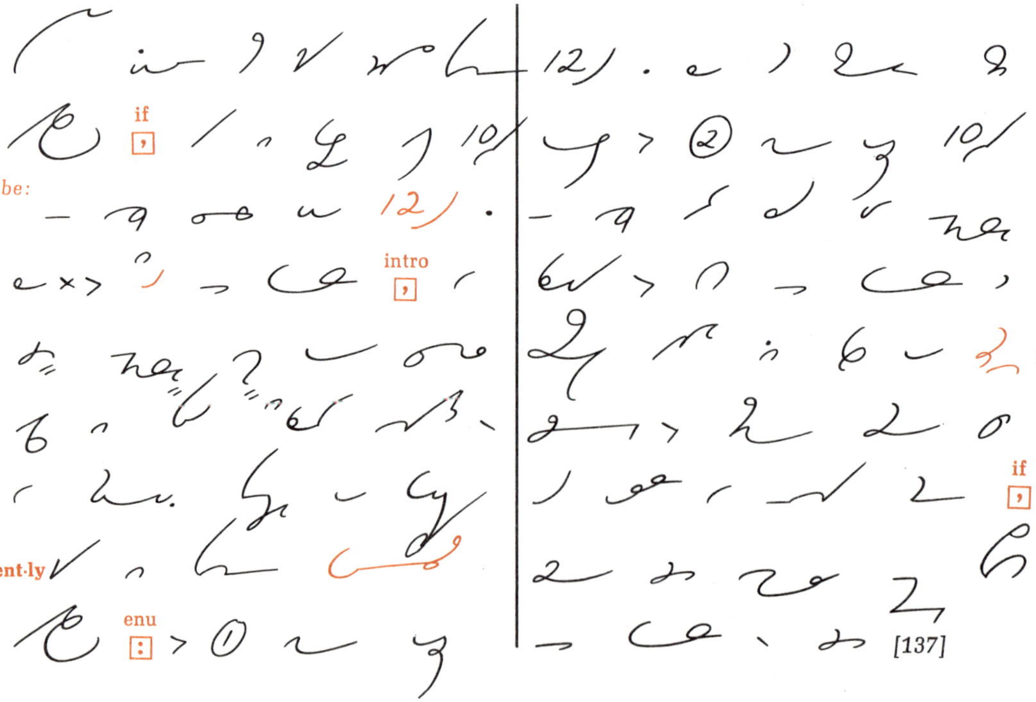

248

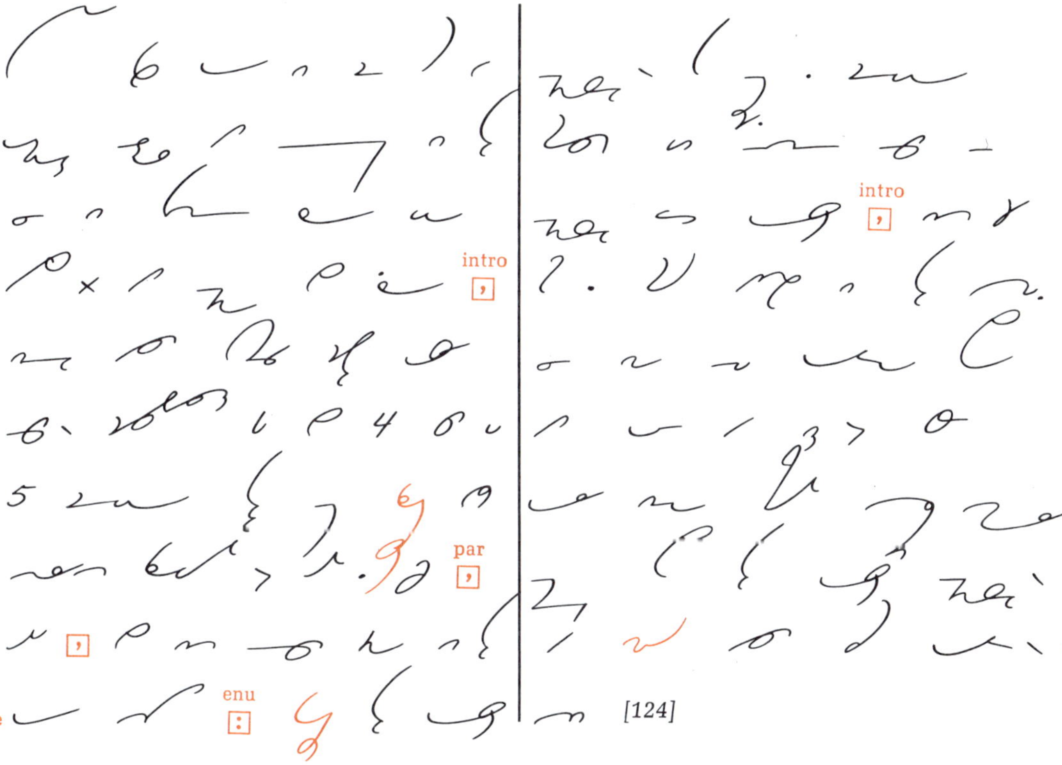

sur·vive

pur·chase intro, par, enu: [124] won't

249
es·sen·tial

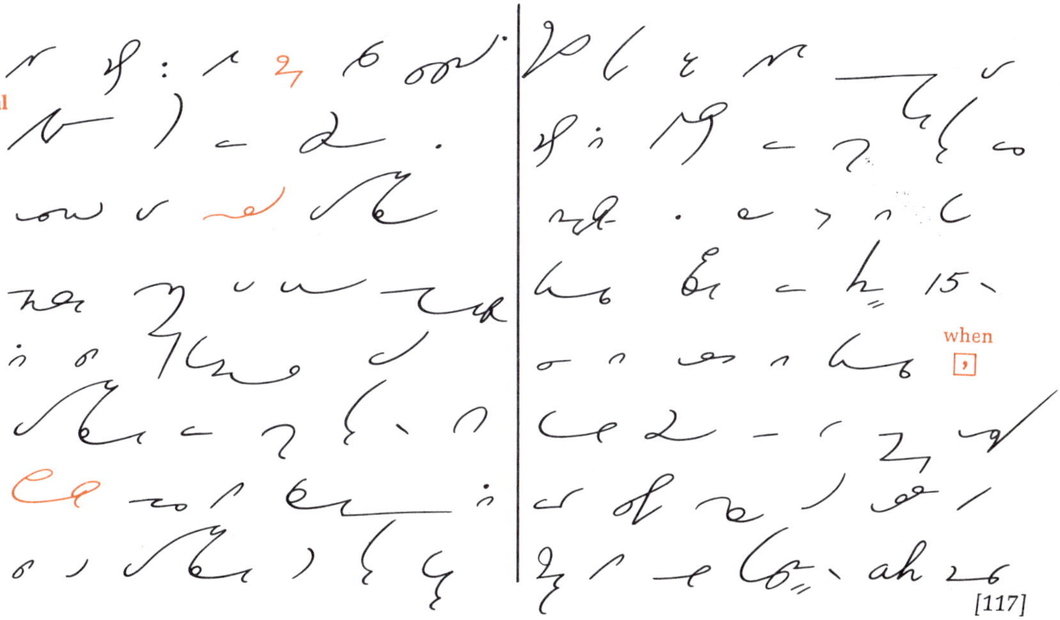

cur·rent

ap·plies when, [117]

LESSON 33 | 181

Building transcription skills

250 OFFICE-STYLE DICTATION | substitutions

Occasionally a businessman will dictate a word or phrase and, on reflection, decide to substitute another word or phrase. He may say:

Your man showed great interest in the plight—make that **welfare**—*of our organization.*

In your notebook you would simply place a heavy downward line through the word *plight* and write *welfare* next to the outline you crossed out, thus:

Sometimes the dictator may change his mind about a word or a phrase after completing a sentence. He may say:

Your man showed great interest in the plight of our organization—make that **welfare of our organization.**

You must be on the alert to notice that it is the word *plight* that is to be changed. You then place a line through *plight* and above it write the word *welfare*, thus:

restorations

There will also be times when the businessman will use a word or a phrase but will change his mind and substitute another word or phrase. Then, on further reflection, he will decide that the first word or phrase was better. He may say:

However, that is where we were wrong—make that **in error;** *oh, perhaps we should leave it* **wrong.**

When the businessman says "make that *in error,*" you will strike a heavy downward line through *wrong* and write *in error.* Then, when he says, "oh, perhaps we should leave it *wrong,*" you will write the word *wrong* again. This is the way it would look in your notes:

Do not try to indicate in your notes that the original *wrong* is to be restored. This may take you longer than writing the word a second time. In addition, it may lead to confusion when you are transcribing.

ILLUSTRATION OF OFFICE-STYLE DICTATION

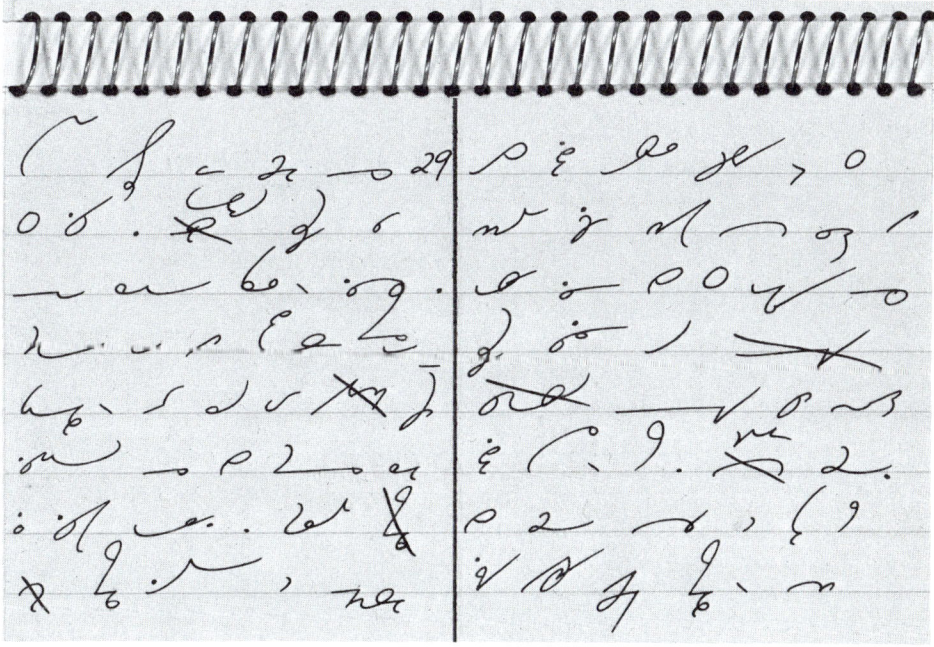

251 | Business vocabulary builder | **status** Position; standing.
exorbitant Excessive.
merger A combining; a consolidation.
imperative Not to be avoided; compulsory.

Reading and writing practice

252

LESSON 34

trans·ferred [54]

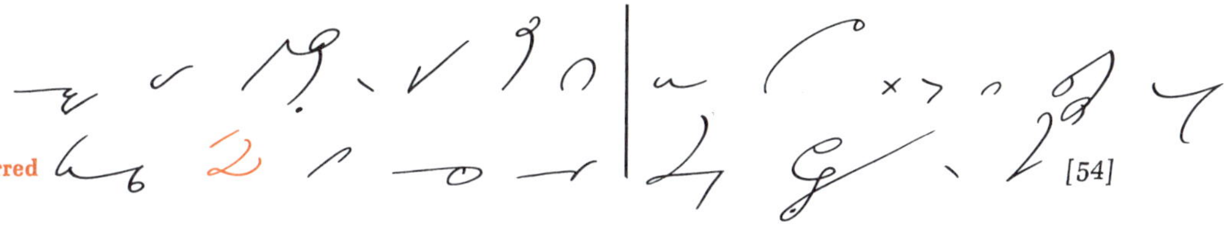

255
ex·or·bi·tant
ap
enu
ser
prac·ti·cal
com·pa·ny's
[103]

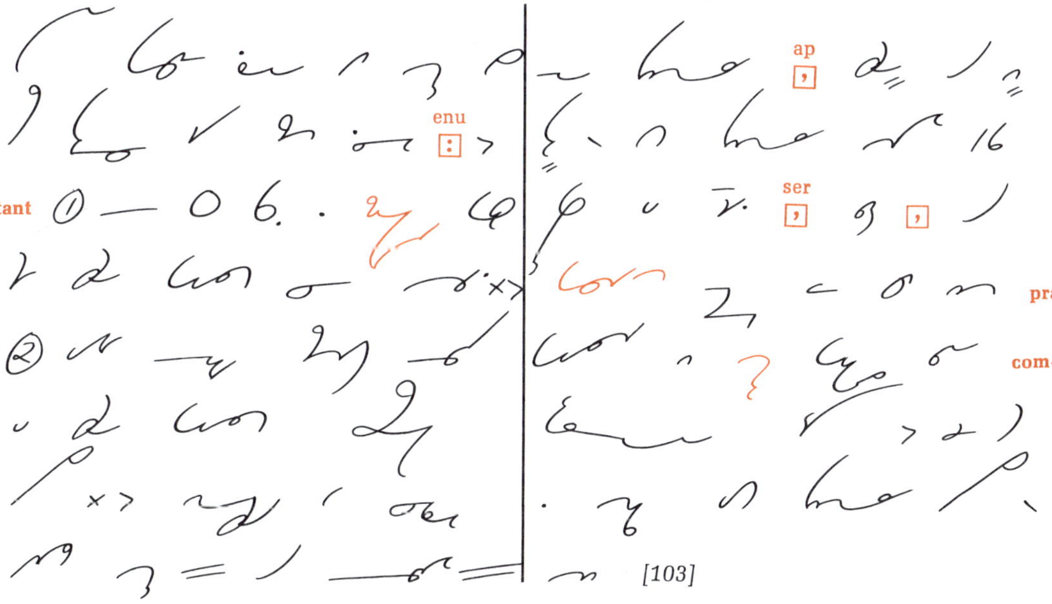

256
at·tor·neys
merg·er
ironed
as
conj
intro
be·gin·ning

LESSON 34 | 185

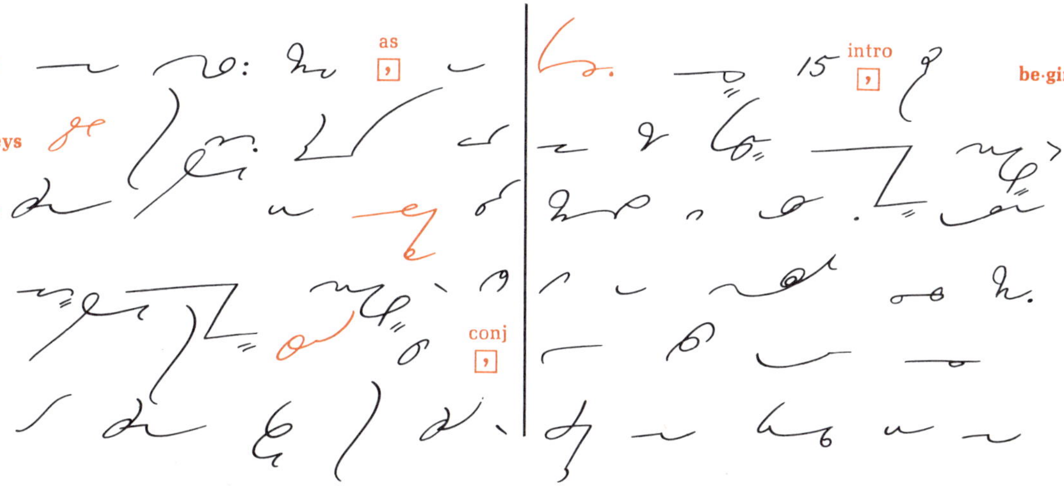

im·per·a·tive

draft [118]

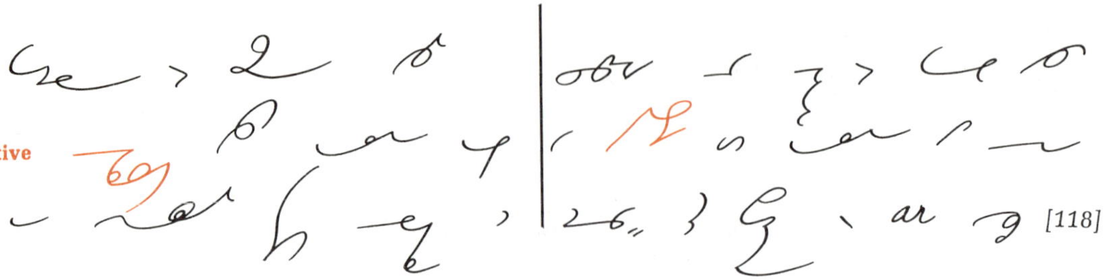

257

Transcribe: 20 percent

its

and o
if
well-trained
hyphenated before noun
isq
conj
iq 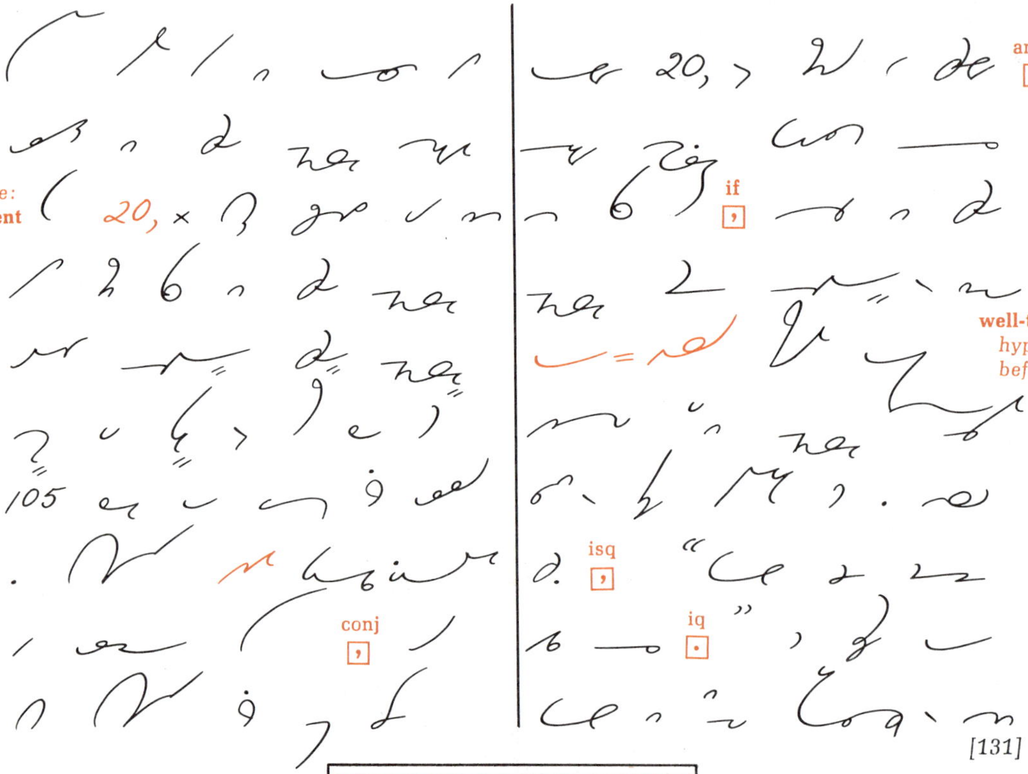
[131]

258

Transcribe: No. 115161

as
if
au·to·mat·i·cal·ly 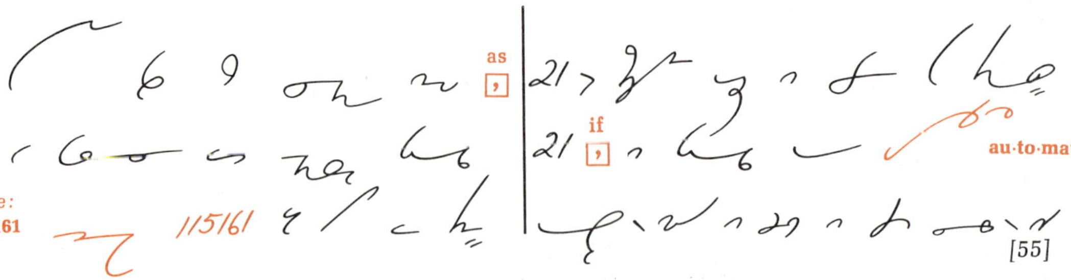
[55]

Building transcription skills

259 WORD CHAIN

Occasionally a businessman may use a word in a sentence and then may not be entirely satisfied with it. For example, he may dictate, "We shall, of course, pay you for the days you lost from your vacation in order to complete the job." Then he may say to you, his secretary, "*Pay* isn't the word I want; it is too cold. What's the word I want?"

The purpose of the Word Chain in this lesson and the Word Chains in following lessons is to enable you to help the dictator select just the right word from a possible five or six, all but one of which almost, but not quite, convey the exact meaning the dictator has in mind. The secretary who can supply the answer to "What's the word I want?" is a valuable person indeed.

An example of a Word Chain is the group of words *pay, compensate, reimburse, satisfy,* and *indemnify*—the Word Chain you will study in this lesson.

All the words in this group have the basic meaning of transferring value from one person or company to another person or company. Each word, however, has a special shade of meaning. Let us consider the meanings of these words:

> **pay** is used when money is given in exchange for goods or services. It is so neutral a word that it may usually be used for any of the other words in this group, although with some loss of exactness of meaning.

He will pay for the goods when he receives them.

> **reimburse** means to pay back or return money that has been already expended.

I am enclosing my check to reimburse you for the expenses you incurred in taking care of my claim.

> **compensate** means to make up for, to make amends for.

We shall certainly compensate you for the many hours of your own time that you spent on the project.

> **satisfy** means to pay a person that which is required by contract or by law.

As soon as we receive your report, we shall take steps to satisfy your claim.

indemnify means to make good a loss suffered by a party as a result of fire, accident, war, and the like.

The United States will indemnify those whose homes were damaged as a result of the explosion.

260

Business vocabulary builder	**statistics** A numerical collection of facts arranged to indicate general trends or theories. **encounter** To meet. **rectify** To make or set right.

Reading and writing practice

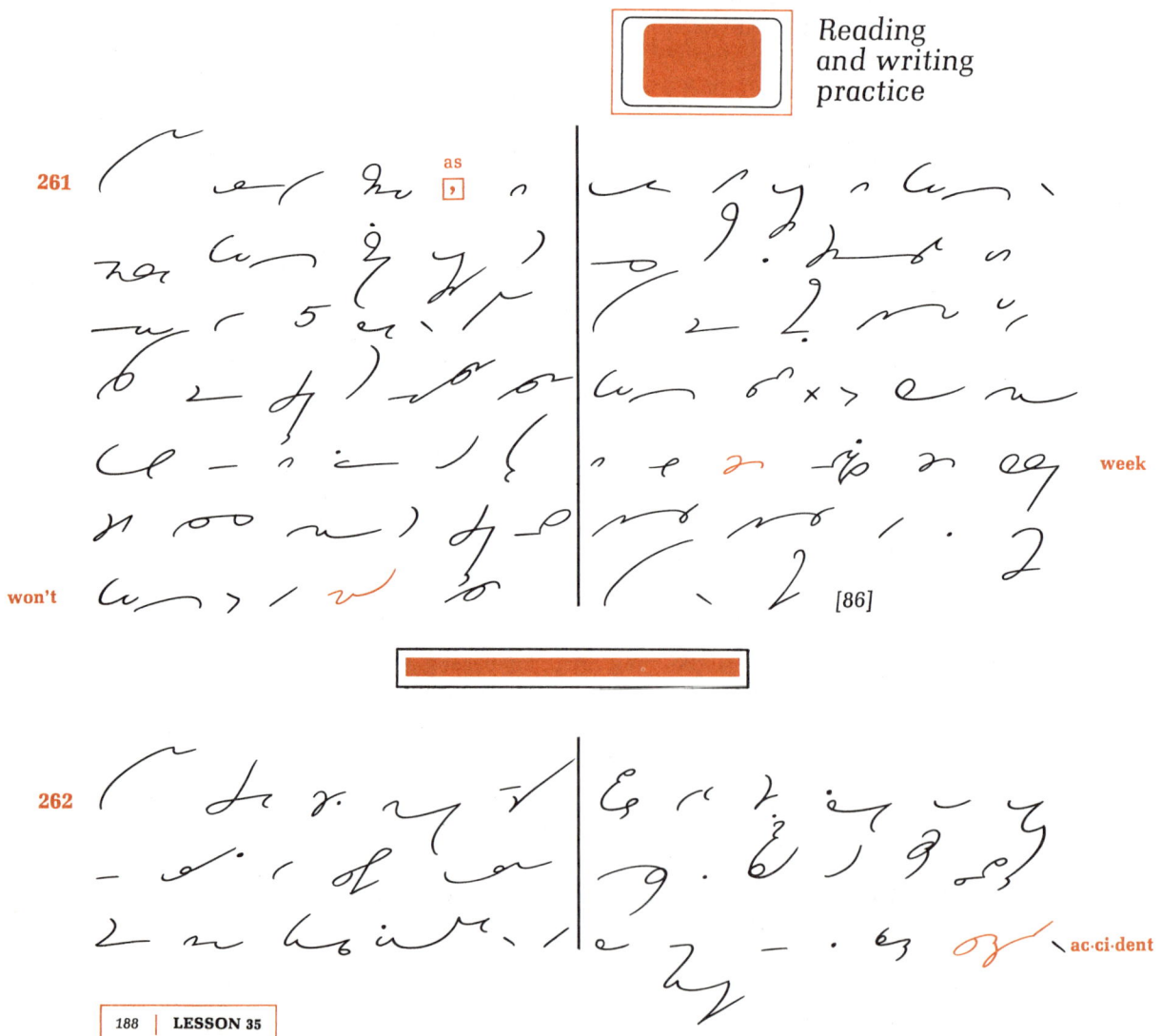

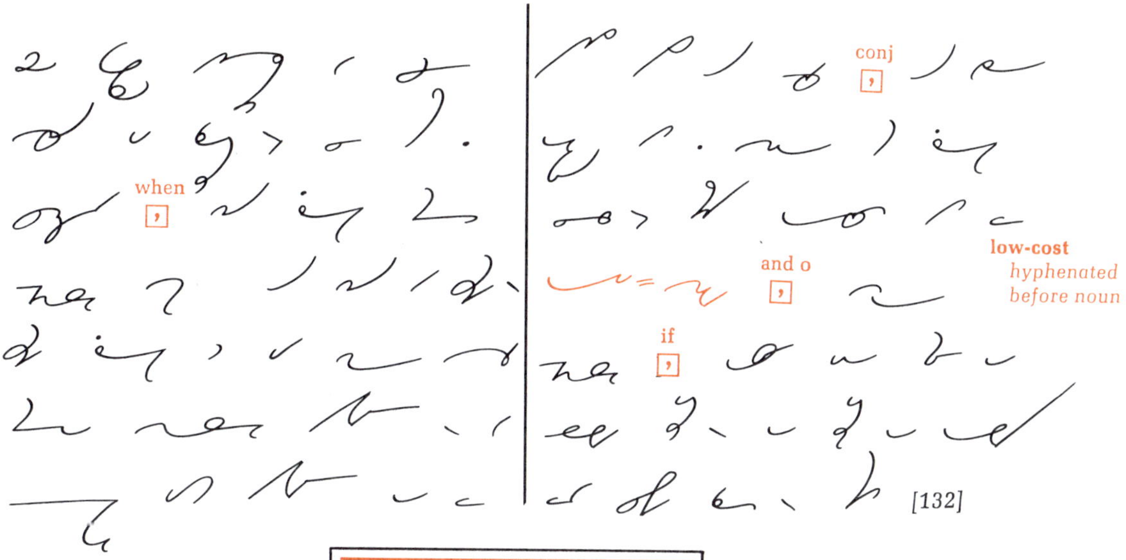
conj
when
and o
low-cost
hyphenated before noun
if
[132]

263

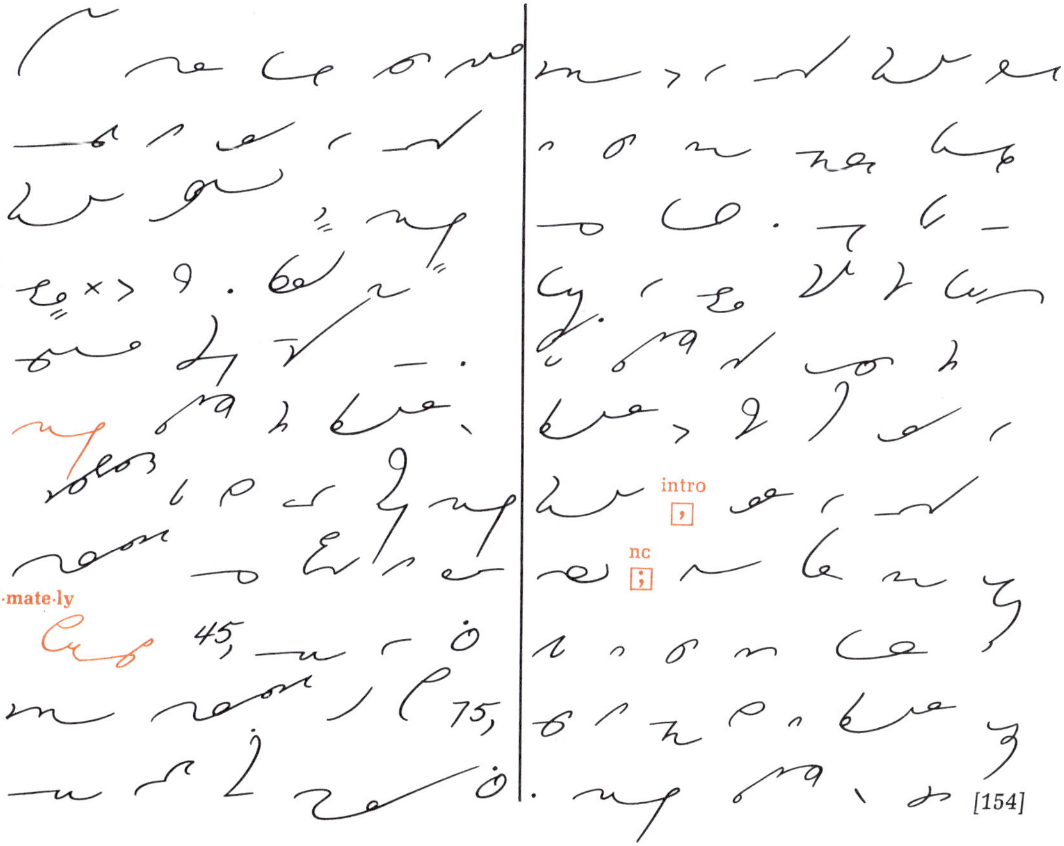
intro
nc
45,
75,
[154]

col·lege

ap·prox·i·mate·ly

264

ours · com·pli·ment · isq · iq · cho·sen · when · [117]

265

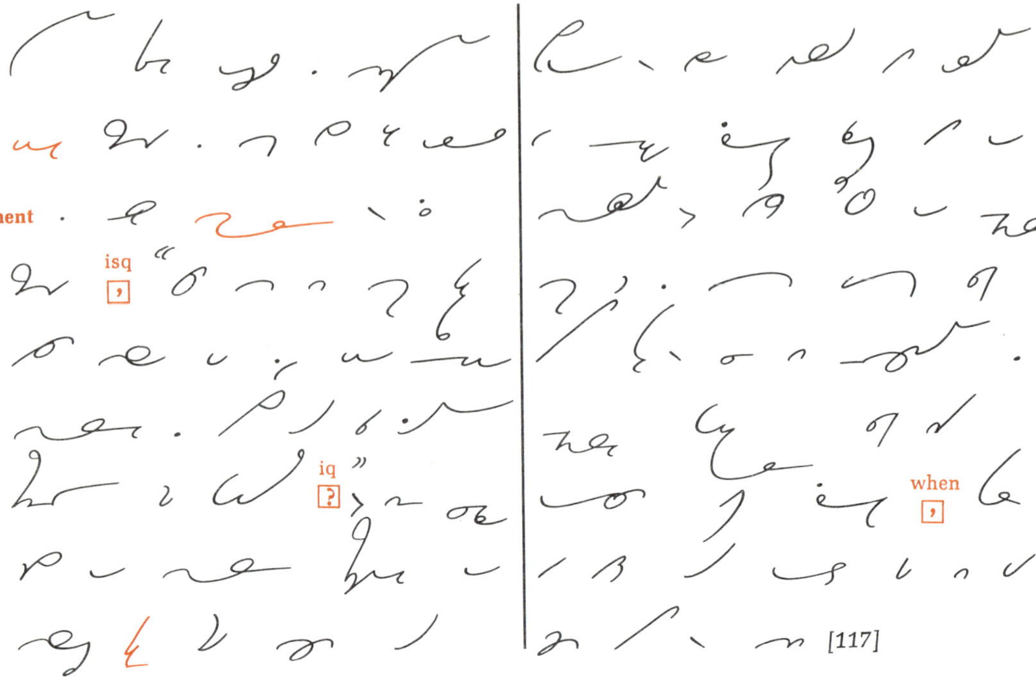

faith·ful·ly · par · intro · nc · lapse · rec·ti·fy · nonr · due · if · [121]

LESSON 35

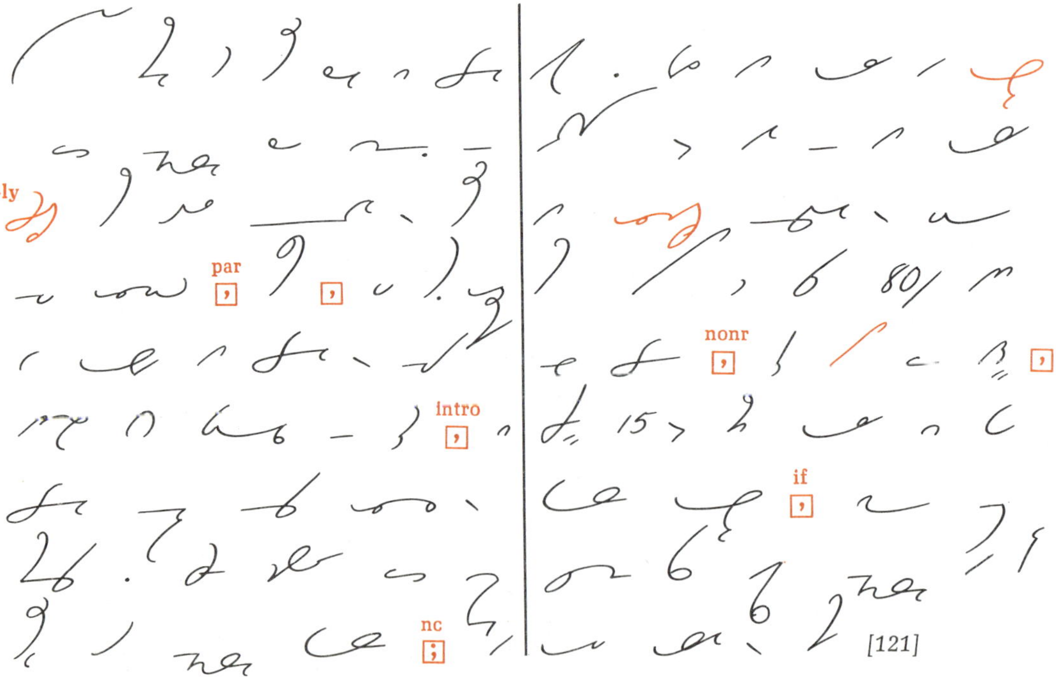

266

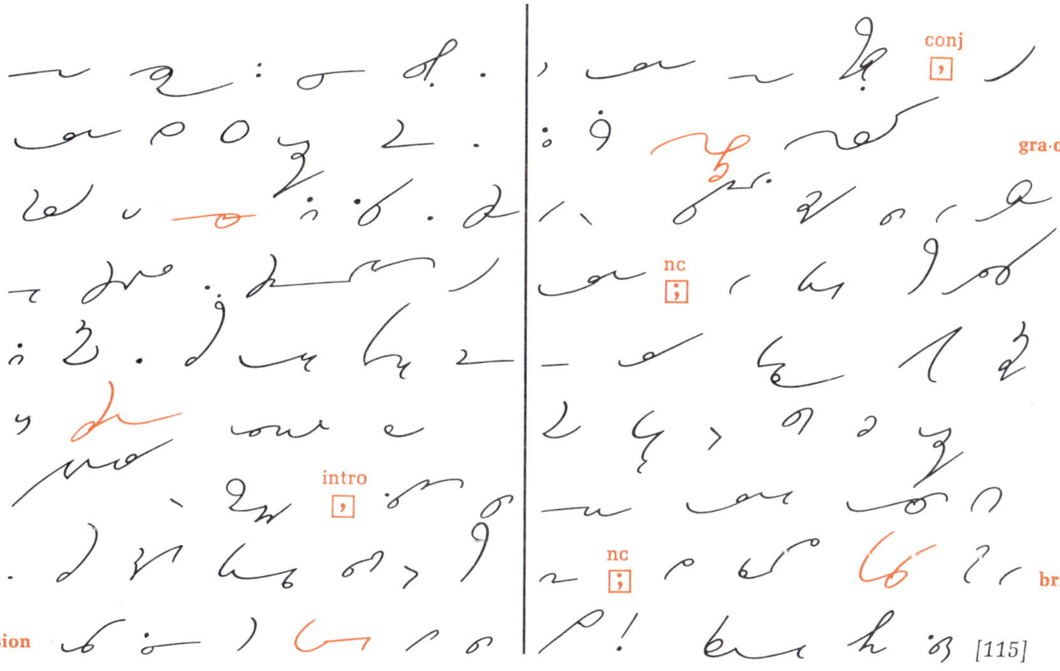

conj

gra·cious·ly

mine

nc

vi·tal

intro

nc

bright·en

per·mis·sion

[115]

267

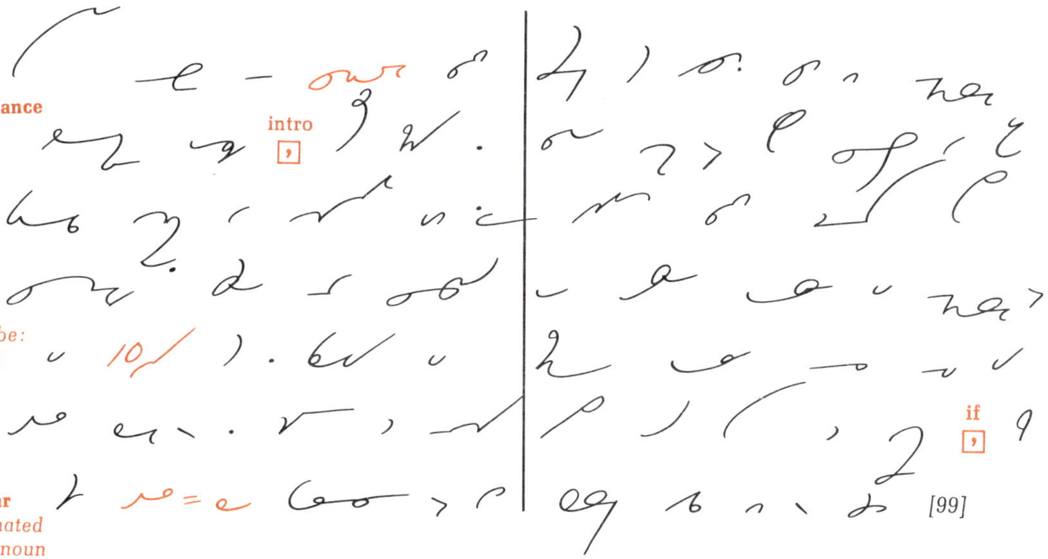

ac·cor·dance

intro

Transcribe:
$10,000

if

three-year
hyphenated before noun

[99]

Interrupting the dictator

Early in her stenographic career, Ellen Gardiner had a sad experience she never forgot.

Mr. Davis was dictating a complicated report and was so absorbed in the subject matter that he did not realize that he was mumbling inaudibly and that Ellen could not hear everything he said. Ellen was not getting it all, but she did not have the courage to stop him. She was afraid that if she stopped him, it would be embarrassing to him and a reflection on her ability. That was her first mistake.

When she sat down to transcribe, she filled in what she thought Mr. Davis had said.

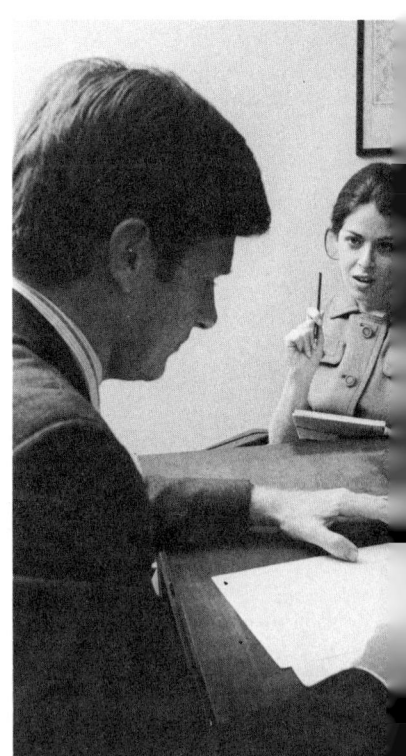

That was her second mistake. When Mr. Davis read the report, he "blew his top," and Ellen dissolved into tears as he stormed:

"In the first place, if you didn't understand me, why didn't you tell me? I know that I concentrate so hard on what I am dictating that I don't realize when I'm mumbling. In the second place, don't ever hand anything to me that doesn't make sense. If you are not sure about something, ask me. Now you will have to do this entire report over."

Ellen never made those mistakes again. Thereafter, whenever Mr. Davis said something she did not hear, she would say, "I'm sorry, but I didn't hear that last sentence." Or if he started to dictate so rapidly that she could not get it, she would say, "I'm sorry, Mr. Davis, but could you dictate a little more slowly." Whenever she wasn't sure whether she had taken something down correctly—that is, it didn't sound right—she would say, "May I read this last sentence to you as I have it." Whenever Mr. Davis used an expression with which she was unfamiliar and that she thought she might not be able to locate in a reference book, she would say, "That expression is new to me. Would you mind spelling it for me." Mr. Davis was always glad to oblige.

A businessman realizes that occasionally a stenographer may have trouble with his dictation, especially if she is a beginner. Consequently, he is always glad to do anything that will enable her to turn out a correct transcript the first time!

Just one suggestion: Some businessmen prefer to be interrupted as soon as the stenographer has a question. Others prefer to complete a sentence or a thought or a letter. Perhaps the wisest thing for you to do as you are about to take your first dictation from your employer is to ask him his preference.

Automobiles

Building transcription skills

268 SIMILAR-WORDS DRILL | break, brake

break To shatter; to fracture.

What would you do if your car were to break down many miles from home?

brake A device for slowing down or stopping motion.

He stepped on the brake to stop the car.

269 | Business vocabulary builder | **detergent** A cleaning substance.
durability Power or ability to last or endure.
ranked Arranged; positioned.

Reading and writing practice

270   ad·just·ment   brakes

[65]

271

en·gine

waste

break

com·plete·ly

intro

intro

intro

par

Harper's de·ter·gent

break

[129]

272

LESSON 36

model
maximum
briefly
its [148]

273
break
garage
assistance
their
receive
mechanics

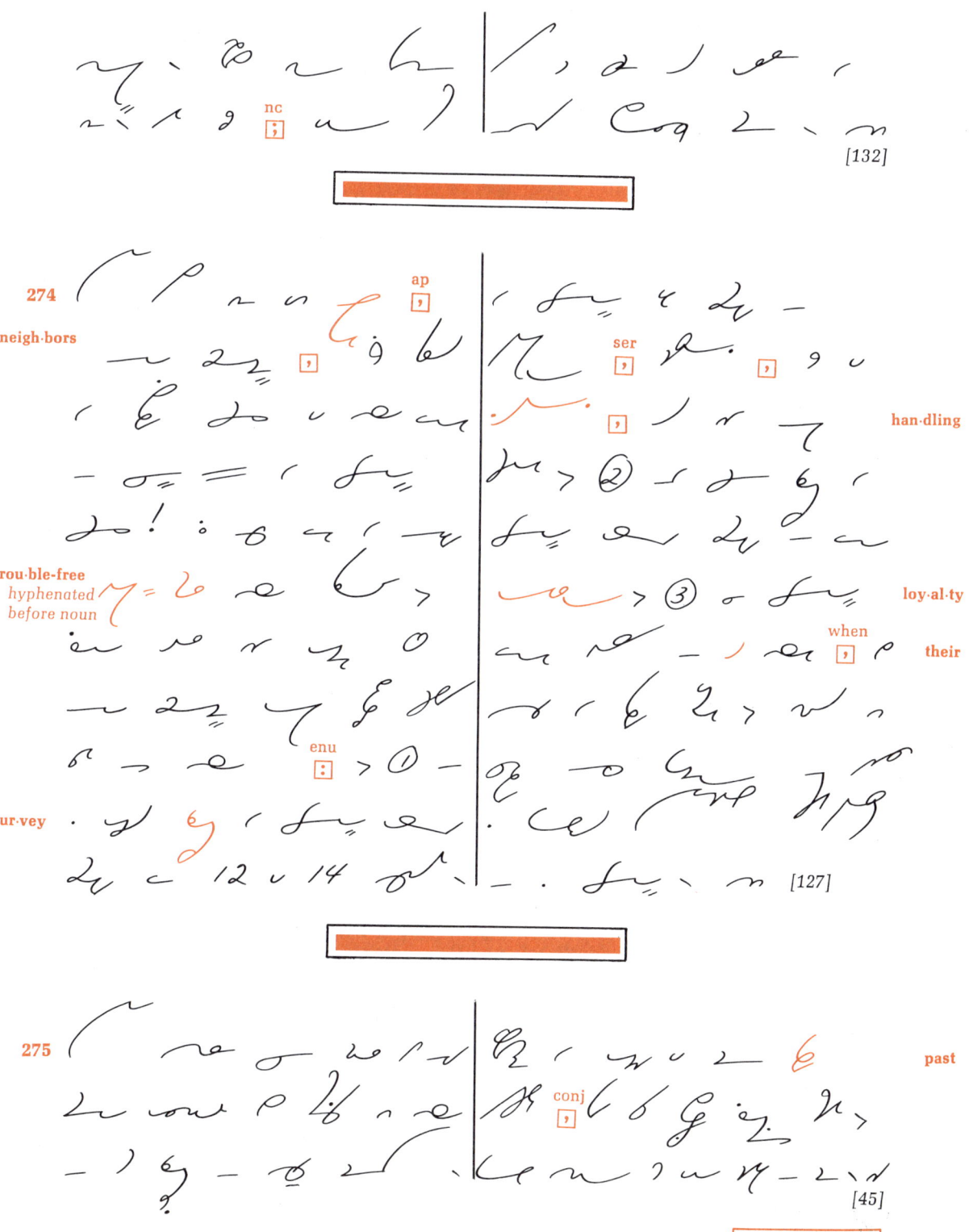

Building transcription skills

276 SPELLING FAMILIES | **-ly added to words ending in e**

Most words ending in e retain the e when the ending -ly is added.

bare·ly	like·ly	scarce·ly
close·ly	name·ly	sin·cere·ly
for·tu·nate·ly	nice·ly	sure·ly
late·ly	safe·ly	unique·ly

But, like most rules, this one has its exceptions. In the following words, the e is dropped when -ly is added:

| whol·ly | tru·ly | du·ly |

277 | **Business vocabulary builder** | **cogent** Forceful; convincing.
countless Cannot be counted; innumerable.
squad car An automobile used by the police and especially equipped with shortwave radiophone.

Reading and writing practice

278

lease
sales·men's
enu
co·gent

equipped

main·te·nance

ser

[110] won't

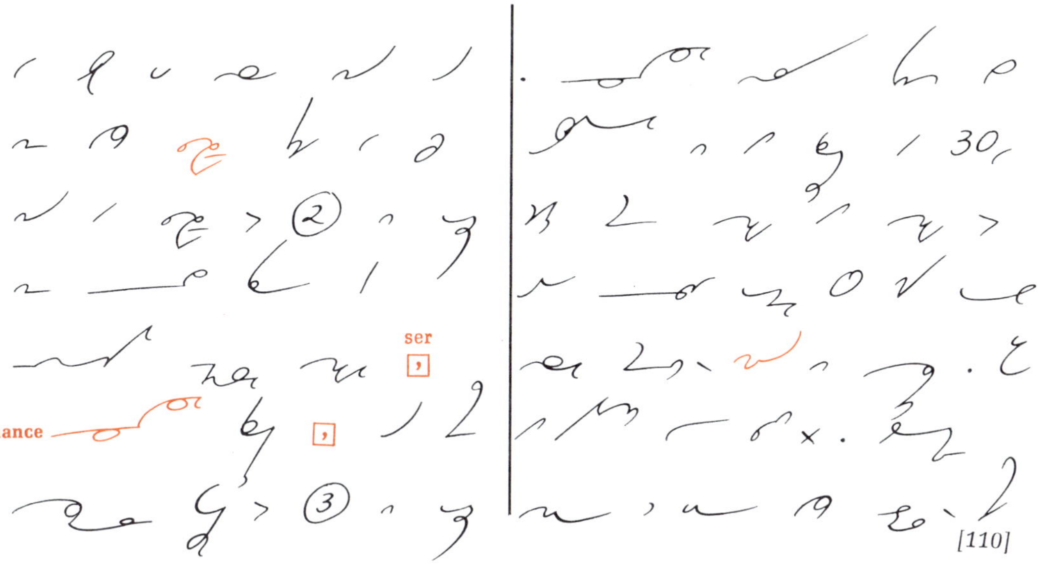

279

coun·try's

com·pa·nies

enu

first-class
*hyphenated
before noun*

air·port

Transcribe:
7 cents

intro

steer·ing

ser

par

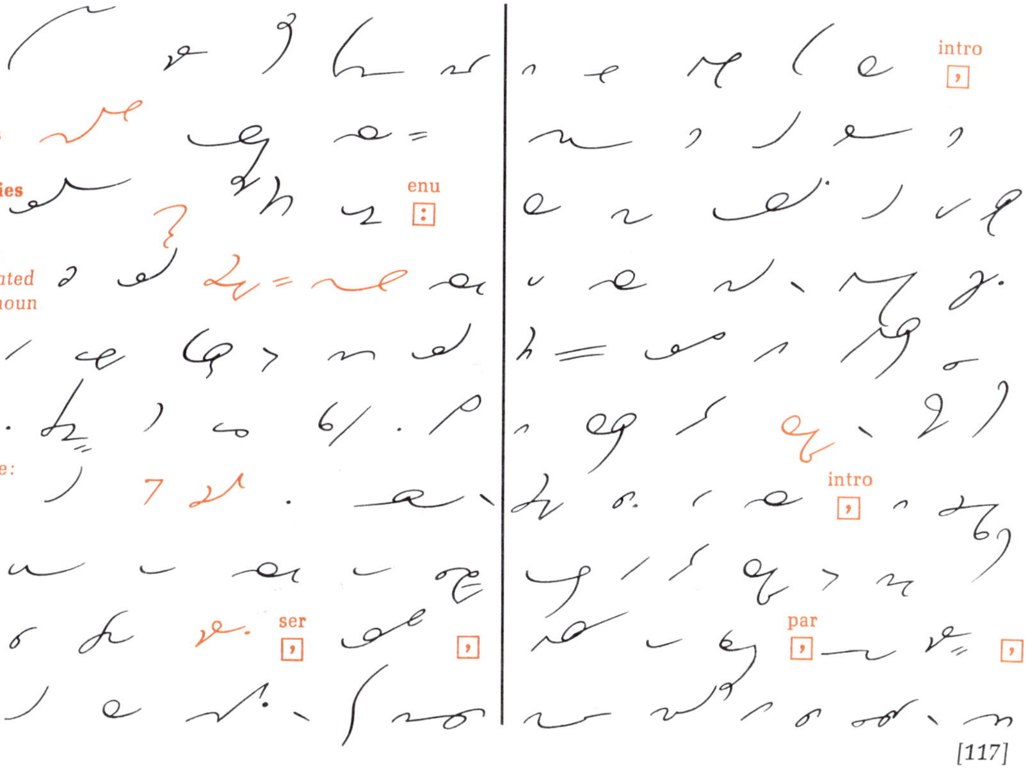

[117]

LESSON 37 | 199

280

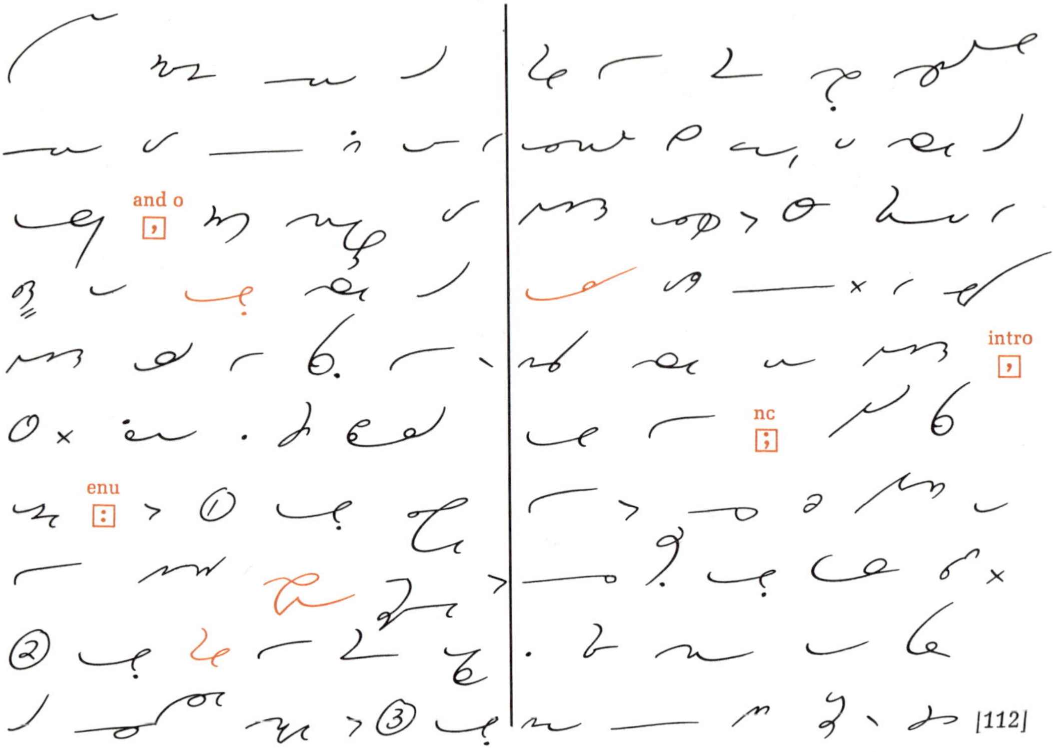

leas·ing

lead

and o

intro

nc

enu

cap·i·tal

frees

[112]

281

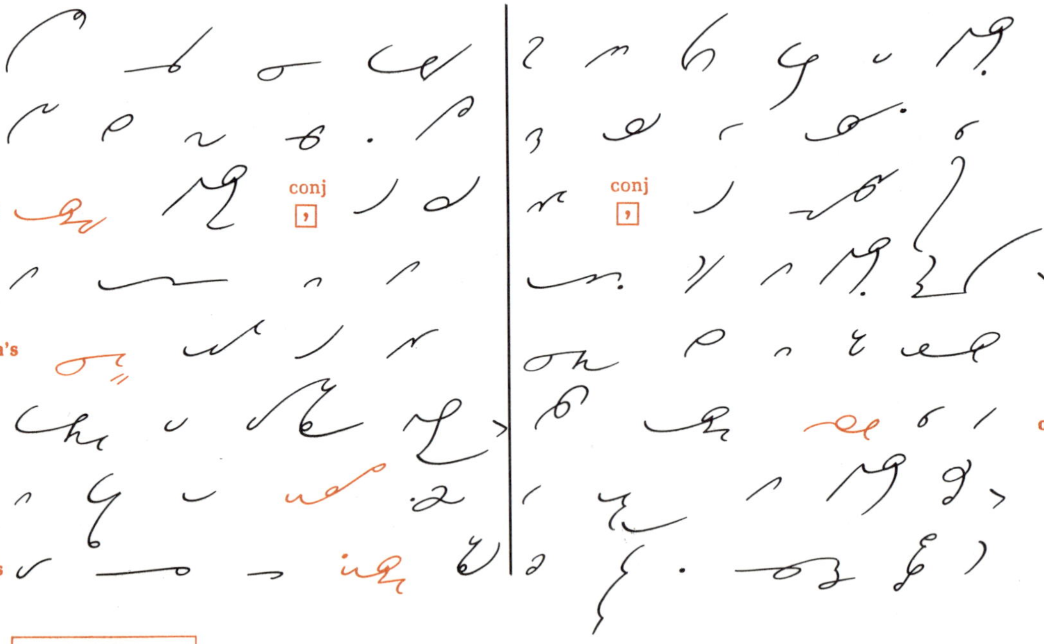

li·censed

conj

conj

Amer·i·ca's

car·ries

al·ready

ho·ri·zons

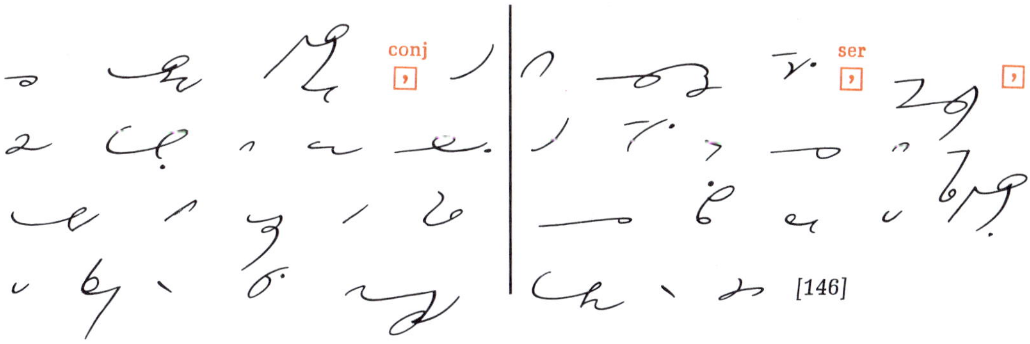

[146]

282

- fleet
- two-way *hyphenated before noun*
- com·pa·ny's
- squad 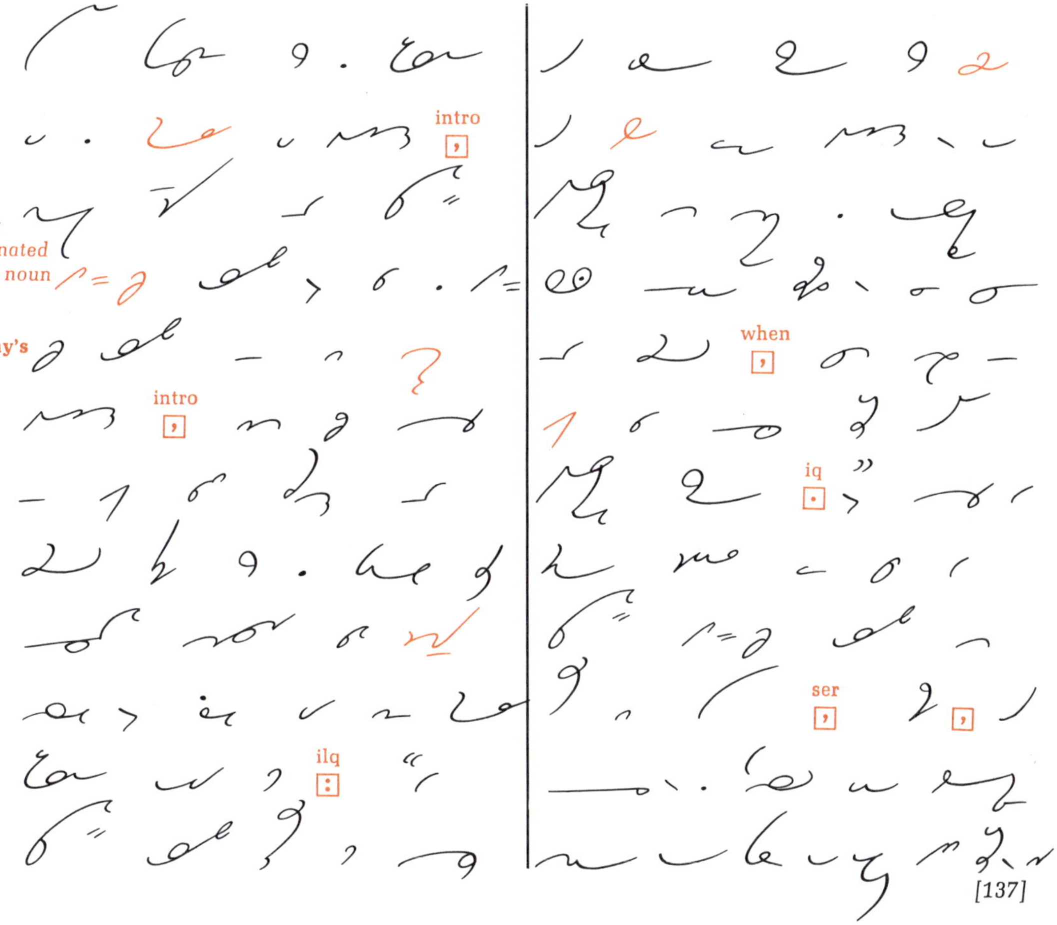
- wear
- tear
- touch

[137]

Building transcription skills

283 ACCURACY PRACTICE

Follow the procedures outlined on page **154** as you work on this Accuracy Practice.

GROUP 1	GROUP 2	GROUP 3
written	get	theirs
regular	gather	ours

practice drill

1 The <u>written</u> agreement is in the safe. The <u>regular</u> agreement is in the safe.
2 I will <u>get</u> the information by noon. I will <u>gather</u> the information by noon.
3 These books are <u>theirs</u>. These books are <u>ours</u>.

284

Business vocabulary builder

filter (noun) A device that strains or purifies.
alterations Changes; modifications.
preview (noun) A private showing or exhibition before its public opening.

Reading and writing practice

285 en·joy·ing if enu par oc·curs fil·ter par and o well-trained *hyphenated before noun* [116]

286 trail·er intro enu shelves al·ready [97]

LESSON 38 | 203

287

its

sight-see·ing

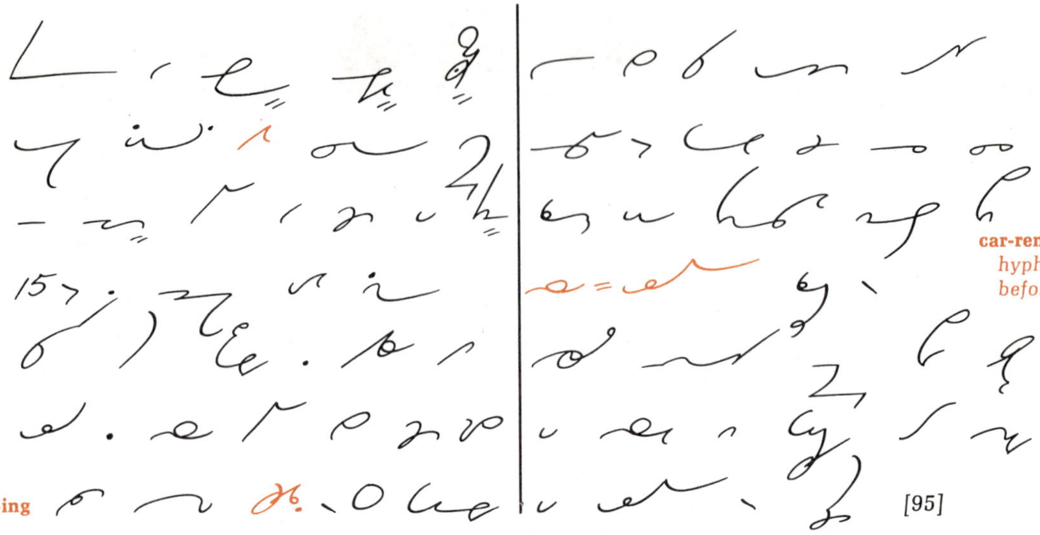

car-rent·al
hyphenated before noun

[95]

288

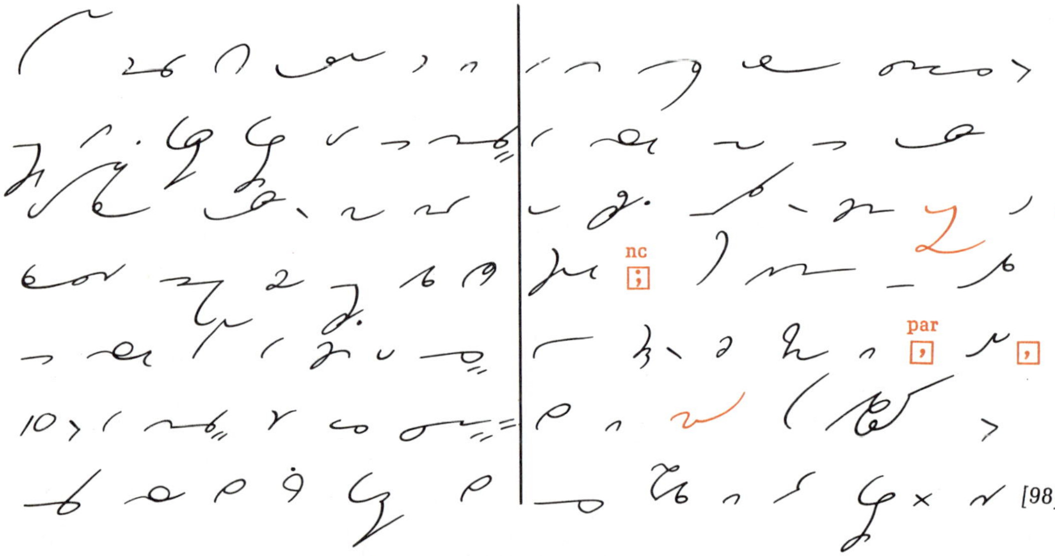

nc
;

re·veal

par
, ,

won't

[98]

289

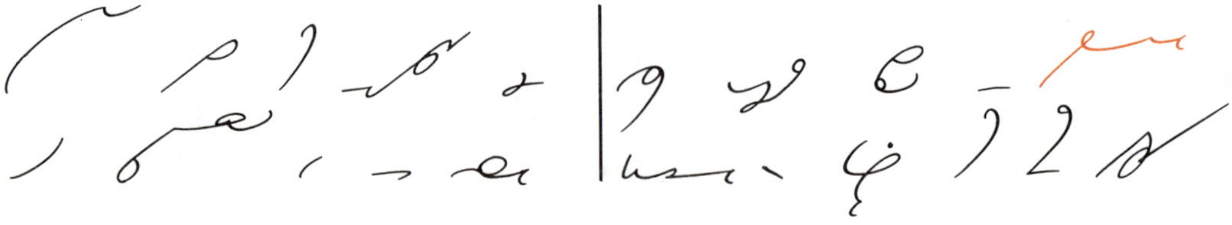

deal·ers'

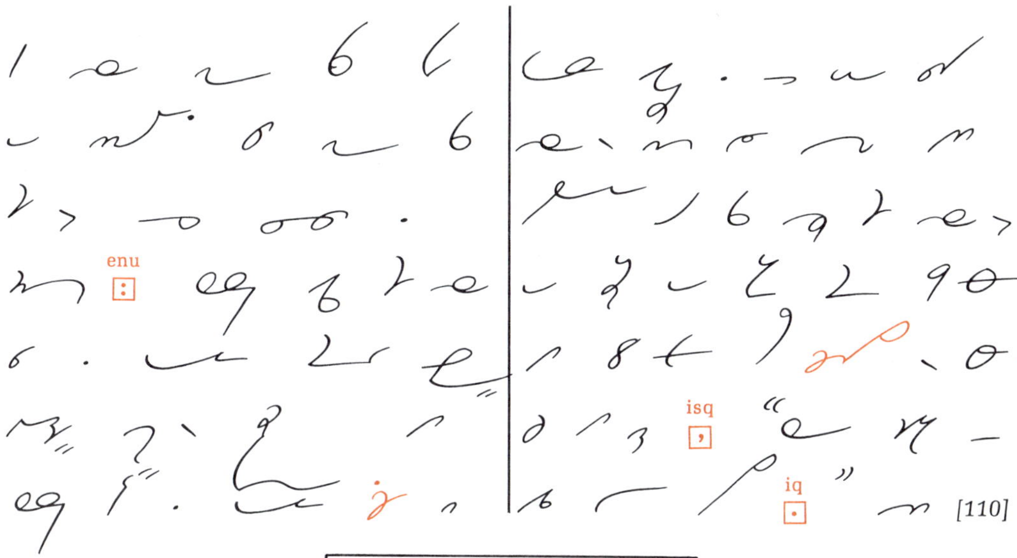

wheth·er

week·day

290 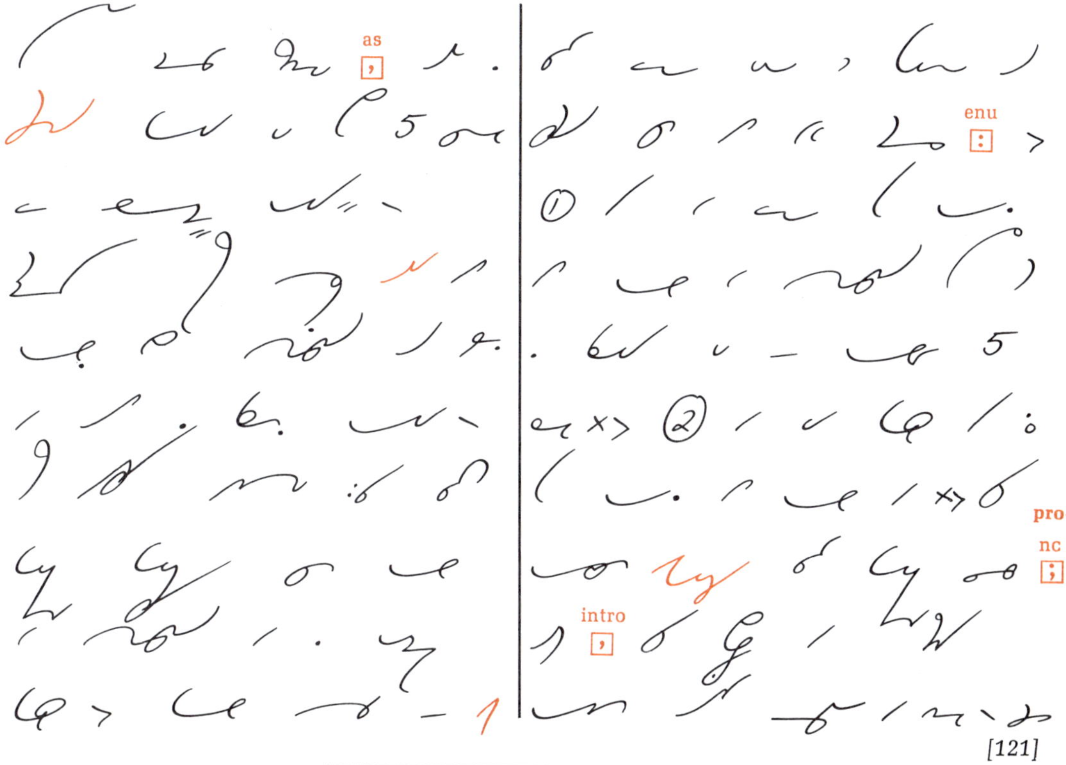
va·cant
thought
touch

pro·ceed

LESSON 38 | 205

Building transcription skills

291 OFFICE-STYLE DICTATION | short transpositions

A businessman may occasionally decide to transpose words or phrases for emphasis or for some other reason. The dictator may say:

We are conducting an advertising campaign for our cars in both weekly and monthly magazines—make that **monthly** and **weekly magazines.**

In your notes, you would indicate the transposition thus:

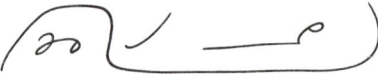

You would then transcribe the word *and* after *monthly.*

long transpositions

Occasionally a dictator will decide that an entire sentence or even a paragraph would be more effective if it were transposed to another part of the letter. When this happens, the simplest way to show the transposition is to encircle the material to be transposed and indicate the new position by an arrow.

▶ **SEE THE OPPOSITE PAGE FOR THE ILLUSTRATION OF OFFICE-STYLE DICTATION**

292

Business vocabulary builder	
prejudiced	Biased; partial.
memorable	Long to be remembered.
justice of the peace	A local magistrate having authority to administer justice in minor cases.

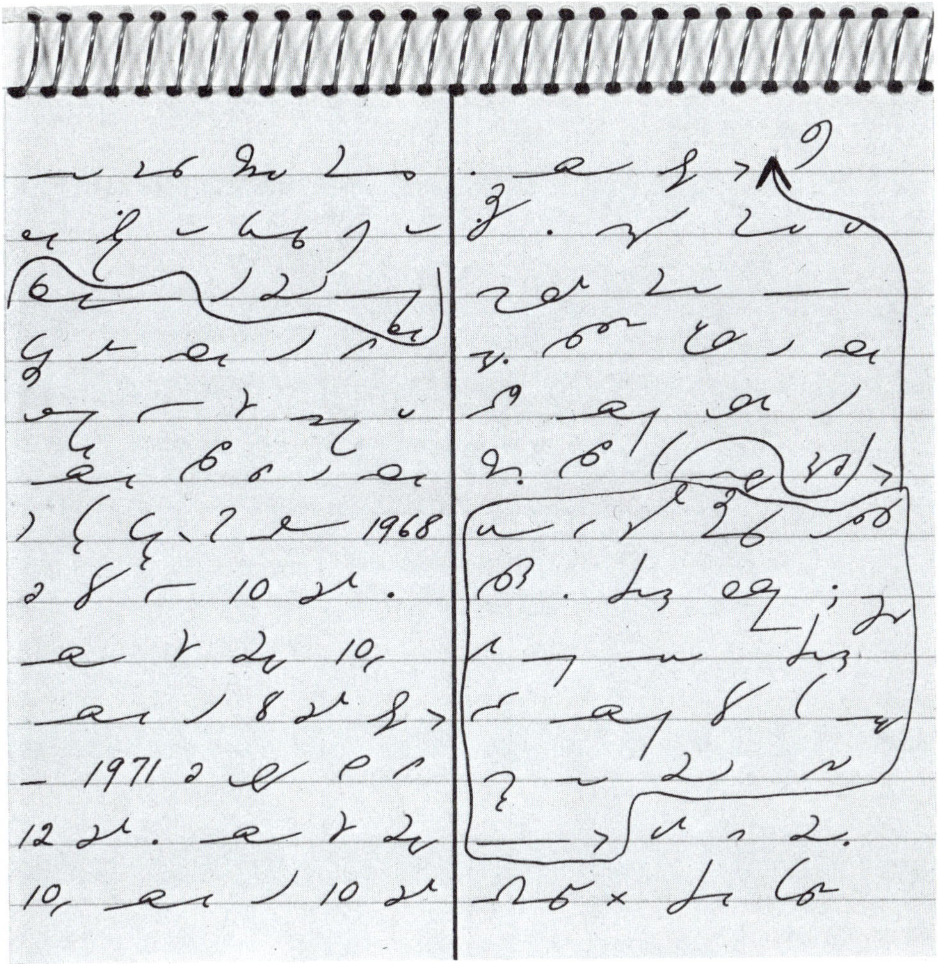

ILLUSTRATION OF OFFICE-STYLE DICTATION

Reading and writing practice

293

LESSON 39

peace

if

nc ;

intro ,

jail

[110]

296

be·gin·ning

high-grade *hyphenated before noun*

intro ,

intro ,

Transcribe: **20 percent**

20,

their

par ,

,

rise

ab·sorbed

intro ,

[134]

297

nc ;

intro ,

hear

LESSON 39

Building transcription skills

299 COMMON PREFIXES | con-

con- The prefix *con-* in many English words means *together.*

connection A joining or fastening together.

conciliate To draw together; to make friendly.

concurrent Running together; happening at the same time.

confer To talk together.

congregate To come together; to meet.

conspire To plan together to do some unlawful act.

consolidate To bring together.

300

Business vocabulary builder	**minor** Not serious.
	impartial Unbiased; fair to all sides.
	conceivable Imaginable.

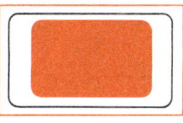

Reading and writing practice

301

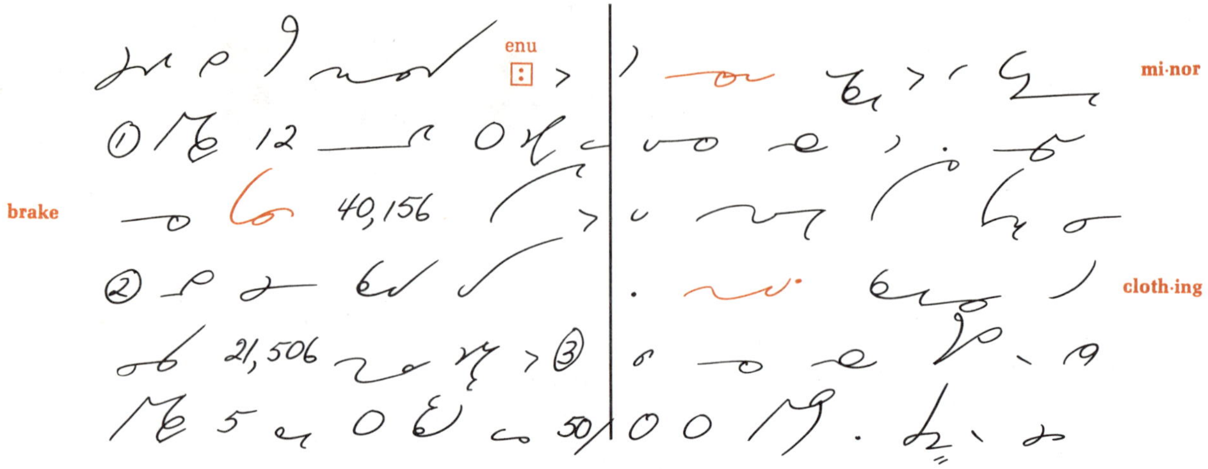
enu
mi·nor
brake
cloth·ing

302

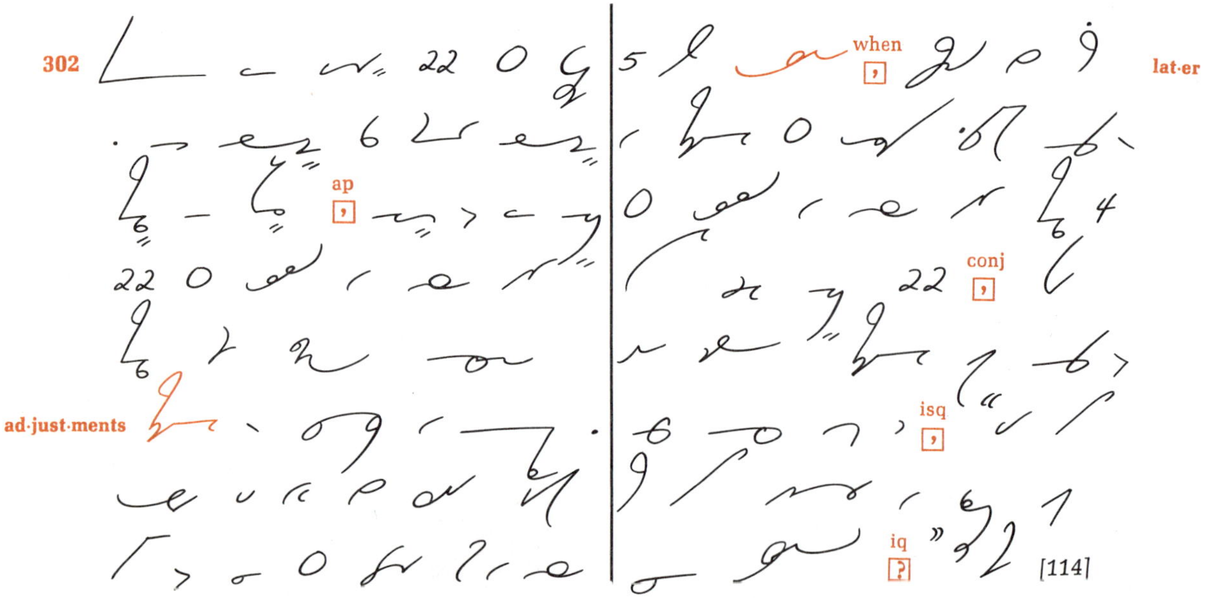
when
lat·er
ap
conj
ad·just·ments
isq
iq
[114]

303

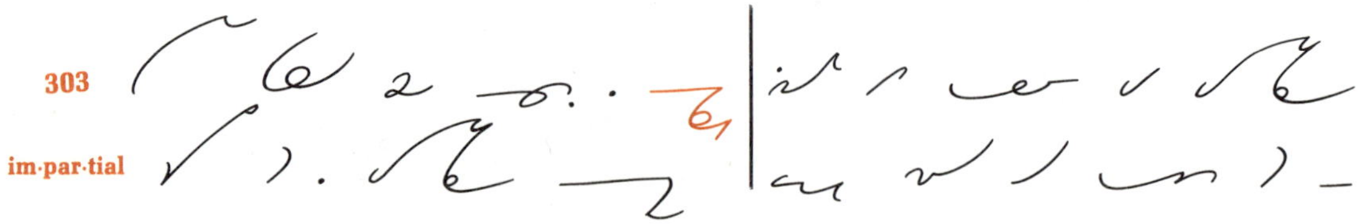
im·par·tial

four-page
hyphenated before noun

4=

cr

intro

re·ac·tion

post·paid

its mod·els

[130]

304

world's

con·fer·ring

par

con·ceiv·able

[131]

own·er's

305

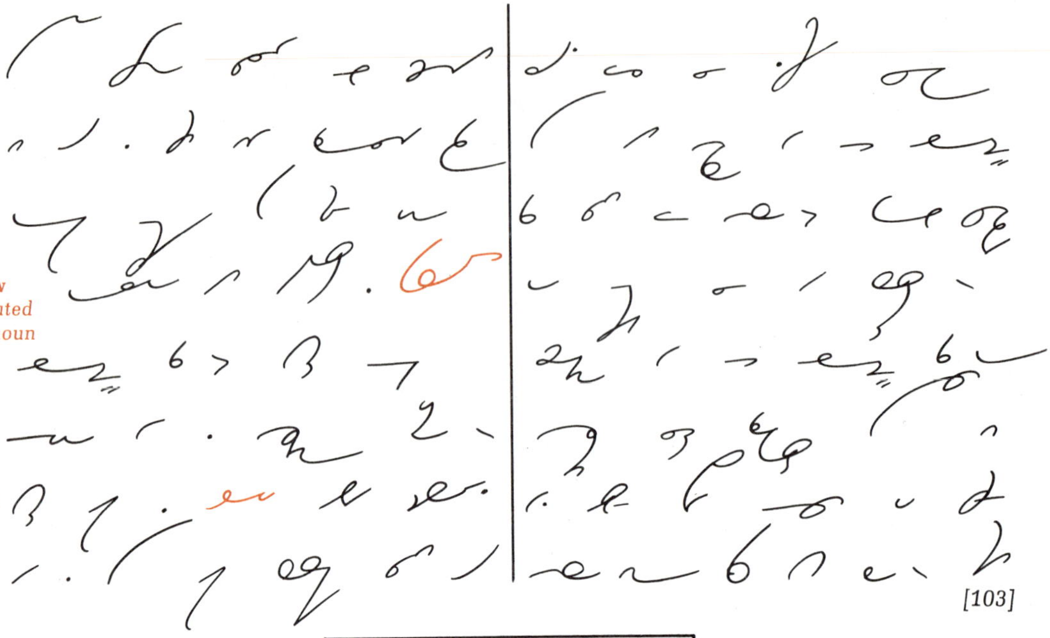

brand-new — hyphenated before noun

thor·ough

[103]

306

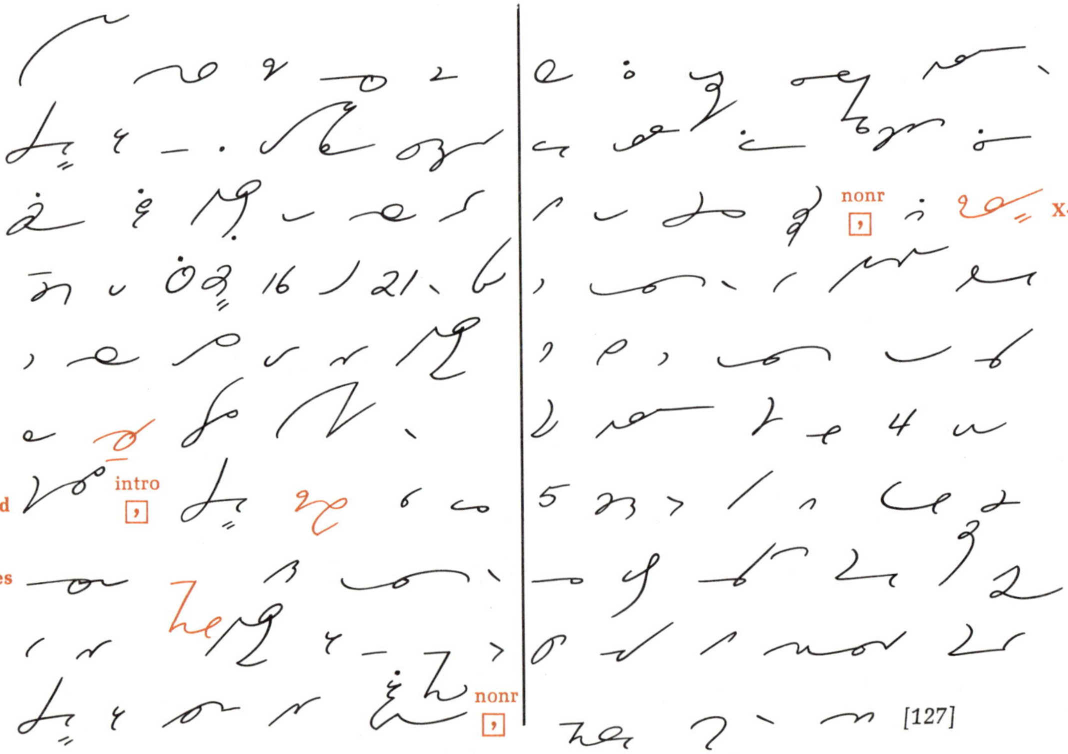

quite

es·caped

in·ju·ries

X-rayed
nonr
intro
nonr

[127]

LESSON 40

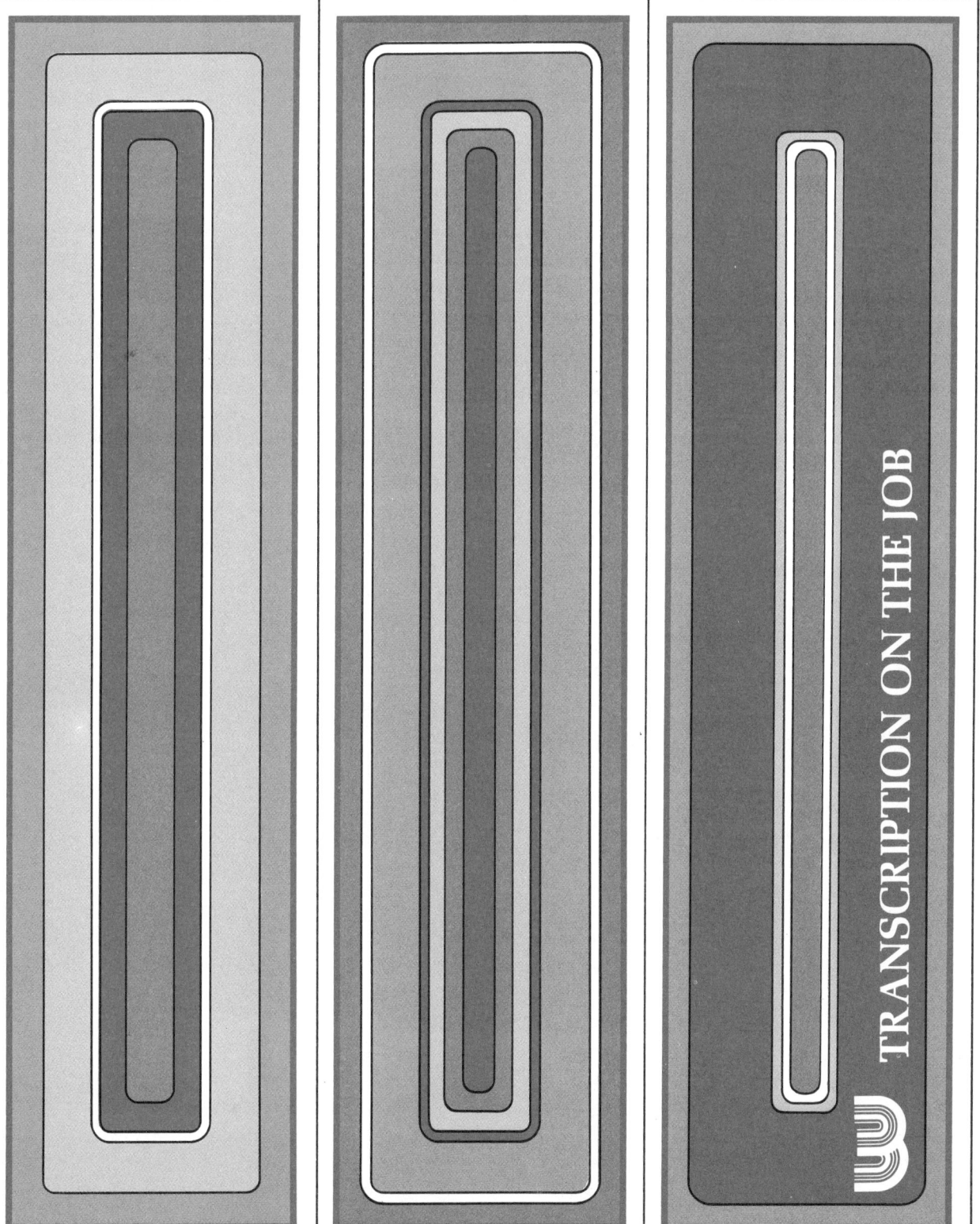

The secretary makes copies

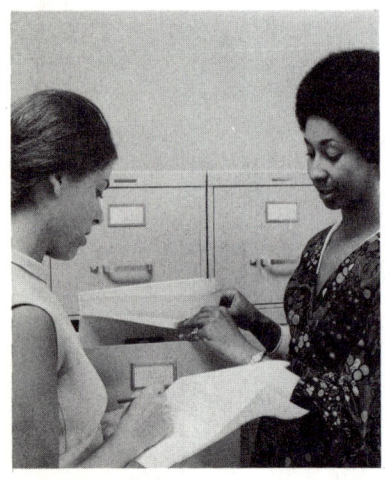

After dictating for a good part of the morning, Mr. Davis finally said, "That will be all." Ellen returned to her desk but didn't start transcribing immediately. So that she could transcribe uninterruptedly, she first gathered all the material and information she would need, such as catalogs and booklets to be enclosed, and checked prices that were to be quoted in the letters. She also looked up the spelling of words that she had encircled in her notes during lulls in the dictation.

Only then did she turn her attention to transcribing.

As she turned to the first letter to be transcribed, her first consideration was the number of copies to make.

Before dictating most of his letters, Mr. Davis says nothing about the number of carbons Ellen should make. When that happens, she makes only one carbon for the files.

When he wishes to keep others informed of what he is writing to a correspondent, he will tell Ellen to "send copies to Jones and Smith." In that case she

makes three carbon copies—one for Mr. Jones, one for Mr. Smith, and one for the files. On the original copy she indicates the names of those who received carbons.

Occasionally he wants a third person to have a copy of his letter to a correspondent, but does not want the correspondent to know about it. In that case Ellen makes two carbons. When she has completed typing the letter, she removes the original from the machine and types on the carbon copies the notation: "bcc: (which means blind carbon copy) Mr. Smith." This notation is usually typed at the top left corner.

After she has determined how many copies she must make, Ellen decides on the type of carbon paper she should use. In making her decision, she takes two things into consideration:

1 The kind of typewriter: standard or electric.

2 The number of copies to be made. (In general, a heavier weight carbon should be chosen when only one carbon is to be made than when four

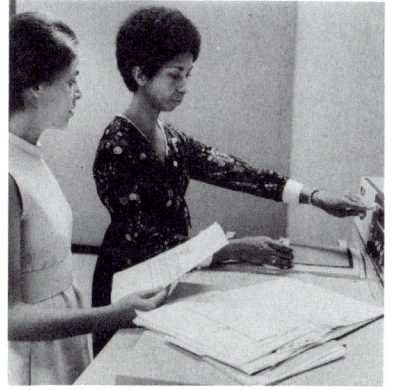

or five carbons are to be made.) Before Ellen actually inserts the carbon paper, she checks to see that it is in usable condition, so that it will give a legible reproduction.

Finally, she inserts the pack into the machine. Before she types a stroke, however, she takes one final precaution: she looks to be sure that the carbon paper has been correctly inserted, with the glossy side against the paper on which the copy is to be made. She would be very much embarrassed, on completing the letter, if she found that she had typed the carbon copy on the back of the original.

Occasionally, Mr. Davis wishes to send copies of his letters to quite a few people. When five or more copies are necessary, Ellen does not make any carbon copies; she types only the original and then runs it through a photocopying machine. This has two advantages. First, it ensures that each person receives a legible copy; second, it saves the time that would be required to correct errors on multiple carbons.

Chapter 9

LESSON 41

Automation and office equipment

Building transcription skills

307 SIMILAR-WORDS DRILL | peace, piece

peace Contentment; freedom from fear.

[shorthand]

Protect your records and obtain peace of mind by installing one of our safes.

piece A part; a portion; a single unit or object.

[shorthand]

I lost the piece of paper.
We shall shortly announce another piece of equipment.

308

Business vocabulary builder	
computerizing	Placing on computers; automating.
survive	To live; to carry on.
intense	Considerable.

Reading and writing practice

309 *[shorthand with "intro" marker]*

won't
nc
when
and o
ac·cu·rate
slight·ly

weighs
hour's
par
reel
too

Transcribe:
9 a.m.
6 p.m.

[136]

310
as
com·put·er·iz·ing
re·ceiv·able
ap
fa·mil·iar·ize

intro
intro
lun·cheon

[114]

LESSON 41 | 219

29 EAST CANYON AVENUE, SANTA FE, NEW MEXICO 87501 Cable: SPLAGAR

SPLANE & GARDNER, INC.

TEL. 445-7890

April 14, 19--

Mrs. Charles R. Gray
   3313 Western Parkway
   Santa Fe, New Mexico 87501

Dear Mrs. Gray:

    I must make a confession. When I came here last fall to take over the Santa Fe branch of Splane and Gardner, Inc., I was sure that it would be easy to sell a great deal of furniture in a short time. The sight of the homes here in Santa Fe must have caused me to be overoptimistic.

    In anticipation of the sales that I expected, I bought large quantities of fine furniture. In spite of the quality of the furniture and the appeal of our low prices, however, sales fell far below my expectations. Now I have a warehouse full of merchandise that must be moved. What's more, there are new shipments on the way from several manufacturers.

    The time for action has come. On Saturday, May 6, you will see in all the Santa Fe papers an announcement of stock-disposal sales. Prices will be low. In many cases, our furniture will be offered at cost and even less. Of course, we expect a great response. Because of this, I feel that you and a few other preferred customers should have the opportunity to shop in comfort before public announcement is made of the sale.

    Therefore, please consider this a personal invitation for you to shop at your convenience on May 3, 4, or 5. When you come, please give the enclosed card to one of our salesmen. He will then take you to the floor on which the sale will be held.

                                 Very truly yours,

                                 SPLANE & GARDNER, INC.

                                 Martin A. Foster

                                 Martin A. Foster
                                    Manager

MAF:RE
Enclosure

Long letter
Indented style
Standard punctuation

311

Transcribe:
18 Street

their

lead [97]

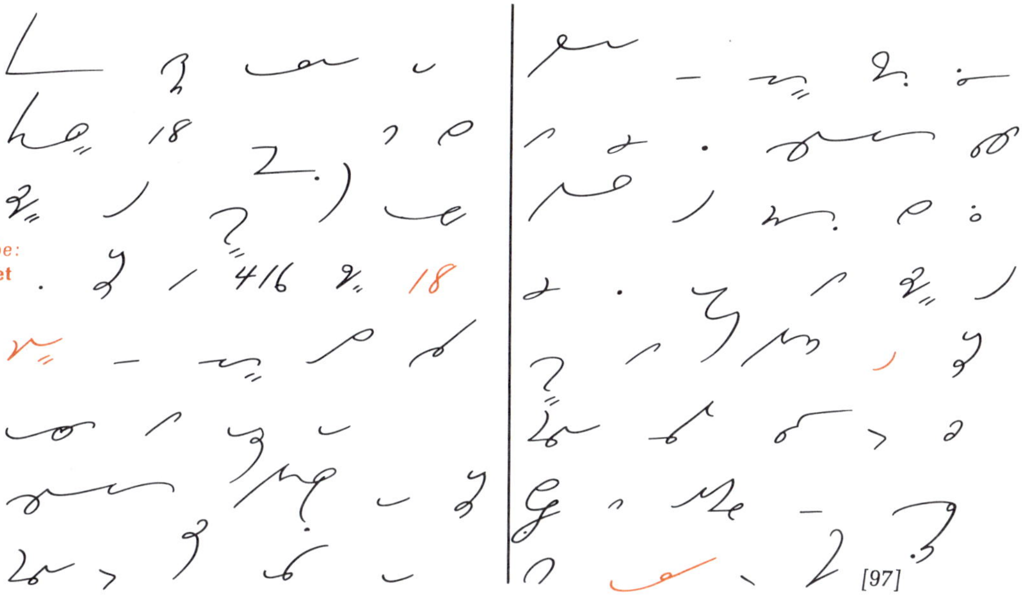

312

well-known
hyphenated before noun

lose

firm's

peace

enu

intro

bur·glar·proof

rec·om·mend [118]

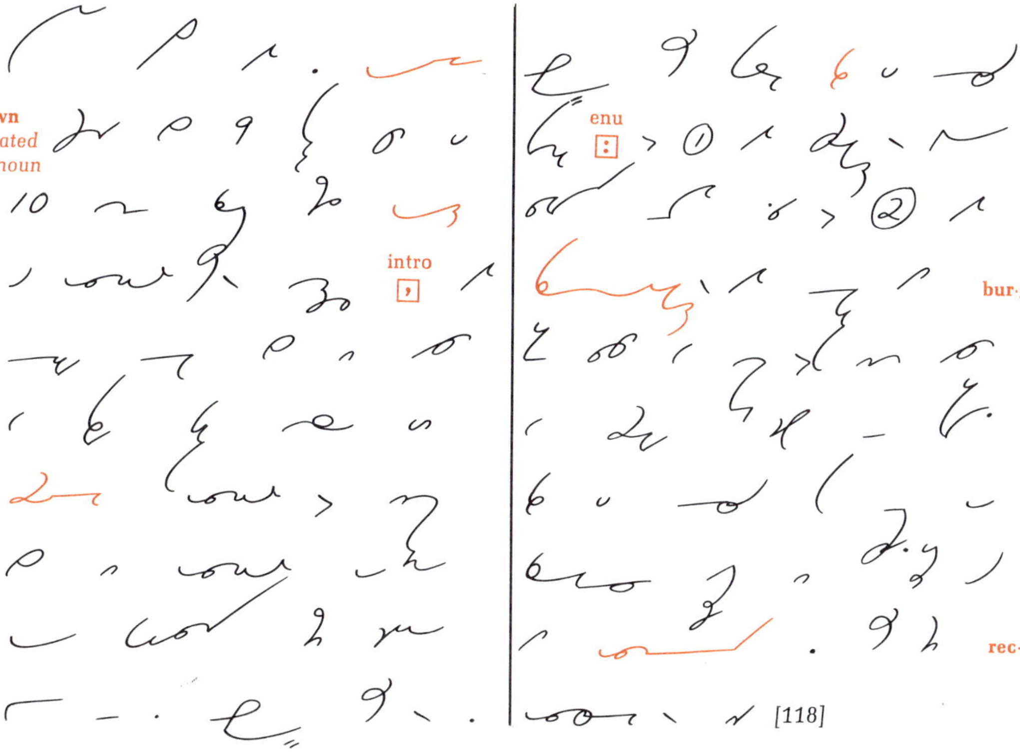

LESSON 41 | 221

313

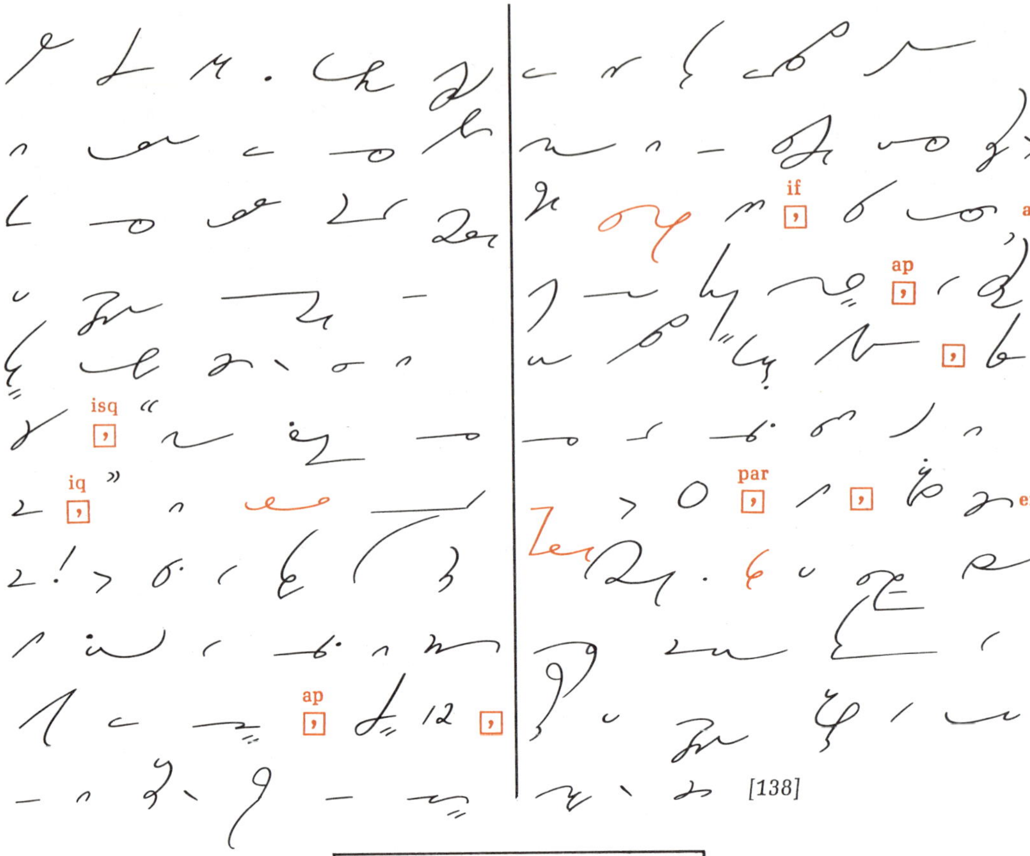

re·al·ly isq iq ap if ap par agree·able en·gin·eers piece

[138]

314

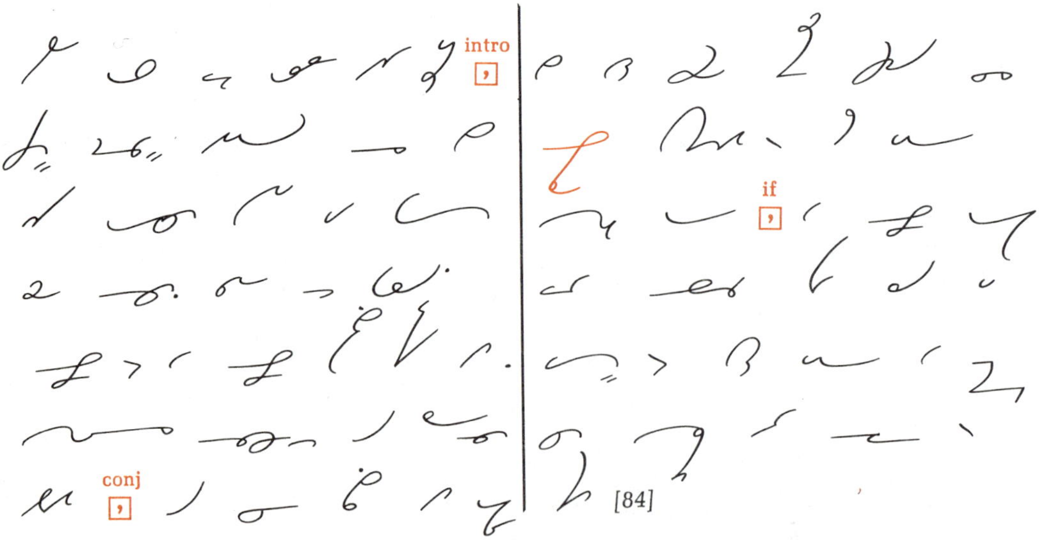

intro conj if ma·jor

[84]

Building transcription skills

315 SPELLING FAMILIES | words in which consonants are doubled

Double trouble!

Words in which consonants are doubled are a frequent cause of misspelling. The following lists contain words in which one or more consonants are doubled, words that are repeatedly misspelled by stenographers.

Double R

| ar·range | em·bar·rass | sur·round·ed |
| trans·fer·ring | in·ter·rupt | oc·curred |

Double N

| in·no·va·tion | per·son·nel | ques·tion·naire |

Double F

| sher·iff | tar·iff | traf·fic |

Double S

| mis·spell | per·mis·sion | pro·cess |
| pos·si·bil·i·ty | pos·ses·sion | suc·cess |

316

| Business vocabulary builder | **tentative** Temporary; not final.
scrapped Discarded.
innovations New ideas, methods, or devices. |

Reading and writing practice

317

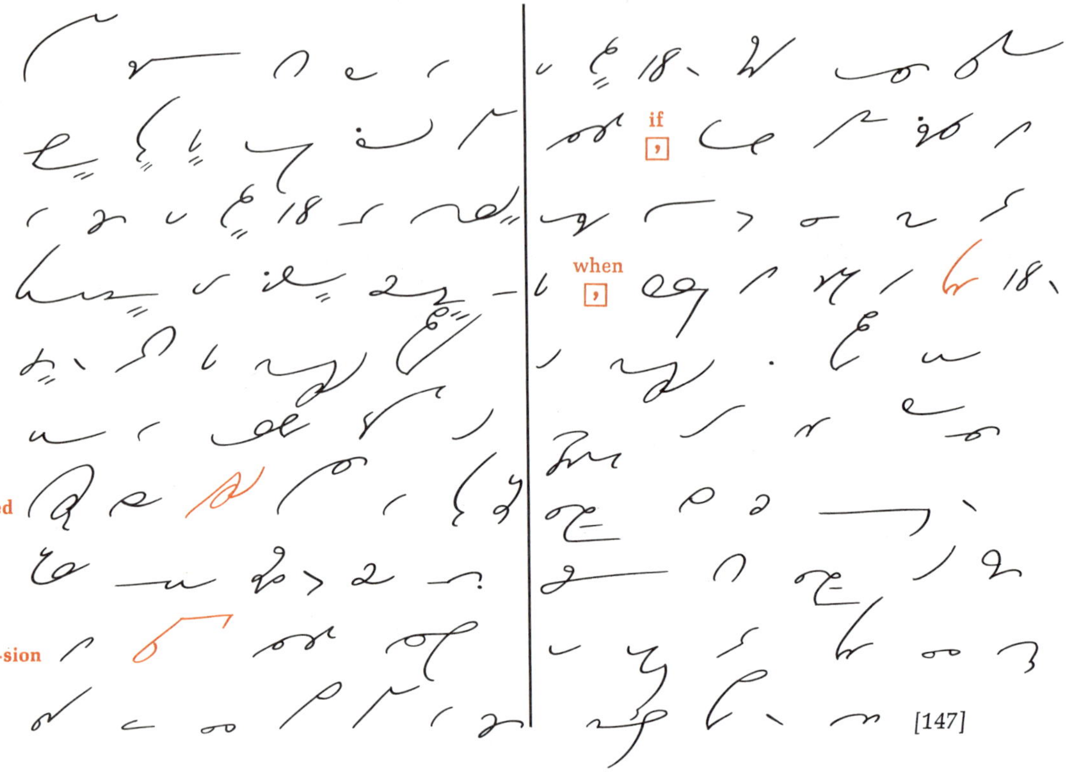

if, when, booth, de·signed, ad·mis·sion

[147]

318

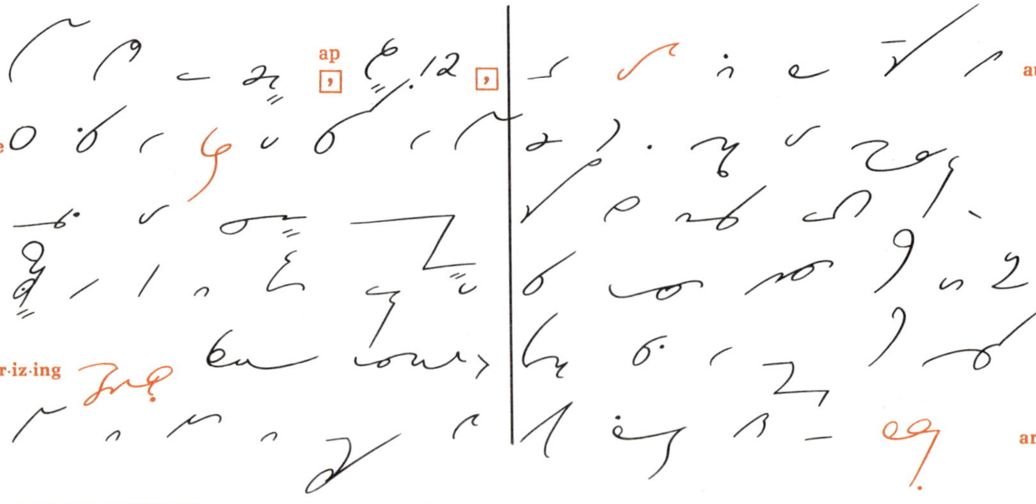

ap, priv·i·lege, au·di·ence, com·put·er·iz·ing, ar·rang·ing

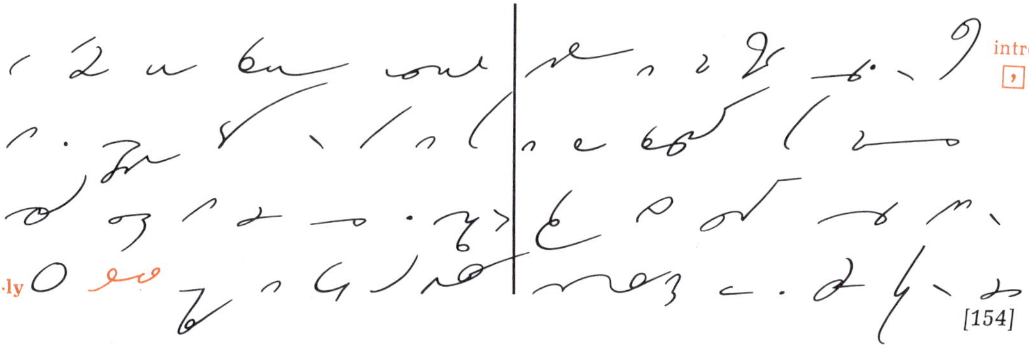

thor·ough·ly [154]

319 scrapped
ex·hib·it·ing
conj
re·main·der
em·bar·rassed [101]

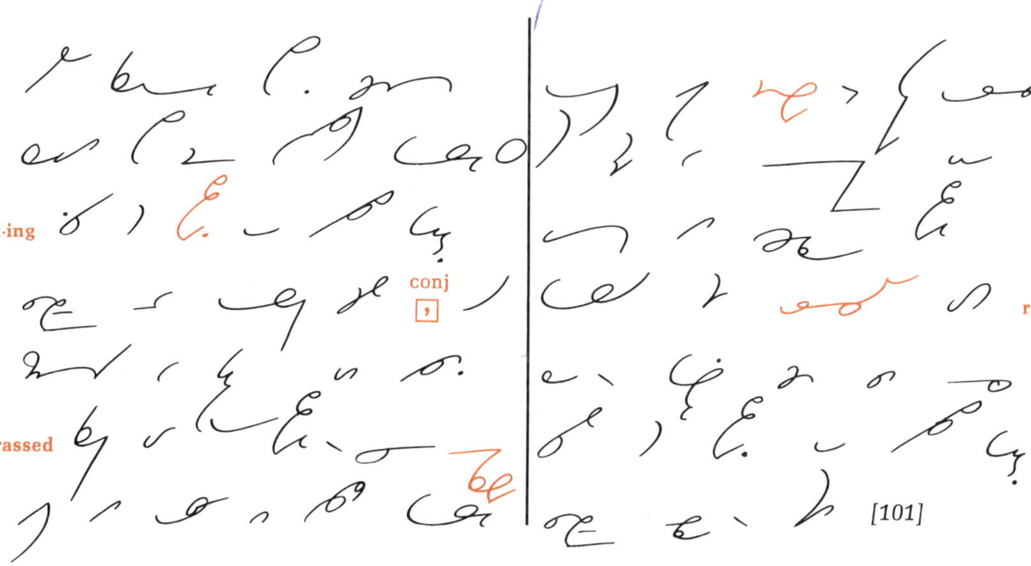

320 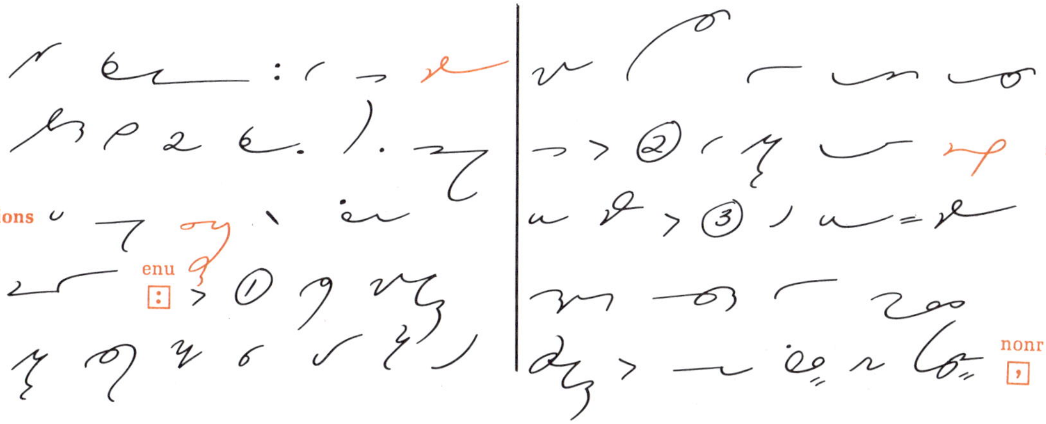
steel
scratch
in·no·va·tions
enu
nonr

LESSON 42

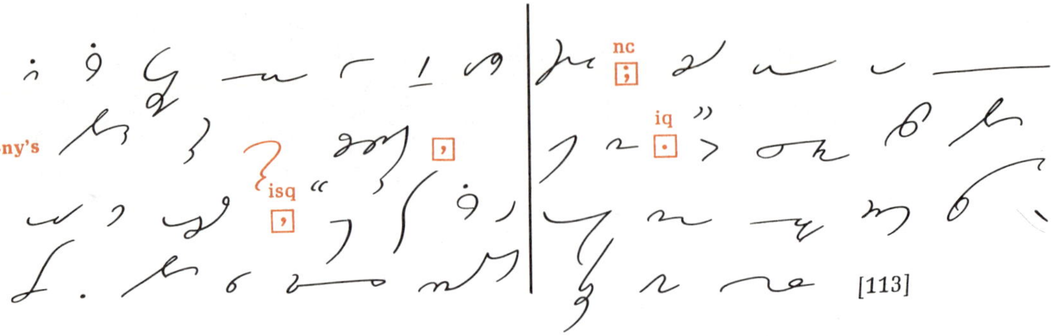
com·pa·ny's
nc
iq
isq
[113]

321

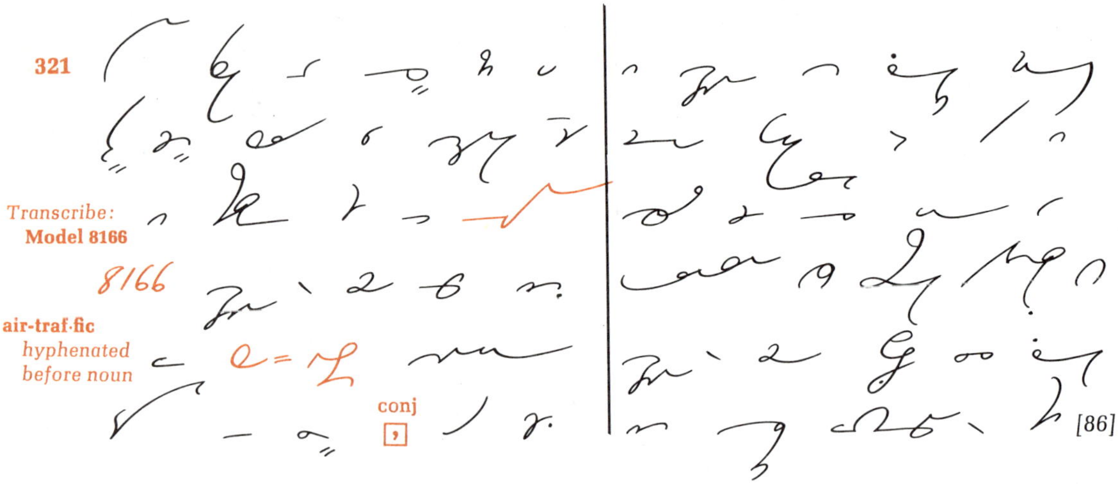
Transcribe: **Model 8166**
air-traf·fic *hyphenated before noun*
conj
[86]

322

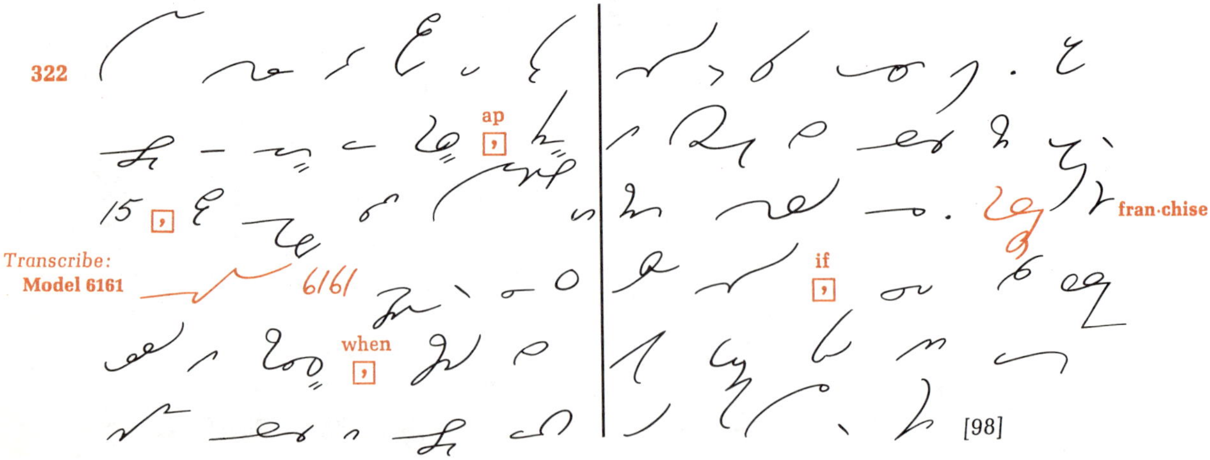
ap
15
Transcribe: **Model 6161**
when
if
fran·chise
[98]

LESSON 43

Building transcription skills

323 GRAMMAR CHECKUP | let, leave

Let and *leave* are two words that people often misuse. You will have no difficulty using these words correctly if you will remember these definitions.

leave To move or go away from; to depart.

I will leave home at 10 o'clock.

let To permit; to allow.

Let (not leave) me help you.

▶ Hint: If you are in doubt as to whether *let* or *leave* is correct, substitute *permit* and *depart*. If *permit* makes sense, use *let*; if *depart* makes sense, use *leave*.

324

Business vocabulary builder	**adjust** To regulate. **warrant** (verb) To justify. **appraise** To place a value on.

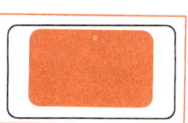

Reading and writing practice

325

bear·er
neph·ew

mas·ter's

LESSON 43 | 227

Au·to·ma·tion — ap — iq — when — guid·ance — par — too [92]

326 — if — and o — lan·guage — ma·jor — en·cour·ag·ing

24-page *hyphenated before noun* — Transcribe: **20 cents** [167]

327

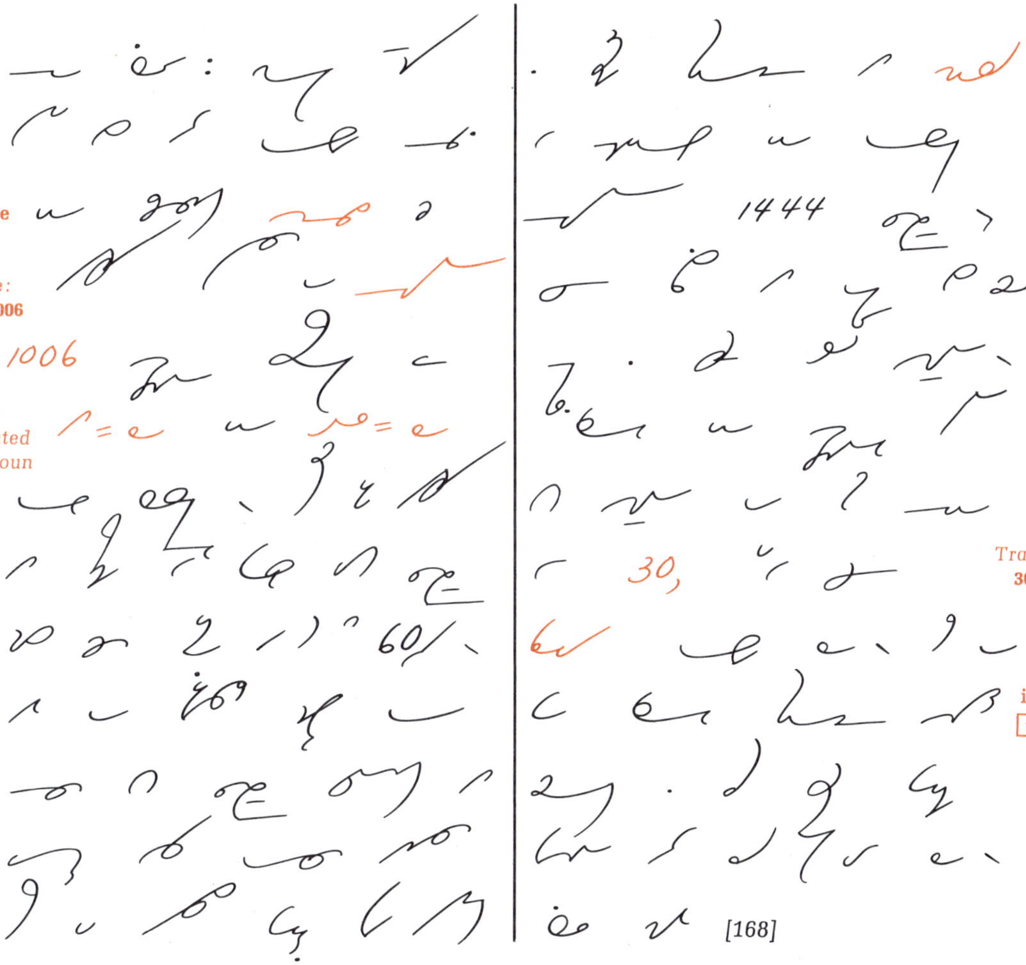

com·mit·tee

Transcribe:
Model 1006

two-year
three-year
hyphenated before noun

war·rant

Transcribe:
30 percent

pe·ri·od

if

[168]

328

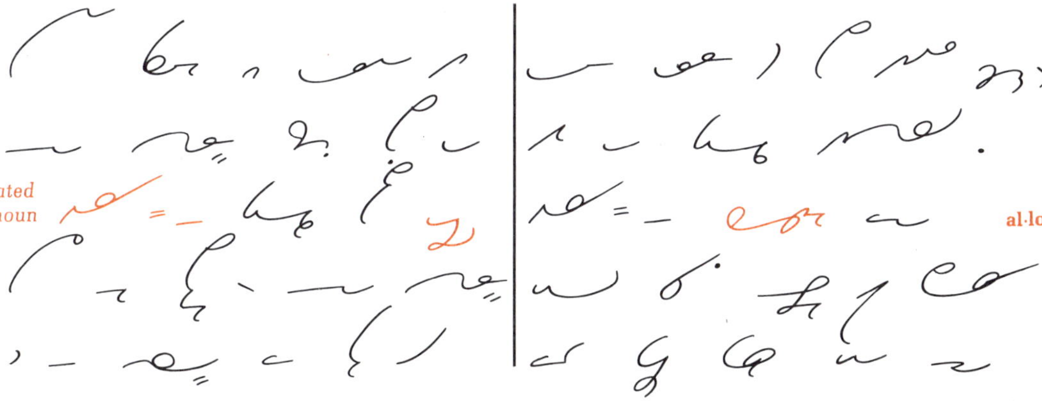

trade-in
hyphenated before noun
re·ferred

al·low·ance

Letter placement
LONG LETTERS

In this lesson you will take up the placement of long letters (those containing more than 200 words).

On page 231 you will find Letter No. 328 of *Gregg Transcription* as Ellen Gardiner wrote it in her notebook and as she transcribed it on her typewriter, which has elite type. The letter contains about 220 words. You will notice that Ellen's notes filled about a column and a quarter of her notebook.

Whenever a letter requires from a column and a quarter up to a column and a half of her notebook, Ellen does three things:

1 She sets her margin stops for 1-inch margins at the left and at the right.

2 She types the date two lines below the last line of the letterhead.

3 She starts the inside address about 3 inches from the top of the paper.

If she is using a typewriter that has pica type, she maintains the same margins but starts the inside address about 2½ inches from the top of the paper.

Copy Letter No. 328 in shorthand and see how much space this long letter requires in your shorthand notebook. Then, if possible, transcribe the letter on the typewriter from your notes, placing it by judgment.

▶ *Caution!* Whenever a letter requires more than a column and a half of her notebook, Ellen considers very carefully whether she should type it as a one-page letter or as a two-page letter. On one occasion she decided to type a letter on one page, only to find, when she completed the body of the letter, that there was not enough space for the closing—so she had to retype the letter.

If you have any doubt whether a letter will fit on one page, play safe—widen your margins and type it as a two-page letter.

VAN WYCK'S • 829 CADILLAC AVENUE • DETROIT • MICHIGAN 48212

July 13, 19--

Mr. George A. Barnes
The Baker College
330 West 16 Street
Indianapolis, Indiana 46205

Dear Mr. Barnes:

    Your letter to Mr. Green asking about our trade-in policies has been referred to me in his absence. Mr. Green is in California on business and will not return for about two or three weeks.

    It is our policy to grant a trade-in allowance on our old adding machines to be applied on the purchase price of our newer models. Before we can tell you how much that trade-in allowance will be, we shall have to see your machine. You may be sure, though, that the allowance will be liberal. If you will indicate on the enclosed card a convenient time for our representative to call to appraise your model, we will arrange a definite appointment. The card requires no postage.

    We think you will be delighted with our new model; it is the product of many years of research and experience on the part of our engineering department.

    This new model is so simple to operate that the average person can learn to use it after a few minutes' instruction. Even though this new model has been on the market for only six months, we have already sold thousands of units.

    If there is any other way in which we can be of service to you, please let us know.

                      Very cordially yours,

                        John L. Burns
                        Sales Manager

JLB:LE

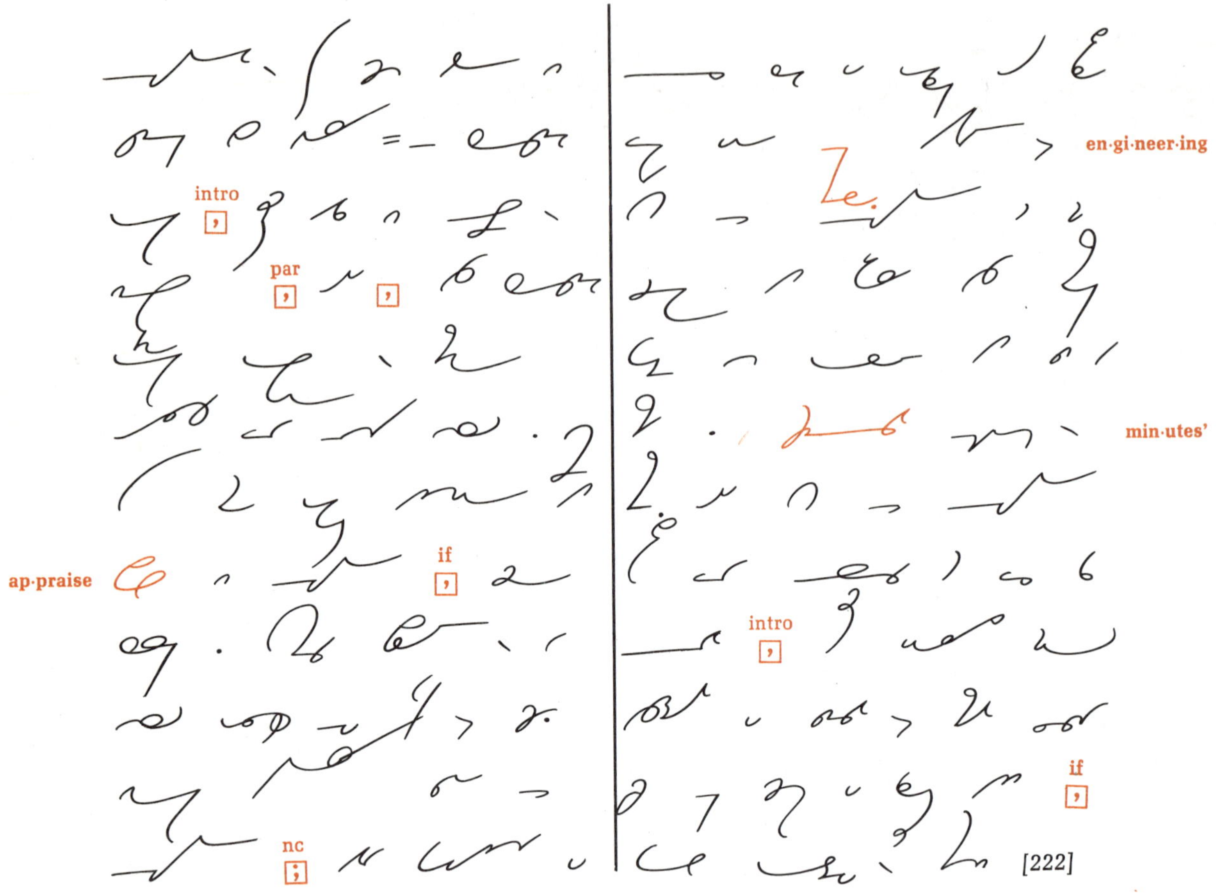

en·gi·neer·ing

intro

par

min·utes'

ap·praise

if

intro

nc

if

[222]

329

as

con·fi·dent

ser

guest

ap

if

[85]

Building transcription skills

330 OFFICE-STYLE DICTATION | short insertions

A common change that a businessman makes in his dictation is the insertion of a word or phrase in a sentence that has already been dictated. The dictator may say:

Our representative will call on you on Friday, June 16—make that **our Chicago representative.**

You must be on the alert so that you can quickly find the point at which the addition is to be made. When you find the point, insert the added word or phrase with a caret, just as you would in longhand, thus:

ILLUSTRATION OF OFFICE-STYLE DICTATION

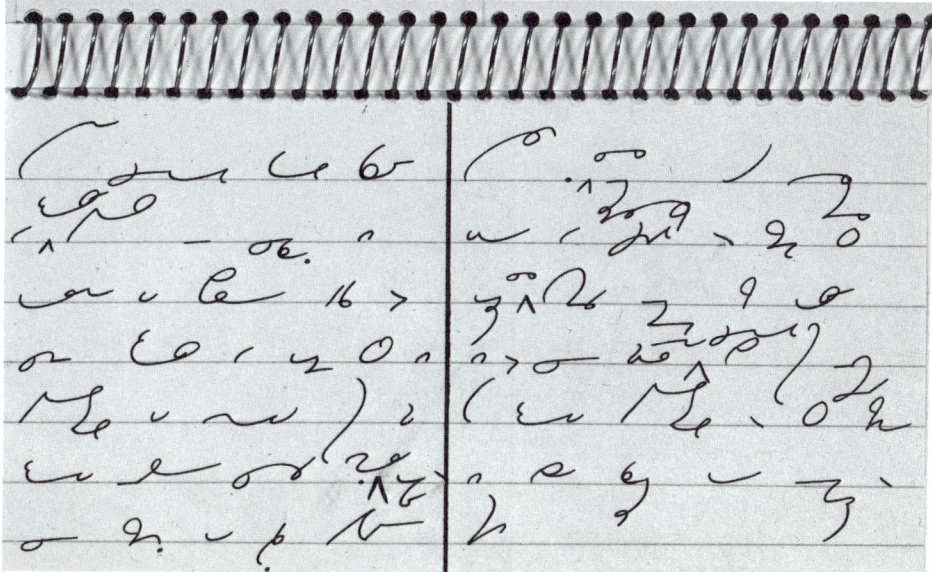

331 Business vocabulary builder

prevailed upon Induced; successfully persuaded.
resolve To solve.
expedite To speed the progress of.

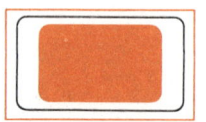

Reading and writing practice

332 Transcribe: No. 116

pre·vailed

won't

[79]

333 Chicago

Transcribe: Model 1151

un·for·tu·nate·ly

cour·te·sy

intro

if

[139]

334

par

its

passed

equip·ment

an·ni·ver·sa·ry

intro

cr

ap

[124]

335

1181

li·cense

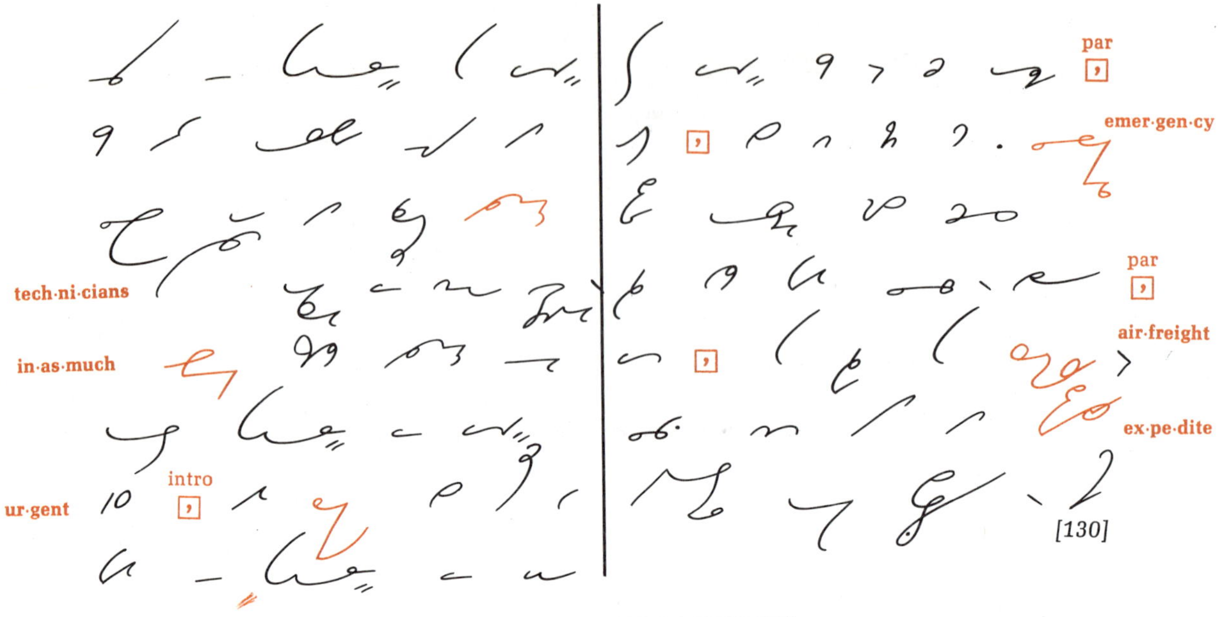

technicians
in·as·much
ur·gent   intro

par
emer·gen·cy
par
air·freight
ex·pe·dite
[130]

336
de·vice 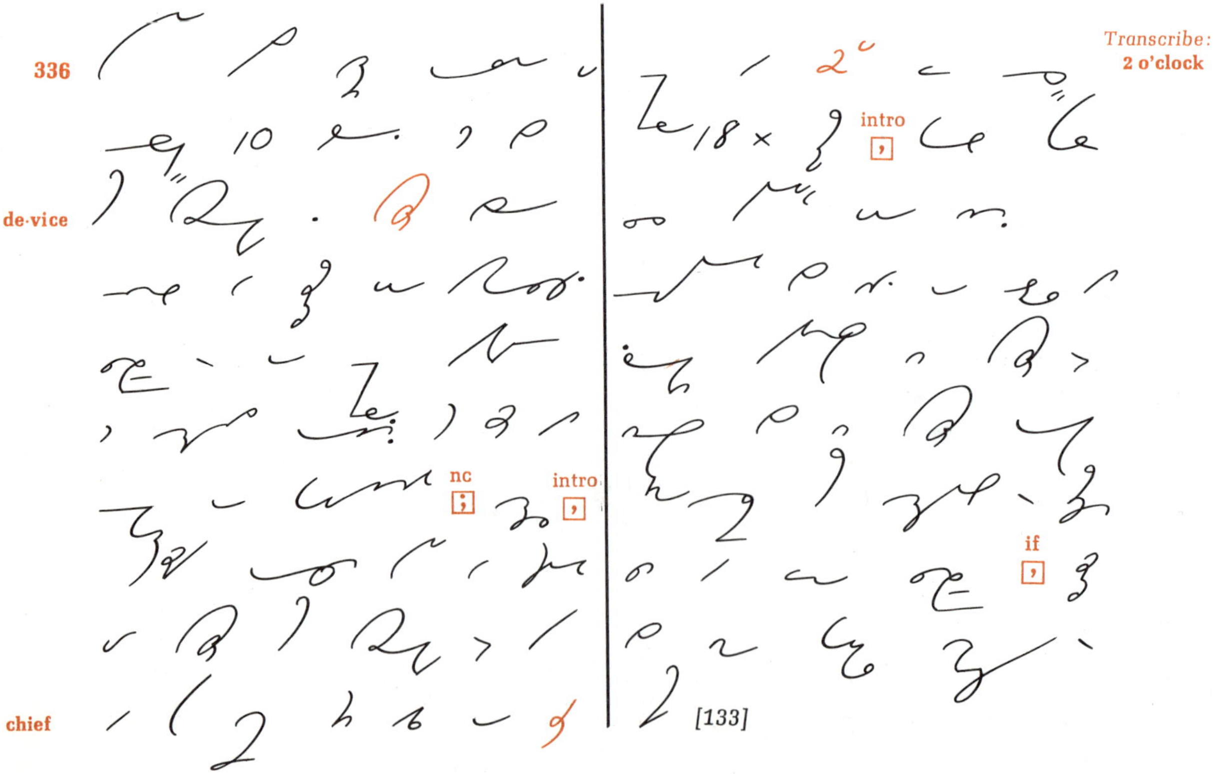

nc intro

chief   [133]

Transcribe:
2 o'clock
intro

if

236 | **LESSON 44**

337 **Transcription Quiz** You are already familiar with the Transcription Quiz from your work with other books in the Diamond Jubilee Series. In *Gregg Transcription*, these quizzes will be more challenging; they will give you an opportunity to test your mastery of all the punctuation rules you have studied up to this point.

As you read each Transcription Quiz, decide what punctuation should be used and what words have been omitted from the shorthand. If any one of a number of words or expressions makes sense at the point of the omission, select the one that makes the sentence read most smoothly.

Then make a shorthand copy of the letter, inserting in your notes the correct punctuation and the missing words.

[132]

Building transcription skills

338 WORD CHAIN

Notice the progression in the intensity of meaning of the words in the following Word Chain from the general idea of *money* to the more exact and specific idea of *legal tender.*

money means metal or paper stamped or printed by a government and used as a medium of exchange.

He does not like to carry large amounts of money with him.

coin refers to metal money as contrasted with paper money.

I have $1.50 in coins and $5 in bills.

cash usually refers to money that is physically in the possession of the person or company, as compared with money in the bank or money owed to the person or company.

I did not have enough cash with me to pay the bill; therefore, I gave the man a check.

currency means all the money that is actually in circulation.

The currency of the United States is accepted in most parts of the world.

legal tender means the kind of money that must be accepted in payment of money obligations.

Nickel and bronze coins are legal tender in the United States for amounts of 25 cents or less.

339

Business vocabulary builder	**interoffice** Between the offices of an organization. **specialty** Subject in which one is particularly well versed or skilled. **shabby** Seedy.

Reading and writing practice

340

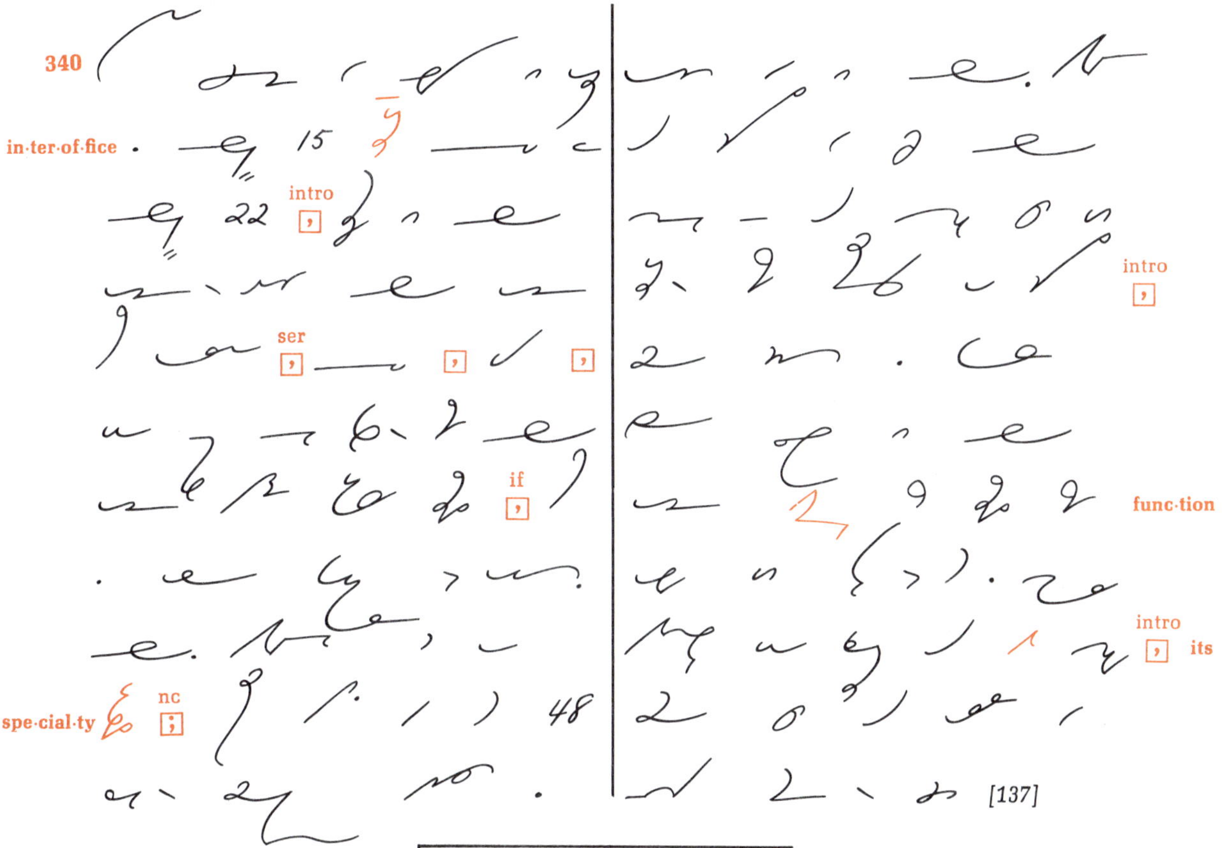

in·ter·of·fice · intro · 22 · intro · ser · if · spe·cial·ty · nc · 48 · intro · function · intro · its · [137]

341

ap · when · 15 · nc · ware·house · conj · em·bar·rassed

year's [100]

342 if fil·ing
oc·curred
 enu
main
cor·re·spon·dence
filed intro
 intro [139]

343 as com·pa·ny's
past

re·spon·si·ble
fill·ing
rec·om·men·da·tions

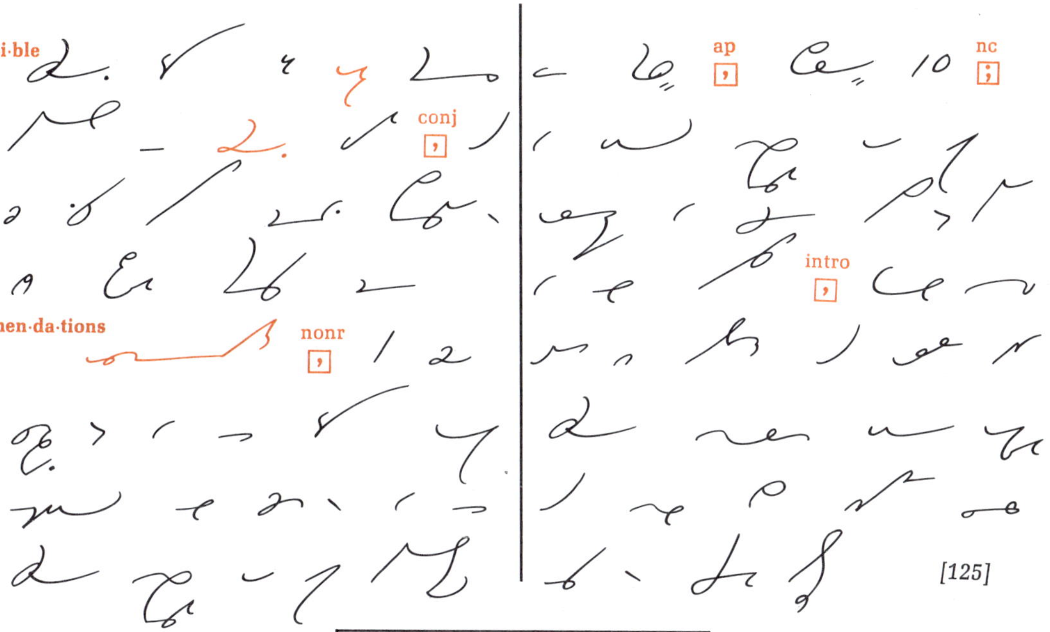

[125]

344
bro·ker·age
Transcribe: LG 401
bro·chures

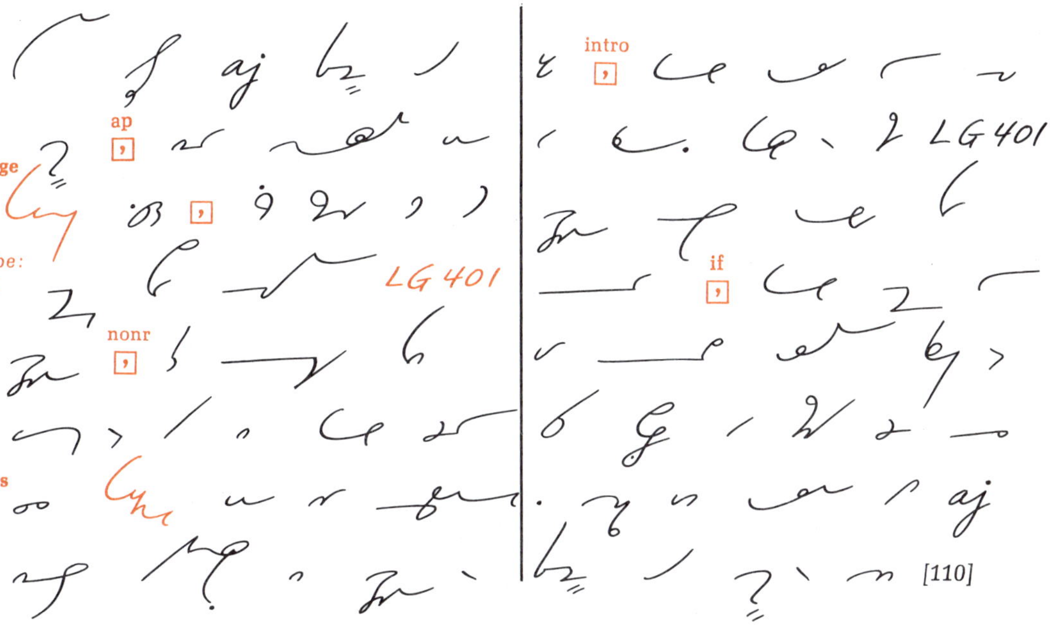

[110]

LESSON 45

The secretary makes corrections

Ellen is a good typist, but she is only human; she occasionally makes a mistake when typing her letters. Ellen realizes, however, that the next best thing to not making a mistake is to correct it neatly and rapidly, *with the emphasis on rapidly*. Here is the technique that Ellen follows:

1 As soon as she realizes that she has struck the wrong key, she moves the carriage either to the right or to the left (so that eraser crumbs do not fall into the typing basket). In order to be able to erase conveniently, she rolls the pack forward a number of lines if the error is not too far down the page or backward if it is near the bottom of the page.

2 She then places a metal eraser guard behind the original copy. (A 5 x 3 card may be used instead of a metal eraser guard. Be sure, however, that it is removed after the erasure has been completed.)

3 She reaches for her sand eraser (which she always keeps in the same place so that she can find it without any loss of time), checks to be sure that it is clean, and erases the incorrect letter on the original copy. She is careful (1) not to press too hard and thus damage the paper and (2) not to smudge any other characters.

4 If she is making only one carbon copy, she removes the guard, reaches for the soft eraser, checks to be sure that it is clean, and erases the carbon copy.

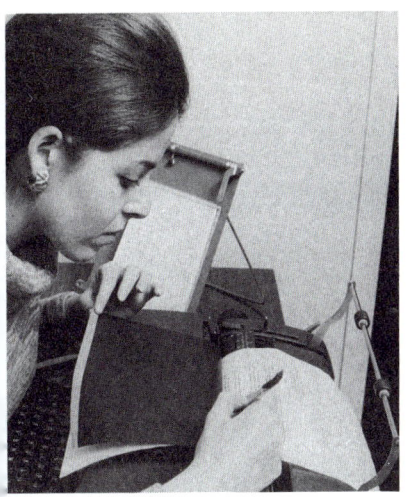

5 If she is making more than one carbon copy, she is careful to place the guard behind each copy on which she is erasing, except the last one.

6 Finally, she types the correct letter in the erased area, using the pressure that matches the rest of her typing. She is careful not to hit the letter too hard, or it will stand out like a sore thumb—a mistake that beginning typists sometimes make.

Through experience Ellen found that there are some typing errors that she can correct without erasing. For example, on her typewriter she can make acceptable, almost undetectable, corrections by lightly striking over:

    c to get e   n to get h
    o to get b   F to get E
    o to get d   , to get ;
    v to get y   . to get ?

Before you use any of these "strikeovers," however, be sure you check to see whether they can be acceptably made on your typewriter.

Note: While the regular erasers are the most commonly used correction devices, others have appeared on the market in recent years. These include:

1 Glass erasers. These are made of glass fibers and can be used on both original and carbon copies.

2 Electric erasers. These can also be used on both original and carbon copies. The tip of the eraser is small so that one letter can be erased at a time.

3 Correction fluid. The correction fluid, which is a quick drying enamel, is placed over the error with a little brush. The correction is then typed over the enamel.

4 Correction paper. This paper is coated on one side with a white, chalklike substance. The coated side is placed over the error. The typist then backspaces and retypes the error thus covering it with the chalklike substance. The correction paper is then removed and the correction typed.

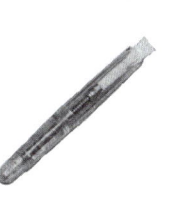

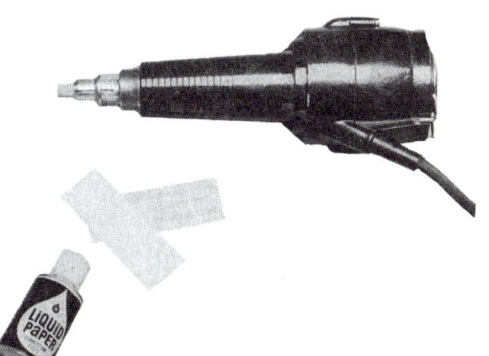

Retailing

Building transcription skills

345 SIMILAR-WORDS DRILL | wait, weight

wait   To stay; to remain; to serve.

You will not have to wait for our salesman to make change.
Our salesman will wait on you soon.

weight   Influence; importance; a measure of heaviness.

What you say carries more weight than anything we might say.
The weight of the package is four pounds.

346

Business vocabulary builder

packaging   Protective covering; wrapping.
appealing   Attractive; interesting.
exhausted   Spent; used up.
French cuffs   Soft cuffs made by turning back part of a wide cuff band and held together by cuff links.

Reading and writing practice

347

iden·ti·fi·ca·tion

car·ry·ing

fa·cil·i·tate

intro

when

iq

conj

wait

proud

[104]

348

re·ceived

in·con·ve·nience

intro

if

LESSON 46

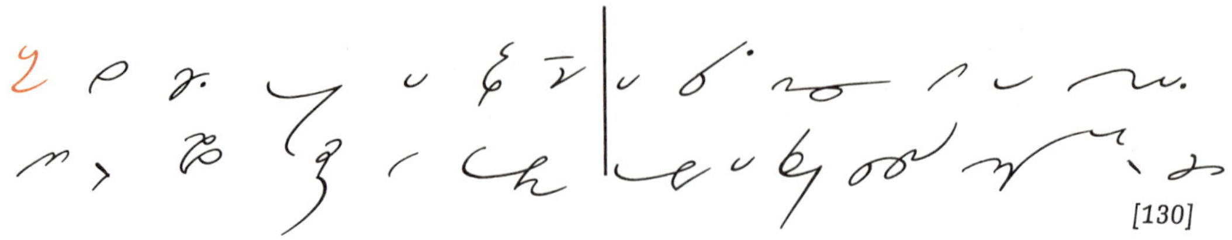

of·fer

[130]

349

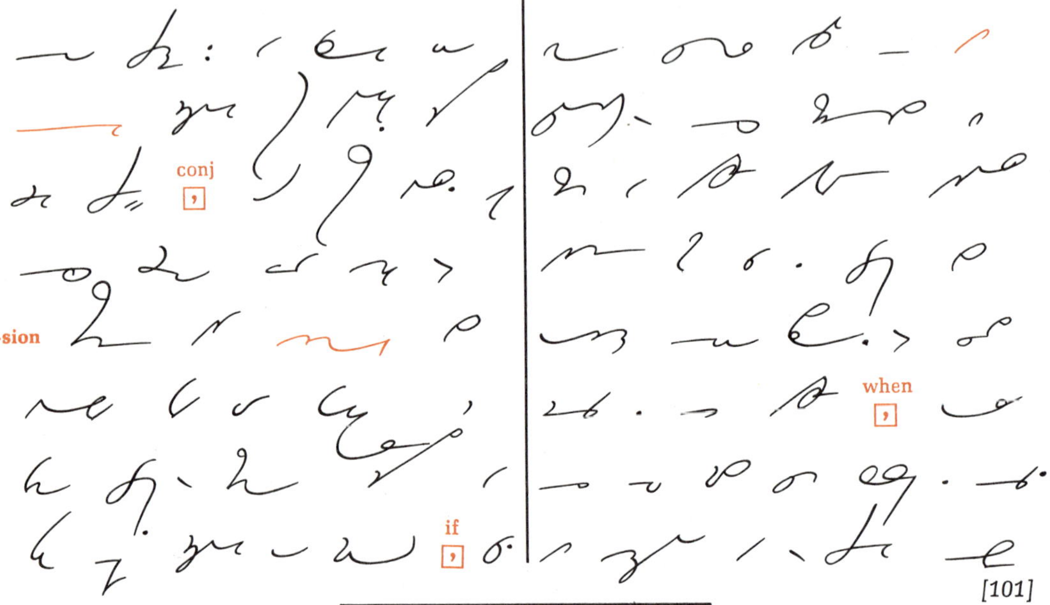

men's

con·clu·sion

too

when

if

[101]

350

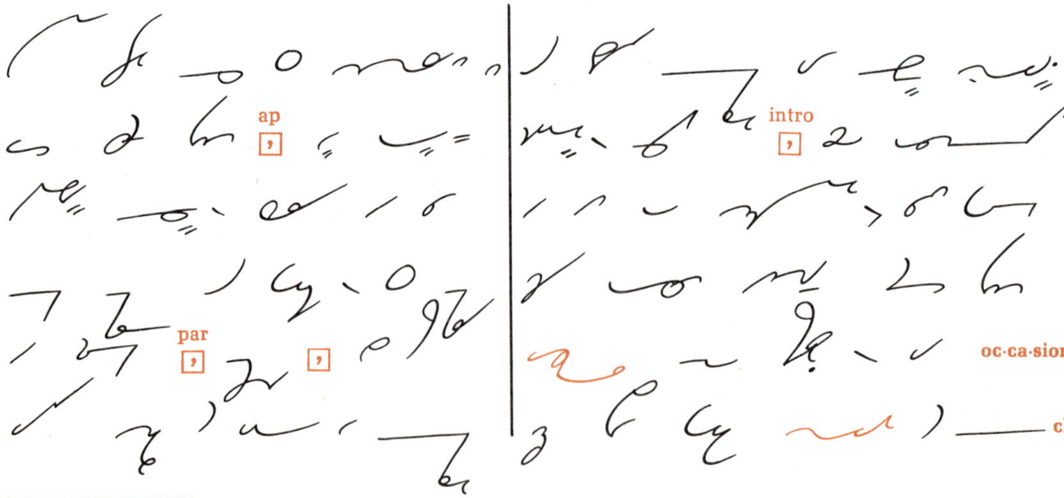

ap

par

intro

oc·ca·sion·al·ly

clothes

LESSON 46

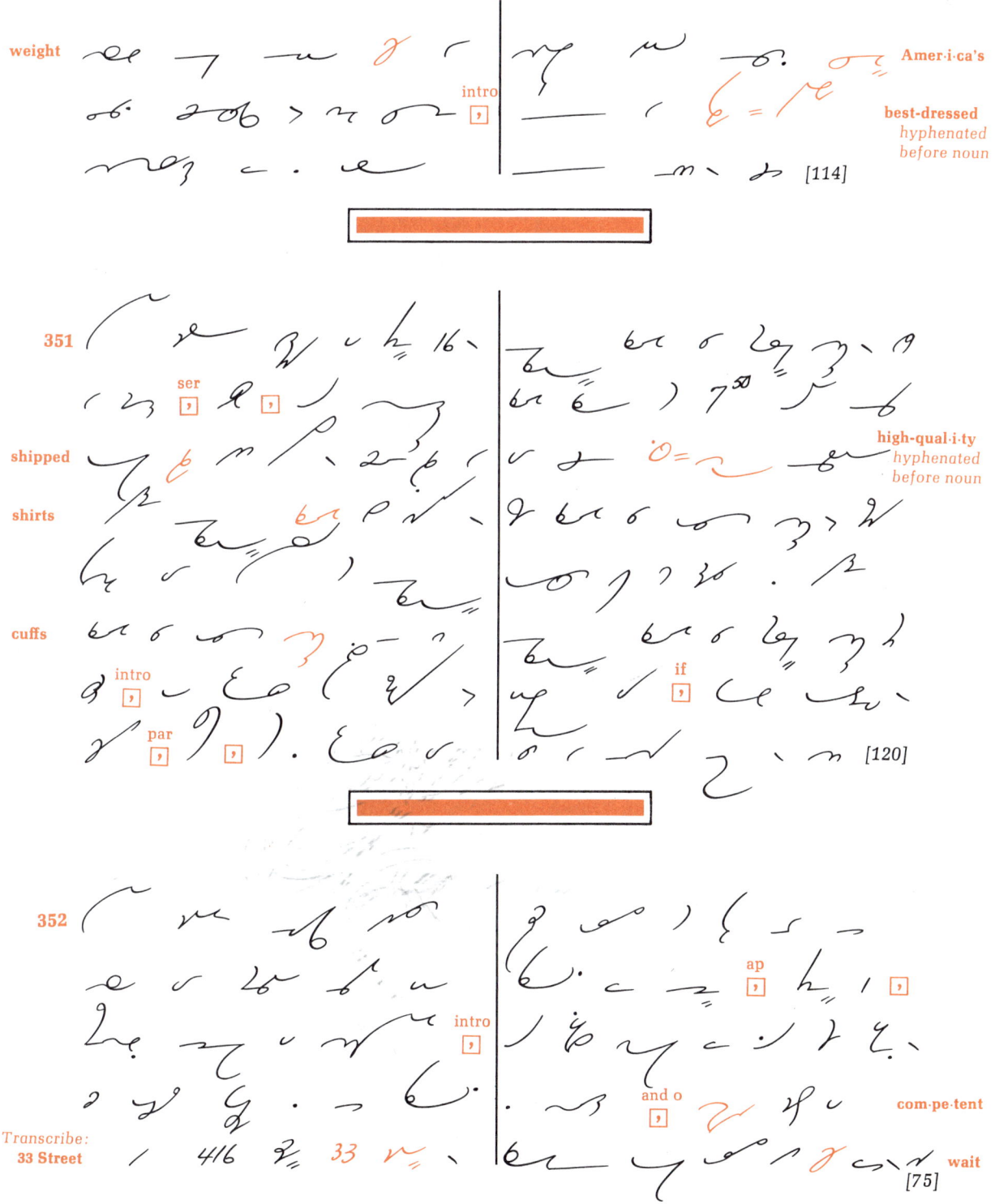

LESSON 46 | 247

Building transcription skills

353 SPELLING FAMILIES | -ible, -able

The problem that probably gives stenographers the biggest spelling headache is deciding whether a word is spelled *ible* or *able*. Unfortunately, there is no rule that tells us when to use *ible* and when to use *able*. In most words in the English language, the ending is spelled *able*, but it is spelled *ible* in a sufficient number of words that you should think twice before you type an *i* or an *a*.

-able

avail·able	ob·tain·able	re·li·able
con·sid·er·able	pay·able	suit·able
de·sir·able	prob·able	un·com·fort·able
dis·agree·able	prof·it·able	un·der·stand·able

-ible

ad·mis·si·ble	im·pos·si·ble	pos·si·ble
de·duct·ible	in·cred·i·ble	re·spon·si·ble
de·fen·si·ble	per·mis·si·ble	sen·si·ble
flex·ible	plau·si·ble	ter·ri·ble

354

Business vocabulary builder	
routine	Relating to a regular course of procedure.
wardrobe	Clothes.
neglected	Omitted.

Reading and writing practice

355

men's   won't   [80]

356

al-ready   par   par   nonr   ship-ping   intro   par   [123]

LESSON 47

357

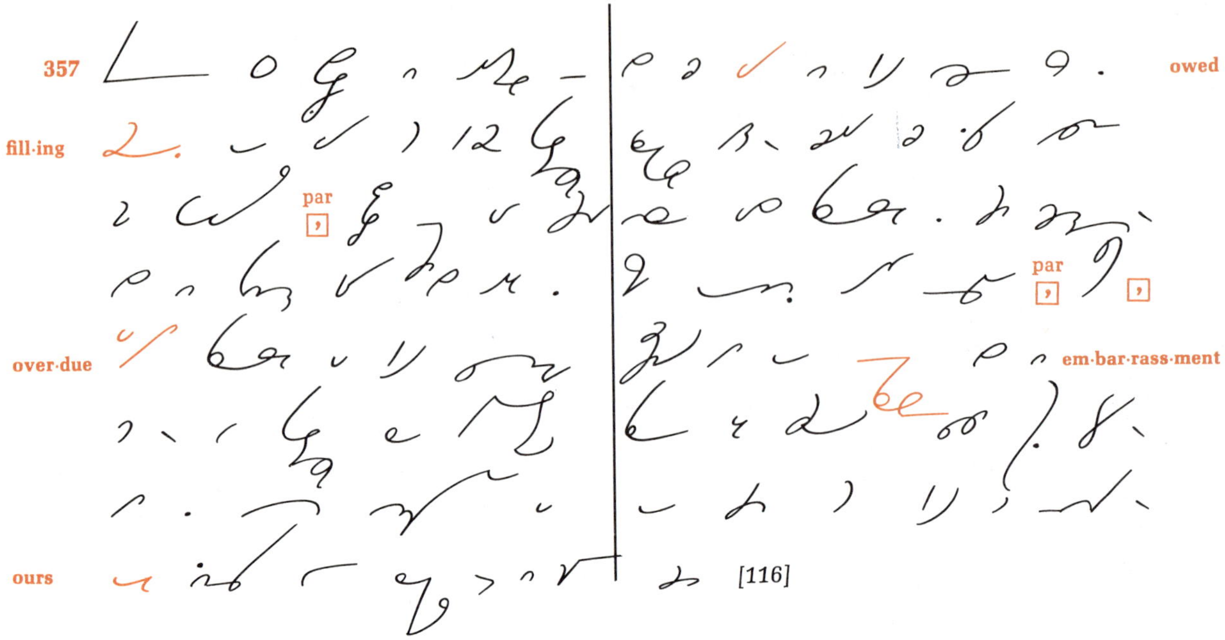

[shorthand content]

358

[shorthand content]

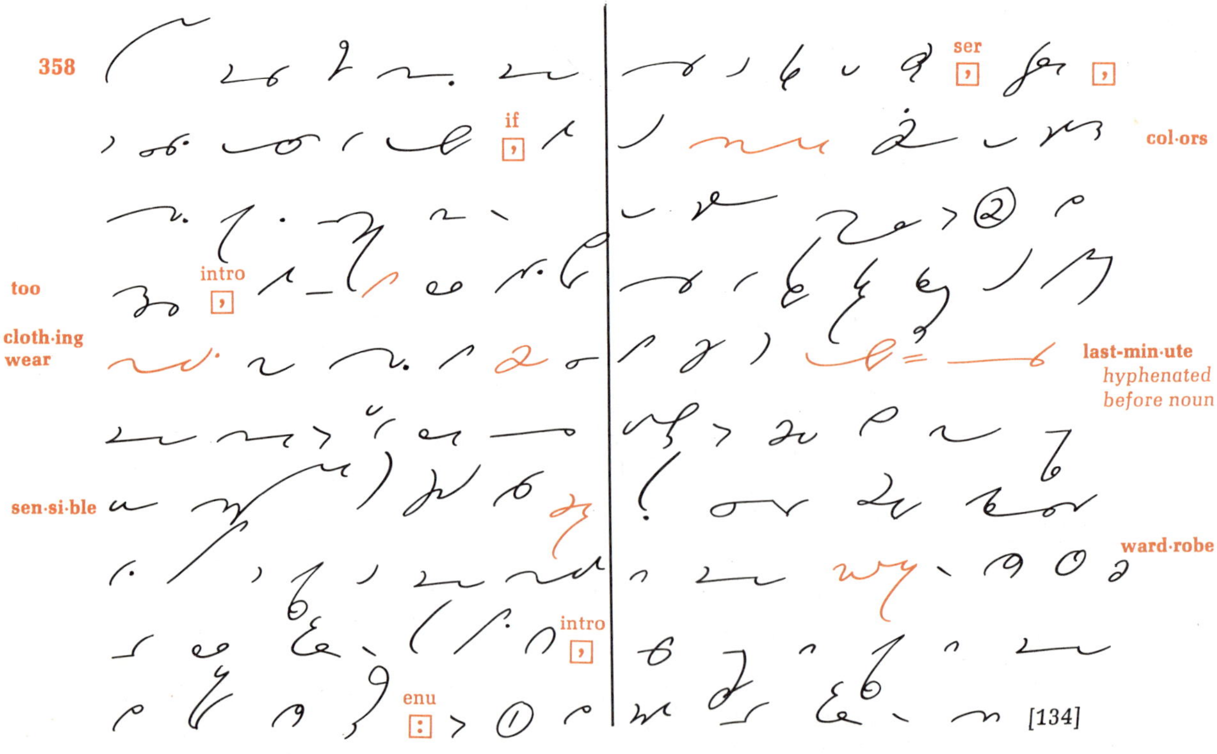

359

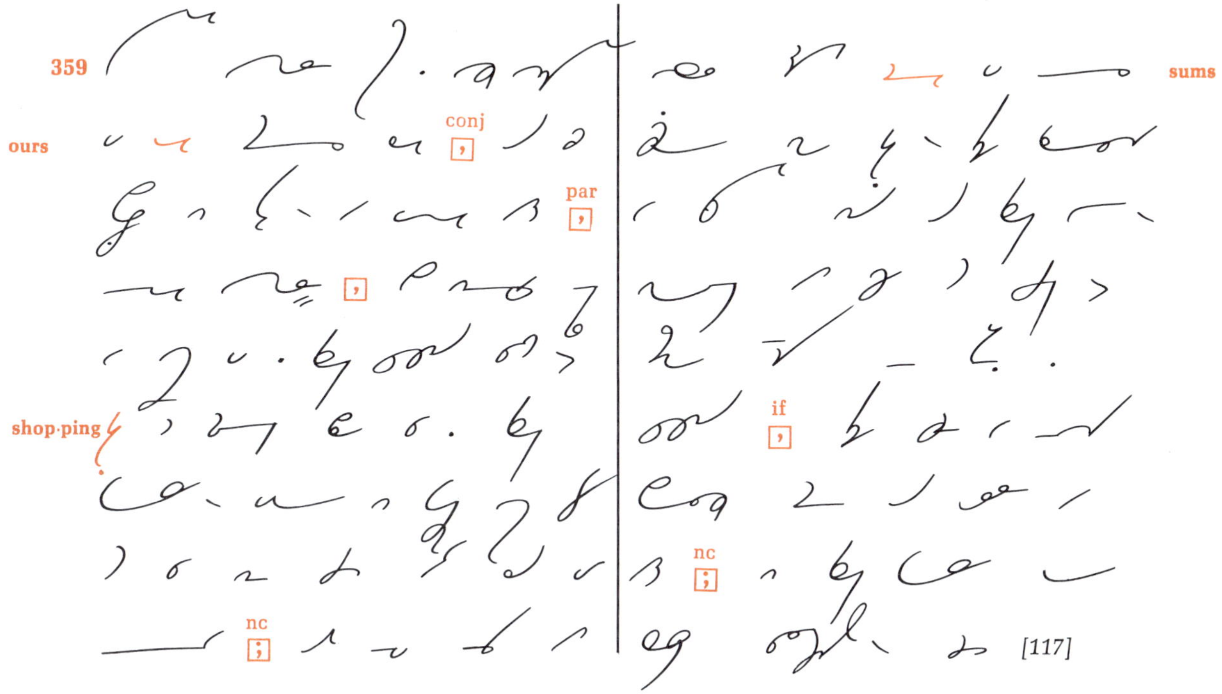
ours
conj
par
shop·ping
if
nc
nc
sums
[117]

360

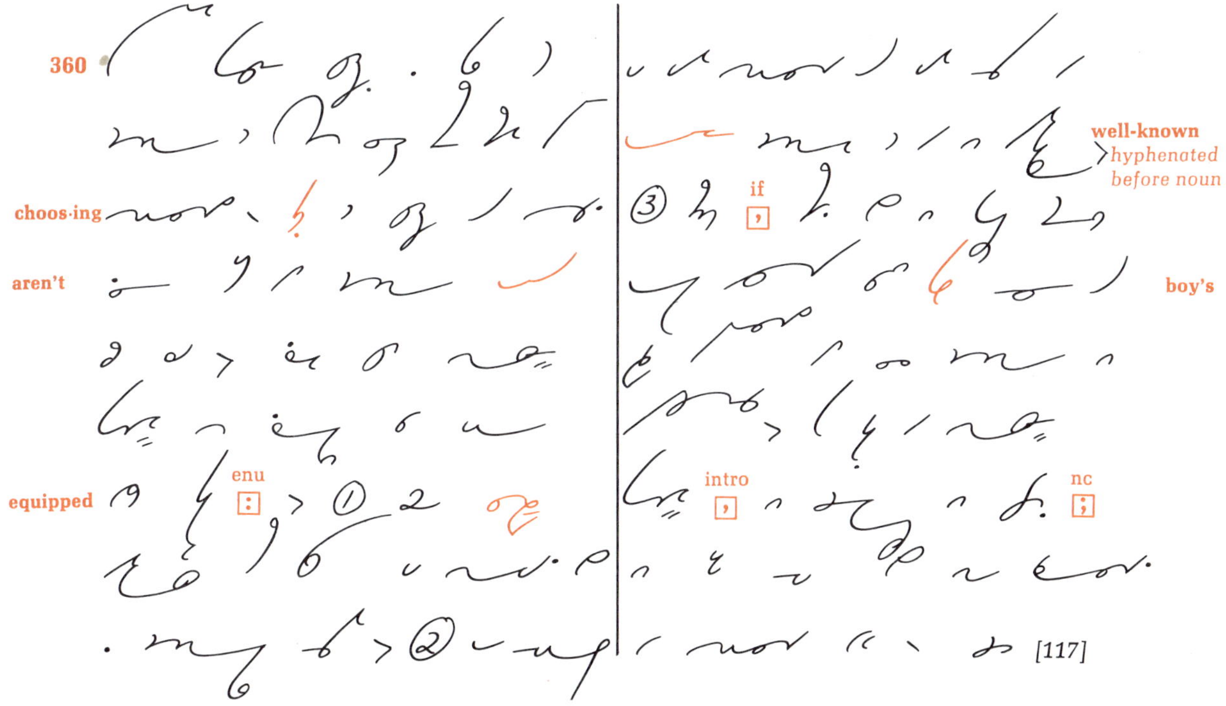
choos·ing
aren't
equipped
enu
if
intro
nc
well-known
hyphenated before noun
boy's
[117]

Building transcription skills

361 ACCURACY PRACTICE

Follow the practice procedures outlined on page 154.

GROUP 1	GROUP 2	GROUP 3
in the	fear	your
at the	feel	this

practice drill

1 I will meet you at the railroad station. I will meet you in the railroad station.
2 I fear that he cannot handle the job. I feel that he cannot handle the job.
3 May I have your report by Monday morning? May I have this report by Monday morning?

362 Business vocabulary builder

comprise Include; contain.

packing list A list of goods to be prepared for shipment or storage.

pertaining Applying or relating to.

chain Several retail stores selling similar merchandise and owned and managed by the same company.

Reading and writing practice

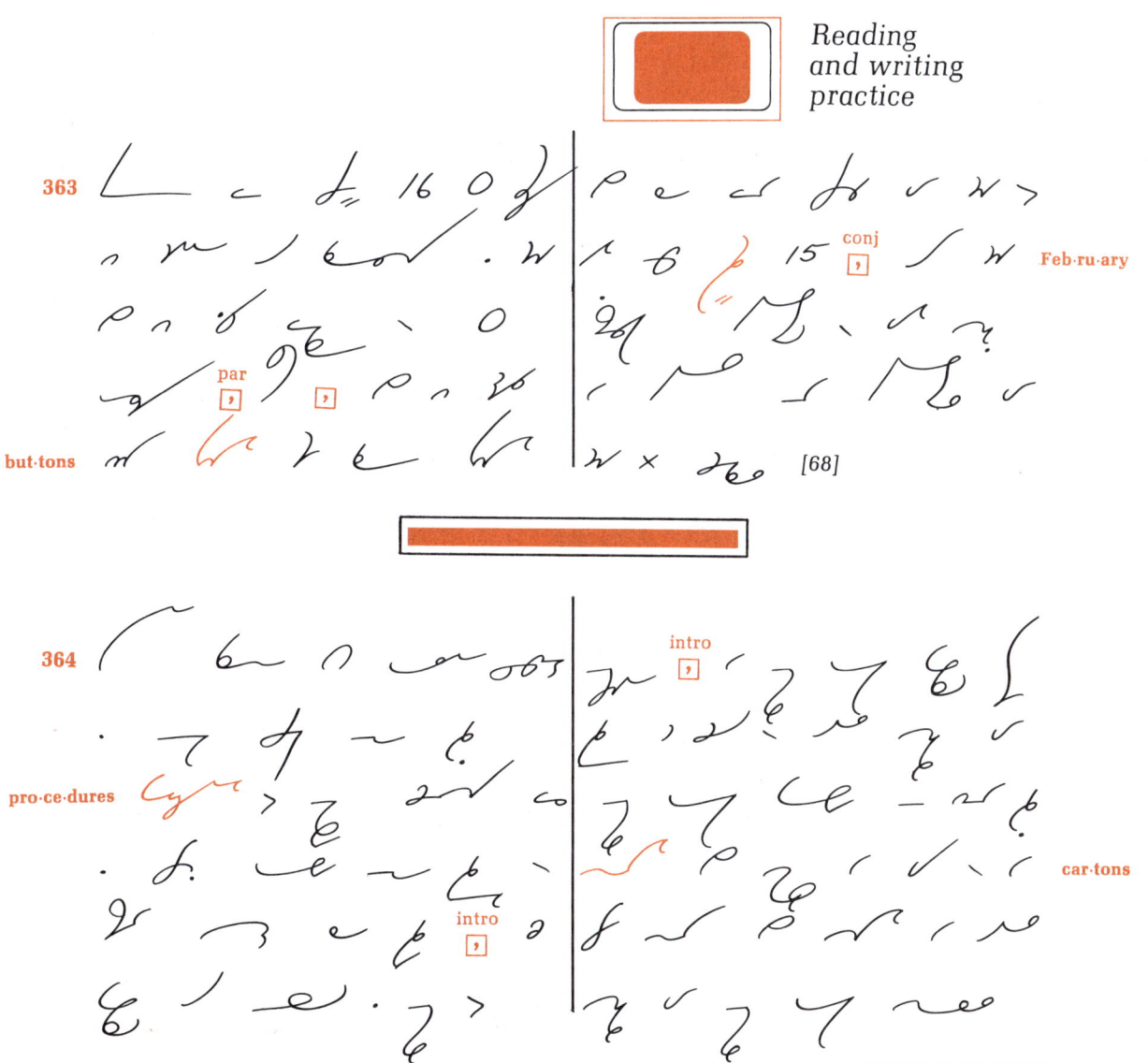

LESSON 48

LESSON 48

Building transcription skills

368 OFFICE-STYLE DICTATION | long insertions

A dictator may sometimes wish to make a long insertion. He may, for example, interrupt his dictation and say, "Go back and insert a sentence after the first one in the letter." When this happens, you should:

1 Write a large A in a circle at the point where the new material is to be inserted.

2 Then draw two heavy lines after the last sentence that you have taken from dictation, to separate the insert from the rest of your dictation.

3 Under the two heavy lines, write "Insert A," encircled; then write the insert.

4 Draw two heavy lines to indicate the end of the insert.

ILLUSTRATION OF OFFICE-STYLE DICTATION

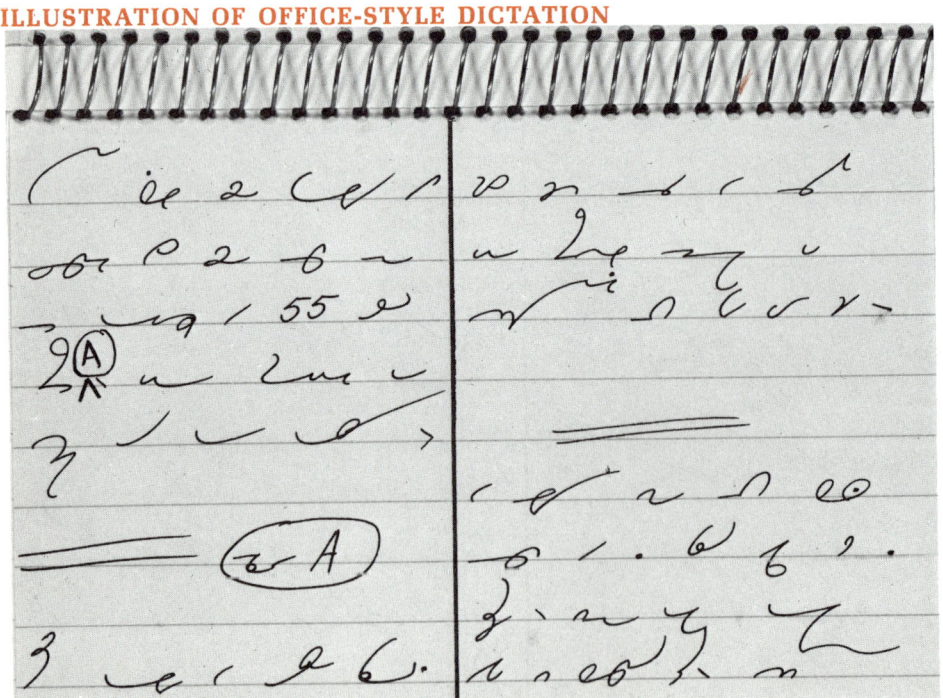

369 | Business vocabulary builder

inferior Lower in quality, value, importance, etc.
supplementary Additional.
transmittal The act of transferring from one person to another.

Reading and writing practice

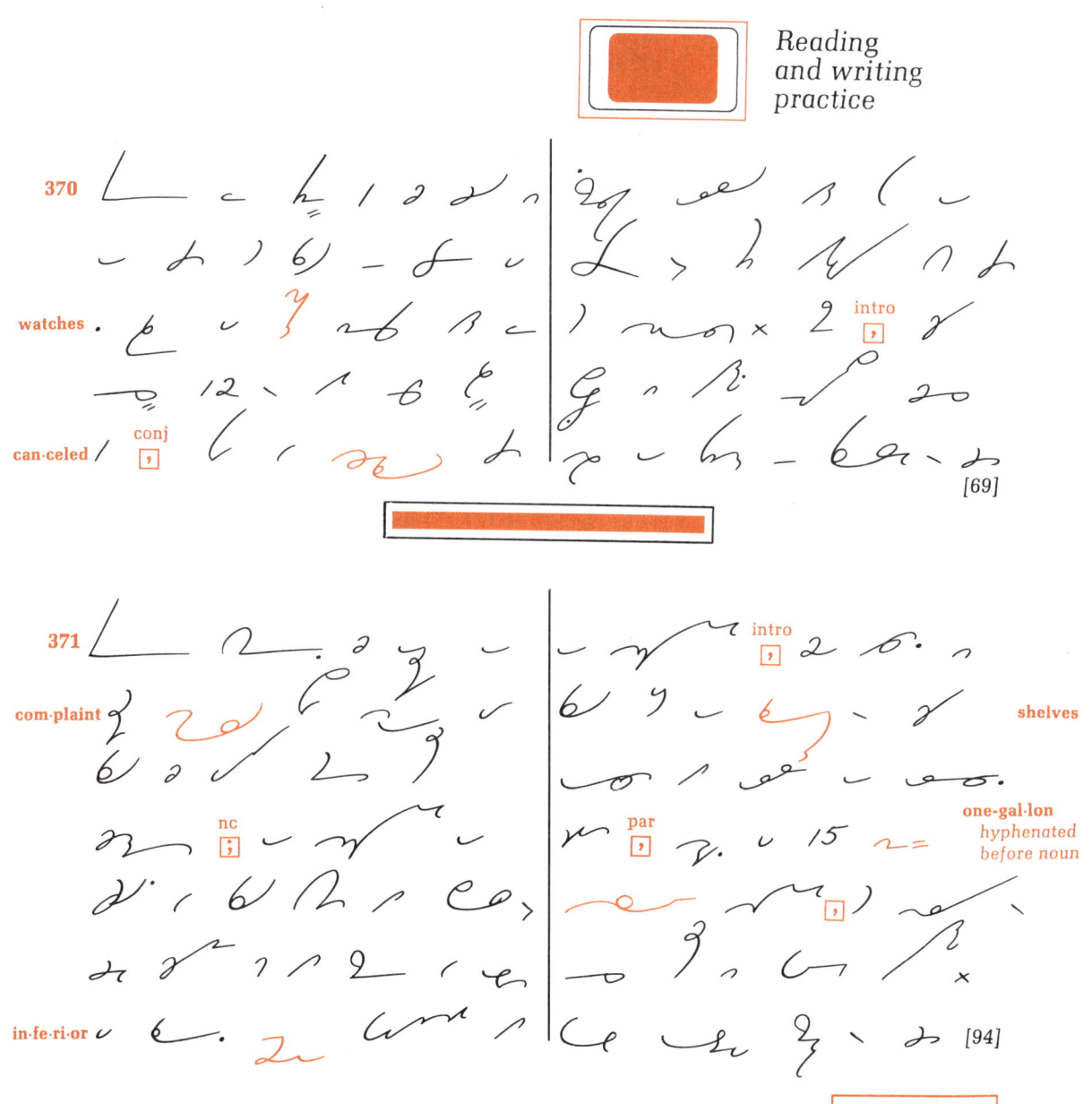

LESSON 49 | 257

372
Transcribe:
No. 16

sup·ple·men·ta·ry   ap   [87]   intro

373 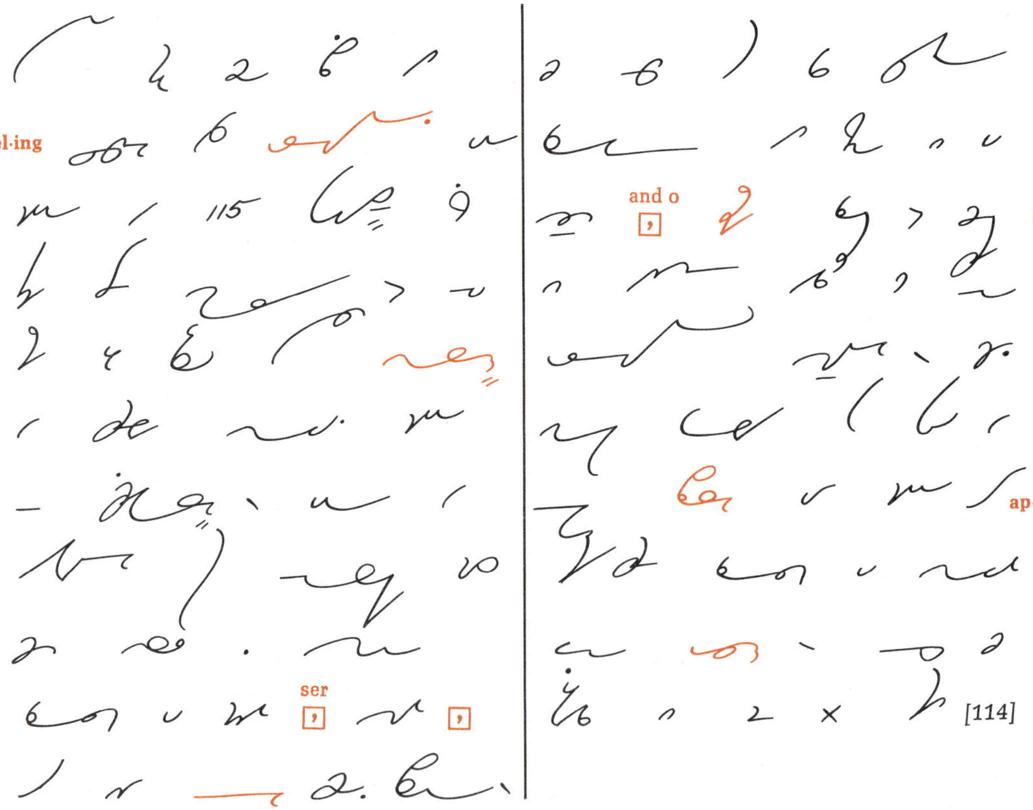
re·mod·el·ing   Clark's   ser   men's   and o   ef·fi·cient   ap·pear·ance   racks   [114]

374

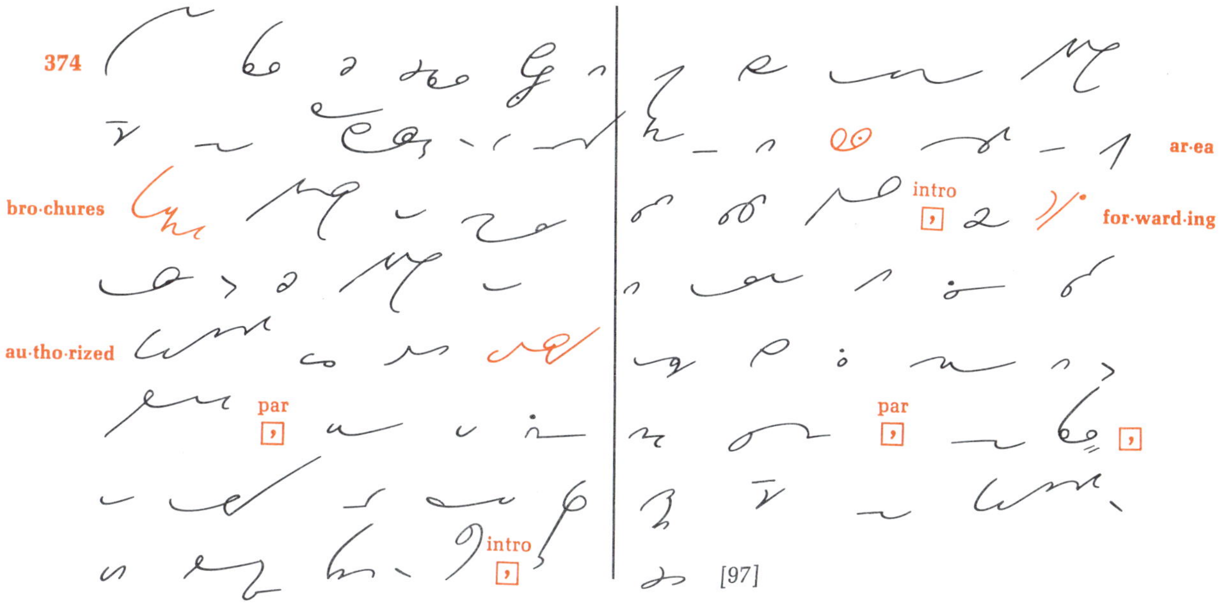

bro·chures   au·tho·rized   par   intro   intro   par   ar·ea   for·ward·ing

[97]

375 Transcription Quiz Supply the missing punctuation and the two words that have been omitted from the shorthand.

[121]

Building transcription skills

376 COMMON PREFIXES | dis-

dis- In many English words, the prefix *dis-* means *not* or *the opposite of* or *the absence of*.

dislike The opposite of *like*; to have an aversion to.

disregard The opposite of *regard*; to pay no attention to.

disloyal Not loyal; unfaithful.

disagreeable Not agreeable; unpleasant.

dissimilar Not similar; different.

377

Business vocabulary builder	**obligated** Obliged; morally or legally bound.
	miniature Tiny; done on a smaller scale.
	possess Own.

 *Reading and writing practice*

378

pur·chase

LESSON 50

Christ·mas

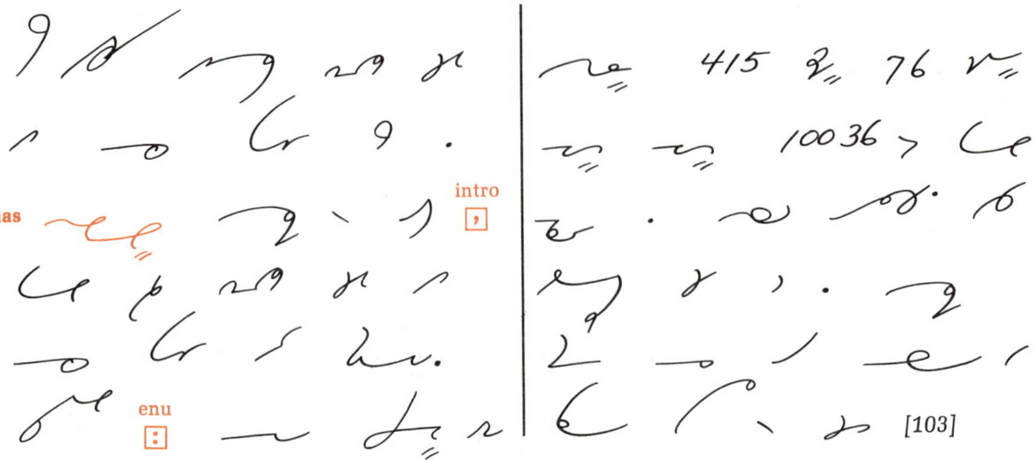

381

sea·shore

don't

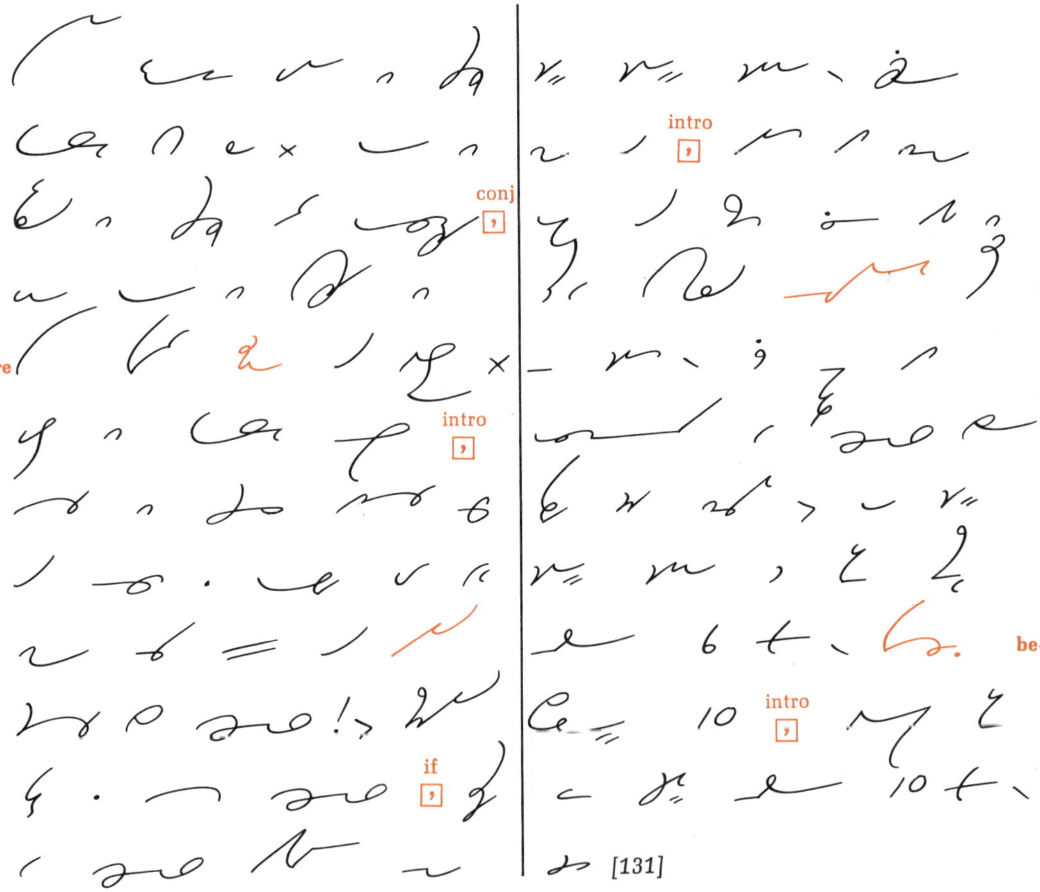

mod·els

be·gin·ning

382

re·fer·ring

par

los·es

dis·agree·able

intro

good·will

nc

par

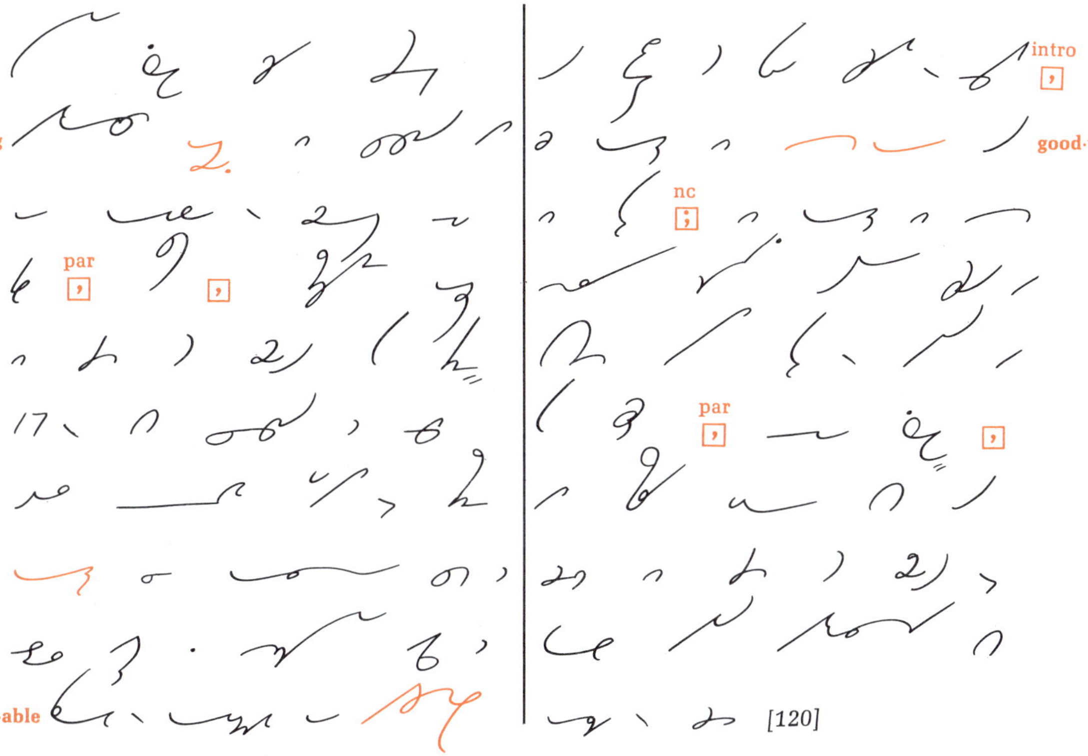

[120]

383

pair

ac·knowl·edg·ment

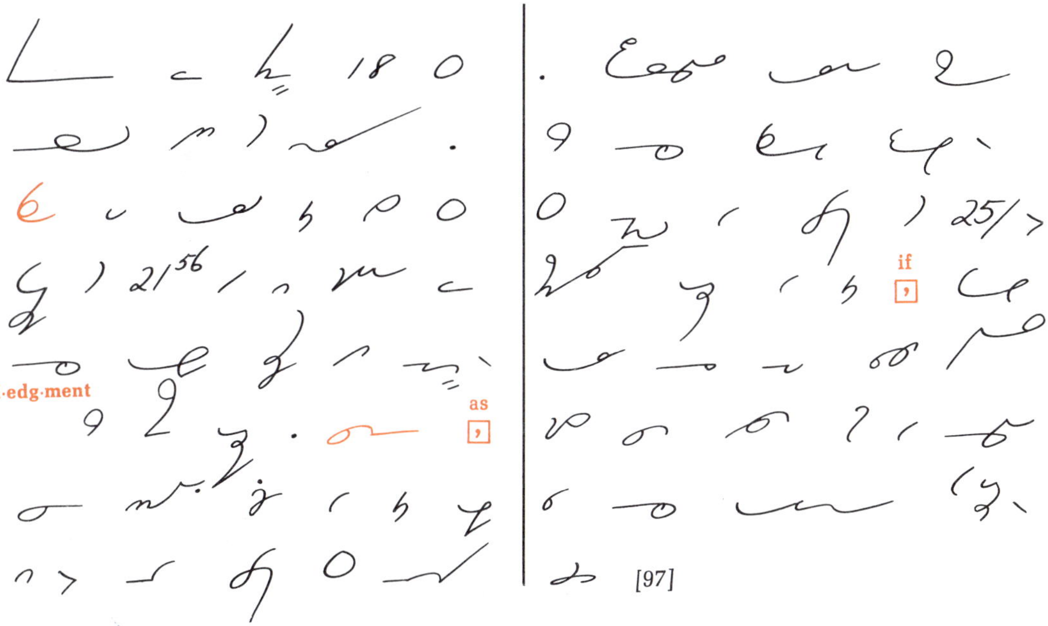

as

if

[97]

LESSON 50

The secretary proofreads

Ellen learned early in her career that it was no disgrace to make an error; the disgrace was in not catching and correcting it. One of the reasons why Ellen is a secretary is the fact that she never submits anything for Mr. Davis's signature until she has proofread it and corrected any mistakes.

Ellen always proofreads her transcripts while they are still in her machine. It is then a simple matter to correct any errors she may find. She knows from experience that making corrections after a letter has been removed from the machine is a much more difficult and time-consuming process.

Ellen learned that she cannot

proofread her transcripts in the same way that she reads ordinary print, where her only purpose is to grasp the writer's meaning. Of course she is interested in the meaning of the transcript, but, in addition, she is interested in the correctness of every stroke she typed.

In her early days as a stenographer, Ellen found that she had to proofread her transcripts almost character by character. Later, she found that she could proofread word by word, reverting to character-by-character reading only when she came to long and unusual words. She is doubly cautious where numbers are involved; she always checks numbers against her notes.

Ellen found that most of her errors fell in four classes:

1   Transpositions—typing recieve for receive; conveneince for convenience.

2   Similar words—typing to rather than too; fair rather than fare; though rather than thought; sale rather than sail. She found that she had a tendency to type the more frequently used member of the pair; that is, instead of too, she would type to; instead of sail, she would type sale.

3   Words in which letters are doubled—typing seel for sell; feel for fell.

4   Numbers, especially those involving a 9 or a 0; a 4 or a 5.

By thus analyzing the types of errors she made—without realizing that she made them while she was typing—she is able to watch for them as she proofreads.

You, too, will be able to make yourself a more efficient proofreader if you try to determine the types of errors that you make most frequently and then watch for them. And, perhaps most important of all, as Ellen proofreads, she makes sure that everything she has transcribed makes sense! If something doesn't "sound right," she checks with Mr. Davis before turning in the transcript.

Travel and transportation

Building transcription skills

384 SIMILAR-WORDS DRILL | **sight, site, cite**

sight Vision; mental perception.

Do not lose sight of this important fact.

site A location.

If you are looking for a site for your new plant, let us know.

cite To quote; to name.

We can cite you many instances that prove our point.

385

Business vocabulary builder	
	roomette A small private bedroom in a Pullman railroad car.
	irreplaceable Cannot be restored.
	utilities Services provided by a public organization, such as light, power, water.
	secondary Of less importance.

Reading and writing practice

386

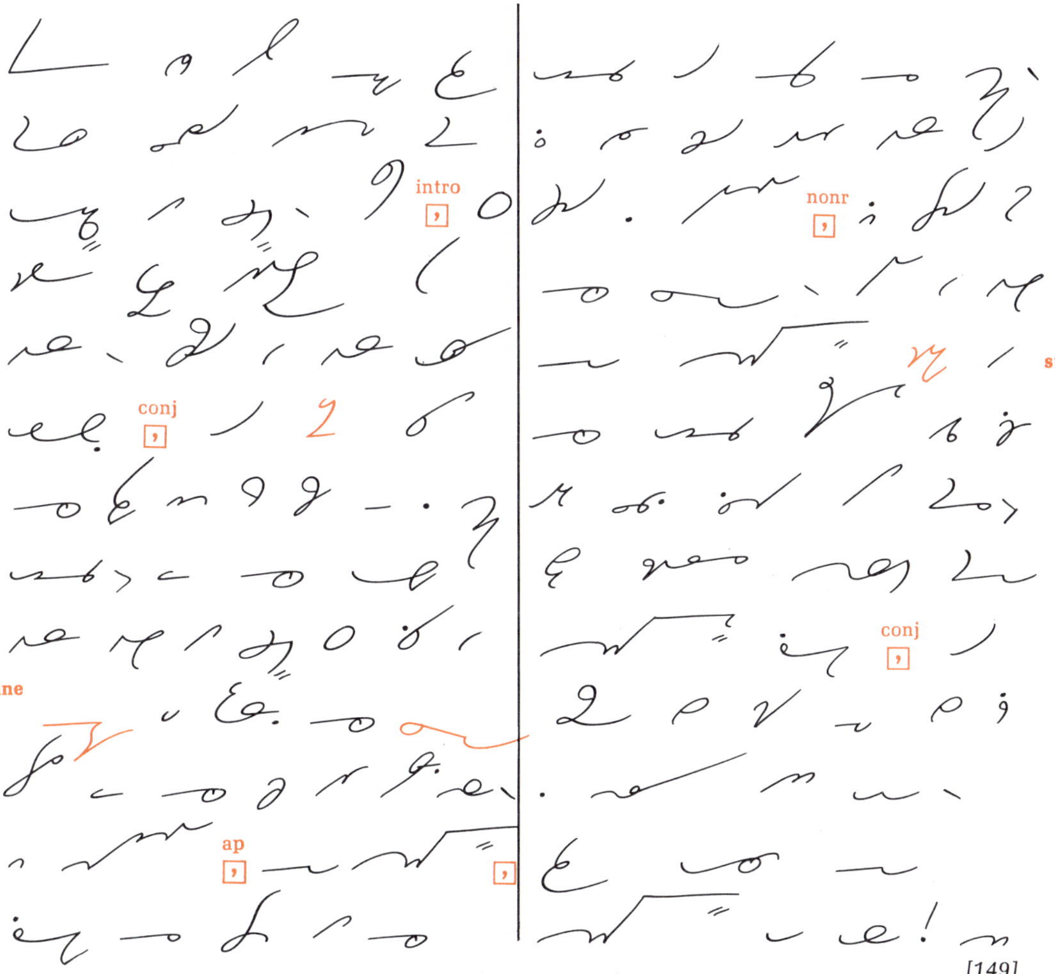

of·ten

mis·for·tune
an·kle

387

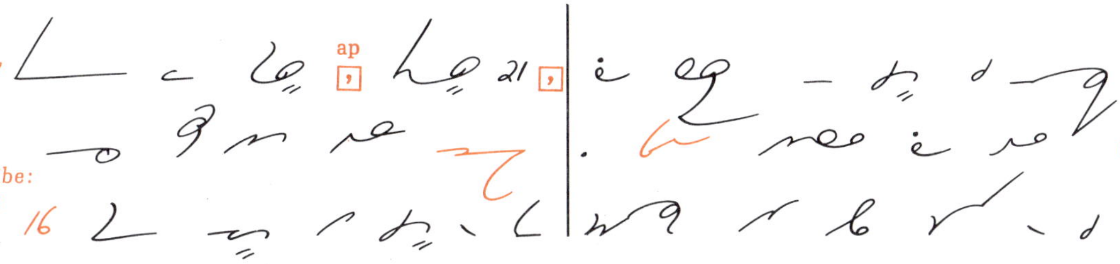

Transcribe:
No. 16

waiting — when — intro — baggage — anxious — irreplaceable — [168]

388 — intro — nc — ser — and o — if — snack — ridden — intro — quiet — [103]

268 | **LESSON 51**

389

fac·tors — par , ,

and ,
round-the-cl[ock]
hyphenated before noun

ser , ,

if , site

pleas·ant

sight

[123]

390

cite

if ,

ser , ,

and o ,

nc ,

up-to-date
hyphenated before noun

site

[118]

LESSON 51 | 269

Building transcription skills

391 SPELLING FAMILIES | forming -ed and -ing derivatives of words ending in l

When the last syllable of a word ending in *l*, preceded by a single vowel, is accented, the *l* is doubled in forming derivatives ending in *-ed* and *-ing*.

com·pel	**com·pelled**	**com·pel·ling**
dis·pel	**dis·pelled**	**dis·pel·ling**
ex·cel	**ex·celled**	**ex·cel·ling**
pro·pel	**pro·pelled**	**pro·pel·ling**

When the last syllable is not accented, the *l* is not doubled.

can·cel	**can·celed**	**can·cel·ing**
equal	**equaled**	**equal·ing**
mod·el	**mod·eled**	**mod·el·ing**
ri·val	**ri·valed**	**ri·val·ing**
to·tal	**to·taled**	**to·tal·ing**
trav·el	**trav·eled**	**trav·el·ing**

392 *Business vocabulary builder*

tourist One who makes a trip for pleasure or culture.
compelled Forced; obliged.
booked to capacity Filled up.

 Reading and writing practice

393 [shorthand] if, board, floats, nonr, beau·ties, one-week *hyphenated before noun* [104]

394 daugh·ter, two-month *hyphenated before noun*, ma·jor, tour·ist, conj [100]

LESSON 52 | 271

395

trav·eled

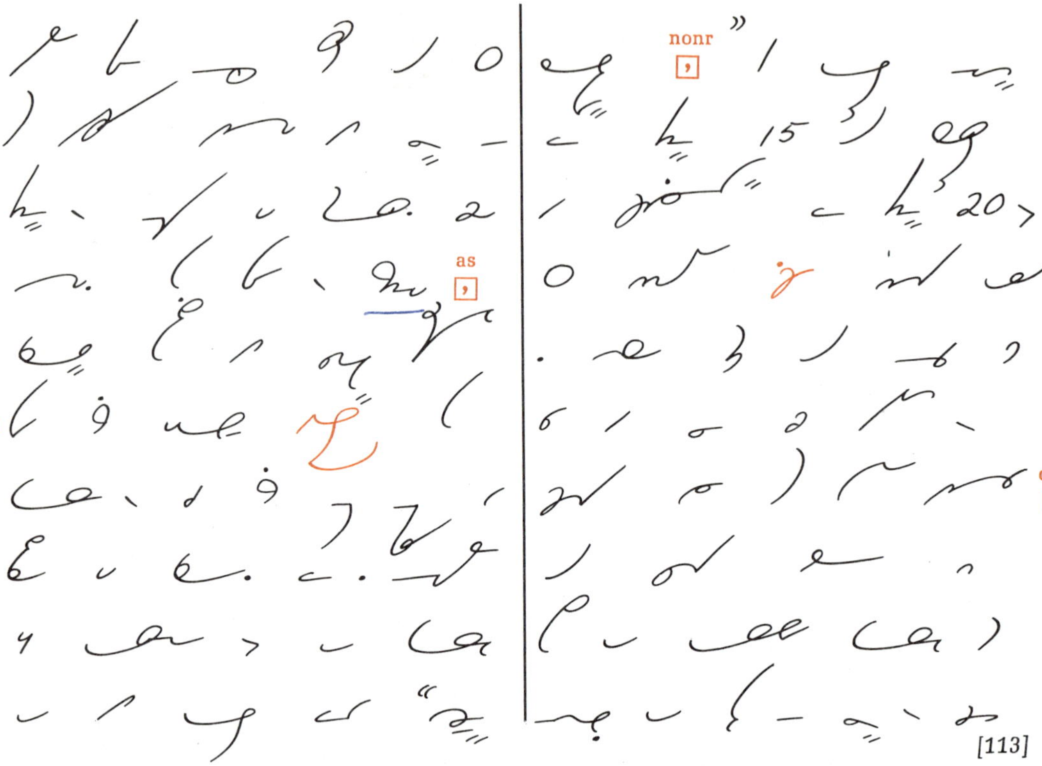

nonr
as
conj
[113]

wheth·er

396

ac·knowl·edge

com·pelled

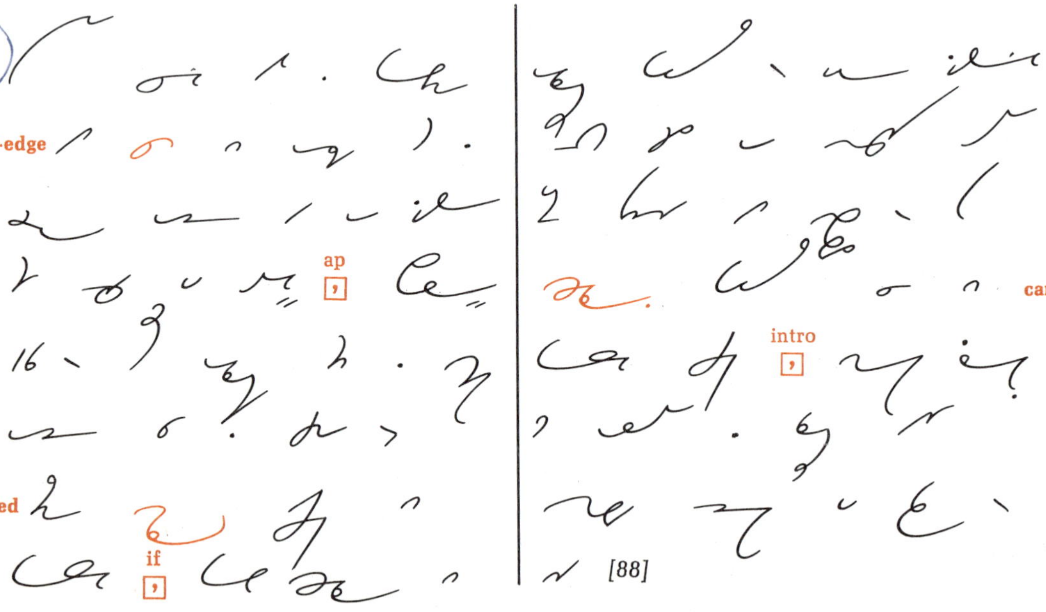

ap
intro
if
[88]

can·cel·ing

397

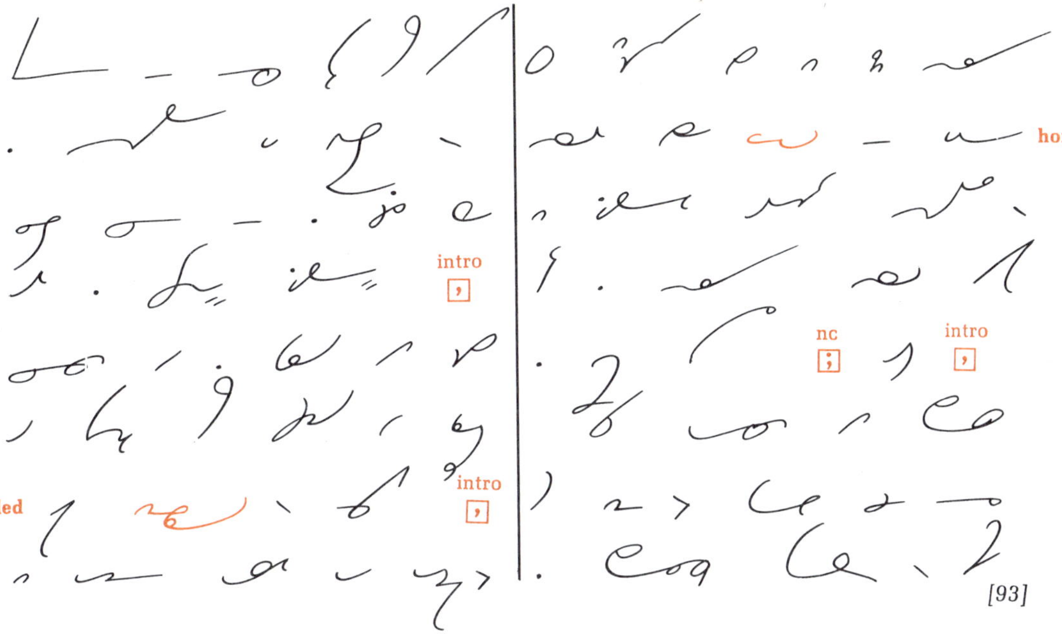

un·ex·celled

hon·ored
intro
nc intro
intro

[93]

398

mu·tu·al
ap
planning

pleasure
par
enu
if

ap

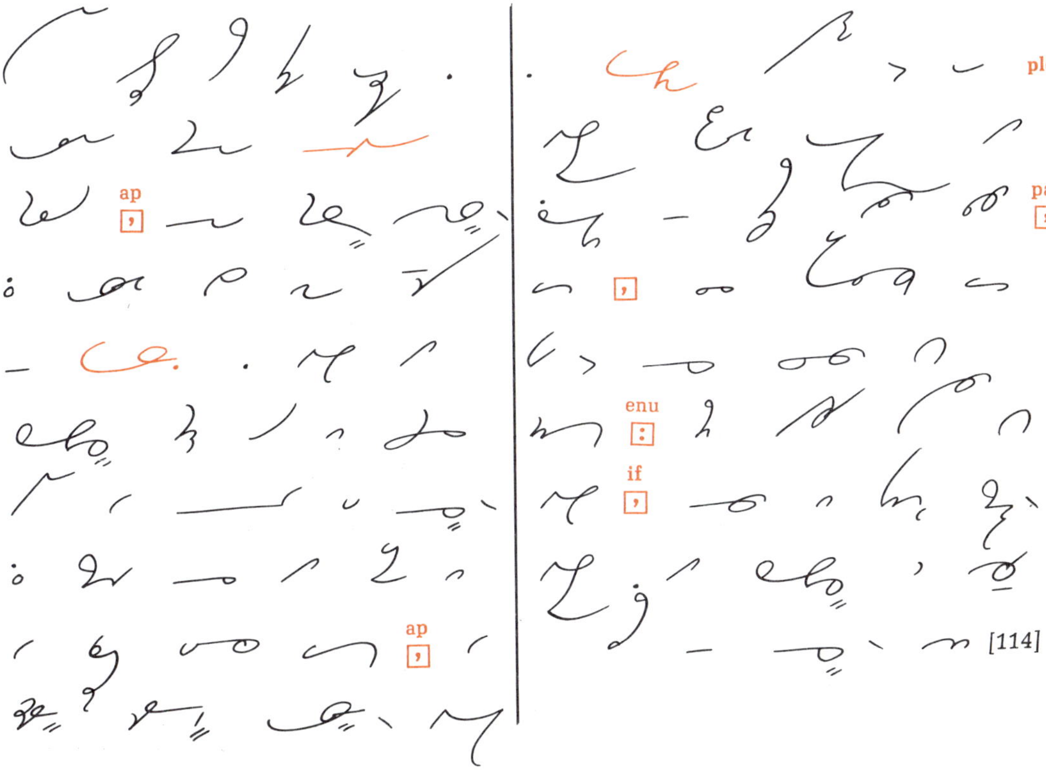

[114]

Building transcription skills

399 GRAMMAR CHECKUP | all right

This expression should always be written as two words. Some unwary transcribers are tempted to spell it *alright* because of the influence of such words as *altogether, always,* and *already.*

A good way to remember that *all right* is spelled as two words is to recall that its opposite is *all wrong*—two words.

It will be all right for you to leave.

400

Business vocabulary builder	**spokesman** One who speaks as the representative of another or others.
	itinerary A record of a journey or trip.
	suitable Fitting; appropriate.

Reading and writing practice

401

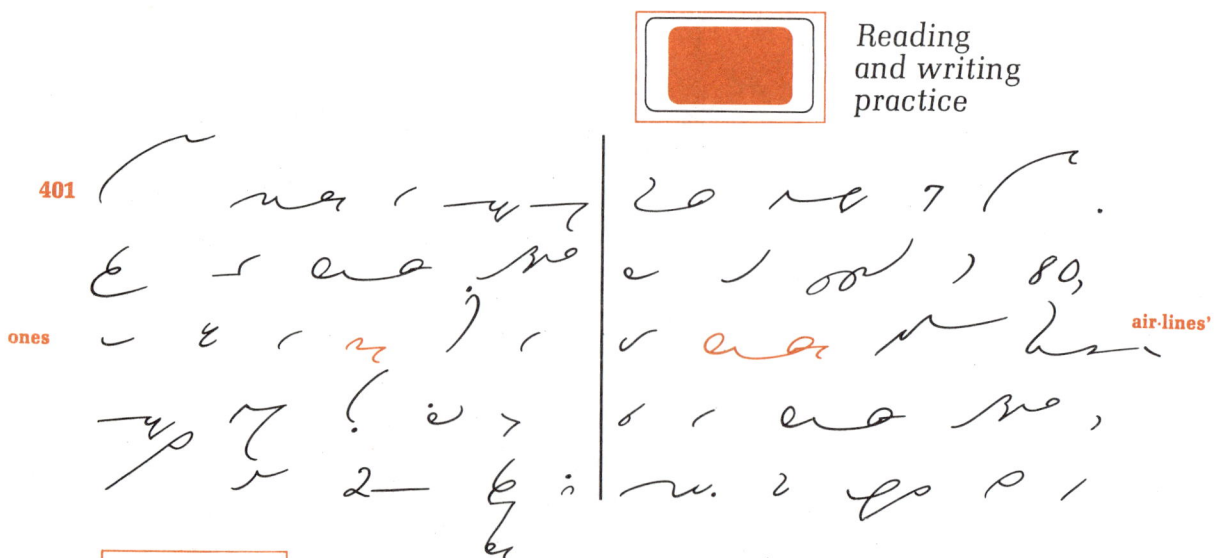

ones

air-lines'

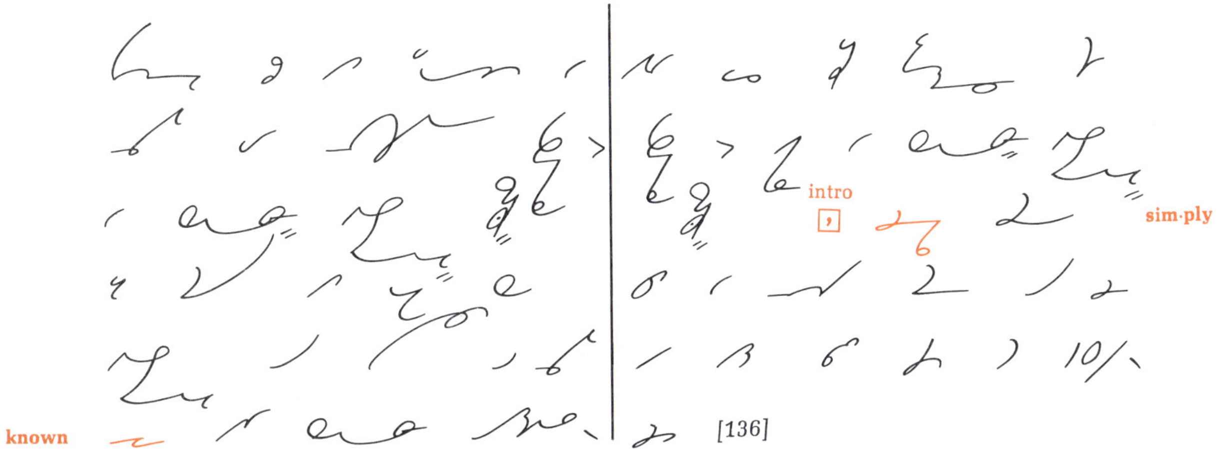

known [136] intro sim·ply

402 ap 4= four-page *hyphenated before noun*
ap
prin·ci·pal avi·a·tion
if
trans·mit·tal [135]

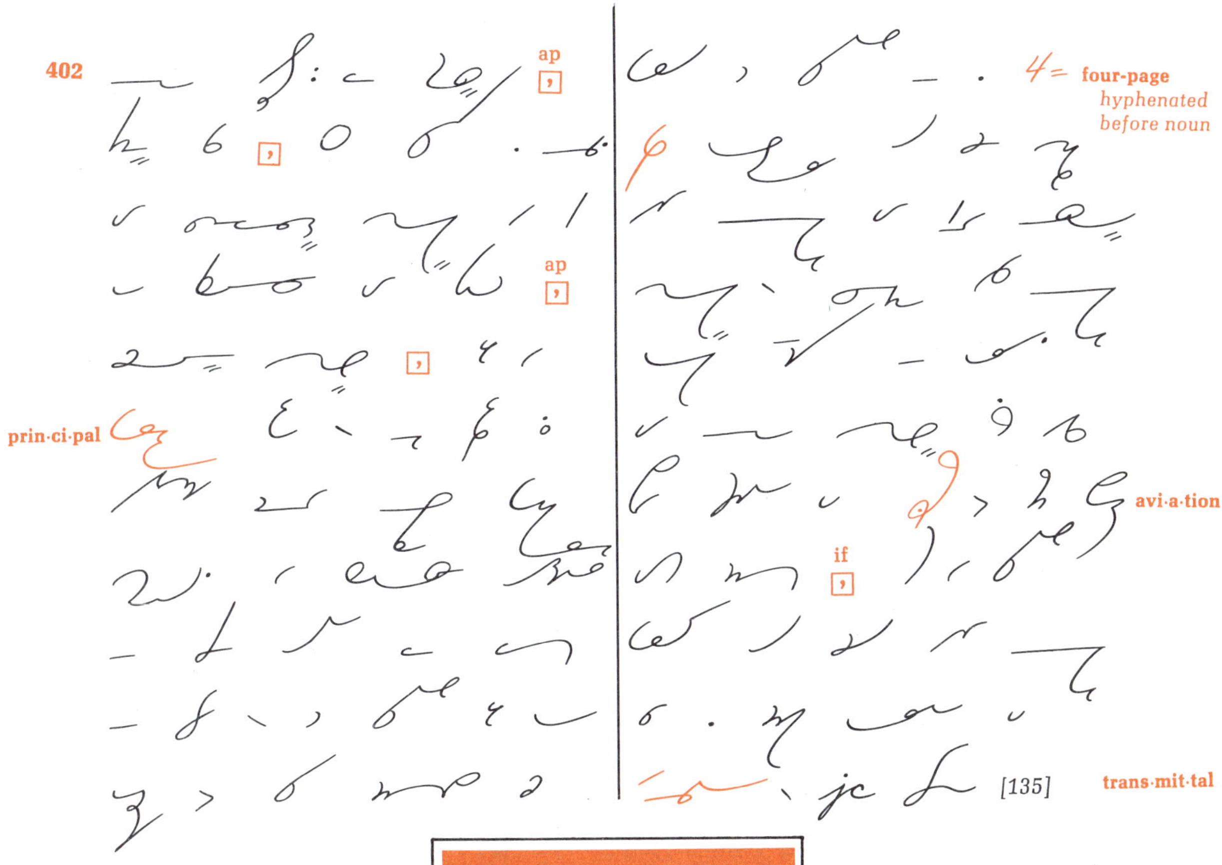

LESSON 53

403

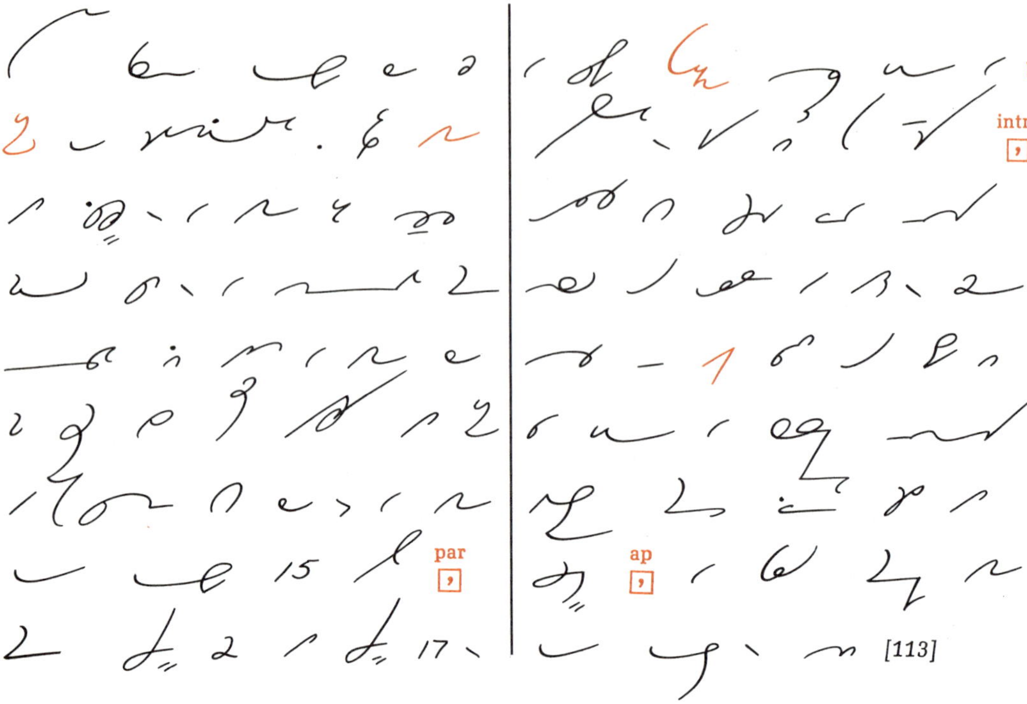

of·fered
tour

bro·chure

intro

touch

par

ap

[113]

404

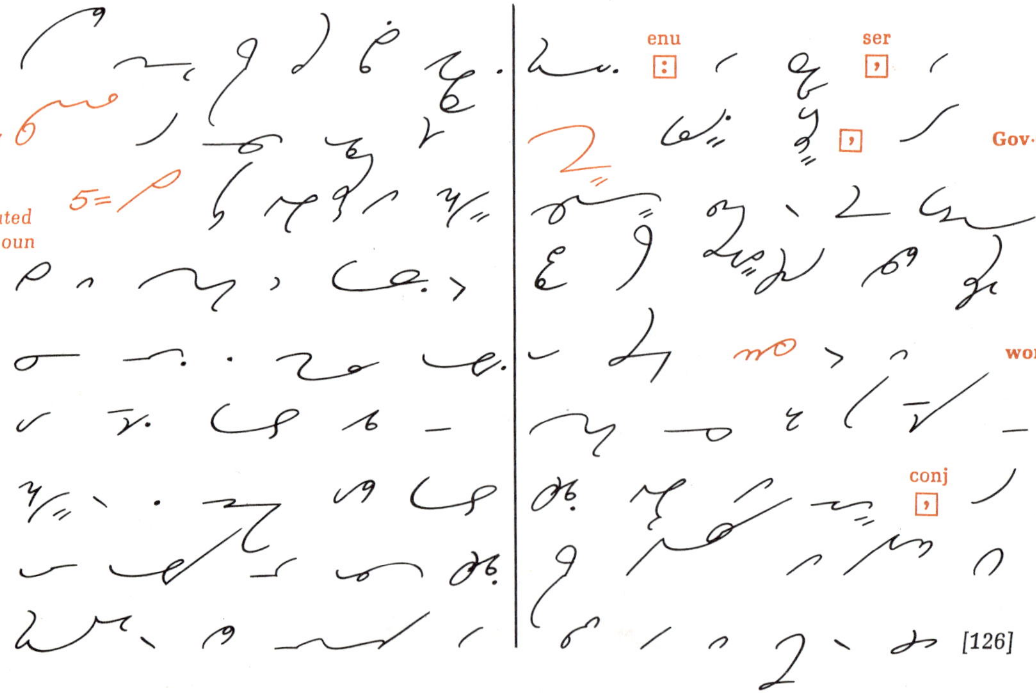

itin·er·ary

five-day
hyphenated before noun

enu

ser

Gov·ern·ment

worth·while

conj

[126]

405

Flight
of·fer·ing
weath·er
can·cel·la·tions
intro, ap, ser
when, in·clem·ent, lis·ten, wheth·er [115]

406

ap, par, if, nc [104]

LESSON 53

Building transcription skills

407 OFFICE-STYLE DICTATION | instructions during dictation

A dictator may occasionally wish to emphasize a word or expression. He may tell you to underscore it or, if he wants to give it strong emphasis, to type it in all capital letters. He may say:

I want the entire staff to attend this meeting—put **entire staff** *all in caps. Notice that the meeting will be held in Room 18—underscore* **Room 18**—*instead of Room 25.*

Draw one line under the expression to be underscored; two lines under the expression to be typed in all capital letters. These sentences would appear in your shorthand thus:

Your transcript would look like this:

I want the ENTIRE STAFF to attend this meeting. Notice that the meeting will be held in Room 18 instead of Room 25.

▶ **SEE THE OPPOSITE PAGE FOR THE ILLUSTRATION OF OFFICE-STYLE DICTATION**

408

Business vocabulary builder	**relatively** *(adverb)* Comparatively.
	rerouted Changed a course that was to be traveled.
	Shannon Airport Airport in Ireland.
	deplaned Got off the plane.

ILLUSTRATION OF OFFICE-STYLE DICTATION

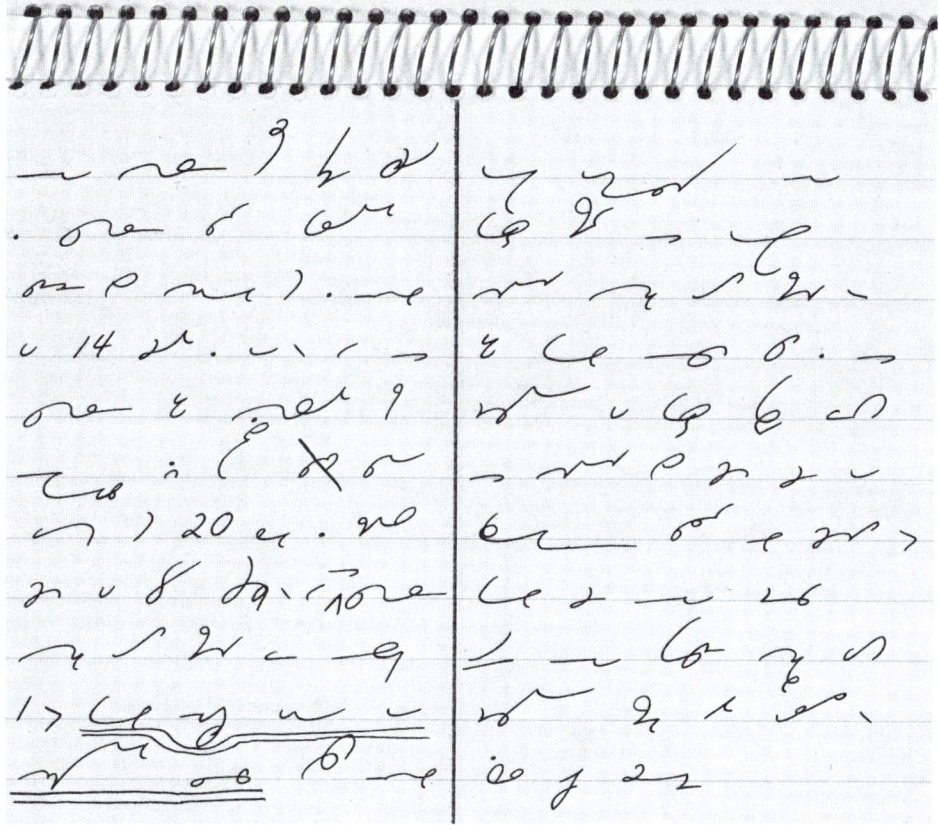

Reading and writing practice

409 Transcribe: Flight 118

280 | LESSON 54

412

LESSON 54

413

im·par·tial

its

pin·ning

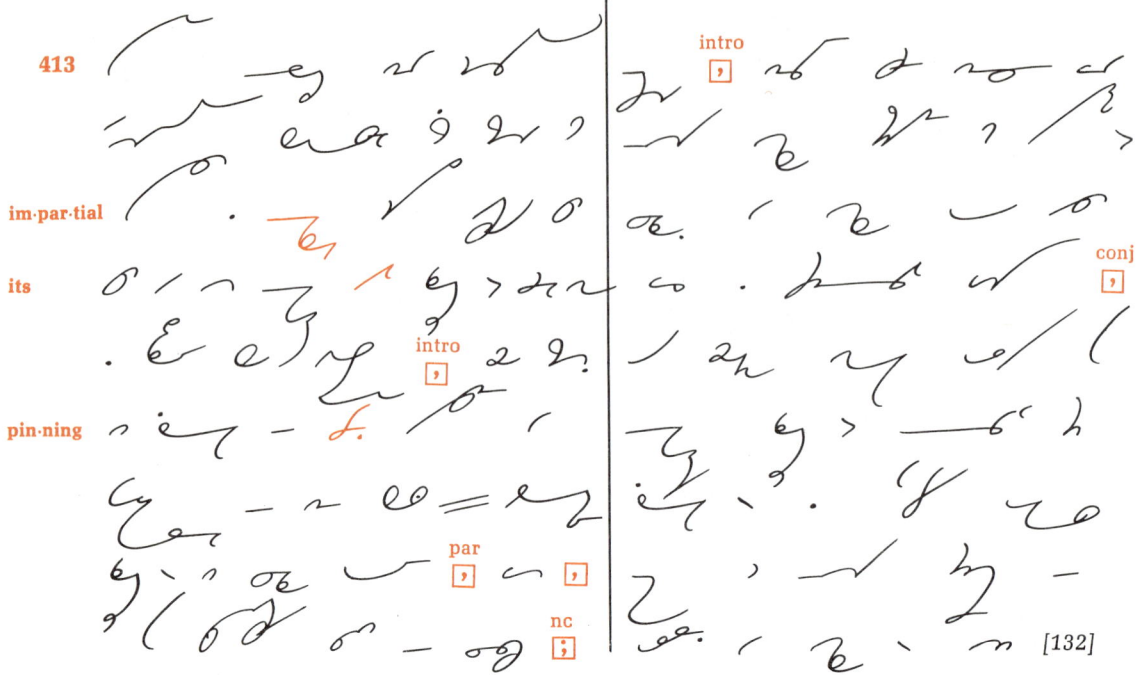

[132]

414 Transcription Quiz Supply the necessary punctuation and the one missing word. (*Hint:* Be sure you do not overlook the question mark called for after one of the sentences. One of the most frequent punctuation errors that stenographers make is to omit the question mark after a direct question.)

[110]

Building transcription skills

415 WORD CHAIN

There is frequent need in business writing for a word that suggests "talk about" in some of its many senses. There are a number of words in this chain, each having a somewhat different meaning.

>**talk about** is the mildest expression in this chain. It implies merely an exchange of opinion or information. *Talk over* is a slightly stronger expression and is almost synonymous with *discuss*.

I should like to talk to you about our plans for the future.

>**discuss** carries the idea of exchanging opinions, as does *talk about*, but it suggests, in addition, an attempt to clarify issues or to test the strength of each party to the discussion.

Please be prepared to discuss your reasons for the changes you wish to make in the plan.

>**argue** is a stronger word than *discuss* and brings in the idea of trying to convince others of the correctness of your own position. You might invite a customer to *discuss* a difference of opinion about an invoice, but you would never suggest that he come in to *argue* about it.

I do not agree with you, but I will not argue the point further.

>**debate** suggests a formal meeting with set speeches.

He feels your position is not well taken, and he would like to debate the issue with you before the entire association.

>**dispute** is even stronger than *argue*; it implies a heated, and usually unfriendly, argument.

No matter how hard you try, you cannot dispute the accuracy of his facts; he has documentary proof.

416 Business vocabulary builder

complimentary Full of praise.
accomplishments Achievements.
decline (noun) A downward slope.

Reading and writing practice

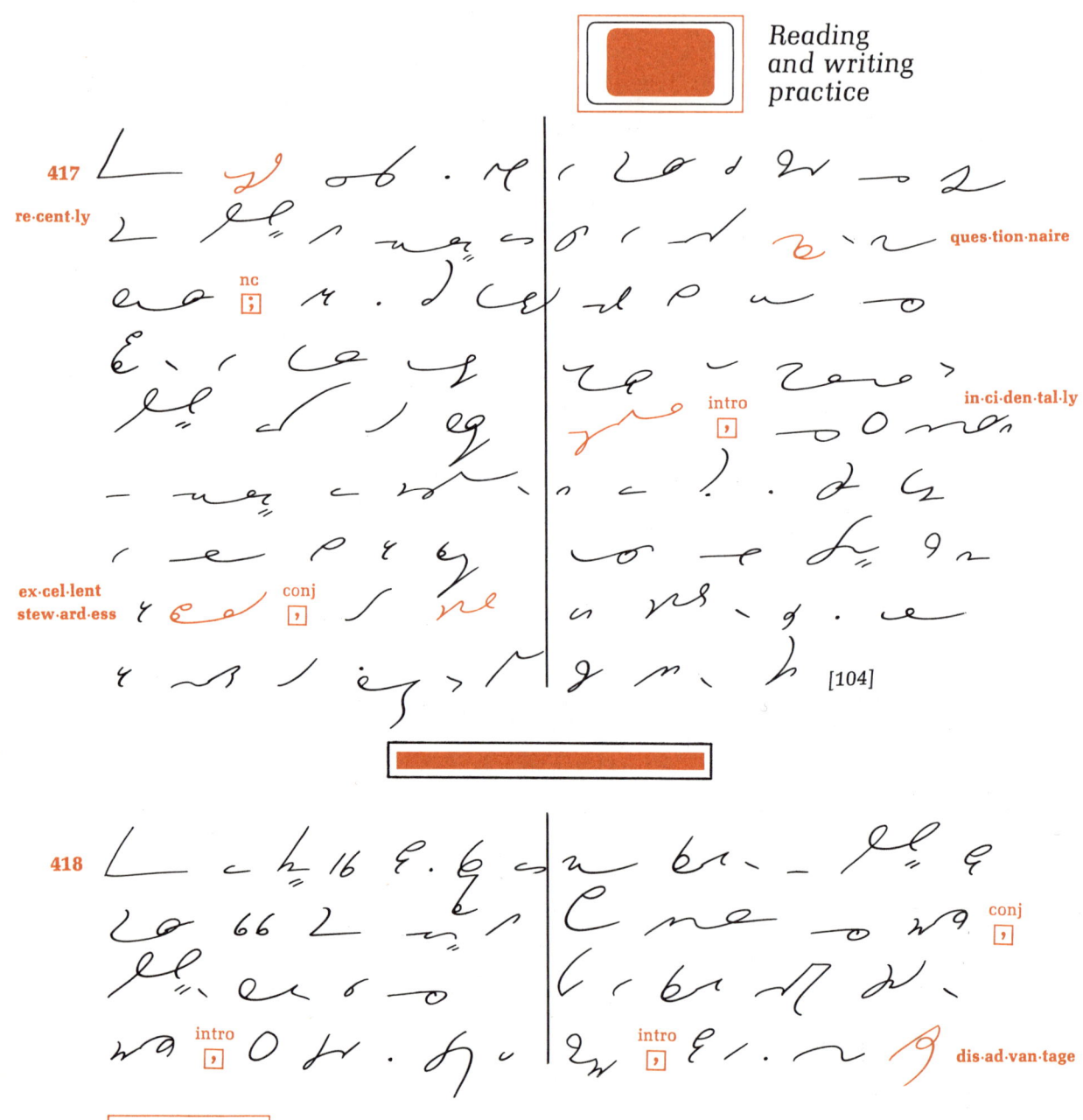

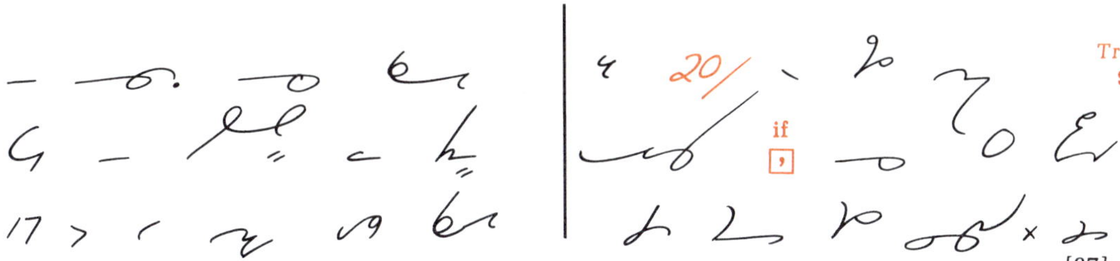

Transcribe: **$20**

[87]

419 Chicago, re·al·ize, some·one, be·hind, hur·ry [134]

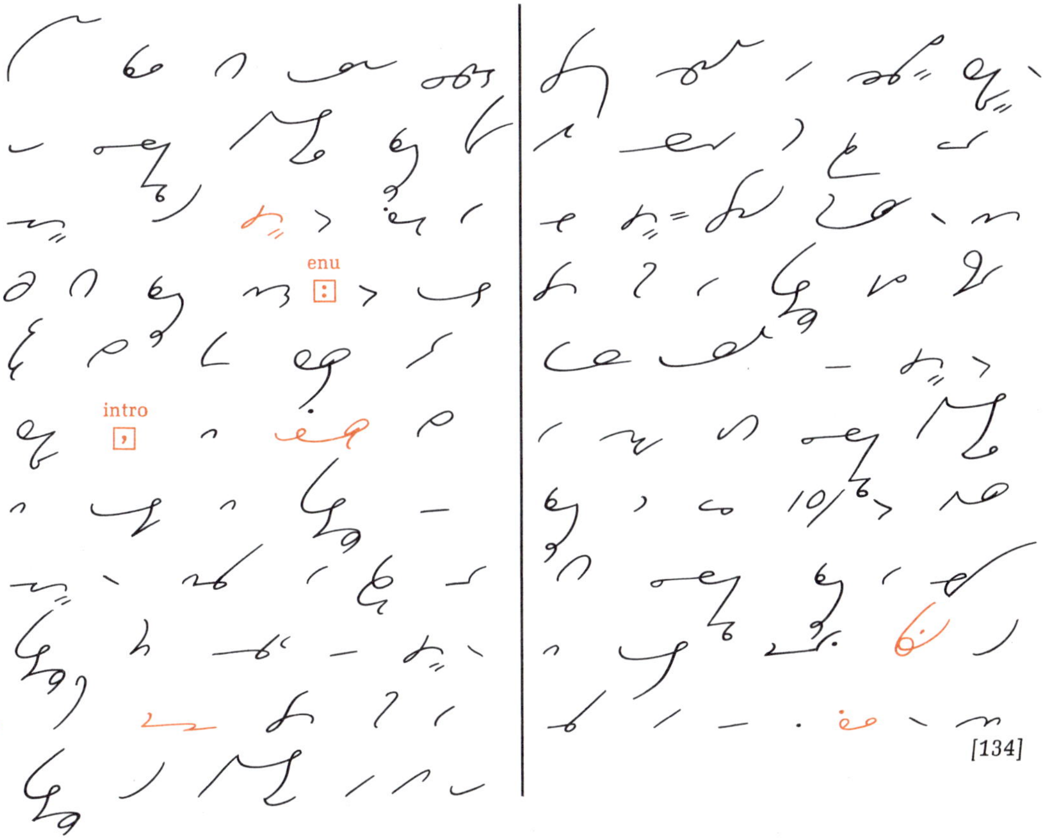

420 ac·com·plish·ments

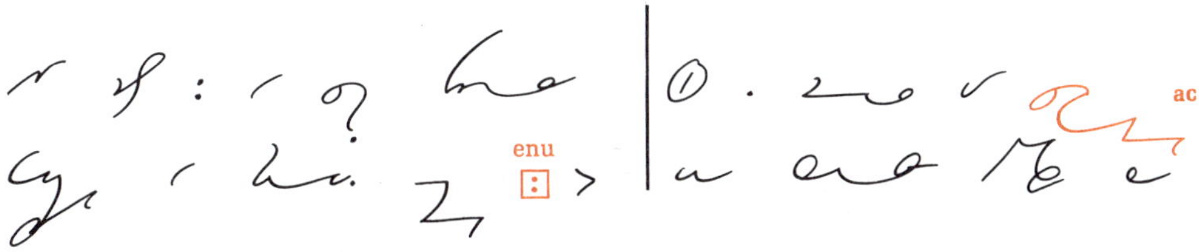

LESSON 55

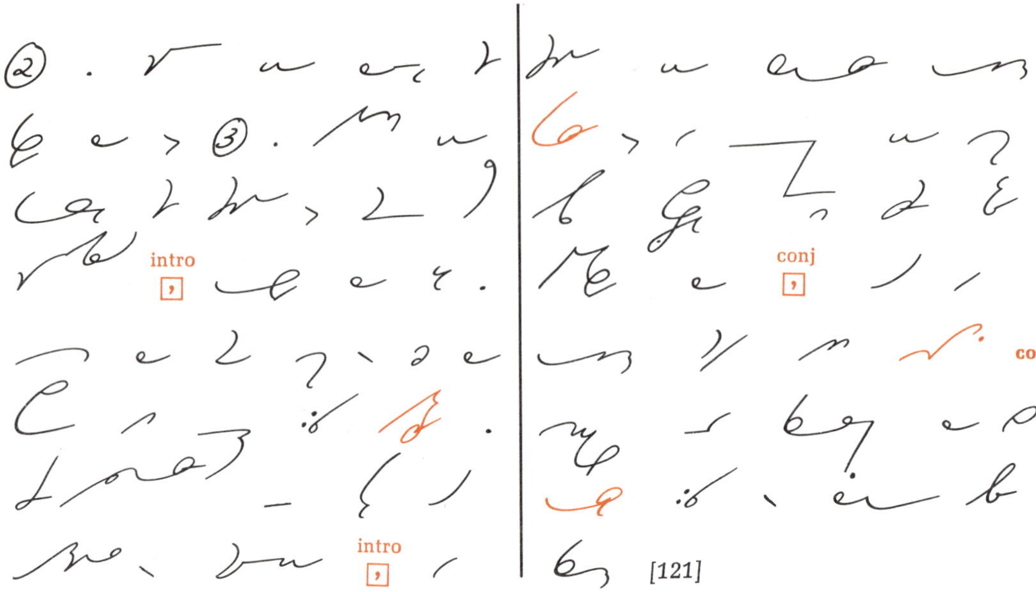

bright
con·tin·u·ing
de·spite
intro
conj
intro
lies
[121]

421
to·ward
ser
en·joy·able 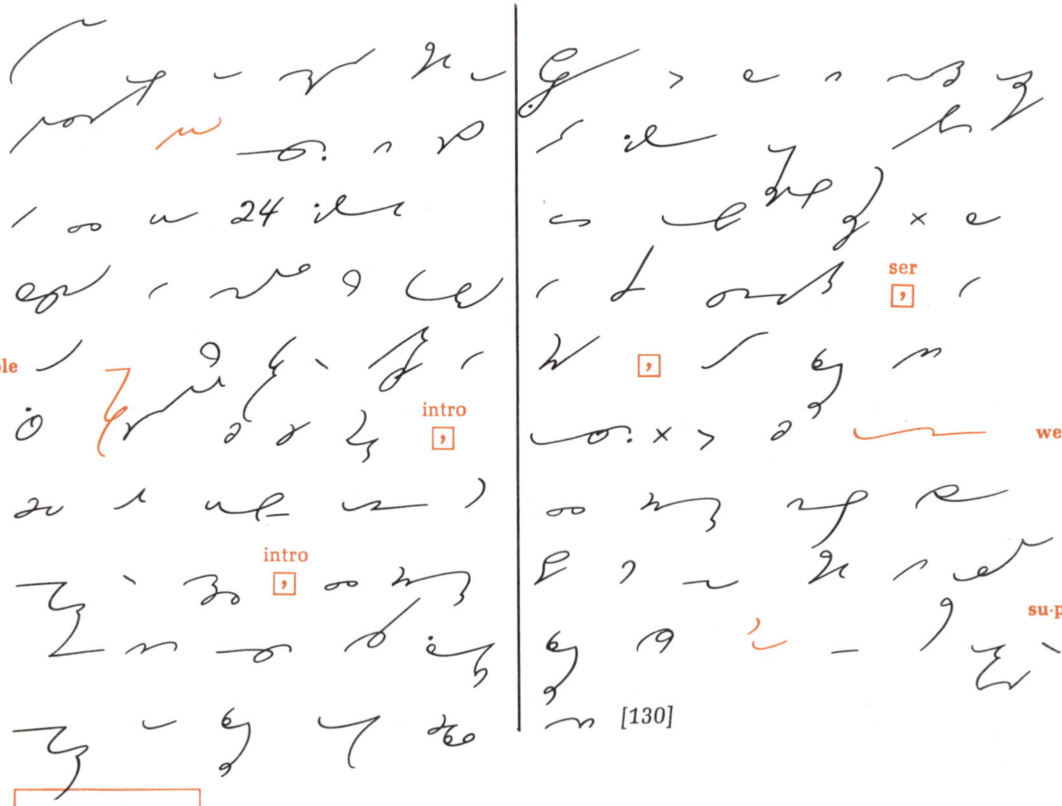
wel·come
intro
intro
su·pe·ri·or
[130]

286 | LESSON 55

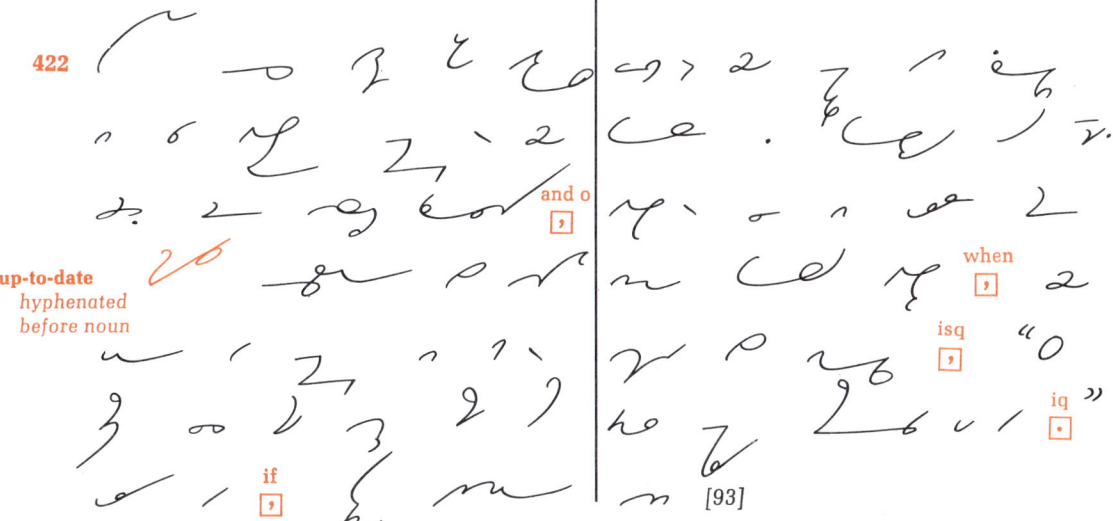

VOCABULARY TIP

A good way to increase your vocabulary is to do a great deal of reading — of books, newspapers, and magazines. Whenever you come across a word in your reading with which you are not familiar, look it up in the dictionary. Some words have several meanings, and you must be careful to select the one that fits the context in which the word occurs.

After you have found the correct meaning of the unfamiliar word, reread the sentence in which you found it to see how the meaning fits the context.

Then, keep a list (in shorthand if you like) of all new words, together with their meanings.

The letter is transcribed

After transcribing and proofreading a letter, Ellen types an envelope. If the letter is more than one page in length or if enclosures are to accompany it, she is careful to select an envelope that will comfortably accommodate all the material.

Then she carefully draws a line through the shorthand notes of the letter she has just transcribed. She is very careful to draw that line through only that transcribed letter. She once had a sad experience when she drew a line through the shorthand notes for a short letter that followed the longer letter she had just finished transcribing. The result was that the short letter was never transcribed—and Mr. Davis

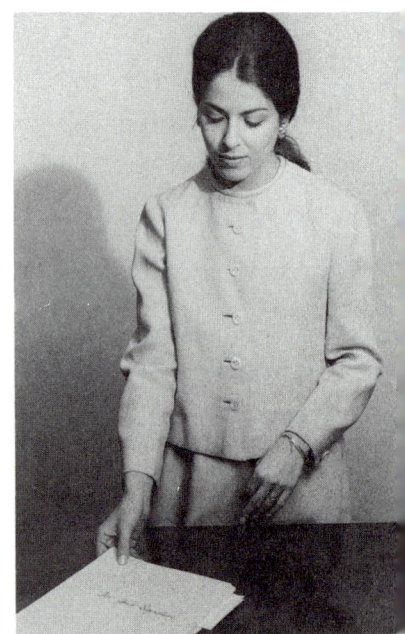

was caused considerable embarrassment.

Then:

1 She picks up the piece of incoming correspondence that has just been answered and places the file carbon on top of it. She then clips (some companies prefer to staple) the two together. Thus the latest communication is always on top.

2 Over all she places the letter to be signed under the flap of the envelope (the address side of the envelope is on top).

3 If the letter is urgent, she immediately takes it to Mr. Davis for signature. If not, she places it in a folder marked "For Your Signature."

Ellen makes it a point to deliver the transcribed letters several times a day rather than all at once toward the end of the workday. In this way her employer can sign them at his convenience instead of in a hurry at the last minute. In addition, Ellen thus protects herself against having to stay after 5 o'clock to retype a letter on which she has made a mistake (which very, very seldom happens) or one on which Mr. Davis wishes to make changes. Mr. Davis frequently pays Ellen the finest tribute that an employer can pay to his secretary or stenographer; he signs routine letters without reading them. But Ellen had to earn that tribute!

Chapter 12

Paper and printing

Building transcription skills

423 SIMILAR-WORDS DRILL | wares, wears

wares (noun)   Goods.

The wares were attractively displayed.

wears   Has on; stands up under use or time.

She always wears smart clothes.
We must determine how well the cloth wears before we can use it on our books.

424

Business vocabulary builder	
priority	Preference; something meriting early attention.
origin	Beginning; source.
peddler	One who travels about with things to sell.
participate	To take part.

425

bul·le·tin

intro ,

[123]

intro , sales·man's

426
Transcribe:
1,000

when ,

intro ,

nc ;

ob·vi·ous·ly

LESSON 56

nc
;
pri·or·i·ty
[90]

427

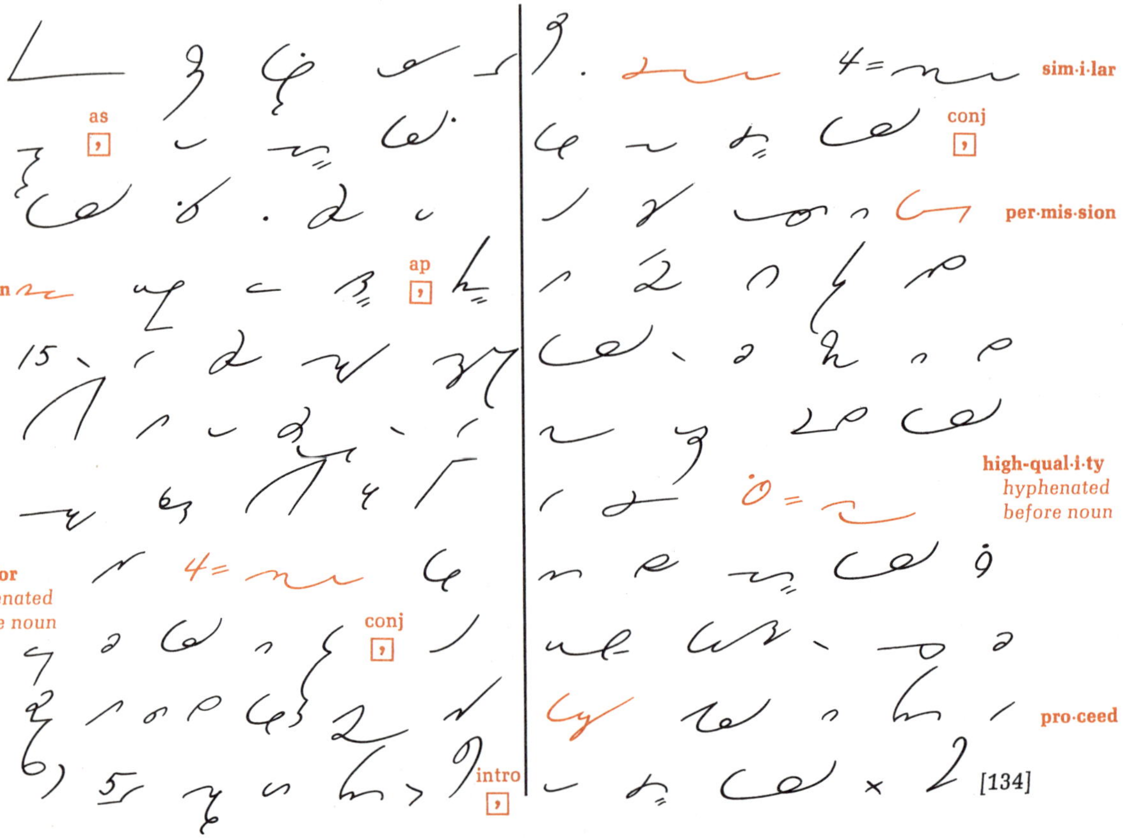
as
,
sim·i·lar
conj
,
per·mis·sion
un·known
ap
,
high-qual·i·ty
hyphenated before noun
four-color
hyphenated before noun
conj
,
pro·ceed
intro
,
[134]

428

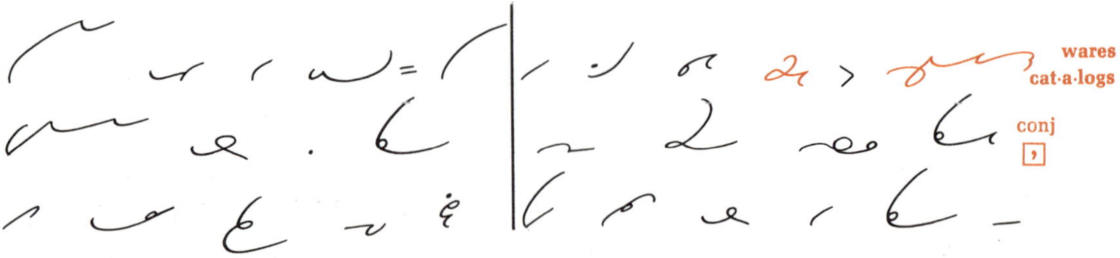
wares
cat·a·logs
conj
,

LESSON 56 | 293

430

LESSON 57

Building transcription skills

431 SPELLING FAMILIES | **forming -ed and -ing derivatives of words ending in t**

When the last syllable of a word ending in *t*, preceded by a single vowel, is accented, the *t* is doubled in forming derivatives in *-ed* and *-ing*.

al·lot	al·lot·ted	al·lot·ting
com·mit	com·mit·ted	com·mit·ting
per·mit	per·mit·ted	per·mit·ting
sub·mit	sub·mit·ted	sub·mit·ting
trans·mit	trans·mit·ted	trans·mit·ting

When the last syllable is not accented, the *t* is not doubled.

ben·e·fit	ben·e·fit·ed	ben·e·fit·ing
cred·it	cred·it·ed	cred·it·ing
prof·it	prof·it·ed	prof·it·ing

When the *t* is preceded by more than one vowel or a consonant, the *t* is not doubled.

ad·just	ad·just·ed	ad·just·ing
cor·rect	cor·rect·ed	cor·rect·ing
greet	greet·ed	greet·ing
in·ter·est	in·ter·est·ed	in·ter·est·ing

432 *Business vocabulary builder*

reams Packages of 500 sheets of paper.
effect (*verb*) To bring about.
centralize To concentrate at one point.

Reading and writing practice

433 no·ti·fied Transcribe: No. 21 intro conj if par sat·is·fac·to·ry anx·ious [115]

434 Transcribe: No. 1156 en·clos·ing as too high qual·i·ty no noun, no hyphen [105]

LESSON 57

[shorthand page — Lesson 57]

Building transcription skills

439 ACCURACY PRACTICE

Follow the practice procedures outlined on page 154.

GROUP 1	GROUP 2	GROUP 3
affect	retain	red
effect	redeem	lead

practice drill

1 The governor's speech may <u>effect</u> the settlement of the dispute. The governor's speech may <u>affect</u> the settlement of the dispute.
2 I will <u>retain</u> the bond. I will <u>redeem</u> the bond.
3 He used a <u>red</u> pencil to indicate his corrections. He used a <u>lead</u> pencil to indicate his corrections.

440

Business vocabulary builder	
discontinued	Stopped.
paramount	Of greatest importance.
deadline	The last moment by which a task must be completed.

Reading and writing practice

441 (shorthand) ex·cel·lent, oc·curred, han·dling, ap, conj [81]

442 loose-leaf (hyphenated before noun), conj, intro, Sta·tio·ner's, nc, par [127]

LESSON 58

443

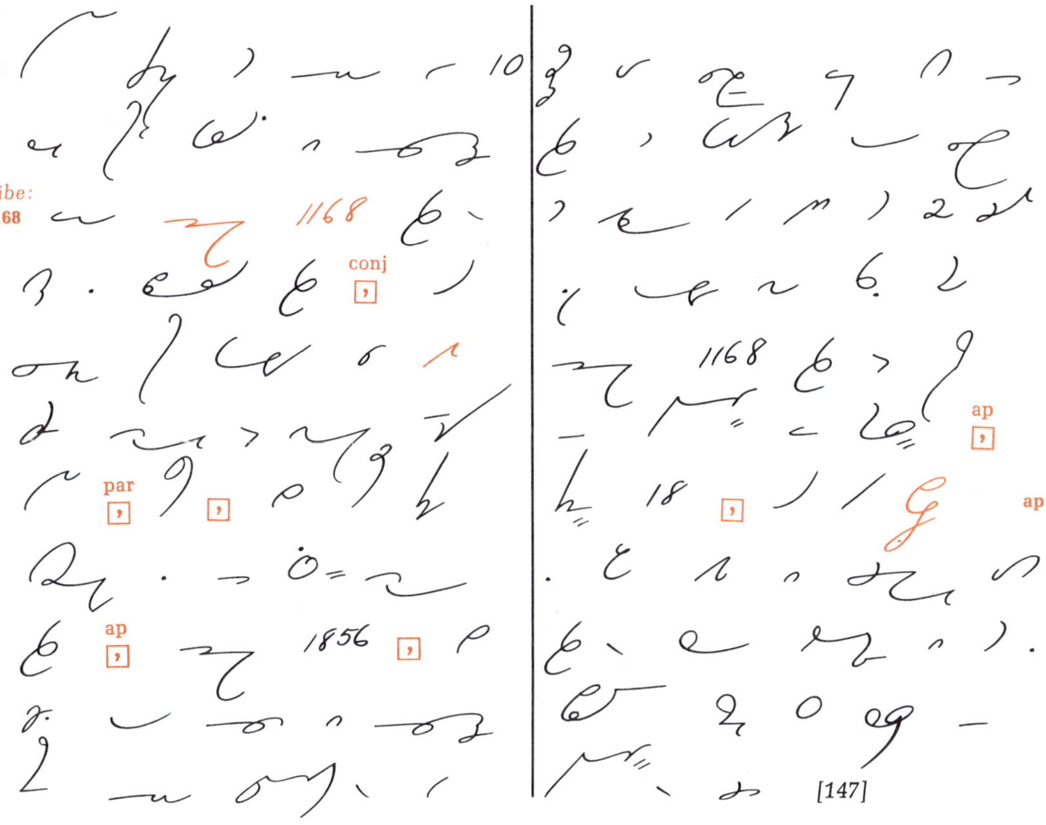

Transcribe:
No. 1168
1168
conj
its
par
ap
1856
1168
ap
18
ap·pre·ci·ate
[147]

444

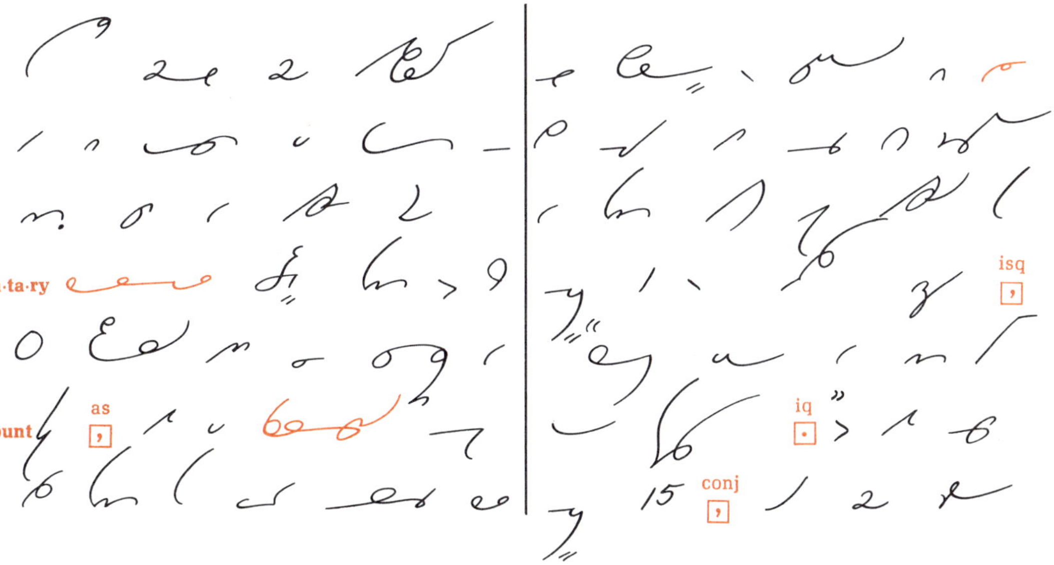

then
el·e·men·ta·ry
par·a·mount
as
isq
iq
15
conj

ti·tle

ser

dead·line

[144]

445 sheets

wel·come

psy·chol·o·gy

oc·curred

four-page
*hyphenated
before noun*

par

[118]

446

Chicago nonr off·set

LESSON 58

PUNCTUATION TIP

If you have been paying careful attention to the punctuation pointers in your textbook, you should be a fairly good "punctuator" by this time.

It is not enough, however, to think about correct punctuation only when you are transcribing business letters in class; you should be thinking about correct punctuation in all the writing you do, whether you are preparing a paper for the history class, corresponding with a friend, or making notes for yourself.

Building transcription skills

447 OFFICE-STYLE DICTATION | instructions during dictation (continued)

One of the best ways to emphasize a few lines of typewritten copy is to indent them. If, for example, the letter is typed with 50 characters to the line, the indented material might be typed on a 40 character line so that it will stand out from the rest of the letter.

If your dictator mentions, *before* he dictates, that the material is to be indented, the shorthand notes can be indented slightly and a large square bracket placed on each side of the material to be indented. If he decides on the indention *after* he has dictated the material, you can place the bracket on each side of the section to be indented. That will remind you, when transcribing, to make the necessary change in the margins.

ILLUSTRATION OF OFFICE-STYLE DICTATION

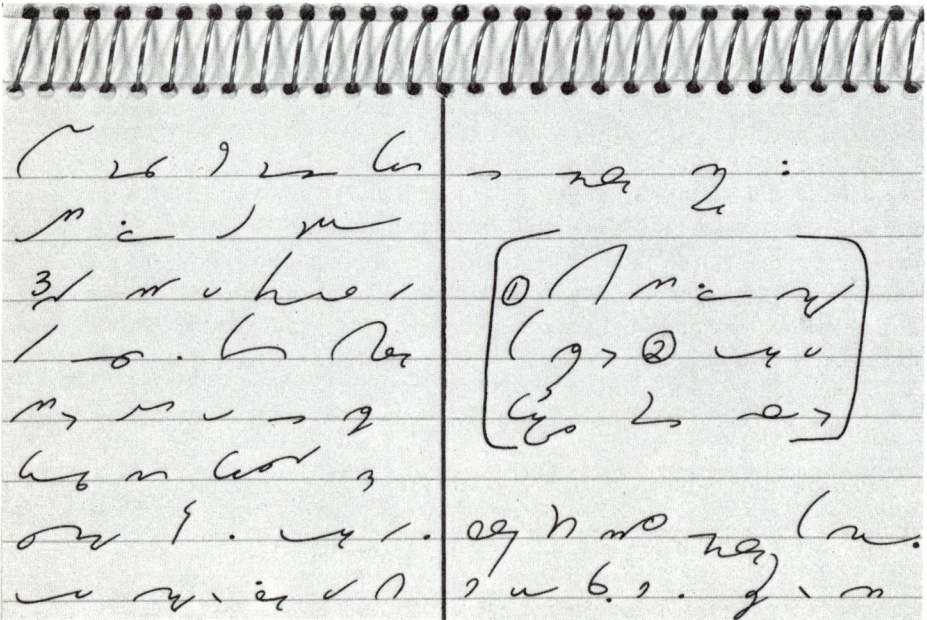

448 Business vocabulary builder

superiority State or quality of excelling.
ads Short for *advertisements*.
initial First.

Reading and writing practice

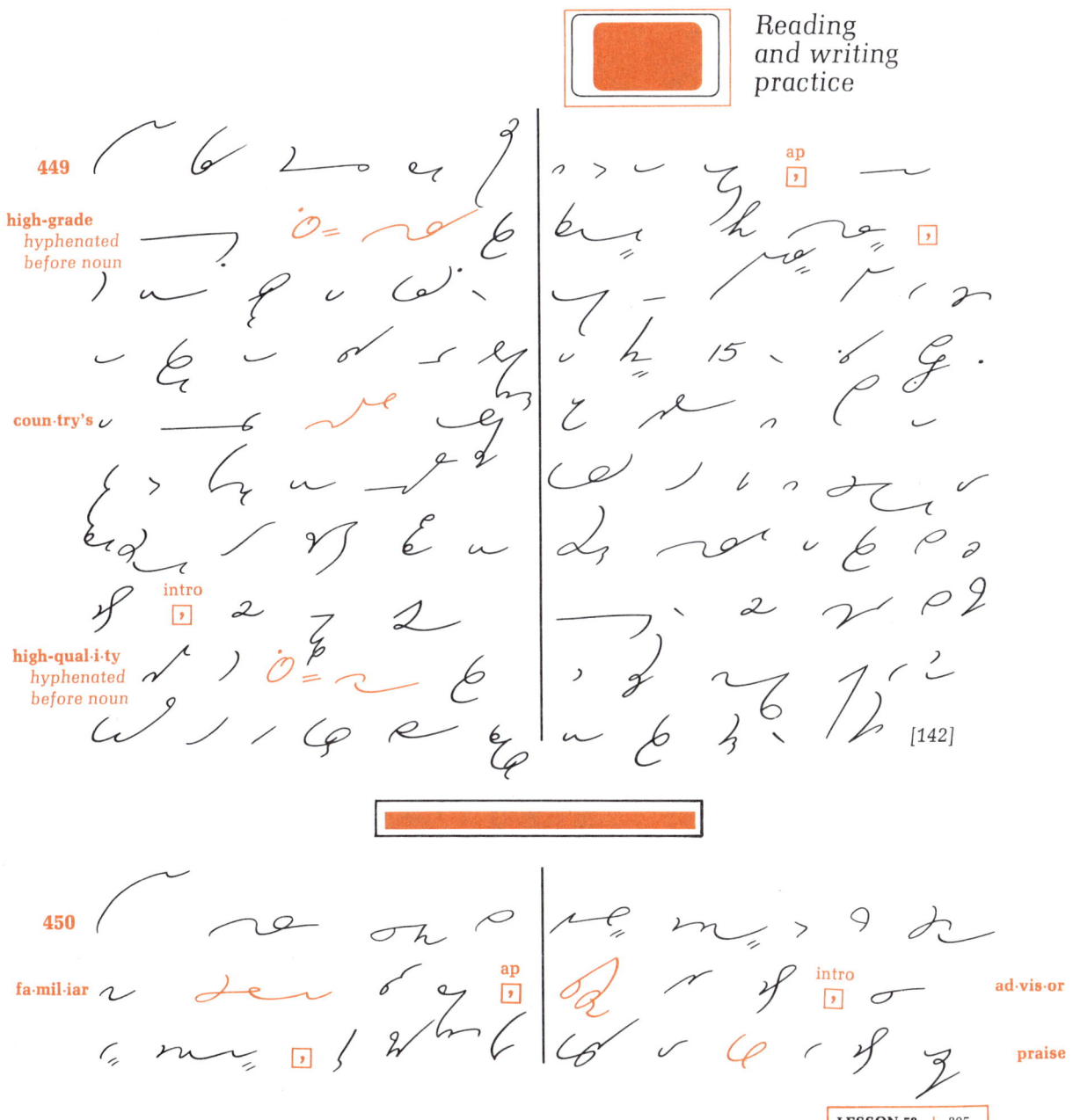

year's — par — as — nc

Transcribe: $2,500 — 25 — 1,230 — par — ads — if — grate·ful [155]

451 ad·vance — ap — ap — their — if — lose [116]

452

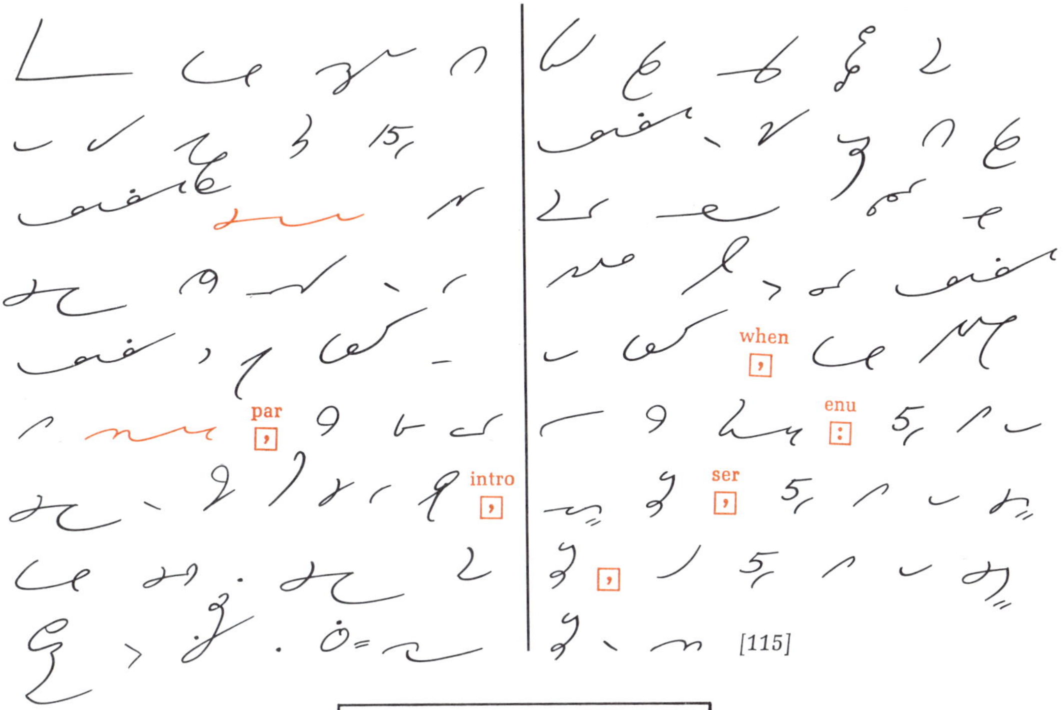

sim·i·lar

col·ors [par,] [intro,]

[115]

453

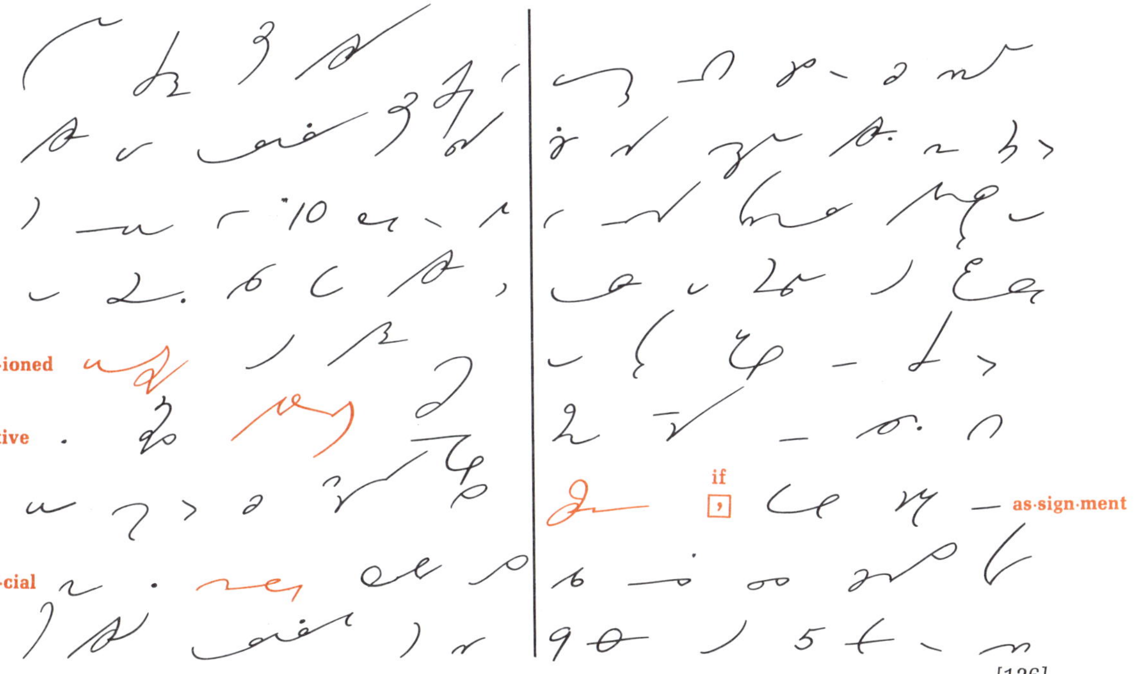

old-fash·ioned
dis·tinc·tive
com·mer·cial

[if,] — as·sign·ment

[126]

LESSON 59

454 Transcription Quiz Supply the necessary punctuation and the two words missing from the shorthand. (Hint: Watch for an omitted question mark.)

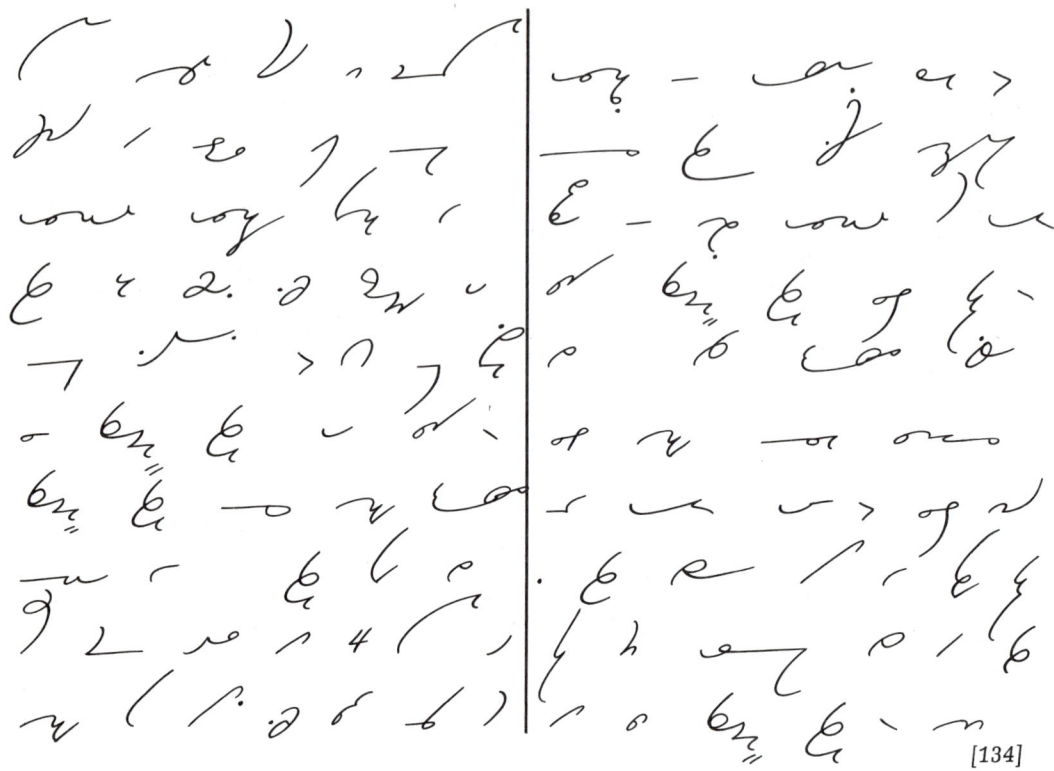

Cheerfulness is contagious! Even over the telephone a pleasant disposition and a friendly tone of voice are easily communicated to the invisible person at the other end of the wire.

Building transcription skills

455 COMMON PREFIXES | ex-

ex- In a great many words, ex- means *from, out, out of*.

exhaust To tire out; to run out of.

exceedingly Going out or beyond the measure of.

exit A way out.

exterior The outside.

expenditure That which is paid out or used up.

456 | Business vocabulary builder | **compositor** The person who sets type.
illustrations Photographs, drawings, etc.
queries Questions.

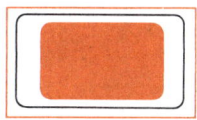

Reading and writing practice

457

ef·fect

print·er's

Transcribe: 40 cents

rais·ing

Transcribe: 15 percent

conj

par

fac·tor

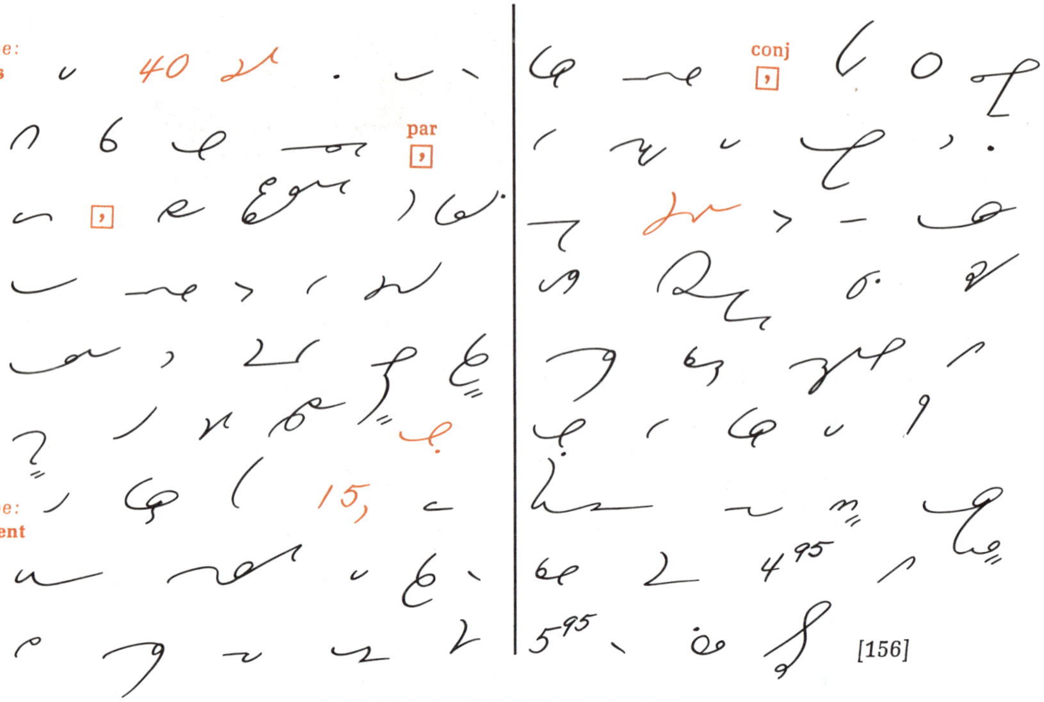

[156]

458

ap

than

nonr

intro

if

cloth

conj

four-page
hyphenated before noun

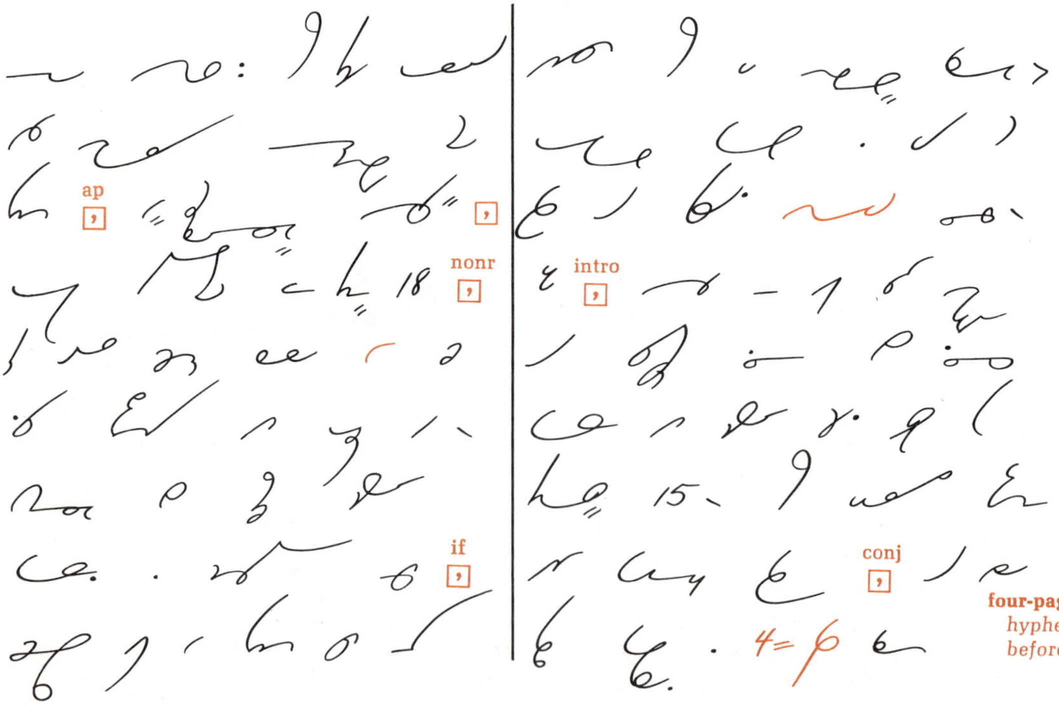

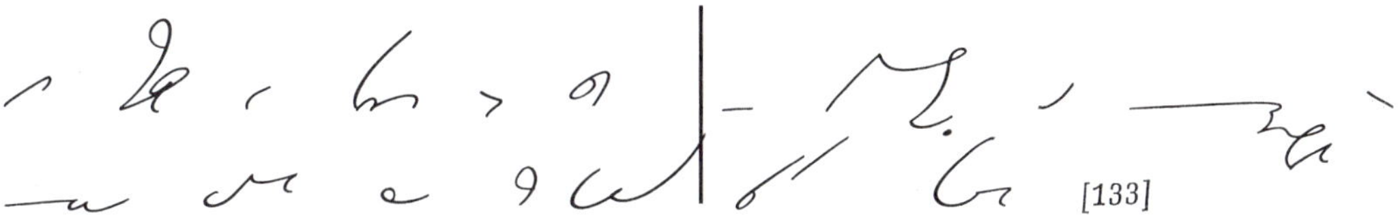

[133]

459

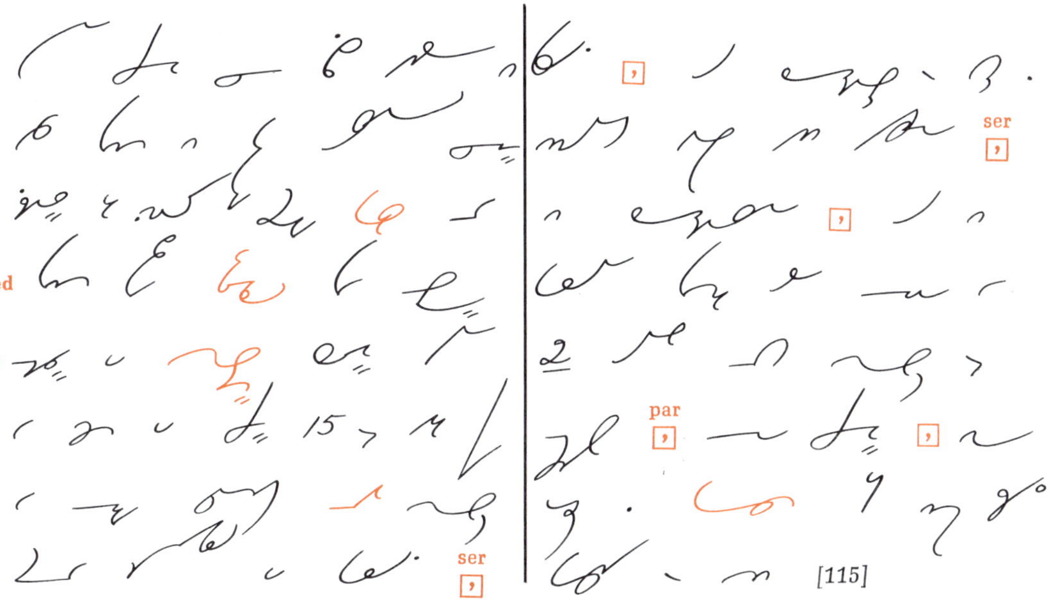

prize

spon-sored

Graph·ic

its

ser

par

plaque

ser

[115]

460

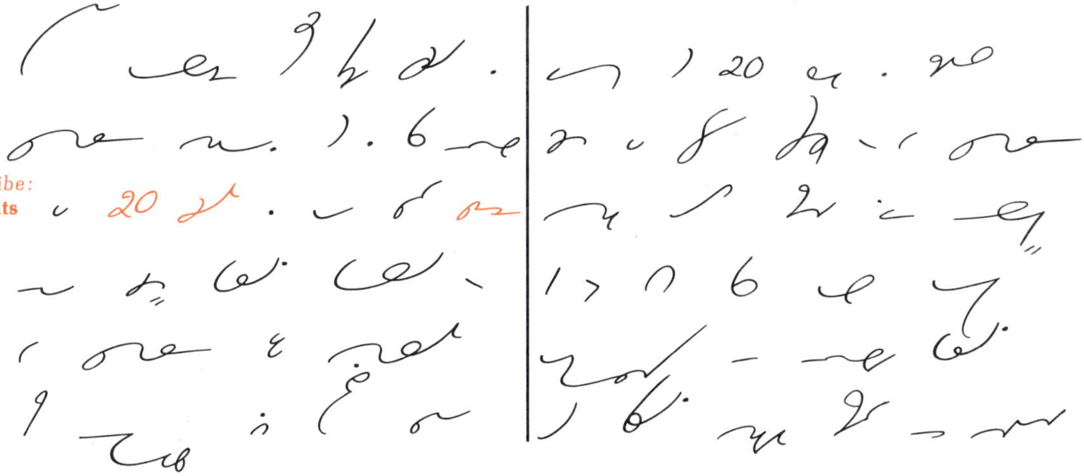

Transcribe:
20 cents
union

LESSON 60

ef·fect

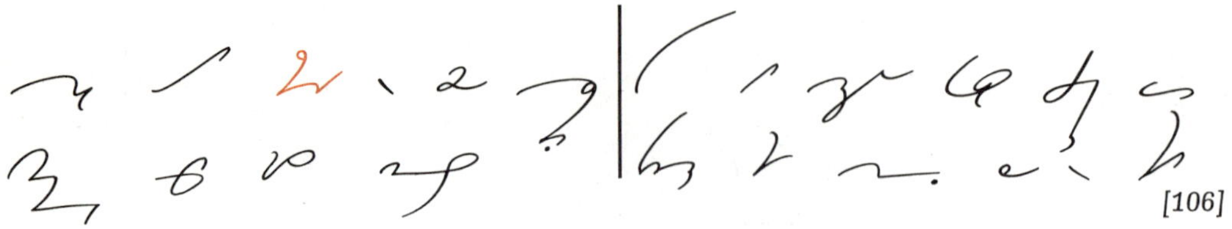

461
intro
foreman
que·ries
[106]

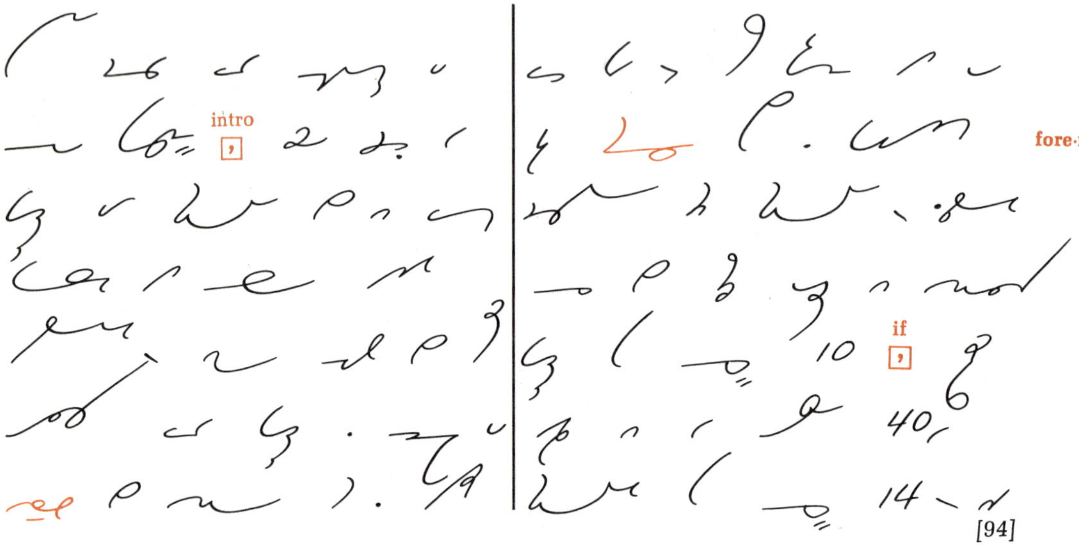

462 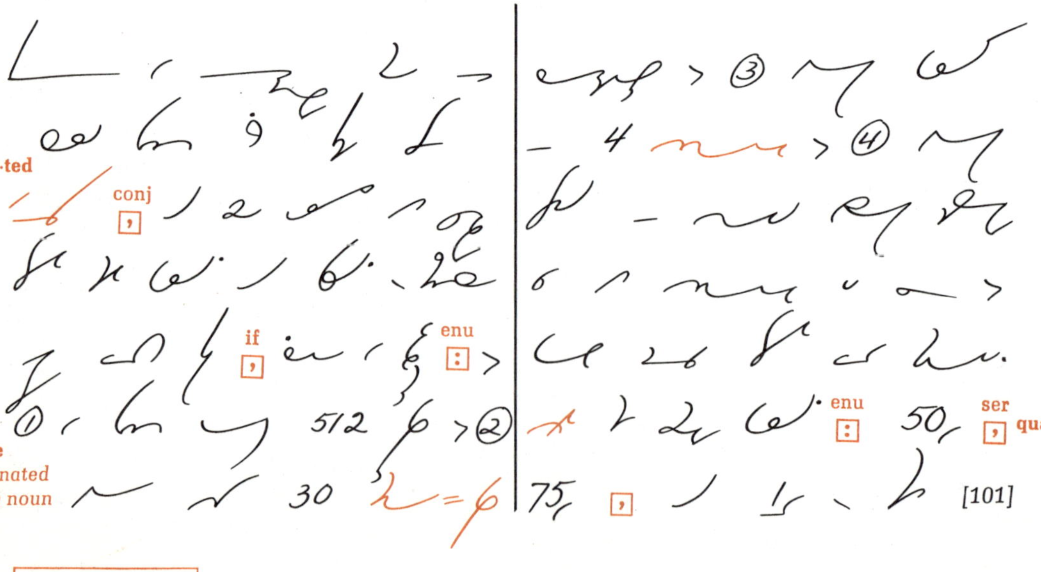
trans·mit·ted
conj
col·ors
if
enu
enu
ser
full-page
hyphenated
before noun
quan·ti·ties
[94]
[101]

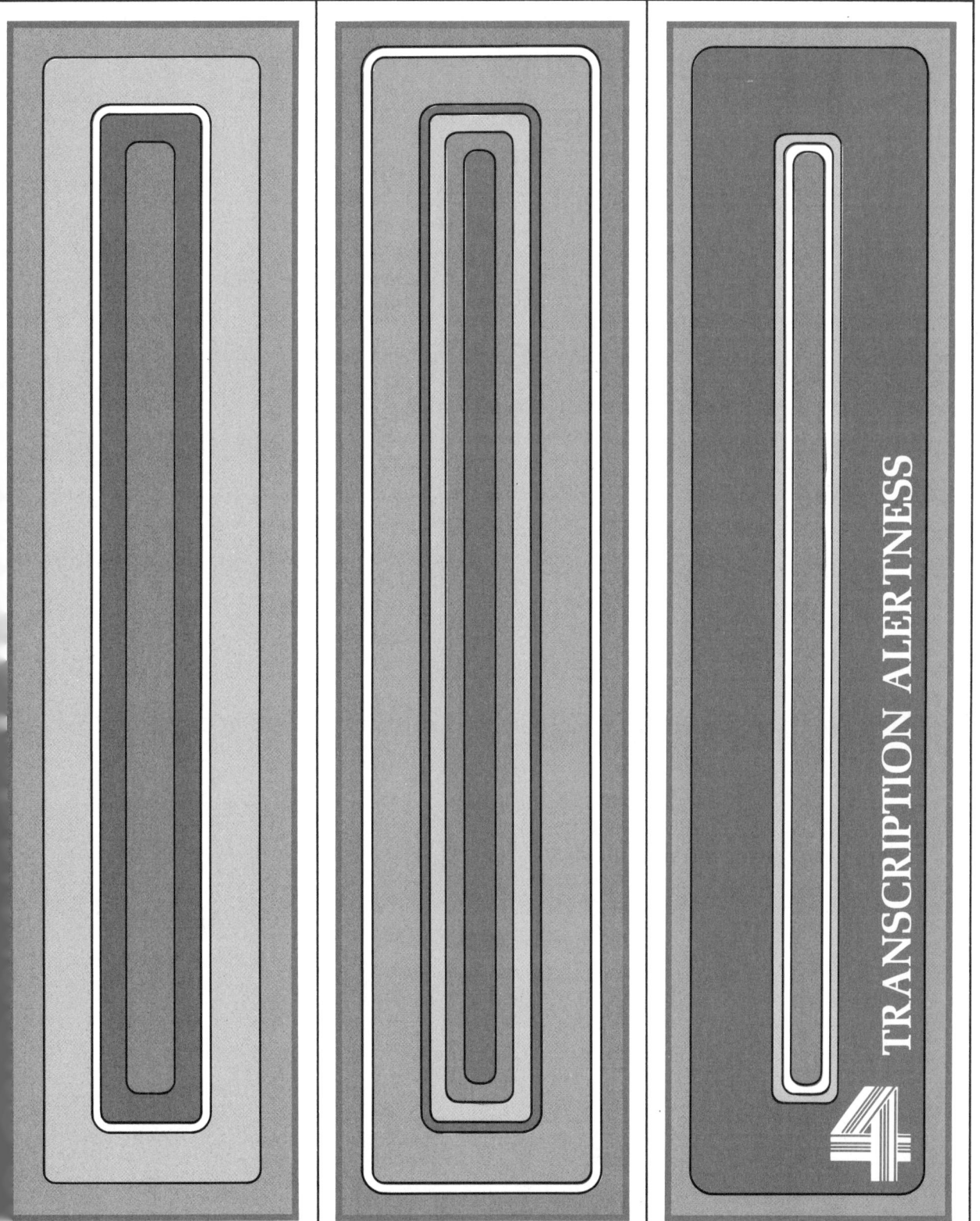

Ellen Gardiner, detective

Mr. Davis expects Ellen to do more than merely take down and transcribe mechanically the material that he dictates. He realizes that occasionally, as he dictates, he makes errors in grammar and even errors in fact. Because he often concentrates so hard on the thought he is trying to express, the verb in his sentence does not always agree with the subject; he sometimes uses a plural pronoun instead of a singular pronoun; he sometimes makes errors in dates, names, amounts, and other important facts.

But he does not worry, for he knows that Ellen is his detective on the lookout for mistakes of that type. He knows that she will correct obvious

mistakes automatically and will ask him when there is a question in her mind about anything.

Mr. Davis knows that Ellen will not simply transcribe a letter as it was dictated and then, when an error is found in it, try to excuse herself by saying, "But that's what you said."

Here are some of the types of dictator's errors that Ellen would change without asking Mr. Davis:

If he should dictate: "Who did you talk with in our company about your proposal?" she would transcribe: "Whom did you talk with in our company about your proposal?"

If he should dictate: "Of the two layouts, I can't decide which is best," she would transcribe: "Of the two layouts, I can't decide which is better."

Most dictators would not make mistakes of this type if their minds were not occupied with more important details than grammar.

Here are some of the types of dictator's errors that Ellen would take up with Mr. Davis, tactfully, of course:

"I will see you on Friday, April 16." (April 16 is a Thursday. Therefore, there is some question whether Mr. Davis means Thursday, April 16, or Friday, April 17.)

In one paragraph Mr. Davis says, "I am sending you two packages of contract forms today, and I will send you another two packages next week." Later he says, "These five packages of forms should meet your requirements for the entire year." (If he sent two packages on one day and two on another, that would make a total of four. Did he mean to send three packages on one of these days, or should he have said, "These four packages"?)

In one paragraph he says, "Mr. Frank Smith was here to see me today." In a later paragraph he says, "Harry Smith impressed me as being a good salesman." (Is the man's name Harry or Frank Smith?)

When Ellen Gardiner discovers errors of this type, she goes to Mr. Davis and says something like this: "Mr. Davis, in my notes I have the statement that you will see Mr. Green on Friday, April 16. I wonder whether it should be Thursday, April 16, or Friday, April 17."

"Mr. Davis, I want to be sure that I have these figures right. Are we to send two packages of contract forms today and two on Wednesday?"

Your employer will expect you, too, to be a detective on the lookout for his mistakes.

Chapter 13 | LESSON 61

Real estate

Building transcription skills

463 SIMILAR-WORDS DRILL | suite, suit

suite (pronounced swēt) A group of rooms occupied as a unit.

The doctor's suite is on the ground floor of the building.

suit (verb) To answer the requirements of.

If the time does not suit you, let me know and I shall change it.

464

| Business vocabulary builder | **real estate taxes** Taxes on buildings and grounds.
converted Changed; transformed.
proceedings Official records of things said and done. |

Reading and writing practice

465

[120]

466 [98]

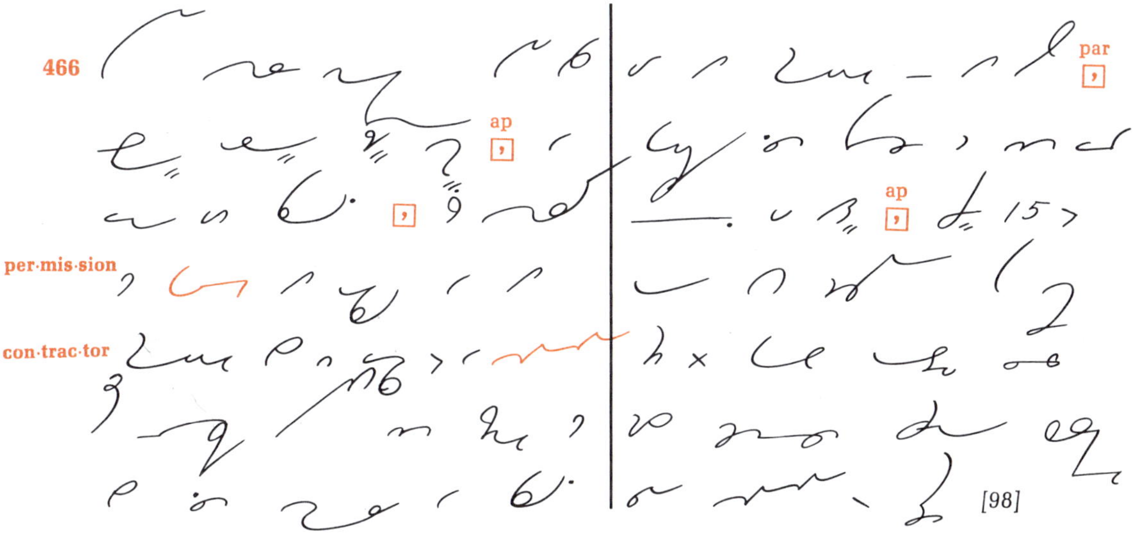

467

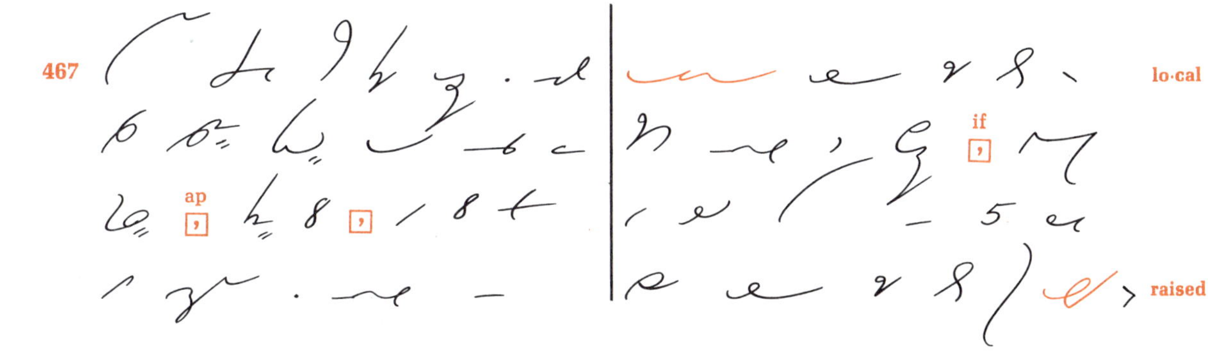

LESSON 61 | 317

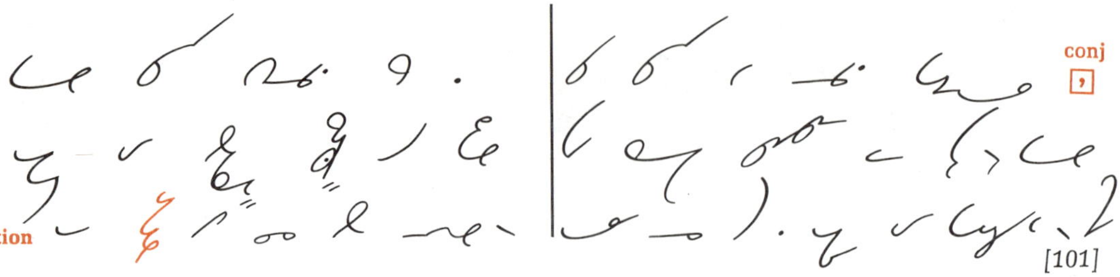

op·po·si·tion

[101] conj

468 doc·tor's suite

five-story
hyphenated before noun

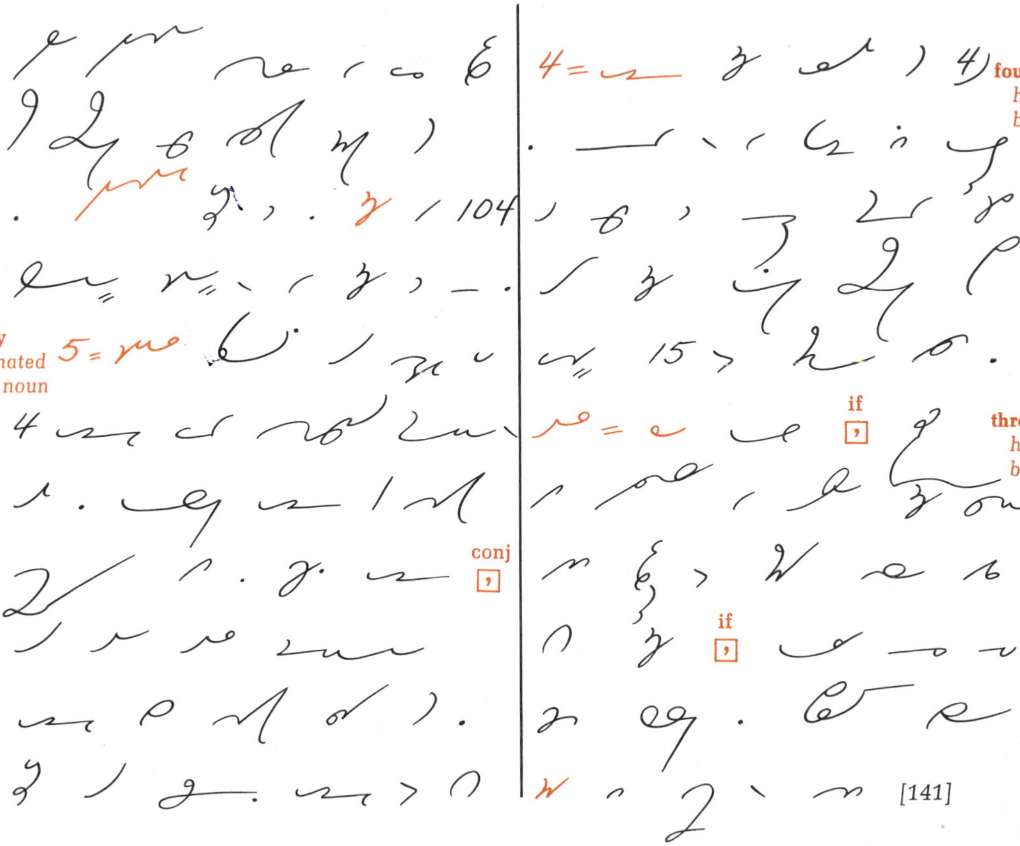

four-room
hyphenated before noun

conj

three-year
hyphenated before noun

conj

if

if

nc

[141] suit

469 kitch·en

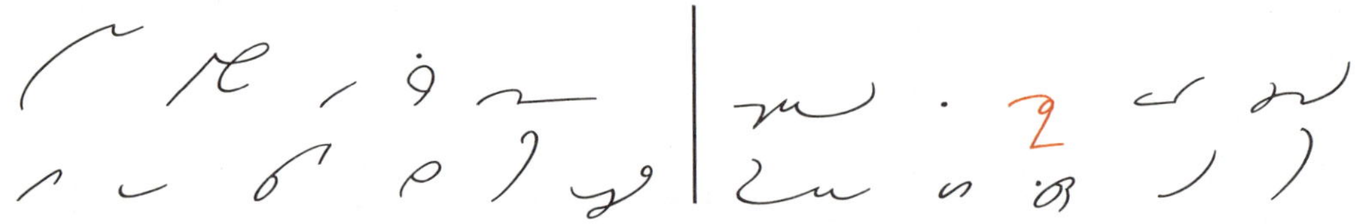

LESSON 61

LESSON 61

470

zon·ing
oc·cu·pan·cy
sub·mit·ted

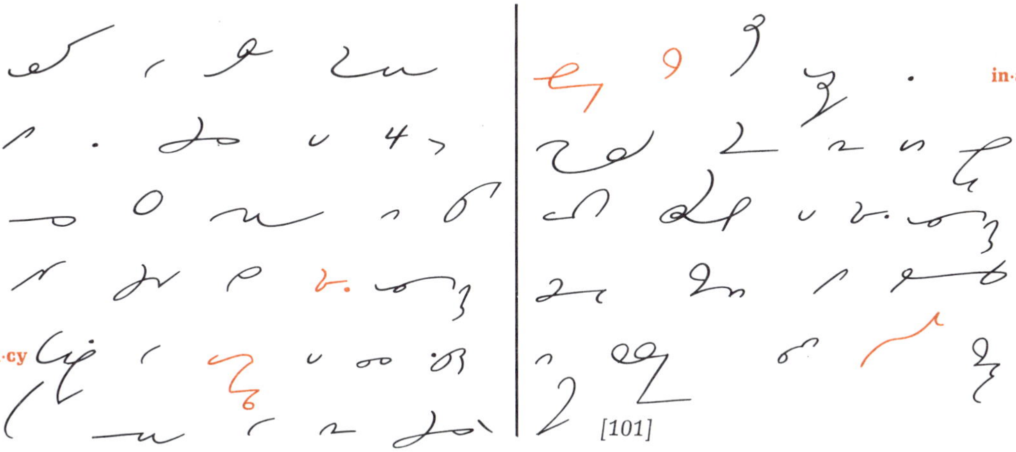

in·as·much as
intro
ten·ants
half-acre *hyphenated before noun*
nonr
of·fered
nonr
conj
re·ac·tion

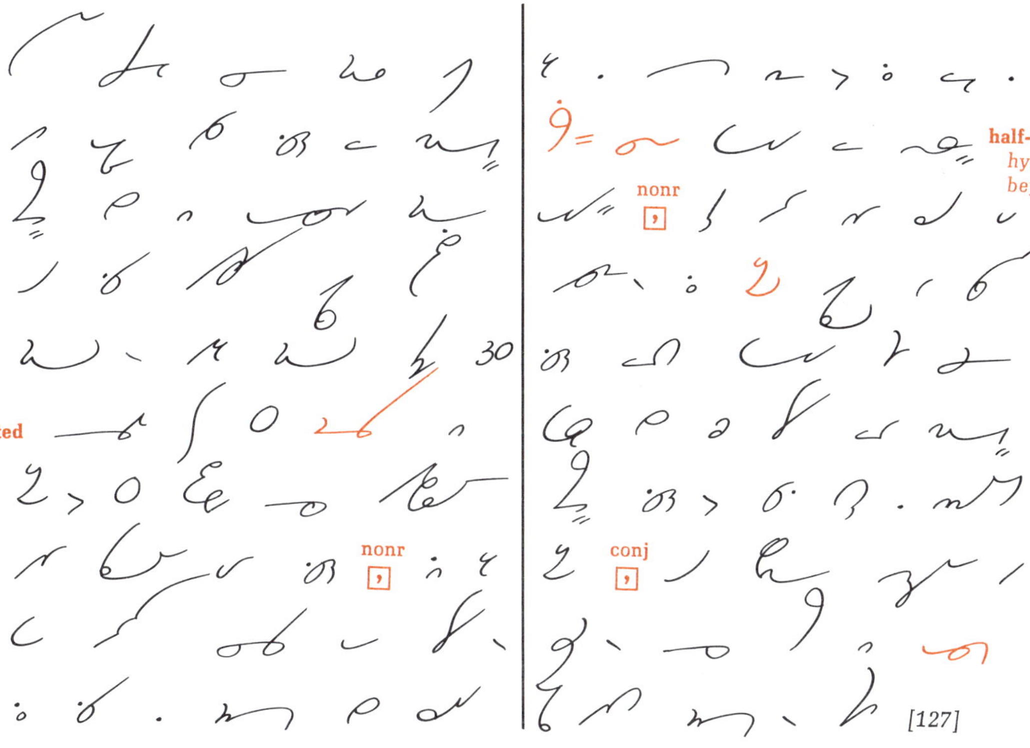

February 22, 19--

Mr. Perry R. Strong, President
Harrison Manufacturing Company
4125 North Fifth Avenue
Denver, Colorado 80208

Dear Mr. Strong:

                         Subject: Employees' Handbooks

I am sending you today by express all the material that we have available on how to prepare an employees' handbook.

You will be interested, I am sure, in our experience in helping the Martin Miller Company prepare its latest handbook. When we were called in, that company already had a handbook but it was out of date. The organization had grown considerably since that handbook was prepared; consequently, the handbook had to be completely rewritten. The new handbook was ready at the end of last year. It benefited by many lessons that had been learned during the work on the first handbook.

While working with the Martin Miller Company, we learned that the following three points are important in preparing a handbook:

    1. It should not be a rule book listing things that should and should not be done by employees.

    2. It should take advantage of the pleasant feeling of satisfaction with which an employee starts a new job. The handbook should play a definite part in maintaining that feeling of satisfaction.

    3. It should set down facts that will make employees feel that they are important parts of the company. It should give them information on every phase of the company's organization and activities.

In the first edition of the handbook we tried to put in a section that was devoted to the history of the company. We had often felt a need for this. We also felt that this objective was not covered fully enough in the first handbook. This handbook was prepared with the employee exclusively in mind.

Mr. Perry R. Strong   2   February 22, 19--

These are just a few thoughts that come to me at this time. I am sure that the Martin Miller Company would be glad to send you a copy of their new handbook. I believe that you may find many suggestions in it that you would be able to use when you prepare your handbook.

Needless to say, we are at your service. If you think that a visit with one of our men would be helpful, please call us. We will be glad to arrange an appointment.

                        Cordially yours,

                        R. L. Kane

                        R. L. Kane, Vice President

RLK:IRT

P. S. I have just learned that Fred Hopkins, the member of our staff who worked with Martin Miller Company, will be in Denver all next week. Would you like to meet him and talk with him?

Two-page letter
Blocked style, with subject line and postscript
Standard punctuation

Building transcription skills

471 SPELLING FAMILIES | dis-, des-

People often pronounce the word beginnings *dis* and *des* alike in words such as *discuss* and *despite*. Consequently, pronunciation will not help you decide whether *dis* or *des* is the correct spelling. The following list contains words with those word beginnings. Study them carefully.

dis-

di·sas·ter	dis·like	dis·pense
dis·close	dis·mayed	dis·pose
dis·cussed	dis·patch	dis·pute
dis·guise	dis·pel	dis·turb

des-

de·scribe	de·spair	de·spon·dent
de·scrip·tion	des·per·ate	des·ti·na·tion
de·sir·able	de·spise	des·ti·tute
des·o·late	de·spite	de·stroy

472

Business vocabulary builder	
impose	To take advantage of.
despaired	Gave up hope.
landlord	The owner of land or of a house, which he rents out to tenants.

Reading and writing practice

473

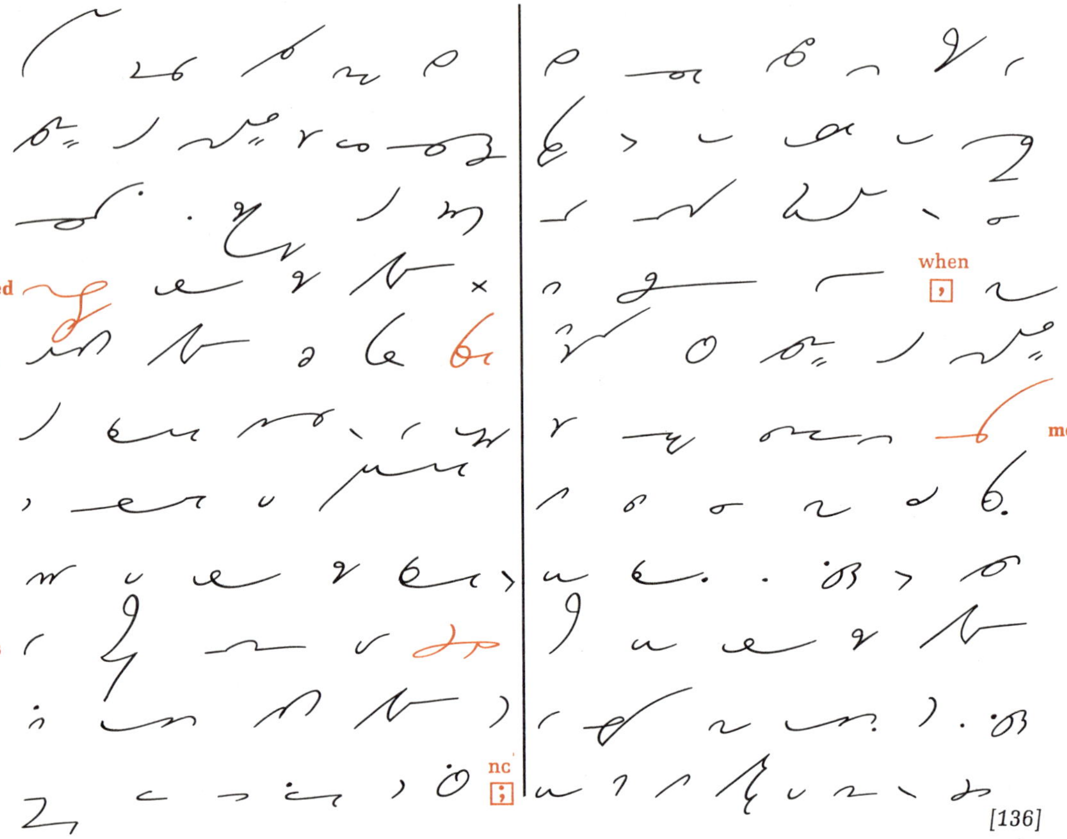

clas·si·fied
buy·ers
fam·i·lies
when
me·di·um

[136]

474

trans·ferred
col·league

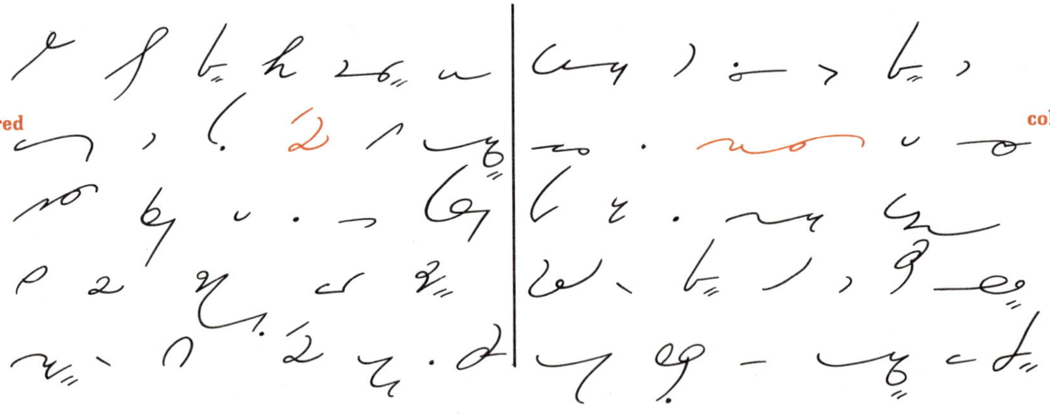

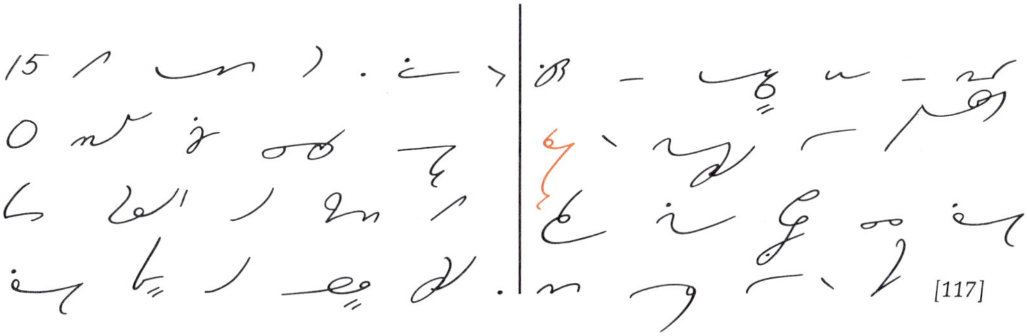
15
[117]

sub·urbs

475

re·ferred

length

mod·ern

per·suade

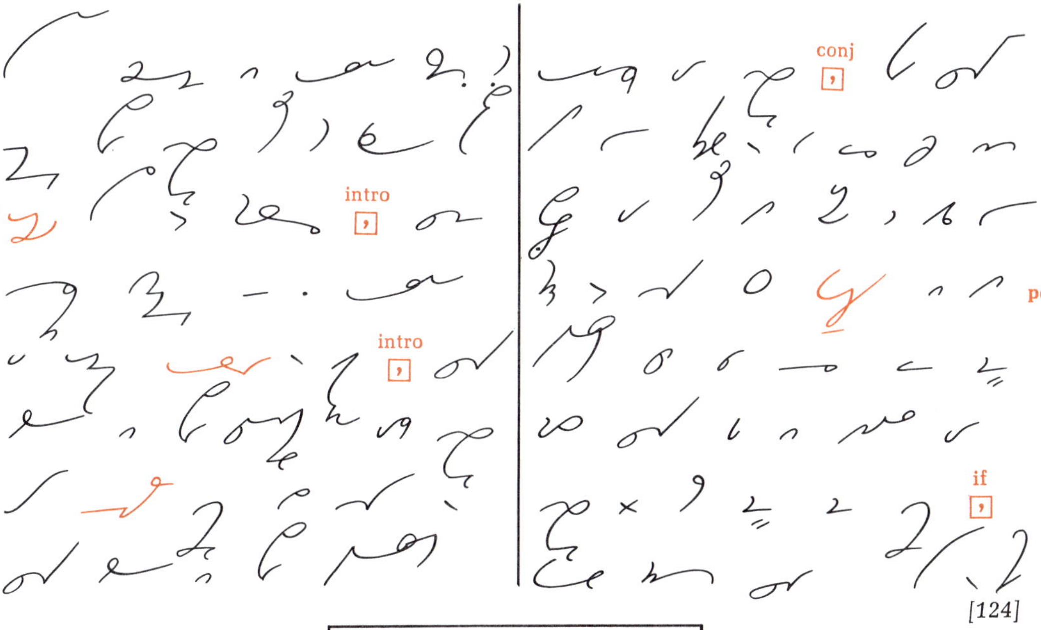
intro
intro
conj
if
[124]

476

pa·tience

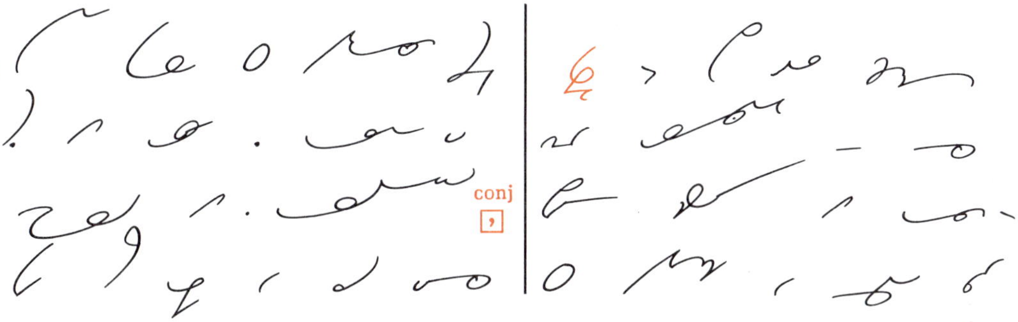
conj

LESSON 62

Building transcription skills

478 GRAMMAR CHECKUP | watch your grammar!

The writer who is careful about his grammar never uses:

party for **person**

> no

The party who called left no message.

> yes

The person who called left no message.

writer for **I**

> no

The writer appreciates your thoughtfulness.

> yes

I appreciate your thoughtfulness.

try and for **try to**

> no

Try and be on time.

> yes

Try to be on time.

the reason is because for **the reason is that**

> no

The reason for his action was because he was confused.

> yes

The reason for his action was that he was confused.

different than for **different from**

    no

The movie was different <u>than</u> any other I have ever seen.

    yes

The movie was different <u>from</u> any other I have ever seen.

those kind for **those kinds**

    no

Those <u>kind</u> of toys appeal to children.

    yes

Those <u>kinds</u> of toys appeal to children.

479

Business vocabulary builder	
resolution	A formal expression of opinion by an official body.
tract	An area of land.
reserved	Saved; kept.
decades	Periods of 10 years.

Reading and writing practice

conj

ef·fect

[143]

481

ap

wel·come

sug·gest·ing

as

as

dis·cussed

intro

ar·ea

ben·e·fit

ser

nonr

par

an·nu·al

[171]

482 [shorthand] set·tled, intro, per·son·al·ly, high-qual·i·ty *hyphenated before noun*, intro, nc [118]

483 tract, bought, site, nonr, piece, when [75]

484 en·gin·eer's   intro   re·fer·ring   if

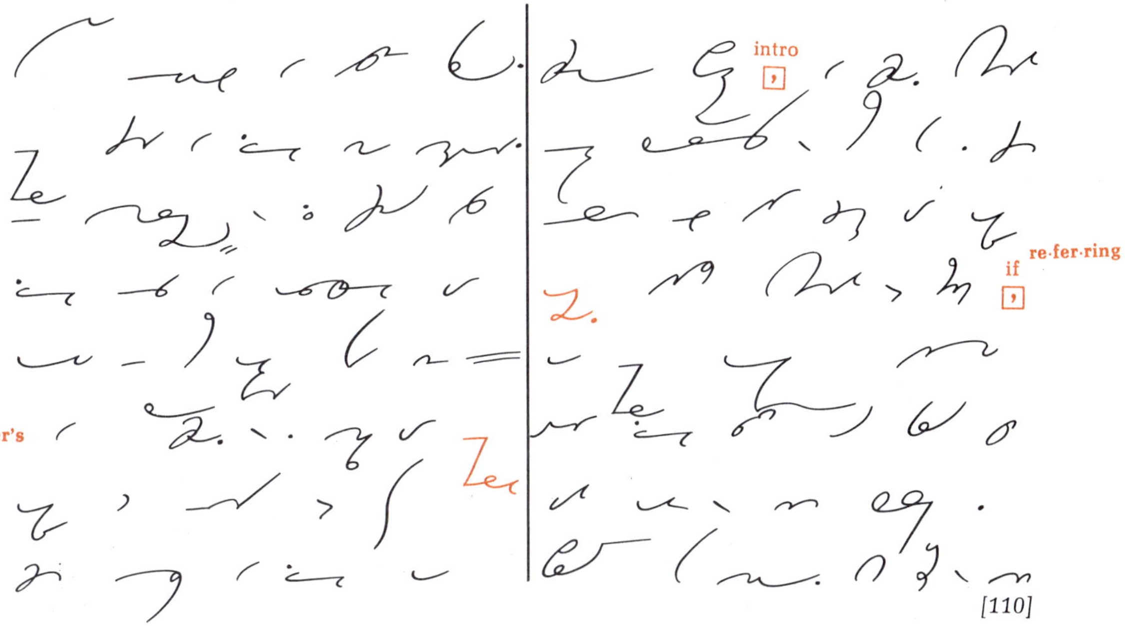

[110]

485

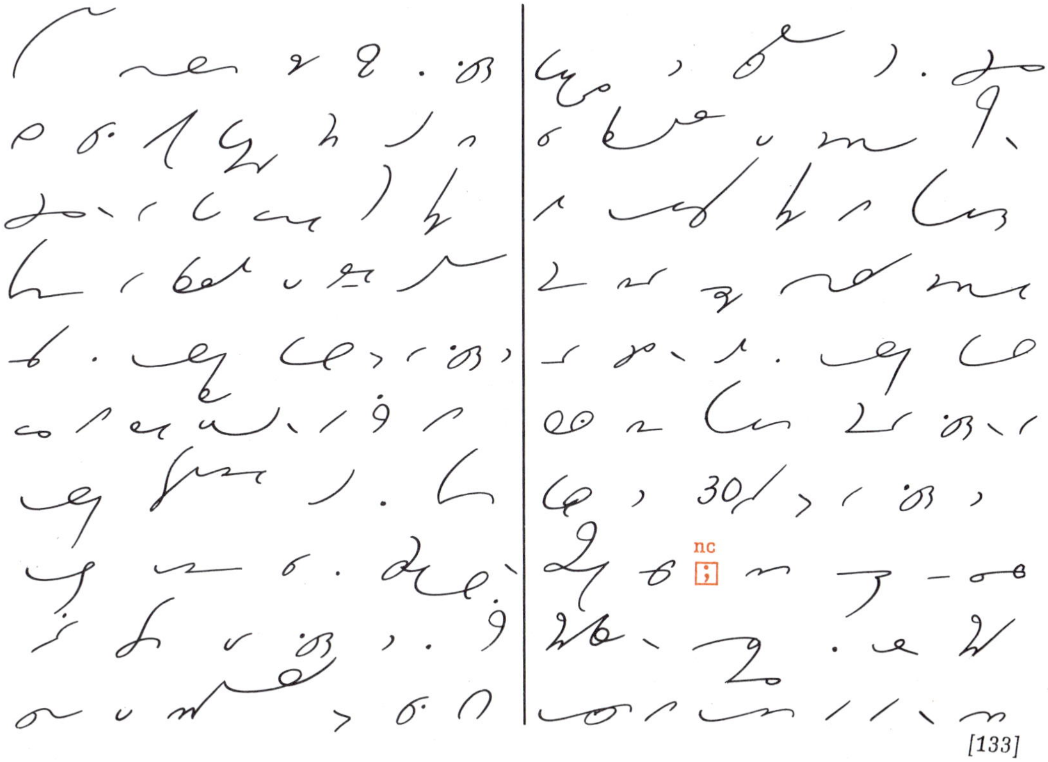

[133]

LESSON 63

Letter placement HINTS

By applying the suggestions for the placement of short, average, and long letters that were presented to you in earlier lessons, you will find that you can place *most* of your letters attractively on the page and *all* of them acceptably.

Occasionally, though, you may find that after typing the complimentary closing, the letter is slightly high on the page. When that happens, you can "pull the letter down" by allowing more space between the complimentary closing and the identification; that is, instead of allowing the customary four spaces between the complimentary closing and the identification, allow five or six; instead of typing the initials two spaces below the identification, type them three or four spaces below.

On the other hand, if you find that after typing the complimentary closing the letter appears to be *low* on the page, you can "lift it" by decreasing the space for the signature between the closing and the identification to three, even two if necessary, blank lines. Also, you can place the initials on the same line as the identification.

Customary

```
If there are any specific questions that I can answer for you regarding
your problem, I hope you will not hesitate to write me.
                                                                        1
                                Very truly yours,                       2
                                                                        3
                                                                        4
                                                                        5
                                John Jones                              6
                                Vice President                          7
                                                                        8
JJ:cb                                                                   9
```

Low

```
If there are any specific questions that I can answer for you regarding
your problem, I hope you will not hesitate to write me.
                                                                        1
                                Very truly yours,                       2
                                                                        3
                                John Jones                              4
JJ:cb                           Vice President                          5
```

High

```
If there are any specific questions that I can answer for you regarding
your problem, I hope you will not hesitate to write me.
                                                                    1
                            Very truly yours,                       2
                                                                    3
                                                                    4
                                                                    5
                                                                    6
                                                                    7
                            John Jones                              8
                            Vice President                          9
                                                                   10
                                                                   11
                                                                   12
JJ:cb                                                              13
```

Also, as you gain experience as a transcriber, you will be able to obtain more attractively placed letters by deviating slightly from the placement suggestions you have received for short, average, and long letters. For example, when a letter contains only 70 or 80 words, your experience will tell you that you will get a better-looking letter by starting the inside address 4½ inches from the top of the paper rather than 4 inches, as suggested for short letters.

When a letter contains 130 words, you will get a better-looking letter by starting the inside address 4 inches from the top of the paper rather than the suggested 3½ inches for average letters.

Building transcription skills

486 OFFICE-STYLE DICTATION | instructions during dictation (continued)

Some dictators interrupt their dictation to give instructions about spelling, punctuation, and other details of transcription. Always record these instructions, no matter how elementary they may seem to you.

If your dictator spells a proper name or a word, record the spelling in longhand immediately above your shorthand outline. If he dictates punctuation, place the marks in your notes, encircling them so that you do not try to read them as shorthand outlines.

ILLUSTRATION OF OFFICE-STYLE DICTATION

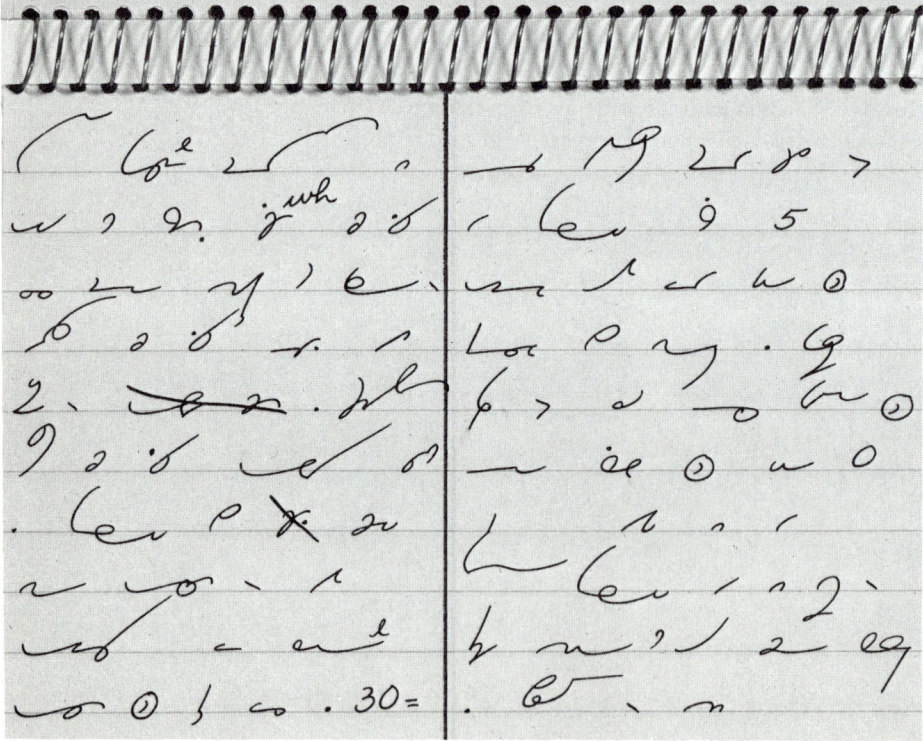

487 Business vocabulary builder

agenda A list of things to be done.
minutes A record of the proceedings of a meeting.
completion Fulfillment.

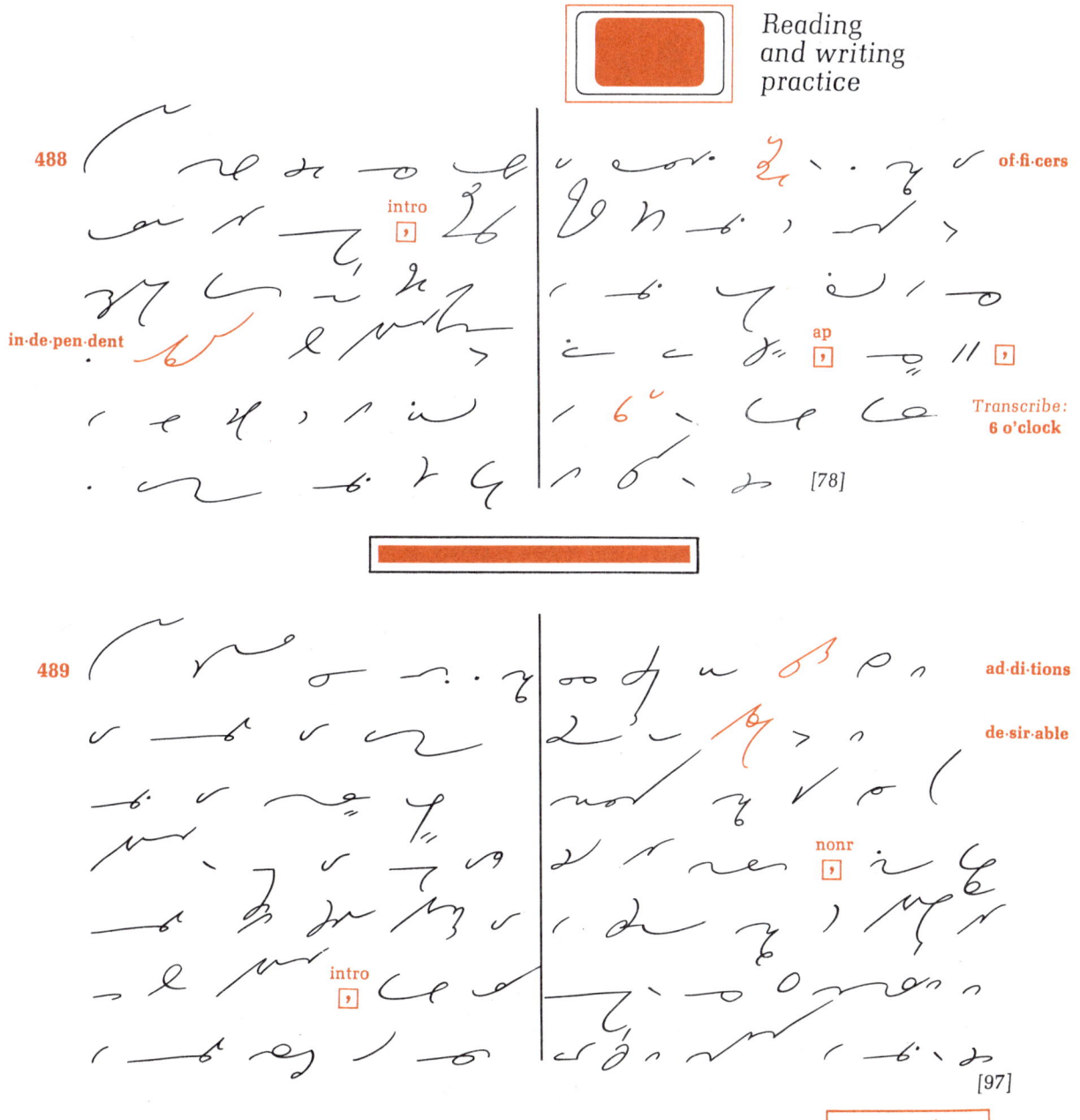

490

[shorthand] intro, and o, welcome, ap, [118]

issuing, if

491

[shorthand] intro, completion, conj

intro, suffered embarrassment, conj

crowd

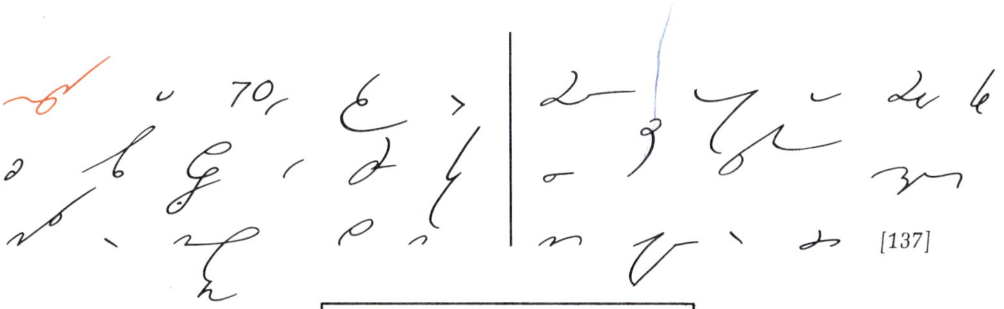

[137]

492

ed·i·tors

as·sis·tant

us·able

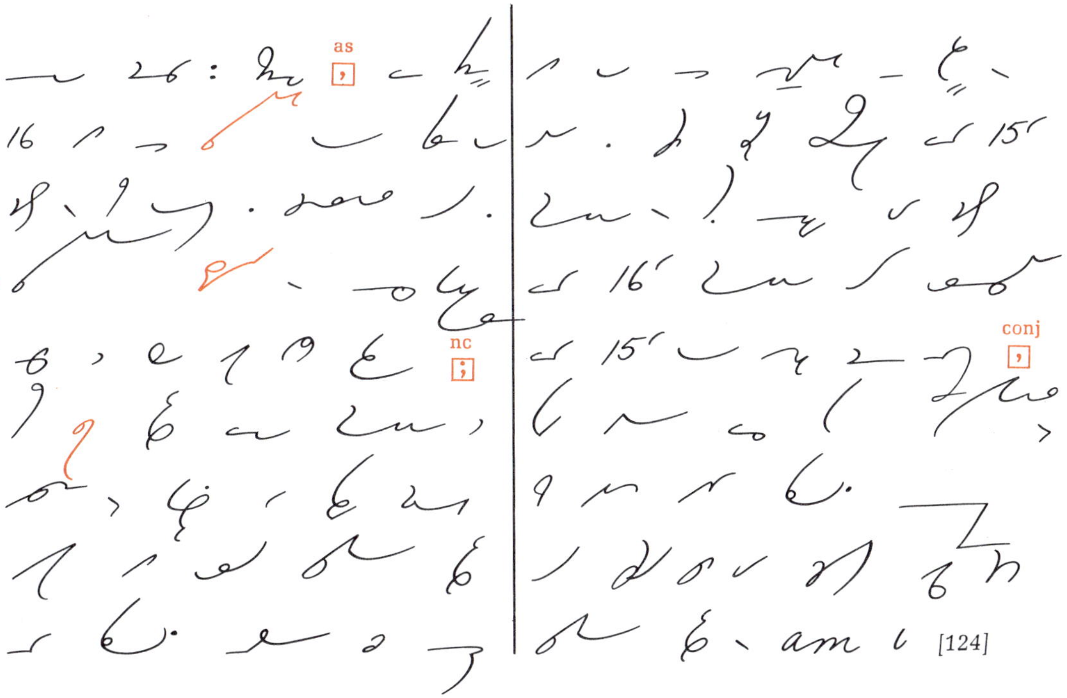

[124]

493

mod·el

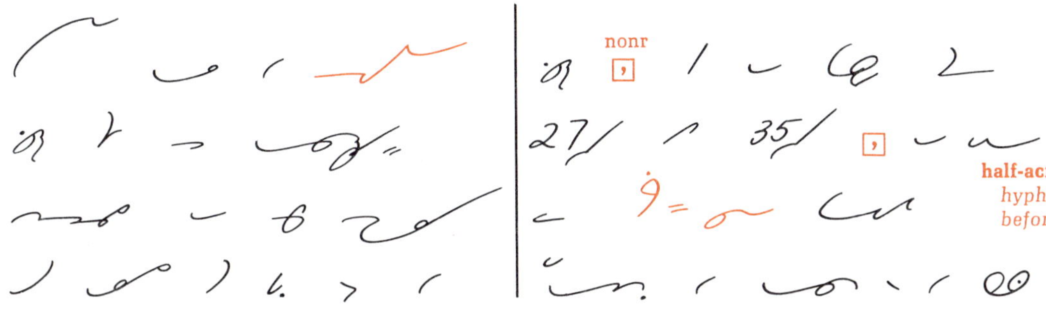

half-acre
*hyphenated
before noun*

LESSON 64

site

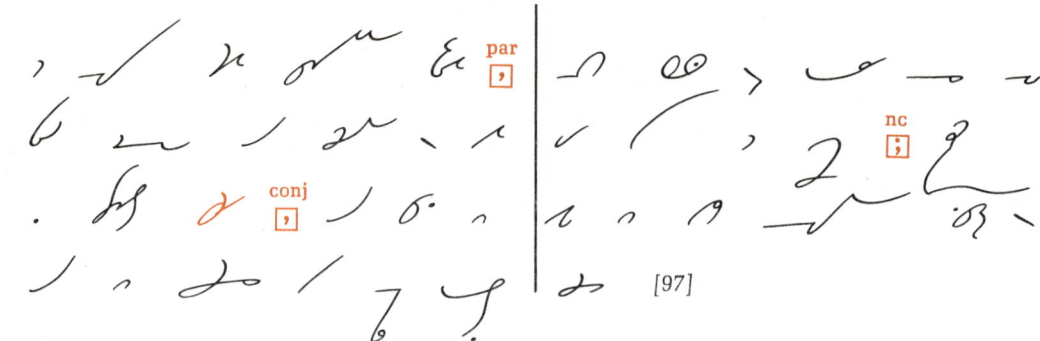

494 Transcription Quiz Can you supply the necessary punctuation and the two words that are missing from the shorthand?

    Also, can you find the mistake that the dictator made in the third paragraph—a mistake that you, as an efficient stenographer, should discover and correct?

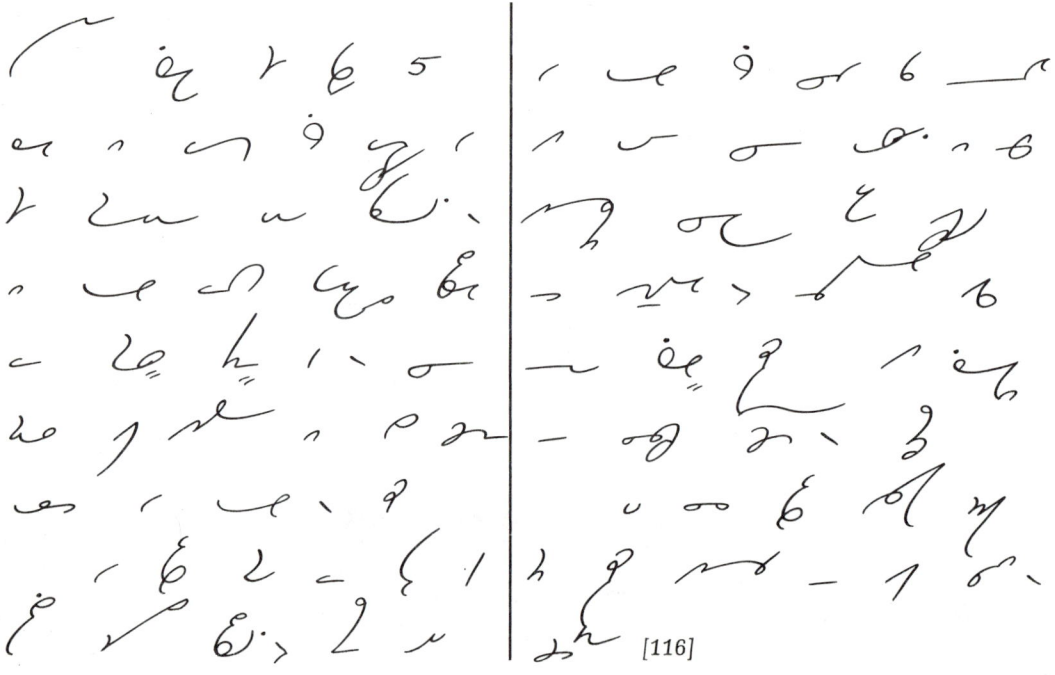

Building transcription skills

495 WORD CHAIN

The words in the following Word Chain refer to "that which a party owes." Notice the difference in the shades of meaning between words in the group.

debt is usually used to mean a definite amount owed for goods or property or services. Not all debts are obligations.

He is $110 in debt.

arrears is used to mean that part of a debt has been paid and that the payment of the remaining part of the debt is overdue.

He made his February and March payments on time, but as of today, his account is $200 in arrears.

indebtedness is used to mean the total amount owed to one creditor or to all creditors.

The indebtedness of the corporation as of January 1 was $3,450,000.

obligation is used to mean a bond or a contract or some similar formal acknowledgment of an amount that is to be paid.

He was under obligation to pay the $600 note by November 6.

496

Business vocabulary builder	
	zoning Dividing an area into sections for specific types of construction.
	counsel Lawyer or lawyers conducting a case.
	reassessment The placing of a new value upon property for the purpose of taxation.

Reading and writing practice

497

498

499

brief·ly
zon·ing

sum·ma·rize

acres

re·zoned

quar·ter-acre
hyphenated
before noun

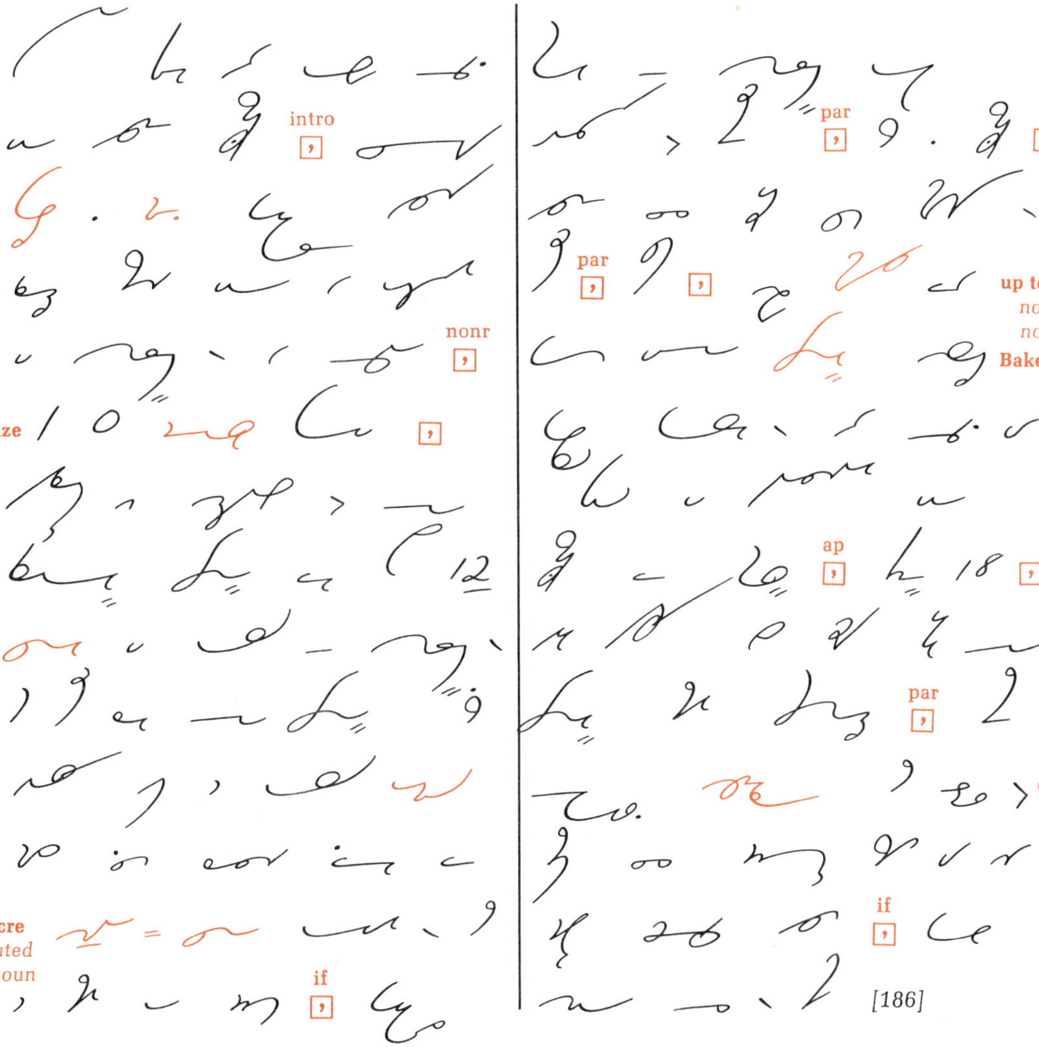

intro
nonr
if
par
par
ap
par
if
[186]

up to date
no noun,
no hyphen
Baker's

coun·sel

500

re·as·sess·ment

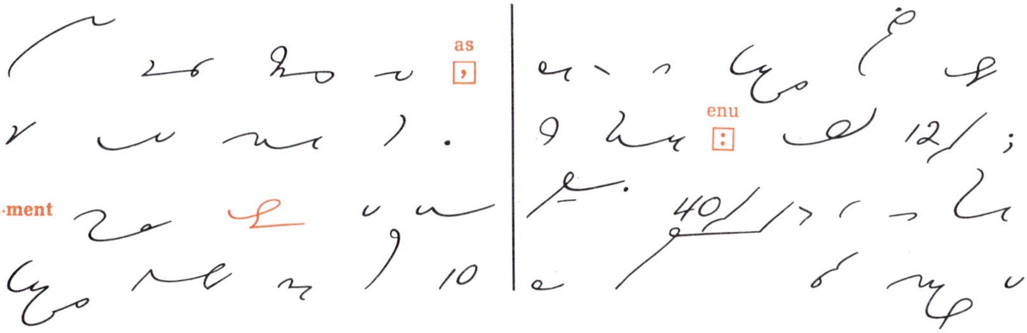

as
enu

lo·cal
ex·haus·tive

nec·es·sar·i·ly

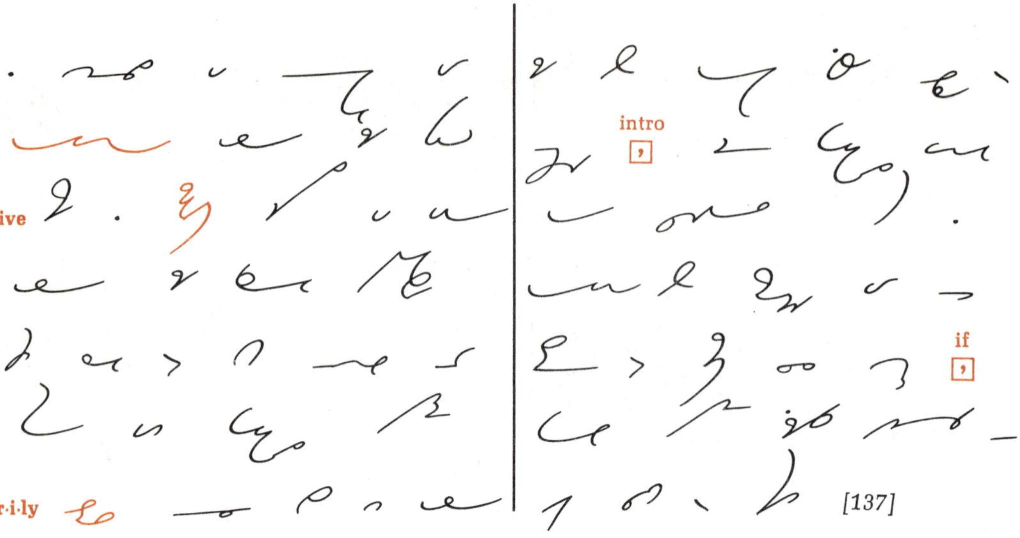

intro

if

[137]

501

fi·nal·ly

piece

conj

de·vel·op·ment

site

enu

when

if

[108]

340 | LESSON 65

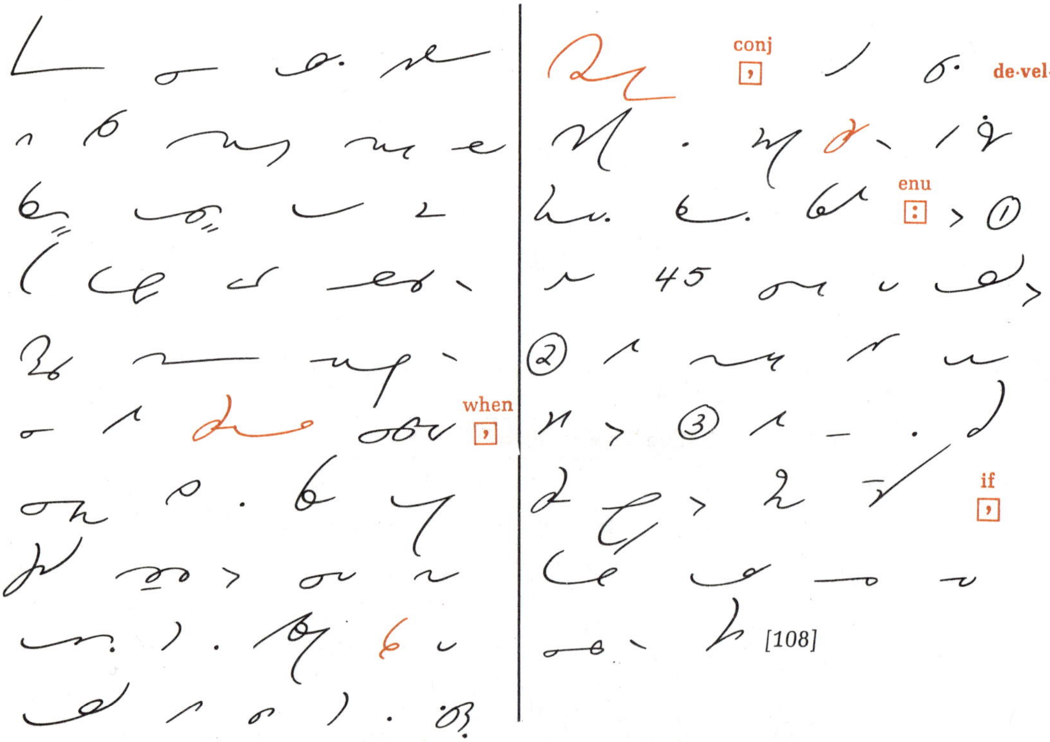

502

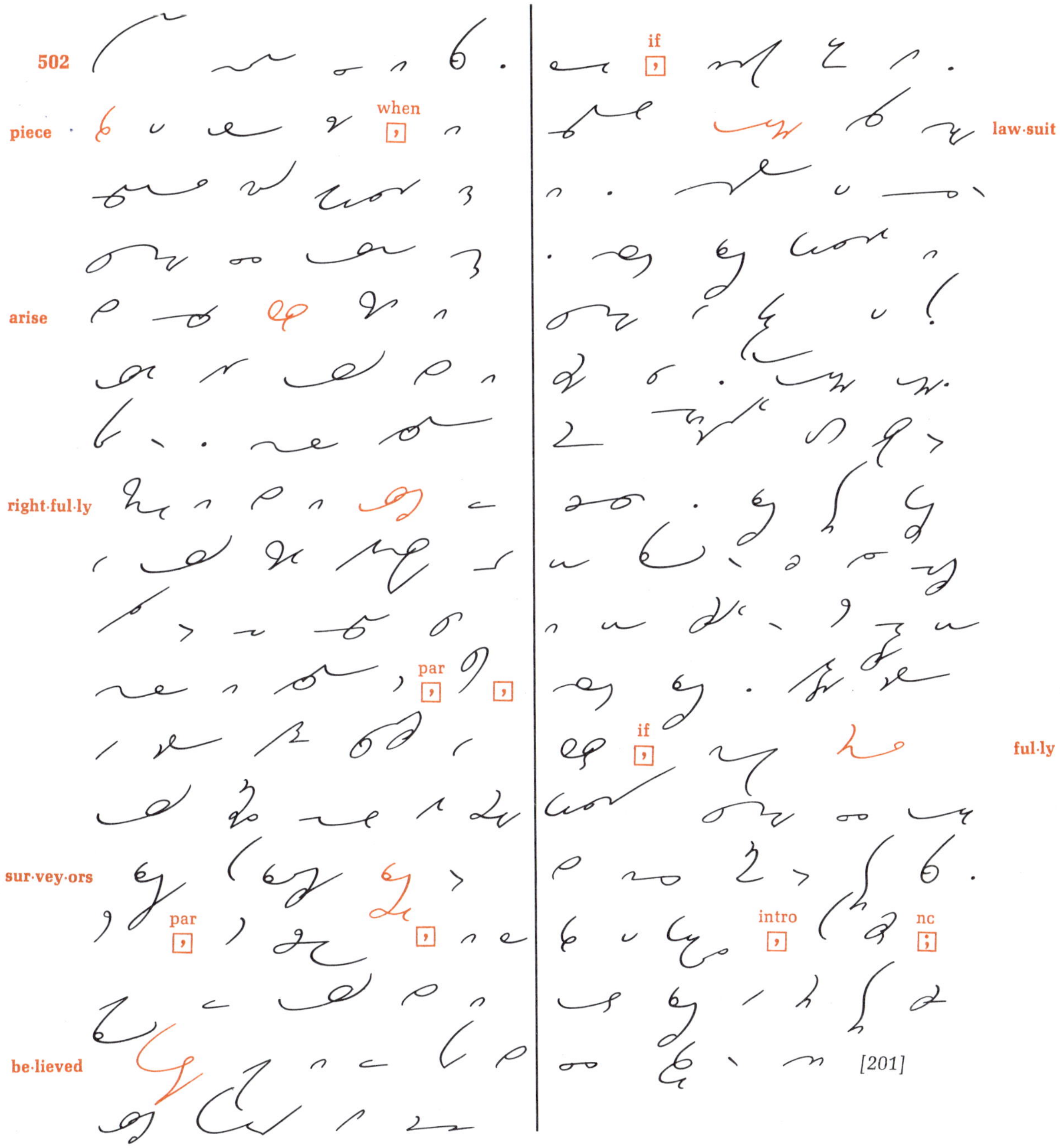

[Shorthand outlines with marginal word hints: piece, when, arise, rightfully, par, surveyors, par, believed, if, law-suit, if, fully, intro, nc]

[201]

LESSON 65

Implied instructions

In the very first letter that Mr. Davis dictated, he mentioned that he was enclosing a booklet that described the company's products. Ellen transcribed the letter accurately but did not enclose the booklet. Her employer signed and mailed the letter without noticing that the booklet had not been enclosed. When the customer received the letter without the booklet, he was considerably annoyed. He had to take time to write another letter, explaining that the booklet had not been enclosed. As the customer represented a very good account, Mr. Davis, too, was considerably annoyed. The results of Ellen's failure to make the enclosure might have been serious.

"When I say that I am enclos-

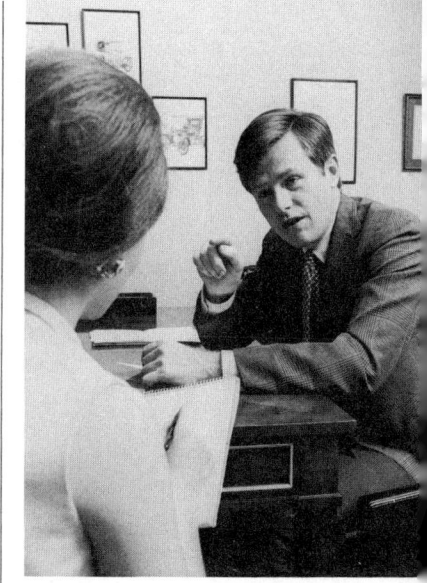

ing something or am going to do something, I don't mean literally that I am going to do it," Mr. Davis told Ellen. "I mean that something is going to be done, and it is your responsibility to do it or to see that it is done."

Thereafter, when her employer dictated:

"I am enclosing a booklet," Ellen made certain that the booklet was in the envelope when she took in the letter to be signed.

"I will see that each salesman gets a copy of the bulletin," she saw to it that the bulletin was duplicated and a copy sent to each salesman.

"I am making a reservation for April 10 at the Nelson Hotel," she either made the reservation herself or placed a memorandum on Mr. Davis's desk reminding him to do so.

"I will meet you at the airport when your plane arrives," she noted the fact on his calendar pad and then reminded him of his engagement in plenty of time for him to meet the plane when it arrived.

After she had carried out the instructions implied in the dictation, she always noted on the carbon the action she took, together with the date.

Some secretaries make doubly sure that they do not forget to take care of implied instructions—they make some indication at the end of the dictated letter to remind themselves, such as, "send catalog"; "send salesmen bulletins"; or "make hotel reservations."

Education

Building transcription skills

503 SIMILAR-WORDS DRILL | **principal, principle**

principal (*noun*)   The amount of money invested or lent on which interest is paid; the head of a school.

The principal amounted to $5,000; the interest on that principal was $100.
Henry Nelson is principal of the high school.

principal (*adjective*)   Main; chief.

My principal job will be addressing high school assemblies.

principle   Rule of action; a law of conduct; a fundamental truth.

I cannot give you any definite principles to guide you.
He is a man of high moral principles.

504

Business vocabulary builder	
novice	Beginner.
tangible	Material; real.
expeditiously	Speedily; rapidly.

Reading and writing practice

505

re·cruit

proud

ser
ap
prin·ci·pals
coun·sel·ors
ca·reers

[94]

506

com·mer·cial
as·sis·tant
than

intro
nonr

when
conj
en·cour·age

LESSON 66 | 345

if

[117]

507

de·scrib·ing

conj

conj

par

New Delhi

[127]

508

as

conj

prin·ci·pal

its

ap

LESSON 66 | 347

Building transcription skills

510 SPELLING FAMILIES | forming -ed and -ing derivatives of words ending in r

When the last syllable of a word ending in *r*, preceded by a single vowel, is accented, the *r* is doubled in forming derivatives in *-ed* and *-ing*.

con·fer	con·ferred	con·fer·ring
in·cur	in·curred	in·cur·ring
oc·cur	oc·curred	oc·cur·ring
pre·fer	pre·ferred	pre·fer·ring
re·fer	re·ferred	re·fer·ring

When the last syllable is not accented, the *r* is not doubled.

dif·fer	dif·fered	dif·fer·ing
flat·ter	flat·tered	flat·ter·ing
hin·der	hin·dered	hin·der·ing
of·fer	of·fered	of·fer·ing

511 **Business vocabulary builder**

alumni Graduates of a school or college.

matriculation fee Fee required to register or enroll in a college or university.

phase Aspect; stage.

Reading and writing practice

512

Transcribe:
2 p.m.

ap

alum·ni
wives

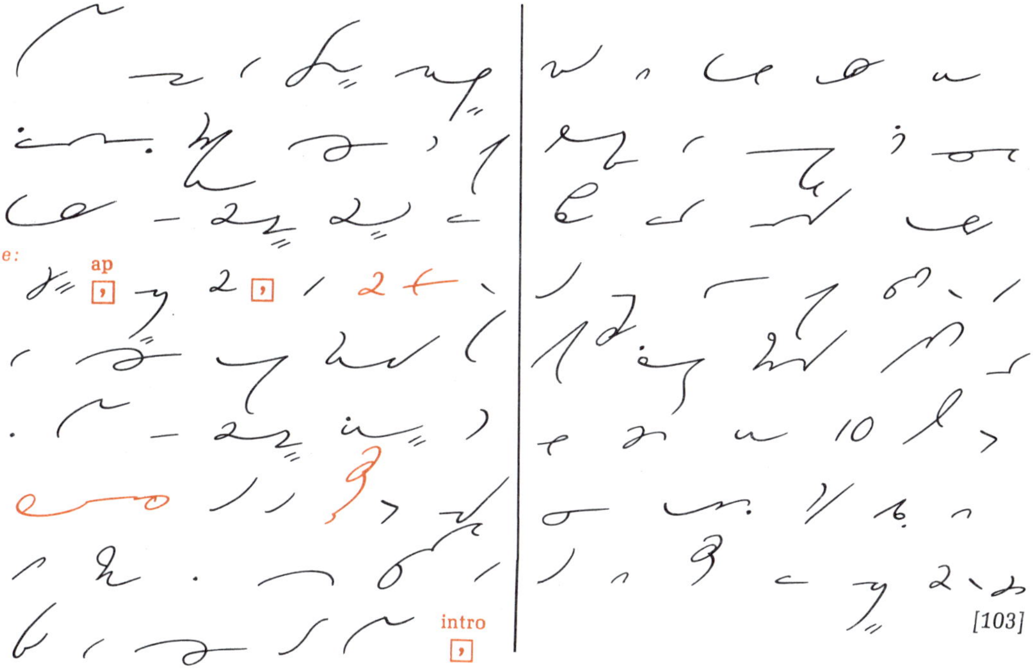

intro

[103]

513

son's

intro

can·cel·la·tions

be·gin·ning

as

if

re·ward·ing

LESSON 67

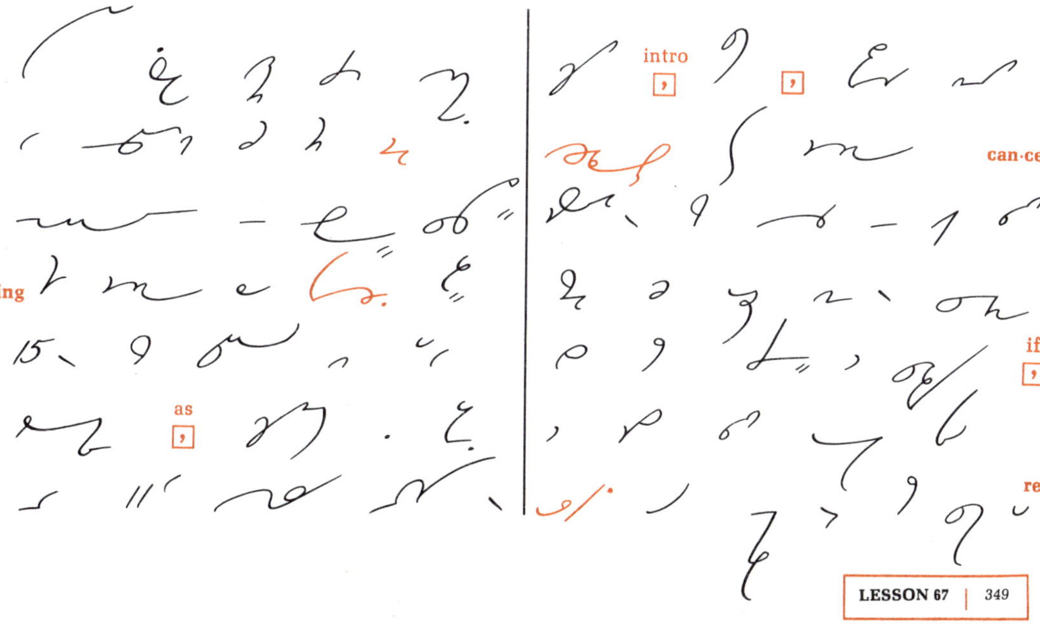

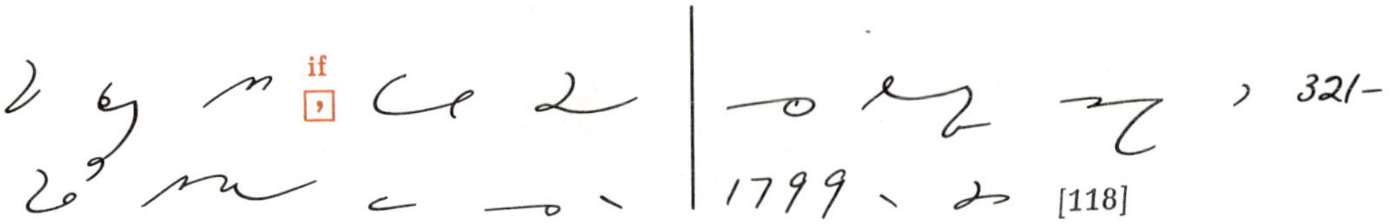

[shorthand content - not transcribable]

350 | **LESSON 67**

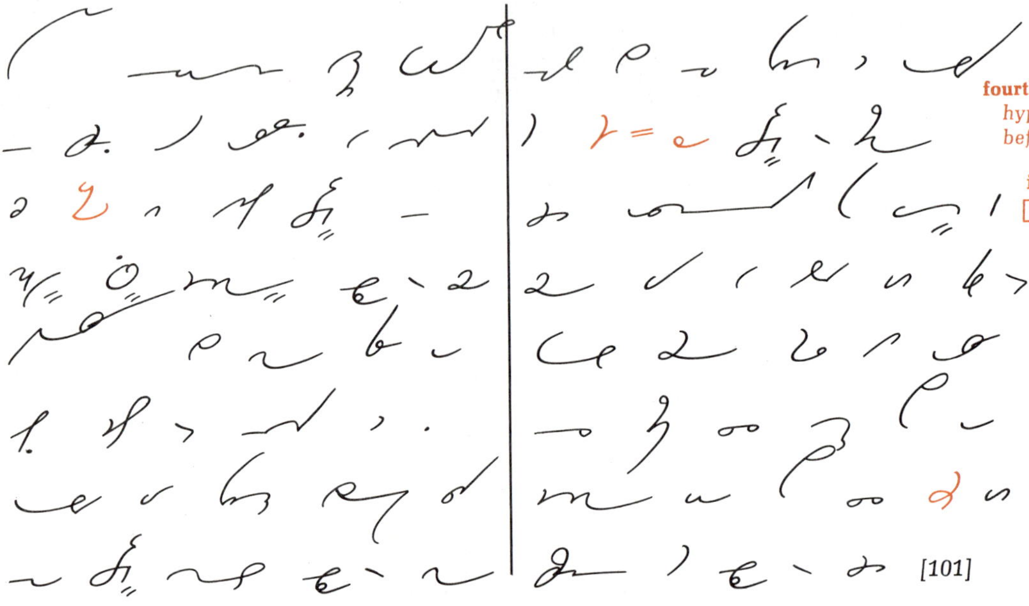

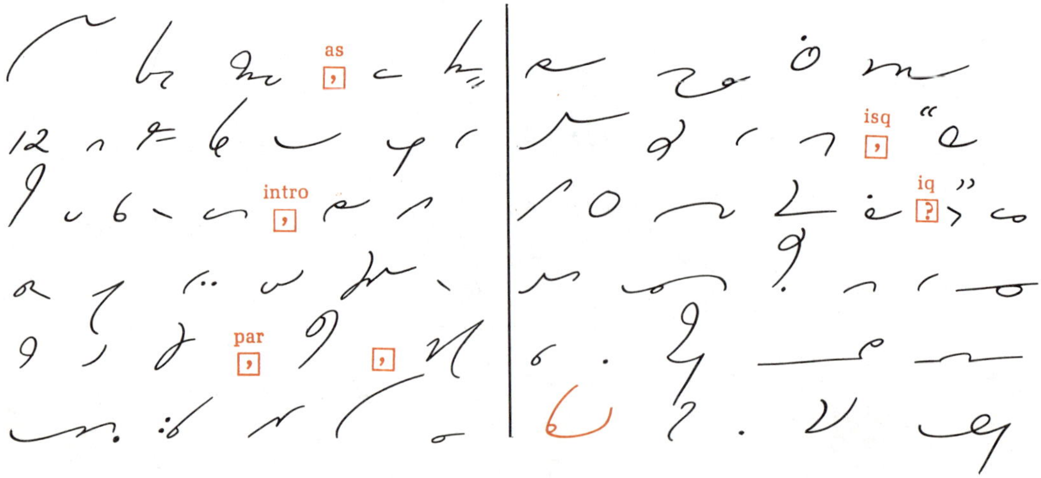

enough [141] pol·i·cies chil·dren's par enu

516 con·fer·ring con·ver·sa·tion ap its if [101]

517 ad·mis·sion [44] con·fi·den·tial

Building transcription skills

518 ACCURACY PRACTICE

Follow the practice procedures outlined on page 154.

GROUP 1	GROUP 2	GROUP 3
office	thick	at least
official	thin	at last

practice drill

1 The office records were destroyed in the fire. The official records were destroyed in the fire.
2 The paper is too thick for our purpose. The paper is too thin for our purpose.
3 I can at least buy my own home. I can at last buy my own home.

519

Business vocabulary builder	
implored	Begged.
sponsoring	Backing; accepting responsibility for.
concise	Brief but complete.

Reading and writing practice

520 his·to·ry, conj, conj, if, when, ap [127]

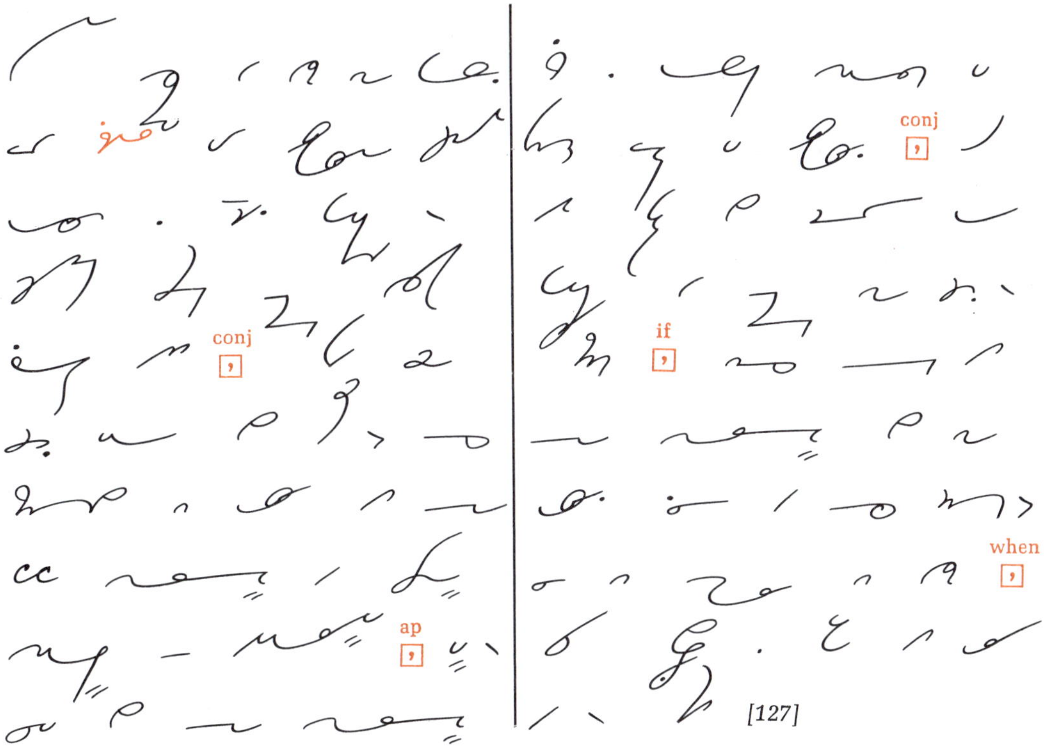

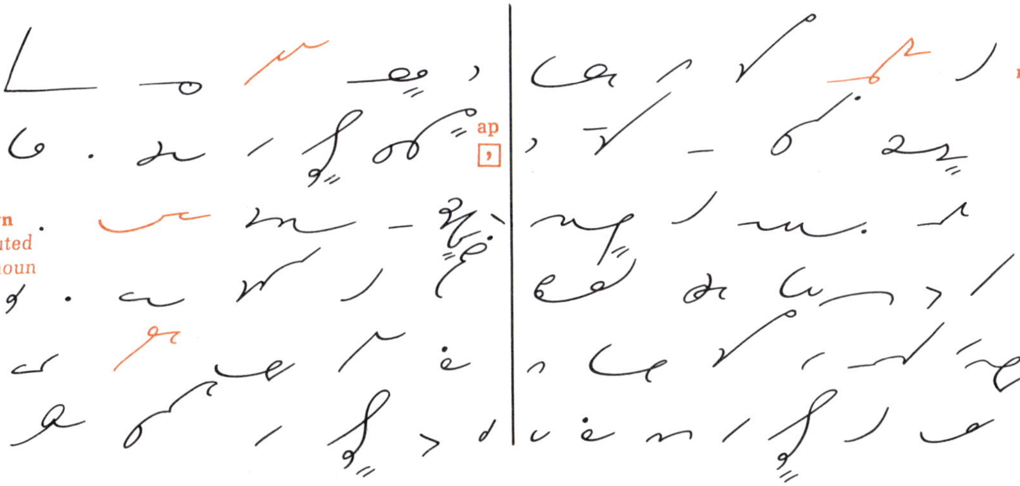

521 daugh·ter, ap, med·i·cine, well-known *hyphenated before noun*, dean's admission [shorthand] if, lacking [113]

522 [shorthand] if, intro, Chicago, hiring, privilege, implored, 743-1212 [133]

523 company's, ser, assistants

[129]

524

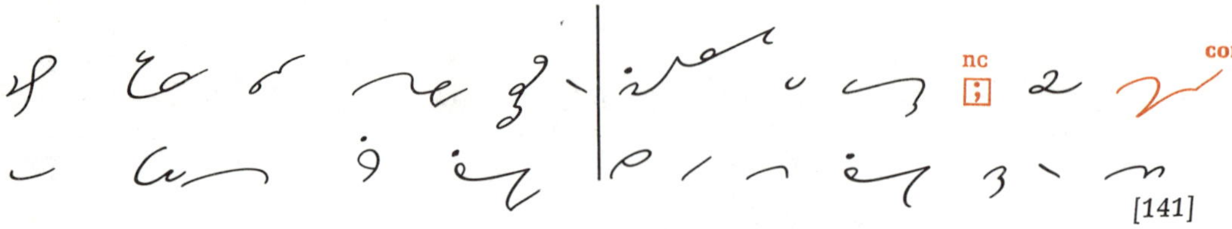

[141]

525
well-planned 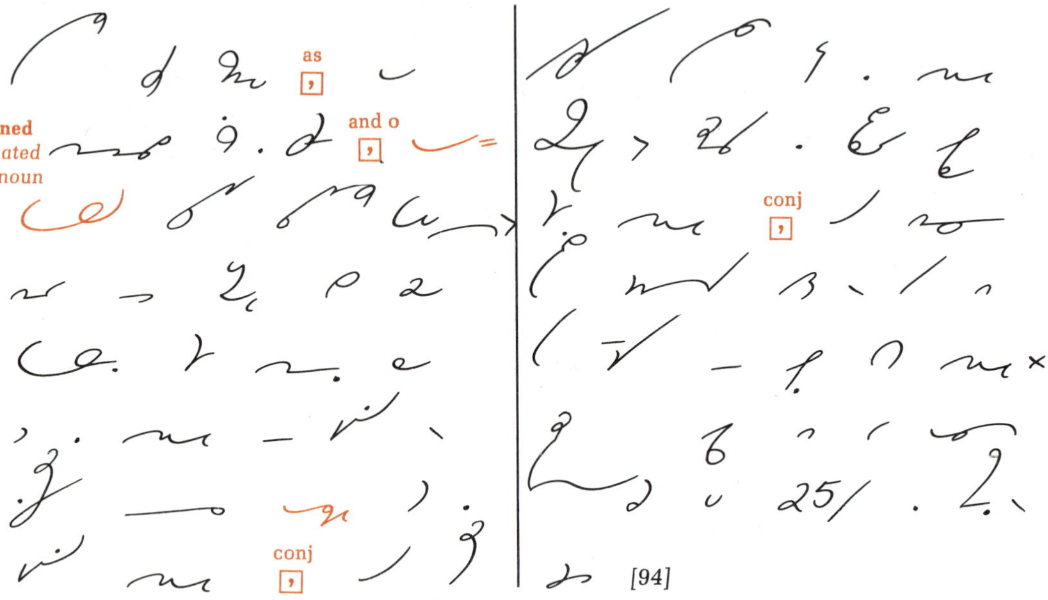
hyphenated before noun

re·quests

[94]

con·fi·dent

356 | LESSON 68

Building transcription skills

526 OFFICE-STYLE DICTATION | **instructions during dictation (continued)**

The types of instructions to which you should pay very close attention are those that require you to do something *before* you transcribe. In the middle of a letter, for example, the dictator may say, "Send a carbon of this letter to Jones." Because you must know this *before* you start transcribing the letter, you should leave a few blank lines at the head of each letter to record this type of information.

ILLUSTRATION OF OFFICE-STYLE DICTATION

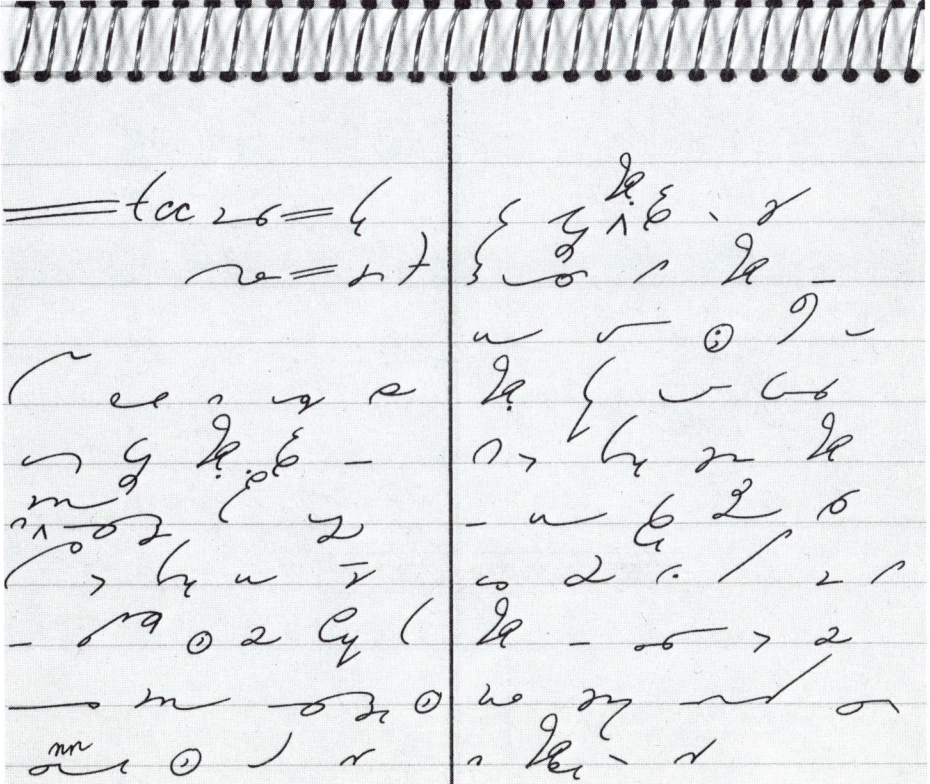

527 Business vocabulary builder

refresher course Course which reacquaints one with material previously studied.
derived Obtained; drawn from.
overwhelming Overpowering.
indispensable Essential; necessary.

Reading and writing practice

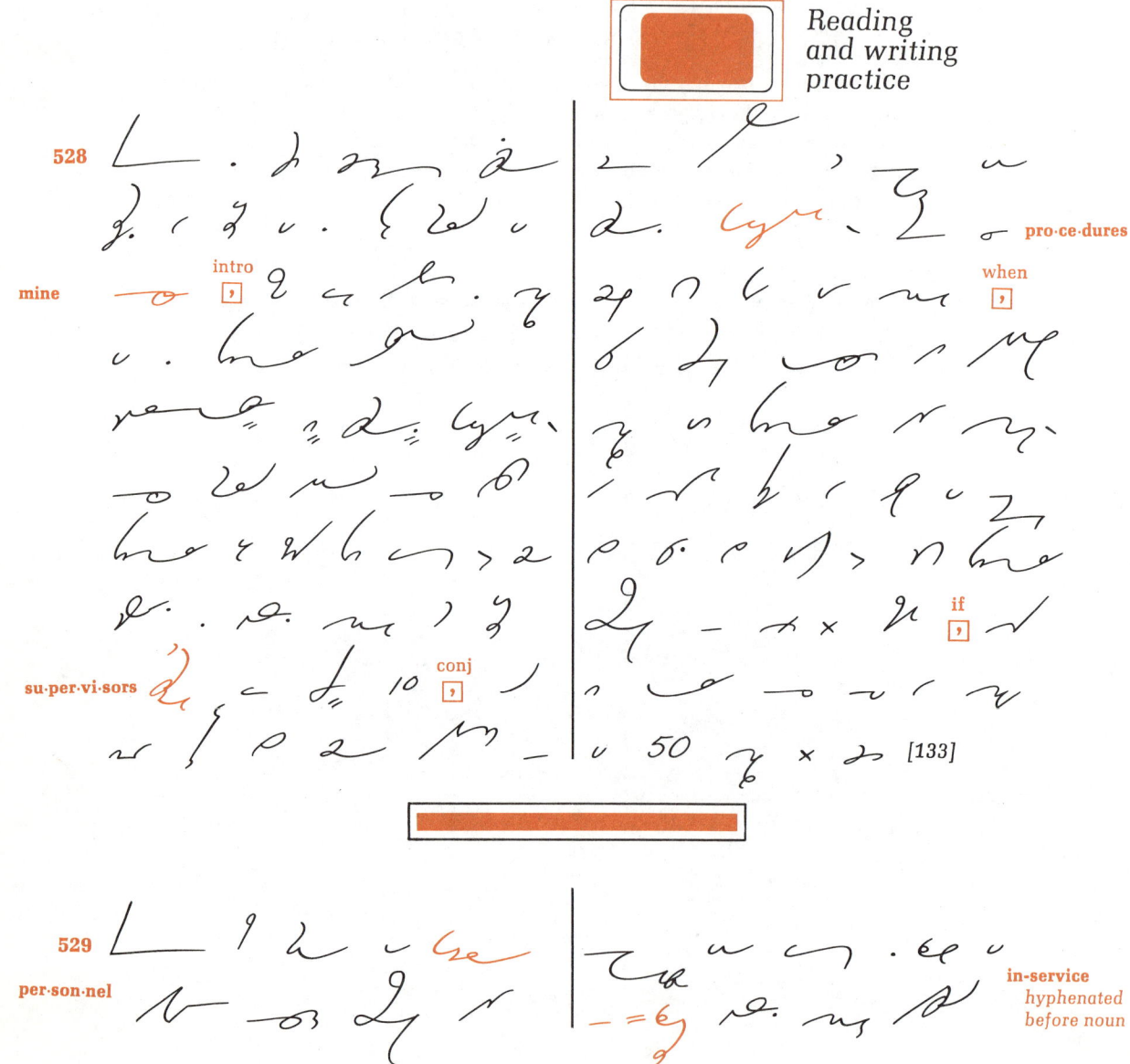

their

tech·niques

sub·scrib·ers   intro ,

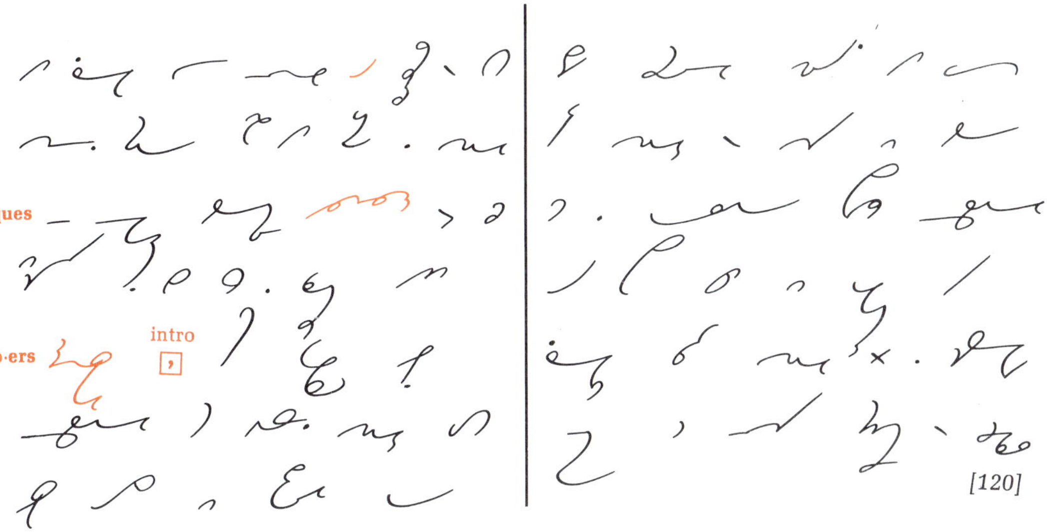

[120]

530

cler·i·cal

hours   conj ,

if ,

[143]

LESSON 69 | 359

Transcribe: $1

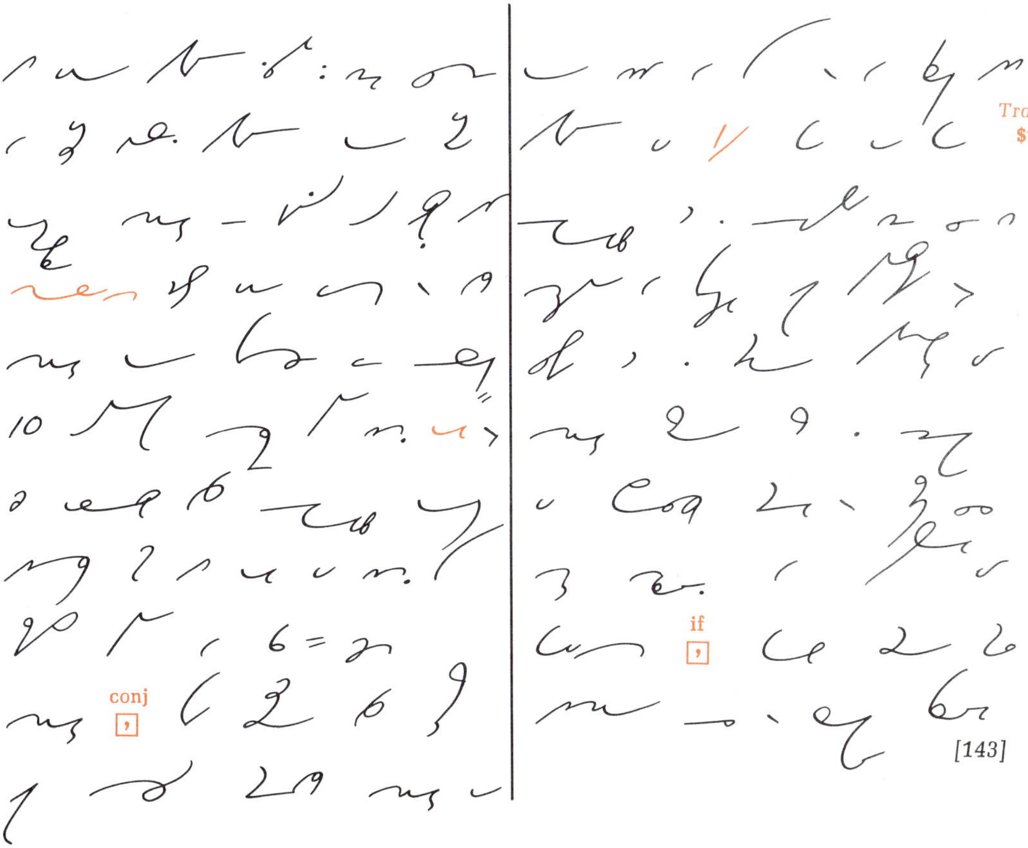

531

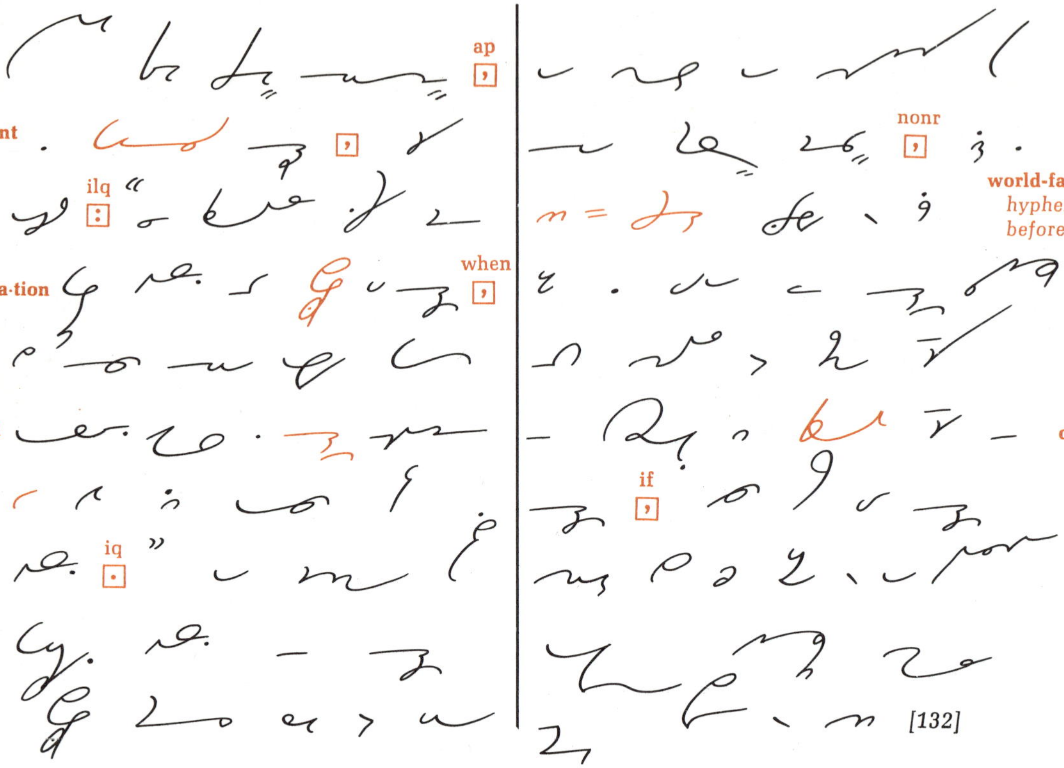

prom·i·nent

ap·pre·ci·a·tion

mu·si·cal

than

world-fa·mous
hyphenated before noun

child's

[132]

532

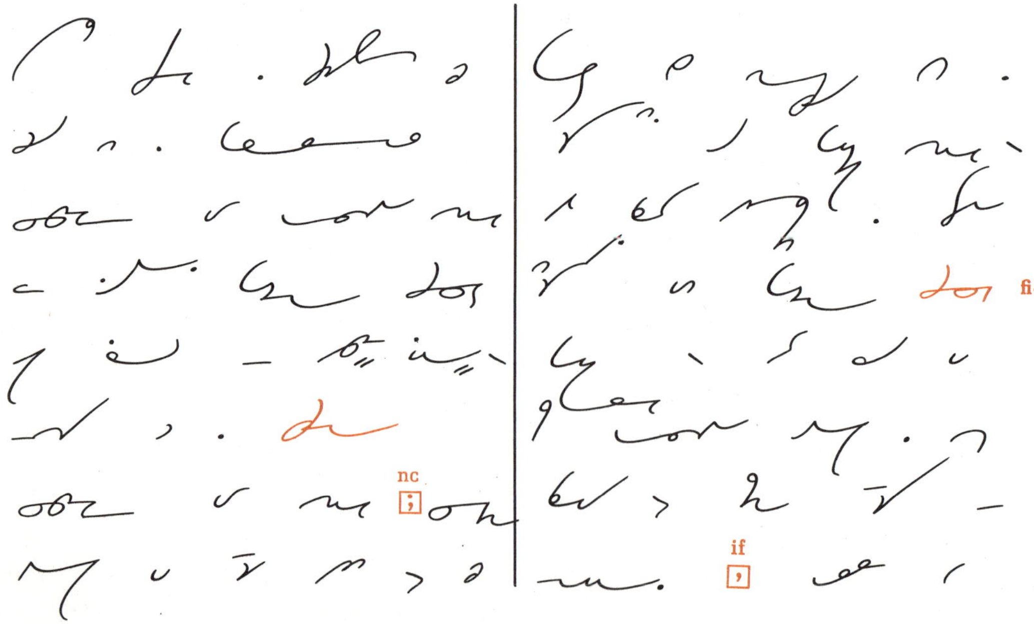

fi·nal

fi·nan·cial

LESSON 69

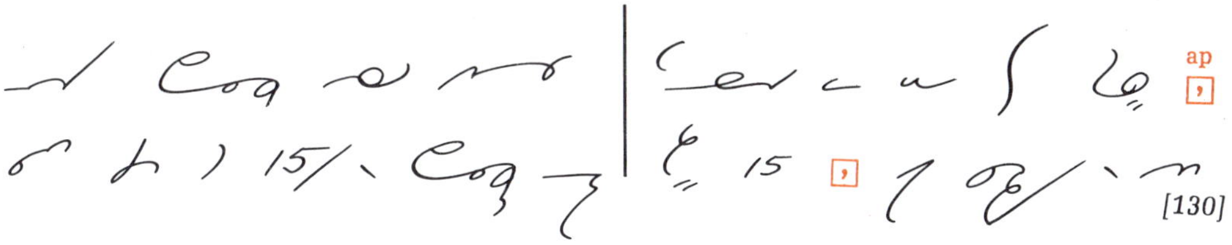

[130]

533 Transcription Quiz Can you supply the correct punctuation and the missing words in this letter?

Also, the dictator made an error in grammar. Can you find it?

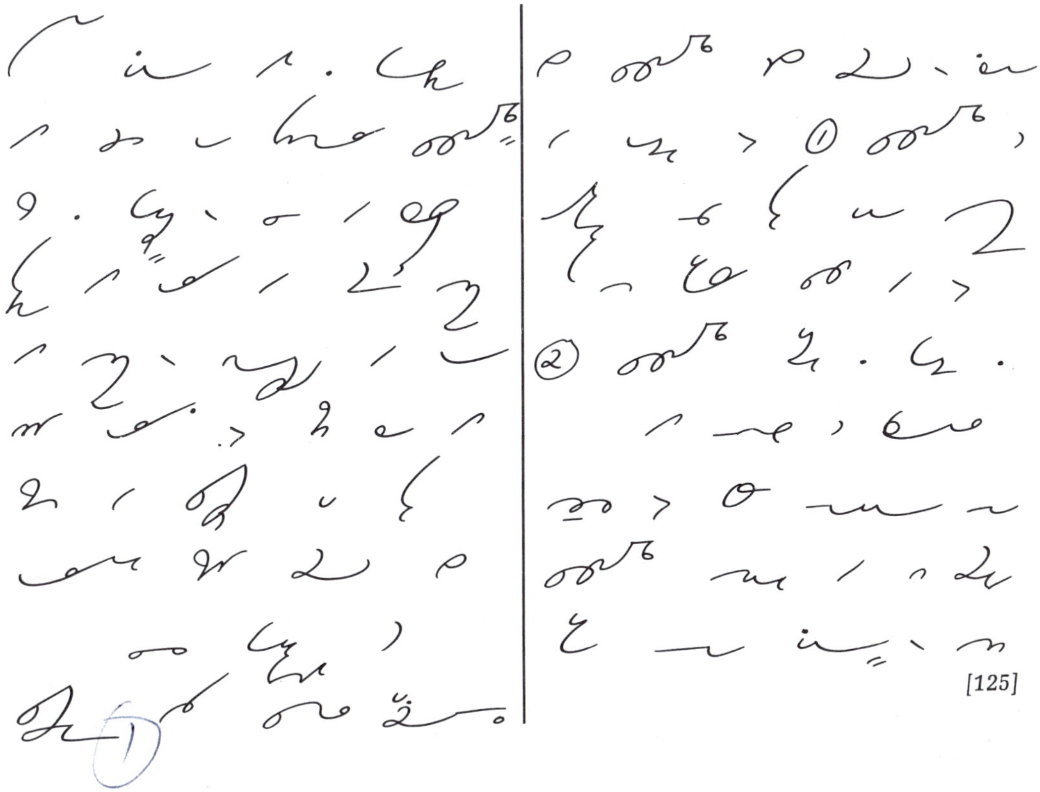

[125]

LESSON 70

Building transcription skills

534 COMMON PREFIXES | pro-

pro- In many words in the English language, *pro-* means *before, ahead, forward, future.*

progress   A moving ahead; a going forward.
produce   To bring forward; to make.
proceed   To go ahead.
program   A plan for the future.
promote   To move ahead.
prospect   A possible future customer.

535

Business vocabulary builder	
probation	A trial period.
violation	Infringement.
behavior	Conduct.

Reading and writing practice

536
per·mis·sion

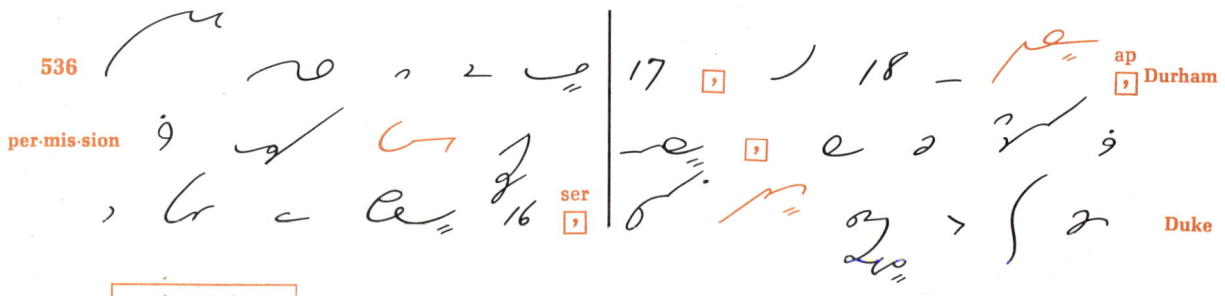

intro

if

[78]

537

conj

be·hav·ior

re·main·der

if

Frank's

[78]

538

daugh·ter

Eas·ter

over·night

re·ply·ing

[86]

539 [shorthand] *Father's* ... [shorthand with annotations: as, ap, 18] | 5:30 p.m. [shorthand with annotations: ap, conj, guest] [138]

540 *an·nu·al*, *caf·e·te·ri·a*, *li·brary* [shorthand with annotations: ap, 18, 6:45] | [shorthand with annotations: ser, prin·ci·pal, ap, 30]

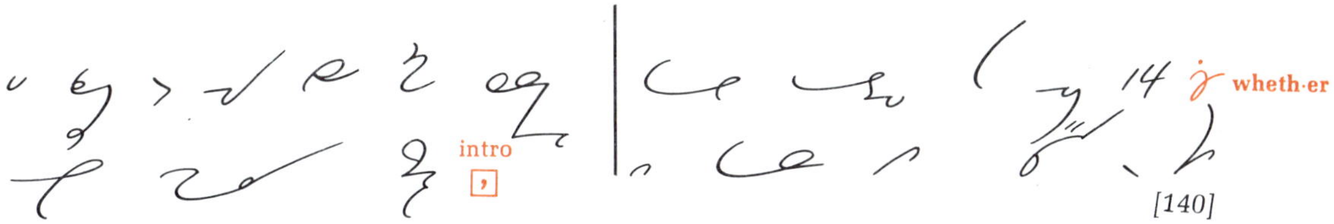

[140] wheth·er

541 prin·ci·pal ap intro par [95] Hoffman's

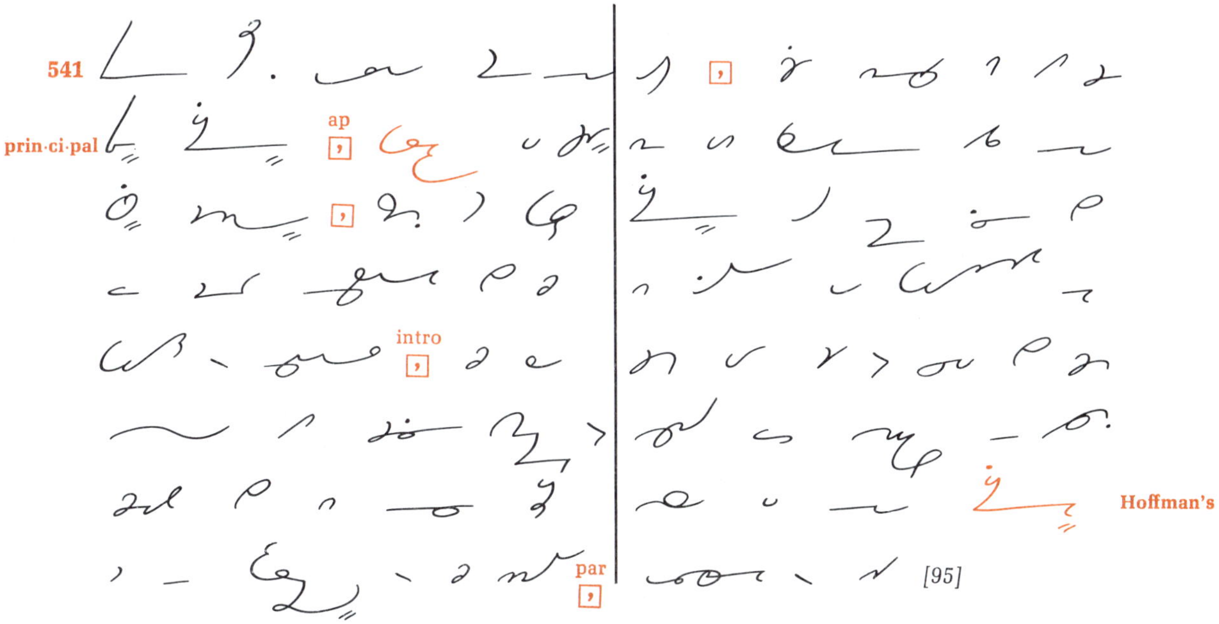

542 ser gram·mar punc·tu·a·tion [77]

LESSON 70

Ellen Gardiner, dictator's helper

One of Ellen's first jobs each morning is to open all of Mr. Davis's mail—all, that is, except letters marked "Personal" or "Confidential." She knows from experience that some of the mail will require immediate attention, some can wait a while, and some can be read at Mr. Davis's leisure. Therefore, she arranges the mail in that order before she places it on his desk.

With some letters she does more than place them on his

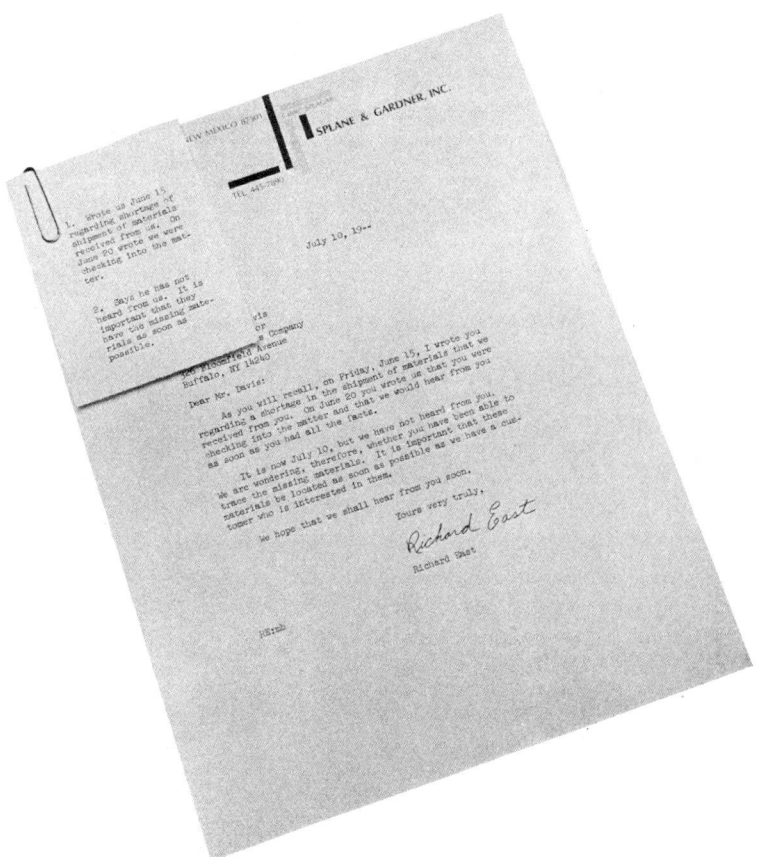

desk: she gathers all the information that her employer needs before he can answer the letters.

For example, when a creditor writes that an overdue bill for $100 for advertising placed in his magazine has not been paid, she checks to see whether a bill was actually received. If it was, she finds out from the accounting department whether it was paid and, if not, why not. She then types this information on a sheet of paper and attaches it to the letter of complaint or jots it down at the foot of the letter. In some cases she even obtains all related correspondence from the file and attaches it to the incoming letter. Thus, when her employer is ready to dictate the answer to that letter, he has all the information he needs at his fingertips.

By gathering all this material beforehand, Ellen is actually helping herself, for she then knows just about what the dictated letter will contain. This information, of course, will be of great help to her when she begins to transcribe the letter.

By gathering all the information necessary to answer certain types of letters and by observing, through Mr. Davis's dictation, how those letters are answered, Ellen can look forward to the thrill one day of hearing her employer say, "You write the letter, Ellen. You know what to tell them."

Chapter 15 · Lesson 71

Marketing and sales promotion

Building transcription skills

543 SIMILAR-WORDS DRILL | affect, effect

affect To act upon; to influence.

These strikes will affect our deliveries to customers.

effect (noun) Result; outcome.

Your failure to pay your bills will have an unfavorable effect on your credit rating.

effect (verb) To bring about; to accomplish.

This is the third letter we have written you trying to effect a settlement of your account.

544

Business vocabulary builder	
imminent	Threatening; impending.
counselor	Adviser.
cosmetic products	Beauty items such as creams, rouge, face powder, etc.
fanfare	Showy outward display.

Reading and writing practice

545

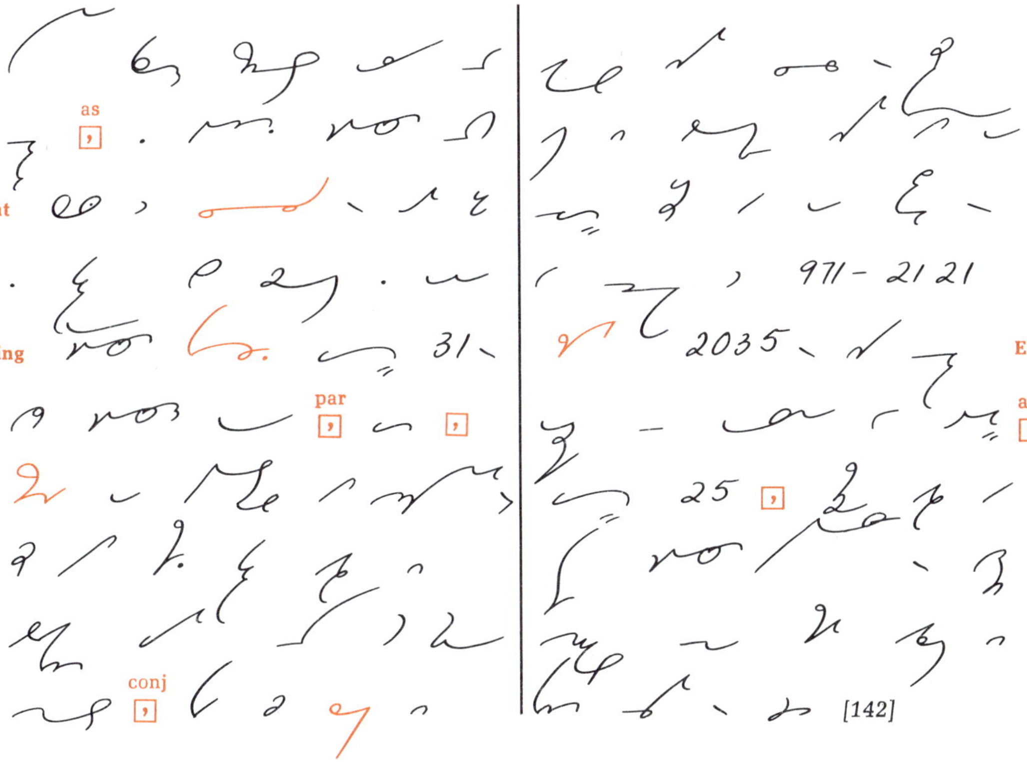

im·mi·nent / as / be·gin·ning / af·fect / par / urge / conj / Ex·ten·sion / ap / [142]

546

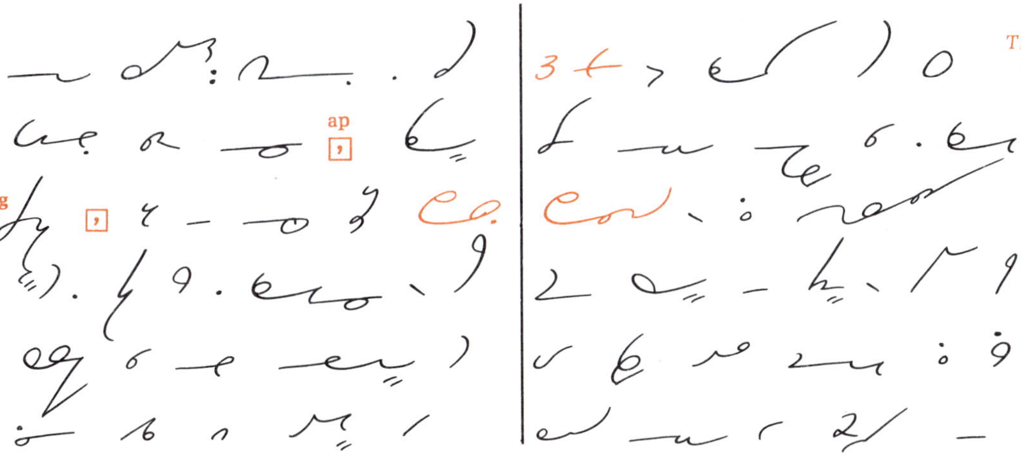

ap·ply·ing / ap / ap·pli·cant / Transcribe: 3 p.m.

door-to-door
hyphenated before noun

[134]

547

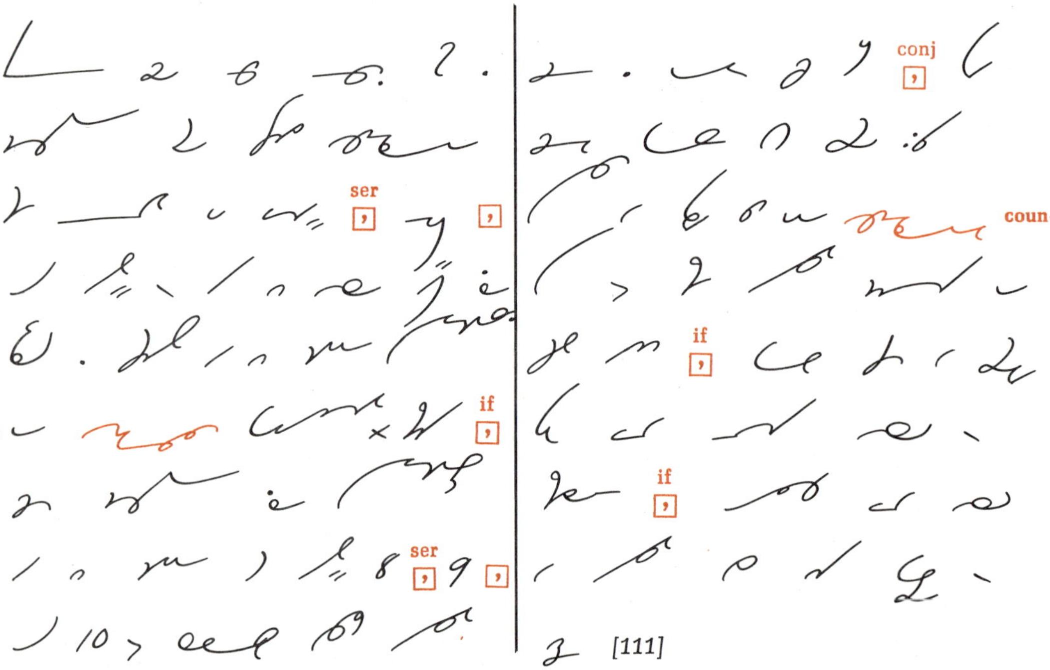

cos·met·ic

coun·sel·or's

[111]

548

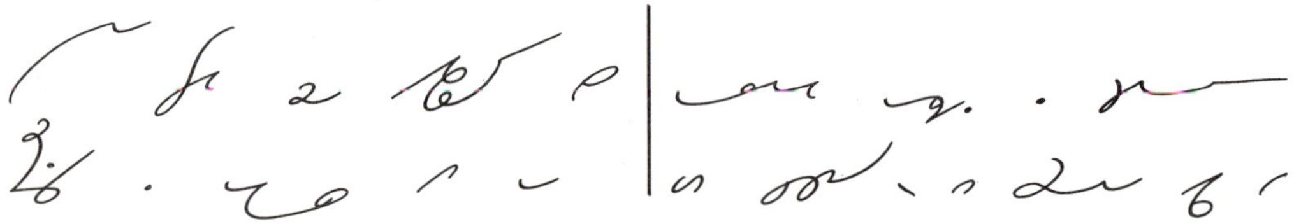

owe
ef·fect
over·due

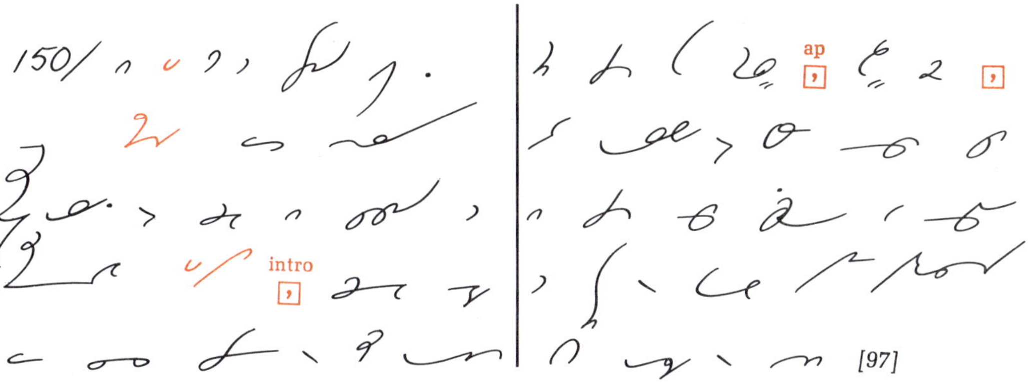

549
fan·fare
if
iq
intro
isq
ap
intro
obviously
pair

[97]
[138]

LESSON 71

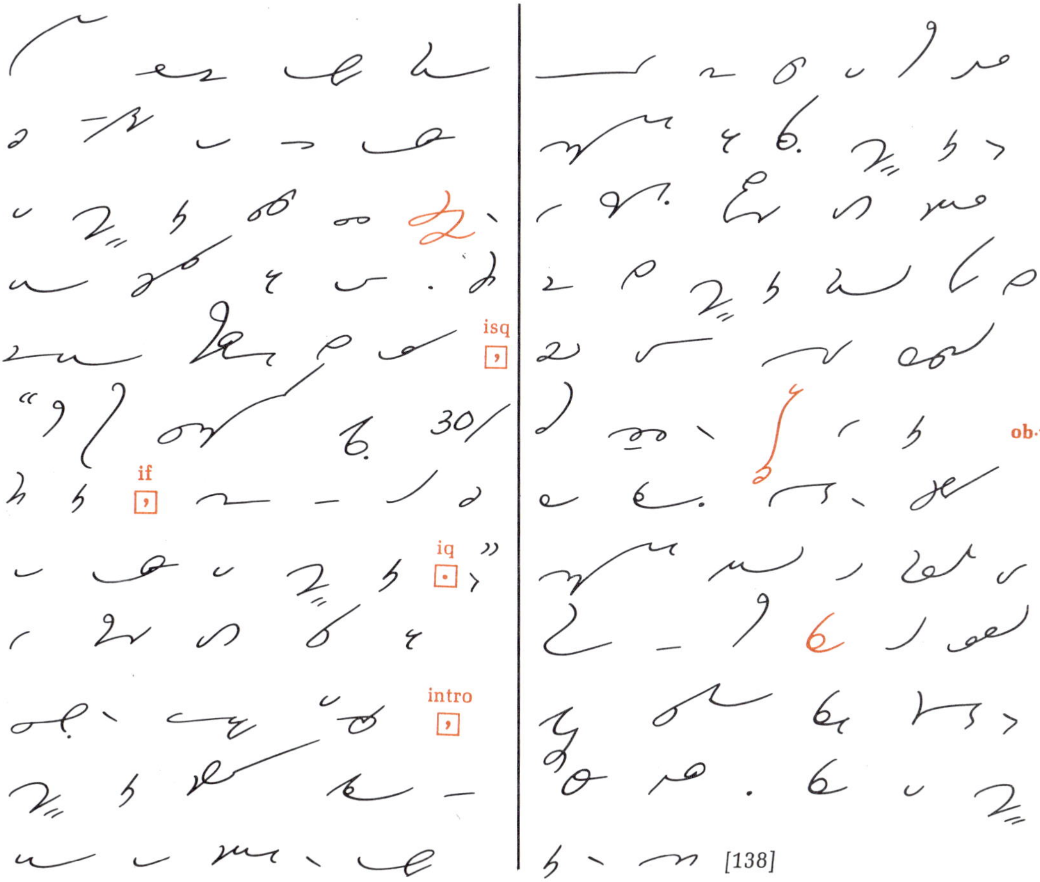

550

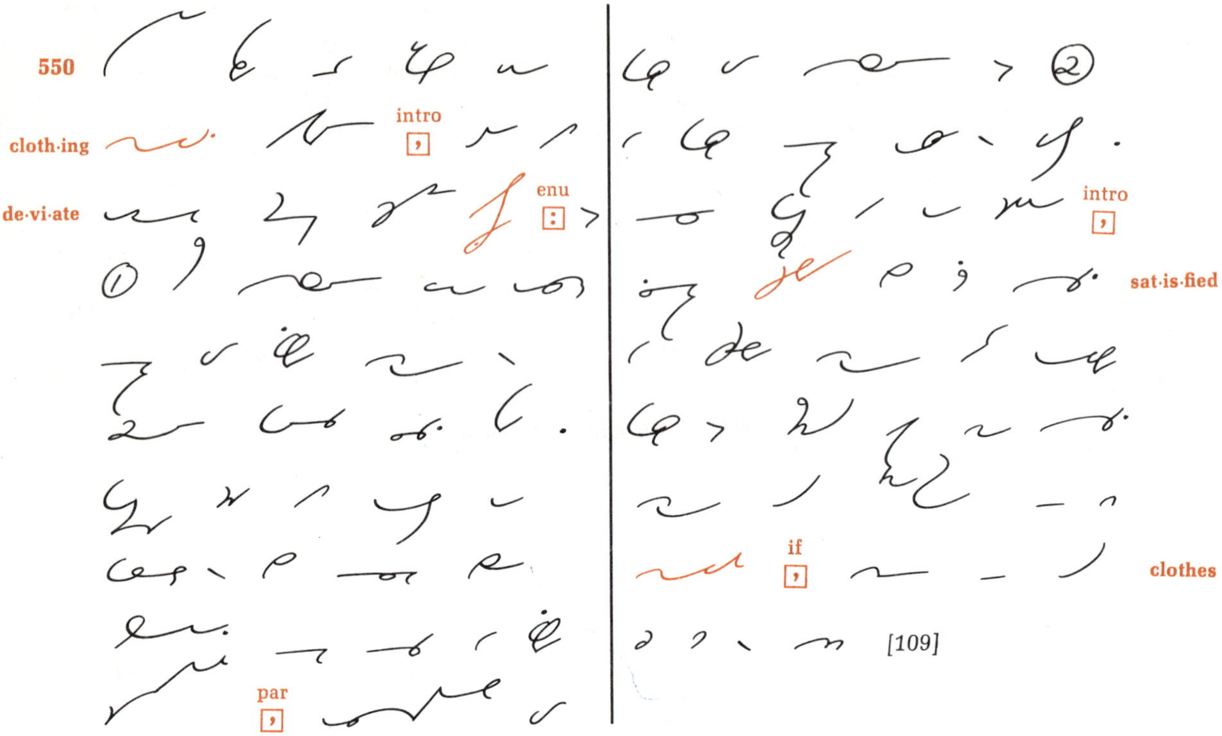

cloth·ing, de·vi·ate, intro, enu, satisfied, intro, if, clothes, par

[109]

"My secretary has been of tremendous assistance to me—first, because of her fine skills; second, because of her ability to do a great number of things on her own without having to trouble me by asking my opinion." *J. D. Silberman, President, White Frost Chemical Company*

LESSON 72

Building transcription skills

551 SPELLING FAMILIES | more double consonants!

More double trouble!
 Here are additional words that are often misspelled because they contain double consonants.

Double M

| com·mit·tee | im·me·di·ate·ly | rec·om·mend |
| com·mu·ni·ty | im·mi·nent | sum·ma·ry |

Double C

| ac·cept | ac·com·pa·ny | oc·cur·rence |
| ac·com·mo·date | oc·ca·sion | suc·ceed |

Double L

| ac·ci·den·tal·ly | es·pe·cial·ly | ca·su·al·ly |
| equal·ly | in·ci·den·tal·ly | prac·ti·cal·ly |

Double G

| ag·gra·vate | bag·gage | lug·gage |
| ag·gre·gate | ex·ag·ger·ate | sug·ges·tion |

552 *Business vocabulary builder*

sizable Large.
atmosphere Surrounding conditions.
encountered Met.

LESSON 72 | 373

553

ca·su·al·ly

buy·er

conj

ser

par

siz·able

[131]

554

re·al·ize

conj

ap

qual·i·fied

Transcribe: $5,000 worth [144]

555 [150]

near-by

LESSON 72

556 par
ac·ci·den·tal·ly
nonr intro
at·mo·sphere equal·ly
in·as·much as
nonr intro
ac·com·mo·dat·ing fair
[144]

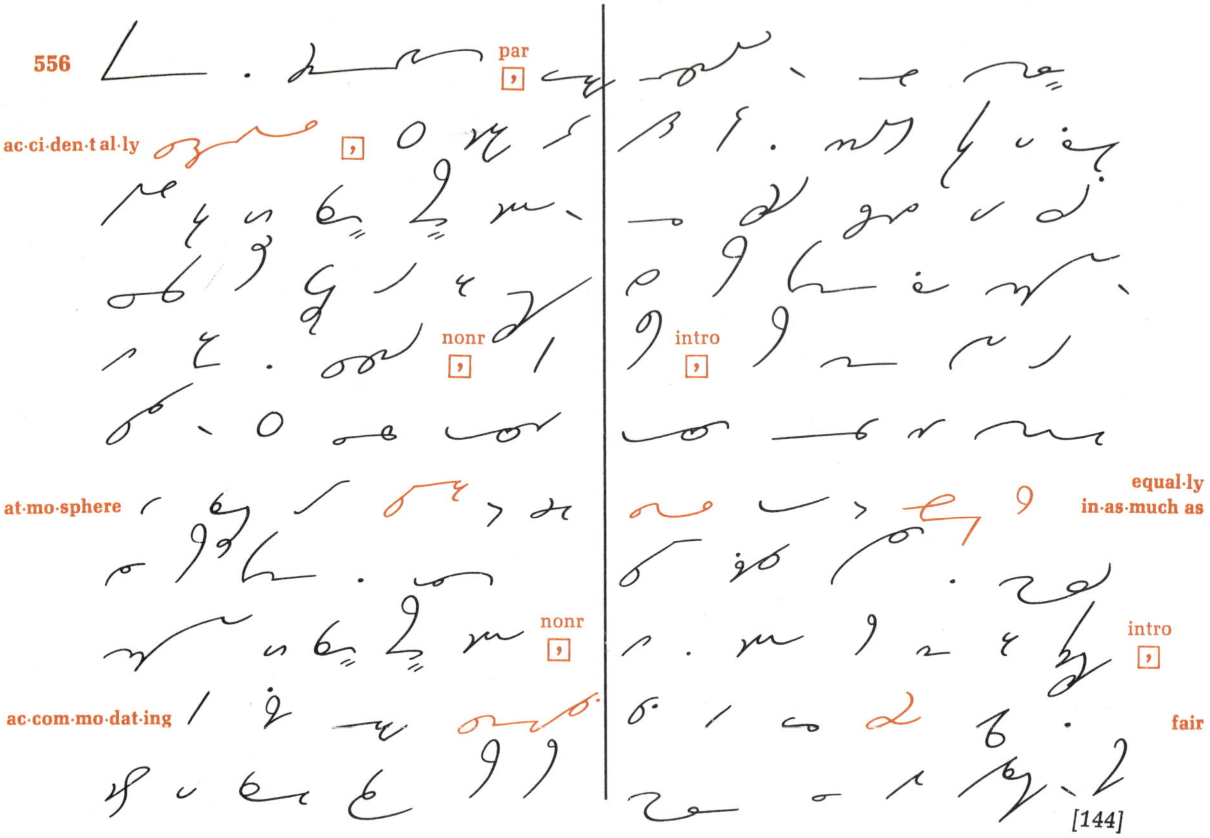

557
intro racks 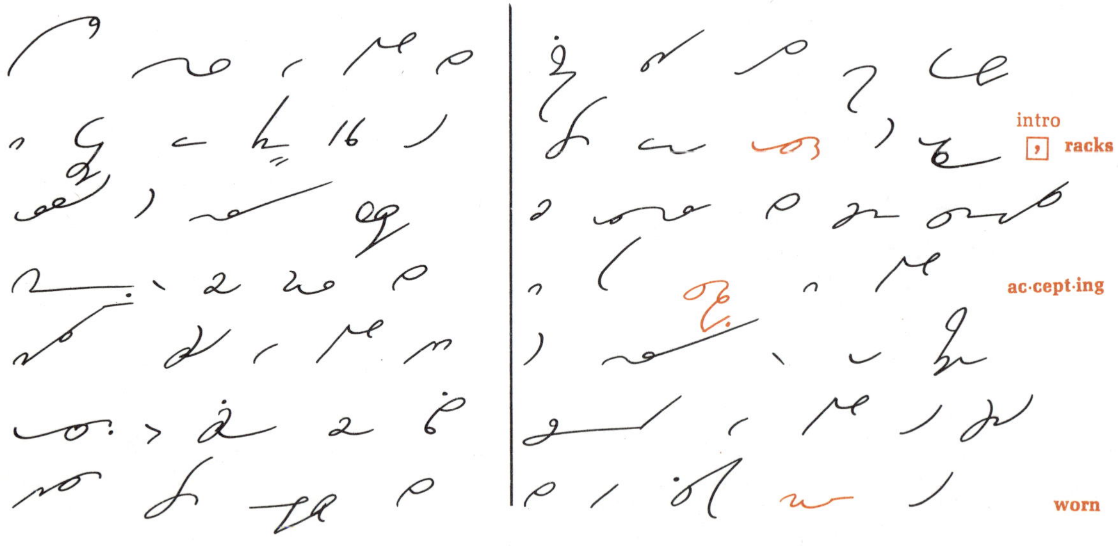
ac·cept·ing
worn

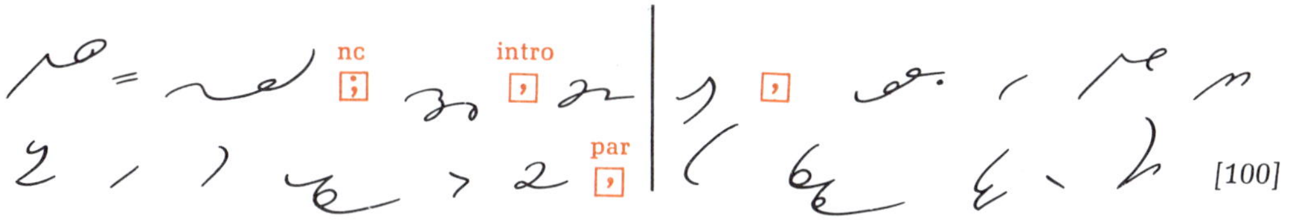
nc
intro
par
[100]

558

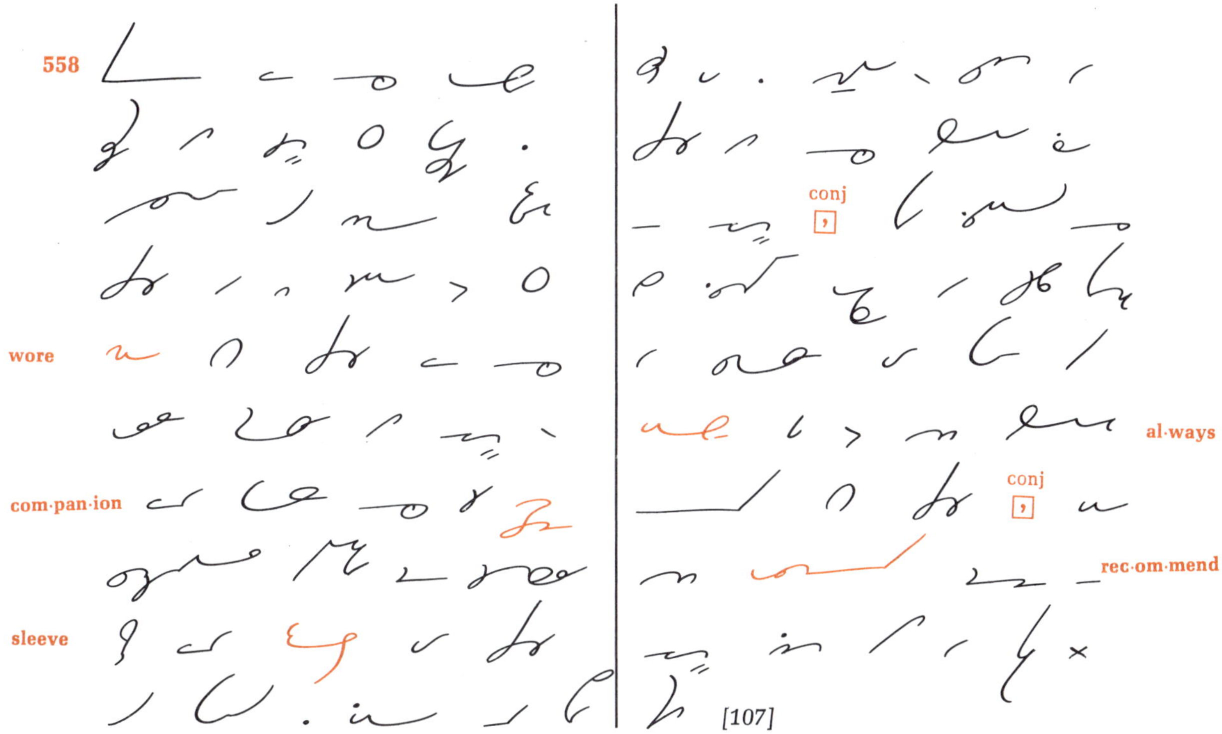
wore
com·pan·ion
sleeve
conj
al·ways
conj
rec·om·mend
[107]

Building transcription skills

559 GRAMMAR CHECKUP | fewer, less

fewer Refers to number.

We received fewer orders (a smaller number) than we expected.

less Refers to degree or amount.

You can type with less effort (a smaller degree of) on an electric typewriter than on a manual machine.

560 Business vocabulary builder

dispelled Cleared up.
fallacy Untruth; false idea.
apparel Clothing; garments.

Reading and writing practice

561 ath·let·ic

LESSON 73

563

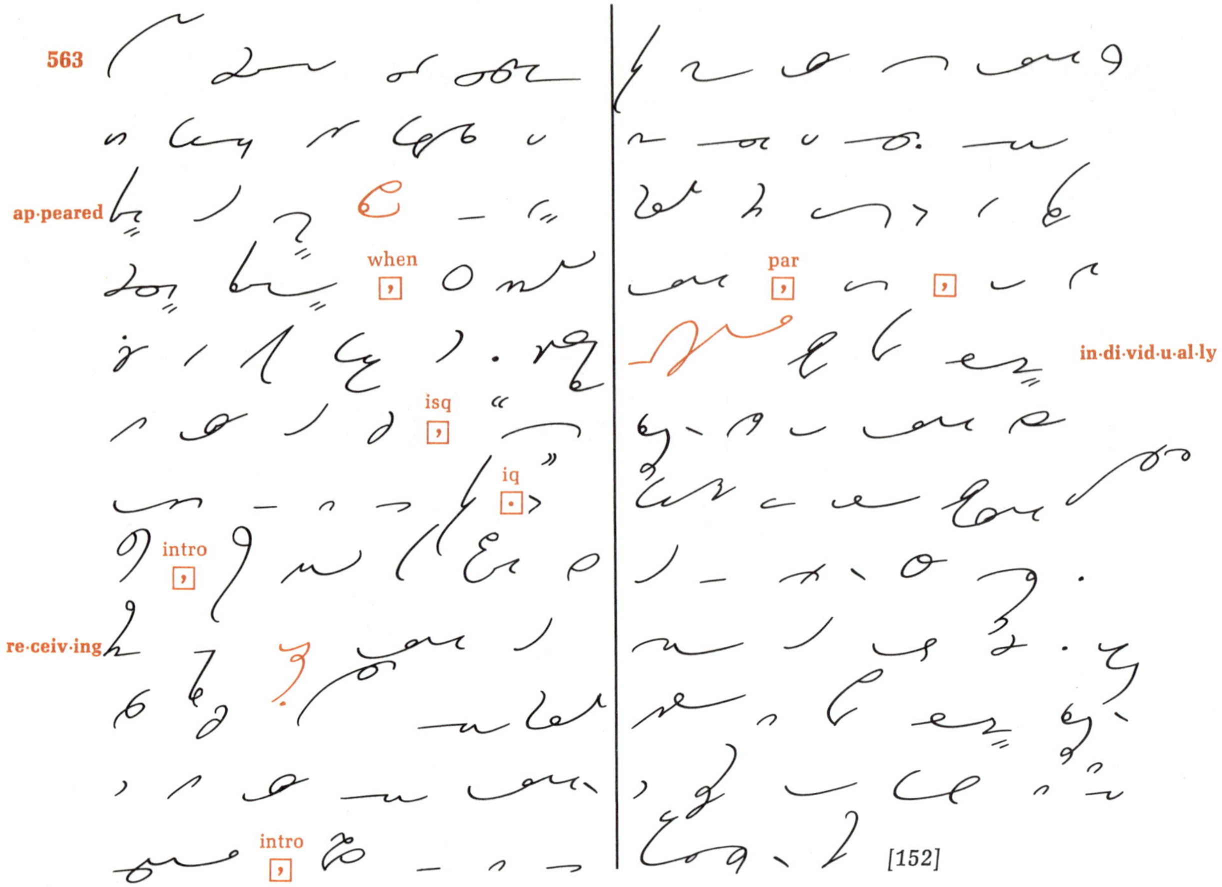

ap·peared / when / isq / intro / re·ceiv·ing / intro / par / in·di·vid·u·al·ly / [152]

564

wom·en's / than / dis·pelled / when / as / par / intro / enu / intro / cloth·ing / be·lieve

[135]

565

Baker's

aunts
un·cles

isq
iq
nonr
intro
[110]

566

ladies'

ap
conj
[44]

LESSON 73

The secretary devises shortcuts

During her first week or two on the job, Ellen found Mr. Davis's dictation somewhat more difficult than the dictation she took in school. For one thing, she was not accustomed to his dictating habits—he puffed on a pipe as he dictated. For another thing, he had a fine command of the English language and often used words with which she was unfamiliar.

During that period Ellen was smart; she wrote each new and unfamiliar word or expression as fully as possible. She was able to do this because she had a good reserve of speed. When she had to take a little time to construct an outline for an unfamiliar word, she could easily catch up.

As Ellen became familiar with the dictating habits of Mr. Davis, she felt more at home with his vocabulary and the terminology of his business. She found that the task of taking dictation was becoming easier.

Furthermore, she took steps to make her task even less difficult. She noticed that Mr. Davis used certain expressions over and over again. During the first week or two she wrote these expressions in full, but she later devised time-saving shortcuts for them. For example, Mr. Davis frequently used the expression "sales promotion campaign." At first Ellen wrote it

When she noticed how often Mr. Davis used the expression, she devised this outline for it

You can quickly see the time and effort she saved thereafter.

In your first secretarial position, you will be smart to follow Ellen's example. But when you are devising a shortcut for any expression, keep in mind these two points:

1 Your dictator must use the expression *very* frequently. A shortcut for an infrequently used word or expression may only cause hesitation in taking dictation and difficulty in transcribing. The shortcut must come to your mind immediately if it is to be of any value. It will come to your mind immediately only if your dictator uses it again and again.

2 The shortcut you devise must be distinctive so that you will not confuse it with some other shorthand outline.

Guard against the temptation to devise too many shortcuts, especially in the early stages of your new job. Some beginners get the mistaken idea that if a few shortcuts will save time and effort and enable them to write more easily, a great many shortcuts will simplify their task even more. That, unfortunately, is not the case.

Here are examples of some shortcuts you might devise if you were working in:

1 A lawyer's office

Testimony, plaintiff, defendant, Supreme Court, abstract of title.

2 A bank

Checking account, bank draft, Federal Reserve Bank, chattel mortgage.

3 An insurance office

Insurance policy, endowment policy, cash value, policyholder.

4 A railroad office

Baltimore and Ohio, Penn Central, freight agent, passenger agent.

5 An accountant's office

Accounts receivable, accounts payable, profit and loss.

6 A publisher's office

Galley proof, page proof, original manuscript, editor-in-chief.

7 A doctor's office

Physical examination, common fracture, hospital.

8 A personnel office

Application blank, personal interview, employment test, in-service training.

▶ *Final caution:* Devise shortcuts *only* for words and expressions that occur over and over again in your dictation.

Building transcription skills

567 OFFICE-STYLE DICTATION | instructions during dictation (concluded)

A dictator will often interrupt his dictation to tell his stenographer or secretary to verify names, amounts, and other data. The businessman may say:

I had a visit from your representative, Mr. Brown—I am not sure whether he spells it **Brown** *or* **Browne.** *Please check the spelling of the name.*

In your notes, this instruction will appear thus:

By indicating immediately above your shorthand outline that you are to check the spelling of the name *Brown*, you will be sure to do so *before* you type the name.

ILLUSTRATION OF OFFICE-STYLE DICTATION

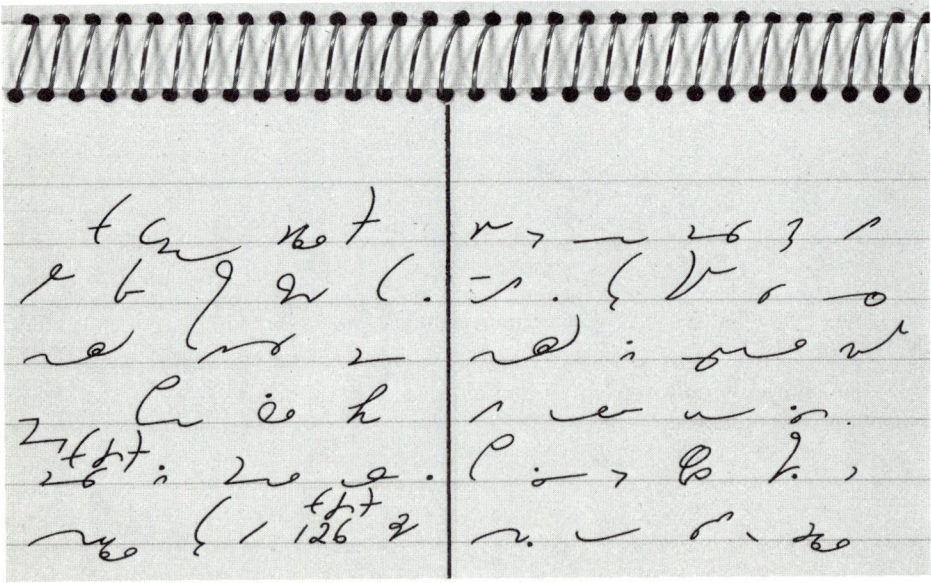

568 Business vocabulary builder

ready-made suit A suit made for general sale.
custom-made suit A suit made for a specific individual, according to his measurements.
grit Soil; dirt.

Reading and writing practice

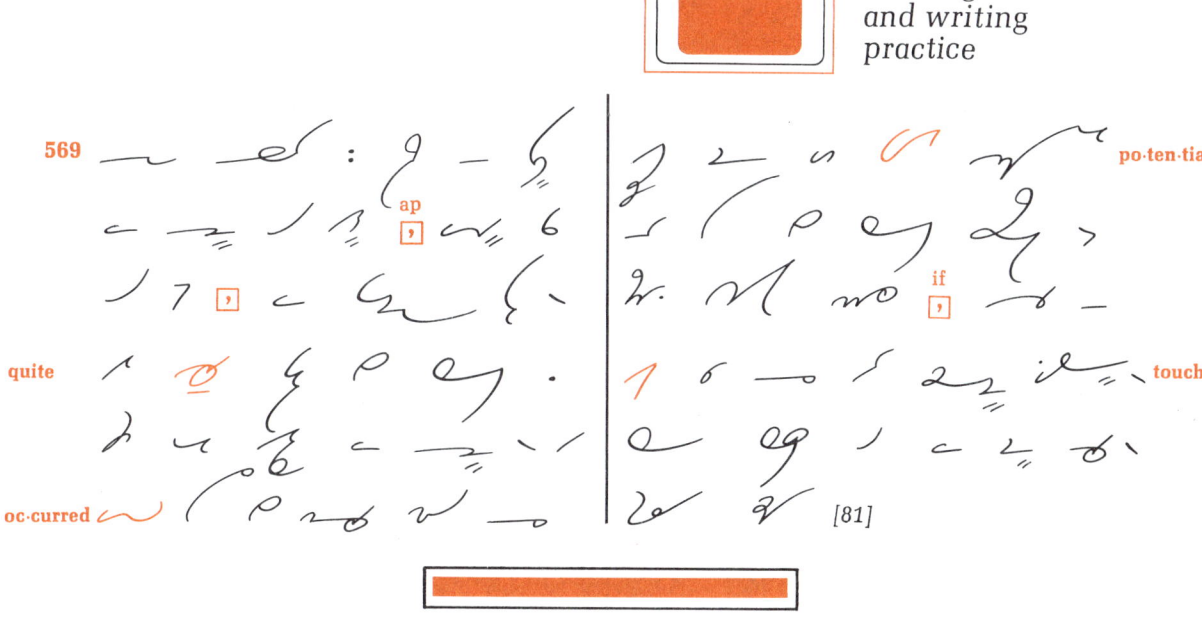

nc ; intro , car·ried

Mon·day's

[113]

571

re·vealed

102

80

intro , if ,

cler·i·cal

off

[133]

572

men's

fi·nal

when

intro

intro

ready-made

cus·tom-made

hyphenated before noun

choos·ing

intro

[158]

573

Tenth

Fifth

intro

pro·ceed

conj

par

[98]

574 Transcription Quiz Supply the necessary punctuation and the missing words.

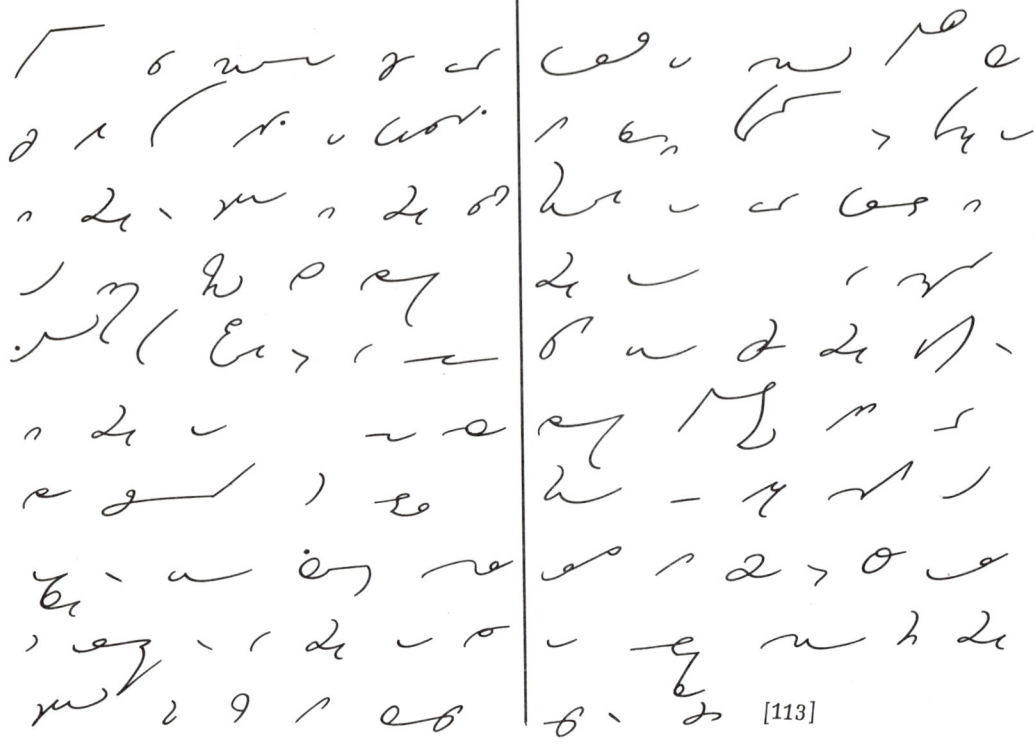

The secretary with an eye to the future takes her responsibilities seriously and gives her best to every assignment.

Building transcription skills

575 WORD CHAIN

This Word Chain consists of a group of words used to convey the meaning of "customer" in different situations.

A **bidder** is one who offers a price for some tangible object.

A **buyer** or **purchaser** is one who buys something tangible.

A **customer** is one who customarily buys from one store, although the word is loosely used to mean one who makes even one purchase in a store.

A **patron** is one who eats in a restaurant or attends a theater, although the word is loosely used to mean one who is a customer of any kind.

A **client** is one who employs the services of a professional person, such as a lawyer, an accountant, or a real estate broker.

A **patient** is one who is under the treatment of a doctor or a dentist or one who is in a hospital. The word comes from a Latin word meaning "to suffer."

A **passenger** is one who is traveling in a public conveyance, such as a train, a plane, a boat, a bus. It is sometimes used in reference to one who is traveling in a private conveyance.

A **depositor** is one who deposits money in a bank.

A **tenant** is one who rents property, thus becoming the "customer" of the landlord.

576

Business vocabulary builder	
expectations	Anticipations; hopes.
curtail	To cut short; to reduce.
footwear	Shoes, slippers, boots, etc.

Reading and writing practice

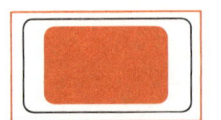

577 (shorthand outline) intro, per·mis·sion, re·main·der, cur·tail, intro, enu, par, co·op·er·a·tion [165]

578 (shorthand outline) ser, pol·i·cies, well-known *hyphenated before noun*

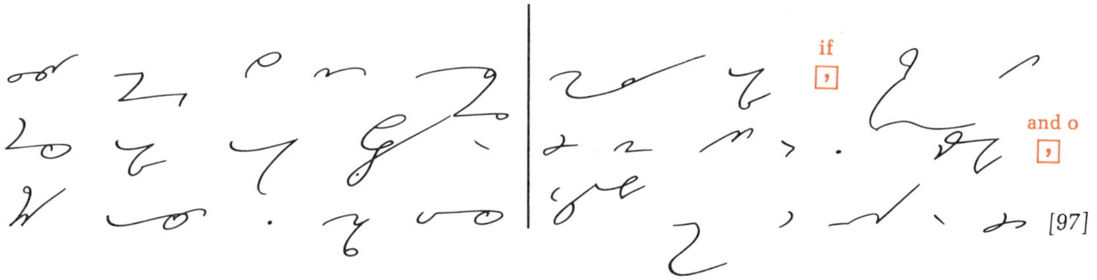

[shorthand content]

LESSON 75

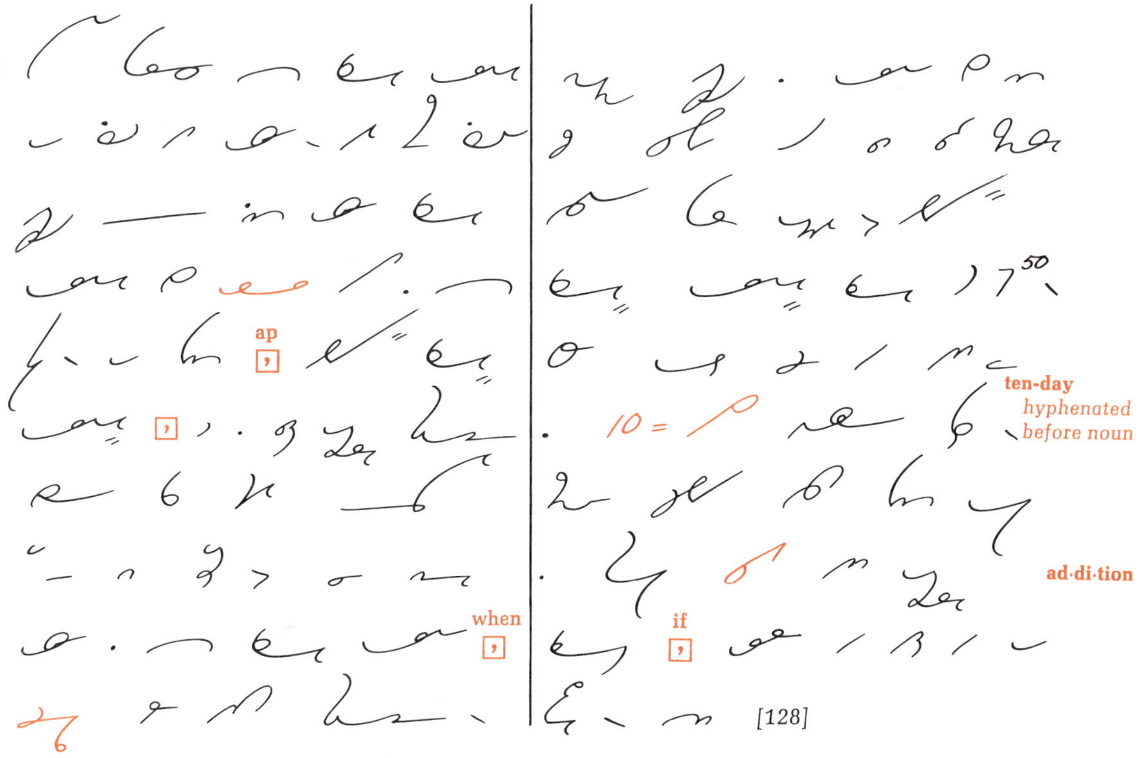

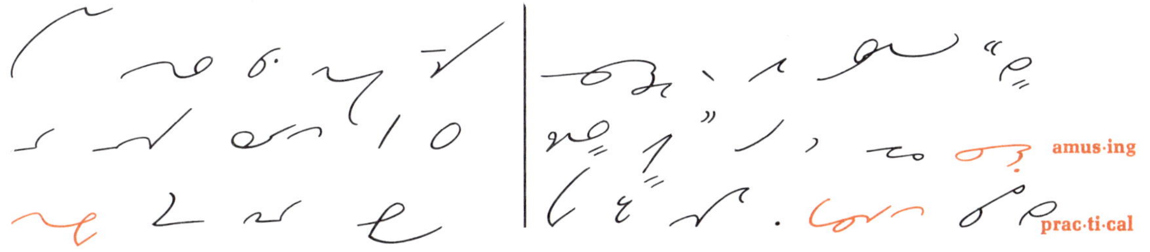

its as ad sew·ing [134]

581 intro

Tenth 855 10¢

their conj [94]

582

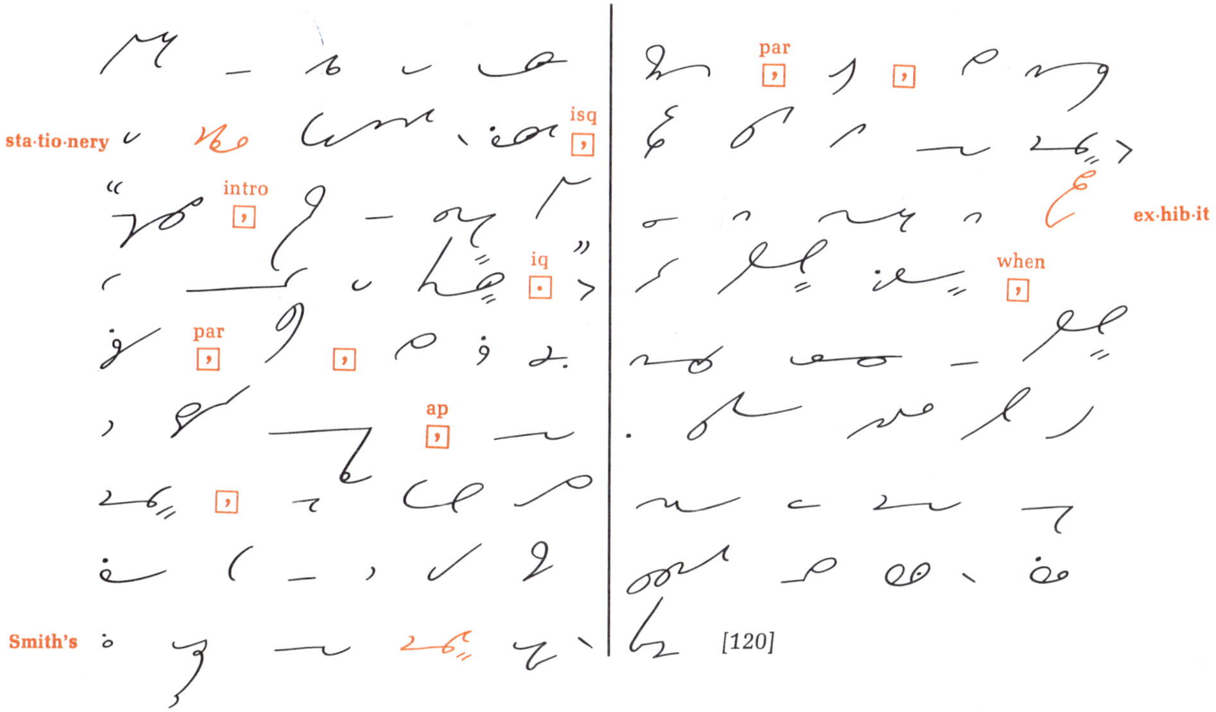

sta·tio·nery   isq
                intro
                par   iq
                par
                        ap
Smith's

par
        ex·hib·it
        when

[120]

Ellen Gardiner, letter writer

Ellen Gardiner first entered Mr. Davis's employ as a stenographer. At the beginning, Mr. Davis dictated only his routine correspondence to her, and he supervised her work very closely.

After Ellen had proved to Mr. Davis that she could transcribe rapidly and accurately and that she was "promotion material," Mr. Davis made her his secretary when the opening arose.

As Ellen learned more and more about the business and its policies and procedures, Mr. Davis found that he could turn over to her the handling of

routine correspondence. The important letters, of course, he continued to dictate. Others he dictated only partially—perhaps a paragraph or two—and Ellen completed the letter from information that she had gathered. For most letters he simply told her what he wanted, and she wrote the letters for his signature. For example, he might say: "Return this proof to Smith, and tell him to correct the errors and submit a revised proof. Ask him to stop in to talk about next year's advertising in his magazine. Suggest April 10 at 10 o'clock. If that is not convenient, tell him to suggest a time."

In her notebook, Ellen wrote in shorthand:

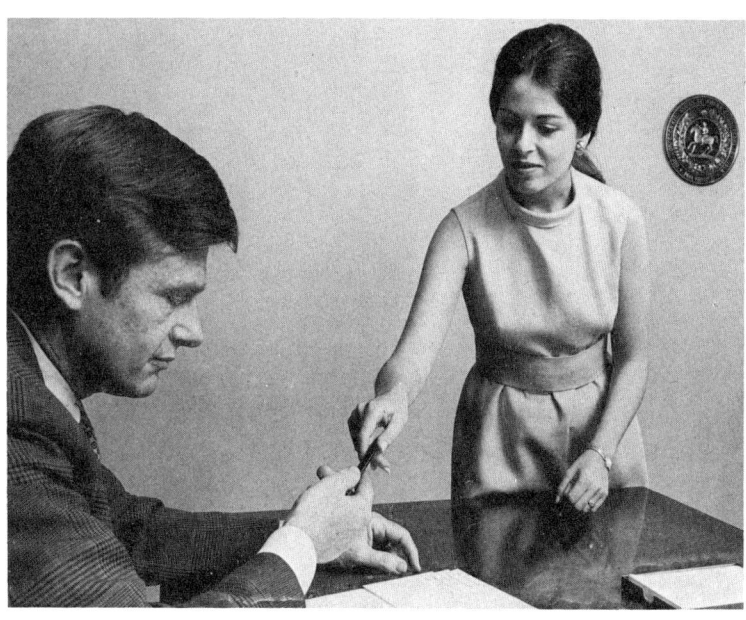

Here is the letter that Ellen placed on Mr. Davis's desk for signature:

    Dear Mr. Smith: I am enclosing the proof you sent me for the ad we are running in the May issue of your magazine. You will notice that there are several errors on it. Please correct the errors and send me a revised proof.

    In a few weeks I must submit to the finance committee my advertising budget and plans for the coming year. Could you stop in to see me on Friday, April 10, at 10 o'clock to discuss what part your magazine may play in these plans? If the time suggested is not convenient, please suggest another time. Sincerely yours,

By relieving Mr. Davis of his routine correspondence in this way, Ellen performs a real service to him: she releases his time for the more important duties of his position.

Chapter 16 · Lesson 76

Investments

Building transcription skills

583 SIMILAR-WORDS DRILL | apprised, appraised

apprised Informed.

He was apprised of our decision last Wednesday.

appraised Set a value on.

The house was appraised at $40,000.

584

Business vocabulary builder	
apt	Likely; liable.
composition	Makeup.
remiss	Negligent; lax.

Reading and writing practice

585

draw·er

intro

ad·e·quate

in·ves·tors

lose

if

se·cu·ri·ties

intro

apt

par

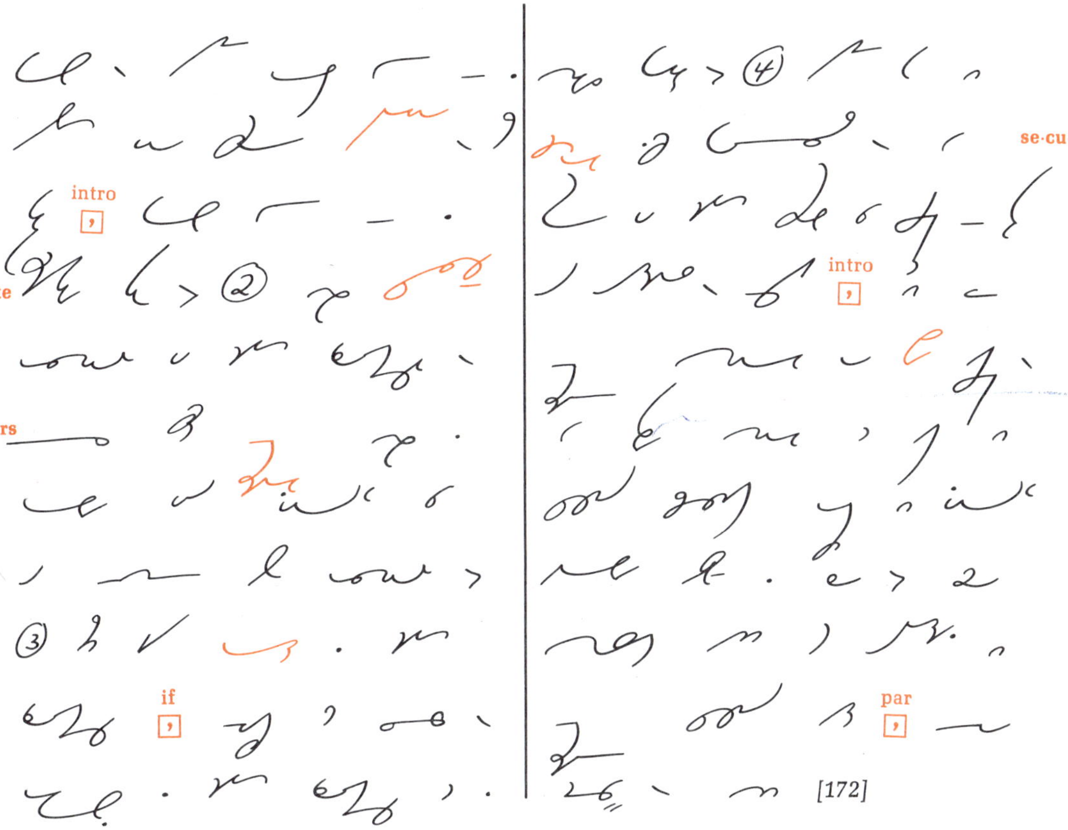

[172]

586

64-page
hyphenated before noun

lei·sure

intro

at·tempts

long-range
hyphenated before noun

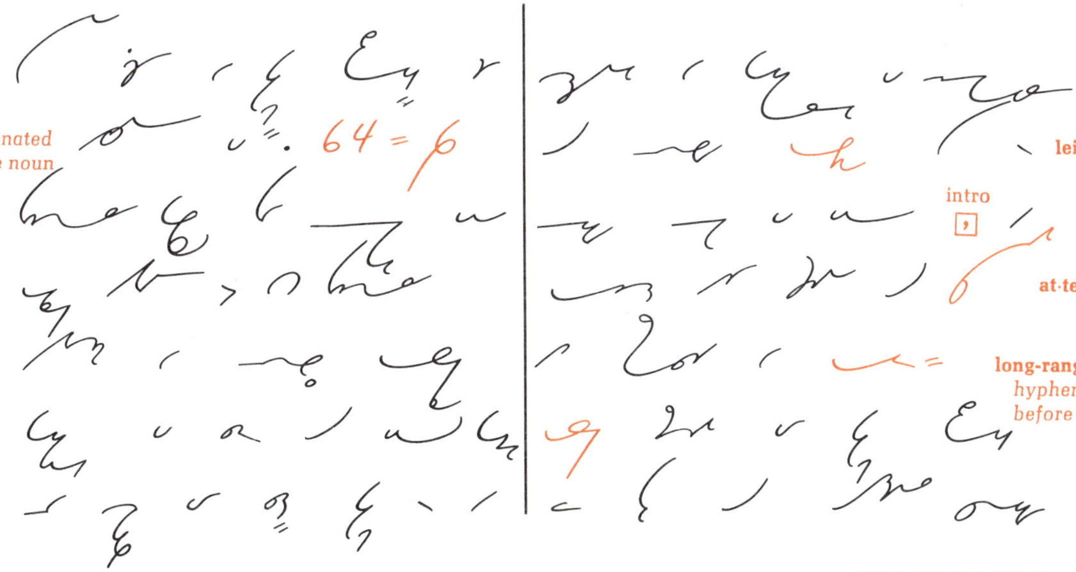

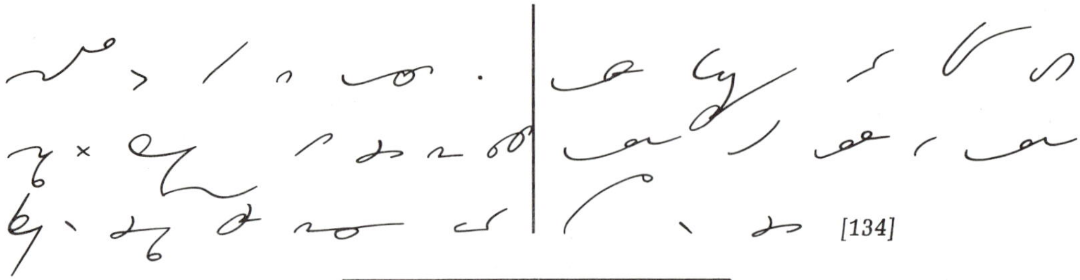

[134]

587 [124]

conj
fac·tors
if
com·mis·sions
if

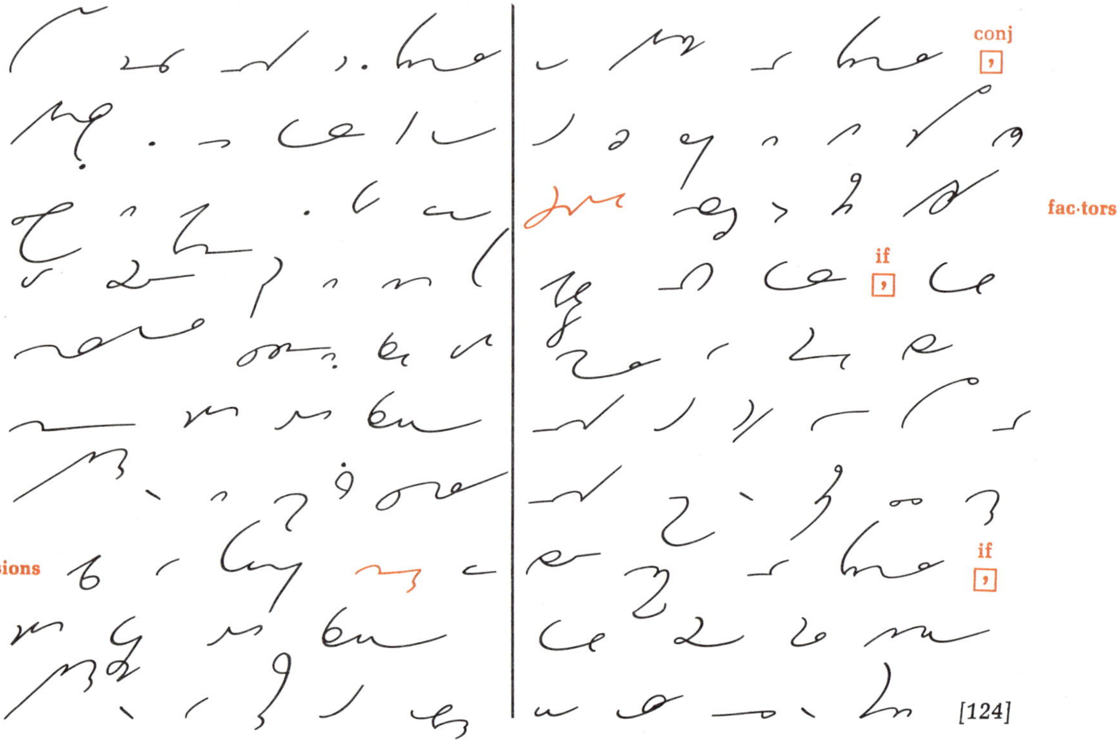

588
ap·prised

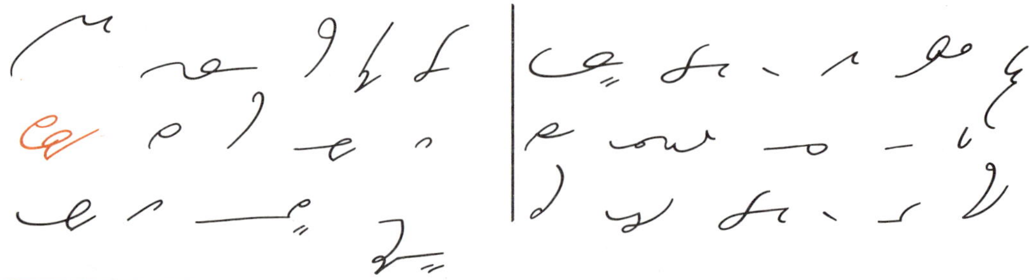

LESSON 76 | 399

Building transcription skills

590 SPELLING FAMILIES | -an, -on, -en

Words ending with an n that is preceded by *a, o,* or *e* have always been a source of spelling difficulty for stenographers. Practice each of the following groups.

-an

| met·ro·pol·i·tan | par·ti·san | sub·ur·ban |
| or·gan | slo·gan | vet·er·an |

-on

but·ton	lun·cheon	sea·son
cot·ton	par·don	sur·geon
les·son *(instruction)*	per·son	wag·on

-en

broad·en	giv·en	les·sen *(decrease)*
bur·den	hid·den	spo·ken
cit·i·zen	kitch·en	writ·ten

A number of these words appear in the Reading and Writing Practice. Watch for them.

591

Business vocabulary builder

critical Crucial; decisive.
over-the-counter securities Stocks unlisted on an organized securities exchange.
facilitate To make easier.

Reading and writing practice

592

crit·i·cal

over-the-coun·ter
hyphenated before noun

if

ap

co·op·er·a·tion
and o

[137]

593

sur·geons
ser

home-study
hyphenated before noun

intro

[112]

594

Transcribe: 15
1,500

intro
im·mense·ly
if
post·paid
[107]

595

An·a·lysts
ap
nonr
as

402 | LESSON 77

LESSON 77

Transcribe:
11 a.m.
tours
ser
intro
nonr
if
at·ten·dance 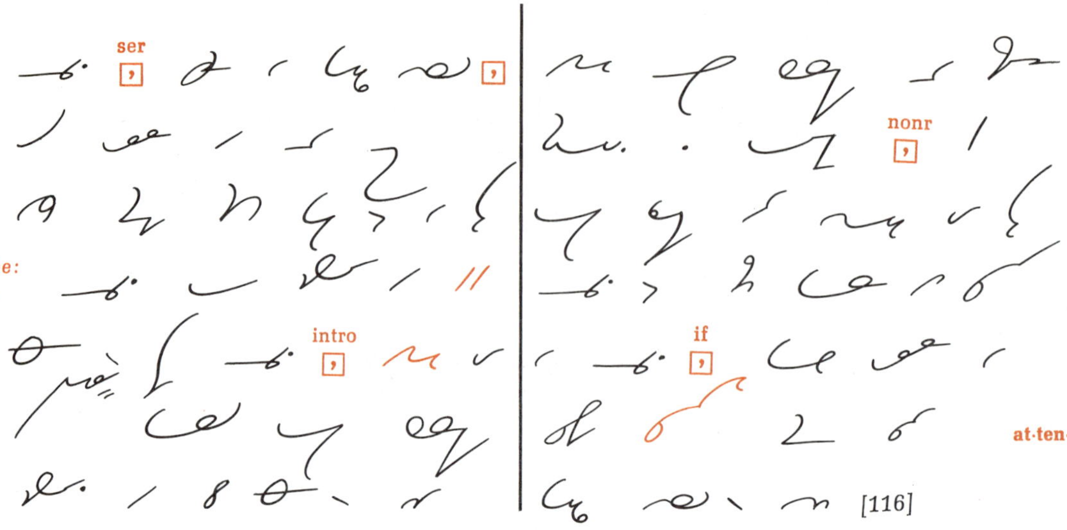
[116]

598
ads
in·her·i·tance
nonr
if 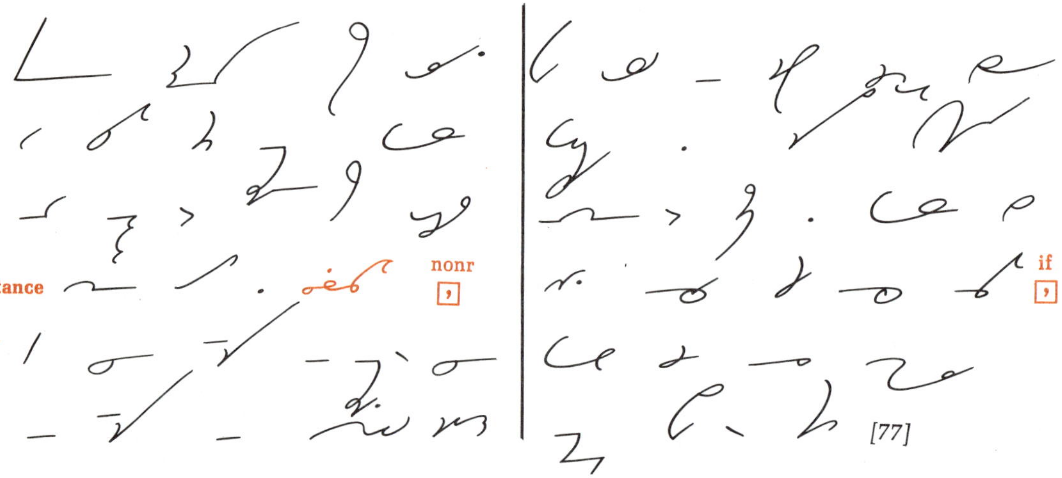
[77]

404 | LESSON 77

Interoffice Memorandum

TO	F. J. Marvin	FROM	A. R. Smith
DEPT.	Personnel Department	DEPT.	Foreign Department
FLOOR	4	FLOOR	39
SUBJECT	Job Replacement	DATE	May 20, 19--

My secretary, Miss Helen A. Hicks, has just informed me that she is to be married on June 15. She plans to leave on June 1.

If it is possible, I should like to get someone to fill the vacancy immediately, so that Miss Hicks can help in the training of the new girl.

As you know, most of my correspondence is with customers in South and Central America. Consequently, it would be a great help to me if you could find a girl who has some degree of proficiency in Spanish.

I shall be in Cleveland on May 21 and 22, but I shall be back on the morning of May 23. I shall, therefore, be able to interview any girls you send me any time after May 22.

A. R. S.

ARS:HH

Interoffice memorandum

Building transcription skills

599 ACCURACY PRACTICE

Follow the practice procedures outlined on page 154.

GROUP 1	GROUP 2	GROUP 3
light	pass	ought
right	base	should

practice drill

1 When you leave, be sure to take the <u>light</u> coat. When you leave, be sure to take the <u>right</u> coat.
2 He will not <u>base</u> judgment on the newspaper stories of the accident. He will not <u>pass</u> judgment on the newspaper stories of the accident.
3 John <u>ought</u> to be happy to go on the trip. John <u>should</u> be happy to go on the trip.

600

Business vocabulary builder	
discreetly	Prudently.
outlook	Perspective; view.
foresight	A look ahead.
objectives	Aims.

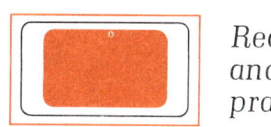

Reading and writing practice

601
re·ceiv·ing

oc·curred

if

par

dis·creet·ly

[104]

602
wom·en
than

fam·i·ly's

wom·an

over·all

if

LESSON 78 | 407

mys·tery ap [140] cou·pon

603 wise·ly as if ser when in·ter·view [133]

604 an·swer·ing if enu fre·quent·ly

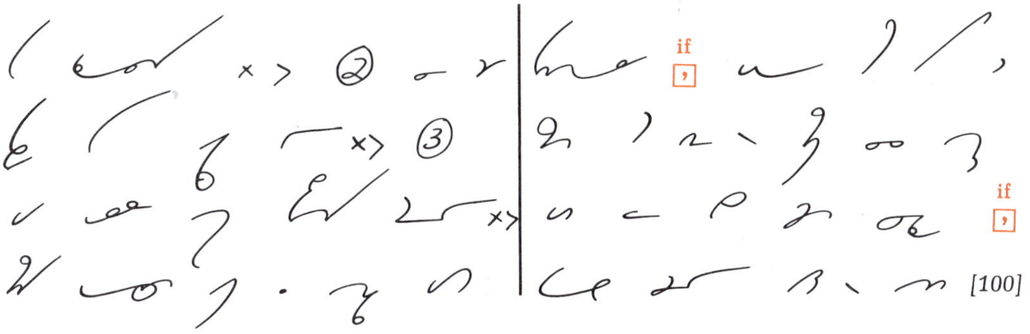

if
if
[100]

605

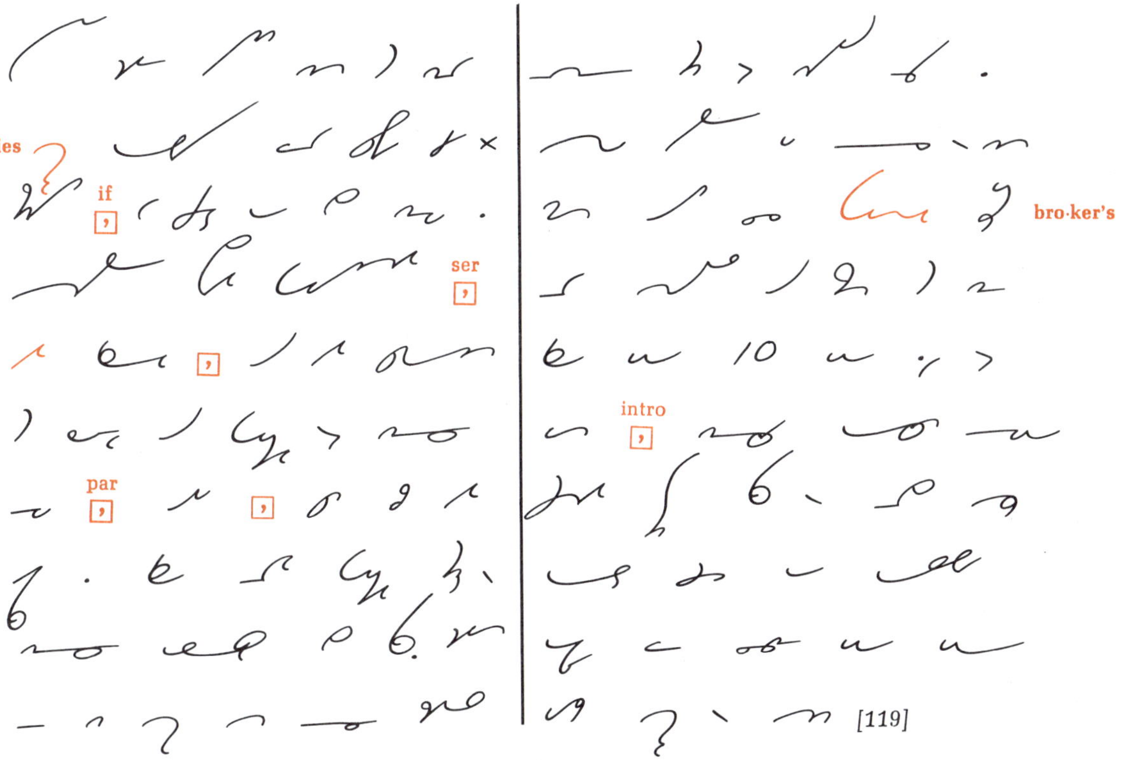

com·pa·nies
if
ser
its
par
intro
bro·ker's
[119]

606

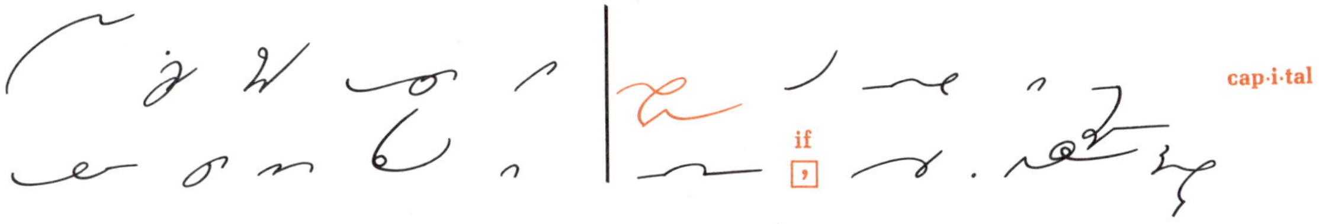

if
cap·i·tal

Week·ly

to·day's

when

fore·sight

intro

isq

iq

[138]

607

in·her·its

when

enu

re·lieve

bank's

[116]

LESSON 78

The secretary types rough drafts

One day after Ellen had been on the job only a short time, Mr. Davis called her into his office and dictated a letter. When he finished, he said to her, "That's an important letter, and I want to be sure that it is just right before we mail it. Just dash off a rough draft, and let me have it as soon as possible."

Ellen either wasn't listening or didn't believe that Mr. Davis really wanted a rough draft. She typed the letter on the company letterhead and made a carbon copy. During the process of transcribing, she made two or three errors that she carefully corrected on both the original and the carbon.

When she handed the letter to Mr. Davis, he was thoroughly annoyed. "Didn't I ask you to dash off a rough draft? Since I dictated the letter, I thought of several other things that should be included, and you will have to retype the letter. You have wasted your time and company money. When I say I want you to dash off a rough draft, I mean just that and not a finished copy ready to sign."

Ellen learned her lesson. Thereafter, when Mr. Davis said he wanted her to dash off a rough draft, she:

1 Typed it on inexpensive manuscript paper and not on letterhead paper.

2 Double-spaced the letter and left wide margins so that Mr. Davis would have plenty of room for corrections or additions.

3 Struck over incorrectly typed letters or x-ed out wrong words (something she would *never* do on a final copy).

4 Submitted it to her employer as soon as she took it out of her machine without even proofreading it (something else she would *never* do with a final copy).

For most dictation, your goal should be to submit for your employer's signature only letters that are mailable—with no errors of any kind. But when your employer says "Dash off a copy"—do just that!

Building transcription skills

608 OFFICE-STYLE DICTATION | **extensive changes**

Most dictators make only an occasional change in their dictation. Some, however, make so many changes that it is advisable to write in only one column of the notebook, leaving the second column for insertions or changes.

ILLUSTRATION OF OFFICE-STYLE DICTATION

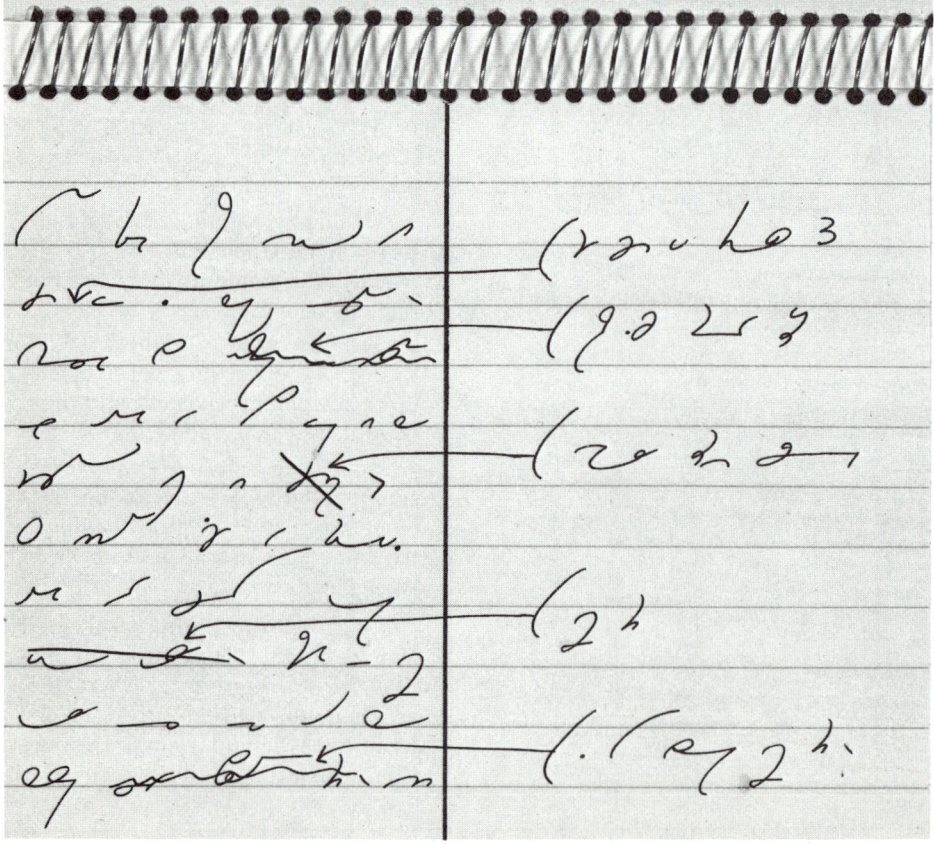

609 Business vocabulary builder

explore Look into.
voluntary Freely chosen.
lucid Clear.

Reading and writing practice

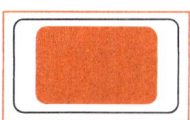

610

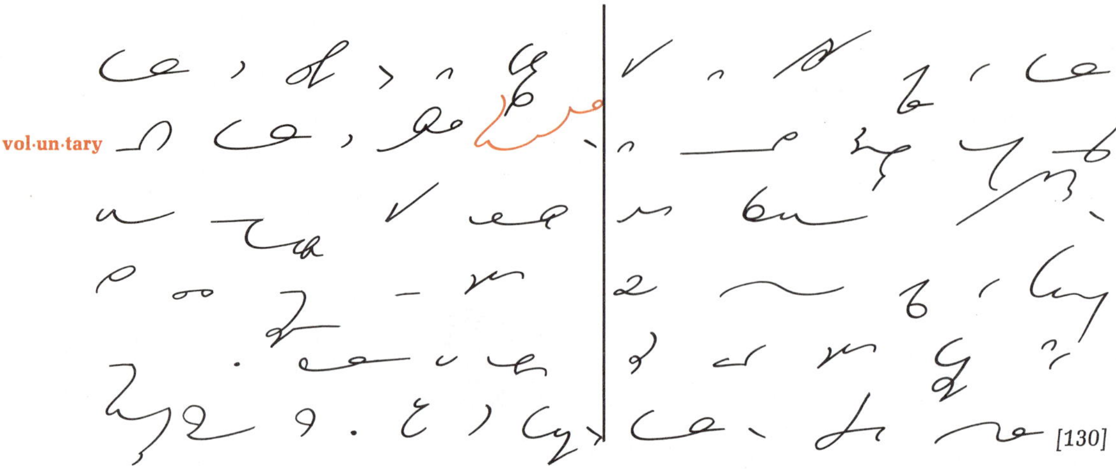

vol·un·tary [130] *intro ,*

612

re·ceive

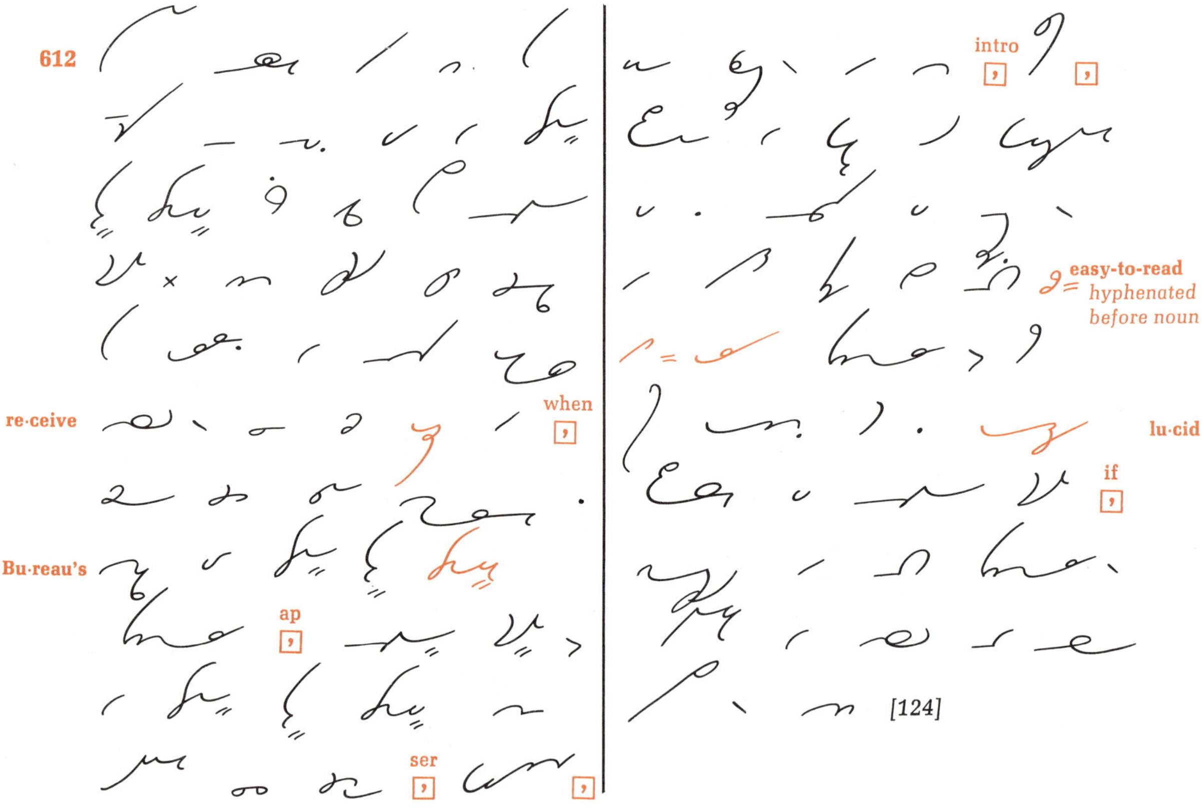

Bu·reau's   *ap ,*   *ser ,*   *when ,*   *easy-to-read = hyphenated before noun*   **lu·cid**   *if ,*   [124]   *intro , ,*

414 | LESSON 79

613

rea·sons

re·al·ly

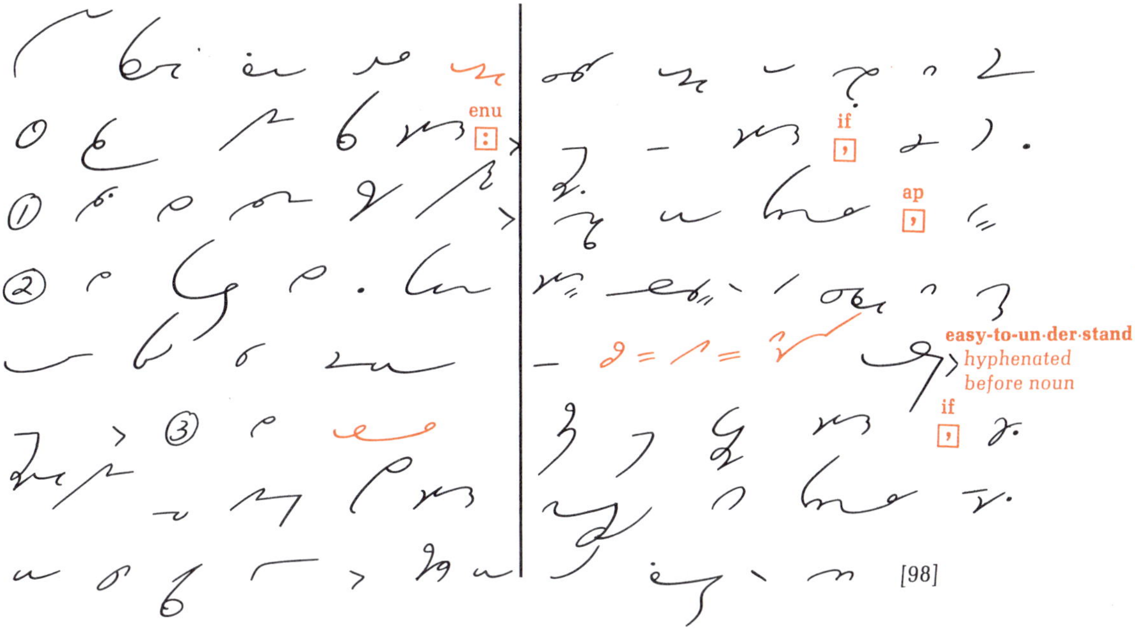

[shorthand content with annotations: enu, if, ap, easy-to-un·der·stand (hyphenated before noun), if]

[98]

614

min·utes'

than

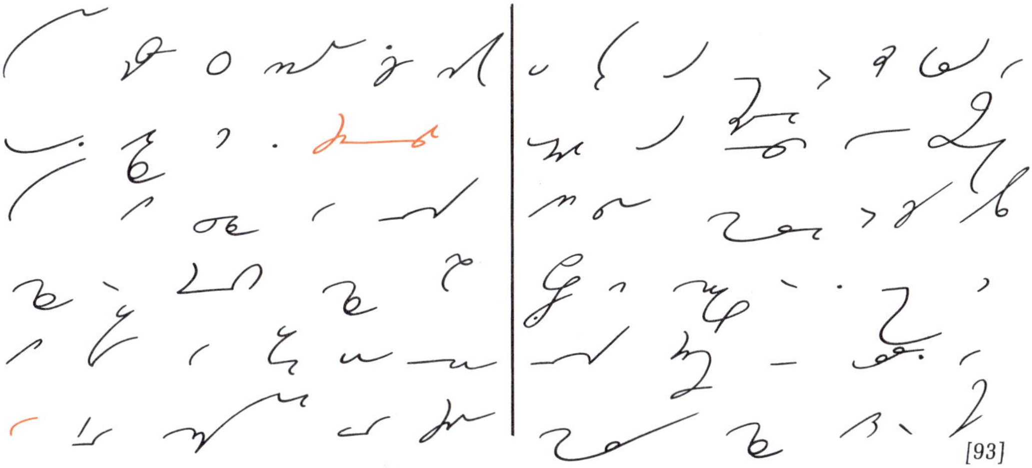

[shorthand content]

[93]

615

[shorthand content with annotation: intro]

LESSON 79 | 415

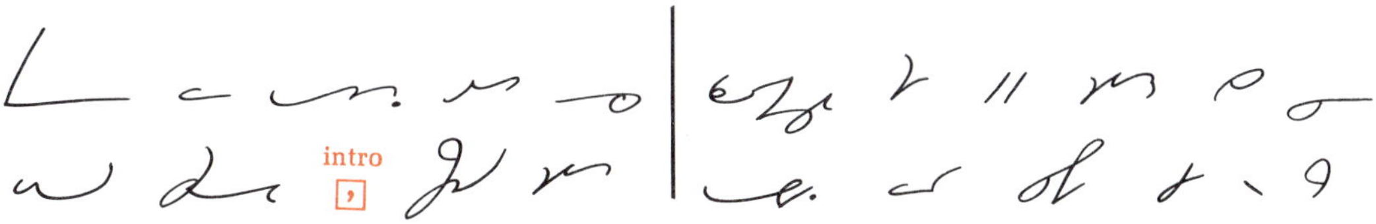

intro

bought

course

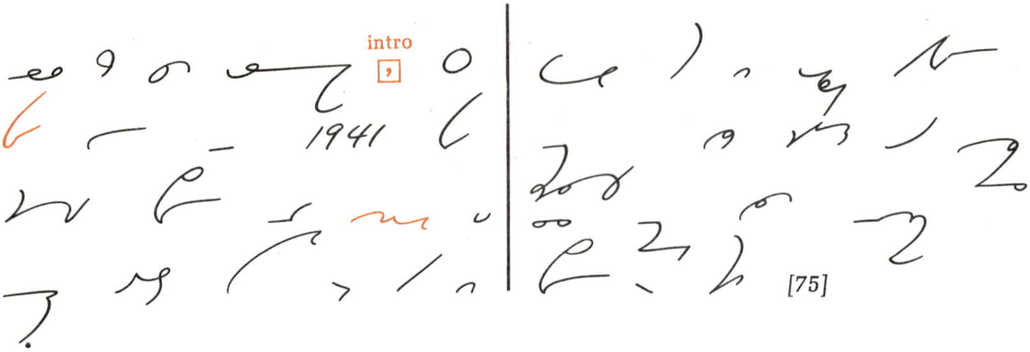

[75]

616 Transcription Quiz *Can you supply all the necessary punctuation and the missing word in this letter?*

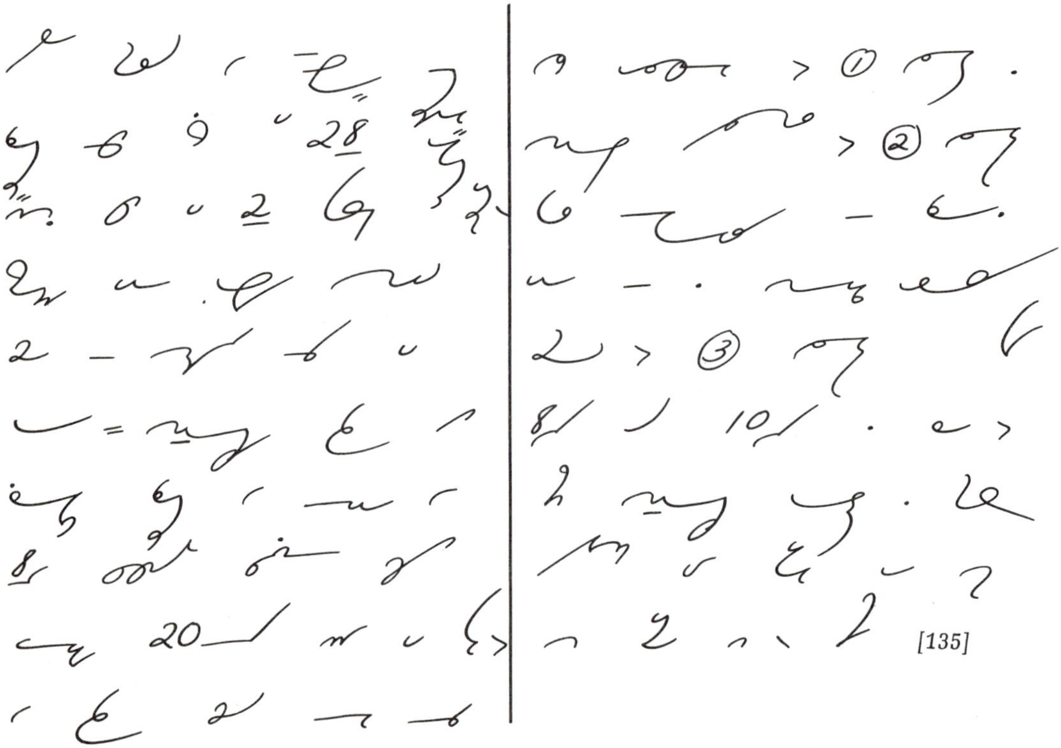

[135]

Building transcription skills

617 COMMON PREFIXES | de-

de- down, away from

    decrease Go down; grow less.

    detract Take away from.

    descend Come down.

    depress Press down; to lower.

    deposit Put down.

    depart Go away from.

618

Business vocabulary builder	
recreation	Amusement.
specific	A particular sort or kind.
affiliated	Connected or associated.
immeasurable	Incapable of being measured.

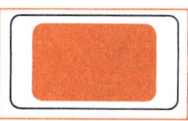 Reading and writing practice

619 [shorthand] rec·re·ation

leisure grown whole industries Forums attendance par if [162]

620 Transcribe: 75 cents 3 cents advise succeed

LESSON 80

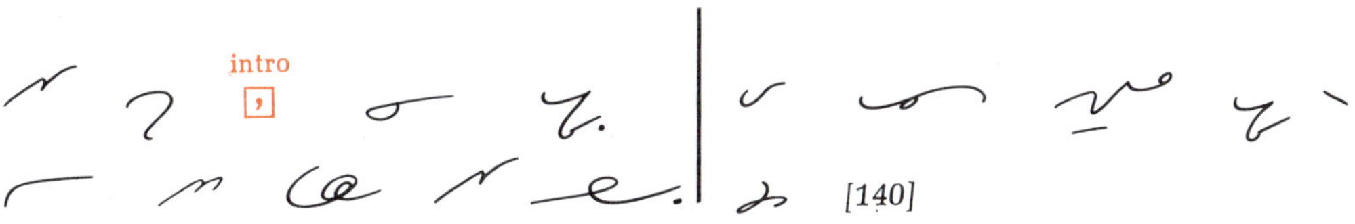

[140]

621 merg·er

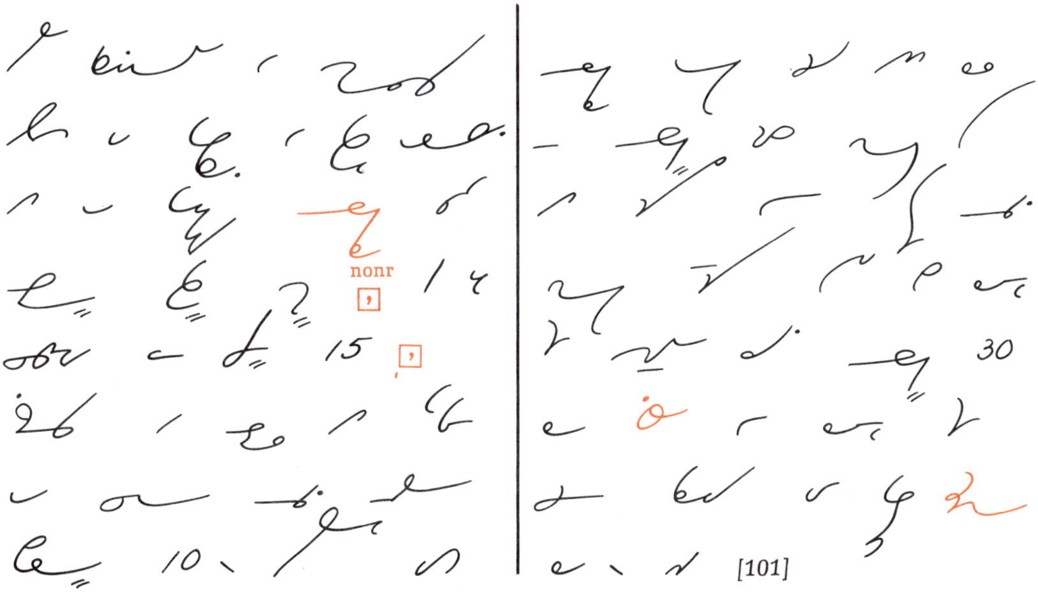

[101] high·er fis·cal

622 bear·er im·mea·sur·able thor·ough·ly

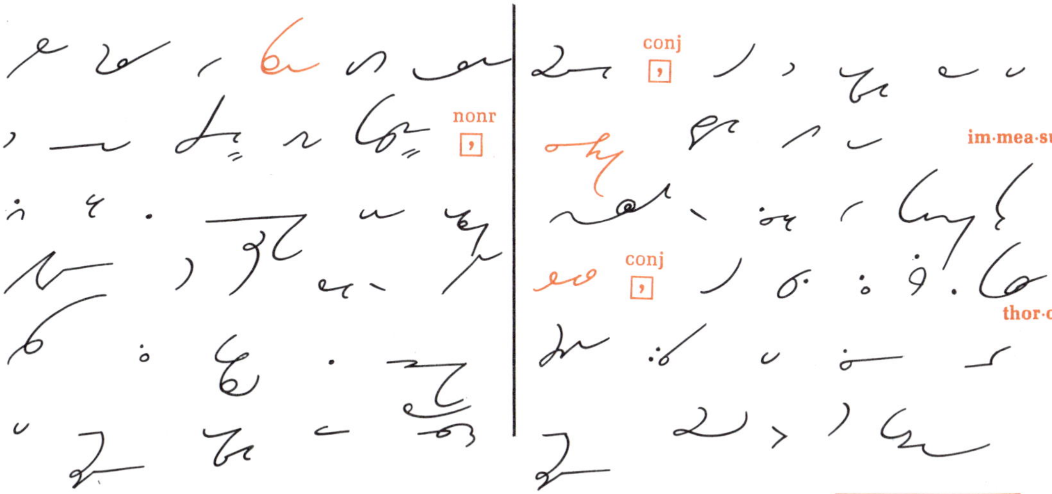

LESSON 80 | 419

LESSON 80

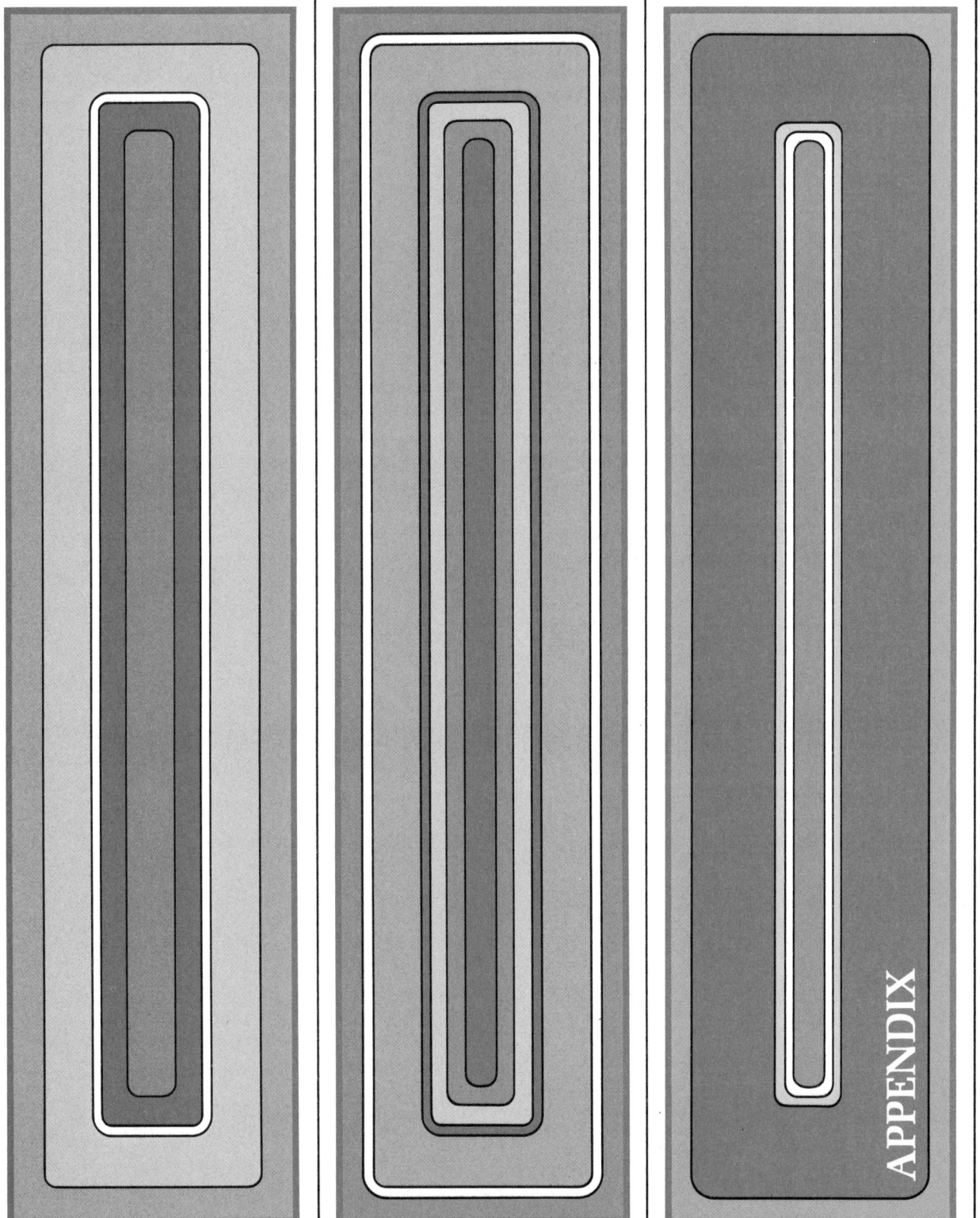

Recall drills

JOINED WORD ENDINGS

1 -ment

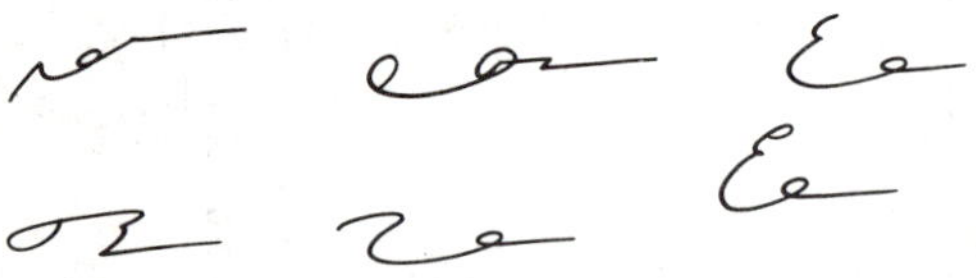

2 -tion

3 -tial

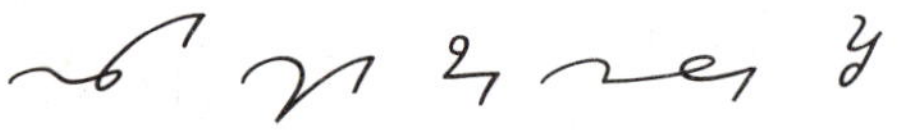

4 -ly

5 -ily

6 -ful

7 -sume, -sumption

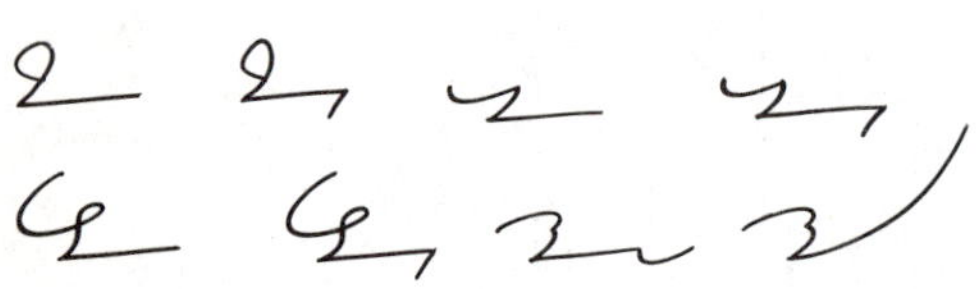

8 -ble

9 -ther

10 -ual

11 -ure

12 -self, -selves

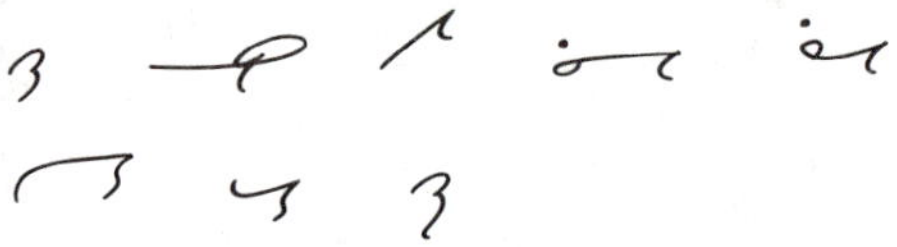

13 -ort

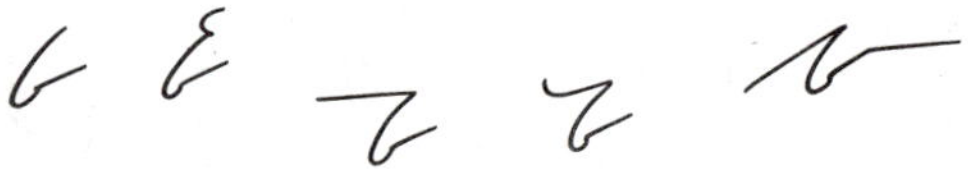

14 -tain

15 -cient, -ciency

DISJOINED WORD ENDINGS

16 -hood

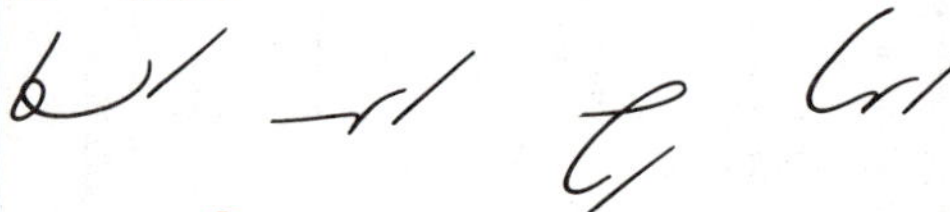

17 -ward

18 -ship

19 -cal, -cle

20 -ulate, -ulation

21 -ingly

22 -ings

23 -gram

24 -ification

25 -lity

26 -lty

27 -rity

JOINED WORD BEGINNINGS

28 Per-, Pur-

29 Em-

30 Im-

31 In-

32 En-

33 Un-

34 Re-

35 Be-

36 De-, Di-	47 Ul-
37 Dis-, Des-	**DISJOINED WORD BEGINNINGS**
38 Mis-	48 Post-
39 Ex-	49 Inter-, Etc.
40 Com-	50 Electr-, Electric
41 Con-	51 Super-
42 Sub-	52 Circum-
43 Al-	53 Self-
44 For-, Fore-	54 Trans-
45 Fur-	55 Under-
46 Tern-, Etc.	56 Over-

PHRASES

57 T for To in Phrases

58 Been Represented by B

59 Able Represented by A

60 Want Preceded by Pronoun

61 Ago Represented by G

62 To Omitted in Phrases

63 The Omitted in Phrases

64 Of Omitted in Phrases

65 A Omitted in Phrases

66 Intersected Phrases

67 Special Phrases

Addresses to be used for mailable transcripts

Chapter 1

LESSON 1

1. Miss Mary C. Green, National Chemical Company, 16 West 56 Street, New York, New York 10040
2. Mrs. James C. Larson, The Atlantic Drug Company, Box 127, Yellow Springs, Ohio 45387
3. Mr. John R. Brooks, 15 Rock Road, Ashland, Maine 04732
4. Miss Helen H. Gordon, Dover Road, Baltimore, Maryland 21202
5. Mrs. Elsa Ellis, Old Orchard Road, Skokie, Illinois 60076
6. Mr. Frank L. Edwards, 76 Reynolds Drive, Meriden, Connecticut 06451

LESSON 2

7. Mr. Thomas J. West, The Star Manufacturing Company, 480 Park Avenue, New York, New York 10022
8. Mr. Mark L. Foster, The National Editors Association, 6511 Arsenal Street, St. Louis, Missouri 63139
9. Mr. Mark L. Foster, The National Editors Association, 6511 Arsenal Street, St. Louis, Missouri 63139
10. Mr. Edward B. Johnson, 180 Main Street, Clifton, New Jersey 07014
11. Mr. Louis C. Black, 25 Park Circle, White Plains, New York 10603
12. Mr. S. J. Allen, 86 Crawford Avenue, Evanston, Illinois 60203

LESSON 3

13. Mr. Harry D. Gates, 310 Valley Street, Burlington, Iowa 52601
14. Mr. Frank E. Byrd, The Brown Furniture Company, 361 West Street, Cincinnati, Ohio 45227
15. Mr. Jacob F. Wise, West Side High School, 1141 Park Street, Los Angeles, California 90022
16. Mr. George Gates, 1561 Clinton Avenue, Los Angeles, California 90022
17. Mr. Herbert G. Mann, Harper and Company, 110 Market Street, Newark, New Jersey 07118
18. Mr. Otis H. Roberts, American Tool & Die Company, 1315 Woodward Avenue, Detroit, Michigan 48207

LESSON 4

19. Mr. Clifford E. Swanson, University of Nebraska, Lincoln, Nebraska 68501
20. Mr. David F. Barnes, Smith and Company, 1168 Bruce Road, Bangor, Maine 04401
21. Mr. David F. Barnes, Smith and Company, 1168 Bruce Road, Bangor, Maine 04401
22. Mr. David F. Barnes, Smith and Company, 1168 Bruce Road, Bangor, Maine 04401

23   Mr. Carl G. Drake, King Office Furniture Company, Inc., 18 Lexington Avenue, Broadview, Illinois   60153

24   Mr. Kenneth B. James, Central Equipment Company, Inc., 315 Beacon Street, Boston, Massachusetts   02215

LESSON 5

25   Mr. Ralph I. Day, Dayton College, 315 Congress Street, St. Paul, Minnesota   55104

26   Mr. Jerome K. West, The Gray Publishing Company, Inc., 5111 Jackson Road, Ann Arbor, Michigan   48106

27   Mr. Donald C. Wilson, The National Education Council, 210 York Avenue, Atlanta, Georgia   30312

28   Mr. Robert F. March, The Davis Manufacturing Company, 416 Commonwealth Avenue, Boston, Massachusetts   02215

29   Miss Rita J. Best, Kerr & Company, 1138 Allen Street, Buffalo, New York   14205

30   Mr. Edward K. Kelly, The Wilson Manufacturing Company, 16 State Street, Clinton, Massachusetts   01510

Chapter 2

LESSON 6

31   Mr. John C. Cummings, American Products Company, Inc., 18 Water Street, Holyoke, Massachusetts   01040

32   National Clothing Stores, 234 West 42 Street, New York, New York   10036

33   Mr. Roger W. Smith, General Sales Manager, The Davis Company, 1027 Broad Street, Philadelphia, Pennsylvania   19107

34   Mr. Paul Y. Kline, 800 East 40 Street, Miami, Florida   33137

35   Mr. George C. Smith, President, Arno Printing Company, Inc., 30 East 115 Street, New York, New York   10019

36   Mr. William A. Johnson, Kent Brothers, Box 4141, Charlotte, North Carolina   28203

LESSON 7

37   Mr. J. C. Carpenter, President, National Manufacturing Company, 116 Baker Road, Springfield, Illinois   62705

38   Mr. Charles J. Baker, The Hunter Publishing Company, Inc., Crawfordsville, Indiana   47933

39   Mr. A. L. Bentley, 610 Third Street, Salt Lake City, Utah   84103

40   Miss Alice C. Day, 1156 Baker Drive, Troy, New York   12180

41   Mrs. Charles I. Quinn, 3415 East 23 Street, Mount Morris, Illinois   61054

42   Mr. C. C. James, James and Company, 16 Wilson Square, Westport, Connecticut   06880

LESSON 8

43   Mr. Thomas J. Barnes, President, Acme Stores, 631 Green Tree Road, Milwaukee, Wisconsin   53209

44 Mr. Frederic C. Meyers, Jones Publishing Company, 114 Flower Street, Portland, Maine 04112
45 Mr. Andrew R. Brown, 415 Broadway, 291 State Street, New Haven, Connecticut 06473
46 Mr. Anthony C. Ash, Wilson Rest Home, 115 Jackson Avenue, Independence, Missouri 64054
47 Mrs. Charles L. Shields, 1177 East 43 Street, Cleveland, Ohio 44114
48 Mr. Howard I. Keating, Davis Manufacturing Company, 702 Second Avenue, Pittsburgh, Pennsylvania 15219

LESSON 9

49 Mr. Harry M. Lee, 1156 Mason Street, Dallas, Texas 75233
50 Mr. Frank C. Lyons, Clark and Company, Inc., Los Angeles, California 90007
51 Mr. Louis B. Paul, 16 College Road, Toledo, Ohio 43608
52 Mr. Thomas C. Mills, 1146 Monroe Street, Chicago, Illinois 60610
53 Mr. Arthur Wolf, The Thompson Products Company, 116 Harper Drive, Little Rock, Arkansas 72205
54 Mr. W. W. Lewis, The National Auto Club, Inc., 115 Bryant Street, Chattanooga, Tennessee 37401

LESSON 10

55 Mrs. Charles R. Green, 115 Marion Avenue, Oregon City, Oregon 97045
56 Mr. David C. James, President, The Grand River Publishing Company, Box 1118, Grand River, Iowa 50108
57 Mr. Donald D. Graham, The Palmer Manufacturing Company, Manchester, New Hampshire 03116
58 Mr. William R. Harris, The Harris Printing Company, 16 Greenwich Avenue, Greenwich, Connecticut 06830
59 Mrs. Alice J. Ray, 515 Madison Street, Billings, Montana 59101
60 Mrs. Clara C. Fenton, 318 Broadway, Racine, Wisconsin 53400

Chapter 3

LESSON 11

61 Mr. Frank Smith, Miami General Hospital, 415 Western Boulevard, Miami, Florida 33137
62 Memorandum to Harry James from Charles Smith
63 Mr. Irving W. Smith, The Baker Company, 516 Main Street, Florence, Alabama 35630
64 Mr. W. W. Edwards, The Johnson Research Corporation, 225 West 57 Street, New York, New York 10019
65 Memorandum to The Staff from William Case
66 Memorandum to Miss West from James R. Dawson
67 Memorandum to The Staff from John Green

LESSON 12

68 Mr. Frederic C. White, Johnson Paper Products, 800 Nelson Avenue, New Bedford, Massachusetts   02740
69 Memorandum from Harold Baker to The Staff
70 Memorandum from Robert J. Mills to The Staff
71 Memorandum from Harry Dexter to The Staff
72 Memorandum from James Wells to The Staff
73 Memorandum from Joseph Wilson to All Executives

LESSON 13

74 Mr. C. C. West, Wilson and Company, 801 Newark Avenue, Elizabeth, New Jersey   07208
75 Memorandum from R. A. Burns to J. C. Jones
76 Memorandum from David Myer, M.D., to The Staff
77 Memorandum from Jack Collins to The Staff
78 Memorandum from Fred A. Bates to All Supervisors
79 Memorandum from James R. Brown to The Staff

LESSON 14

80 Memorandum from Charles R. Smith to Mr. Brown
81 Memorandum from James Stacy to The Staff
82 Memorandum from Frank Lopez to Mr. Stone
83 Memorandum from Charles Wilson to The Staff
84 Memorandum from Frank Davis to The Staff
85 Personnel Department, Oxford Manufacturing Company, Inc., Clinton Road, Garden City, New York   11530
86 Memorandum from James C. Brown to The Staff

LESSON 15

87 Memorandum from Sam Jones to Mr. Willis
88 Memorandum from Harry Myers to J. C. Phillips
89 Memorandum from James Denton to The Staff
90 Memorandum from Harry Davis to The Staff
91 Memorandum from John C. Drake to All Supervisors
92 Memorandum from A. B. Simmons to The Sales Staff
93 Memorandum from Harry Jones to The Staff

Chapter 4

LESSON 16

94 Mr. Charles J. James, Harper Industries, 114 Park Avenue, New York, New York   10013
95 American Bookbinding Company, 2804 Fourth Street, Flagstaff, Arizona   86001
96 Professor Edward A. James, National College, Nashville, Tennessee   37219

97 Memorandum from James Watson to All Managers
98 Mr. David J. Smith, President, G. & C. Industries, 116 Pratt Street, Baltimore, Maryland 21202
99 Mr. D. D. Ray, Graphic Printing Company, 114 Main Street, Dallas, Texas 75207

LESSON 17

100 Mr. Herbert L. Taylor, Wilson Department Stores, 214 M Street, N.W., Washington, D.C. 20037
101 Mr. Adam J. Love, Western Electronics Company, 200 State Street, Chicago, Illinois 60607
102 Mr. John K. Parker, Case Electronics, Inc., 1130 Davis Street, Denver, Colorado 80205
103 Mr. Edward M. Davis, Weston Retail Distributors, Inc., 307 East 15 Street, Cincinnati, Ohio 45202
104 Graphic Arts, Inc., 141 Herman Street, York, Pennsylvania 17404
105 Memorandum from Robert L. Day to The Staff
106 Mr. Walter J. Star, 945 Larch Street, Elmhurst, Illinois 60125

LESSON 18

107 Mr. J. J. Best, Union Book Company, Inc., 415 Congress Street, Boston, Massachusetts 02210
108 Mr. John L. Foster, United Manufacturing Company, 4151 Davis Avenue, Pittsburgh, Pennsylvania 15213
109 Mr. Donald J. Baker, The Madison Publishing Company, 115 West 56 Street, New York, New York 10035
110 Mr. Barry C. Green, 320 North Zeeb Road, Ann Arbor, Michigan 48106
111 Mr. Russell K. Little, United Book Company, 815 Avenue B, San Antonio, Texas 78206
112 Dr. Harry L. Smith, The College of Commerce, 318 Bruce Street, Greenwich, Connecticut 06830
113 Mr. Allen N. Carter, Western Products Company, 326 West 48 Street, Topeka, Kansas 66603

LESSON 19

114 Mr. John R. Casey, Davis Publishing Company, 2902 Division Street, Los Angeles, California 90065
115 Mr. Rex C. Morgan, American Equipment Company, 15 Park Place, St. Louis, Missouri 63146
116 Mr. Jerome R. Harper, Noble Manufacturing Company, 481 Lafayette Street, New York, New York 10003
117 Mr. Benjamin P. Lyons, 1415 P Street, Lincoln, Nebraska 68501
118 Young & Brown, Inc., 220 Western Avenue, Covington, Kentucky 41011
119 Mr. Lee R. Conley, Nickelson & Company, 124 Wilshire Avenue, Fullerton, California 92632
120 Mr. Harold H. Jack, 315 Praline Street, Lake Charles, Louisiana 70601

LESSON 20

121. Mr. Frank C. Paul, 279 Madison Avenue, Memphis, Tennessee 38101
122. Mr. R. J. Foster, 3218 Long Beach Road, Oceanside, New York 11572
123. Mr. M. C. Anthony, Davis Manufacturing Company, 628 Hancock Street, Caribou, Maine 04736
124. Mr. Wilbur L. Fay, Williams Clothing Company, 125 West End Avenue, New York, New York 10023
125. Mr. Steven T. Taylor, Indianapolis Printing Company, 114 West Street, Indianapolis, Indiana 46220
126. Mr. Lauren C. Best, President, American Investment Company, 400 Superior Street, Detroit, Michigan 48219
127. Mr. Leslie J. Parker, 405 Pine Bluff, Hillsdale, Wyoming 82060

Chapter 5

LESSON 21

128. Mr. Ralph C. Taylor, American Publishing Company, 316 West Street, Chicago, Illinois 60610
129. The Mann Marketing Services, Inc., Ridge Road, Cliff Lake, Montana 59720
130. Mr. Harvey C. Willis, The Hill Publishing Company, 318 Lexington Avenue, Miami, Florida 33112
131. Mr. Harvey C. Willis, The Hill Publishing Company, 318 Lexington Avenue, Miami, Florida 33112
132. Mr. Henry Q. Charles, The National Travel Magazine, 315 Wilson Boulevard, Yonkers, New York 10714
133. Mr. Donald J. McKenzie, 31 Main Street, Concord, New Hampshire 03303
134. Mr. Howard L. Lincoln, 2151 South Street, New Orleans, Louisiana 70109

LESSON 22

135. Mr. Arnold Swanson, The American Chemist, 322 Rogers Road, Kingston, Rhode Island 02836
136. Mr. Eric L. Barnes, American Business, Inc., 818 Marian Avenue, Mason City, Iowa 50401
137. Mr. William J. James, The Reader's Monthly, 717 Jackson Street, Independence, Missouri 64050
138. Professor Harvey L. Smith, Baker University, 540 North Street, Fort Worth, Texas 76108
139. Memorandum from Jim Stacy to Mr. Smith.
140. Memorandum from Harold J. Smith to The Staff
141. Mrs. Charles H. Paul, 43 Osage Street, Denmark, Kansas 67206

LESSON 23

142. Mr. C. C. Harris, Johnson Printing Company, Inc., 204 Cooper Street, Windham, New York 12496

143 Mr. Otto S. Day, The Wilson School of Management, 15 Main Street, Jacksonville, Florida   33120

144 Miss Alice C. Kay, Fisher and Company, 642 Forrest Street, Wichita, Kansas   67206

145 Mr. Samuel C. Barry, 643 Randolph Street, Richmond, Indiana   47374

146 Mr. Kevin L. Murphy, The Edison Manufacturing Company, 165 Lee Avenue, Fall Church, Virginia   22040

147 Mr. Herman A. White, West High School, 316 Main Avenue, Freemont, Nebraska   68025

148 Mr. Ernest C. Miller, Warren Publishers, Inc., 1800 Clark Road, Salem, Oregon   97301

LESSON 24

149 Mr. Daniel C. Baker, C.P.A., National Bank Building, 151 Broadway, New York, New York   10056

150 Mr. Harvey J. Green, Eastern School of Business, 101 Anderson Avenue, New Rochelle, New York   10802

151 Miss Mary L. Gold, Johnson School of Business Training, 3187 Clinton Avenue, Medina, Ohio   44256

152 Mr. Frank C. Larson, United Manufacturing Company, 216 Carroll Street, Alton Park, Tennessee   37401

153 Mr. Alexander J. Gordon, Walsh School of Business, 617 Lansing Street, Maywood, New Jersey   08330

154 Miss Margaret Casey, Central High School, Helena, Montana   59601

155 Miss Kay Frank, National Secretaries Association, 315 Brewer Street, Bisbee, Arizona   85603

LESSON 25

156 Mr. Chester C. Gray, East High School, 2600 Broad Road, Hartsville, South Carolina   29550

157 Miss Jane L. West, Central High School, 31 Church Road, Huntington, Indiana   46750

158 Memorandum from James R. Green to Mr. Jones

159 Mr. Dell H. Temple, 415 Seminole Street, Tampa, Florida   33612

160 Mr. Frederic J. Thomas, Smith Publishing Company, 15 Post Road, Scarsdale, New York   10583

161 Miss Louise L. James, 415 Cross Boulevard, Hoboken, New Jersey   07030

162 Memorandum from Charles C. Wilson to Mr. Wallace

Chapter 6

LESSON 26

163 Mr. Spencer L. James, 21 Church Lane, Tarrytown, New York   10591

164 Mr. Kermit N. Green, 106 Lake Drive, Marquette, Wisconsin   53947

165 Harry C. Jones, Esq., 316 Main Avenue, Marquette, Wisconsin   53947

166   Mr. Kermit N. Green, 106 Lake Drive, Marquette, Wisconsin   53947
167   Mrs. Kenneth A. Smith, 980 Decatur Road, Grand River, Iowa   50108
168   Mrs. Mary J. Deems, 36 Farmer Road, Southport, Indiana   48786
169   Mr. Jack L. Pierce, 471 Raleigh, Burlington, West Virginia   28710

LESSON 27

170   Mr. George H. Young, 1 Shawnee Avenue, La Crosse, Wisconsin   54601
171   The National Tree Company, 961 Franklin Avenue, Columbus, Ohio   43211
172   Eastern Appliance Company, Inc., 410 Market Street, Newark, New Jersey   07118
173   Mr. Melvin C. Hughes, 118 Garden Road, West New York, New Jersey   07093
174   Mrs. Grace H. Wilson, 94 Main Street, White Plains, New York   10601
175   Mr. Roger N. Bronson, 1461 Avenue J, Elkhart, Indiana   46514
176   Mr. Howard M. Ford, 714 Meadow Lane, Craftsbury, Vermont   05826

LESSON 28

177   Mrs. Frederic J. West, 684 White Plains Road, Pelham, New York   10566
178   Mr. C. C. Morris, 28 Parker Road, Westerly, Rhode Island   02891
179   Mr. David C. Green, 15 West 18 Street, Ossining, New York   10562
180   Mrs. Clayton C. Mills, 116 Lake Road, Dallas, Texas   75214
181   Mrs. Adam Y. Wilson, 116 Shelby Street, Somerset, Indiana   46984
182   Mr. Elmer C. Jackson, 39 Stone Street, Springfield, Massachusetts   01131
183   Mrs. C. C. Murray, 361 Baylor Street, Omaha, Nebraska   68119

LESSON 29

184   Stratford Home Supplies Company, 51 Main Street, Stratford, Connecticut   06497
185   Mr. Donald J. Smith, Baker Construction Company, 14 Southview Avenue, Bridgeport, Connecticut   06496
186   The American Home Magazine, 150 Main Street, Dover, New Jersey   07801
187   Mr. Harry C. Moore, 15 Baker Street, Fargo, North Dakota   58103
188   Mr. Walter R. Wall, 1246 Beechtree Road, Atlanta, Georgia   30314
189   Mr. Frank R. Pace, 156 Eagan Avenue, Walla Walla, Washington   99362
190   Mr. Jerry L. Smith, 28 Park Lane, Tacoma, Washington   98411

LESSON 30

191   Mrs. Mildred J. Drake, 96 East Street, Paris, Mississippi   38949
192   International Machines Company, 156 Knox Avenue, Fort Madison, Iowa   52627
193   Mr. D. C. Cooper, 117 Day Street, Osage, Minnesota   56570
194   Mr. Charles C. Dix, 141 West 61 Street, Wilmington, Delaware   19804
195   The Little River Home Appliance Company, 40 Wilcox Avenue, Little River, Alabama   36550
196   Mr. Paul J. Frost, 16 Calhoun, Fairmont, West Virginia   26550
197   Mrs. Hubert G. Hughes, 116 Jackson Road, Bisbee, Arizona   85603

Chapter 7

LESSON 31

198 Memorandum from James C. Brown to Mr. Curtis
199 Mr. Jacob C. Deems, 156 Palm Tree Drive, Miami, Florida   33125
200 Mr. Chester L. James, 47 Clay Road, Robbins, Illinois   60472
201 Mr. Randolph J. Krause, Morgan Manufacturing Company, Inc., 8 West Pine Street, Chattanooga, Tennessee   37401
202 Mr. Emery S. Abbey, 64 Ward Street, Wichita Falls, Texas   76301
203 Dr. E. John Smith, 28 South Street, Birmingham, Alabama   35201
204 Mr. Alan D. Grace, Jackson and Company, 16 Farrier Street, Charleston, West Virginia   25303

LESSON 32

205 Mr. Gerald C. Strong, 15 State Street, Albany, New York   12225
206 Mrs. J. P. Hunter, 61 Snow Street, Nome, Alaska   99762
207 Western Insurance, 16 Ocean Drive, Honolulu, Hawaii   96817
208 Mr. Abraham Roberts, 1415 Bryant Avenue, Boise, Idaho   83706
209 Mr. Albert C. Sheridan, 116 Mountain Road, Reno, Nevada   89502
210 Mr. Willis A. Franklin, 15 Main Street, Albuquerque, New Mexico   87112
211 Mr. Frank C. Davis, 116 Austin Avenue, Tulsa, Oklahoma   74127

LESSON 33

212 Mr. Theodore Hughes, 115 Simons Road, Rochester, New York   14014
213 The Empire Insurance Company, 64 Hudson Street, Garden City, New York   11530
214 Mr. Harry J. Gates, 115 South Boulevard, Pierre, South Dakota   57501
215 Mr. Henry L. Arnold, 441 Michigan Avenue, Detroit, Michigan   48207
216 Mr. John C. Morris, Morris and Brown, 401 Butler Avenue, Cleveland, Ohio   44104
217 Mr. Phillip S. Bailey, Wilson and Bailey, Inc., 61 Federal Street, Portland, Maine   04106
218 Miss Marlene A. Riley, 14 Harper Drive, Seattle, Washington   98112

LESSON 34

219 Mr. Clinton C. Davis, Lewis & Davis, 8 Lowell Street, Providence, Rhode Island   02932
220 Mr. Martin A. Baker, 181 Market Street, Philadelphia, Pennsylvania   19150
221 Miss Louise Perez, 42 Capstan Road, Oceanside, California   92054
222 Mr. Edwin C. Briggs, 84 Pine Street, Oak Grove, Wisconsin   53925
223 Mr. Morton J. Green, 46 East Street, Pueblo, California   81009
224 Mr. Abraham J. Klein, 119 Black Street, Wilkes-Barre, Pennsylvania   18714
225 Mr. Michael C. Sims, 146 Ridge Road, Cliff Lake, Montana   59720

LESSON 35

226 Mr. Jay R. Barnes, The Eastern Insurance Company, 614 West Main Street, Bloomsburg, Pennsylvania   17815
227 The Hartford Insurance Company, 46 Market Street, Hartford, Connecticut   06117
228 Mr. Myron J. Green, 215 Oneida Street, Lewiston, Idaho   83501
229 Mr. Morris Rosen, 151 Kent Street, Wilmington, Delaware   19801
230 Mr. Arthur B. Johnson, 416 Grant Street, Silver City, New Mexico   88061
231 Mr. Wilford A. May, 690 Pine Bluff, Hillsdale, Wyoming   82060
232 Mr. David L. West, 320 Cedar Street, Sioux Falls, South Dakota   57107

Chapter 8

LESSON 36

233 Mr. Andrew C. Casey, 29 Bliss Road, El Paso, Texas   79906
234 Mr. David D. Ball, 206 Main Street, Freedom, Wyoming   83120
235 Mr. P. T. Baker, 209 Adams Street, Menasha, Wisconsin   54952
236 Mr. Donald C. Dawson, 720 Country Road, Milton, Delaware   19968
237 Mr. Irving Moses, 74 Erie Street, Albany, New York   12216
238 Mr. Whitney Kramer, 100 King Street, Clarksburg, West Virginia   26301

LESSON 37

239 Memorandum from James Wilson to Mr. Grace
240 Mr. Frederic Bailey, 96 Hamilton Avenue, Baltimore, Maryland   21208
241 United Manufacturing Company, 360 Oak Street, Nashua, New Hampshire   03060
242 Stone Lumber Company, 26 Canyon Avenue, Estes Park, Colorado   80517
243 Mr. V. R. Richards, Wilson and Company, 500 Calvert, Cumberland, Maryland   21501
244 Mr. Herbert C. Hamilton, Western Printing Company, 84 Horse Pike, Laramie, Wyoming   82070
245 Mr. Douglas G. Grant, 81 Simpson Street, Laurel, Mississippi   39440

LESSON 38

246 Mr. Morris G. Klein, 38 Main Street, Chatham, New Jersey   07928
247 Mr. Horace G. Lee, 96 Clinton Avenue, Sandusky, Ohio   44870
248 Mr. Thomas G. Watson, President, National Retail Stores, 315 West 16 Street, New York, New York   10018
249 Mr. Harmon P. Henry, 15 Palmer Avenue, Miami, Florida   33112
250 Mr. Alan G. Keith, 24 Park Lane, Bristol, Connecticut   06010
251 Mr. Everett Baker, 1158 South Mason, Houston, Texas   77015
252 Mr. Herbert C. Peters, 390 Essex Street, Greensboro, North Carolina   27404

LESSON 39

253 Acme Tire Company, 341 Western Avenue, Springfield, Ohio   45512
254 Mr. C. C. Stern, 14 Ocean Avenue, Asbury Park, New Jersey   07712

255 Mr. Edward J. Booth, 750 Pershing Avenue, Las Vegas, Nevada   89108
256 Mr. Henry L. Gates, National Trucking Company, 771 Warren Street, Belleville, New Jersey   08502
257 Mr. Phillip R. Lawrence, 145 Carroll Street, Alton Park, Tennessee   37401
258 Mr. R. M. Wall, 41 Decatur Avenue, Memphis, Tennessee   38109
259 Mr. Douglas L. Drake, 2616 Euclid Avenue, Cleveland, Ohio   44150

LESSON 40

260 Mr. Arnold J. Smith, 480 Knox Avenue, Bennington, Nebraska   68007
261 Mr. C. C. West, 1617 Nelson Avenue, Albany, New York   12203
262 The American Car Company, 366 Woodward, Detroit, Michigan   48207
263 The American Car Company, 336 Woodward, Detroit, Michigan   48207
264 Mr. James C. Percy, 450 Harris Avenue, Reading, Pennsylvania   19607
265 Mr. Jacob L. Wilson, 761 Clinton Avenue, Buffalo, New York   14264
266 Mr. Amos C. Samson, 43 Mill Run, Ashland, Pennsylvania   17921

Chapter 9

LESSON 41

267 Memorandum from James C. Joseph to Miss Davis
268 Mr. Roscoe G. Day, The American Data Processing Corporation, 155 Madison Avenue, New York, New York   10037
269 Jones Office Furniture Company, 315 West 18 Street, 1512 Fifth Avenue, New York, New York   10036
270 Mr. Harry J. Barton, Broadway Printing Company, Las Cruces, New Mexico   88001
271 Mr. Ronald L. Benson, Merritt Clothing Company, 47 Fredrick Avenue, Hagarstown, Maryland   21740
272 Mr. Howard G. Tracy, First National Bank, 153 Bayou Boulevard, St. Petersburg, Florida   33706
273 Mr. Graham A. Harvey, Harper Publishing Company, 31 East Boulevard, Minneapolis, Minnesota   55410

LESSON 42

274 Memorandum from Fred Harvey to Mr. Smith
275 Mr. James C. Simmons, The Jones Appliance Company, 42 Alger Street, Grand Rapids, Michigan   49528
276 Mr. Lawrence G. Sims, 90 West Street, Rapid City, South Dakota   57701
277 Mr. Charles R. Sanders, 1415 Park Place, Kansas City, Missouri   64109
278 Mr. Grant C. James, 34 Cliff Street, Shaker Heights, Ohio   44150
279 Mr. Tracy R. Collins, Gates Manufacturing Company, 67 Day Street, Seattle, Washington   98112
280 Mr. William S. Temple, The Topeka Men's Shop, 300 Oakland Street, Topeka, Kansas   66617

LESSON 43

281   Mr. James Abbey, 100 North Avenue, Waterbury, Connecticut   06709
282   The National Automation Institute, 16 Hamilton Street, Macomb, Illinois   61455
283   Memorandum from William G. Hart to Mr. Watts
284   Mr. Addison G. James, 461 South Street, Elizabeth, New Jersey   07215
285   Mr. C. C. Irving, Park Paper Company, 450 Hartwell Avenue, Cincinnati, Ohio   45225
286   Mr. Daniel C. Smith, Johnson Envelope Company, 16 East 42 Street, New York, New York   10082

LESSON 44

287   Mr. Lawrence G. Banks, White Printing Company, Inc., Bowling Green, Kentucky   42101
288   Memorandum from James C. Smith to Harry S. Parsons
289   Adams Electronics, Inc., 61 Burnham Road, Worcester, Massachusetts   01626
290   Mr. Earl G. Snyder, Davis Printers, Inc., Buffalo, New York   14250
291   Mr. David G. Jones, Day Paper Company, 61 Lafayette Court, Fall River, Massachusetts   02720
292   Mr. C. J. Towers, Gates Women's Shop, 900 Railroad Avenue, Toledo, Ohio   43610
293   Mr. Frank L. Thompson, 117 Lenoir Avenue, Gastonia, North Carolina   28052

LESSON 45

294   Memorandum from Harry Burns to Mr. Baker
295   Memorandum from Charles C. Stone to James Gates
296   Mr. Albert C. Binns, The Western Publishing Company, 112 Newton Street, Little Rock, Arkansas   72203
297   Mr. Carlos Perez, Darwin and Company, 24 Fourth Street, Mount Kisco, New York   10549
298   Mr. J. C. Drake, Casey Stationery Company, 222 Western Avenue, Covington, Kentucky   41011
299   Mr. Edwin C. Jackson, National Glass Company, 315 Harper Street, Baton Rouge, Louisiana   70802
300   Mr. Harold S. Martin, New York Publishing Company, 115 Broadway, New York, New York   10044

Chapter 10

LESSON 46

301   Larson Women's Shop, Inc., 315 Monroe Street, Chicago, Illinois   60614
302   The Illinois Supply Company, 38 Second Avenue, Macomb, Illinois   61455
303   Memorandum from Harry Jackson to James Mason
304   Mr. Willis Long, 37 Marquette Street, Green Bay, Wisconsin   54304
305   Carr Hardware Store, 14 Wheeler Street, Mount Wilson, California   91023

306 Mr. Henry J. Benson, 37 Hillside Avenue, Hudson, New York   12534
307 Mr. R. R. Simms, National Clothing Stores, 115 Park Place, Gary, Indiana   46409

LESSON 47

308 Mr. E. C. Bates, 156 Mason Street, Linwood, North Carolina   27299
309 Albany Appliance Company, 15 State Street, Albany, New York   12205
310 Mr. C. C. Carter, Parker Stores, Inc., 316 Franklin Avenue, Brooklyn, New York   11224
311 Mr. Charles E. Hamilton, 1446 River Drive, Bangor, Maine   04401
312 Draper Clothing Stores, 1445 Sixth Avenue, Lexington, Kentucky   40505
313 Mr. C. E. Case, 151 South Street, Cullman, Alabama   35055
314 Mr. Arthur Putnam, 145 Willis Avenue, New York, New York   10046

LESSON 48

315 Mrs. Gertrude G. Peters, 115 Mead Lane, Ironwood, Michigan   49938
316 Western Products Company, Inc., 74 Worth Street, Grand River, Iowa   50108
317 Mr. Ira G. Hart, Hart Department Store, 166 Parsons Boulevard, Moline, Illinois   61265
318 Mr. George H. Simons, 3146 Lenox Avenue, Rye, New York   10580
319 Mr. Wilson C. Sherman, Gray Manufacturing Company, 116 Broadway, New York, New York   10018
320 Harris Men's Shop, 116 Essex Street, Gloucester, Massachusetts   01930
321 Mr. Samuel G. Blackton, National Printing Company, 615 Vine Street, Dallas, Texas   75214

LESSON 49

322 The Western Textbook Company, 316 Potter Place, Omaha, Nebraska   68119
323 Mr. George H. West, West Hardware Store, Granby, Connecticut   06035
324 Mr. Ellis H. Baker, Meadow Binding Service, 2116 Harwood, Dallas, Texas   75215
325 Harson Hardware Company, Inc., 317 Davis Drive, Racine, Wisconsin   53400
326 Mr. Edgar Casey, Hunter Stationers, Shelbyville, Indiana   46176
327 Mrs. Alice H. Mason, 118 Bruce Park, Stroudsburg, Pennsylvania   18360
328 Mr. Cyrus Jackson, 110 Henry Street, Madisonville, Kentucky   42431

LESSON 50

329 Harrison Department Stores, 316 Crawford, Evanston, Illinois   60203
330 Mr. R. R. Perry, Perry Department Stores, 116 Clay Street, Minneapolis, Minnesota   55401
331 Mr. Henry C. Green, 155 West 60 Street, New York, New York   10018
332 Mr. Edward G. Sharp, 128 Wilshire Avenue, Fullerton, California   92632
333 Mrs. Charles H. Travis, 200 South Street, Norristown, Pennsylvania   19401
334 Mrs. Kenneth G. James, 14 West Fourth Street, Mount Kisco, New York   10549
335 Mr. Solomon G. Bloom, 360 Baylor Avenue, Omaha, Nebraska   68119

Chapter 11

LESSON 51

336 Mrs. Marian G. Gifford, 7 West 48 Street, Los Angeles, California   90022
337 Mr. C. C. Richards, 14 Ohio Street, Chicago, Illinois   60614
338 Mr. Frederic C. Leonard, 156 Lexington Avenue, New York, New York   10048
339 Dr. C. C. Green, 316 East 72 Street, New York, New York   10041
340 Mrs. Janice G. Flood, 561 Western Avenue, Lincoln, Nebraska   68500
341 Mrs. G. G. Smith, 615 Forrest Road, Nashville, Tennessee   37204
342 Mr. Clark A. Nelson, 61 Edison Avenue, Philadelphia, Pennsylvania   19117

LESSON 52

343 Mr. Jeffry Morris, 240 Park Avenue, Hicksville, New York   11802
344 Mr. Gordon C. Nelson, 600 Camera Avenue, St. Louis, Missouri   63126
345 Mr. Frank D. Deems, The American Products Company, 166 Wood Street, Braintree, Massachusetts   02184
346 Mr. D. C. Schmidt, 81 Maiden Lane, Milwaukee, Wisconsin   53212
347 Mr. C. C. Day, 716 Jackson Avenue, Bloomfield, Connecticut   06002
348 Mr. J. C. Barlow, 16 Washington Avenue, St. Louis, Missouri   63101
349 Mr. Edward G. Starr, Box 1181, Benton Harbor, Michigan   49022

LESSON 53

350 Mr. John H. Collins, 416 East State Street, Rockford, Illinois   61104
351 Mr. Wallace G. Potter, 100 Columbus Avenue, Boston, Massachusetts   02116
352 Mr. Donald H. Parker, 816 Avenue B, San Antonio, Texas   78206
353 Mr. Samuel J. Allen, 216 Eddy Street, Providence, Rhode Island   02903
354 Mr. Andrew C. Finley, 308 Stokes Avenue, Trenton, New Jersey   08638
355 Miss Rosemary Carson, 216 Dixwell Avenue, Hamden, Connecticut   06514
356 Mr. William C. Tarr, 1916 Shepard Road, St. Paul, Minnesota   55116

LESSON 54

357 Mr. Edwin G. Davis, 315 West 16 Street, New York, New York   10031
358 Memorandum from William C. Barnes to Mr. James
359 Memorandum from John Abbey to Mr. Jacobs.
360 Mr. Martin Allen, The Gray Manufacturing Company, 100 Park Avenue, New York, New York   10017
361 Mr. Del C. Barton, Gordon Industries, Inc., 2950 Division Street, Los Angeles, California   90065
362 Mr. Howard Masters, W. R. Baker and Company, Inc., 116 Federal Street, Chicago, Illinois   60605
363 Mr. Carlos H. Doyle, 100 Hillcrest Drive, Marion, Illinois   62959

LESSON 55

364 Mr. Charles H. Robins, 315 Tyler Street, Collinston, Louisiana   71229

ADDRESSES | 439

365   Mr. Lauren G. Grace, 37 East 18 Street, New York, New York   10003
366   Mr. Frederic R. Daly, 21 Park Row, New York, New York   10016
367   Mr. Clarence H. Richards, 1423 Salina Street, Syracuse, New York   13201
368   Mr. Casper L. Jones, 15 Scull Street, Lebanon, Pennsylvania   17042
369   Mr. Cecil B. Abbey, 16 North Road, Poughkeepsie, New York   12601
370   Mr. Edgar C. Taylor, 415 Pike Street, Cincinnati, Ohio   45202

Chapter 12

LESSON 56

371   Mr. Ira G. West, Johnson and Baker, Inc., 315 Forrest Lane, Storrs, Connecticut 06268
372   Lowell Manufacturing Company, 114 Main Street, Kansas City, Missouri   64108
373   Wilson Printing Company, 14 Webster Street, Newark, New Jersey   07104
374   Wilcox Associates, Box 116, Montpelier, Vermont   05602
375   Mr. Clarence H. Dobbs, World Hardware Company, 61 Maple Road, Greensburg, Pennsylvania   15601
376   Wilson Printing Company, 61 Third Street, Salt Lake City, Utah   84103
377   Mr. Jason C. Harper, Burns Clothing Company, 16 First Street, San Francisco, California   94105

LESSON 57

378   Mr. Samuel G. Green, Hudson Paper Company, 19 Lawrence Street, Denver, Colorado   80202
379   Mr. Marvin C. Bates, Washington Rug Company, 146 Main Street, Maynard, Massachusetts   01754
380   Mr. A. B. Lamb, American Magazine, 16 Arch Street, Philadelphia, Pennsylvania   19107
381   Mr. Fred Linton, General Electronics, Inc., 839 Pearl Street, Jackson, Michigan   49202
382   Jacobs Publishing Company, 141 West 41 Street, Charlotte, North Carolina   28201
383   Mr. Frank Johnson, Leslie and Jones, Inc., 2906 El Camino, Palo Alto, California   94304
384   Baker Paper Company, 311 Second Avenue, Spokane, Washington   99204

LESSON 58

385   Mr. James R. Williams, Oliver Publishing Company, Inc., 1015 Duane Street, New York, New York   10013
386   Wilson Stationers, 41 Davis Place, Greenwich, Connecticut   06830
387   Mr. Orson C. Grayson, National Paper and Printing Company, 67 Monroe Drive, Atlanta, Georgia   30324
388   Mr. D. L. Mason, New England Paper Company, Box 617, Boston, Massachusetts   02102
389   Mr. Oliver Herbert, 7 South Lane, Oklahoma City, Oklahoma   73104

390 Parker Paper Company, 16 Grand Boulevard, Detroit, Michigan 48211
391 Jones Printing Company, Inc., 2156 Arthur Avenue, Elk Grove, Illinois 60007

LESSON 59

392 Memorandum from Charles H. Green to Mr. Grace
393 Mr. Howard H. Macy, Thomas School, 681 Clark Road, Helena, Montana 59601
394 Mr. Homer J. Bates, The Medical Journal, 115 Wilson Avenue, Linwood, North Carolina 27299
395 Mr. Steven J. Jones, The Western Publishing Company, 600 Main Street, Little Rock, Arkansas 72204
396 Mr. Louis Jackson, The Hill Publishing Company, 400 Hancock Street, Lake Charles, Louisiana 70601
397 Mr. Thomas C. Day, Edison Watch Company, Inc., 61 Main Avenue, Hyattsville, Maryland 20780
398 Mrs. David C. Taft, Bell Publishing Company, 116 Brewer Avenue, Fairview, New Jersey 07022

LESSON 60

399 Mr. J. C. Winston, 764 Butler Road, Selma, Ohio 45364
400 Memorandum from Charles C. Gray to Edward Burns
401 Memorandum from Harry C. James to The Staff
402 Mr. Louis A. Swanson, Butler and Company, Inc., 716 West 14 Street, Los Angeles, California 90022
403 Mr. Simon G. Boyle, Irving and Palmer, Inc., 60 Amherst Avenue, Staunton, Virginia 24401
404 Mr. A. A. Parker, Western Publishing Company, Inc., 141 Wheeler Street, Mount Wilson, California 91023
405 Mr. George H. Harms, Prescott Manufacturing Company, 915 Jewett Street, Muskeegon, Michigan 49440

Chapter 13

LESSON 61

406 Mr. Harry C. Casey, 140 Main Street, Maynard, Massachusetts 01754
407 Memorandum from James Green to The Staff
408 Mr. Charles G. West, 41 Post Road, Deal, New Jersey 07723
409 Mr. G. C. Elliott, 14 West 16 Street, Tampa, Florida 33610
410 Mr. and Mrs. John Alden, 161 Wilson Avenue, Greenfield, Massachusetts 01301
411 Mr. James C. Parker, 115 Avenue J, Kingsport, Tennessee 37662
412 Mr. Frank C. Cooper, 424 Oxford Street, Eastport, Maine 04631

LESSON 62

413 Town and Country, 67 Washington Avenue, Houston, Texas 77021
414 Mr. Fred G. Wall, 102 Broad Street, Philadelphia, Pennsylvania 19107
415 Mr. Howard C. Wilson, 60 North Street, Medina, Ohio 44256

416   Mr. Leo G. Tyrone, 48 Fanning Street, Moultrie, Virginia   31769
417   Mr. Roger J. Mason, 42 Smith Drive, Richmond, Indiana   47374
418   Mr. C. C. Gill, 116 Main Street, Springfield, Massachusetts   01109

LESSON 63

419   Mr. C. C. Jones, 15 Glen Ridge Park, Greenwich, Connecticut   06830
420   Mr. David R. Wilson, 82 Church Lane, Greenwich, Connecticut   06830
421   Mr. Edward G. Carr, 14 Western Avenue, Westfield, Massachusetts   01085
422   Mr. Lawrence C. Dennis, 41 Church Street, Greenwich, Connecticut   06830
423   Mr. Ralph C. Abbey, 414 West 68 Street, New York, New York   10031
424   Mr. Leonard A. West, 14 Lake Avenue, Springfield, Massachusetts   01109
425   Mr. Homer R. Brady, 31 Hudson Street, New York, New York   10032

LESSON 64

426   Mr. C. C. George, 41 Glen Ridge, Greenwich, Connecticut   06830
427   Mr. Clarence G. Green, 81 Glen Ridge, Greenwich, Connnecticut   06830
428   Mr. Harry J. Davis, Chamber of Commerce Building, 116 Fifth Avenue, Springfield, Illinois   62704
429   Mr. Clarence G. Green, 81 Glen Ridge, Greenwich, Connecticut   06830
430   Mr. D. C. Ford, 63 Madison Street, Cullman, Alabama   35055
431   Mr. Gordon L. Clay, 314 Kings Highway, Lexington, Kentucky   40505
432   Mr. Andrew Kline, Wilson and Company, Inc., 315 State Street, Chicago, Illinois   60607

LESSON 65

433   Mr. George R. Kline, Kline Real Estate Company, 116 Pine Road, Tampa, Florida   33610
434   The Daily Times, 116 Nelson Drive, Miami, Florida   33125
435   Mr. Ralph Jones, 316 Elm Drive, Greenville, North Carolina   27834
436   Mr. Harold C. Reese, 60 West Douglas Avenue, Omaha, Nebraska   68119
437   Mr. Otis R. Thomas, 42 Cumberland Road, Martin City, Missouri   64144
438   Mr. Fred G. Rose, 316 Central Avenue, Trenton, New Jersey   08608
439   Mr. A. R. Harms, 126 Harmon Street, Durham, North Carolina   27701

Chapter 14

LESSON 66

440   Mr. Ernest C. Tuttle, State College, Durham, North Carolina   27701
441   Miss Oleen Edison, 461 Euclid Avenue, Cleveland, Ohio   44128
442   Mr. Fred G. Harvey, 116 Jackson Avenue, Trinidad, Colorado   81082
443   The Norris Data Processing Company, 146 Graham Road, Harrison, New York   10528
444   Mr. Milton J. Barnes, 118 White Plains Road, White Plains, New York   10601

445   Memorandum from James C. Casey to The Staff
446   Mr. Sidney J. Malone, 21 Main Street, Stratford, Connecticut   06497

LESSON 67

447   Mr. August C. Mann, 14 Dade Boulevard, Miami, Florida   33125
448   Mr. Russell C. Harper, 600 Friendship Street, Huntington, Indiana   46750
449   Mr. William J. Baker, Principal, Washington High School, 41 Smith Street, Morristown, New Jersey   07960
450   Mr. Henry M. Green, 125 Beacon Street, Boston, Massachusetts   02129
451   Mr. Martin N. Donnelly, 460 Monroe Street, Indianapolis, Indiana   46225
452   Mr. Frank C. David, 45 Liberty Street, Little Ferry, New Jersey   07643
453   Mr. Charles R. Meade, 84 Memorial Drive, Cambridge, Massachusetts   02140

LESSON 68

454   Mr. Jerome H. West, National Machines Company, Inc., 315 Broadway, Woodstock, Vermont   05091
455   Mr. Ross I. Jones, 511 Spring Avenue, Pawtucket, Rhode Island   02860
456   Mr. Joseph C. Carter, Star Printing Company, Inc., 11 Dean Street, Canton, Ohio   44106
457   Mr. Douglas A. Rich, 314 River Road, Alexandria, Virginia   22301
458   Mr. Melvin H. Todd, 31 Shore Drive, Seattle, Washington   98112
459   Miss Janet J. Pine, 41 West Street, Rapid City, South Dakota   57701
460   Miss Julia Russell, 1617 Fifth Avenue, Grand Rapids, Michigan   49528

LESSON 69

461   Mr. David C. Pine, Personnel Manager, Fox Manufacturing Company, 111 Houston Street, New York, New York,   10018
462   Mr. Bernard G. Horn, National Paper Products, 67 Lexington Avenue, Lewiston, Maine   04240
463   Memorandum from James C. Green to The Staff
464   Mr. Robert A. Abbott, Sales Manager, Morris Publishing Company, Inc., 315 Third Street, Pittsburgh, Pennsylvania   15247
465   Memorandum from A. R. Brown to Mr. Gray
466   Mr. Allen L. Melvin, Myers Chemical Products Company, 415 Shelby Street, Somerset, Indiana   46984
467   Mr. Frederic L. Archer, Davis Publishing Company, 415 Manhattan Avenue, New York, New York   10058

LESSON 70

468   Mr. F. R. Richards, Harris Military Academy, Tampa, Florida   33610
469   Mr. Frank Parker, Wilson Military Academy, 14 Dade Avenue, Miami, Florida   33125
470   Mrs. Charles E. Morton, 47 Fulton Street, Brattleboro, Vermont   05301
471   Mrs. Charles E. Morton, 47 Fulton Street, Brattleboro, Vermont   05301

472 Mr. Howard I. Lewis, 156 Califa Street, Van Nuys, California 91401
473 Mrs. Mary I. Gold, 600 Avalon Boulevard, Los Angeles, California 90003
474 Mrs. David M. Green, 115 Avenue J, Benton Harbor, Michigan 49022

Chapter 15

LESSON 71

475 Memorandum from A. J. Harris to The Sales Staff
476 Memorandum from John Andrews to Fred Ames
477 National Cosmetics Company, Inc., 155 South Street, Garwood, New Jersey 07027
478 Mr. Ralph Sinclair, The Woods Engraving Company, 3346 Quail Street, Albany, New York 12206
479 Mr. Clinton C. Sloan, Brooks Department Store, 300 Burnett Road, Union City, New Jersey 07087
480 Mr. Arthur A. Harper, American Publishing Company, 416 West 18 Street, York, Pennsylvania 17402
481 Mr. William L. Baldwin, Central High School, 321 Main Avenue, Concord, New Hampshire 03301

LESSON 72

482 Mr. C. C. Wilson, 71 Avenue de Villiers, Paris 17, France
483 Memorandum from Ted Easton to James C. Cranford
484 Memorandum from David Green to Mr. C. C. Jones
485 Memorandum from James C. Barker to The Sales Staff
486 Memorandum from James Browning to Mr. Grace
487 Memorandum from James Gray to Mr. Ellis
488 Mr. Eric G. Smith, Sales Manager, Burns and Company, Inc., 416 West 118 Street, Augusta, West Virginia 26704

LESSON 73

489 Memorandum from A. H. Lipton to Mr. Day
490 Mr. Samuel C. Cooper, Davis and Company, Inc., Box 4156, Tulsa, Oklahoma 74130
491 Memorandum from J. H. Smith to Mr. Green
492 Mr. Morris D. Banks, National Metal Products Company, 104 South Hanover Street, Baltimore, Maryland 21201
493 Mr. Edward K. Hughes, Benson Manufacturing Company, Inc., 16 Broad Street, Rahway, New Jersey 07065
494 Mr. Lawrence H. Jones, Crane Processing Company, Box 166, Princeton, New Jersey 08540
495 Davidson Service Corporation, 110 West 56 Street, Portland, Oregon 97209

LESSON 74

496 Memorandum from John Martin to Fred Weston
497 Memorandum from Fred J. Harvey to Charles Burns

498 Memorandum from Harry Baker to James Wolfson
499 Memorandum from John Green to Mr. Elliott
500 Mrs. Harriet G. Smith, 160 Macklind Avenue, St. Louis, Missouri   63110
501 Mr. Frank C. James, 41 Webster Street, Newark, New Jersey   07104
502 Mr. C. C. West, 3116 Manor Road, Burlington, Iowa   52601

LESSON 75

503 Memorandum from Harry C. Bates to The Staff
504 Miss Alice A. Albert, 44 Lane Avenue, Crawfordsville, Indiana   47933
505 Memorandum from James R. Brennan to Mr. Harper
506 Memorandum from A. C. Ramsey to Mr. Jones
507 Mr. Henry L. Sims, Box 487, Barnstable, Massachusetts   02630
508 Mr. Jason R. May, 115 Camden Avenue, Danville, New York   14437
509 Mr. William L. Gray, 116 Osborne Avenue, Marion, Illinois   62959

Chapter 16

LESSON 76

510 Harris Investment Company, Inc., 44 Monroe Street, Chicago, Illinois   60655
511 Mr. Harvey J. West, Smith, Brown, and Baker, 244 East 19 Street, New York, New York   10017
512 Mr. Jack J. Smith, 315 Ash Street, Scranton, Pennsylvania   18509
513 Mr. Harold G. Gray, 141 Commerce Street, Nashville, Tennessee   37219
514 Mr. Wilbur A. Day, 316 Forest Park, St. Louis, Missouri   63108
515 Mr. Joseph C. Wallace, 46 Gold Street, Havre, Montana   59501
516 Mr. Glen A. Ellis, 150 Church Lane, Wilmington, Delaware   19801

LESSON 77

517 Memorandum from Sal Perez to Mr. James
518 Mr. Gordon C. Elliott, 47 Montgomery Lane, Bethesda, Maryland   20014
519 Mr. Edward L. Weeks, 74 Varick Street, New York, New York   10013
520 Mr. Clay L. Swanson, 14 East Avenue, Bay City, Michigan   48706
521 Mr. Edgar S. Smith, Kimball Road, DeWitt, Nebraska   68341
522 Mr. George H. Rule, 43 Osage Road, Denmark, Kansas   67486
523 Mr. Emory C. Farmer, 67 Salmon Avenue, Colfax, Washington   99111

LESSON 78

524 Mr. Edward L. Lance, 361 North Avenue, Brooklyn, New York   11201
525 Mrs. Ann Smith, 61 Jackson Street, Philadelphia, Pennsylvania   19148
526 New York Investment Company, 315 Wall Street, New York, New York   10016
527 Mr. Albert C. West, 13 North Huron Street, Toledo, Ohio   43601
528 Mr. Charles L. Raymond, 6 Flagg Street, Lancaster, Massachusetts   01561
529 Mr. Carl D. May, 16 Adams Avenue, New Bern, North Carolina   28560
530 Mr. Robert H. West, 66 Draper Road, St. Paul, Minnesota   55151

LESSON 79

531 Larson Lumber Company, 116 Second Avenue, Oakland, California   94612
532 Memorandum from Harry C. Wilson to Mr. James
533 Memorandum from Charles Brown to Mr. Baker
534 Mr. Carl Francis, 441 Locust Street, Shelbyville, Indiana   46176
535 Mr. Anthony C. Rizzo, 116 Parker Drive, Milwaukee, Wisconsin   53202
536 Mr. Armond C. Archer, 56 Liberty Street, Jacksonville, Florida   32202
537 Mr. Don C. Blake, Box 982, Dayton, Ohio   45401

LESSON 80

538 Memorandum from Charles C. Barnes to Mr. Davis
539 Mr. James Smith, Williams and Company, 14 Nelson Avenue, Binghamton, New York   13902
540 Mr. C. C. James, 116 Avenue C., San Antonio, Texas   78206
541 Mr. Allen G. Sands, Old Hook Road, Sharon Hill, Pennsylvania   19079
542 Mr. Lee R. Barnes, 136 Lakeside Avenue, Beaver Falls, New York   13305
543 Mr. Paul S. Gordon, 2415 South Vail Avenue, Los Angeles, California   90054

Index to transcription helps

The number next to each entry refers to the page in the text in which the entry appears.

ACCURACY PRACTICE

affect, effect	299
as, if	154
at least, at last	352
fear, feel	252
get, gather	202
in the, at the	252
light, right	406
office, official	352
order, audit	154
ought, should	406
pass, base	406
red, lead	299
retain, redeem	299
say, see	154
theirs, ours	202
thick, thin	352
written, regular	202
your, this	252

GRAMMAR CHECKUP

All right	274
Bring, take	178
Common errors	325
Let, leave	227
fewer, less	378

COMMON PREFIXES

con-	211
dis-	260
ex-	309
inter-	164
de-	417
pro-	362

LETTER PLACEMENT

Average letters	134
Hints	330
Long letters	230
Short letters	30

MODEL LETTERS

Average letter	123
Interoffice memorandum	405
Long letter	220
Short letter	22
Two-page letter	320

OFFICE-STYLE DICTATION

Deletions	158
Extensive changes	412
Instructions during dictation	278
	304
	332
	357
	384
Long insertions	256
Long transpositions	206
Restorations	182
Short insertions	233
Short transpositions	206
Substitutions	182

PUNCTUATION PRACTICE

Apostrophe	67
—COLONS	
Enumeration	129
Introducing long quote	140
—COMMAS	
And omitted	16
Apposition	15
As clause	42
Conjunction	16
If clause	42
In numbers	93
Inside quote	136
Introducing short quote	136
Introductory	42
Nonrestrictive	42
Parenthetical	15
Series	16
When clause	42
Courteous request	66
Hyphens	66
—PUNCTUATION WITH QUOTATION MARKS	
Colon introducing long quote	140
Comma inside quote	136
Comma introducing short quote	136
Period inside quote	136
Question mark inside quote	136
—SEMICOLONS	
No conjunction	68

SIMILAR WORDS

adverse, averse	170
affect, effect	368
apprised, appraised	396
brake, break	194
cite, sight, site	266
week, weak	146
peace, piece	218
principal, principle	344
suit, suite	316

wait, weight 244
wares, wears 290

SPELLING FAMILIES

-able, -ible 248
-al, -el, -le 174
-an, -on, -en 400
-ense, -ence 150
des-, dis- 321
Forming -ed, -ing derivatives of words ending in *l* 270
Forming -ed, -ing derivatives of words ending in *r* 348
Forming -ed, -ing derivatives of words ending in *t* 295
-ly added to words ending in *e* 198
Words in which m, c, l, g are doubled 373
Words in which r, n, f, s are doubled 223

TRANSCRIPTION SUGGESTIONS

Advance information 90
Devising shortcuts 382
Dictation tools 64
Helping dictator 366
Implied instructions 342
Interrupting dictator 192
Interruptions in dictation 168
Letter writing 394
Making copies 216
Making corrections 242
Notebook techniques 118
Proofreading 264
Reference books 40
Rough drafts 411
Secretary's desk 12
Transcribed letters 288

Watching for errors 314
Writing positions 144

TYPING STYLE STUDIES

Addresses 92
Amounts 92
Commas in numbers 93
Dates 93
Expressions of time 93
Titles 120
Numbers at the beginning of a sentence 94

WORD CHAINS

buyer 389
debt 337
money 238
pay 187
talk about 283

BRIEF FORMS OF GREGG SHORTHAND
IN ALPHABETICAL ORDER

	A	B	C	D	E	F	G
1							
2							
3							
4							
5							
6							
7							
8							
9							
10							
11							
12							
13							
14							
15							
16							
17							
18							
19							